THE HANDBOOK OF CRITICAL LITERACIES

The Handbook of Critical Literacies aims to answer the timely question: what are the social responsibilities of critical literacy academics, researchers, and teachers in today's world? Critical literacies are classically understood as ways to interrogate texts and contexts to address injustices and they are an essential literacy practice. Organized into thematic and regional sections, this handbook provides substantive definitions of critical literacies across fields and geographies, surveys of critical literacy work in over 23 countries and regions, and overviews of research, practice, and conceptual connections to established and emerging theoretical frameworks. The chapters on global critical literacy practices include research on language acquisition, the teaching of literature and English language arts, Youth Participatory Action Research, environmental justice movements, and more.

This pivotal handbook enables new and established researchers to position their studies within highly relevant directions in the field and engage, organize, disrupt, and build as we work for more sustainable social and material relations. A groundbreaking text, this handbook is a definitive resource and an essential companion for students, researchers, and scholars in the field.

Jessica Zacher Pandya is Professor of Teacher Education and Liberal Studies at California State University, Long Beach, USA.

Raúl Alberto Mora is Associate Professor in the School of Education and Pedagogy and Chair of the Literacies in Second Languages Project research lab at Universidad Pontificia Bolivariana, Medellín, Colombia.

Jennifer Helen Alford is Associate Professor in the Faculty of Creative Industries, Education and Social Justice at Queensland University of Technology, Australia.

Noah Asher Golden is Assistant Professor of Secondary Education at California State University, Long Beach, USA.

Roberto Santiago de Roock is Assistant Professor of Learning Sciences & Technology at the University of California, Santa Cruz, USA.

THE HANDBOOK OF CRITICAL LITERACIES

EDITED BY JESSICA ZACHER PANDYA, RAÚL ALBERTO MORA,
JENNIFER HELEN ALFORD, NOAH ASHER GOLDEN, AND
ROBERTO SANTIAGO DE ROOCK

Routledge
Taylor & Francis Group

NEW YORK AND LONDON

First published 2022
by Routledge
605 Third Avenue, New York, NY 10158

and by Routledge
2 Park Square, Milton Park, Abingdon, Oxon, OX14 4RN

Routledge is an imprint of the Taylor & Francis Group, an informa
business

© 2022 Taylor & Francis

The right of Jessica Zacher Pandya, Raúl Alberto Mora, Jennifer Helen
Alford, Noah Asher Golden, and Roberto Santiago de Roock to be
identified as the authors of the editorial material, and of the authors for
their individual chapters, has been asserted in accordance with sections 77
and 78 of the Copyright, Designs and Patents Act 1988.

Library of Congress Cataloging-in-Publication Data
A catalog record for this book has been requested

ISBN: 978-0-367-90260-5 (hbk)
ISBN: 978-0-367-90259-9 (pbk)
ISBN: 978-1-003-02342-5 (ebk)

DOI: 10.4324/9781003023425

Typeset in Bembo
by Apex CoVantage, LLC

CONTENTS

Contents

PREFACE

This handbook aims to answer a historic but ever-pressing question: What is the social responsibility of critical literacy academics, researchers, and teachers in today's world? As the chapters suggest, this question is at the forefront of our minds. We five editors—living in Australia, Colombia, Singapore and the United States when we began our collaboration—met because of our ability as global academics to travel and present our research. Out of ongoing dialogues, we began the Transnational Critical Literacy Network (TCLN), aiming to bring researchers together from around the world to share perspectives and forge new alliances. At first, this consisted of inviting colleagues near and far to join the venture via a Google Docs (https://docs.google.com/document/d/19PK5Fz6I4x8-u2CZMW6zQEIWLWjzi5rXzaeLNZf6Yuk/edit?usp=sharing). As the network grew in numbers and ideas, we began drafting a joint paper (with the entire network of over 100 scholars) as well as thinking of other shared projects. The Network now has over 140 members from about 20 countries including Argentina, Australia, Brazil, Canada, Chile, Colombia, England, Hong Kong, Indonesia, Iran, Japan, Mexico, Palestine, New Zealand, Norway, Puerto Rico, Saudi Arabia, Scotland, Singapore, South Africa, Sweden, Uganda, and the United States. Members are preservice teachers, classroom teachers, graduate students, new professors, and more established as well as emeritus professors. As members shared the occasional conference call, journal call, or began asking for potential research collaborators, we began to conceive of this project. The five of us decided on a handbook of critical literacies, an undertaking done both in homage to our own critical literacy mentors—Barbara Comber, Hilary Janks, Allan Luke, and Vivian Maria Vasquez—and in a deliberate attempt to broaden and diversify the scholars who might find intellectual homes under a revitalized critical literacy umbrella. We have called it the *Handbook of Critical Literacies*.

When we put the invitation to help craft the handbook proposal to the Network/TCLN, we hoped to interest the members and garner potential authors; we generated an incredible amount of supportive and honest commentary that led directly to this book. Those who spoke against participating in a handbook project had different kinds of objections. They said that handbooks privilege those who can afford to access or buy them; handbooks *are* expensive and our aim in the future is to transform the chapters into more accessible and affordable platforms. Some members also said that handbook chapters mattered less in their retention, tenure, and promotion processes. This is changing in a lot of contexts as the value of various forms of publishing is accepted, but we acknowledge that this practice is often tied to privilege where those who are already well published and promoted can afford to deviate from the norm.

However, for us, the book itself is a space like no other, and after weighing the pros and cons, we decided to proceed with the handbook as a way of bringing a host of experienced and emerging scholars together on a single, defining collaborative, generative project, one that would help emerging scholars gain recognition for their work. It is our hope that the handbook will also see critical literacy claim an important territory with a well-recognized publisher. We asked those who did want to participate—despite the real issues we've just discussed—to go far out of their comfort zones. We set up a Google Doc for chapter ideas we had, invited more ideas, and kept refining it until we felt we had a workable structure. This included a section of the handbook on established critical literacy traditions, which we originally referred to as the section on critical literacy over time; one on the different traditions and epistemological variations of critical literacy around the world; and a third area that asked authors to push the boundaries of critical literacy further out and further into the future. We took a partial table of contents, made another Google Docs, and asked network members to sign up for any and all chapters they wanted to work with/in/on. We tried to make every single chapter (all 50 of them) jointly authored so that no one person would be the sole voice of authority on a given topic, country, region, or emerging idea. We asked people to find authors who brought different perspectives than their own on the same problem, to find younger or older scholars, people from other countries, institutions, language backgrounds. If authors wanted help finding a coauthor, we helped; we also turned to the larger Network to ask for additional authors, ideas, and leads. We discussed the project with our mentors and asked their guidance about structure and content.

We mention these linkages and these complicated flows to highlight that this really has been a group project, if not a collective one. None of us five editors feels we are qualified, capable, or arrogant enough to define critical literacy on our own, much less decide what topics should be included and what should not. We had to do it together, and together we have done it! From all of us to you, our readers, welcome to the conversation, welcome to the Network!

Jessica Zacher Pandya, Raúl Alberto Mora, Jennifer Helen Alford,
Noah Asher Golden, and Roberto Santiago de Roock

INTRODUCTION TO AREA 1

Jessica Zacher Pandya

In Area 1, authors—delve into the antecedents and current configurations of critical literacy work. The area begins with the editors' introduction (Chapter 1), which outlines the history of this collection and lays out some of our editorial hopes, fears, and dreams. Lina Trigos-Carrillo, Rebecca Rogers, and Miriam Jorge begin their exegesis of the global histories and antecedents of critical literacy in **Chapter 2** with autobiographical poems that invite their readers to think creatively and with emotion about these deeply theoretical constructs. Like many chapters, this one ends with questions to push our own work in this field further, but authors also ask us to consider how we contribute to inequalities in the publishing and grant writing industries, perhaps at the cost of doing our own social justice work. In **Chapter 3**, Rohit Mehta, Csilla Weninger, and David Martínez-Prieto methodically lay out connections between neoliberalism, ethnonationalism, and transnationalism, arguing that critical literacies are the antithesis of neoliberal literacies. They ask us to examine the impact of neoliberalism on literacy education, especially as it influences transnational flows of people, ideas, and literacy practices in online and in person spaces.

Four chapters in this area take up issues of pedagogy and teaching directly. The first of these is **Chapter 4**, in which Chris K. Chang-Bacon, Nihal Khote, Robin Schell, and Graham V. Crookes take up the relationship between English language teaching (ELT) and critical literacies. They ask readers to consider two purposes for criticality in ELT, a pedagogical one to promote critical engagement with texts and lifeworlds in language classrooms and a larger one about English itself. They interrogate the global nature of English language teaching and ask us to ask: Why English? And, whose English? Betina Hsieh and Susan Cridland-Hughes describe the evolution of critical literacy work in teacher education and in K–12 classrooms in **Chapter 6**, discussing dispositions of teachers and teacher educators, then moving on to examples of critical literacy in practice. They ask us to reflect on the roles of our local school districts and partners, as well as teacher education programs, in making critical literacy practices not only sustainable but also more central to language arts education. **Chapter 8** focuses our attention on queer critical literacies. Navan Govender and Grant Andrews draw on a dense body of past work to offer a pedagogical tool: a framework for queering and queer critical literacy. In **Chapter 9**, Anwar Ahmed and Saskia Van Viegen address the rich history of the relationship between writing and critical literacy. They argue that creating and maintaining a critical writing pedagogy can further critical literacy and move us toward equity and justice in classrooms around the world.

Another three chapters focus on youth experiences of and with critical literacy. In **Chapter 5**, Robert Petrone, Nicole Mirra, Steve Goodman, and Antero Garcia outline the intersections of critical literacy work, youth activism, and civic participation. They define key terms, offer citations of landmark and more recent YPAR-related work, and ask us to question the boundaries and benefits of YPAR for youth and their communities. **Chapter 7** describes past and present work in critical literacies from an embodiment perspective, considering the ways children's and youth's bodies as social texts are written and performed. Elisabeth Johnson, Grace Enriquez, and Stavroula Kontovourki review work on children remaking selves, engaging critically in their social worlds, and press readers to remember how much bodies and representations still matter in an increasingly post-humanist world. The last chapter in Area 1, **Chapter 10**, reviews work at the nexus of critical literacies and critical media production or critical media literacies. Olivia G. Stewart, Cassandra Scharber, Jeff Share, and Anne Crampton argue that as academics we need to continually teach criticality in media spaces and suggest that academics must do this as they create their own media and as they create spaces for children and youth to critically create and consume media.

1.1

INTRODUCTION TO THE HANDBOOK OF CRITICAL LITERACIES

The Current State of Critical Literacy Around the World

Jessica Zacher Pandya, Raúl Alberto Mora, Jennifer Helen Alford, Noah Asher Golden, and Roberto Santiago de Roock

This is an expansive handbook on the past, present, and future of critical literacies on a transnational scale. Critical literacies, as they are classically conceived, offer people ways of interrogating texts and contexts and of writing and rewriting texts and realities to address injustices. They are, or ought to be, a key skill in any literate individual's repertoire of literacy practices (cf. Comber & Simpson, 2001; Janks, 2010; Luke, 2014; Vasquez, 2005). We define them in this Handbook as literate practices individuals need in order to survive and thrive in the world, foregrounding the concept that information and texts are never neutral; they afford the ability to produce powerful texts that address injustices in our lived worlds. This formulation is sometimes known by other names in the Global South, particularly in Latin America and Africa. As chapters in Area 2 of the Handbook will show, it can be seen in research on language acquisition, the teaching of literature and English language arts, Youth Participatory Action Research, environmental justice movements, and more. As the notion of "critical" has become increasingly commonplace, we as editors fear that, without reflexivity, the term has sometimes become too diluted or misconstrued to mean much at all, especially as terms like "critical thinking" become part of the neoliberal educational vocabulary. We are also concerned that the deeply contextualized meanings of critical literacy in different places and spaces around the globe may be lost even before coming to light. In the Handbook, we intentionally draw on multiple critical epistemologies, including European, Black, and Indigenous thinkers from the Global South and the Global North. At a time when post-truth paradigms influence the ways education is understood and enacted, and misinformation and disinformation increasingly shape unfolding events and evolving structures of power, critical literacies feel more relevant and crucial than ever.

Transnational issues of literacy are central to the resurgence of authoritarian forces and thus critical approaches have never been more important. As we write, we are experiencing the COVID-19 pandemic, whose ravages highlight the very inequalities and power arrangements that critical literacies research highlights. The pandemic's death toll is exacerbated by years of intensifying ethno–racialized notions of citizenship and nationhood across the world, which some among us see as resurgent fascisms. This has included strong anti-science discourses and right–wing populist support, all based on broad-based consumption of misinformation and disinformation (often called "fake news") spurred on by the architecture of and people's use of social media. Additionally, existential threats due to climate genocide and nuclear proliferation

DOI: 10.4324/9781003023425-2

are increasingly pressing, with significant repercussions for our biosocial and material worlds. Within education, we are also seeing increasingly narrow conceptualizations of literacy serving the interests of standardization, measurability, and accountability (Pandya, 2011) and a concomitant rise of edu-businesses that profit from literacy education. At the same time, the nature of texts and textual flows are rapidly transforming via media manipulation and the algorithms underlying digital platforms, altering the ways humans and nonhumans interact, produce, and consume knowledge, experience text(s), and experience racism (Benjamin, 2019; de Roock, 2021). If not for the everyday and collective resistance that is ongoing and necessary, such as the Black Lives Matter uprisings of 2020, or the recent protests taking place across Latin America or Asia, to name two regions, for the past two years, it would be easy to feel that critical literacies educators are losing the battle.

In response to this complex confluence of change driving humanity toward homogenization in the name of control and profit, this Handbook provides a heterogeneity of current interpretations and applications of critical literacy by scholars from across the globe. We seek to demonstrate the diversity of uptake within critical literacy research communities; to strengthen our critical literacies praxis and international collaborations; and to present a stronger collective and heteroglossic front. We see a strong need for collaborations across borders and foresee the generative possibilities of such collaborations. As oppressive discourses, institutions, and forces are increasingly transnational, and as socioeconomic injustices grow and inequities widen, research and organizing that responds to oppression must also grow and diversify. We purposefully use the term "transnational" to signal our own perspectives on our places in the world and our own lived realities. Transnationalism as a term "came into existence at that moment in time when successful nation-state building 'contributed to the creation of large numbers of people' out of place—that is, crossing over the national boundaries erected in the last two centuries" (Roudometof, 2005, p. 119). Attention has shifted "from state and macro-actors to the micro-level of globalization and to civil society movements" (Duscha, Klein-Zimmer, Klemm, & Spiegel, 2018, p. 3) creating opportunities for refocusing the loci of voice and power. The Handbook is an attempt to capture disparate voices about critical literacy as a kind of collective civil movement.

This Handbook grew out of the Transnational Critical Literacies Network (TCLN), which was named to reflect our senses of being transnational academics and teachers, both in and out of place, and our awareness that our positionings allow us to decenter our own ways of knowing. As part of this commitment, we sought to highlight what counts as critical literacy work in diverse sociocultural contexts to counter the often-Eurocentric foundations of its academic lineage. In each of the chapters that follows, regardless of topic, area, or theme, we have asked authors to write about their social responsibilities as critical literacy researchers in this world. We decided early on that ideally no one person should write a chapter on their own, and that no one could write more than one. In the end, only three chapters are single-authored. Some authors knew each other before they began writing, while others were total strangers, connected through the TCLN and through their desire to write about this work. We took this approach to diversify the voices in these pages and to ensure that we had authors engaged in dialogue as they wrote. We have all reached far beyond our comfort zones to ask each other uncomfortable questions about whose voices should structure each section and how we should make decisions about inclusion and exclusion. One of our major preoccupations has been the languages we would use in this Handbook. We were not allowed to publish chapters in two languages—such as the authors' preferred language and English—but as readers will see as they read the Handbook, we succeeded in arguing that many varieties of English were welcome. Readers will also encounter a wide variety within the structures we created; some authors chose to focus more on their home or adopted countries in a chapter on a geographic region, and some authors chose to focus on emerging instead of canonical work. Additionally, we have not required certain terms or acronyms (e.g., readers will see both "multilingual learner" and "emergent bilingual" in use in different places). The variation readers will encounter is intentional and reflects our vision for this Handbook as a space for diversity of experimentation, change, and intellectual rigor.

Form and Structure of the Handbook

As we hinted in the Preface, the Handbook is laid out in three Areas, allowing us to engage in three related projects mirrored in its areas: the antecedents and current state of critical literacies in Area 1; a global survey of critical literacy in praxis, examining work in 23 countries and geographical regions in Area 2; and finally, the chapters in Area 3 highlighting work that has pushed and continues to push the boundaries of critical literacies. We describe below some of the key concepts, theoretical frameworks, and areas of research in the three areas.

Area 1: Critical Literacies Over Time: Antecedents and Current Configurations

The first area addresses substantive definitions of critical literacies across fields and geographies, including historical surveys and deep theoretical dives. We have conceived of this first area as one about *time*; chapters describe and summarize critical literacy research over time in its different guises and subfields. Chapters also tackle critiques of critical literacy and questions about how it can be of use in neoliberal contexts and spaces. The authors of Chapter 1.2 experiment with the form and structure of the Handbook chapter. They begin by delving into critical literacy in action in three separate contexts, from the educational practices of a community of former guerilla members, through a "pedagogy of the earth" course in Brazil, to a U.S. grassroots teacher activist network. They trace connections between popular education—as Freire and others have described and enacted it—and our more current conceptions of critical literacies. What those authors do in poetry and prose, subsequent chapter authors take up more forthrightly, offering definitions of neoliberalism and ethnonationalism; English language teaching, bi/multilingualism, and translanguaging; youth, participatory, action, and research (as "YPAR"); embodiment, the disciplined body, the body as social text, the feeling/sensing body, the intra/acting body, and embodied literacies; identities, heteronormativity, practices of queering, and queering critical literacy; and critical media consumption and production.

The authors in Area 1 draw on a wide range of historical and current theoretical framings, as befits the wide scope of the Handbook. Readers will engage with sociocultural, poststructuralist, and post-humanist approaches. They will be reminded of the contributions of systemic functional linguistics and critical discourse analysis and be asked to take up queer perspectives on literacies, writing, and the world. Multiliteracies, participatory culture, and connected learning are also referenced in these chapters. Reading across the chapters is a reminder of how we as researchers and teacher educators draw on widely different traditions and theories to make sense of the critical literacies in which we engage to make sense of our worlds.

We asked authors to undertake reviews of and implications for research in their separate chapters. Reading across them shows the impact of neoliberal policies on literacy education, illuminating how such policies shape and exclude on a transnational scale (Chapter 1.3). It also shows us how children and youth can engage in critical literacies at all language levels, emphasizing the relevance of critical literacies to the lived realities of multilingual students (Chapter 1.4); we are reminded that critical literacy practices in the ELT classroom can facilitate language proficiency, motivation, and engagement, whether or not that is the original goal. Teachers are at the center of some chapters, where we see how teacher preparation contexts can be inimical to, or can foster, the uptake of critical literacy practices by teachers in preservice classes and their own classrooms (Chapter 1.6), and how teachers' work facilitates critical literacies for English learners (Chapter 1.4).

We are reminded of the ways Youth Participatory Action Research (YPAR) privileges youth identities, epistemologies, and literacy practices, and of how YPAR challenges formal classroom learning methods and practices, as well as how it may transform the ways teachers are educated

(Chapter 1.5). These challenges are reiterated and viewed through the lens of embodiment in Chapter 1.7, where adult objectives for literacy learning are interrogated alongside youth's own perspectives and goals, and where authors see critical engagement in the exploration of youth's embodied literacy practice. We see how queering critical literacy entails the questioning of the representation of queer peoples' experiences, as well as questioning how we police (a)gender and (a)sexuality through our literacy practices (Chapter 1.8). We are asked to consider the role of writing in critical literacy education (Chapter 1.9). We are introduced to competing, overlapping, and contradictory approaches to media literacy, from critical digital literacies to critical computational literacies to pedagogies of invention (Chapter 1.10).

Area 2: Critical Literacies Across Space: A Global Survey of Critical Literacy Praxis

The second area addresses the question: What does critical literacy pedagogy look and sound like around the world? We conceived of this area as a collection of critical literacies praxis across *space*. We brought together surveys of critical literacy work that cover all continents, blending research on long-standing and recognized traditions together with research in regions with emergent or less recognized traditions. We were specifically interested in exploring what it means to engage in transnational critical literacy work (both country- and region-specific), especially teasing out the tensions involved in indexing these global concepts and theories in local contexts. Contributions contest any monolithic sense of critical literacy, pushing for a more expansive and transnational critical literacy project.

We were invested in highlighting countries or regions typically left out of discussions on critical literacy pedagogy, ultimately including both country- and region-specific surveys. The hope was to have all regions covered in some way. However, many regions are missing, not because there is not work being done there but due to a combination of limitations in our networks and lack of time for those we invited (especially given the COVID-19 pandemic). The term "critical literacy" also is far from universal, and even when similar work is being done, it more often than not goes by different names.

The scope and organization of this area was far from straightforward, especially given our commitment to remain sensitive to the histories, politics, and tensions embodied in geographical divisions. The process illustrates the ways textual practices are always political. Puerto Rico, for example, is a colony of the United States rather than an independent country, but we have chosen to list it with countries. Similarly, there was a question of whether Hong Kong should have its own chapter or be grouped with Taiwan, Macao, and Tibet under a greater China chapter. There was debate about how to approach the Caribbean, especially given the ways languages at play (Spanish, French, English, Dutch) come with distinct histories, flows, and debates. In the end, these chapters (Chapters 2.11, 2.17, and 2.18) coalesced through conversations with the authors, who were best positioned to stake claims, especially given what they felt capable and qualified to write about. We remain aware, however, that these are clearly political decisions, and that not all readers will be happy with them.

The configuration of the chapter authors was a broad palette. Some of the chapters included research teams that are working together to create a research body or make sense of it all within one institution (Australia [Chapter 2.2], Brazil [Chapter 2.3], Canada [Chapter 2.4], Colombia [Chapter 2.5], Indonesia [Chapter 2.7], Norway and France [Chapter 2.20], Russia [Chapter 2.12], Singapore [Chapter 2.13]) or across different institutions (Aotearoa New Zealand [Chapter 2.1], Mexico [Chapter 2.10], Nordic Countries [Chapter 2.19], South Africa [Chapter 2.14], United Kingdom [Chapter 2.15], United States [Chapter 2.16]). Some chapters mixed scholars situated both in the Global South and North, joined by a common topic (e.g., India [Chapter 2.6], Iran

[Chapter 2.8], Japan [Chapter 2.9], Puerto Rico [Chapter 2.11], South Asia [Chapter 2.21]). Some chapters bookended years of collaborative work, some chapters encompassed budding partnerships, and sometimes, serendipity brought the authors together (e.g., Uganda and Congo [Chapter 2.22]).

Some of the driving questions for the chapters in this section include: What forces are driving definitions and redefinitions of critical literacy? How is it thought about in different spaces? What local and global historical factors are reshaping definitions? What are the barriers to enacting critical literacy pedagogy in these countries? We suggested structuring chapters into six sections to identify major issues surrounding critical literacy on a global scale: (i.) An overview of the geographical space in its sociopolitical contexts; (ii.) An overview of the geographical space's educational system(s); (iii.) A survey of critical literacy work (including theory and pedagogy) by researchers and practitioners in the country, with some comparison to international work and lineage; (iv.) Visions for moving into more transnational and critical work from the perspective of that country; (v.) Conclusions/findings/suggestions for further research and practice; and (vi.) Implications for our social responsibility as academics.

This transnational work is ongoing, partial, and incomplete; we see it as a push for the field to both recognize and work for the expansion of critical literacies praxis. Covering every country or even region was a nearly impossible task and therefore this Handbook is not, in that sense, comprehensive. We see it as a conversation starter for our authors, readers, and the field. It represents an opening to look at emerging issues not only in these countries, but also on every continent. Whether addressing their country or region, contributing authors, made efforts to situate the conversations in their chapters as part of ongoing regional or continental issues that deserve more attention in years to come.

Area 3: Pushing the Boundaries: Critical Literacies in Motion

In the third area, authors set up a spirited agenda for critical literacies, pushing current boundaries with explicit calls to action for practitioners and researchers around extant and future critical literacy projects. The goal is to showcase critical literacy in motion. Chapters capture moving versions of critical literacies practice or invitations to connect critical literacy with emerging or under-explored bodies of thought and practice. Each chapter presents work that forges new territory in the field, reporting on varied contexts with a range of far-reaching implications. The projects they explore highlight the ongoing importance of the critical, as well as the unique and at times challenging directions in which contemporary practitioners and researchers are taking this work. This section is a collection of bold calls to continue the evolving relevance of critical literacy to today's complex education agenda and the broader social, cultural, political, economic, and material life in which we are always enmeshed.

We asked authors in Area 3 to invite us into their subfields by defining key concepts and acknowledging and contending with critiques of critical literacies in their domains. As for Areas 1 and 2, we wanted to know the implications of these approaches for our pedagogies, ongoing scholarship, and, perhaps most importantly, for our social responsibility as academics. The agenda that emerges from these chapters invites us to reflect on the limitations of past work in critical literacies as we forge new possibilities, and this rich agenda offers no single approach as we work to respond to conditions shaped by transnational and translocal concerns. The issues engaged through these critical literacy practices in motion are varied and many: chapter authors in Area 3 take up systems of domination grounded in anti-Blackness and other forms of racism; the unfolding climate crisis; the impacts of datafication; social hierarchies produced through deeply problematic exchanges and readings of linguistic capital; the unfurling loss of Indigenous languages; misrecognitions of people; deficit framings of identities; rising nationalisms and xenophobia; and textual practices that limit our ability to form imaginaries that may engender possibilities for new social and material relations. These are indeed weighty concerns.

Critical literacy scholars have long resisted the notion of any single approach or methodology that could fix whatever might be seen in a given moment as the "literacy problem" a society or community is facing, recognizing decades ago that:

> [l]iteracy refers to a malleable set of cultural practices shaped and reshaped by different—often competing and contending—social institutions, social classes, and cultural interests ... how and when literacy became a problem had as much to do with economic, cultural, and social change as it did with anything that might go on in schools and classrooms.
>
> *(Luke & Freebody, 1999, p. 2)*

The more important question is what literacies can do to help create sites of possibility and transformation in the economic, cultural, and sociopolitical flows that delineate current affordances and limitations—flows that are increasingly transnational. Just as there is no single approach to fix a "literacy problem" in formal education, there is no one critical approach to textual analysis or multimodal production that has a monopoly on possible interruptions of the contemporary and future-oriented weighty concerns taken up in this area. Thankfully, the spirited agenda in **Area 3: Critical Literacies in Motion** offers multiple approaches to the enactment of critical literacies, all directed toward these contemporary and ongoing issues.

These approaches include analysis of contemporary literatures to question and make sense of "the sociopolitical systems through which we live our lives" (Chapter 3.1) and the impact of our choices for textual analysis (Chapter 3.3). These approaches also include multimodal arts-based methods to access emotions and rich imaginaries (Chapter 3.2). Readers are invited to pay attention to emergent situated discourse in classrooms to cocreate moments of critical analysis (Chapter 3.13), and encouraged to view the decentering White and hegemonic gazes as a process as we engage in dialogue and activism in youth-led spaces (Chapter 3.14). Chapter authors detail approaches to navigating the beneath-the-screen, less visible software space and datafication to help people better understand new cultural and commercial relations (Chapter 3.5) and explore how everyday relations are shaped by digital media and technologies, positing ways critical digital literacies can broaden understandings of how language, literacy, and power are mediated in these contemporary digital ecologies (Chapter 3.8). Authors argue for the limitations of current frameworks as they entice readers to embrace posthuman and new materialist methodologies in an effort to encourage planetary literacies that offer new understandings of subjectivity—understandings may help to address the urgency of the unfolding climate crisis (Chapter 3.4). We are invited to open our work to "everything, everyone, every moment" as authors propose a politics of immediation for literacy studies (Chapter 3.12). Generative cross-fertilization of critical literacies with dis/ability studies are suggested as a means to disrupt global, ableist hegemonies as we readers are encouraged to center on the experiences of minoritized youth given special education disability labels (Chapter 3.6). Teacher education programs can develop new understandings of schools as embedded within community systems, and teacher educators are invited to see community members as partners in the work of supporting new literacy educators (Chapter 3.15). We see the possibilities in recent work on translanguaging in Additional Language Teaching (Chapter 3.9), and the ways critical literacies can further English Language Teaching (Chapter 3.11). We are invited into Indigenous youth's use of social media to resist the loss of Indigenous languages (Chapter 3.10). To interrupt rising nationalisms, xenophobia, continuing colonialism, and social hierarchies grounded in racial identities, we are offered approaches to cosmopolitan critical literacies (Chapter 3.16), border literacies (Chapter 3.17), and abolitionist literacies (Chapter 3.7).

No single thread connects the theoretical frameworks, framings, and associated pedagogies and research programs present through the chapters of Area 3. There are chapters that resist the notion of "giving voice" to minoritized people, instead recognizing that people already have voices and seeking to affirm these voices by centering on these people's knowledges and experiences (e.g., Chapters 3.7, 3.15). There are chapters proposing new theoretical frames, arguing contemporary frameworks cannot attend to the politics of affect (Chapter 3.12), environmental crises (Chapter 3.4), or digital ecosystems (Chapter 3.5). We read about new views of translanguaging (Chapter 3.9), ways to engage the critical in and through contemporary literatures (Chapter 3.1) and the arts (Chapter 3.2), and the need to see beyond our comfort zones while recognizing the current limitations of them (Chapter 3.3). This rich pastiche of approaches shows the current state of the field, and where critical literacies are going. Throughout, we, the readers, are invited to move beyond neoliberal academic production to engage, organize, disrupt, and build as we work for more sustainable social and material relations.

Conclusion

We, as editors, are awed, inspired, and bolstered by the chapters we have jointly collected, curated, and supported as they arrived in these pages. Our collective futures might involve the creation of websites, listservs, more handbooks, articles, and research studies; it might also include grassroots activism, or active engagement with teachers and students, or with policymakers and curriculum developers. In all cases, we will continue to question our own privilege, our own linguistic and cultural capital, and ask: Where are we going from here? We hope readers feels similarly, and are left with this thought: it is always time to do the work, and let's do the work.

References

Benjamin, R. (2019). *Race after technology: Abolitionist tools for the New Jim Code*. Polity Press.

Comber, B., & Simpson, A. (Eds.). (2001). *Negotiating critical literacies in classrooms*. Lawrence Erlbaum Associates.

de Roock, R. S. (2021). On the material consequences of (digital) literacy: Digital writing with, for, and against racial capitalism. *Theory Into Practice*. https://doi.org/10.1080/00405841.2020.1857128

Duscha, A., Klein-Zimmer, K., Klemm, M., & Spiegel, A. (2018). Understanding transnational knowledge. *Transnational Social Review*, 8(1), 2–6. https://doi.org/10.1080/21931674.2018.1427680

Janks, H. (2010). *Literacy and power*. Routledge.

Luke, A. (2014). Defining critical literacy. In J. Z. Pandya & J. Ávila (Eds.), *Moving critical literacies forward: A new look at praxis across contexts* (pp. 19–31). Routledge.

Luke, A., & Freebody, P. (1999). Further notes on the four resources model. *Reading Online*, 1–4. Retrieved from www.readingonline.org/research/lukefreebody.html

Pandya, J. Z. (2011). *Overtested: How high-stakes accountability fails English language learners*. Teachers College Press.

Roudometof, V. (2005). Transnationalism, cosmopolitanism and glocalization. *Current Sociology*, *53*(1), 113–135. https://doi.org/10.1177/0011392105048291

Vasquez, V. (2005). *Negotiating critical literacy*. Lawrence Erlbaum Associates.

1.2

CRITICAL LITERACY
Global Histories and Antecedents

Lina Trigos-Carrillo, Rebecca Rogers, and Miriam Jorge

Current Conditions and Genealogical Roots

Globally, in the second decade of the twenty-first century, we are living in an era of widening gaps in wealth, power, and income; environmental crisis worsens as some governments deny their existence and risk. There is a continued violation of human rights (racism, homo/transphobia, detainment of children/youth, human trafficking, lack of access to health care/education; violent response to social protest). Fear is used to control economies, continue wars, and increase military budgets worldwide.

In Latin America, in 2020, people experience panic about the expansion of the coronavirus as the dollar price skyrockets affecting local economies; migrants travel across the continent for different reasons, including hunger and violence; the instability of peace and democracy is latent as popular protests face repressive and increasingly militarized tactics. In Brazil, the dubious impeachment (Snider, 2018) of the democratically elected female president Dilma Rousseff in 2016 was followed by antidemocratic events that led to the election of a President who celebrates the brutality of military dictatorship (Schipani, 2017) and condemns human rights. After achieving the historical milestone of leaving the UN World Hunger Map for the first time in 2014, food insecurity returned to the country in 2020.

In the United States, we are experiencing a surge of anti-immigrant, anti-Black rhetoric, policies, and practices that infuse every domain of public life. Under the direction of the US Secretary of Education, we see the continued usurping of public funds for private education, de-professionalization of educators, and detainment or separation of children and families at the border for profit. All of this is coupled with surging gun violence, in schools and communities.

In the midst of this global–local, sociopolitical stage lies the struggle for/with educational literacies as now more than ever global dynamics have a direct impact on local action, and many communities experience the effects of "glocalization" (Brooks & Normore, 2010). We situate our work with critical educational literacies within these larger geographical, social, political, racial, linguistic, and economic forces that work on and against public schools, teachers, children/youth, families, and communities.

Critical Autobiographical Poems: Becoming Scholars of Critical Literacy

Before we delve deeper into critical literacy, we each share a poem from our own roots and routes to becoming critical literacy scholars. We do this to emphasize the relationships that exist within each

DOI: 10.4324/9781003023425-3

of our stories and the ways in which our narratives intersect in concentric circles. Even though we were raised in different decades and in different countries, there are similarities in our narratives that highlight how pervasive social problems are and how social inequities inspire the desire for change. The continuing push toward consumerism and public apathy is reinforced through individualism, alienation, and isolation. These principles are reinforced in school curricula that emphasize teaching isolated facts, without situated context, or relationships (e.g., for a critique of this, see Zinn, 2005). But without hope education cannot exist.

Lina

> *Raised in a working-class neighborhood*
> > *in Bogota, Colombia,*
> > *a point on the map*
> *Becoming aware of the faces of poverty and violence.*
> *The 80s, the decade of terror*
> *the war against drug cartels.*
> > *La Violencia*
> *No mass shootings or police brutality,*
> *Sporadic bombs to random buildings in cities and towns,*
> > *kidnappings,*
> > > *murders,*
> > > > *massacres.*
> > *We all were vulnerable.*
> *My home, political involvement.*
> *Votation day with mi abuelo,*
> *I put my finger into a red-ink container (the color of the liberal party)*
> *I symbolically voted.*
> *My home. Reading.*
> *Filled with secondhand books wall-to-wall wooden shelves.*
> *At fifteen, discovered horror literature and philosophy*
> > *Aristotle, Sartre, Marx, Hannah Arendt*
> *Existence was volatile.*
> *My home. Education for a woman*
> > *shielded from domestic work*
> > *and other female-dominated activities*
> > *in my patriarchal Colombia.*
> *Being a privileged mestiza, becoming una mujer, becoming empowered.*
> *At Universidad Nacional de Colombia*
> *eager to learn more*
> *about the world, language, education,*
> *all socioeconomic and ethnic backgrounds,*
> > *all regions around the country*
> > *living together.*
> *Later, an encounter with Paulo Freire and Henry Giroux.*
> *Appealing ideas but not entirely new.*
> *Critical praxis transpired in the environment.*
> *In my early thirties, life took a turn,*
> > *A baby boy, a partner, and two pieces of luggage*

in an empty apartment in the US Midwest
 being a student again, a doctoral student.
Seven years, being transnational, speaking another language,
discovering my new identity as a Latina, as the Other.
An encounter with "critical literacy."
My home.
The tenets of critical literacy and critical pedagogy
embodied
 in the streets,
 en el barrio,
 in the university,
 in my native country.
Becoming a critical literacy scholar
the fluidity of my identity:
 a Latina in the US
 a privileged mestiza in Colombia.
Encounters with communities in Mexico, Costa Rica and Colombia,
 multilingual and migrant families in the US,
 former guerrilla members and their families in rural Colombia.
Transnational. Educator.

Miriam

Growing up in Brazil I lived and learned
 Racism
 Classism
 Sexism
Those were times of oppression
Songs of Chico Buarque, Milton Nascimento and Geraldo Vandré
Songs I sang as a child; lyrics I understood in college
I want to be a teacher! Nice to meet you, Freire!
Times to unlearn
 Racism
 Classism
 Sexism
It's democracy again!
Seize the day: learn, teach, pair, share!
Remember those bedtime stories?
 Your grandmother, goodness
 Your mother, strength
 Your uncles, struggle
 Your father, love
 Your sisters . . . inspiration
Be strong and disobedient:
 Learn English
 Live abroad
 Learn, teach, pair, share!
 Publish and inspire
 Be a teacher educator

Critical literacies for better schools
Language education for everyone
Racial Democracy
    a fallacy
Dictatorship, never more!
    Teach, learn, teach
Times to confront
    Racism
    Classism
    Sexism
Social Justice, Critical Pedagogies
Long live the Northeast of Brazil!
Viva Freire!
Ghosts from the past
Haunting our futures
Are they planning to come back?
And silence our voices, denying the existence of
    Racism
    Classism
    Sexism
No.
Not him. Not them again
We hope
We act
We continue singing
Chico Buarque, Milton Nascimento, Geraldo Vandré
And we
    teach
    learn
    unlearn
    share

Rebecca

For hundreds of years
my people have lived on Haudenosaunee lands
becoming white at different times
some ancestors changed their names and language
while working
        in factories, mines
others started the schoolhouse that required language be lost
Growing up in the 1970's and early 80's
dominant culture in the United States
had enough with human rights for womyn and People of Color
the air thick with the unregulated freedoms of businesses
Violence circulated around us
"War on Drugs" (the US manufactured and profiled youth of Color and Immigrant youth)
"Cold War" (the imminent threat of nuclear war with the former Soviet Union)
Disappearance of Indigenous people

Yet we experienced
relative safety and privilege
in the schools of thought
created by and for our people
education converted to property
Three decades stood between me
and
Sisters in Spirit by Sally Roesch Wagner
Indigenous People's History by Roxanne Dunbar-Ortiz
Ain't I a Woman by bell hooks
Faces at the Bottom of the Well by Derrick Bell
An American Sunrise by Joy Harjo
As a young girl, feelings of unfairness
different academic expectations for boys
      girls banned from serving at the altar in the Catholic Church
          Burned within me
From my mother
apprenticed into acting with charity
Donating clothes
   to children at school
      to womyn with mental illness,
An unspoken lesson: We could make lives better, even in a small way.
   A spirit of volunteerism awoke within me
      I became a Literacy Volunteer
         as a teenager
Something bigger than myself.
I worked several jobs to pay for a car
and commute to the University
   earn college degrees
I wrote poetry by the Mohawk River
and traveled great distances with ideas
Still, I had not seen a Person of Color in front of the class
nor a white educator with a critical racial lens
This absence is part of my herstory
By day, I worked at Literacy Volunteers of America
organizing people, money, and programs
and at night,
I studied with critical materialist feminist scholars
Who promised "by the end of the semester, you will swim in this theory we read."
Sitting in a circle, we deliberated the teachings of
Karl Marx, Homi Bhabha, Rosemary Hennessy, Teresa Ebert, Terri Eagleton
This desire to dismantle
   capitalism, patriarchy, and colonialism
      grew stronger in a group
I encountered the concept of critical literacy
when a Professor in graduate school encouraged me to read
Paulo Freire's "Pedagogy of the Oppressed"
and
"And Also Teach Them to Read: The National Literacy Crusade of Nicaragua"

sacred encounters
>*social movements come alive through words*
>>*words create movements*
>>>*uniting people across time, place, and difference*

Border crossings as awakenings
St. Louis, Caracas, New Market, Cuernavaca, Detroit
geo-political realities of life in a hyper-segregated city
Gracias neoliberalismo, for my yearning to organize,
be part of a group,
to fight profit-making, racism, and patriarchy
in classrooms, schools, and communities
Fuels my desire to link arms and create a better world
—otra vez y otra vez—
as an academic, activist/organizer, y madre.

***

We created these critical autobiographical poetic encounters deliberately to witness our own diverse routes to critical literacy education. We arrived at critical literacy in our lives through critical praxis before we encountered the theoretical foundations of the concept. This is a dynamic we have seen in communities where action and reflection come before or even without a formal theory. This may be due to the fact that action and transformation play a central role in the ways people embrace and embody critical literacy. Before Paulo Freire wrote about literacy from a critical perspective, he worked with the community and reflected about their social actions. Freire's personal history paved the ground to his theory as he learned early in life about the social injustices and political struggles Brazilian people faced through conversations with his father (Schugurensky, 2011). He learned from his parents how to read and write, and his first teacher, Eunice Vasconcelos, was also a model of teaching (Schugurensky, 2011). Elza Freire, a primary school teacher and Paulo's spouse, introduced education in his life (Spigolon, 2016). These experiences were the foundations of Freire's approach to rely on the learners' vocabulary as a departing point for building meaning and literacy, through the work with generative themes and words (Freire, 1970). Elza was fundamental in the elaboration, systematization, and the reasoning of the Paulo Freire method (Spigolon, 2016). Elza and his mother influenced his decision to be part of progressive Catholic movements that based their actions in the liberation theology (Schugurensky, 2011). During a decade of work at SESI (Serviço Social da Indústria), Freire entered into contact with the realities of working-class people in Brazil (Schugurensky, 2011). Although his theoretical antecedents were mostly authors from the Global North (e.g., Dewey, Marx, and Hegel), his experience in the Global South shaped his approach to critical literacy and popular education (Roberts, 2015). We want to address this relationship before we move forward with the conceptualization of critical literacy.

Popular Education and Critical Literacy

Critical literacies are closely tied to popular education because they both constitute ethical and political proposals for social transformation. Rooted in Latin American thought and realities, the popular education movement has its foundations in the independentist efforts and struggles. The ideas of Simón Rodríguez, Simón Bolívar's teacher, planted the seed of what he called popular education: (1.) an education to become American, instead of European (South and North America as a whole continent); (2.) an education to reach freedom; and, (3.) an education to be able to work and live independently (Mejía, 2011). During the first half of the twentieth century, popular education universities were founded in Mexico, El Salvador, and Peru to educate the working class with a strong consciousness about their place and role in history and organization as a principle to defend their rights (Mejía, 2011). In Bolivia and Peru, movements to create schools based on indigenous thinking, such as the Ayllu de Warisata School, posed the need for an education grounded in the indigenous culture and epistemologies, which consider education as movement and as a process of cultural creation and social transformation that happened in the community (Mejía, 2011). In the 1960s, Paulo Freire started the Movement of Popular Culture and developed his pedagogy for popular education. Torres-Carrillo (2016) defines popular education as a set of social and discursive educational practices intended to center people from popular segments in society so that they become protagonists of social transformation based on their own interests and emancipatory visions of the future.

Knowing the origins of popular education is important to understand the tenets of critical literacy because literacy education was interwoven in the movements of popular education as its leaders worked with communities who were illiterate. The epistemological foundations of literacy education lay on the power of social transformation and not on the functional purposes of literacy. This, tied to the particular sociopolitical circumstances in which popular education emerged, pushed toward critical approaches to literacy education. Critical literacy's departing point is the reality of the people and the critical reading of that reality; it crosses the walls of the school; it takes into account the power dynamics in the ways of knowing; and it is an ethical and political initiative to achieve social transformation (Mejía, 2011). Teaching in the context of critical pedagogies and popular education in Latin America is characterized by a pedagogy of dignity; teaching rooted in hospitality and generosity; teaching to preserve the memory and history of communal identity; teaching that centers historical knowledge to build historical consciousness, to rethink the present, and radically imagine the future to transform unjust social structures; and a pedagogy based on processes of cultural negotiation, confrontation, and dialogue of "saberes" (knowledges/wisdom) (Cappellacci et al., 2018; Quintar, 2018).

The group-centered spirit of popular education has deep roots in the United States as well. Popular education was at the core of the Highlander Center in New Market, Tennessee, which was the hub of labor rights (1930s) and civil rights organizing (1950s) and, currently focuses on immigrant rights. The popular education process relies on horizontal relationships between people who jointly inquire and analyze a social problem, plan, take action, and reflect.

For example, the goal of the Citizenship Schools—and teachers such as Bernice Robinson, Septima Clark, and Alice Wine—was for African Americans to achieve voting rights by passing literacy tests required at polling places during Jim Crow. To do this, organizers/educators used voter registration materials as the basis for literacy education across the south (Bell, Gaventa, & Peters, 1990; Stokes-Brown, 1990). Together, they engaged in a problem-posing, problem-solving method of education.

Critical Literacy in Action

According to Menezes de Souza (2007) in the first volume of the journal *Critical Literacy: Theories and Practices*, if literacy is "a socio-culturally situated practice involving the ongoing negotiation of meaning in continuously contested sites of meaning construction, then all literacy in a certain sense ought to be 'critical'" (p. 4). However, the emphasis on the word "critical" relates to a major attention "to literacy in issues relating to citizenship education, development education, foreign-language education and teacher education as sites of various socio-cultural crises in the form of continuously contested meaning construction and negotiation" (p. 4).

From our own experiences, we share three examples of critical literacy in action. Each of these vignettes emphasize the critical, creative, and collective forms of practice, reflection, theorizing, and acting that are necessary to imagine and build hopeful futures. They represent "glocalized" flows of knowledge, power, and organizing; that is, energies that are both local and global. For example, the global politics on climate change impacts food security in Latin America and Africa. Finally, literacies are positioned in a dialectical relationship with social movements—part of the texts, talk, interactions, signs, songs, and ever-reaching multimodal landscape—that create and represent social movements. Within each of these snapshots of global critical literacy praxis, we draw attention to the intellectual roots that have informed and inspired this work.

Vignette 1: Popular Education in a Community of Former Guerrilla Members and Their Families

In 2016, the FARC-EP, one of the oldest guerrilla groups in Latin America, and the Colombian government signed a peace agreement to put an end to more than 50 years of armed conflict. The peace negotiation focused on six major topics: integral rural reform, political participation, the end of the armed conflict, a solution to drug trafficking, victims' compensation, and implementation and verification mechanisms. Nearly 3,000 guerrilla members who endorsed the peace agreement moved to the 24 Territorial Spaces for Training and Reincorporation (ETCR in Spanish) that were created to support the transition process. In La Montañita, Caquetá, almost 300 guerilla members and their families started the reintegration process at ETCR Héctor Ramírez. This community, committed to maintaining and strengthening peace, has managed to buy this land and built the Centro Poblado Héctor Ramírez. The town is organized around a community cooperative that manages the income obtained through sustainable productive projects, such as pineapple, passion fruit, and coffee crops, fishing, and ecotourism.

In 2020, around 250 adults and 60 children live in the community, which is organized around the indigenous philosophy of "Buen Vivir" (Good Living), "conceptualized as collective and integrative well-being, where the subject of wellbeing is not the individual, but the relation between an individual and his/her specific cultural-natural environment" (Chaves, Macintyre, Verschoor, & Wals, 2018, p. 153; Morin & Delgado, 2014). Buen Vivir philosophy in the community looks for equitable education, health, housing, and food for everyone. Community people possess deep knowledge about the plants and the land, the animals, and their ecosystems, the weather and agriculture, among other things, developed during the years living in the mountains. Education is highly important. Among the educational initiatives, a library named after former guerrilla member Alfonso Cano—a leader of critical education—was opened in 2018. In the process of peacebuilding, the library has become a thinking center and the space for the design and implementation of educational activities.

Even though people in this community have not read Paulo Freire, they live and embody a critical consciousness and the main tenets of critical literacies in their daily life. The community organized an Education Committee, in a horizontal alliance with a university, to co-construct a relevant and own educational model for the community. This model is characterized by: (1.) the recognition of local knowledges, practices, and identities; (2.) a critical lens toward rural education; (3.) transformative praxis and political commitment in education; and (4.) education that works to achieve *Buen Vivir* in the community.

In this context, critical literacies take different forms; for example, the town houses are decorated with murals that contest dominant narratives about the former guerrilla members and their identity; ex-combatants write their own stories and visions of the future in *crónicas*; children learn about the history of the armed conflict and rural traditions through theater and playwriting; children learn about the importance of the land and its conservation through an analysis of the global forces that influence their relationship with the land as well as local practices of sustainable food production; the popular library Alfonso Cano organizes activities and events to promote a critical reading of social reality in the process of peacebuilding; and, finally, children and youth create their own critical means of communication through a community newspaper and a local radio, where they offer analysis and versions of the news that resist stereotyped representations of the community on the dominant media. With this, the community uses literacy beyond its functional purposes, as a praxis to read, rewrite, and transform their rural social realities.

Vignette 2: Pedagogy of the Earth and the Landless Movement

In 2005, a group of Brazilian peasants, members of social movements, entered the undergraduate Pedagogy of the Earth course at the Federal University of Minas Gerais, Brazil (UFMG). The teacher education program was the result of a partnership between the Ministry of Agrarian Development, the Landless Movement, the Via Campesina social movement, and the National Institute of Colonization and Agrarian Reform (Incra). The graduates from the program would be able to work as teachers in their communities of origin (campings and settlements) as teachers of Language Arts (including foreign languages); mathematics; life and natural sciences; social sciences; and humanities.

The program curriculum was based on the pedagogy of alternation, which combines classroom and distance education. The academic year was organized into classroom and non-classroom modules, or school-time and community-time for students to engage in learning in the city (university/ school) and the country (community). The "community time" was spent in each of the students' communities, settlements, or occupied encampments, where families wait to be settled for an unknown amount of time. Despite the communities being under-resourced, the pedagogy of the earth was coherent with the social movement education premise that students need to engage in socially beneficial work.

Caldart (2009) states that the movement's agenda included education as a result of the lack of schools in the settlements where the militants lived, or camps where landless families lived while fighting for the right to the land. The movement's educational perspective criticized the "rural" approach to education, which did not reflect their peasant identities. However, it was necessary to transform public schools for the achievement of the movement's educational goals, a "transition within the MST—from a movement of popular educators to a movement of public school teachers" (Tarlau, 2015, p. 5). A new pedagogy is developed within the movement, firmly based on Freire's critical pedagogy and the liberation theology, as well as the thoughts of Gramsci and Florestan Fernandes. Our teacher education program was a response to the need to educate teachers of the movements to teach in (more appropriately named) "country" schools. All the students were peasants—activists fighting for the redistribution of land, the conditions to produce food, and live a dignified life (Tarlau, 2015). Thus, the Pedagogy of the Earth represents an ethical and political approach to transformative education led by activists concerned with critically reading their reality for transformational actions. Critical literacies are enacted through the constant analysis of the texts originated in the university's discourses, challenging potential asymmetrical power relations regarding different ways of knowing and doing within the university and the social movement.

According to Leher and Vittoria (2015), the education of the landless movement converges popular education and Marxist Critical Pedagogies. Every day during the school-time immersion on the university campus, students prepared a mystical introduction to the day (*mística*), which summarized the previous day's experiences. The *mística* is understood as a symbolic political representation, a cognitive praxis, and a social movement frame for the interpretation and articulation of counterhegemonic alternatives (Issa, 2007). The *místicas* were the dramatic enactment of significant events, represented through written texts, drawings, and elements of their work and struggle, such as seeds, earth, tools, and agricultural tools. After a long day of class, the students got together to make sense of the education provided by college professors within the movement's pedagogy for country schools.

Vignette 3: A Grassroots Teacher Activist Group

In the early 2000s teachers across the United States faced the growing pressures of neoliberal forces: school closures, high-stakes tests, decreased autonomy of teachers, dramatic reductions in school spending. It was during this time that grassroots teachers' groups sprouted up around the United States—from Chicago to New York City, Washington DC, and San Francisco to St. Louis. What united many of these groups was the agency of educators to envision and create alternative realities for public education; realities infused with social justice pedagogy. In 2000, Mary Ann Kramer and I, Rebecca, started a teacher inquiry group focused on generating critical literacies in classrooms across the lifespan. We invited a diverse group of teachers to collaboratively move through the cycle of popular education, inquiring, reflecting, and acting together. Over time, this small group grew into a network called Educators for Social Justice (ESJ), which includes over 1,000 educators and many dedicated leaders (including a current majority Womyn of Color Board). This group was born out of the need to reinvigorate a critical project in literacy education—linking literacy education to social and political struggles.

For years, we worked together to create classroom- and community-based instances of critical literacy practice. Whether advocating for human rights at the Old Court House, designing a campaign for adult literacy education, creating Teach-Ins to support racial justice, supporting adult education students in their efforts to keep their school open, hosting a Banned Books celebration, or crafting Solidarity Statements—we knew that literacy teaching and activism were interconnected; one infusing the other. As we organized for social movements, we drew on and created powerful literacy practices to change social conditions.

In our individual and collective social movement organizing and activism—from the womyn's movement, civil rights movement, anti-nuclear movement, immigrant rights movements to organizing within schools and for environmental rights—we collectively discerned that group-centered leadership and popular education were central principles guiding our work. Several of us attended organizing workshops at Highlander, a popular education center in New Market, Tennessee. We drew on the wisdom of organizers and educators such as John Berry Meachum and Mary Meachum and the abolitionist teaching on the Freedom Schools in the Mississippi River (Webster Moore, 1973), Ella Baker and the Student Non-violent Coordinating Committee and Black Freedom Movement (Ransby, 2003), Septima Clark, Joann Robinson, Myles Horton and the Citizenship Schools (Stokes-Brown, 1990). They offer examples of group-centered leadership that are strategic and have historical roots that continue to impact the education for liberation movement today.

In 2009, participants in this group collectively wrote a book which features both case examples of critical literacy practice across the lifespan and also theoretical and pedagogical for enacting critical literacy education (Rogers, Mosley, Kramer, & LSJTRG, 2009). This model includes the elements of building community, developing critical stances, critical inquiry and analysis, and action. At the heart of this framework is the popular education cycle which is committed to a horizontal relation of power whereas people engage in a problem-posing, problem-solving process. In a community, teachers can practice criticality and take action to change the material conditions of their classrooms, schools, and communities. We reframe the "teaching of critical literacy" to "organizing for social justice" and, in this process, critical literacies emerge.

Along the way, there have been debates about the amount of emphasis placed on awareness raising and social action. ESJ has done both. There have been material differences made through this collective work. The network itself was a material outcome of critical literacy praxis. That is, the building of a network is a form of organizing from which critical literacies emerge. Adult literacy teachers and students organized to keep a school open. For 15 years, teachers organized a social justice conference at a local school. We have organized rapid-response Teach-Ins to speak out about continued police brutality. In these forums, educators learn how to address racial violence as part of the literacy curriculum. We continue to work in coalition with regional organizations to change school district policy around the suspension of Children of Color from school. These efforts matter to keep children in school and #BTP (#Break the School to Prison Pipeline). ESJ creates a counter-narrative that showcases educators who have reclaimed professional development and are leading the grassroots educational reform.

The network continues to live outside of formalized institutions of teacher education and higher education. Through teacher-led, radical professional development, ESJ provides a "meeting space" for educators across the region and across the life span to connect, inspire, and organize for social justice in their schools.

***

The three vignettes highlight transformations in the way people enact and embody critical literacy around the globe. First, these initiatives are born in the community out of a necessity for social change. That is, there is a sense of urgency as they respond to current social concerns. Second, the vignettes represent communal efforts with horizontal power relationships, where participation, learning, and collaboration take place. Third, across the vignettes there is a link between the materiality of organizing for social justice and critical literacy praxis. In these contexts, critical literacy is not an intentional practice planned by a teacher or leader, it is the organic result of social action. It moves beyond critical awareness and installs itself at the core of social organization. Finally, the three vignettes center epistemologies of the South by moving Black, indigenous, rural/country knowledges/values to the heart of social organization and praxis. They occur in the everyday, in-and-out of school, communal experience of people who are already empowered to take over social action.

Critiques of Critical Literacy

In our own work as critical literacy scholars, we have been aware of the continued debates about the role of critical literacies in social transformation. Freire's life and legacy are often used interchangeably with critical literacy. Tuck and Yang (2012) make the point that Freire situates the work of liberation in the minds of the oppressed without comprehensive recognition of settler colonialism. They argue that liberation, in this sense, becomes a metaphor of the mind and the "rest will follow." Put in this way, the project of critical literacy needs to include awareness raising and joining together with social justice movement organizing to avoid "settler harm reduction" (Tuck & Yang, 2012, p. 21). Consciousness raising without struggle to change material conditions that reproduce systemic inequities will not contribute to collective liberation. Some critical literacy frameworks address this reality and insist on a social action component which links educational literacies with movement building (e.g., Lewison, Leland, & Harste, 2007). Given the sociopolitical contexts discussed at the start of this chapter, it is not without surprise that the action component gives educators a great deal of uncertainty. Perhaps, this is one of the reasons that critical literacy has failed to take off in any kind of comprehensive way in teacher education.

Morgan (1997) provides an overview of critiques of critical literacy which come mainly from poststructuralists and feminists: (1.) they question the authority of truth as connected with ideological distortions; that is, people coming to understand their "true" oppression/liberation; (2.) trusting radical pedagogical theorists to drive social change is difficult when their arguments are made through dense academic discourses accessible only to the elite; (3.) the conceptions of power as "power-over" or "empower" is problematic; (4.) and, finally, the unproblematic celebration of student difference, life experiences, and voice in the "innocent" concept of "dialogue," which is often associated with Freirean methods, could be ineffective to achieve social transformation because of the power relations at play. These critiques are a reminder that critical literacy practices must continually be held up for reflexive analysis.

Further, discourses of individuality (ironically) surround critical literacy. This is problematic given the genealogy of critical literacy can be traced to indigenous leaders working in community, freedom fighters, abolitionists, etc. Important in these global antecedents is the role of group-centered leadership and womyn-led efforts. Yet, in current scholarship of critical literacy, the default major citations are given to white men from the Global North (e.g., Giroux, McLaren, Ira Shor, Aronowitz, and Colin Lankshear) (Freire and Allan Luke as an exception in this group).

The analysis of the vignettes offers some insights about the new trajectories and challenges of critical literacy in action. Vignette 1 presents a case where critical pedagogies and literacy emerged organically from the community desire to achieve *Buen Vivir* in the context of peacebuilding. This vignette shows a grassroot organization where social action truly involves communal organization and resistance as they want to maintain their identity while working toward peace amidst the challenges of rural Colombia. The role of academia in this process is to learn, collaborate, and accompany the process in a horizontal relationship, where the community takes responsibility for their needs and desires; scholars are open to learn from the community; and social transformation is embodied collectively in everyday practices. In this context, critical literacy is part of building, reflecting, resisting, creating awareness, and transforming social reality. It also implies a physical and epistemological connection between the urban and rural Other.

Vignette 2 shows a case where learners would subvert the traditional approaches to higher education. The after-class meetings and the *místicas* allowed students to occupy the large estate (latifundio) of knowledge. Members of social movements planned together their future as teachers who would implement bottom-up pedagogies in the mainstream schools of the rural area. These pedagogies were the basis for educating children and youth to resist agro-imperialism and foster sustainable agriculture, fair trade, farmworkers' rights, and food sovereignty. On the other hand, in a dialogical relation with social movements, the universities had to question power relations across a curriculum. The learners were quite aware of how they wanted to reconstruct and redesign education in their sociopolitical realities, and the university had to invent new ways of teaching, learning, and impacting society.

Vignette 3 offers perhaps a typical example of the kind of social justice organizing that occurs from teacher-led groups across the United States. Many of the teachers in the inner circle/leadership were from privileged school contexts (either schools with resources or from higher education). There have been pockets of what could be considered substantive action and modest changes (changes to practice, changes to identity, changes in narratives). Yet, teachers remain undervalued and underpaid, schools are inequitably funded and segregated, and the school-to-prison pipeline still exists. Critical literacy practitioners must connect with social justice unionism to make lasting reforms.

Radically Imagining a Future for Transnational Critical Literacy Scholarship

Many overviews of critical literacy have been written that have influenced our own understanding of the field (see, Luke, 2012; Morgan, 1997; Morrell, 2008; Vasquez, Janks, & Comber, 2019). In this chapter, we have paid tribute to and push beyond Freire's work to examine embodied social theories that have guided people in their quest for freedom across time and place. There is a rising push of recent scholarship generated from the Global South that emphasizes the global presence of critical literacy praxis around the world. For example, in Brazil, as part of the National Literacies Project (Monte Mor, 2019), Menezes de Souza (2011) suggests a redefinition of critical literacy that encompasses the pedagogical task of preparing learners for confrontations with differences of all kinds. In his perspective, the Freirean concept of listening acquires vital importance. More than learning to listen to each other, it is essential to learn to listen to ourselves listening to the other (Menezes de Souza, 2011). Careful and critical listening leads to looking for other forms of interaction that are not even direct confrontation nor the pursuit of the harmonious elimination of differences. Duboc and Ferraz (2018) problematize orientations for critical literacies in fostering language education for social change. These orientations include embracing the contradictions and acknowledging the needs of revision in the field of critical literacies; overcoming the dichotomy between the micro and macro levels of spaces for change; exploring the possibilities of social media for new ways of activism; and emphasizing a sense of belonging among language teacher professional communities.

Yet, what if we are not in need of any more scholarship? What if what we need is more strategic organizing and networking as we are engaged in with the Transnational Critical Literacy Network? Our own work for this chapter is a case in point—for many weeks we met across time and place—to consider the lived realities in Colombia, Brazil, and the United States. We shared and listened to each other's stories, struggles, and experiences. In this process of radically imagining the future of critical literacy, we offer a list of "what ifs" as a starting point to move the field forward.

- What if scholars collectively wrote an open letter to professional organizations describing the scholarly integrity and impact of social justice organizing connected to schools, community centers, and institutions of higher education? This letter could make a case for this kind of engaged scholarship and ways to examine its value outside of commonly used academic metrics.
- What if we learn from social movements already taking place globally and strengthen action-oriented partnerships to imagine new routes for education?
- What if we change the competitive, individualistic work in academia for community goals and desires?
- What if we disrupt the logic of academic prestige through publication and start valuing outreach engagement activities?
- What if we learn from and accept other forms of language and discourse in knowledge building?
- What if we reflect with the community on their own visions so that our collaboration works toward dignity and generosity?
- What if we challenge neoliberal perspectives on development that position rural, indigenous, and Global South peoples as deficient?
- What if we work to build historical memories shaping narratives of marginalized groups that are meaningful for the communities and their realities?
- What if we take critical literacy education out of the classroom through lasting engagements and commitments with communities?
- What if . . .

References

Bell, B., Gaventa, J., & Peters, J. (1990). *We make the road by walking: Conversations on education and social change: Myles Horton and Paulo Freire.* Temple University.

Brooks, J. S., & Normore, A. H. (2010). Educational leadership and globalization: Literacy for a glocal perspective. *Educational Policy, 24*(1), 52–82.

Caldart, R. S. (2009). Educação do campo: notas para uma análise de percurso. *Trabalho, Educação e Saúde, 7*(1), 35–64.

Cappellacci, I., Guelman, A., Loyola, C., Palumbo, M., Said, S., & Tarrio, L. (2018). Disciplinar indómitos y acallar inútiles: la Educación Popular y las Pedagogías Críticas interpeladas. In A. Guelman, F. Cabaluz, & M. Salazar (Eds.), *Educación Popular y Pedagogías Críticas en América Latina y el Caribe* (pp. 27–42). CLACSO.

Chaves, M., Macintyre, T., Verschoor, G., & Wals, A. (2018). Radical ruralities in practice: Negotiating buen vivir in a Colombian network of sustainability. *Journal of Rural Studies, 59*, 153–162.

Duboc, A., & Ferraz, D. de M. (2018). Reading ourselves: Placing critical literacies in contemporary language education. *Revista Brasileira de Linguística Aplicada, 18*(2), 227–254.

Freire, P. (1970). *Pedagogy of the oppressed*. Seabury Press.

Issa, D. (2007). Praxis of empowerment: Mística and mobilization in Brazil's landless rural workers' movement. *Latin American Perspectives, 34*(2), 124–138.

Leher, R., & Vittoria, P. (2015). Social movements and critical pedagogy in Brazil: From the origins of popular education to the proposal of a permanent forum. *Journal for Critical Education Policy Studies, 13*(3), 145–162.

Lewison, M., Leland, C., & Harste, J. (2007). *Creating critical classrooms: K-8 reading and writing with an edge*. Routledge.

Luke, A. (2012). Critical literacy: Foundational notes. *Theory into Practice, 51*(1), 4–11.

Mejía, M. (2011). Educación y pedagogía en América Latina, una práctica con historia. En Viceministerio de Educación Alternativa y Especial (Eds.), *Educaciones y pedagogías críticas desde el sur: Cartografías de la educación popular* (pp. 15–35). CEAAL.

Menezes de Souza, L. M. (2007). Editor's preface. *Critical Literacy: Theories and Practices, 1*(1), 4–5.

Menezes de Souza, L. M. (2011). Para uma redefinição de letramento crítico: conflito e produção de significação. In R. F. Maciel & V. A. Araújo (Eds.), *Formação de Professores de Línguas: ampliando perspectivas* (1st ed., pp. 128–140). Paco Editorial.

Monte Mor, W. (2019). Formação Docente e Educação Linguística: uma perspectiva linguístico-cultural-educacional. In W. M. Silve & R. Muñoz Campos (Eds.), *Desafios da Formação de Professores na Linguística Aplicada* (pp. 187–206). Pontes.

Morgan, W. (1997). *Critical literacy in the classroom: The art of the possible*. Routledge.

Morin, E., & Delgado, C. (2014). *Reinventar la educación: hacia una metamorfosis de la humanidad*. Multiversidad Real Edgar Morin.

Morrell, E. (2008). *Critical literacy and urban youth: Pedagogies of access, dissent, and liberation*. Routledge.

Quintar, E. (2018). Crítica teórica, crítica histórica. Tensiones epistémicas e histórico políticas. In A. Guelman, F. Cabaluz, & M. Salazar (Eds.), *Educación Popular y Pedagogías Críticas en América Latina y el Caribe* (pp. 15–26). CLACSO.

Ransby, B. (2003). *Ella Baker and the Black freedom movement*. University of North Carolina Press.

Roberts, P. (2015). Paulo Freire and Utopian education. *Review of Education Pedagogy and Cultural Studies, 37*(5), 376–392.

Rogers, R., Mosley, M., Kramer, M., & LSJTRG. (2009). *Designing socially just learning communities: Critical literacy education across the lifespan*. Routledge.

Schipani, A. (2017). Rightwing populist firebrand eyes presidency in Brazil. *FT.Com*. Retrieved from http://ezproxy.umsl.edu/login?url=https://search-proquest-com.ezproxy.umsl.edu/docview/1975513675?accountid=14595

Schugurensky, D. (2011). Intellectual biography. In B. Richard (Ed.), *Continuum library of education thought Paulo Freire* (pp. 10–48). Continuum.

Snider, C. M. (2018). "The perfection of democracy cannot dispense with dealing with the past": Dictatorship, memory, and the politics of the present in Brazil. *The Latin Americanist, 62*(1), 55–79.

Spigolon, N. (2016). "Escritos Íntimos" e Escrita de si: Por entre as páginas e a vida de Elza Freire. *Revista Brasileira De Pesquisa (Auto)Biográfica, 1*(2), 254–268.

Stokes-Brown, C. (Ed.) (1990). *Ready from within: A First person narrative of Septima Clark and the civil rights movement*. Africa World Press.

Tarlau, R. (2015). How do new critical pedagogies develop? Public education, social change, and landless workers in Brazil. *Teachers College Record, 117*(11).

Torres-Carrillo, A. (2016). *Educación Popular y Movimientos Sociales en América Latina*. Biblos.

Tuck, E., & Yang, W. K. (2012). Decolonization is not a metaphor. *Decolonization: Indigeneity, Education, & Society, 1*(1), 1–40.

Vasquez, V., Janks, H., & Comber, B. (2019). Critical literacy as a way of being and doing. *Language Arts, 96*(5), 300–311.

Webster Moore, N. (1973). John Berry Meachum (1789–1854): St. Louis Pioneer Black abolitionist, educator, and preacher. *Missouri Historical Society Bulletin, 29*(2), 94–103.

Zinn, H. (2005). *A people's history of the United States*. Harper Perennial Modern Classics.

1.3

LITERACIES UNDER NEOLIBERALISM

Enabling Ethnonationalism and Transnationalism

Rohit Mehta, Csilla Weninger, and David Martínez-Prieto

Introduction

Critical literacies, in a Freirean sense, are acts of subversion of texts to question historical and social constructions and enforcements of power differentials in the world (Freire, 2018; Shor, 1999). In youth discourses, critical literacies are manifested through critiques of dominant ideologies and political systems, active engagement in sociopolitical and cultural discourses, participation in exploration and creation of complex self-identities, and expressions of solidarity with others who have been socially or systemically marginalized (Goodman & Cocca, 2014; Luke, 2014). Historically, the liberating agency of critical literacies has been seen as a threat to the status quo by the powerful private interests who benefit from the extant social and economic systems (Chomsky, 1999; Goodman & Cocca, 2014). These interests—commonly associated with neoliberalism by its academic critics—prefer the state's assistance in the privatization of public sectors and creation of free markets for them to commoditize and profit from public spheres such as education, postal services, or health care (Giroux, 2014; Hursh, 2005). In this chapter, we share examples of critical literacies that challenge neoliberal and ethnonationalist interests and complicate transnationalism.

In recent decades, educational institutions across the world have reconstituted themselves to operate based on hyper-capitalist market models. The growing corporate push to monetize teaching and learning has perpetuated neoliberal values, ideals, and principles into youth literacies and discourses, and language education (Giroux, 2014; Schmeichel, Sharma, & Pittard, 2017). In formal settings, this has meant, among other things, the introduction of corporate management systems and accountability, evident in the prevalence of high-stakes testing as well as ranking and performance monitoring systems. Within education, the neoliberal model has reduced literacies to the mercy of decontextualized skills training and standardized assessments that claim to measure the quality of their product: students, who are both commodity and labor for the market (Apple, 2000; Au, 2016). Building standards and monolithic curricula to control youth literacies and produce new labor for the global market can be compared to a form of colonization proliferated through digital technologies, fueled by neoliberal globalization (Reyes & Segal, 2019; Sah, 2020). In more informal settings, with digital technologies and the internet, more youth are engaging in new literacies on social media platforms to market themselves as brands (influencers)—where they make and become marketable products transacted within a digital free market.

More recently, when COVID-19 pushed a transition to online work and education across the world, the internet became an even more crucial space for civic engagement and critical literacies,

DOI: 10.4324/9781003023425-4

24

while at the same time pulling more consumers into a neoliberal global economy. Neoliberalism in the digital age raises major concerns not only for literacies and language education but also for local and global citizenship and identity. As users of a corporate-controlled internet grow and education is being privatized, these neoliberal ontologies are showing potential to colonize what is left of indigenous and local literacies—those historically marginalized by dominant ways of being, knowing, and doing (Au, 2016; Cazden, 2002; Salas & Portes, 2017)—especially in the "Global South." Further, to keep global control and maintain power, neoliberal values, ideals, and principles have even been found intersecting with global nationalistic forces, such as ethnonationalism and transnationalism, in ways that have repercussions for individual and social freedom and dignity.

As a challenge to neoliberal influence, transnational critical literacies scholarship calls for critique of current policies and practices in literacies and language education and counter the marginalization and dehumanization of those without sociopolitical and economic power (Siebers, 2019). We review the extant literature that dissects the role of neoliberalism in education and discuss current concerns for literacies under neoliberalism. We present instances from global discourses to demonstrate the active role of critical literacies in countering neoliberalism. Framing our argument around digital technology and its role in enabling ethnonationalism and shaping transnationalism, we follow with possible attempts to counter the potential effects of neoliberalism on literacies education and, more broadly, global citizenship.

Definitions of Key Concepts

Literacies

As the form of the word implies, *literacies* denote a pluralistic conceptualization of what it takes for people to successfully function as meaning-makers in diverse communicative situations. This plurality characterizes several aspects of literacies. First, being literate is not merely an individual's cognitive ability to read and write but entails close familiarity with the textual conventions, histories, values, and identities of social groups whose everyday practices occasion the need for reading and writing (Gee, 2008; Street, 1995). Second, being literate cannot simply entail competence in reading and writing print. Digital technology has diversified the notion of *text* and also made traditional understandings of authorship more complex. *Literacies* not only recognizes the legitimacy of diverse semiotic modes and technologies of meaning-making (such as visual, embodied, digital. or multimodal) and authorship but also advocates their inclusion in formal education (New London Group, 1996). Third, because *literacies* see meaning-making as always situated within sociocultural groups engaged in communicative practices, it also underscores the diverse histories, conventions, and practices of various communities. In this conceptualization, elite codes that are often expected and taught in formal institutions are only one of many co/existing, valid systems of meaning-making. Such a pluralistic conceptualization does not mean an uncritical celebration of multilingualism or diversity (Kubota, 2016). It entails an acute awareness of the unequal social valuation of different forms of literacy and the resulting inequalities among social groups based on access to and mastery of these literacies. Consequently, *literacies* also necessitate a critical stance toward itself, or, toward a singular *literacy* as an ideological instrument of institutional private interests that can be used to establish and justify social hierarchies and to maintain the status quo.

Neoliberalism

Neoliberalism is a set of economic and social policies and processes based on the principle that markets can and should be in charge of social goods (Rogers, Mosley, & Folkes, 2009; Thorsen, 2010). It values competitive markets and the freedom of individual choice within them. It discourages governmental attempts to interfere in the market unless governmental involvement is needed in setting up systems, structures, and standards that create spaces for the free market to transact (Hursh, 2005). Neoliberalism today is not simply an economic policy; it is a foundational logic that uses market principles to organize all aspects of social and cultural life, including education (Schmeichel et al., 2017). As one of the few remaining public spaces in the United States, education has been a prime target for privatization. For instance, in 2016–2017, approximately 89% of all K–12 school children in the United States were enrolled in public schools, with school revenues totaling $736 billion (National Center for Educational Statistics, n.d.)—making education a tempting sector for privatization.

Ethnonationalism

Ethnonationalism and neoliberalism have formed a transactional relationship, each providing for the needs of the other. Neoliberalism has increasingly benefited from enabling ethnonationalist sentiments in parts of the world (Agbaria, 2018; Baruah, 2012; Rodgers, 2018), pledging a future with individual liberty to participate in and profit from the free market—with minimal interference from the state. Neoliberal utopia is sold as an auspicious opportunity in times of economic instability. However, in policy and practice, private interests exploit the free markets to serve big businesses over public interest (Bessner & Sparke, 2017). A role for ethnonationalist states, here, is to divert public attention away from the exploitation (Shtern, 2016; Zia, 2020). It diverts by attaching an ethnic identity to the national identity, branding the latter as an epitome of ethnonationalist values and principles, marketed to the public as the voice of unity and harmony, though it is actually an alarming attempt at homogenization (Arthur, 2015). Any public dissatisfaction with the state of the free market can be dissolved through media portrayals of the "other" as a threat to economic prosperity, offering "answers" for hurdles to individual power and wealth (e.g., in Nazi Germany othering Jews, or, ironically, in Jewish ethnonationalism in Israel othering Palestinians (Shtern, 2016)).

Transnationalism

The connotation of *transnationalism* can vary drastically depending on the context and is an evolving concept, especially with rapidly changing demographics in the United States. In the context of Latin America, the analysis of transnationalism has emphasized the hegemonic dominance of the United States among populations south of its border in terms of corporate dominance and rapacious capitalism (Briggs, McCormick, & Way, 2008; Galeano, 2013), the negative impact of neoliberal practices among disadvantaged populations (Hernández-Zamora, 2017), and the perpetuation of social disparities through educational practices (Zúñiga, Hammann, & Sánchez García, 2016). Transnationalism has also been defined as the international connections that individuals have across communities divided by policies and borders (Sánchez, 2007). This understanding has transformed with the changing global demographics in the United States (Salas & Portes, 2017) and Latin American countries, which have experienced waves of return migration in the last decade (Alcántara-Hewitt, 2013). Transnationalism has been associated with technology to highlight how the identity construction of transnationals is not limited by physical contact of communities and transforms with digital communication (Christiansen, 2015). Additionally, transnationalism has been defined as a migration process which involves emotional costs to individuals (Oliveira, 2018). Incorporating these varying conceptualizations, Skerrett (2020) describes *transnationalism* as a "phenomenon wherein people, through a mix of necessity and choice, live their lives across two or more countries. This lifestyle generates cross-national familial, social, educational, cultural, economic, sociopolitical, and other networks, with their associated benefits and challenges" (p. 501).

Historical, Current, and/or Emerging Theory

Impact of Neoliberalism on Literacies and Literacy Education

The reconceptualization of education in market-economic terms has its roots in Human Capital Theory (HCT) (Becker, 1962). HCT postulates that there is a causal relationship between a person's educational experience and their socioeconomic power (their income) (Gillies, 2011). These beneficial economic effects are claimed to also impact at the societal level so that higher overall levels of education will positively impact a country's national economy. At the center of the HCT model is the individual as a rational, enterprising agent who devises courses of action to maximize their economic benefits (Tan, 2014). Importantly, this *Homo economicus* is understood as themselves a form of mobile capital—a bundle of knowledge, skills, and dispositions that is accumulated through education and valued on the (global) economic market (Attick, 2017).

Literacy as the ability to read and write has always been associated with economic development and upward social mobility, even if such positive association has not consistently been observed (Graff, 1979). Nevertheless, one clear effect of a marked economic framing of literacies has been the touting of effective communication as an important "soft skill" for successful participation in an increasingly service-oriented economy (Fairclough, 1999; Weninger & Kan, 2013). Language and literacy as the pillars of "effective communication" are generally understood to refer to codified, elite systems of meaning-making, whose mastery must be verified through standardized language assessment. Literacy, in this iteration, has become a commodity.

The commodification of literacy has had a number of effects on how it is defined and taught. First, there has been an increasing penetration of commercial interest into the public education domain through the provision of testing, data analytics, teacher professional development, educational technologies, and even content in the form of literacy programs (Au, 2016; Ball, 2017). Such private-market educational "products" often demand strict compliance with narrowly defined goals and processes that fail to meet the needs of diverse groups of educators and learners (Freebody, 2000; Pandya, 2014). Second, given the global economic currency of standard English, there has been an exponential growth of the private business sector that caters to the training and assessment of English language skills (Foteini-Vassiliki, 2016). Testing in particular has become a multibillion-dollar industry that reinforces colonial structures of domination through its emphasis on native-speaker varieties (Tupas, 2020). What we see through these developments is a narrowing of the notion of literacy (Weninger, 2019); away from the pluralistic conceptualization defined earlier toward one where (singular) literacy is equated with internationally intelligible English (or other major "global" languages) used primarily for effective communication within transaction-oriented encounters.

Literacies in the Web of Neoliberal Ethnonationalism

In ethnonational contexts, literacies play a dual role: as propaganda machine for the state and critical agent for dissent and social justice. As a long-term propaganda device for ethnonationalism, states have been revising textbooks erasing histories and narratives that do not feed their agendas (Kumar, 2014; Peled-Elhanan, 2012), instead pushing a dominant singular literacy as a standard to re-educate and assimilate. For instance, in 2015, *Al Jazeera* news reported that, "Hindu nationalists have been rewriting school textbooks in some states and holding training camps for teenage boys and girls in an apparent attempt to inculcate children into their cause." When blocked by previous standards, textbooks revised by Hindu nationalists are being offered as "supplementary material," which students frequently use to work on projects, even though they "deviate vastly from the guidelines by relying heavily on religious subjects and mythology" (Kumar, 2014, p. 10). Since COVID-19 caused a transition to online education, in the guise of relaxing curricular expectations the Indian government mandated that government-run schools no longer have to teach chapters on "democratic rights, secularism, federalism, and citizenship," among other topics (Sanghera, 2020, p. 3). Revising curriculum provides an opportunity to curb dissent early and align students with a monolithic, dominant literacy. In Israel, Peled-Elhanan (2012) noted textbooks are returning to a blunt, nationalistic, nonscientific presentation of the world, of Israel, and of the political context, convincing young children to serve in the military. In textbooks, portrayals of marginalized groups such as Muslims (or Palestinians in Israel's case) ranges from absent to negative, "imbued with some form of extreme nationalism" (Kestler-D'Amours, 2012).

To some extent, the internet offers a space to counter ethnonationalist discourses through critical literacies. Unfortunately, critical examination and analysis of multimodal texts, such as fabricated visuals and facts, has become the responsibility of the individual meaning-maker (Mehta & Guzman, 2018), many of whom do not have access to or knowledge of critical literacies resources—let alone a formalized education on new and digital media. In such cases, the state can brand "the nation" as it pleases to serve its own economic and religious agendas (Siebers, 2019), reaching more people through social media than educational institutions. Social media, which was once heralded as a platform for free and independent speech, especially dissent, has rapidly become an unsafe environment for marginalized voices, attacks on whom have no longer been restricted to the safety of the internet but have been transferred to physical violence to silence dissent (Figure 1.3.1, Joshi, 2020b), giving ethnonationalist states more control over discourses in the media. Focus on ethnonationalist discourses helps shift the public attention away from failing promises of free market, economic growth, employment, and development—benefits of which have been going only to a few big corporations and ultrawealthy individuals interested in maintaining the status quo.

Transnational Influence of Neoliberalism on Literacies: The Example of Mexico

Unlike the United States, in which the extant educational system has been described as a tool to maintain the status quo of the privileged (Apple, 2000; Gee, 2008), in parts of Central and Latin America, such as Mexico and Colombia, education was originally intended and designed to

Figure 1.3.1 Photograph of a bleeding university student in Delhi, India who was beaten up by state-backed hoodlums after having protested ethnonationalist policies and laws.

Source: Posted on 5 January 2020, by journalist Faye D'Souza on Instagram.

accomplish the social justice goals of people's revolutions (Levinson, 2001). Nonetheless, through transnational influence and irreflective implementation of neoliberal practices in higher education, educational institutions in Central and Latin America have been diverted far from their original goals.

Education in Mexico, for instance, has also been severely impacted by neoliberalism. After a series of economic crises, Mexico adopted a neoliberal educational system (Czarnecki & Chanes, 2018). Unlike previous Mexican educational systems, which aimed to form reflective professionals, neoliberalism in Mexico is focused on creating a qualified labor force to satisfy local and global market needs (Torres, 2009). After the 2008 economic crisis and the increase in nationalism and xenophobia against Mexicans residing in the United States, many Mexicans decided to go (back) to Mexico with their school-aged children, now that it too offered U.S.-like economic growth paths through education. For this reason, the number of Mexican transnationals—that is, Mexican individuals who were educated in U.S. schools and returned to Mexico—pursuing higher education degrees has increased significantly, especially in English language teaching degrees. To their advantage, transnational English speakers get a superior treatment over those who learned English as a second language (Martínez-Prieto & Lindahl, 2019). However, despite this salient nativism, Mexican transnationals pursuing a degree in English Language Teaching are not completely successful in terms of adapting to a new school system. In this regard, some of the main constraints that transnationals face when adapting to the Mexican educational system relate to their own lack of academic digital literacies due to their unfair and uneven educational experience in the United States.

In general, compared to their Mexican counterparts, U.S. schools have better access to technology. However, not all students in U.S. schools are provided with equal opportunities. Gee (2008) pointed out that neoliberalism in U.S. schooling *a priori* divides students according to their future role in the U.S. economy. Even though many Mexicans living in the United States are highly involved in their children's education in spite of their lack of formal educational background (Olivera, 2018), access and social mobility for many Mexicans studying in the United States are limited due, in part, to an unfair U.S. educational system that intentionally does not address the needs of transnational students (Skerrett, 2020). Regardless of the contingent nature of transnationalism, exposure of transnationals to different educational and ideological systems of the dominant classes received through formal education can impact their educational trajectory across borders (Martínez-Prieto, 2020). In other words, ideologies prevalent in some formal education systems, such as neoliberal and ethnonational perspectives, are pivotal to understanding transnationalism.

Reviews of and Implications for Research

The Impact of Neoliberalism on Literacies and Literacy Education

Researchers have been documenting how neoliberal reframings of education and specifically literacy have impacted policy and practice, highlighting tensions and contradictions that the infusion of market logic, private interest, as well human capital perspectives have spawned in various local contexts. In policy, these tensions have been generated partly by the fact that education policy is increasingly being formulated at the global level, by technical experts who move between public, private, and third-sector spheres (Ball, 2017). Tracing policy network connections and influences in the United States, Brass (2014) posited that the Common Core State Standards movement epitomizes neoliberal education policy—designed by a network of venture philanthropists, nongovernmental organizations, and educational businesses with the primary goal of creating an educational service market. The resultant narrowing of educators' professional roles to that of compliant service providers creates tensions as teachers try to reconcile accountability with the ethics of care many see as a core value of the profession (Loh & Liew, 2016).

Weninger (2019) similarly explored how the global policy initiative for twenty-first-century skills, specifically digital literacy, was vernacularized (Rizvi & Lingard, 2010) within the Singapore context. She argued that, on the one hand, digital literacy sits uneasily at the nexus of empowerment discourses of democratic citizenship and creativity and, on the other, bolsters economic arguments for the ICT upskilling of a compliant workforce. She examined policy and curricular positioning of digital literacy and analyzed surveys from English teachers as well as students' reported engagement with various media. Her results indicated that while creativity and digital literacy were coveted skills within national economic policy initiatives, creative expression—as an important aspect of digital literacy connected to personal empowerment—was practically nonexistent in curricula and teachers' conceptualization and was only minimally evident in students' out-of-school digital media use. Instead, in curriculum and practice, there seemed to be a disproportionate emphasis on ethics, responsibility, and cyber wellness, in line with the country's compliant educational ethos. Weninger argues that Singapore teachers find themselves unable to reconcile the economic mandate for creativity with the narrow curricular definition of digital literacy. These tensions throw into sharp relief the seemingly unproblematic rationalization of neoliberal literacy policies as tools for both democratic empowerment and economic productivity (Black, 2018).

Researchers have also documented the impact of neoliberal educational policies and education governance on teaching, teachers, and learners. An important line of scholarship has concerned standardized testing and high-stakes exams as ubiquitous elements of the accountability systems that underpin literacy education. The washback effect of testing was revealed in Pandya's (2011) year-long ethnography of a U.S. elementary classroom. She noted how a significant amount of classroom time was taken up by practicing for tests, the discussion of test-taking strategies as well as subsequent in-class discussion and evaluation of test performance. Comber (2012) and Hardy (2015) observed similar trends in Australian classrooms in the wake of the country's introduction of national assessments in literacy. As Hardy noted, teachers' whole professional practice shifted to pivot around aspects of the national assessment, so that a "logic of enumeration" became the central organizing principle to not only schooling practice but also teachers' habits (p. 335). Perhaps, even more worryingly, Holloway and Brass's (2018) research with English teachers in the U.S. clearly indicates the normalization of a new teacher subjectivity that embraces the marketized logic of education. Their analysis demonstrated that while teachers in the early 2000s reacted to federal standards-based policy mandates with suspicion and viewed them as impositions on their professional identity, English teachers one decade later readily accepted accountability, performance management, and a marketized notion of education as neutral mechanisms to aid their and their students' self-improvement.

Researchers have also begun to examine how the shifting realities of teaching are impacting learner subjectivities. Hickey's (2016) study documented some of the ways in which a neoliberal school culture impacted U.S. elementary emergent bilingual students' perspectives and experiences of academic literacy. She found that students felt anxious and pressured by the desire to do well in tests and regularly used terms associated with assessment discourse to talk about themselves and their experiences during interviews with the researcher. The children often framed their in-school literacy experiences as labor: tasks to be accomplished that had little to do with enjoyment or curiosity. In a world where language and literacy are viewed as commodities, learners are interpolated to be resourceful, strategic risk-takers who seek out "valued" opportunities and overcome challenges to achieve the desired proficiency (De Costa, 2016; de Costa, Park, & Wee, 2016). It is precisely this desire, theorized in terms of investment (Norton, 2013), that points to the complex social and political entanglements of motivation, literacy learning, power, and identity; entanglements that call for critical examination and engagement.

Neoliberalism, Transnational Exclusion, and Digital Literacies: A Case Study

To better explain the impact of neoliberalism and transnationalism on literacies, we share the case of a Mexican transnational student pursuing a degree in English Language Teaching, Mariana. Because of the neoliberal influence over educational practices in the United States and Mexico, she was systematically marginalized in her educational journey. Specifically, we concentrate on neoliberal values of efficiency, proficiency, quantification, and standardization to demonstrate how her transnational status entangled with discriminatory educational practices in both countries to negatively impact her digital literacies.

In 2014, David, the third author of this chapter, returned to central Mexico to teach in TESOL (Teaching English to Speakers of Other Languages) Teacher Preparation Programs. Through his experience, he learned that Mexican universities had unreflectively adopted neoliberal policies, where accountability had become a pivotal factor in higher education. Professors were now being evaluated according to the quantity of their work over quality of their research. A redesign of internal policies in university programs had relegated critical thinking and reflection to secondary roles. In most public universities, classes were now being designed so students produce "a quantifiable product," or *evidencias* (teaching evidence), so professors' performance could be quantified.

During David's second semester as a teacher in a public university in the state of Tlaxcala, all professors were requested by the university authorities to have students submit an inter-class *evidencia*; that is, a learning product produced by all the students who were taking the same classes regardless of the section in which they were enrolled. In theory, these *evidencias* would represent uniformity in the teaching preparation of future second language teachers. All of the junior preservice teachers (fifth–sixth semesters) were requested to create a series of wikis, videos, and online pedagogical material as part of their final *evidencia*, which accounted for 25–40% of their final grade in *all* of their classes.

David examined whether teacher candidates' digital literacies were appropriate to accomplish their *evidencia* task. Exploring preservice teachers' access to the internet and digital devices, while quantitative results showed no significant difference among preservice teachers with and without access to the internet and devices, qualitative results suggested that students without internet access struggled more to accomplish the tasks. More concerningly, one transnational preservice teacher, Mariana, decided to abandon the qualitative tasks. "*I'm sorry, David, I just can't,*" she said.

Describing her experience in the United States, Mariana mentioned she did not have access to technology classes even though she had a computer lab in her school: "*We had to share a blue computer, an old one . . . but the teachers never taught us anything . . . they didn't care.*" U.S. schooling did not prepare Mariana to use technology as part of academic preparation. In one of their tutorials, David told her that it is common in Mexico to believe that schools in the United States are better equipped in terms of technology and that students are more digitally literate than most Mexicans, to which she replied:

> Well, that's true . . . I mean, we didn't really have internet at home, my parents were very poor, that's why my father sent us back [to Mexico] . . . but in general, with my phone, I could use Facebook and Snap [chat] before all of my cousins here [in Mexico].

Mariana's teachers in the United States did not promote the use of technology for academic purposes, even if they were aware of her social media literacies. Instead, she had to learn to incorporate technology into academic work by herself:

> So, that's why it is so difficult to do [the *evidencia* task] . . . they never taught us anything [in the U.S.] . . . and my professors here [in Tlaxcala] are always in a rush to finish

the *evidencia* . . . maybe they think I know already because I lived there [in the United States] . . . but I really don't.

In early 2018, Mariana dropped out of the program. For her, educational systems in both countries had neglected to offer her academic opportunities to develop her digital literacy skills. Her case illustrates how uncritical implementation of neoliberal approaches to teacher education programs hindered her successful participation. Her educational experiences did not provide her with opportunities to connect her social media–related/derived digital practices to her educational development. Although transnational language teachers in Mexico are believed to have advantages over their Mexican national peers in terms of their bilingual and bicultural skills (Martínez-Prieto & Lindahl, 2019), some transnationals are also disadvantaged by transnational neoliberal practices. In other words, different faces of neoliberalism in the United States and Mexico frustrated Mariana's pursuit of a teaching certificate and diminished her chances of a better quality of living in her reincorporation to Mexico.

Recommendations and Forward Thinking

Critical Literacies: The Antithesis of Neoliberalism

Critical literacies are a strong contender to challenge the neoliberal assumptions governing the lives and relationships of teachers and students alike. For those oppressed by the state, critical literacies act as an agent for dissent and social justice. Educational institutions—mostly liberal higher education spaces—expose students to diverse voices and perspectives that encourage pluralism and secularism and afford youth access to literacies for social and political participation (Chomsky, 1999; Giroux, 2014). Universities are privileged spaces where educators can use their privilege to facilitate critical dialogue and transformative social action through their research, teaching, and community engagement work. Critical literacies provide the tools to create dialogue around justice, equity, and identity (Ranieri, Fabbro, & Frelih, 2016), all of which are deemed an antithesis to ethnonationalist and neoliberal private interests (Magklara, 2018; Schmeichel et al., 2017).

One important argument from critical literacies research stresses the need to reconnect (critical) literacies to communities' sociocultural practices and to identify social change as the core concern for literate identities (Albury, 2018; Comber, 2016; Luke, 2012). It is important to recognize that despite its ideological dominance in (literacy) education, the contradictions and inconsistencies of neoliberalism can also open up "spaces of action" (Goodman & Cocca, 2014, p. 210) for transformative human agency and practice. Attick (2017) urges that teachers, teacher educators, and students must engage in self-directed critical literacies and question the "dominant paradigm of the market while engaging each other in a pedagogy of interdependency" (p. 47). Roach and Stewart (2011) argued for classrooms that "engender an awareness of students' larger roles as participants in the construction of communities local and global" (p. 135). Manan (2020) noted how teachers play an agentive role in critical literacies and activism through transformative pedagogy.

Yet, not everyone has access to privileged spaces that offer them the possibility to both wield and critique the various forms of capital afforded to them (Goastellec & Välimaa, 2019). Social media remains a powerful space for critical literacies to amplify dissenting voices and thus engender transformation of perspective and action. The potential of subversive discourses to spread, especially in contexts where more traditional avenues for critical thought (the free press and universities) have largely fallen prey to neoliberal and ethnonational pressures, can be seen in some current contexts of India/Kashmir and Israel/Palestine.

Digital Literacies as Resistance

Recently, the right-wing Hindu nationalist government in India removed the autonomous status of Kashmir—the only Muslim-dominant state in India. Instead of acknowledging the attack on indigenous Kashmiri existence, the state argued in favor of economic development and prosperity of Kashmir, which arguably had been blocked by its ex-special status. Zia (2020) argued that this guise of development is "embedded in a structure of neocolonialism based on fundamentalist Hindu ethnonationalism or Hindutva and fueled by neoliberalism in which even Muslims living in India are cast as invaders and foreigners" (p. 60) (Figure 1.3.2). Further, she reminds:

> Kashmiri, doubly marked as the Other: first as Muslims and second as seekers of self-determination, fear their loss of territorial sovereignty will pave way for settler colonialism, dispossession of indigenous people and rampant exploitation of resources resulting in neocolonial maldevelopment.
>
> *(p. 60)*

Similar acts of settler colonization are on the rise in northeast India, a mélange of diverse tribal communities, where Hindu nationalists have already successfully entered schools and have actively been assimilating indigenous people—most of whom had been previously converted to Christianity by missionaries—into Hindutva through Hindi language and literacy education (Joshi, 2020a). In Israel, too, Agbaria (2018) and Shtern (2016) have highlighted how neoliberal ideals have enabled ethnonationalism to further marginalize and ghettoize Palestinians. Literacy education, here too, is at the center of assimilation through highly standardized and decontextualized endeavors; as Peled-Elhanan (2012) has pointed out, textbooks and school curricula have been weaponized to indoctrinate Israeli youth with anti-Palestinian sentiments.

Since "offline" acts of resistance are met with similar violence and suppression (see Figure 1.3.2 which shows similarities in Israel and India' approach to silencing critical voices), the biggest threat

Figure 1.3.2   Stand with Kashmir, an activist group recently blocked in India, shared on their Instagram account a video showing similarities between Israel and India's approach to suppressing critical voices.

Source: Posted by *Stand with Kashmir* on Instagram

to such ethnonationalist acts of assimilation are critical literacies that have found their home in social media spaces (see Figures 1.3.3–1.3.6). Youth are using digital spaces to create and share multimodal texts to critique dominant ideologies and practices.

In India, artist Manek D'Silva, for instance, designed a multimodal piece (Figure 1.3.3) as a representation of the suppressive measures taken by the ethnonationalist state, such as policing social media accounts and in-person gatherings that encourage critical discourses. In Figure 1.3.4, transnational artist and activist Shilo Shiv Suleman created a multimodal artwork indicating an intercultural woman as an expression of India's long oppressed women (who have been facing increased acts of rape), saluting secular roots and inclusivism, accompanied with a poem stating "I am of here".

Figure 1.3.3 Instagram post commenting on silencing of students at liberal universities in Delhi portraying Hindu nationalists and the police as brain-eating zombies and Prime Minister Narendra Modi as the evil behind it.

Source: Posted by artist *Manek D'Silva* on Instagram

Figure 1.3.4 Multimodal artwork on Instagram as an expression of India's secularism and inclusivism.

Source: Posted by artist *Shilo Shiv Suleman* on Instagram

Figure 1.3.5 A Palestinian kid shared a rap song on Instagram showing solidarity with George Floyd and the shared oppression of African Americans and Palestinians.

Source: Posted on *Wear the Peace* on Instagram

Figure 1.3.6 Instagram post from a clothing brand that uses its sales to fund charities helping refugees.

Source: Posted on *Wear the Peace* on Instagram

Figure 1.3.5 shows an Instagram post of a Palestinian kid rapping in solidarity with the African American community in the United States, paying his tribute to George Floyd.

With roots in Pakistan and South Asia, *Baude-e-sabaa* is a digital magazine run by transnational young activists, artists, and writers who are using Instagram to engage South Asian diaspora in critical and independent publishing and art. In the United States, *Decolonize This Place* is an Instagram account dedicated to "an action-oriented movement: Indigenous struggle, Black liberation, free Palestine, workers, degentrification, dismantle patriarchy." There is a plethora of international examples of critical literacies that exist on Instagram alone, which allows for flexible multimodal creativity and engagement. Through social media, such critical youth voices have been at the core of literacy practices countering ethnonationalism and neoliberalism.

Social media spaces have even allowed critical voices to not only counter ethnonationalism but in fact also use social media's embedded neoliberal practices to fund their campaigns. For instance, Figure 1.3.6 shows an Instagram post from a small clothing business that uses their sales to support charitable organizations that work with refugees in Western Asia, Europe, and Africa. This example highlights how critical literacies and practices of activism and resistance are also intertwined with the neoliberal approaches reflective of the social media spaces in which they exist. The examples from Figures 1.3.3–1.3.5 are sometimes difficult to differentiate from other similar art-based Instagram accounts that, at times, engage in influencer culture practices of delivering consistent content, designing a marketable social media image, commodifying self as a marketable product, and inviting lesser-known accounts to pay for wider audience reach—all practices that can be used to generate capital. Given the contentious nature of the work, more research is needed around activist and critical literacy practices against ethnonationalist nation states and their relation to neoliberalism.

Implications for Our Social Responsibility as Academics

As academics, we must first of all recognize that we are complicit in this neoliberal project; as teachers, teacher educators, as well as researchers. There is a host of contradictions we must reconcile: the need for our students to have access to the academic literacy of the powerful with the necessity to situate that acquisition within a critical framework that simultaneously denaturalizes (singular) literacy's ideological basis. Situated within neoliberal institutions, we need to continually work to align literacy teaching and research with learners' social milieu while fostering global consciousness. We need to apply our social-constructionist epistemological stance to counter with the positivism that underlies the metrics that determine our and our students' advancement. And, finally, we need to navigate the tension between framings of our research according to narrowly defined criteria of funding agencies and the imperative to engage in collaborative, transdisciplinary, and transnational research with real positive social impact on real communities.

Specifically, since solely "offline" life is no longer a choice in many contexts, critical literacies researchers and educators have important next steps in terms of social responsibility. First, we must develop and adopt pedagogical approaches that actively counter standardization and big-data-driven assessments and testing through an emphasis on creativity, play, and imagination as powerful tools in the construction of new realities. As part of this pedagogic plan, we must also enable the development of learner identities beyond that of future labor in a capitalistic market. Our curriculum, classroom pedagogy, and teacher persona must be "designed" to inspire students to experience and thus to believe that literacy is power. Second, shifting demographics demand a reconsideration of how we conceptualize language learning, underscoring a need to move away from "English" as being at the center of academic communities and publications in literacies research (e.g., NCTE) to new, often unimagined realities where language is independent of colonial labels that marginalize transnational students and academics. On the one hand, this could mean fully embracing multilingualism in our classrooms through supporting translanguaging and linguistic experimentation. On the other hand, this is a call for us as editors and reviewers to put into practice our beliefs in the plurality of linguistic expression when it comes to evaluating research for funding or for publication. Third, there is an urgent need to not only use digital technologies that counter neoliberal practices and policies but also to participate in the creation of new technologies rooted in anti-colonial and indigenous epistemologies. Finally, a need that cuts across all responsibilities is to actively challenge existing educational institutions we partake in and change policies to create new futures where inclusion of historically marginalized and erased populations is more than performative rhetoric—supported with shifts in power and leadership.

References

Agbaria, A. K. (2018). The 'right' education in Israel: Segregation, religious ethnonationalism, and depoliticized professionalism. *Critical Studies in Education*, *59*(1), 18–34. https://doi.org/10.1080/17508487.2016.11856 42

Albury, N. J. (2018). "If we lose their language we lose our history": Knowledge and disposition in Māori language acquisition policy. *Journal of Language, Identity & Education*, *17*(2), 69–84.

Alcántara-Hewitt, A. A. (2013). *Migration and schooling: The case of transnational students in Puebla, Mexico* (Publication No. 3599860) (Doctoral dissertation). New York University. Pro-Quest LLC.

Al Jazeera. (2015). *India's Hindu fundamentalists*. Retrieved from www.aljazeera.com/programmes/peopleand-power/2015/10/indias-hindu-fundamentalists-151008073418225.html

Apple, M. W. (2000). The cultural politics of home schooling. *Peabody Journal of Education*, *75*(1–2), 256–271. https://doi.org/10.1080/0161956X.2000.9681944

Arthur, J. (2015). Extremism and neo-liberal education policy: A contextual critique of the Trojan Horse affair in Birmingham schools. *British Journal of Educational Studies*, *63*(3), 311–328. https://doi.org/10.1080/000 71005.2015.1069258

Attick, D. (2017). *Homo Economicus* at School: Neoliberal education and teacher as economic being. *Educational Studies*, *53*(1), 37–48. https://doi.org/10.1080/00131946.2016.1258362

Au, W. (2016). Meritocracy 2.0: High-stakes, standardized testing as a racial project of neoliberal multicultural-ism. *Educational Policy*, *30*(1), 39–62. https://doi.org/10.1177/0895904815614916

Ball, S. J. (2017). Laboring to relate: Neoliberalism, embodied policy and network dynamics. *Peabody Journal of Education*, *92*(1), 29–41.

Baruah, S. (2012). *Ethnonationalism in India: A Reader*. OUP India.

Becker, G. (1962). Investment in human capital: A theoretical analysis. *The Journal of Political Economy*, *70*(5), 9–49.

Bessner, D., & Sparke, M. (2017). Nazism, neoliberalism, and the Trumpist challenge to democracy. *Environment and Planning A: Economy and Space*, *49*(6), 1214–1223. https://doi.org/10.1177/0308518X17701429

Black, S. (2018). From 'empowerment' to 'compliance': Neoliberalism and adult literacy provision in Australia. *Journal of Critical Education Policy Studies*, *16*(1), 104–144.

Brass, J. (2014). English, literacy and neoliberal policies: Mapping a contested moment in the United States. *English Teaching: Practice and Critique*, *13*(1), 112–133.

Briggs, L., McCormick, G., & Way, J. T. (2008). Transnationalism: A category of analysis. *American Quarterly*, *60*(3), 625–648.

Cazden, C. B. (2002). A descriptive study of six high school Puente classrooms. *Educational Policy*, *16*(4), 496–521.

Chomsky, N. (1999). *Profit over people: Neoliberalism and global order*. Seven Stories Press.

Christiansen, M. S. (2015). Mexicanness and social order in digital spaces contention among members of a multigenerational transnational network. *Hispanic Journal of Behavioral Sciences*, *37*, 3–22.

Comber, B. (2012). Mandated literacy assessment and the reorganization of teachers' work: Federal policy, local effects. *Critical Studies in Education*, *53*(2), 119–136.

Comber, B. (2016). *Literacy, place and pedagogies of possibility*. Routledge.

Czarnecki, L., & Chanes, D. V. (2018). Welfare regime, neoliberal transformation, and social exclusion in Mexico, 1980–2015. *Social Welfare Responses in a Neoliberal Era*, 72–87. https://doi.org/10.1163/978900438 4118_005

De Costa, P. I. (2016). *The power of identity and ideology in language learning: Designer immigrants learning English in Singapore*. Springer.

De Costa, P. I., Park, J., & Wee, L. (2016). Language learning as linguistic entrepreneurship: Implications for language education. *The Asia-Pacific Education Researcher*, *25*(5–6), 695–702.

Digest of education statistics, 2019. (n.d.). National Center for Education Statistics. Retrieved October 1, 2020, from https://nces.ed.gov/programs/digest/d19/tables/dt19_105.50.asp

Fairclough, N. (1999). Global capitalism and critical awareness of language. *Language Awareness*, *8*(2), 71–83.

Foteini-Vassiliki, K. (2016). *Indiscipline in young EFL learner classes*. Palgrave Macmillan.

Freebody, P. (2000, October). Crafting a mix: Programs and packages in literacy education. *Newsletter of the Australian Literacy Educators' Association*. Retrieved February 24, 2020, from www.alea.edu.au/documents/item/60

Freire, P. (2018). *Pedagogy of the oppressed*. Bloomsbury Publishing USA.

Galeano, E. (2013). *Las Venas Abiertas de América*. Siglo Veintiuno Ediciones-Edición Kindle.

Gee, J. P. (2008). *Social linguistics and literacies: Ideology in discourses*. Routledge.

Gillies, D. (2011). State education as high-yield investment: Human capital theory in European policy discourse. *Journal of Pedagogy*, *2*(2), 224–245.

Giroux, H. A. (2014). *Neoliberalism's war on higher education*. Haymarket Books.

Goastellec, G., & Välimaa, J. (2019). Access to higher education: An instrument for fair societies? *Social Inclusion*, *7*(1). https://doi.org/10.17645/si.v7i1.1841

Goodman, S., & Cocca, C. (2014). "Spaces of action": Teaching critical literacy for community empowerment in the age of neoliberalism. *English Teaching: Practice and Critique*, *13*(3), 210–226.

Graff, H. J. (1979). *The literacy myth: Literacy and social structure in the nineteenth-century city*. Academic Press.

Hardy, I. (2015). A logic of enumeration: The nature and effects of national literacy and numeracy testing in Australia. *Journal of Education Policy*, *30*(3), 335–362.

Hernández Zamora, G. (2017). Historias de migrantes retornados. In G. Hernández Zamora, P. Sánchez, & G. Ramírez (Eds.), *20 Años después: Jóvenes migrantes en Norte América* (pp. 47–85). UAM-ITESO-UNAM.

Hickey, P. J. (2016). "They always keep us in line": Neoliberalism and elementary emergent bilinguals. *Journal for Critical Education Policy Studies*, *14*(2), 14–40.

Holloway, J., & Brass, J. (2018). Making accountable teachers: The terrors and pleasures of performativity. *Journal of Education Policy*, *33*(3), 361–382.

Hursh, D. (2005). Neo-liberalism, markets and accountability: Transforming education and undermining democracy in the United States and England. *Policy Futures in Education*, *3*(1), 3–15.

Joshi, S. (2020a, January 3). *An Indian minister wants all students to learn Hindu religious texts so they don't 'go abroad and eat beef'*. Vice. Retrieved from www.vice.com/en_in/article/wxe8py/an-indian-minister-wants-all-students-to-learn-hindu-religious-texts-so-they-dont-go-abroad-and-eat-beef

Joshi, S. (2020b, January 6). *This is how Indians are reacting after a masked mob beat up students and teachers at a Delhi University*. Vice. Retrieved from www.vice.com/en_asia/article/qjdpmb/this-is-how-indians-are-reacting-after-a-masked-mob-beat-up-students-and-teachers-at-a-delhi-university

Kestler-D'Amours, J. (2012, May 26). Militarising education in Israeli schools. *Al Jazeera*. Retrieved from www.aljazeera.com/indepth/features/2012/06/2012624854285479.html

Kubota, R. (2016). The multi/plural turn, postcolonial theory, and neoliberal multiculturalism: Complicities and implications for applied linguistics. *Applied Linguistics*, *37*(4), 474–494.

Kumar, R. (2014, November 4). Hindu right rewriting Indian textbooks | India | Al Jazeera. *Al Jazeera*. Retrieved from www.aljazeera.com/indepth/features/2014/11/hindu-right-ideology-indian-textbooks-gujarat-20141147028501733.html

Levinson, B. U. (2001). *We are all equal: Student culture and identity at a Mexican secondary school, 1988–1998*. Duke University Press Books.

Loh, C. E., & Liew, W. M. (2016). Voices from the ground: The emotional labour of English teachers' work. *Teaching and Teacher Education*, *55*, 267–278.

Luke, A. (2012). After the testing: Talking and reading and writing the world. *Journal of Adolescent and Adult Literacy*, *56*(1), 8–13.

Luke, A. (2014). Defining critical literacy. In J. Pandya & J. Avila (Eds.), *Moving critical literacies forward: A new look at praxis across contexts* (pp. 19–31). Routledge.

Magklara, M. (2018). *Policy change in literacy education: A multi-dimensional approach to the production of the 2010 Greek-language syllabus in Cyprus*. King's College London.

Manan, S. A. (2020). Teachers as agents of transformative pedagogy: Critical reflexivity, activism and multilingual spaces through a continua of biliteracy lens. *Multilingua*, *0*(0). https://doi.org/10.1515/multi-2019-0096

Martínez-Prieto, D. (2020). *The ideological impact of U.S. curricula on Mexican transnational pre-service language teachers* (Publication no. 13164) (Doctoral dissertation). University of Texas at San Antonio. ProQuest Dissertations Publishing.

Martínez-Prieto, D., & Lindahl, K. (2019). (De)legitimization: The impact of language policy on identity development in an EFL teacher. *MEXTESOL Journal*, *43*(2), 1–11.

Mehta, R., & Guzmán, L. D. (2018). Fake or visual trickery? Understanding the quantitative visual rhetoric in the news. *Journal of Media Literacy Education*, *10*(2), 104–122.

New London Group. (1996). A pedagogy of multiliteracies: Designing social futures. *Harvard Educational Review*, *66*(1), 60–92.

Norton, B. (2013). *Identity and language learning: Extending the conversation*. Multilingual Matters.

Oliveira, G. (2018). *Motherhood across Borders*. New York University Press.

Pandya, J. (2011). *Overtested: How high-stakes accountability fails English language learners*. Teachers College Press.

Pandya, J. (2014). Standardizing, and erasing, critical literacy in high-stakes settings. In J. Zacher Pandya & J. Avila (Eds.), *Moving critical literacies forward: A new look at praxis across contexts* (pp. 160–173). Routledge.

Peled-Elhanan, N. (2012). *Palestine in Israeli School Books: Ideology and Propaganda in Education*. Tauris Academic Studies Year: 2012.

Ranieri, M., Fabbro, F., & Frelih, M. (2016). Making sense of students' media literacy and civic agency across media analysis and production. In M. Ranieri (Ed.), *Populism, Media and Education: Challenging discrimination in contemporary digital societies* (pp. 127–146). Routledge.

Reyes, M., & Segal, E. A. (2019). Globalization or colonization in online education: Opportunity or oppression? *Journal of Teaching in Social Work, 39*(4–5), 374–386.

Rizvi, F., & Lingard, B. (2010). *Globalizing education policy*. Routledge.

Roach, T., & Stewart, B. (2011). Teaching homo economicus. *Academic Exchange Quarterly, 14*(2), 130–136.

Rodgers, D. (2018). The uses and abuses of "neoliberalism." *Dissent, 65*(1), 78–87. https://doi.org/10.1353/dss.2018.0010

Rogers, R., Mosley, M., & Folkes, A. (2009). Focus on policy: Standing up to neoliberalism through critical literacy education. *Language Arts, 87*(2), 127–138.

Sah, P. K. (2020). Reproduction of nationalist and neoliberal ideologies in Nepal's language and literacy policies. *Asia Pacific Journal of Education*, 1–15. https://doi.org/10.1080/02188791.2020.1751063

Salas, S., & Portes, P. (Eds.). (2017). *U.S. Latinization: Education and the New Latino South*. SUNY Press.

Sánchez, P. (2007). Cultural authenticity and transnational Latina youth: Constructing a metanarrative across borders. *Linguistics and Education, 18*(3–4), 258–282.

Sanghera, T. (2020). *Modi's textbook manipulations* [News]. Foreign Policy. Retrieved from https://foreignpolicy.com/2020/08/06/textbooks-modi-remove-chapters-democracy-secularism-citizenship/

Schmeichel, M., Sharma, A., & Pittard, E. (2017). Contours of neoliberalism in US empirical educational research. *Curriculum Inquiry, 47*(2), 195–216.

Shor, I. (1999). What is critical literacy? *Journal of Pedagogy, Pluralism, and Practice, 1*(4), 2.

Shtern, M. (2016). Urban neoliberalism vs. ethno-national division: The case of West Jerusalem's shopping malls. *Cities, 52*, 132–139. https://doi.org/10.1016/j.cities.2015.11.019

Siebers, H. (2019). Are education and nationalism a happy marriage? Ethno-nationalist disruptions of education in Dutch classrooms. *British Journal of Sociology of Education, 40*(1), 33–49. https://doi.org/10.1080/01425692.2018.1480354

Skerrett, A. (2020). Transnational students and educational change. *Journal of Educational Change, 21*(3), 499–509. https://doi.org/10.1007/s10833-020-09369-0

Street, B. V. (1995). *Social literacies: Critical approaches to literacy in development, ethnography and education*. Longman.

Tan, E. (2014). Human capital theory: A holistic criticism. *Review of Educational Research, 84*(3), 411–445.

Thorsen, D. E. (2010). The neoliberal challenge—What is neoliberalism? *Contemporary Readings in Law and Social Justice, 2*(2), 188–214.

Torres, C. A. (2009). *Globalizations and education: Collected essays on class, race, gender, and the state*. Teachers College Press.

Tupas, R. (2020). The coloniality of English language testing. In S. A. Mirhosseini & P. I. De Costa (Eds.), *The sociopolitics of English language testing*. Bloomsbury.

Weninger, C. (2019). *From language skills to literacy: Broadening the scope of English language education through media literacy*. Routledge.

Weninger, C., & Kan, K. H. Y. (2013). (Critical) Language awareness in business communication. *English for Specific Purposes, 32*(2), 59–71.

Zia, A. (2020). The haunting specter of Hindu ethnonationalist-neocolonial development in the Indian occupied Kashmir. *Development*. Retrieved from https://link.springer.com/article/10.1057/s41301-020-00234-4

Zúñiga, V., Hammann, E. T., & Sánchez García, J. (2016). Students we share are also in Puebla, Mexico: Preliminary findings from a 2009–2010 survey. In H. D. Romo & O. Mogollon-Lopez (Eds.), *Mexican migration to the United States* (pp. 248–265). University of Texas Press.

1.4

CRITICAL LITERACY IN ENGLISH LANGUAGE TEACHING, BI/MULTILINGUALISM, AND TRANSLANGUAGING

*Chris K. Chang-Bacon, Nihal Khote, Robin Schell,
and Graham V. Crookes*

Language and literacy research is fraught with contradictions. Although the field increasingly recognizes broader definitions of language and its use, a growing number of named languages are listed as endangered or have been altogether wiped out. In many educational circles, teachers and scholars are challenging restrictive language policies and language hierarchies. Yet, in a range of political contexts, monolingual orientations continue to gain traction in a time of emboldened nativism and anti-immigrant sentiment. Global literacy rates are the highest in recorded history. Nevertheless, the current era of so-called *post-truth* brings into question our collective ability to discern truth from falsehood in what we read.

These contradictions are not new, particularly in relation to critical literacies. In our view, critical literacies are inherently multilingual and transnational. Nevertheless, the scholarly literature on implementational and instructional paradigms for critical literacies tends to prioritize publications in English, a trend we recognize is extended by this very chapter. Yet, it is this dominance of English that compels us to focus on critical literacies in relation to the global enterprise of English language teaching (ELT) and its relation to bi/multilingualism and translanguaging. Such tensions reflect those inherent to the very notion of language education: Does language learning primarily function to foster engagement with an extended range of audiences or to promote asymmetrical linguistic assimilation?

It is our view that critical literacies offer a productive, albeit imperfect, avenue to taking up such questions in relation to language education. The purpose of this chapter is to explore the manifestation of critical literacies in ELT, bi/multilingualism, and translanguaging. Although, for the purpose of this chapter, we focus specifically on English, its global dominance, and its prevalence in the literature on critical literacies, we encourage readers to explore additional research on critical literacies beyond English (e.g., Macedo, 2019). We begin by defining our key concepts and terminologies. Next, we explore historical and emerging theories of critical literacies in relation to ELT, bi/multilingualism, and translanguaging. We then review past empirical work on critical literacies in multilingual contexts to highlight its implications. Finally, we offer recommendations for the field moving forward and reflect on the social responsibility of critical scholars.

DOI: 10.4324/9781003023425-5

Definitions and Key Concepts

In recent decades, scholars of language have engaged in productive discussion about the labels we use in our field and have begun troubling the boundaries of named languages themselves (Makoni & Pennycook, 2007; Otheguy, García, & Reid, 2015). For the purposes of this chapter, we discuss the field commonly described as ELT. Within ELT, we include (1.) English-dominant contexts where English is taught as a second or additional language, commonly referred to in the United States as English as a Second Language (ESL); and (2.) ELT in contexts where English is not widely spoken, often denoted as English as a Foreign Language (EFL). All of the student groups we describe in this chapter, and in the reviewed research, are engaged in learning one or more additional languages. We use the term *multilingual learners* to acknowledge the vast range of language practices students bring to classrooms.

Naturally, when engaging with ELT through a critical lens, one must engage with the history of English as a colonial language. It is accordingly important to understand ELT not as a neutral endeavor of simply teaching a language but as a global enterprise connected to specific histories of imperialism, colonialism, and racism (see Motha, 2014; Phillipson, 2009). What's more, this history reflects a process in which English continues to exert influence and privilege certain populations and their language practices over others. In light of these dynamics, we articulate critical literacies in relation to ELT and language teaching overall as having a dual purpose. The first purpose is pedagogical—to promote classrooms in which students and teachers critically engage with peers, texts, and the world around them multilingually. The second purpose is to foreground critical questions of language education writ large: Why teach *this* language? *Whose* particular language use is being taught as "standard?" Who *benefits* from the teaching of this language? These dual purposes are brought together throughout this chapter as we ask how teachers and students can critically engage with a language while learning the language itself.

Historical, Current, and Emergent Theory

The ability to exert one's criticality is an inherent part of what it means to be human, and thus critical literacy should be seen as a natural part of being literate. While we often think of critical literacies as a modern endeavor, it is important to note the long, even ancient, history of critical thinking across multiple cultures and languages as a fundamentally human endeavor (not one solely associated with modernity). In a detailed account, Abednia and Crookes (2019) identify examples of this in the early history of literacy. For example, scholars have noted that Plato was critical of some of the traditions of Homer, and that the pre-Socratic Greek philosophers Xenophanes and Heraclitus "denounce the fact that the ancient poets [Homer and Hesiod] have not been examined critically" (Caizzi, 1999, pp. 337–338). Critical reading, in some form or another, shows up at various points in the history of literate traditions such as the Islamic and the Chinese, though examples are usually not associated with critical theories of society in any modern sense. Modern critical literacy traditions generally trace a lineage to the work of Freire (1975/1996) in Brazil, which was then built upon by other language specialists, explored as follows.

Critical Literacies and Theories of Language

Although Freire's work is seen as foundational to critical literacy, it has been critiqued as lacking a specific theory of language or a recommended approach for linguistic and textual analysis (Luke,

2012). A range of scholars in linguistics and language education have thus sought to apply the central principles of critical literacies to the study of language, notably by taking up explorations of how power permeates interactions in bi/multilingual contexts and in the enterprise of language learning more broadly. Any attempt to provide a strictly linear account of the development of critical thought in literacy would be misleading as multiple lines of thought emerged over time. Here, however, we highlight three theories of language that are often used within the field to analyze language learning through a critical lens: Systemic Functional Linguistics, Critical Discourse Analysis, and Translanguaging. Importantly, this is not an exhaustive list of linguistic theories to have taken up critical approaches, and it should not be assumed that *all* (or even most) scholarship within these approaches takes up a critical lens. Nevertheless, these fields provide productive examples of how critical approaches can be applied within linguistic theory.

Systemic Functional Linguistics (SFL). In the 1970s, Halliday and Hasan first developed Systemic Functional Linguistics (SFL), a language-based theory of learning (Halliday, 1994; Hasan, 1996). Halliday explored institutionalized linguistic biases related to minoritized youth arising from differences between students' language practices and the language varieties privileged at school. Halliday's SFL approach conceived of language as a context-dependent system of linguistic choices that language users can deploy to express three interrelated levels of meanings: the message and discourse, interpersonal relations and status, and organizational resources to construe a cohesive text. In this way, SFL provided examples of metalanguage that could be used to interrogate and challenge texts. Hasan (1996) proposed a critical frame to teaching and learning in what she called *reflection literacy*, where "we not only use language to shape reality, but we also use it to defend that reality against anyone whose alternative values might threaten ours" (p. 34). Theorists of the Sydney School of SFL suggest that students expanded their linguistic repertoires by deploying grammatical features of typical written genres of schooling to engage with challenging disciplinary texts in resistant, often critical, ways (Christie & Derewianka, 2008; Martin & Rose, 2003).

Critical Discourse Analysis (CDA). Related forms of linguistic analysis evolved within the field of Critical Discourse Analysis to highlight the relationships between language, text, and power (Fairclough, 1989/2013; Van Dijk, 2015). Fairclough (2013) described CDA as consisting of three levels of analysis: *description* of the text, *interpretation* of that text in relation to discursive interaction, and *explanation* of that interaction in relation to social context. In this approach, language is understood to construct messages that maintain and reproduce social inequities and asymmetrical power relations in texts. Janks (1991) proposed a similar approach, described as *critical language teaching*. She posited that students are empowered when armed with linguistic knowledge in order to unmask the lexical choices that foreground or hide certain discourses that marginalize or silence them. Janks (2000) also identified and cautioned against the "paradox of access"—the perceived need to provide students access to dominant linguistic forms that simultaneously contributes to maintaining the dominance of these forms—a paradox that resonates particularly profoundly in relation to ELT.

Translanguaging. Recent scholarship on *translanguaging* has been productive in moving the field toward critically interrogating its fundamental conceptions of language and language learning. While not specifically aligned with the critical paradigm, we see promise in emergent scholarship that maps translingual perspectives on to critical literacies (see the section Recommendations and Forward Thinking later in the chapter). The term *translanguaging* was originally conceptualized as a pedagogical practice in which multilingual learners used a variety of linguistic modes to express messages in more fluid and effective ways (Williams, 1996). More recent scholarship in translanguaging challenges the view of languages as separate and compartmentalized entities, but instead it refers to the complex ways in which multilingual learners deploy one unitary and integrated linguistic repertoire, particularly by troubling the "one language only" or "one language at a time" ideologies of monolingual and traditional bilingual language education classrooms (García & Wei, 2014, p. 67). This theory of language thus shares a degree of common ground with SFL and CDA in its systematic analysis of language variation in ways that expose normative and racialized hierarchies (Khote & Tian, 2019). However, it is again important to note that none of these theories, in and of themselves, are inherently critical (see Jaspers, 2018). In this way, it remains important for individual researchers and educators to consider deeply what it means to take up critical analysis that foregrounds the power dynamics of language and language learning within a range of linguistic approaches.

Reviews of and Implications for Research

In this section, we explore how the aforementioned theories, and critical literacies in general, have been incorporated into empirical research on ELT, bi/multilingualism, and translanguaging. While certainly not an exhaustive review (for more detailed reviews, see Abednia & Crookes, 2019; Bacon, 2017; Luke & Dooley, 2011), we provide an overview of five key themes, representing claims that have been repeatedly documented across decades of research. As critical literacies is a field that constantly seeks to question and reinvent itself, we should never consider any debates to be fully "settled" within the critical paradigm. Nevertheless, the themes we highlight here represent a foundational body of knowledge, representing principles for the field to build on, and even to challenge, in future research.

Engagement at All Language Levels

Students can engage in critical literacies at all language levels (leveraging their full linguistic repertoires). Perhaps, one of the most consistent queries in relation to critical literacies in language education is whether or not students can engage in critical literacies in a language they are still learning. The emphatic answer from the literature is *yes, they can*. Though there are certainly complexities involved with engaging critical literacies in a language learning setting—as there are with any topic in a new language—the field has generated strong evidence that students can engage with, and indeed benefit from, critical engagement in language learning (Brown, Schell, & Ni, 2018; Lau, 2012; Souryasack & Lee, 2007). Souryasack and Lee (2007), for example, conducted a study of Laotian students learning English in a U.S. middle school. The study found critical literacy pedagogies, such as problem-posing and culture circles, shifted what students had previously perceived to be disconnected language exercises toward engaging explorations of topics relevant to students' lived experience.

It should, however, be made obvious that all learners engage most readily in critical analysis through a language with which they are comfortable. Thus, multilingual approaches that allow students to critically engage through both the language they are learning and their preferred language(s) are recommended—and represent a clear solution to any concern that students may not be "ready" to critically engage in the target language. Unfortunately, monolingual orientations often deny students the opportunity to engage in critical literacies in both ESL and EFL contexts (Bacon, 2017). Recognizing the importance of multilingual engagement lays the groundwork for designing critical language learning experiences that engage students' full linguistic repertoires as a matter of regular practice (see Lau, Juby-Smith, & Desbiens, 2016).

Relevant to the Lived Realities of Multilingual Students

Critical literacies are deeply relevant to the lived realities of multilingual students. Research has highlighted the particular relevance of critical literacies to the lived realities of students engaged in language learning. Many students, especially students of color from immigrant or refugee backgrounds, are not only compelled to learn a socially dominant language (i.e., English in ESL contexts) but are simultaneously exposed to "embodied experiences of discrimination" (Dooley, 2009, p. 15) involving nationalism, racism, and other forms of intolerance. It is a principle of critical literacy that all students have the right to read and write their own realities through critical engagement (Luke, 2004). In such cases, engaging in critical literacies provides a structure for students to critique the social inequities with which they already engage on a daily basis. Batista-Morales, Salmerón, and DeJulio (2019), for example, found bilingual Latinx students in the second grade "already reading their worlds and naming spaces where they wanted to effect change" (p. 487). Critical literacies, therefore, offer an important avenue for teachers and students to engage with the various power hierarchies of language, race, and class that impact the lived realities of all language users and multilingual learners in particular.

The relevance of critical literacies also extends to students learning English in contexts where it is not widely spoken (i.e., EFL contexts), particularly as the notion of English as a globally dominant language continues to exert influence (Phillipson, 2009). Language and power are intertwined in EFL classrooms, as are critical questions of why students are compelled to learn English, who gets to participate, and who ultimately benefits from this endeavor. A range of critical scholarship has addressed the first question, demonstrating that students are compelled to learn English to compete for social and economic advantage (Kubota, 2011; Ricento, 2015). This can be true even in contexts and professions where English is not actually useful for communicative purposes but is prioritized for entrance exams or as a marker of prestige (Leong & Dodge, 2015). As English learning has become a privatized commodity, the notion of *who has access* to English learning becomes increasingly stratified by social class. Nevertheless, students in such contexts exert a keen awareness of these dynamics and are able to critically engage with the role English learning plays in their local and global contexts, even while learning the language (Bacon & Kim, 2018; Vasilopoulos, 2015).

Facilitates Language Proficiency, Motivation, and Engagement

Although it is not the main goal of critical literacies, critical engagement can facilitate language proficiency, motivation, and engagement. There is also evidence that engaging in critical literacies can help to facilitate language learning. While documenting observable changes in language proficiency is not generally a primary goal of critical literacies, it is useful to note that such learning exists as an ancillary benefit. Derince (2011), for example, studied a one-year English prep class for students entering Turkish universities that was taught through a critical framework, finding that critical pedagogy helped to facilitate deeper English proficiency. Similarly, Okazaki's (2005) case study of four students in an intensive English program at a provincial U.S. public university demonstrated that students engaged in critical dialogue made gains in English proficiency in both speaking and writing.

There is also evidence that the introduction of critical literacy pedagogies can increase learner motivation and engagement (Kuo, 2013; Lee & Runyan, 2011). Lee and Runyan (2011) followed three students aged 9–10 who had been labeled as "resistant readers" in classrooms that emphasized "functional skills and surface-level interpretations" (p. 28). The authors found that, when critical literacy-oriented instruction was introduced, students' resistance could actually be used as a springboard for critical engagement and deeper understanding of the text. Similarly, Kuo (2013) found that Taiwanese college freshmen in a general English class were willing to spend more time previewing and reviewing texts that emphasized critical reflection and self-discovery. One student in the study reported that "[t]his activity not only helped me develop my English ability but also made me become more willing to pay attention to my life and people around me" (Kuo, 2013, p. 555).

Teachers' Role in Facilitating Critical Literacies

Across all of the examples provided, it is important to note the key role played by teachers in relation to critical literacies. Although students are the primary drivers of critical engagement, in the existing research, it is most often teachers who create space for critical engagement in their class-rooms. Due to the pressures of high-stakes testing, teachers are often compelled to focus on students' literal comprehension of texts rather than on questioning deeper underlying textual implications (Masuda, 2012; Pandya, 2011). Many teachers, however, have found ways to engage with critical literacy practices that simultaneously create meaningful language learning opportunities while pri-oritizing critical dialogue, students' lived experiences, and social justice issues (Abednia & Izadinia, 2013; Kuo, 2013; Lau, 2012). As critical literacy is rarely a mandated (or even encouraged) practice, a teacher's choice to engage critical perspectives plays a crucial role in facilitating students' engage-ment with critical literacies.

Criticality Not Limited to Specific Cultural Contexts

Due to the relevance of critical literacies across such a range of language learning experiences, it is important that critical engagement not be considered as a project limited to specific contexts. In particular, we highlight the erroneous assumption that teachers and students of particular cultural backgrounds are more or less amenable to critical literacies. Again, criticality is a fundamentally human endeavor. However, the notion of "critical thinking" is often used to argue a supposed superiority of Western education systems based on inaccurate, and frankly racist, assumptions about teachers and learners in other global contexts. Of course, there exist certain governments or school systems that discourage and even punish the questioning of political authorities or deviance from a prescribed curriculum (Nuske, 2017). However, these restrictions should not be generalized to the intellect or critical consciousness of students and teachers themselves (Shin & Crookes, 2005). Huang (2011) explored critical literacies in Taiwan, a country whose students, she notes, are often stereotyped as reluctant to question authority. Nevertheless, the students in Huang's (2011) study exerted an eagerness to engage in critical literacies, and reported the practices as beneficial to both their academic goals and political consciousness. Abednia and Izadinia (2013) incorporated criti-cal, problem-posing, literacy techniques into an English reading comprehension course in Iran, a country known for curricular conservatism, and found students motivated and adept at engaging in critical analysis. While we reiterate that cultural and political contexts must be taken into account when engaging in critical literacies, the field has demonstrated that learners across a range of cultural contexts are able and eager to engage in critical literacies toward transformational outcomes.

Recommendations and Forward Thinking

The study of critical literacies in relation to language learning has made substantial contributions to our understanding of language, how it is learned, and how language learning and critical engage-ment can be mutually reinforcing. However, several questions still persist. In particular, tensions remain between critical literacies' foundational principle of questioning dominant systems, and the perpetuation of one such dominant language system through the very enterprise of ELT. In this sec-tion, therefore, we offer three recommendations for the field around *infusing, sustaining*, and *expand-ing* criticality in future research and critical pedagogy.

Infusing Criticality

Much of the work reviewed throughout this piece involved teachers, researchers, and students ques-tioning traditional modes of language instruction and infusing them with critical perspectives. For example, critical SFL-informed pedagogy (see Accurso & Gebhard, 2020; Harman, 2018) has been used to engage students' critical perspectives while also fostering disciplinary literacy practices in a range of contexts (Gebhard, 2019; Schleppegrell, 2004) as well as in foreign language teaching

(Macedo, 2019). However, future work must grapple with the continued tensions of attempting to infuse critical practices into a largely normative paradigm of language learning that asks students to replicate, rather than interrogate, language practices seen as "standard" within a given language (see Baker-Bell, 2020). What might it look like for ELT, and language teaching more broadly, to approach language from a critical paradigm that asks "why am I learning this language?" or "why am I learning this particular dialectal variety?" and to situate these questions in relation to colonial histories, neoliberal priorities, and racial/linguistic/class biases? Ultimately, while there are obvious benefits to learning a widely used language, critical perspectives compel us to ask why students are most often the ones expected to adapt to the linguistic preference of their school systems rather than the other way around.

Sustaining Criticality

A separate but related challenge is sustaining criticality as once-radical approaches become more commonly accepted, and more often than not, watered down. Edelsky and Cherland (2006) identified this phenomenon as *the popularity effect* in which the term "critical" is applied to practices far more traditional than the original emancipatory intents of critical literacies. In relation to language learning, we see this frequently occurring with innovative program models becoming co-opted to serve elite populations. This has been critiqued recently in relation to bilingual and dual language education, originally intended to serve linguistically minoritized populations but increasingly popularized to serve the needs of wealthy, English-dominant clientele (Valdez, Freire, & Delavan, 2016). Thus, scholars have called for developing critical consciousness in relation to dual language and bilingual education programming (Cervantes-Soon et al., 2017). Here, we see the potential for productive synergies between the fields of bi/multilingual education and critical literacies for grappling with power dynamics across both languages and literacies toward a paradigm of *critical biliteracies* (Colomer & Chang-Bacon, 2020).

Expanding Criticality

As demonstrated by the literature reviewed throughout this piece, the field of critical literacies in language learning is not monolithic. In fact, many approaches often described as falling within the critical literacies paradigm may not necessarily self-identify with that designation (including Freire, 1975/1996). The field must ask what can be learned from other critical approaches that may not align themselves specifically with critical literacies. Oftentimes, these approaches are theorized and applied toward a specific form of oppression—a degree of focus critical literacies can be justifiably critiqued as lacking. Fields such as Critical Race Theory, LatCrit, DisCrit, and Queer Theory apply critical perspectives with the aim of disrupting specific oppressions imposed onto specific groups. Work in the wider field of critical literacies often operates under a theory of change that presumes, once students learn to critically engage with texts, they will know how to identify, engage with, and disrupt specific forms of oppression. Today, the sustained presence, and even emboldenment of racism, sexism, ableism, and homo/transphobia brings this theory of change into question. As such, the field of critical literacies has much to gain from critical approaches that name and focus on particular forms of oppression to explore the nuanced ways in which power and inequity manifest in specific contexts. We encourage scholarship on language learning to engage with this full range of critical approaches.

Implications for Our Social Responsibility as Academics

It is a basic assumption of critical literacies, and critical pedagogies more widely, that a heightened awareness of injustice will eventually result in some form of action. Having read *the word*, students will consider how to and act in order to read *the world* differently. In this way, a key aspect of social responsibility for academics and teachers in relation to critical literacies would be to ask whether or not our basic assumptions around critical literacies and resultant social change hold true in ways that tangibly improve the lives of our students and marginalized peoples, more broadly. Documenting this change is difficult, however. As with all forms of education, drawing direct causal links between what happens in a given class or course, and what an individual student does, perhaps years later as an adult, is nearly impossible. Regardless, the enactment of critical literacies beyond the classroom is perhaps the least documented aspect of critical literacy in relation to language learning (even though critical pedagogy more generally can show some strong examples, for example, Campano, Ghiso, & Welch, 2016; Duncan-Andrade & Morrell, 2008).

In fact, critical literacy is usually on its guard against charges of imposition, and teachers acting out of this position rightly concern themselves with the matter. That is why we problem-pose, not problem solve, and use projective devices like Freirean *codes* (e.g., pictures or other realia that enable students to articulate the problems they themselves, see Wallerstein, 1983) to allow students to articulate their views or concerns and should acquiesce when students deny the relevance of an issue to their lived experiences. Although teachers have an essential role of providing space for critical engagement in the classroom, as critical literacies strive to be a mutual enterprise, teachers should not view themselves as the sole causal agents of action.

However, it is also a key case of social responsibility to acknowledge that multilingual learners have often been deprived of critical literacy practices across a range of educational contexts. This is particularly true in language learning, a field especially susceptible to the overemphasization or simple replication of dominant linguistic forms, disengaged from the use of reading and writing as a tool for social change and from understanding its historical power dynamics (Macedo & Bartolome, 2019). Capturing this view, hooks (1995) says that "it is not the English language that hurts me, but what the oppressors do with it, how they shape it to become a territory that limits and defines how they make it a weapon that can shame, humiliate and colonize" (p. 167).

Recognizing the social and academic needs of students, there is a particular need for further work in critical literacies to foster classroom spaces that move toward legitimizing all varieties of student languaging. In addition, we see the need for educators to be armed with theories of language that facilitate moving beyond teaching for communicative and academic purposes to create opportunities for students to grapple with the ways language can be used to silence, misrepresent, or marginalize particular individuals or communities. Though the use of language to oppress rather than liberate is an ever-relevant dynamic, critical literacy advocates optimism that the historical lineage of the field, coupled with advances in the study of language and its social correlates, will continue to push our field forward in productive ways.

References

Abednia, A., & Crookes, G. V. (2019). Critical literacy as a pedagogical goal in English language teaching. In X. A. Gao (Ed.), *Second handbook of English language teaching* (pp. 255–275). Springer.

Abednia, A., & Izadinia, M. (2013). Critical pedagogy in ELT classroom: Exploring contributions of critical literacy to learners' critical consciousness. *Language Awareness, 22*(4), 338–352.

Accurso, K., & Gebhard, M. (2020). SFL praxis in the US teacher education: A critical literature review. *Language and Education.* Advance online publication. https://doi.org/10.1080/09500782.2020.1781880

Bacon, C. K. (2017). "Multi-language, multi-purpose": A literature review, synthesis, and framework for critical literacies in English language teaching. *Journal of Literacy Research, 49*(3), 424–453. https://doi.org/10.1177/1086296X17718324

Bacon, C. K., & Kim, S. Y. (2018). "English is my only weapon": Neoliberal language ideologies and youth metadiscourse in South Korea. *Linguistics and Education, 48*, 10–21. https://doi.org/10.1016/j.linged.2018.09.002

Baker-Bell, A. (2020). *Linguistic justice: Black language, literacy, identity, and pedagogy.* Routledge.

Batista-Morales, N. S., Salmerón, C., & DeJulio, S. (2019). Their words, their worlds: Critical literacy in bilingual spaces. *Bilingual Research Journal, 42*(4), 471–490. https://doi.org/10.1080/15235882.2019.1675804

Brown, C. L., Schell, R. F., & Ni, M. (2018). Powerful participatory literacy for English learners. *Journal of Adolescent and Adult Literacy, 62*(4), 369–378.

Caizzi, F. D. (1999). Poetics of early Greek philosophy. In A. A. Long (Ed.), *The Cambridge companion to early Greek philosophy* (pp. 332–362). Cambridge University Press.

Campano, G., Ghiso, M. P., & Welch, B. J. (2016). *Partnering with immigrant communities: Action through literacy.* Teachers College Press.

Cervantes-Soon, C. G., Dorner, L., Palmer, D., Heiman, D., Schwerdtfeger, R., & Choi, J. (2017). Combating inequalities in two-way language immersion programs: Toward critical consciousness in bilingual education spaces. *Review of Research in Education, 41*(1), 403–427.

Christie, F., & Derewianka, B. (2008). *School discourse: Learning to write across the years of schooling.* Continuum.

Colomer, S. E., & Chang-Bacon, C. K. (2020). Seal of biliteracy graduates get critical: Incorporating critical biliteracies in dual language programs and beyond. *Journal of Adolescent and Adult Literacy, 63*(4), 379–389. https://doi.org/10.1002/jaal.1017

Derince, Z. M. (2011). Language learning through critical pedagogy in a "brave new world". *International Review of Education, 57,* 377–395.

Dooley, K. T. (2009). Re-thinking pedagogy for middle school students with little, no or severely interrupted schooling. English Teaching: *Practice and Critique, 8,* 5–20.

Duncan-Andrade, J. M. R., & Morrell, E. (2008). *The art of critical pedagogy: Possibilities for moving from theory to practice in urban schools* (Vol. 285). Peter Lang.

Edelsky, C., & Cherland, M. R. (2006). A critical issue in critical literacy. In K. Cooper & R. E. White (Eds.), *The practical critical educator: Critical inquiry and educational practice* (pp. 17–33). Springer.

Fairclough, N. (1989/2013). *Language and power.* Longman.

Freire, P. (1975/1996). *Pedagogy of the oppressed* (new revised ed.). Penguin Books. (Original English translation published 1970).

García, O., & Wei, L. (2014). *Translanguaging: Language, bilingualism and education.* Basingstoke: Palgrave Macmillan. https://doi.org/10.1057/9781137385765_4

Gebhard, M. (2019). *Teaching and researching ELLs' disciplinary literacies: Systemic functional linguistics in action in the context of U.S. school reform.* Routledge.

Halliday, M. A. K. (1994). *An introduction to functional grammar.* Edward Arnold.

Harman, R. (Ed.) (2018). *Bilingual learners and social equity.* Springer.

Hasan, R. (1996). Literacy, everyday talk and society. In R. Hasan & G. Williams (Eds.), *Literacy in society* (pp. 377–424). Longman.

hooks, b. (1995). "this is the oppressor's language/yet I need it to talk to you": Language, a place of struggle. In A. Dingwaney & C. Maier (Eds.), *Between languages and cultures: Translations and cross-cultural texts* (pp. 295–301). University of Pittsburgh Press.

Huang, S.-Y. (2011). Reading "further and beyond the text": Student perspectives of critical literacy in EFL reading and writing. *Journal of Adolescent & Adult Literacy, 55*(2), 145–154.

Janks, H. (1991). A critical approach to the teaching of language. *Educational Review, 43*(2), 191–199. https://doi.org/10.1080/0013191910430207

Janks, H. (2000). Domination, access, diversity, and design. *Educational Review, 52,* 175–186.

Jaspers, J. (2018). The transformative limits of translanguaging. *Language & Communication, 58,* 1–10.

Khote, N., & Tian, Z. (2019). Translanguaging in culturally sustaining systemic functional linguistics: Developing a heteroglossic space with multilingual learners. *Translation and Translanguaging in Multilingual Contexts, 5*(1), 5–28. https://doi.org/10.1075/ttmc.00022.kho

Kubota, R. (2011). Questioning linguistic instrumentalism: English, neoliberalism, and language tests in Japan. *Linguistics and Education, 22*(3), 248–260.

Kuo, J. (2013). Implementing critical literacy for university freshmen in Taiwan through self-discovery texts. *Asia-Pacific Education Researcher, 22*(4), 549–557.

Lau, S. M. C. (2012). Reconceptualizing critical literacy teaching in ESL classrooms. *The Reading Teacher, 65*(5), 325–329.

Lau, S. M. C., Juby-Smith, B., & Desbiens, I. (2016). Translanguaging for transgressive praxis: Promoting critical literacy in a multi-age bilingual classroom. *Critical Inquiry for Language Studies, 14*(1), 1–29. https://doi.org/10.1080/15427587.2016.1242371.

Lee, A. C., & Runyan, B. (2011). From apprehension to critical literacy. *The Journal of Educational Thought, 45,* 87–106.

Leong, P., & Dodge, P. (2015). Situating English as a lingua franca in context: Narratives from Japanese and Chinese classrooms. *Intercultural Communication Studies, 23*(3), 50–63.

Luke, A. (2004). Two takes on the critical. In B. Norton & K. Toohey (Eds.), *Critical pedagogies and language learning* (pp. 21–29). Cambridge University Press.

Luke, A. (2012). Critical literacy: Foundational notes. *Theory into Practice, 51*(1), 4–11.

Luke, A., & Dooley, K. T. (2011). Critical literacy and second language learning. In E. Hinkel (Ed.), *Handbook of research on second language teaching and learning* (Vol. 2, pp. 859–867). Routledge.

Macedo, D. (Ed.). (2019). *Decolonizing foreign language education: The misteaching of English and other colonial languages*. Routledge.

Macedo, D., & Bartolome, L. I. (2019). Dual language teachers as a potentially democratizing force in English learner education. In M. Pacheco, P. Zitali Morales, & C. Hamilton (Eds.), *Transforming schooling for second language learners: Theoretical insights, policies, pedagogies, and practices* (pp. 43–59). Information Age Publishing.

Makoni, S., & Pennycook, A. (2007). Disinventing and reconstituting languages. In S. Makoni & A. Pennycook (Eds.), *Disinventing and reconstituting languages* (pp. 1–41). Multilingual Matters.

Martin, J., & Rose, D. (2003). *Working with discourse: Meaning beyond the clause*. Continuum.

Masuda, A. (2012). Critical literacy and teacher identities: A discursive site of struggle. *Critical Inquiry in Language Studies, 9*(3), 220–246.

Motha, S. (2014). *Race, empire, and English language teaching: Creating responsible and ethical anti-racist practice*. Teachers College Press.

Nuske, K. (2017). Novice practitioners' views on the applicability of post-method and critical pedagogy in Saudi EFL contexts. In *Language, identity and education on the Arabian Peninsula: Bilingual policies in a multilingual context* (pp. 199–219). Multilingual Matters.

Okazaki, T. (2005). Critical consciousness and critical language teaching. *Second Language Studies, 23*(2), 174–202.

Otheguy, R., García, O., & Reid, W. (2015). Clarifying translanguaging and deconstructing named languages: A perspective from linguistics. *Applied Linguistics Review, 6*(3), 281–307.

Pandya, J. Z. (2011). *Overtested: How high-stakes accountability fails English language learners*. Teachers College Press.

Phillipson, R. (2009). *Linguistic imperialism continued*. Oxford University Press.

Ricento, T. (Ed.). (2015). *Language policy and political economy: English in a global context*. Oxford University Press.

Schleppegrell, M. (2004). *The language of schooling: A functional linguistics perspective*. Lawrence Erlbaum Associates.

Shin, H., & Crookes, G. (2005). Exploring the possibilities for EFL critical pedagogy in Korea—a two-part case study. *Critical Inquiry in Language Studies, 2*(2), 112–138.

Souryasack, R., & Lee, J. S. (2007). Drawing on students' experiences, cultures and languages to develop English language writing: Perspectives from three Lao heritage middle school students. *Heritage Language Journal, 5*(1), 79–97.

Valdez, V. E., Freire, J. A., & Delavan, M. G. (2016). The gentrification of dual language education. *The Urban Review, 48*(4), 601–627.

Van Dijk, T. A. (2015). Critical discourse analysis. In D. Tannen, H. E. Hamilton, & D. Schiffrin (Eds.), *The handbook of discourse analysis* (pp. 466–485). Wiley.

Vasilopoulos, G. (2015). Language learner investment and identity negotiation in the Korean EFL context. *Journal of Language, Identity & Education, 14*(2), 61–79.

Wallerstein, N. (1983). *Language and culture in conflict: Problem-posing in the ESL classroom*. Addison Wesley.

Williams, C. (1996). Secondary education: Teaching in the bilingual situation. In C. Williams, G. Lewis, & C. Baker (Eds.), *The language policy: Taking stock* (pp. 39–78). CAI.

1.5

YOUTH CIVIC PARTICIPATION AND ACTIVISM (YOUTH PARTICIPATORY ACTION RESEARCH)

Robert Petrone, Nicole Mirra, Steve Goodman, and Antero Garcia

At a practical level, nearly every form of civic participation[1] is a manifestation of literacy practice. Whether informing oneself about candidates' platforms, discussing current events, or addressing local concerns, meaning-making about society is taking place through the medium of language. Yet, at the conceptual level, civics in the United States[2] is often aligned with the disciplines of history and social science rather than with literacy or English. Civic education standards are embedded within social studies curricula in all 50 states, and the term "civic literacy" in policy documents largely refers to functional knowledge of content and skills regarding democratic institutions and procedures rather than fundamental understandings about the social nature and purpose of communication (Garcia & Mirra, 2019). When establishing predictors for civic engagement, researchers often cite literacy proficiency—as defined by narrow, standardized indicators—as a key variable; this, in effect, suggests that literacy and civic engagement are separate entities and that the former precedes and predicts the latter.

Critical literacy dismantles this arbitrary distinction in definition, practice, and purpose. In definition, critical literacy is grounded in the Freirian mantra that reading the word is reading the world (and vice versa) as engagement with text in any form represents an interaction with the public sphere. In practice, critical literacy advocates for the analysis of social issues as central to literacy teaching and learning. In purpose, it insists upon interrogation of structural inequities and commitments to equity and humanization. Thus, critical literacy is inextricably linked with civic participation (Goodman & Cocca, 2014).

This chapter goes into depth about one such manifestation of critical literacy—Youth Participatory Action Research (YPAR). YPAR positions young people as the subjects (rather than the objects) of critical inquiry about social and political issues that matter to/for them, and it offers a window onto ways critical literacy challenges normative understandings of whose voices are valued in public life, how civic understandings are expressed, and what the purpose of literacy is in transforming the world. These underpinnings of YPAR are particularly noteworthy given how demonstrative youth-led activism and literacies are in raising consciousness within the current sociopolitical climate of global pandemic, rampant anti-blackness, and environmental assault (Mirra & Garcia, 2020; Watson & Petrone, 2020).

In this chapter, we begin by teasing apart the elements of the YPAR acronym to demonstrate the challenges each of these components offers to traditional academic research and literacy education. While we explore common underlying concepts, we also acknowledge the uneven and unequal

DOI: 10.4324/9781003023425-6

social, political, and institutional conditions in which YPAR is practiced, as well as the range of ways authentic participation is fostered and relationships between research and action are negotiated. We then explore the intellectual lineage of YPAR before surveying key research in the field. Our exploration of the possibilities and tensions generated by YPAR leads us to suggest new directions and provocations for the broader critical literacy community.

Key Concepts

Youth

The distinctive feature of YPAR is that it centers youth. Based on the principle "No research on us without us" (Fine & Torre, 2019), YPAR repositions youth from the objects to the subjects of research. Thus, YPAR draws attention to and critiques the adult-centricism inherent, though rarely mentioned, within dominant research epistemologies. Adult(hood) is assumed as the norm when it comes to research(er) and most knowledge production in academia.

In addition to drawing attention to youth-adult power dynamics, YPAR implies a reconceptualization of both the concept of "youth" and the people the moniker represents. Though dominant notions of youth within education are rooted in biological and psychological developmentalist frameworks (Lesko, 2012), YPAR operates from a theory of youth that recognizes it as a historically contingent, socially produced category that has material effects for the people it represents, as well as adults, including educators and researchers. In other words, YPAR understands that how young people are known—even, at times by themselves—has as much to do with ways they are positioned by discourses and social structures (including schools) as it does with their developing bodies. Moreover, YPAR's conceptions of youth emphasizes young people's active engagement in and abilities to impact the world. Therefore, YPAR's recalibration of youth actively works against the deficit orientations of youth that operate as normative in public discourse, media, and education.

Participatory

The participatory aspect of YPAR addresses both *who* counts as researcher and *how* research gets conducted. Participatory approaches center the people most affected by their circumstances as experts and work toward collaborations between these people and outside researchers. Thus, relational approaches that build collaboratives are integral to a participatory research paradigm (Carr & Kemmis, 1986). By overtly addressing power dynamics, participatory approaches shift normative understandings of research being done *on/for* people to research being done *with/by* people.

The participatory nature also necessitates an ongoing negotiated process of identifying the need for research, establishing questions, designing a project, collecting and analyzing data, and disseminating results. This shared governance ensures that the people who are closest to the issues have a central and active role and also helps mitigate researcher biases. This is especially significant given how participatory research is mainly carried out by/with people from marginalized communities whose epistemologies, modes of dissemination, and perspectives have historically been marginalized and/or denigrated by academia and professional researchers (Brayboy, 2005).

In YPAR, participatory means that youth and adults are engaged in intergenerational collaborative work that seeks to create a space where all voices are needed, respected, and heard. These "contact zones" (Fine & Torre, 2019) require authentic self-reflective dialogue and transparency that acknowledge differences and challenges. Moreover, YPAR demands that the adults involved make an ethical commitment to stand alongside and in solidarity with youth researchers. Ultimately, an aim of YPAR is that the space created evolves into a community of practice where learning is situated, youth develop identities as active co-researchers, and knowledge is distributed.

Action

The action aspect of YPAR speaks directly to questions of *why* research is being conducted. Action research is carried out to draw attention to and address specific issues within local contexts and situations (e.g., Lewin, 1997). Therefore, action research tends to be more practical and specific in nature. Within education, for example, a common type of action research is for teachers to identify a problem of practice, design and carry out a systematic inquiry to understand the problem, and then develop a plan of action to redress the situation. Often, action research is iterative whereby a first cycle would be followed by another inquiry to further develop understandings of the initial problem identified. In this way, action research recognizes that change happens over time and facilitates incremental steps toward transformation. In short, action research is carried out to simultaneously understand and change the world.

Inspired by the Freirian critical pedagogy of praxis, this connection between learning, critical literacy, and action can take a wide variety of forms and have multiple outcomes depending on the particular project. For example, student action emerging from YPAR projects in schools and communities include: conference presentations on race and educational equity in California schools (Mirra, Morrell, Cain, Scorza, & Ford, 2013), coauthored policy papers and legal briefs addressing LGBTQIA issues and "dignity schools" nationally (Fine & Torre, 2019), screenings and discussions of student "know your rights" documentaries on police violence and ICE raids in New York City schools (Goodman, 2018), and meetings, marches, and sit-ins at the Arizona statehouse to save the Ethnic Studies program in a Tucson high school (Palos & McGinnis, 2011). In some cases (e.g., projects with undocumented youth and/or other vulnerable communities), action may be limited to the youth making their voices heard within their collaborative.

Research

In addition to recalibrating questions of who, why, and how, YPAR also calls into question *what* counts as research. Not simply a method, it is, as Fine (2008) describes, "a radical epistemological challenge to the traditions of social sciences, most critically on the topic of where knowledge resides" (p. 215). YPAR critiques the notion of research as the detached, "objective" pursuit of knowledge conducted by professional outsiders studying and extracting knowledge from (disadvantaged) communities.

In general, YPAR is guided by the principles that (1) research should be applied to solving social problems of injustice, and (2) research should be conducted in collaboration with those who have been the most impacted by those injustices. Following these principles, YPAR engages young people as active researchers and draws upon their insights and insider perspectives on the problems they experience. Borrowing from diverse fields including anthropology, sociology, and social journalism, YPAR uses a range of research techniques including surveys, interviews, focus groups, oral histories, participant observation, and audiovisual documentation. In some cases, youth may access and interpret legal, policy, and other "official" documents from local institutions such as schools, police, or housing departments.

Historical, Current, and Emerging Theory

The practices and principles of participatory action research with youth are drawn from the broader tradition of Participatory Action Research (PAR), which has roots in adult popular education, community development, organizing campaigns emerging in the mid-twentieth century in England and the United States, and in anti-colonial and liberation theology inspired struggles in Latin America, Asia, and Africa. Across these manifestations, members of oppressed communities partner with activist scholars in a praxis of collective inquiry, action, and reflection toward a shared goal of justice.

As Fals-Borda and Rahman (1991) describe, PAR is a *vivencia*, an open-ended process of life and work requiring an ethical commitment to structural transformation.

Rooted in the pedagogy of critical literacy (Freire, 1970), PAR develops participants' capacity to collaboratively gather, question, make sense of, and use language and texts to make their voices heard about the systemic problems they experience. It is based on the understanding that language and literacy are never neutral but always carry political implications that can either legitimize and reinforce systems of oppression or empower people to resist and overcome them. As a manifestation of critical literacy, PAR is a radical form of civic education. Engaging participants in public inquiry, dialogue, and action, it links the process of becoming literate to the process of political struggle.

In early examples of PAR in the United States, Appalachian communities investigated absentee land ownership, toxic mining, and industrial chemicals in their workplace and water. In doing so, they learned to read real-estate tax records and medical textbooks to understand who owned the land and the public health dangers of chemicals in their community (Gaventa, 1991). For disenfranchised African Americans participating in Citizenship Schools and Freedom Schools in the Jim Crow South of the 1950s and 1960s, learning to read their state's constitution and election laws was linked to learning about local political party power and the possibility of changing it (Carson, 1981; Charron, 2009). This adult literacy education was key for political liberation since it not only prepared people to pass racist literacy tests and vote for the first time, but it also empowered many to become active in the voter registration civil rights movements.

In these and other examples, practicing a critical literacy approach through PAR meant empowering "ordinary" people to access and analyze previously restricted official information. Blending the methods and discourses of those in power with the culture and language of the local community, PAR collaboratives disseminated their findings through multimodal counter-narratives (e.g., art, music, drama, video, photography, poetry, storytelling) to provoke dialogue with audiences.

PAR began to emerge as a methodological approach in formal academic scholarship as researchers in multiple fields—notably public health—sought to normalize the idea that those meant to be the beneficiaries of public-facing inquiry should be invited to participate in its design and implementation. In education, these beneficiaries are young people, which added a new level of theorizing to the practice. While PAR, by definition, already involves individuals of any age who participate in action research, the unique history by which the construct of youth has been operationalized in U.S. educational institutions to infantilize young people and discount their perspectives led educational researchers to consciously begin adding the Y to PAR to specifically highlight the tensions and possibilities of integrating youth into critical inquiry praxis (e.g., McIntyre, 2000).

While the label of YPAR could be affixed to many previous efforts, a watershed moment occurred in educational research in 2008 when two influential texts were published demonstrating the urgency of YPAR as a tool to transform scholarship, policy, and practice in the field. In *Revolutionizing Education* (2008), Julio Cammarota and Michelle Fine gathered a group of practicing YPAR scholars to make a collective statement about YPAR as a methodology for conducting educational research. In the same year, Jeffrey Duncan-Andrade and Ernest Morrell introduced *The Art of Critical Pedagogy* (2008), which explored YPAR as both an innovative methodology and a literacy *pedagogy* with implications for both informal *and* classroom literacy learning. While impossible to pinpoint the exact moment at which YPAR gained traction in education, it is undeniable that references to YPAR in the field's scholarly literature increased exponentially after 2008 (Caraballo, Lozenski, Lyiscott, & Morrell, 2017).

Reviews of and Implications for Research

Considering the surge of YPAR research since 2008, an exhaustive review of scholarly literature in education is beyond the scope of this chapter. Instead, we review four major themes related to critical literacy that consistently emerge across recent YPAR scholarship.

YPAR Privileges Youth Identities, Epistemologies, and Literacy Practices

A recent literature review found the majority of YPAR scholarship comprised studies focusing on how engaging in inquiry impacts youth's sense of agency as knowledge producers, as well as their developing academic, interpersonal, and civic identities (Anyon, Bender, Kennedy, & Dechants, 2018). Researchers who document YPAR dedicate a great deal of analysis to interrogating the concept of "youth," telling rich ethnographic stories that illuminate what it looks like in practice to privilege young people's perspectives in the processes of research, and how situating them as experts transforms their sense of self in multiple areas of their lives. These studies often operationalize the conceptualization of youth by exploring the intersection of age and other social constructs (e.g., race, national origin) to interrogate the marginalization of minoritized communities and advocate for YPAR as a means by which young people can assert their humanity and counter oppression (Cammarota, 2017; Wagaman & Sanchez, 2017).

Intertwined with honoring the perspectives of young people is the commitment to amplify expression of youth epistemologies in more expansive literacy forms than are often accepted in the dominant research community (Fox, 2012; Mirra, Garcia, & Morrell, 2016). Instead of relying upon traditional research reports written in stiff academic language and filled with citations from credentialed adult researchers, YPAR studies document how youth and their adult supporters creatively develop and produce texts to represent their knowledge for a wider audience (Goodman, 2018). For instance, youth have been shown to consider personal or family *testimonios* as forms of embodied data alongside observations and survey results, and to express what they have learned in literacy forms as varied as tweets, blogs, spoken word, documentaries, music, and public presentations (Garcia, Mirra, Morrell, Martinez, & Scorza, 2015; Greene, Burke, & McKenna, 2018; Marciano & Warren, 2018).

The push within YPAR scholarship to forefront the identities, epistemologies, and literacy practices of youth as they conduct community inquiry has surfaced tensions about the appropriate role of adults within the YPAR process (Bautista, Bertrand, Morrell, Scorza, & Matthews, 2013). Researchers have documented the steps adults have taken to attempt to decenter their own perspectives, move from hierarchical transmission of knowledge to one of collaborative problem–posing, and utilize their social positioning and resources to broaden the scope and audience for student inquiry (Caraballo & Soleimany, 2019).

YPAR Challenges and Reconstructs Formal Classroom (Literacy) Instruction

A growing body of YPAR research has turned to exploring the possibilities and drawbacks of integrating YPAR into classroom instruction. This focus has grown both from a recognition of YPAR's aforementioned benefits and from the desire to make formal classroom instruction more authentic, relevant, and culturally sustaining for young people (Warren & Marciano, 2018). Because the tenets of YPAR challenge hierarchical forms of teaching and learning, research has revealed a great deal of contestation and conflict.

Many studies stress the potential fit of YPAR into literacy instruction in particular because so many elements of the inquiry process map well onto standards; for example, YPAR takes the traditional research paper assignment to a deeper level (Kornbluh, Ozer, & Allen, 2015). Researchers and practitioners explore how YPAR can complement and extend common ELA classroom activities in ways that achieve the critical social analysis and civic purpose called for by critical literacy (DeJaynes & Curmi-Hall, 2019; DeJaynes, Cortes, & Hoque, 2020; Mirra, Filipiak, & Garcia, 2015).

Nonetheless, this research almost always returns to the difficulties that emerge, both logistically and philosophically, from attempts to integrate a radical set of principles into the context of schooling. Logistical concerns include a school bell schedule organized by discrete subject areas, which works against interdisciplinary collaboration; the prevalence of high-stakes standardized test-ing, which has a deterministic effect on curriculum and instructional time; and the constraints of the classroom space itself, which can stifle field work in community sites.

Often more pressing, however, are the tensions that surface when youth critical inquiry upsets prevailing views of power in schools. Researchers document instances whereby school administra-tors who initially support YPAR recoil or block student inquiry when the research challenges poli-cies or practices put in place by adults or encourages students to explore controversial social issues (Buttimer, 2018). Studies in educational leadership explore the difficulty that many school leaders have in taking youth seriously, which loops back to the deficit conceptualization of youth that YPAR challenges (Bertrand, 2019).

These contentious instantiations of YPAR in schools have raised questions about the extent to which YPAR is a viable practice at all in formal educational contexts and the extent to which the compromises made to make it fit within these contexts inherently rob the practice of its radical roots (Brion-Meisels & Alter, 2018). This debate demonstrates the centrality of YPAR to exposing fun-damental tensions between education and schooling and to sparking continued dialogue regarding what it takes to put critical literacy into action.

YPAR Transforms How Teachers are Educated

A developing line of inquiry has emerged that examines the intersection of YPAR and teacher education. Teacher educators who embrace YPAR suggest that preservice and in-service educators who understand and value its tenets constitute a necessary link to better integrating the practice into school instruction, and, by extension, transforming schooling into a force for critical literacy praxis (Brown & Rodriguez, 2017; Mirra & Morrell, 2011; Zenkov, Pellegrino, & Sell, 2014).

Research in this area has highlighted the role of YPAR to actualize the stated commitments of many teacher education programs to equity and social justice (Lac, 2019). When preservice teachers participate in YPAR collectives, researchers suggest that they can engage in anti-colonial models of teacher development (Lyiscott, Caraballo, & Morrell, 2018) that encourage them to critically analyze their own assumptions and biases about the hierarchical teacher/student rela-tionship, adopt asset-based perspectives toward young people and the communities in which they live, and encourage a justice orientation to curriculum planning (Rubin, Abu El-Haj, Graham, & Clay, 2016).

YPAR Connects Critical and Traditional Literacies

While the central values of critical literacy are enacted through YPAR, the liberatory processes through which participatory research unfolds are filled with literacy practices that can look rote and unimaginative. These literacies—such as students preparing presentations to be delivered in stand-ard academic English, conducting survey-based data collection, or drafting an email requesting an interview with a school administrator—resist the critical slide toward developing "militant illiterates" (Morrell, 2010). Examples of how these seemingly traditional literacies thrive within YPAR projects include a focus on functional, pragmatic forms of communication.

Looking across many examples of YPAR projects discussed throughout this chapter, there is a common theme that may be unspoken: in order to "do" YPAR, there are elements of planning, note-taking, developing presentation slides, coordinating meetings via email, sending text messages, and myriad other forms of literacies at work. These forms of coordination spread the gamut of tra-ditional text-based literacies to the multimodal practices that hinge on emerging technologies. Such practices reflect the "syncretic" conceptualizations of literacies that weave academic and sociocultural spaces of learning together (Gutiérrez, 2014).

Recommendations and Forward Thinking

YPAR researchers acknowledge various tensions inherent in this work. These tensions can emerge between the researcher and the researched, popular and official knowledge, written and oral/visual modes of communication, hegemonic and counter hegemonic narratives, educational institutions and community, research and action. Moreover, epistemological questions may also surface regarding ownership, value, and purpose of the knowledge that is produced as YPAR scholars may publish their collaborative research and present at conferences. Additional tensions may arise in professional development initiatives that can expand the impact of YPAR in K–12 schools while also bumping up against the bureaucratic and ideological obstacles that inequitable systems can produce.

To navigate through these tensions and develop sustainable partnerships, YPAR activist academics must commit to a practice of humility, transparency, and accountability in their collaborative work with youth, where contradictions are named and subject to debate through ongoing dialogue and a praxis of action and self-reflection. We highlight three of these areas as we consider recommendations and forward thinking for the field.

Role of Adults in YPAR

Recent scholarship has documented various ways adult researchers have attempted to mitigate the hierarchical power dynamic inherent in YPAR between youth and adults. We suggest that YPAR scholarship continue to focus on the complex and shifting role of adults and relations they develop with youth through this work. Research is also needed into the praxis of work that is moving beyond the adult–youth binary toward CPAR (Critical Participatory Action Research) and IPAR (Intergenerational Participatory Action Research). CPAR is an epistemology that draws on

> [C]ritical theory (feminist, critical race, queer, disability, neo-Marxist, indigenous, and post-structural) . . . [and] challenges hegemonic conceptions of where social problems originate, cultivates deep participation, produces evidence designed to awaken a sense of injustice and seeks to provoke collective engagement.
>
> *(Torre, Fine, Stoudt, & Fox, 2010, pp. 171, 182)*

Torre and Fine (2008) also suggest that researchers consider the individuals, communities, and ecologies that make up the "contact zone" (p. 23) of YPAR projects in order to more explicitly enact solidarity and knowledge production across intergenerational collectives. Such efforts, following the model of the New York City-based program Cyphers for Justice, should explore adults' roles in partnership with youth not only as coresearchers and coproducers of new knowledge but also as audiences in positions of power who are worthy of, and in respectful dialogue with, youth presenting their work (Caraballo & Lyiscott, 2018).

In fact, if there is any single recommendation it would be to remind adult YPAR researchers to interrogate their own positionality, with an emphasis on (re-)centering youth perspectives in dialogue with youth who can hold them accountable. How do youth, for example, experience the decentering of adult power and authority, particularly given how youth have been trained by schooling and social structures to look to and for adults for guidance? What suggestions might they have for the role of adults in YPAR projects?

YPAR Within the System

The resistance of schools to YPAR raises questions concerning the compatibility of a pedagogy that challenges the status quo within institutions that are designed to reproduce it. Research is needed to illuminate how a complex mix of ideology, school leadership, structures, and culture create conditions that can nurture, smother, or co-opt YPAR. This can provide a deeper understanding of the roadblocks erected in defense of institutional prerogatives that critical educators and academic partners must navigate. Studies can examine the process where YPAR can also produce a potential loss of criticality, exploitation, and co-optation for the normative aims of the institutions. How might YPAR grow from and build upon more student-centered, culturally responsive sustaining pedagogies that link classroom learning to real-world social justice issues, particularly within the current context of youth-led anti-racist protest movements? This can include examining the crossover of relationships and projects that YPAR participants develop with other liberatory sites of possibility in alternative and credit recovery schools that lift up silenced and marginalized student voices such as DREAMer clubs, restorative justice programs, and GSAs (Goodman, 2018).

YPAR in Teacher Education

As YPAR scholarship demonstrates its value as a component of teacher education, it also illuminates some of the challenges of this work, highlighting, in particular, how YPAR projects can be "discounted, discredited, and disbelieved" (Brown & Rodriguez, 2017, p. 88) by future teachers on the basis of youth not being "qualified" researchers, as well as other factors, many of which, including use of "appropriate" language, are code for racialized discrimination (Brown & Rodriguez, 2017; Rodriguez & Brown, 2018).

Because, as part of YPAR projects focused on teacher education, youth of color often interface with Primarily White Institutions (PWIs), it is important for scholarship to attend to factors that facilitate and/or enable the success of these endeavors, including preparation done in advance with pre-service teachers and the debriefing done with youth researchers. Because of the overwhelmingly white demographic of future teachers, it is especially important to understand the myriad ways race/ism may be factoring into these experiences for both preservice teachers and the youth researchers. Therefore, questions for consideration include: How are the youth researchers being debriefed from their experiences, particularly if they did not go well? In what ways might these experiences help "reveal ways white supremacy may be operating within teacher education and/or how to work against it?" (Petrone & Rink, 2020, p. 250).

A concern here is that youth researchers brought into a PWI, particularly when they may already have a negative history of participation in/with schools, may be set up for a recapitulation of harm done by/in school (Petrone & Rink, 2020). In this way, we raise questions related to not only enabling and/or inhibiting factors but also ethics to be taken into consideration as research continues to investigate the intersection of YPAR and teacher education.

Our Social Responsibility as Academics

We note that we write this chapter in a historical moment of white supremacist, carceral neoliberalism that presses upon our work. We question—for the critical literacies field writ large—How do we teach and do research *with* our students at a time when we ourselves, these youth, and their families and communities are under siege?

Engaging in YPAR means not just crossing borders that traditionally separate academia from marginalized communities but also actively working to erode them. With these efforts comes a commitment to not only share resources and expertise but also to infuse our work with an analysis of the current sociopolitical context. This means recognizing that, in addition to the problems of under-resourced, inequitable, and segregated schools, many youths live in communities that are under siege from, and engaged in resistance to mass incarceration and deportation, police violence, limited health care, gentrification and homelessness, and more.

Having a critical analysis of these conditions means YPAR scholars are not only working alongside youth to analyze these injustices but also standing in solidarity with them to act upon these issues. Academics who take this commitment seriously must be intentional about forming partnerships with schools and communities and be creative in using their research to attack these problems and their resources to build a sense of agency among youth. Simultaneously, the popularity of YPAR has led to a slipperiness of the label. As YPAR is taken up more broadly in mainstream settings, it is at risk of losing its fundamental criticality. It is the social responsibility of YPAR scholars to uphold and to continually reassess the critical dimensions at the heart of this work.

Finally, we note that YPAR—as an identifiable and named research tradition—is itself part of the adult academic world that has potential negative effects on/for youth. Many youth who are not part of YPAR projects are also active researchers and change agents in the world. That they are not considered engaging in YPAR provokes several questions: What (doesn't) count(s) as YPAR? When and how does "youth research" become "youth participatory action research"? Is YPAR only YPAR when adults name it as such or are involved in it? We raise these questions to draw attention to how the nomenclature and increasing entrenchment within academia of YPAR authorizes and bolsters particular knowledge production and renders marginal/invisible other youth work.

Despite the fact that we must actively work to reshape the world of the academy to be one where the issues and full humanity of historically marginalized youth not only find purchase but are amplified, we must do so in ways that will—for now—be legible by academic constituents. Challenging systemic racism and structural inequalities require a both/and iterative approach that stakes a claim for YPAR epistemologies and methodologies within the academy while simultaneously deconstructing the power of the academy to credential knowledge in the first place. In this way, the civic explorations of YPAR are not only about imprinting acts of literacy on the sociopolitical world but also transforming the interpretations and sense of ownership around critical knowledge through continually agitating the spaces in which YPAR is heard, interpreted, and expanded.

Notes

1. Our definition of civic participation encompasses engagement in formal structures of local, state, and national democratic politics and the informal structures of shared community life. It explicitly pushes back on legal interpretations of citizenship that exclude members of the U.S. civic community.
2. We acknowledge that because the expertise of the authors is confined to the U.S., this chapter does not sufficiently consider international perspectives.

References

Anyon, Y., Bender, K., Kennedy, H., & Dechants, J. (2018). A systematic review of youth participatory action research (YPAR) in the United States: Methodologies, youth outcomes, and future directions. *Health Education & Behavior, 45*(6), 865–878.

Bautista, M. A., Bertrand, M., Morrell, E., Scorza, D., & Matthews, C. (2013). Participatory Action Research and City youth: Methodological insights from council of youth research. *Teachers College Record, 115*, 1–23.

Bertrand, M. (2019). "I was very impressed": Responses of surprise to students of color engaged in youth participatory action research. *Urban Education, 54*(9), 1370–1397.

Brayboy, B. (2005). Toward a tribal critical race theory in education. *The Urban Review, 37*(5), 425–446.

Brion-Meisels, G., & Alter, Z. (2018). The quandary of youth participatory action research in school settings: A framework for reflecting on the factors that influence purpose and process. *Harvard Educational Review, 88*(4), 429–454.

Brown, T., & Rodriguez, L. (2017). Collaborating with urban youth to address gaps in teacher education. *Teacher Education Quarterly, 44*(3), 75–92.

Buttimer, C. (2018). The challenges and possibilities of youth participatory action research for teachers and students in public school classrooms. *Berkeley Review of Education, 8*(1), 39–81.

Cammarota, J. (2017). Youth participatory action research: A pedagogy of transformational resistance for critical youth studies. *Journal for Critical Education Policy Studies, 15*(2), 188–213.

Cammarota, J., & Fine, M. (Eds.). (2008). *Revolutionizing education: Youth participatory action research in motion.* Routledge.

Caraballo, L., Lozenski, B., Lyiscott, J., & Morrell, E. (2017). YPAR and critical epistemologies: Rethinking education research. *Review of Research in Education, 41*, 311–336.

Caraballo, L., & Lyiscott, J. (2018). Collaborative inquiry: Youth, social action, and critical qualitative research. *Action Research, 0*(0), 1–18.

Caraballo, L., & Soleimany, S. (2019). In the name of (pedagogical) love: A conceptual framework for transformative teaching grounded in critical youth research. *Urban Review: Issues and Ideas in Public Education, 51*(1), 81–100.

Carr, W., & Kemmis, S. (1986). *Becoming critical: Education, knowledge, and action research.* Falmer Press.

Carson, C. (1981). *In struggle: SNCC and the black awakening of the 1960s.* Harvard University Press.

Charron, K. M. (2009). *Freedom's teacher: The life of Septima Clark.* University of North Carolina Press.

DeJaynes, T., Cortes, T. Hoque, I. (2020). Participatory action research in schools: Unpacking the lived inequities of high stakes testing. *English Teaching: Practice & Critique, 19*(3), 287–301.

DeJaynes, T., & Curmi-Hall, C. (2019). Transforming school hallways through critical inquiry: Multimodal literacies for civic engagement. *Journal of Adolescent & Adult Literacy, 63*(3), 299–309.

Fals-Borda, O., & Rahman, M. A. (Eds.). (1991). *Action and knowledge: Breaking the monopoly with participatory action research.* The Apex Press.

Fine, M. (2008). An epilogue, of sorts. In J. Cammarota & M. Fine (Eds.), *Revolutionizing education: Youth participatory action research in motion* (pp. 213–234). Routledge.

Fine, M., & Torre, M. E. (2019). Critical participatory action research: A feminist project for validity and solidarity. *Psychology of Women's Quarterly, 43*(4).

Fox, M. (2012). Literate bodies: Multigenerational participatory action research and embodied methodologies as critical literacy. *Journal of Adolescent & Adult Literacy, 55*(4), 343–345.

Freire, P. (1970). *Pedagogy of the oppressed.* Continuum.

Garcia, A., & Mirra, N. (2019). "Signifying nothing": Identifying conceptions of youth civic identity in the English Language Arts Common Core State Standards and the National Assessment of Educational Progress' Reading Framework. *Berkeley Review of Education, 8*(2), 195–223.

Garcia, A., Mirra, N., Morrell, E., Martinez, A., & Scorza, D. (2015). The council of youth research: Critical literacy and civic agency in the digital age. *Reading & Writing Quarterly, 31*(2), 151–167.

Gaventa, J. (1991). Toward a knowledge democracy: Viewpoints on participatory research in North America. In O. Fals-Borda & M. A. Rahman (Eds.), *Action and knowledge: Breaking the monopoly with participatory action research* (pp. 121–131). The Apex Press.

Goodman, S. (2018). *It's not about grit: Trauma, inequity, and the power of transformative teaching.* Teachers College Press.

Goodman, S., & Cocca, C. (2014). Spaces of action: Teaching critical literacy for community empowerment in the age of neoliberalism. *English Teaching: Practice and Critique, 13*(3), 210–226.

Greene, S., Burke, K., & McKenna, M. (2018). A review of research connecting digital storytelling, photovoice, and civic engagement. *Review of Educational Research, 88*(6), 844–878.

Gutiérrez, K. (2014). Integrative research review: Syncretic approaches to literacy learning. In P. Dunston, L. Gambrell, K. Headley, S. Fullerton, & P. Stecker (Eds.), *Leveraging horizontal knowledge and expertise: 63rd literacy research association yearbook* (pp. 48–61). Literacy Research Association.

Kornbluh, M., Ozer, E., & Allen, C. (2015). Youth participatory action research as an approach to sociopolitical development and the new academic standards: Considerations for educators. *Urban Review: Issues and Ideas in Public Education, 47*(5), 868–892.

Lac, V. (2019). The critical educators of color pipeline: Leveraging youth research to nurture future critical educators of color. *Urban Review: Issues and Ideas in Public Education, 51*(5), 845–867.

Lesko, N. (2012). *Act your age! A cultural construction of adolescence.* Routledge.

Lewin, K. (1997). *Resolving social conflicts and field theory in social science.* American Psychological Association.

Lyiscott, J. J., Caraballo, L., & Morrell, E. (2018). An anticolonial framework for urban teacher preparation. *The New Educator.* https://doi.org/10.1080/1547688X.2017.1412000

Marciano, J., & Warren, C. (2018). Writing toward change across youth participatory action research projects. *Journal of Adolescent & Adult Literacy, 62*(5), 484–494.

McIntyre, A. (2000). Constructing meaning about violence, school, and community: Participatory action research with urban youth. *The Urban Review, 32*(2), 123–154.

Mirra, N., Filipiak, D., & Garcia, A. (2015). Revolutionizing inquiry in urban English classrooms: Pursuing voice and justice through youth participatory action research. *English Journal, 105*(2), 49–57.

Mirra, N., & Garcia, A. (2020). *The profound civics lessons kids are getting from the U.S. government's response to the covid-19 pandemic.* Retrieved from www.washingtonpost.com/education/2020/05/06/profound-civics-lesson-kids-are-getting-us-governments-response-covid-19-pandemic/

Mirra, N., Garcia, A., & Morrell, E. (2016). *Doing youth participatory action research: Transforming inquiry with researchers, educators, and students.* New York: Routledge.

Mirra, N., Morrell, E., Cain, E., Scorza, D., & Ford, A. (2013). Educating for a critical democracy: Civic participation re-imagined in the Council of Youth Research. *Democracy & Education, 21*(1), Article 3.

Mirra, N., & Morrell, E. (2011). Teachers as civic agents: Toward a critical democratic theory of urban teacher development. *Journal of Teacher Education, 62*(4), 408–420.

Morrell, E. (2010, April). *Praxis and problem-posing pedagogy: Utilizing critical theory as a transformative tool in urban schools across disciplines.* Paper presented at the American Educational Research Association annual meeting, Denver, CO.

Palos, A. L., & McGinnis, E. I. (Producer). (2011). *Precious knowledge: Fighting for Mexican American studies in Arizona schools.* Dos Vatos Productions, Inc.

Petrone, R., & Rink, N. (with Speicher, C.). (2020). From talking *about* to talking *with*: Integrating native youth voices into teacher education via a repositioning pedagogy. *Harvard Education Review, 90*(2), 243–268.

Rodriguez, L. F., & Brown, T. (2018). Toward transformative practices in teacher development: Lessons from research with youth of color. In E. A. Lopez & E. L. Olan (Eds.), *Transformative pedagogies for teaching education: Moving towards critical praxis in an era of change.* Information Age Publishing.

Rubin, B., Abu El-Haj, T. R., Graham, E., & Clay, K. (2016). Confronting the urban civic opportunity gap: Integrating youth participatory action research into teacher education. *Journal of Teacher Education, 67*(5), 424–436.

Torre, M., & Fine, M. (with Alexander, N., Billups, A. B., Blanding, Y., Geneno, E., Marboe, E., Salah, T., & Urdang, K.). (2008). Participatory action research in the contact zone. In J. Cammarota & M. Fine (Eds.), *Revolutionizing education: Youth participatory action research in motion* (pp. 23–44). Routledge.

Torre, M., Fine, M., Stoudt, B., & Fox, M. (2010). Critical participatory action research as public science. In P. Camic & H. Cooper (Eds.), *Handbook of research methods in psychology* (pp. 171–184). American Psychology Association.

Wagaman, M. A., & Sanchez, I. (2017). Looking through the magnifying glass: A duo ethnographic approach to understanding the value and process of participatory action research with LGBTQ youth. *Qualitative Social Work, 16*(1), 78–95.

Warren, C., & Marciano, J. (2018). Activating student voice through youth participatory action research (YPAR): Policy-making that strengthens urban education reform. *International Journal of Qualitative Studies in Education, 31*(8), 684–707.

Watson, V. W. M., & Petrone, R. (2020). "On a day like this": How a youth epistemological approach can shape English education. *English Teaching: Practice & Critique, 19*(3), 245–251.

Zenkov, K., Pellegrino, A., & Sell, C. (2014). Picturing kids and "kids" as researchers: Preservice teachers and effective writing instruction for diverse youth and English Language Learners. *New Educator, 10*(4), 306–330.

1.6

TEACHERS ENACTING CRITICAL LITERACY

Critical Literacy Pedagogies in Teacher Education and K–12 Practice

Betina Hsieh and Susan Cridland-Hughes

Critical literacy in K–12 contexts is not limited to a specific set of practices for particular students (Lee, 2011). Rather, implementation comes through dynamic and adaptable techniques that are context-dependent (Gregory & Cahill, 2009; McLaughlin & DeVoogd, 2004) and can be enacted with young children (Bourke, 2008; Ciardiello, 2004; Souto-Manning, 2009) as well as secondary students (Bean & Moni, 2003; McLaughlin & DeVoogd, 2004; Wood, Soares, & Watson, 2006) across a range of achievement levels (Lee, 2011).

Further, critical literacy is not simply critical thinking practices in the liberal–humanist tradition (Cervetti, Pardales, & Damico, 2001). The goal of liberal–humanist grounded critical reading practices is to promote claims based on evidence and higher order thinking (Cervetti et al., 2001; Lee, 2011). While critical literacy necessitates critical thinking, critical literacy also considers power, both in text and context (Gregory & Cahill, 2009; Shor, 1992). Janks (2000, 2012, 2014) discusses critical literacy as a way to understand power by examining how texts have been constructed, whose interests are served in their authoring, and how those messages work to produce our identities. In their examination of research and professional literature on critical literacy in teacher practice, Lewison and her colleagues (2002) found four dimensions central to critical literacy: disrupting the commonplace; interrogating multiple viewpoints; focusing on social political issues; and taking action to promote social justice. In other words, critical literacy extends beyond identifying textual meaning or even recognizing sociopolitical contexts that give texts and symbols particular meanings in sociohistorical moment; it also emphasizes the ability to take action in response to the subtexts of the word and the world (Morrell, 2008).

In defining critical literacy for teaching and teacher learning contexts, we consider how critical literacy has often been misrepresented and oversimplified in pedagogical contexts. Literacy, itself, in fact, is often reduced to encompass only reading and writing. This reduction masks the inherent sociopolitical and ideological nature of being literate in particular ways that allow people to access power, independence, and flexibility within particular societies (Gregory & Cahill, 2009). While textual analysis of written texts and the production of traditional forms of writing are certainly part of critical literacy, as a construct, critical literacy is not limited to reading and writing traditional forms of text (Lee, 2011). In fact, Freire (1985) defines critical literacy as going beyond reading the word (written text) to support students in reading and interpreting the world around them. Freire and Macedo (1987) extend this idea to emphasize the importance of developing communities of critically literate people who understand both how meaning is socially constructed and the political

DOI: 10.4324/9781003023425-7

and economic contexts surrounding texts, thereby recognizing the role of literacy in their own emancipation.

Freire's work on critical literacy focused primarily on the role of adult facilitators coming to know and critique their own worlds in community. However, the transfer of these ideas from community-based learning spaces into governmental agencies such as K–12 schools, and to teachers' work in formal settings, has been less clear. To address this gap, this chapter examines research on enacting critical literacies in K–12 classrooms and our own classroom practice as teacher educators in promoting critical literacies pedagogies. First, we discuss how preservice teachers learn about critical literacy and how teacher candidates and teacher educators might support one another to enact critical literacy in practice through critical collaborative learning environments. We then look at the literature around the enactment of critical literacies in classroom spaces with two lived examples from our own work with educators. Finally, we end with considerations for future work in teacher preparation and professional learning that can support rich and varied critical literacy practices in K–12 classrooms and our responsibility in that work as both academics and teacher educators.

Introducing and Supporting Critical Literacy Practices for K–12 Teachers: An Evolving Perspective

Two major foci that emerge from the literature on teacher learning about and enacting critical literacy are developing critical literacy dispositions through reflective practice and explicit choice-making by teachers and teacher educators to engage in the work of critical literacy. The work on preservice teacher education highlights the need to explicitly address teacher beliefs and teacher positioning vis-à-vis students who may have different cultural, linguistic, and literacy experiences than their own (Heydon & Hibbert, 2010; Jones & Enriquez, 2009). To engage in critical literacy, teacher candidates and teacher educators must consider the places from which they read the word and the world (Freire & Macedo, 1987) and reflect on their own experiences as starting points to consider larger sociopolitical contexts based on identities related to gender, race, social class, and dis/ability (Heydon & Hibbert, 2010; Jones & Woglom, 2016). To become more critically literate, educators' taken-for-granted beliefs must be explicitly and intentionally disrupted, prompting conscious, guided reflection on their practice, including the ways in which literacy is taught and learned in schools (Heydon & Hibbert, 2010). Teacher educators can begin this work by asking teacher candidates to consider texts, the culture of schooling, and assessments through critical frameworks and supporting candidates to relate these experiences to their own literacies and learning, as spaces from which to challenge dominant practices (Riley & Crawford-Garrett, 2015).

As teachers enter the field, they must be aware that texts and schooling situations are cloaked in sociopolitical rhetoric and historical contexts, and they must develop analytical tools of critical literacy in order to fully understand, interpret, and deconstruct these interwoven constellations of rhetorical standpoints (O'Quinn, 2005). New teachers must also be willing to critically examine the way that their own practices demonstrate evidence of critical literacy practice (Luna et al., 2004). Teachers transitioning from preservice to teaching in their own classrooms must move beyond a critical literacy stance intellectually grounded in theory, to adopt, instead, morally grounded beliefs about the importance of critical literacy as a process involving continuous authentic reflection on the teacher's position and students' roles, representation, participation, and voices in the classroom (Jones & Enriquez, 2009). For teachers to embrace critical literacy, they must engage in both intellectual and moral shifts that allow them to teach children who move through and interpret worlds different from their own.

Critical collaborative inquiry, a tool for both teachers and teacher educators to reflect on integrating critical literacy practices as part of teacher learning, emerged as a particularly salient way by which to develop critical literacies (Crawford-Garrett & Riley, 2016; Luna et al., 2004; Riley, 2015; Riley & Crawford-Garrett, 2015). Additionally, integrating texts and ethnographic work that center multiple perspectives, including voices often left out of traditional curriculum (Crawford-Garrett & Riley, 2016; Jones & Woglom, 2016; Mosley, 2010) into literacy preservice education classes can promote critical literacy practices. Beginning as teacher candidates, educators can examine and acknowledge the inherent power in their positions as future teachers and the political nature of teaching as a profession (Jones & Enriquez, 2009).

Exploring Enactments of Critical Literacies in Preservice and K–12 Contexts

We organize the remainder of the chapter by examining themes related to teacher enactment of critical literacy practices including: considerations of student identities, teacher agency, and the use of texts and tools to support critical literacies. We first discuss the literature, then offer two lived examples from our own teacher education practice as illustrations of the enactment of critical literacies in teacher learning spaces.

Critical Literacies for Whom: Considering and Engaging Student Identities

The literature on critical literacy pedagogies often focuses upon the ways teachers help students to understand power, contexts, and subtexts related to texts with which students identify. A subset of this literature, however, highlights the importance of student identities when engaging in critical literacy practices. Literacy practices that center Black male experiences (Wood & Jocius, 2013) by giving Black male students opportunities to engage in socially conscious ways with texts that are culturally relevant to them can be one example of considering student identities in ways that promote critical literacy. Critical literacies are strengthened through the use of culturally responsive pedagogies like text collaboration and critical conversations in contexts that honor Black male students' rights to express their truths and challenge the truths of others (Wood & Jocius, 2013). A second example centers around a teacher's work with young students from low-income backgrounds in Australia (Comber, Thomson, & Wells, 2001). Primary students were asked to draw wishes, worries, and things that angered them in relation to both local and global contexts, then walked their neighborhood in order to author solutions, which were then sent to local organizations. In this example, the teacher drew from the community-based knowledge of students then supported them to read, interpret, and take notes on the world around them before moving into local action.

Teacher facilitation of critical literacy development, however, may require (uncomfortable) shifts in teacher perspectives and practice. Hagood (2002) explores the ways in which teachers ascribe particular identities to students which, when taken up, contribute to particular readings of the world that may be problematic. She argues that we must consider both students' perceptions of their own identities and the subjective perceptions of others, particularly teachers, in relation to reading the world when examining critical literacy in K–12 school contexts. Teachers must be willing to change their own thoughts about students in order to engage in work that can develop and consider student identities. Another example, from a rural primary setting, was that of a first-grade teacher who moved beyond her comfort in teaching "happy" texts to her first graders (Leland, Harste, & Huber, 2005), by introducing texts that engaged issues with which they were familiar (e.g., poverty and isolation) through experiences beyond their rural environments (e.g., urban homelessness and Japanese American incarceration camps). These studies portray teachers as important actors who set up learning opportunities that either support or detract from students' development of critical literacy practices.

Teacher Agency: Enacting Critical Literacy Practices

In addition to considering student identity and positioning within classrooms, the literature notes the role of teachers' stance itself. This section examines the ways in which teachers enact their roles in the classroom to promote students' critical engagement in and beyond classroom spaces.

One foundational principle that teacher educators discuss with K–12 teachers is the power of everyday curricular choices they make, particularly in text selection within their classrooms. Luke (2012) argues that literacy and access to texts have always been "struggles over the control of information and interpretation" and that "wherever textual access, critique, and interpretation are closed down . . . human agency, self-determination and freedom are put at risk" (p. 5). Using preservice teacher education to engage the question of access and denial of marginalized identities in the official curriculum, and of simultaneous welcoming and unwelcoming structures within a particular school context, is central to preparing teachers to make decisions in real classrooms that hold space for all. The literature includes multiple examples of using young adult fiction (Bean & Moni, 2003), multimodal texts (Morrell, 2002, 2008), and multicultural children's literature (Souto-Manning, 2009) to engage K–12 students, as well as the adoption of critical literacies stances toward reading (Locke & Cleary, 2011; McLaughlin & DeVoogd, 2004). Introducing diverse text types and modalities to preservice candidates and teachers who may have had more traditional literacy experiences creates space for critical literacy practices.

However, text selection alone is not enough for teachers to set up authentic opportunities for critical literacy development. In examining storytelling as critical literacy pedagogy, Enciso (2011) demonstrates how teachers in traditional classroom settings can inadvertently shut down students' connections to texts and to one another. To prevent this, teachers must vigilantly counter hegemonic norms of schooling that may silence students and instead establish contexts that allow for students to be heard. By creating opportunities for multivocal engagement with community issues grounded in power, belief, representation, and knowledge, critical literacies work can take place (Enciso, 2011). Similarly, Aukerman (2012) asserts that dialogic engagement which decenters teachers as the primary textual authority is a rarely considered, but integral, part of critical literacy. The decentering of self is likely rare because it is uncomfortable. To create dialogic environments of authentic student interaction, teachers must reconsider traditional roles in which they exert control over narratives and interactions in the classroom. By repositioning themselves as members of a community of learners and storytellers rather than at the center, teachers give up control of classroom discourse, thereby creating spaces in which critical literacies practices are more likely to emerge.

K–12 teachers must also be willing to reconsider what critical literacy practices may look like when taken up by students. When focusing exclusively or predominantly on textual interpretation, teachers may miss students' powerful embodied or performative critical literacy practices (Johnson & Vasudevan, 2012; Lopez, 2011) or critical literacy emerging from unexpected connections between events in students' worlds and the words they are reading (Hagood, 2002). Again, this requires teachers to push beyond traditional notions of literate practices and center students' ways of knowing.

Finally, teachers must be able to consider their role in promoting student agency through critical literacy practices in and beyond the classroom. Examples of this from practice include exploring social studies and social justice issues through critical lenses (Ciardiello, 2004; Reidel & Draper, 2011; Soares & Wood, 2010) that engage students as social actors, as well as through modeling stances of activism and agency in constructing curriculum (Lopez, 2011). In cases like this, while critical literacy may begin through reading and writing in classrooms, teachers extended the reach of critical literacy into communities and societies. This required additional commitments to enactment on the part of teachers, but afforded more authentic critical literacy opportunities for students.

Multimodal Texts and Tools to Promote Critical Literacies

In considering urban youth identities, practices drawing from New Literacy Studies (The New London Group, 1996), with its focus on social context, diversity, multimodality, and honoring youth identities and experiences, provide salient ways to enact critical literacies pedagogies in K–12 classrooms and center student voices. Enacting critical literacies can come through nontraditional textual responses to traditional text formats (Mosley, 2010), through centering nontraditional texts such as hip-hop rap, spoken word, popular film, television, media and social media (Morrell, 2002, 2008), and through promoting multimodal practices to accomplish socially responsive goals within classroom communities in response to community social issues (Silvers, Shorey, & Crafton, 2010).

Using critical media literacy frameworks and popular culture texts as an approach to teach critical literacies, particularly for adolescents, is not a new idea (Alvermann & Hagood, 2000; Morrell, 2002). However, in terms of teacher learning and digital literacies, research indicates that teacher educators must explicitly ground digital literacy courses and opportunities for practice (e.g., projects) in critical literacy frameworks in order for teacher candidates to move beyond a comfort zone of simply using technology as an innovative tool to support practice (Myers & Beach, 2004; Robertson & Hughes, 2012). Thoughtful digital and media literacies can empower educators to design and enact practices promoting greater community agency and critical consciousness. Integrating critical literacy-based multimodal learning opportunities, however, also requires shifts on the part of educators (and teacher educators) away from deficit views of digital literacies as taking away from literacy learning and toward a view of twenty-first-century tools and literacies as powerful ways to engage with both the words and worlds around us (Avila & Moore, 2012; Kingsley, 2010; Stewart et al., 2021 see also Stewart, Scharber, Share, and Crampton, this volume).

Preservice Example: Taking Up Critical Literacy Practices in Lesson Design

The literature can help us consider the following lived example of a preservice candidate in Betina's secondary literacy course. In this course, candidates designed lesson plans incorporating twenty-first-century literacies to support student learning. While no explicit integration of critical literacies was required, the course was taught from a framework that centered identity in relation to literacies and asked candidates to consider literacy broadly and in the context of students' lives and society. Texts (both traditional and digital) used in class centered perspectives of traditionally marginalized subgroups, with a focus on humanization, empathy, and understanding perspectives of those who differ from us within a context of power, and the class incorporated multiple digital tools for students to use.

Cinthia (pseudonym), a Latina preservice English teacher, submitted a high school lesson plan with the essential question: *What is power?* In designing her plan, Cinthia used multiple multimodal texts and digital tools to enhance development of critical literacy for her future students. Cinthia's chosen texts for the lesson included multiple perspectives on the idea of power, and she highlighted Yalitza Aparicio, an indigenous Mexican actress featured in *Time's* 100 Most Influential People of 2019 as an example (Cuarón, 2019). She also included a Macklemore video (Macklemore LLC, 2013) and TED-Ed talk (Liu, 2014) as other multimodal and nontraditional classroom texts. These texts allowed for relevant and varied examinations of power taken from popular culture, often not centered in academic spaces. Cinthia incorporated these texts in a "digital gallery walk" through the digital platform Padlet, a strategy and tool previewed in the methods class. Further, Cinthia integrated both traditional and nontraditional response formats in her plan, requiring both written responses to two pins on the Padlet board, as well as a Flipgrid recorded response synthesizing students' ideas about power and ideas shared with them by a partner in class.

Cinthia used critical literacy as a way to support future students in interrogating notions of power by synthesizing tools and activities that she had been exposed to in preservice literacy coursework. Cinthia adapted the digital gallery walk activity from Betina's model in class on US agricultural movements. Betina's model centered the experiences of women and people of color, including images for young mothers in the Dust Bowl era, braceros, the farm workers' movement, and recent farm labor strikes against fast food restaurants. Further, Betina had used other multimodal texts including digital stories, spoken word, graphic novels, and music videos with Cinthia's class. These nontraditional texts centered on themes such as intergenerational relationships among immigrant mothers and daughters and bullying and were contemporary texts chosen to represent Latinx and Asian American experiences (matching program demographics). Betina's choices in designing her preservice course considered who students were and integrated multimodal texts that asked them to consider identity, literacy, and themes relevant in the world as well as through texts. Cinthia's lesson plan demonstrates the ability of a preservice teacher candidate to take up modeled practices and integrate tools, texts, and principles for critical purposes when such texts, tools, and critical literacy perspectives are a foundational part of preservice coursework.

From Preservice to the Classroom: Living Critical Literacies in the Day-to-Day Work of Teaching Texts

Lesson plans like Cinthia's demonstrate how instruction grounded in critical literacy perspectives can impact candidate lesson design, but it remains difficult to determine how much conversations around critical literacies that occur in the methods coursework influence the texts, methods, and critical orientations that teachers use once they enter their own classrooms. Rogers, Wetzel, and O'Daniels (2009) focus on the apprenticing into critical literacy that occurs as preservice teachers move into the classroom, practicing critical literacy and demonstrating what that looks like for both the students in their classrooms and for the novice teachers who come after them. Susan's secondary English methods course and local district experience offer an example of how one former student enacted "teacher critical literacy" in order to apprentice both K–12 students and preservice teachers into critical literacy.

Fall semester of their senior year, English Education majors take a course focused on designing and implementing a unit of study. While preparing to design the unit, students read articles on dialogic practices and critical literacy and on the need for diverse representation in literature (Cridland-Hughes, 2012; We Need Diverse Books, 2020). Conversations in the class explore the intersection of power and identity in the design of curriculum with explicit advocacy for candidates to read widely, read diversely, and bring those varying perspectives into the classrooms where they teach. Graduates from the English Education program often go on to teach in local school districts where preservice teachers in Susan's program are placed. This was the case for Parker (pseudonym), a White teacher who had graduated from Susan's program three years earlier and started her teaching career in a diverse high school in a small rural district, and Chelsea (pseudonym), a preservice teacher placed with a cooperating teacher at Parker's school. As part of Parker's curriculum for the 2019–2020 school year, she created a unit focused on *The Hate U Give* (Thomas, 2017). When Parker began asking for resources to teach the text, the district curriculum director brought Parker's unit to the attention of the school board. The school board placed a moratorium on the teaching of all novels not on the approved list until they made a decision related to Parker's unit. Chelsea's unit on literature circles could not be started until a decision was reached regarding Parker's *THUG* unit. One week later, all English teachers in the district were notified that they were to teach only the officially sanctioned novels. Chelsea's attempts to navigate this challenge became a source of ongoing discussion in Susan's Monday night class, as both Susan and the other students provided support to Chelsea while she revised her unit.

The first part of this story demonstrates how the system resists challenges to official knowledge and the curriculum. What Parker did next, however, created space for both her students as learners and herself as an instructor. Instead of teaching the novel, Parker taught excerpts, choosing to interpret the moratorium as only applying to full-length novel studies. Parker's agency was democratizing in her focus on the needs and interests of her students over a prescribed curriculum and activist in circumventing attempts to restrict her power. In their analysis of how teachers develop critical literacy stances, Rogers et al. highlight three aspects of critical literacy: "discourses of action, discourses as action, and discourses in action" (2016; p. 307), with activism as "the dialogue between an individual's conscience and inequitable social conditions that prompt one to act" (p. 308). Parker engaged in a critically literate navigation of the system. Through this act, she also provided an example to Chelsea, apprenticing her into how teachers can hold space for their students and themselves, modeling teaching as both agentive and resistant. This notion of apprenticeship into advocacy, of showing both students and colleagues how to be authentically engaged in critical action through our actions and our discussions, offers a frame for how to expand practices of critical literacy that challenge power in and beyond classrooms.

Moving Critical Literacies Forward in Teacher Education and Teacher Enactment

Both lived examples illuminate the importance of professional models and intentionality in text and pedagogical choices to promote the development of critical literacy practices for K–12 teachers. Betina served as a professional model for her preservice students. Being able to engage with a variety of multimodal texts that were chosen to reflect perspectives often left out of the curriculum, in a variety of ways, supported Cinthia in developing a lesson plan centering the idea of power and drawing upon similar types of texts and modalities. In Susan's example, Parker enacted critical literacy practices introduced in her preservice coursework by navigating district administrative attempts to prevent her from teaching a relevant young adult text with important themes around race and police brutality. In doing so, Parker enacted activist critical literacies that created space for curricular critical literacy while serving as a model for Chelsea of how to resist curricular limits.

While the studies featured in this chapter demonstrate that critical literacies can and are being enacted by teacher educators and teachers in K–12 spaces, there is work to be done in moving critical literacies practice forward in these areas. One notable trend across both the examples and the studies reviewed is that the work focuses on the efforts of individuals, either within teacher education contexts or within K–12 site contexts. Collaboration through reflective practice helps K–12 teachers develop and strengthen their ability to enact critical literacies; however, the research in this area does not offer systemic or structural approaches to integrating critical literacies in teacher education contexts, K–12 sites, or during the transition between credential programs and classroom teaching.

As reflected in other chapters of this handbook, there is clear knowledge about critical literacies implementation in a variety of contexts. We recommend that critical literacies be extended to teacher education and K–12 contexts through more cohesive, coherent models of teacher learning. These might include embedding critical literacies practices throughout multiple courses in a teacher education program or making critical literacies the focus of extended professional learning work within a department or across a K–12 school site. Considering the myriad ways in which critical literacies can be conceptualized and integrated into classroom practice, focusing on critical literacies as a framework for professional learning can be a powerful way in which to move the work beyond individual agency and individual educators to become a lens through which educators consider their pedagogical and curricular practices. Further research on the enactment of critical literacies across teacher education programs, K–12 sites, and districts is critical to extending the reach of critical literacies.

A second focal area for research in K–12 critical literacies implementation is the induction period. As preservice teachers move to their beginning practice, what supports might be introduced to build more cohesion between teacher education programs, induction programs, and novice teacher learning? Susan's example of Parker's experience demonstrates the powerful actions of a single teacher navigating oppressive institutions and also raises the question of how many new teachers face challenges to their desire to implement critical literacies practices and then back down. With more cohesive systems of support and connections between teacher education programs and school districts, perhaps new teachers like Parker would either face less resistance from school districts or be better equipped to navigate situations like the one we described.

We Must Move the Work Forward Together

As academics and teacher educators, we see our role as supporting critical literacies in teacher education praxis and through K–12 partnerships. As scholars who have done research on our individual practice and who are interested in critical literacies enactment, we must begin to move beyond our own classrooms and candidates to look for openings and partnerships within broader teacher education contexts. Our critical literacies work must move toward collective enactment, with the knowledge that this collective enactment will not be possible without strong understanding of and commitment to critical literacy practices. Given the major shifts in curriculum, teacher positioning, pedagogies, and active agency required to enact critical literacies, this work will be complex, but it is essential to move the work forward in more powerful ways.

Further, we must deepen and extend partnerships and teacher learning opportunities to strengthen the impact of critical literacies practices. As teacher educator academics, we must make concerted efforts to follow our preservice candidates from our classrooms into their practicum placements and professional practice to support them as they navigate professional environments that may not support the development or enactment of their critical literacy practices. Finally, we must leverage our positions and power in our work with schools and districts to advocate for supportive professional learning that can strengthen the understanding and enactment of critical literacies practices. In supporting a reconceptualization of the work of teaching through a lens of critical literacies, we can contribute to empowerment and change through teaching and learning.

RELATED TOPICS: Youth civic participation and activism; Critical literacies and writing; Critical media production, Critical literacy and English language teaching, Situated critical literacy pedagogy and classroom discourse, Culturally sustaining pedagogies and critical literacies.

References

Alvermann, D. E., & Hagood, M. C. (2000). Critical media literacy: Research, theory, and practice in "New Times". *The Journal of Educational Research, 93*(3), 193–205.

Aukerman, M. (2012). "Why do you say yes to Pedro, but no to me?" Toward a critical literacy of dialogic engagement. *Theory into Practice, 51*(1), 42–48.

Avila, J., & Moore, M. (2012). Critical literacy, digital literacies, and common core state standards: A workable union? *Theory into Practice, 51*(1), 27–33.

Bean, T. W., & Moni, K. (2003). Developing students' critical literacy: Exploring identify construction in young adult fiction. *Journal of Adolescent & Adult Literacy, 46*(8), 638–648.

Bourke, R. T. (2008). First graders and fairy tales: One teacher's action research of critical literacy. *The Reading Teacher, 62*(4), 304–312.

Cervetti, G., Pardales, M. J., & Damico, J. S. (2001). A tale of differences: Comparing the traditions, perspectives, and educational goals of critical reading and critical literacy. *Reading Online, 4*(9), 80–90.

Ciardiello, A. V. (2004). Democracy's young heroes: An instructional model of critical literacy practices. *The Reading Teacher, 58*(2), 138–147.

Comber, B., Thomson, P., & Wells, M. (2001). Critical literacy finds a "place": Writing and social action in a low-income Australian grade 2/3 classroom. *The Elementary School Journal, 101*(4), 451–464.

Crawford-Garrett, K., & Riley, K. (2016). Living and learning in the here-and-now: Critical inquiry in literacy teacher education. *Journal of Language and Literacy Education, 12*(2), 33–55.

Cridland-Hughes, S. (2012). Literacy as social action in City Debate. *Journal of Adolescent and Adult Literacy, 56*(3), 194–202.

Cuarón, A. (2019, December). Yalitza Aparicio. *Time 100: The most influential people of 2019*. Retrieved from https://time.com/collection/100-most-influential-people-2019/5567863/yalitza-aparicio

Enciso, P. (2011). Storytelling in critical literacy pedagogy: Removing the walls between immigrant and non-immigrant youth. *English Teaching: Practice and Critique, 10*(1), 21–40.

Freire, P. (1985). Reading the world and reading the word: An interview with Paulo Freire. *Language Arts, 62*(1), 15–21.

Freire, P., & Macedo, D. (1987). *Literacy: Reading the word and the world*. Routledge.

Gregory, A., & Cahill, M. A. (2009). Constructing critical literacy: Self-reflexive ways for curriculum and pedagogy. In *Critical literacy: Theories and practices*.

Hagood, M. C. (2002). Critical literacy for whom? *Literacy Research and Instruction, 41*(3), 247–265.

Heydon, R., & Hibbert, K. (2010). "Relocating the personal" to engender critically reflective practice in pre-service literacy teachers. *Teaching and Teacher Education, 26*(2010), 796–804.

Janks, H. (2000). Domination, access, diversity and design: A synthesis for critical literacy education. *Educational Review, 52*(2), 175–186.

Janks, H. (2012). The importance of critical literacy. *English Teaching: Practice and Critique, 11*(1), 150–163.

Janks, H. (2014). Critical literacy's ongoing importance for education. *Journal of Adolescent & Adult Literacy, 57*(5), 349–356.

Johnson, E., & Vasudevan, L. (2012). Seeing and hearing students' lived and embodied critical literacy practices. *Theory into Practice, 51*(1), 34–41.

Jones, S., & Enriquez, G. (2009). Engaging the intellectual and the moral in critical literacy education: The four-year journeys of two teachers from teacher education to classroom practice. *Reading Research Quarterly, 44*(2), 145–168.

Jones, S., & Woglom, J. F. (2016). From where do you read the world? A graphic expansion of literacies for teacher education. *Journal of Adolescent & Adult Literacy, 59*(4), 443–473.

Kingsley, K. V. (2010). Technology-mediated critical literacy in K–12 contexts: Implications for 21st century teacher education. *Journal of Literacy and Technology, 11*(3), 2–39.

Lee, C.-j. (2011). Myths about critical literacy: What teachers need to unlearn. *Journal of Language and Literacy Education, 7*(1), 95–102.

Leland, C., Harste, J., & Huber, K. (2005). Out of the box: Critical literacy in a first-grade classroom. *Language Arts, 82*(4), 257–268.

Lewison, M., Seely Flint, A., & Van Sluys, K. (2002). Taking on critical literacy: The journey of newcomers and novices. *Language Arts, 79*(5), 382–392.

Liu, E. (2014, November 4). *TED-Ed: How to understand power—Eric Liu* [Video]. Retrieved from www.youtube.com/watch?v=c_Eutci7ack

Locke, T., & Cleary, A. (2011). Critical literacy as an approach to literary study in the multicultural, high-school classroom. *English Teaching: Practice and Critique, 10*(1), 119–139.

Lopez, A. E. (2011). Culturally relevant pedagogy and critical literacy in diverse English classrooms: A case study of a secondary English teacher's activism and agency. *English Teaching: Practice and Critique, 10*(4), 75–93.

Luke, A. (2012). Critical literacy: Foundational notes. *Theory into Practice, 51*(1), 4–11. https://doi.org/10.1080/00405841.2012.636324

Luna, C., Botelho, M. J., Fontaine, D., French, K., Iverson, K., & Matos, N. (2004). Making the road by walking and talking: Critical literacy and/as professional development in a teacher inquiry group. *Teacher Education Quarterly, 31*(1), 67–80.

Macklemore LLC. (2013, April 17). *Macklemore & Ryan Lewis—can't hold us feat*. Ray Dalton (Official Music Video) [Video]. Retrieved from www.youtube.com/watch?v=2zNSgSzhBfM

McLaughlin, M., & DeVoogd, G. (2004). Critical literacy as comprehension: Exploring reader response. *Journal of Adolescent & Adult Literacy, 48*(1), 52–62.

Morrell, E. (2002). Toward a critical pedagogy of popular culture: Literacy development among urban youth. *Journal of Adolescent & Adult Literacy, 46*(1), 72–77.

Morrell, E. (2008). *Critical literacy and urban youth: Pedagogies of access, dissent, and liberation*: Routledge.

Mosley, M. (2010). Becoming a literacy teacher: Approximations in critical literacy teaching. *Teaching Education, 21*(4), 403–426.

Myers, J., & Beach, R. (2004). Constructing critical literacy practices through technology tools and inquiry. *Contemporary Issues in Technology and Teacher Education, 4*(3), 257–268.

O'Quinn, E. J. (2005). Critical literacy in democratic education: Responding to sociopolitical tensions in US schools. *Journal of Adolescent & Adult Literacy, 49*(4), 260–267.

Reidel, M., & Draper, C. A. (2011). Reading for democracy: Preparing middle-grades social studies teachers to teach critical literacy. *The Social Studies, 2011*(102), 124–131.

Riley, K. (2015). Enacting critical literacy in English classrooms: How a teacher learning community supported critical inquiry. *Journal of Adolescent & Adult Literacy, 58*(5), 417–425.

Riley, K., & Crawford-Garrett, K. (2015). Reading the world while learning to teach: Critical perspectives on literacy methods. *Teacher Education Quarterly, 42*(3), 59–79.

Robertson, L., & Hughes, J. (2012). Surfacing the assumptions: Pursuing critical literacy and social justice in preservice teacher education. *Brock Education Volume, 22*(2), 73–92.

Rogers, R., Kramer, M., Mosley, M., & The Literacy for Social Justice Teacher Research Group. (2009). *Designing socially just learning communities: Critical literacy education across the lifespan.* Routledge.

Rogers, R., Wetzel, M., & O'Daniels, K. (2016). Learning to teach, learning to act: Becoming a critical literacy teacher. *Pedagogies: An International Journal, 11*(4), 292–310. https://doi.org/10.1080/15544 80X.2016.1229620

Shor, I. (1992). *Empowering education: Critical teaching for social change.* University of Chicago Press.

Silvers, P., Shorey, M., & Crafton, L. (2010). Critical literacy in a primary multiliteracies classroom: The hurricane group. *Journal of Early Childhood Literacy, 10*(4), 379–409.

Soares, L., & Wood, K. (2010). A critical literacy perspective for teaching and learning social studies. *Reading Teacher, 63*(6), 486–494.

Souto-Manning, M. (2009). Negotiating culturally responsive pedagogy through multicultural children's literature: Towards critical democratic literacy practices in a first-grade classroom. *Journal of Early Childhood Literacy, 9*(1), 50–74.

Stewart, O., Hsieh, B., Pandya, J.Z., & Smith, A. (2021). What More Can We Do? A Scalar Approach to Examining Critical Digital Literacies in Teacher Education. *Pedagogies: An International Journal, 16*(2), 125–137. https://doi.org/10.1080/1554480X.2021.1914054

The New London Group. (1996). A pedagogy of multiliteracies: Designing social futures. *Harvard Educational Review, 66*(1), 60–92.

Thomas, A. (2017). *The hate u give.* Balzer and Bray.

We Need Diverse Books. (2020, February 19). *About WNDB.* Retrieved from https://diversebooks.org/about-wndb/

Wood, K. D., Soares, L., & Watson, P. A. (2006). Research into practice: Empowering adolescents through critical literacy. *Middle School Journal, 37*(3), 55–59.

Wood, S., & Jocius, R. (2013). Combating "I hate this stupid book!": Black males and critical literacy. *The Reading Teacher, 66*(8), 661–669.

1.7

CHILDREN'S AND YOUTH'S EMBODIMENTS OF CRITICAL LITERACY

Elisabeth Johnson, Grace Enriquez, and Stavroula Kontovourki

Keywords

Embodiment—Broadly, embodiment refers to an ontological, experiential, and/or material quality, expression, or representation of discursive reality. The term *embodiment* is used widely to describe what happens through, by, within, and to the material body. Some scholars use the term for general description and macroanalysis; others use it to refer literally and specifically to the human body in parts or constituted as a whole.

Disciplined body—The notion of the disciplined body recognizes that the human body is both object and subject of power. As object, the body can be viewed and analyzed for its material constitution and actions. As subject, the body is regulated through discursive ways of being, feeling, and acting in order to produce a specific kind of ideal subject or identity.

Body as social text—Conceptualizing the body as social text acknowledges that bodies are both perceived through social discourses and that social discourses materialize through bodies. To this extent, bodies represent and mediate the social discourses at play in a given context. Likewise, such discourses provide the lenses through which bodies are read.

Feeling/sensing body—Registering the feeling/sensing body acknowledges that human bodies are more than just their material makeup. The body is a medium through which we feel, sense, and respond to physical–social–historical–political contexts in which we exist and flow. Our decisions, actions, and knowledge within a particular context are shaped by emotions discourses into affective practices. The degree of emotional response within, through, and by the body are assessed as affective intensities.

Intra/acting body—Highlighting the intra/action of the body emphasizes how the boundaries and borders between humans and nonhumans are constantly enmeshed, fleeting, indeterminate, and impossible to truly disentangle, assembling with emotion, discourse, matter, movement, and tension. Such intra/action invites opportunities to reshape, re-matter, and re-story bodies and thereby interconnectedness with the world.

Embodied literacies—These encompass the various assemblages of literacies and bodies. Literacy is multimodally conceived (hence, the plural *literacies*) to include the multiple modalities through which we read and compose the world, and the body is the medium through which such reading and composing transpire. We propose four frameworks for embodied literacies: literacy practices as a mechanism for disciplining bodies, bodies that are read and (re)fashioned as social texts, literacy practices that circulate and mobilize bodies to make meaning through

 DOI: 10.4324/9781003023425-8

material-discursive and affective engagements, and the mutually indeterminate, mobile realities of bodies and literacies.

Historical, Current, Emerging Theory

Children and youth bodies have been the focus in studies of their multimodal meaning-making as early as the 1980s (e.g., Harste, Woodward, & Burke, 1984), and this contrasts policies and pedagogies that have depended upon understandings of the mind over the body, and language over other ways of sense-making. Valuing children's embodiments of literacy echoes a broader "body" turn in social and human sciences. In our edited volume (Enriquez, Johnson, Kontovourki, & Malozzi, 2016), we acknowledged how dualistic tendencies are challenged through the recognition of the inseparability of the mind–body–social, the entanglement of stuff, sensations, and affects, and the concurrent possibility of fixity and emergence. We proposed that the embodiment of literacy serves as a construct to expose how literate bodies are simultaneously disciplined and disciplining; lived, feeling, and affective; social texts that are impossible to represent but also possible to re-present; and thus mobile and indeterminate (Johnson & Kontovourki, 2016). Acknowledging recent developments in new materialist and post-humanist work (e.g., Kuby & Gutshall Rucker, 2016; Stornaiuolo, Smith, & Phillips, 2017), we added that literacy is not only of subjective feelings, material bodies, or produced subjectivities but also expands to the ways in which bodies are always intra-acting with human and nonhuman, material and immaterial entities (un)bounded in spaces and times; risking and affirming recognition (Kontovourki, Johnson, & Enriquez, forthcoming).

That bodies are disciplined has been a recurring theme in earlier studies of children's embodiment of literacy in institutional spaces like school classrooms. Luke's (1992) analyses of pedagogies in early literacy classrooms focus on children's bodies inscribing broader configurations of power, discourse, and authority. Drawing on Foucault's technologies of the self and Bourdieu's notion of habitus, Luke (1992) traces how children's bodies become both objects and subjects as they are repeatedly arranged (physically and corporeally) via pedagogical truth claims that produce an ideal literate subject. The deconstruction of this material subject denaturalizes literacies and subjectivities through concepts of discursive power, moral regulation, and social reproduction. Likewise, Dixon (2011) suggested that school literacy learning is permeated by discourses that shape children as particular types of literate subjects that emerge in education policy, classroom practices, and arrangements of time and space. Drawing on performativity theory, Enriquez (2016) concurs, arguing that readers' classroom transactions with texts are surveilled, regulated, and recognized differently, and this affects their meaning-making and recognition as literate subjects.

Children's and youth's embodiments of literacy also identify how they concurrently take up and destabilize discourses inscribed on and inscribing their bodies. Analyzing children's embodied performances in classroom spaces, Kontovourki (2014) noticed how these were fragmented, manifold, and open to redefinition. Muhammad and Haddix (2016) reach similar conclusions in their review of Black girls' ways of knowing, where they argue that bodies may be read as "reimagined text in action" (p. 315) that reference historicized discourses of, in this case, race and gender. As such, bodies are social texts perpetually made and potentially remade. This possibility of re-representation is often assumed to be discursively constructed and non-discursively performed, as children's and youth's bodies and adornments become material resources to remake selves, engage critically in social worlds, and craft spaces of belonging (Blackburn, 2016; Johnson, 2011; Wager & Perry, 2016).

This view of the body destabilizes literacy, always in flux and necessarily felt, lived, and emotive. Emotive responses may be differentially recognized or ignored in social spaces like school classrooms (Lewis & Crampton, 2016), indexing the material-discursive effects that lie dormant in schooled bodies (Jones, 2016) and spill out of classed, gendered bodies entangled in territorializing academic practices (Thiel, 2016). Attention to bodies as affective can also imply a nonrepresentational view of literacy; unhinged from stable grammars of design that permeate movement toward a goal, product, or text (e.g., Ehret, 2016; Leander & Boldt, 2013) instead focused on the coming-togetherness of people, things, and the unknowingness of emergence (Ehret & Leander, 2019; Wargo, 2015). The Handbook authors Ehret and Rowsell (Chapter 3.12) further explore the potential of affect to untether literacy from social and political historical time; reimagining a perpetually reconfigured, reimagined politics as feelings. What counts as political unfolds moment-to-moment anew. In this sense, (critical) literacy becomes indeterminate, impossible to pin down and always becoming. Recent post-humanist theorizations of critical literacy echo this contingent politics, conceptualizing children's and youth's bodies in classrooms as more-than-human assemblages of material and immaterial forces (Lenters & McDermott, 2020).

Reviews of and Implications for Research

Much literacy research that explicitly claims a social justice orientation connects critical literacy and embodiment. Scholars in this vein draw on critically focused theories (e.g., CRT, feminism, poststructuralism) to highlight ways bodies engage with discursive relations, power inequities, and identities like gender (e.g., Kirkland, 2009; Shannon & Labbo, 2002), race (e.g., Rogers & Mosley, 2006; Muhammad & Haddix, 2016), socioeconomic class (e.g., Dutro, 2009; Jones, 2006), dis/ability (e.g., Goodley, 2013), language (Esquivel, 2019), and their various intersections. Embodied identities are also conceptual tools that erode critical literacy as a rationalist act. Janks (2002) presented a case study of a South African restaurant chain's attempts at humorous advertising to argue that "identity investments" in discourse take us into a "territory beyond reason" where embodied knowledge, desire, and identification can work against . . . cold, distanced, and disembodied critical analysis of text" (p. 9). Other frameworks treat "embodiment" as an ontological, experiential stance necessary for identifying and analyzing discourses of power, situating critical literacy as an attitude or frame of being (Shor, 1999; Rogers & Mosley, 2006; Vasquez, Janks, & Comber, 2019).

However, identity, embodiment, and criticality do not always line up predictably. Following two graduate students into their full-time roles as classroom teachers, Jones and Enriquez (2009) found that embodying critical literacy practices can fluctuate. Using Bourdieuian constructs of field, habitus, doxa, and capital, they argue that how one embodies criticality may look different in varying contexts as those constructs intersect. Specifically, "embodied intellectual and moral dispositions toward critical literacies might produce situated pedagogical practices in response to children" (p. 162). Similarly, applying critical discourse analysis, Rogers's (2002) ethnography of an African-American mother and daughter revealed a discursive and ideological disconnection between their proficient negotiation of language and literacy at home versus at school. As such, literate subjectivities are often fragmented, where one might have "acquired-and embodied-two contradictory subjectivities" (p. 266).

This fragmentation can be a resource when diverse funds of knowledge (Moll, Amanti, Neff, & Gonzalez, 1992) are valued in classrooms. Through critical discourse analysis, Esquivel's (2019) case study found that social justice pedagogy infused with culturally responsive pedagogy enabled Latinx emergent bilingual students to utilize the discourses they brought to their bilingual elementary classroom, thus cultivating their criticality via engagement in examinations of power within texts. Such embodiment does not necessarily manifest itself corporeally, but through a broader sense of being, feeling, emoting, moving, and intra/acting within a human and nonhuman assemblage, allowing both the body and context to be reshaped, re-mattered, and re-storied toward social justice.

While embodiment is central to criticality, the two converge in complex ways, depending largely on who is setting the critical objective. Noticing that this is particularly the case when working with youth, we review work that theoretically conceptualizes both criticality and literacies as embodied, first in research where adults set the critical objective and, then, as emerging in embodied youth literacies.

Adults Setting Critical Objectives Supple to Youth Embodiment

In designing and assigning critical literacy work with youth, educators and researchers set an agenda with varying results. Whether designed as classroom instruction or out-of-school activity, such work often invites youth to deconstruct the texts of their world and reconstruct them toward social justice goals. Many studies deliberate how teacher-directed critical literacy pedagogy positions bodies as texts to be discursively analyzed, mobilized, and rewritten. Many of those projects include explorations of curricular practices as well as practitioner research with children's literature, websites, and artifacts of children's and youth's pop culture. Researchers focused on multiliteracies, particularly those interested in popular culture and critical media literacy (e.g., (Alvermann, Moon, & Hagood, 1999; Hagood, 2002) and drama pedagogy (e.g., Medina, Coggin, & Weltsek, 2014) are concrete in their discussions about embodiment, recognizing the material body's appearance, movements, and gestures as a semiotic system that could be read and remade critically like any other text. Other studies encompass the body into broader directives for critically examining texts and the subjectivities evoked when encountering them. Specifically calling out the young Black female body, Richardson (2013) showed how pervasive dominant discourses about Black female sexuality were in the reception of the narratives of two tween girls in an afterschool setting designed to empower Black women and girls. Indeed, Jones and Decatur-Hughes (2011) posit that bodies must be regarded seriously, centrally and critically when engaging in justice-oriented pedagogy. They advocate a "critical body pedagogy" to explore, critique, and reconstruct the meaning-making junctions of bodies and texts.

Even when the body itself is not the focus of critical analysis, researchers have found that it materializes because of its capacity for being read and reinscribed. For Caffrey and Rogers (2018), the body can be moved, manipulated, and repositioned to invite critical literacy. In a museum exhibit assignment for a unit on "Exploring Identity," Caffrey and Rogers found that students purposefully designed displays that solicited the body to take an active role in the display experience. Fox (2011/2012) found the same necessity to incorporate embodied methods of processing text in a critically focused, multigenerational participatory action research project. Through embodied methodologies, particularly drama-based techniques, participant-researchers were able to make "room for different experiences and multiple interpretations" in support of critical literacy understandings (p. 345).

Toward these assertions, such studies affirm the "body as a tool for narration and a resource for critical literacy" (Doerr-Stevens, Lewis, Ingram, & Asp, 2015, p. 28). Expanding the ontological-experiential to include the material, Comber, Thompson, & Wells (2001) maintain that critical consciousness rises from one's being and sensing of place, but it is also entwined with kinesis, or movement (Comber, 2013). Furthermore, place is a relational, ever-in-flux concept as one's sense of belonging in any place is under constant negotiation. Mills, Comber, and Kelly (2013) illustrate this assertion via sensory ethnographic methods that explored the digital media productions of children:

> The active participation of children's whole bodies—the eyes, the ears, the feet, the hands and other organs—as well as an active mind, are involved in making sense of place, and of representing perceptions and knowledge of the world.
>
> *(p. 25)*

Bodies, accordingly, are pivotal not just for their sensory utility but for positioning in a way to feel, live, and move within the critical and social justice issues of a given place.

As these feelings and movements disrupt *adult* notions of critical literacies, explorations of these unanticipated encounters can generate insights for research, theory, and practice. Petrone and Bullard (2012) note that student resistance is rarely explored in *English Journal* projects designed with critical literacy objectives. Though "within critical literacy, student resistance may actually be generative" (p. 127). (Teacher)-researchers attuned to youth's embodied, critical literacies can illustrate youth's contingent efforts to revise, recognize, and reconfigure the features of (Enriquez, 2016; Krone, 2019), conditions within (Wager & Perry, 2016) and perpetual means through which (Lewis & Dockter Tierney, 2011; Ehret, Hollett, & Jocius, 2016) students' embodied counter-narratives take place amidst critical curriculum and pedagogy. Indeed, Vander Zanden and Wohlwend (2011) posited that critical literacy practices are strengthened when we see their relationship to embodied classroom and school routines and the procedural texts that accompany them (e.g., anchor charts outlining "rules" for an activity). To that end, some critical literacy work traces how youth's embodied performances intra/act with modes, genres, and places to challenge, disrupt, or denaturalize power relations in and beyond school spaces where adults endeavor to set objectives or engage students in critical (media) literacy practice (Alvermann et al., 1999; Johnson, 2011; Lewis & Crampton, 2016).

Youth's critical, embodied pushback on adults' objectives also extends to instructional experiences intended to be critically focused. Sometimes, pushback stems from the power of affect. Extending Rosenblatt's concept of aesthetic reader-response, which asserts how the nexus of feeling, thought, and experience impact textual response, Enriquez (2016) highlighted students' unsanctioned embodied performances to a whole-class read-aloud. Enriquez found that these *body-poems* can signify disconnection with the text that discloses discursive relations between text and student. Likewise, Lewis and Dockter Tierney (2011) describe the pushback of Vanessa and Shannon, two African American high school students who disagreed with a teacher-provided article that attempted to critically analyze the 1995 Disney animated film, *Pocahontas* while upholding reified racist views of Black female sexuality. Youth's body-poems and mobilized emotion indicate embodied critical literacy work that may or may not be sanctioned by classroom norms for textual response or anticipated by adamant advocates of social justice pedagogy.

Some researchers make unanticipated encounters' boundary work visible, displaying roles prefigured methodologies play in constraining, provoking, and negotiating representations of youth's critical literacies. Krone (2019), a White female university researcher, examines six Black seventh grade boys' embodied refusals of racial binaries she proffered as part of her initial inquiry into their collaborative composition process. Turning to choreographic criticalities renders auteurs choreographing *Mute*, a raceless faceless superhero who shared power on the basketball court. Participants assumed *and* refused racialization; imagining beyond erasure. In contrast, Wager and Perry's (2016) critical ethnography of a Vancouver youth-led theatre production *assumed* embodiment *and* resistance, analyzing moments of resistance to "explore the negotiations of power, desire, and space within . . ." (p. 258). After scripting and rehearsing a play about recent closures of underage safe houses, cast members refused to memorize personal experience scripts instead improvising scenes to play one another, social workers and hospital staff; changing histories, responses, and social positions. As teacher–artist–researchers render contingent negotiations of critical objectives, youth's embodied refusals demand contingent pedagogical and methodological shifts that can *become* inquiry, findings, and implications.

Exploring Embodied Youth Literacies Turns Up Critical Engagement

In contrast to setting critical literacy objectives at the start of a project, some research into children and youth embodiments of (critical) literacies frame the literate body—and decidedly, the student body—as both a medium recognized for its potential for critical literacy work *and* an agent already in the throes of criticality (Wohlwend & Lewis, 2011). In some of this work, researchers conceptualize literacies as intra-actionally formed, entangled, assembled amidst and across **bodies**–things–texts–sounds–feelings–places. While decentering the language of critical *literacies*, we include it here as it draws on critical literacies work while endeavoring to reconfigure it. Returns to dominant discourses and literacy practices, while attempting to disrupt them, are vital given their durable, disciplinary, material constraints on youthful bodies living at the intersections of marginalized identities, (e.g., race, social class, gender, dis/ability, etc.) (Dernikos, Ferguson, & Siegel, 2019; Nichols & Campano, 2017).

Several scholars of embodied literacies of socially and structurally marginalized youth render embodied critical literacies as part of youth's everyday lives, to survive, thrive, and be. Johnson and Vasudevan (2012) cast critical literacy as performed, positioned, and produced by youth and find that what youth wear on their bodies as well as *ir*rational responses, are embodiments of everyday texts; critical literacy performances youth engage in daily. Kirkland (2009) reads Derreck's tattoos as literacy artifacts that enflesh symbolic stories of struggle, help Derreck navigate challenges and perpetually connect Derreck to his past. Inking a life journal visible to all, Derreck renders *personal* events and identities undervalued in school. In a case study of Simone, a tenth-grader who assembled gestures, movements, sounds, and silences, Johnson (2011) illustrated how youth use such embodied performances to assert and sometimes shroud criticality as a means to maintain a critical identity along with multiple other identities. Blackburn (2016), too, recognized this constructive notion of performance, as her case study of Kira, a biracial, lesbian adolescent girl, showed how bodies can be refashioned and re-presented, a site where both imagination and action have potential. Thomas and Stornaiuolo (2016) looked at youth's online bending of mainstream texts via social media. This kind of re-storying, or refashioning narratives to reflect diverse perspectives and experiences is marked by the bending of popular children's and young adult media to "manifest embodied, lived realities and identities" via race (p. 315). Critical valence accumulates as youth position themselves—consciously and subconsciously—as critical agents in their learning and identity (re)presentation across spaces.

Humor as embodied, affective, improvisational practice is another means by which youth play with anticipated performances of critical literacy. Juxtaposing "hot-spots," in two separate studies, McDermott and Lenters (2019) proffer assemblages of humor-sacred "objects" and youth as emergent critical literacies. They illustrate how African-American and Muslim youth's unanticipated connections in the moment (between MLK and a roast and a hijab as blindfold in a classroom comedy sketch) incited laughter or play that reconfigured patterned social roles, sedimented boundaries, sociocultural narratives, and white school adult expectations for sanctioned topics in learning encounters, thereby operating as critical literacies.

Without context and history, youth's embodied critical literacies risk invisibility and romanticization. Thiel (2015) illustrates critical *engagement* during a time when a costume provoked curiosity and affect that continued, uninterrupted without "challenge or frustration"; leveraging Zack's (a young regular at the Awesome Club House, an out of school art-making space) inclusion in a peer group. Zapata (Zapata, Kuby, & Thiel, 2018) renders an assemblage of linguistic and nonlinguistic resources in a translanguaging event where English–Japanese–Arabic assemble amidst markers, a graffiti board, an open space for composing on a campus mourning and reacting to police violence against black community members, and an audience (Zapata et al., 2018). Decentering youth's agentic actions, im/material non/linguistic interactants surrounding play, inclusion, and a translanguaging moment become objects of exploration in these studies. Critical valence comes with the marginalized statuses afforded "Awesome Club House" community youth-thing-place engagements (like Zack's) whose doing-being-knowing beyond discursive constraint are critical literacies. Critical valence *is* "powerful, infidel heteroglossia," in an English-dominant space for a student with a history of linguistic marginalization.

Scholars who study youth's composition *processes* as embodied literacies find queer innovations and material-discursive boundary-making across time, place, things, feelings, and bodies. Wargo

(2015) finds that 16-year-old Ben's composing via Snapchat is techno-embodied, that is, selves and composing processes are continuous. Snapchat Stories, an inherently queer practice, enfolds past and present so time is felt during and beyond events as Ben moves to compose new stories in response to past stories that evince audiences' felt experience of his present. Critical valence comes as embodied mobile composing queers linear, disembodied, disconnected conceptions of time, space, and the composition process. Through "idea tracing," Ehret et al. (2016) follow five adolescents' ideas expressed across three physical locations, field notes, video and audio of student work, interviews, researcher feelings, and side conversations to idea actualization in the production process and product of a digital book trailer. They find youth making media across places and things are always already engaged in the continuous emergence of boundaries that produce exclusion and motivation. In this sense, such work to document embodied literacies of youth saves critical literacy pedagogy from becoming a potentially colonizing practice on students by teachers.

Researchers exploring youth embodiments and (critical) literacies in a post-human world encourage adults with critical objectives to slow down, watch closely, listen intently, intervene less, follow more, and document widely across unplanned space–times. They find that critical engagements emerge. To that end, but enacted differently, Woodard, Vaughan, and Coppola (2020) distribute agency for the *object of inquiry and findings* across the bodies of school-involved stakeholders, (i.e., youth, teachers, and youth caregivers) in a school–university partnership study of embodied writing. Drawing on Enriquez et al.'s (2016) embodiment framework as methodology, Woodard et al. (2020) inquire into (a) students' writing practices produced by and from their bodies and (b) writing practices' effects on their own and others' embodied actions. When students write by and from their bodies, their bodies operate as modes of representation with things like hijab or Quran, and they write to counter-narrate negative experiences like hijab discrimination.

These works affirm that purposeful positioning of the physical body engaging in critical literacy activities is already happening. The pedagogical challenge rests in educators' methods for valuing the intrinsic, embodied critical literacy engagement of youth. Acknowledging such activity levels authority for defining critical literacy beyond the teacher or explicit curriculum, and assumes that youth are fully capable of exploring and exposing the ways power circulates, potentially across under-recognized communication modes (genres, things, feelings) and events.

Forward Thinking

Critical literacy scholarship embraces embodiment as requisite for criticality; central in deconstructing dominant discourses, reconstructing narratives, and mobilizing action. As technologies of discipline or texts of social identity, bodies are signifiers of discursive dominance and marginalization while sites of promise, sensors of place-based matters, circulators of emotion, shifters of identity, critics of normative routines and ways of knowing, story-benders, and space–time travelers.

And while youth reimagine critical literacy daily, independent of adult intervention, "traditional" critical literacy work is still important as youthful bodies are still being read, relegated, and positioned in ways that uphold dominant discourses about race, gender, language, dis/ability, sexual orientation across on and offline worlds with durable, material, inequitable consequences (Nichols & Campano, 2017). Indeed, as Wager and Perry (2016) illustrate, without the external imposition of their critical drama-based pedagogical project, improvisations that rethink staid narratives impacting homeless youth would remain invisible for stakeholders positioned to revise educational opportunities for homeless youth. While representations of critical literacies in their embodied contingency and indeterminacy are impossible to predict, within that boundary-work alongside minoritized youth, retheorizations of critical literacy via praxis take place and social and civic actions transpire. Woodard et al. (2020) embody this boundary work in their collaborative inquiry into youth's embodied writing with a local network of cross-generational school stakeholders working toward curricular and pedagogical transformation. Next steps for youth embodiments of critical literacies theory, research, and pedagogies might enmesh this embodied method with practices like collaborative, retrospective "idea tracing" (Ehret et al., 2016) across data gathered with multigenerational stakeholders. How does power circulate bodies–feelings–things–places as we trace from identifying the embodied problem of practice to embody findings as curricular/pedagogical revision? Collaborative, cross-generational methodologies in groups with power to constrain, recognize, and reimagine youth's daily school experiences assumes and enfolds critical literacies' recognition into research processes and pedagogical practices in *real* time, heeding the call to act *and* think with theory (Dernikos et al., 2019).

Implications for Social Responsibility as Academics

After reviewing current research on embodiment and critical literacies, we are left wondering who gets to eschew the binary or deconstructionist approach to children's and youth's embodiments of critical literacy? Who gets to eschew representation when we still live in a world where representations do material harm? While there is work arguing toward the impossibility of representation in research, there are researchers working the intersections of these boundaries, doing both and, using their lived histories as resources when following children and youth across contexts, crafting, curating, and rendering lived critical literacies as performatives, engagements, encounters, and more (e.g., Thiel, 2015). Franklin-Phipps and Rath (2019) frankly position themselves as reluctant post-humanists, "unwilling to concede a category we've never been allowed to fully occupy: full humanist subject" (p. 147). Together, they point out the material consequences of post-humanist literacy frameworks that lean toward *becoming* in lieu of anti-racist *action*; emphasizing instead "the mixological putting-into-relation of putatively incongruent components" as opposed to the "philosophical unseeing of racial assemblages" (Weheliye, 2014, p. 65 in Franklin-Phipps & Rath, 2019). Racial literacy, for example, forces a reckoning with time and academic responsibility to render and bend before deconstructing representation of children's and youth's embodiments of critical literacies. And this extends to the boundaries academics have constructed around age and the time within which we follow and render youth to include transitions to adulthood often expedited for Black youth (Goff, Jackson, Di Leone, Culotta, & DiTomasso, 2014) while materially deferred for adults with dis/Abilities (Midjo & Aune, 2017). As Muhammad and Haddix (2016) note, Black girls' literacies are simultaneously multiple, tied to identities, historical, collaborative, political/critical. We close with the knowledge that scholarship on the literacies of Black Indigenous youth and Children of Color is, in and of itself, research on embodied critical literacies given the racialized discourses, identities, and systems Black youth inherit, bend, deconstruct, counter, transcend, live, and breathe.

References

Alvermann, D., Moon, J., & Hagood, M. (1999). *Popular culture in the classroom: Teaching and researching critical media literacy*. International Reading Association.

Blackburn, M. (2016). Traditionally marginalized bodies make space through embodied literacy performances. In G. Enriquez, E. Johnson, S. Kontovourki, & C. Mallozzi (Eds.), *Literacies, learning, and the body: Putting theory and research into pedagogical practice* (pp. 170–181). Routledge.

Caffrey, G., & Rogers, R. (2018). Students taking social action: Critical literacy practices through school-as-museum learning. *Berkeley Review of Education, 8*(1), 83–114.

Comber, B. (2013). Schools as meeting places: Critical and inclusive literacies in changing local environments. *Language Arts, 90*(5), 361–371.

Comber, B., Thompson, P., & Wells, M. (2001). Critical literacy finds a "place": Writing and social action in a low-income Australian grade 2/3 classroom. *The Elementary School Journal, 101*(4), 451–464.

Dernikos, B., Ferguson, D. E., & Siegel, M. (2019). The possibilities for "humanizing" posthumanist inquiries: An intra-active conversation. *Cultural Studies Critical Methodologies, 0*(0), 1–14.

Dixon, K. (2011). *Literacy, power, and the schooled body: Learning in time and space.* Routledge.

Doerr-Stevens, C., Lewis, C., Ingram, D., & Asp, M. (2015). Making the body visible through dramatic and creative play: Critical literacy in neighborhood bridges. In M. Perry & C. L. Medina (Eds.), *Methodologies of embodiment: Inscribing bodies in qualitative research* (pp. 28–52). Routledge.

Dutro, E. (2009). Children's testimony and the necessity of critical witness in urban classrooms. *Theory Into Practice, 48,* 231–238.

Ehret, C. (2016). Moving off-screen: Pathways for understanding an adolescent's embodied experience of new media making. In G. Enriquez, E. Johnson, S. Kontovourki, & C. Mallozzi (Eds.), *Literacies, learning, and the body: Putting theory and research into pedagogical practice* (pp. 136–151). Routledge.

Ehret, C., Hollett, T., & Jocius, R. (2016). The matter of new media making: An intra-action analysis of adolescents making a digital book trailer. *Journal of Literacy Research, 48*(3), 346–377. https://doi.org/10.1177/1086296X16665323

Ehret, C., & Leander, K. M. (2019). Introduction. In K. M. Leander & C. Ehret (Eds.), *Affect in literacy learning and teaching: Pedagogies, politics and coming to know.* Routledge.

Enriquez, G. (2016). Reader response and embodied performance: Body-poems as performative response and performativity. In G. Enriquez, E. Johnson, S. Kontovourki, & C. Mallozzi (Eds.), *Literacies, learning, and the body: Putting theory and research into pedagogical practice* (pp. 41–56). Routledge.

Enriquez, G., Johnson, E., Kontovourki, S., & Malozzi, C. (Eds.). (2016). Literacies, learning, and the body: Bringing research and theory into pedagogical practice. In J. Rowsell & C. Lewis (Series Eds.), *Expanding literacies in education series.* Routledge.

Esquivel, J. (2019). Embodying critical literacy in a dual language classroom: Critical discourse analysis in a case study. *Critical Inquiry in Language Studies.* https://doi.org/10.1080/15427587.2019.1662306

Fox, M. (2011/2012). Literate bodies: Multigenerational participatory action research and embodied methodologies as critical literacy. *Journal of Adolescent & Adult Literacy, 55*(4), 343–345.

Franklin-Phipps, A., & Rath, C. L. (2019). Collage pedagogy: Toward a posthuman racial literacy. In C. Kuby, K. Spector, & J. Thiel (Eds.), *Posthumanism and literacy education: Knowing/becoming/doing literacies* (pp. 142–155). Routledge, 2018.

Goff, P. A., Jackson, M. C., Di Leone, B. A. L., Culotta, C. M., & DiTomasso, N. A. (2014). The essence of innocence: Consequences of dehumanizing Black children. *Journal of Personality and Social Psychology, 106*(4), 526–545. https://doi.org/10.1037/a0035663

Goodley, D. (2013). Dis/entangling critical disability studies. *Disability & Society, 28*(5), 631–644. https://doi.org/10.1080/09687599.2012.717884

Hagood, M. C. (2002). Critical literacy for whom? *Reading Research and Instruction, 41*(3), 247–266.

Harste, J., Woodward, V., & Burke, C. (1984). *Language stories and literacy lessons.* Heinemann.

Janks, H. (2002). Critical literacy: Beyond reason. *Australian Educational Researcher, 29*(1), 7–27.

Johnson, E. (2011). "I've got swag": Simone performs critical literacy in a high-school English classroom. *English Teaching: Practice and Critique, 10*(3), 26–44.

Johnson, E., & Kontovourki, S. (2016). Introduction: Assembling research on literacies and the body. In G. Enriquez, E. Johnson, S. Kontovourki, & C. Mallozzi (Eds.), *Literacies, learning, and the body: Putting theory and research into pedagogical practice* (pp. 3–19). Routledge.

Johnson, E., & Vasudevan, L. (2012). Seeing and hearing students' lived and embodied critical literacy practices. *Theory Into Practice, 51*(1), 34–41.

Jones, S. (2006). Language with an attitude: White girls performing class. *Language Arts, 84*(2), 114–124.

Jones, S. (2016). When the body acquires pedagogy and it hurts: Discursive practices and material affects of round robin reading. In G. Enriquez, E. Johnson, S. Kontovourki, & C. Mallozzi (Eds.), *Literacies, learning, and the body: Putting theory and research into pedagogical practice* (pp. 75–89). Routledge.

Jones, S., & Decatur-Hughes, H. (2011). Speaking of bodies in justice-oriented, feminist teacher education. *Journal of Teacher Education, 63*(1), 51–61.

Jones, S., & Enriquez, G. (2009). Engaging the intellectual and the moral in critical literacy education: The four-year journeys of two teachers from teacher education to classroom practice. *Reading Research Quarterly, 44*(2), 145–168. https://dx.doi.org/10.1598/RRQ.44.2.3

Kirkland, D. (2009). The skin we ink: Tattoos, literacy, and a new English education *English Education, 41*(4), 375–395.

Kontovourki, S. (2014). Reading (through) bodies: Students' embodied performances of poetry and testing. *Pedagogies: An International Journal, 9*(2), 133–154.

Kontovourki, S., Johnson, E., & Enriquez, G. (2020). Guest editorial: Embodiment and literacies: Teaching, learning, and becoming in a post- world. *English Teaching: Practice & Critique, 19*(4), 381–388. https://doi.org/10.1108/ETPC-11-2020-191

Krone, B. (2019). Embodied refusals and choreographic criticalities. *English Teaching Practice and Critique, 18*(4), 415–428.

Kuby, C.-K., & Gutshall Rucker, T. (2016). *Go be a writer! Expanding the curricular boundaries of literacy learning with children.* Teachers College Press.

Leander, K., & Boldt, G. (2013). Rereading "A pedagogy of multiliteracies": Bodies, texts, and emergences. *Journal of Literacy Research, 45*(1), 22–46.

Lenters, K., & McDermott, M. (2020). Introducing affect, embodiment, and place in critical literacy. In K. Lenters & M. McDermott (Eds.), *Affect, embodiment, and place in critical literacy: Assembling theory and practice* (pp. 1–18). Routledge.

Lewis, C., & Crampton, A. (2016). Literacy, emotion, and the teaching/learning body. In G. Enriquez, E. Johnson, S. Kontovourki, & C. Mallozzi (Eds.), *Literacies, learning, and the body: Putting theory and research into pedagogical practice* (pp. 105–121). Routledge.

Lewis, C., & Dockter Tierney, J. (2011). Mobilizing emotion in an urban English classroom. *Changing English, 18*(3), 319–329.

Luke, A. (1992). The body literate: Discourse and inscription in early literacy learning. *Linguistics and Education, 4*(1), 107–129.

McDermott, M., & Lenters, K. (2019). Youth reassembling difficult topics through humour as boundary play, *Pedagogy, Culture & Society.* https://doi.org/10.1080/14681366.2019.1700299

Medina, C. L., Coggin, L., & Weltsek, G. (2014). Foregrounding emergence, embodiment, and critical practices: Performance pedagogies in literacy methods. In J. Brass & A. Webb (Eds.), *Teaching the English language arts methods: Contemporary methods and practices* (pp. 70–82). Routledge.

Midjo, T., & Aune, K. E. (2017). Identity constructions and transition to adulthood for young people with mild intellectual disabilities. *Journal of Intellectual Disabilities, 22*(1), 33–48.

Mills, K., Comber, B., & Kelly, P. (2013). Sensing place: Embodiment, sensoriality, kinesis, and children behind the camera. *English Teaching: Practice and Critique, 12*(2), 11–27.

Moll, L. C., Amanti, C., Neff, D., & Gonzalez, N. (1992). Funds of knowledge for teaching: Using a qualitative approach to connect homes and classroom. *Theory into Practice, 31*(2), 132–141.

Muhammad, G. E., & Haddix, M. (2016). Centering Black girls' literacies: A review of literature on the multiple ways of knowing of Black girls. *English Education, 48*(4), 299–336.

Nichols, T. P., & Campano, G. (2017). Posthumanism and literacy studies. *Language Arts, 94*(4), 245–251.

Petrone, R., & Bullard, L. (2012). Reluctantly recognizing resistance: An analysis of critical literacy in English journal. *English Journal, 102*(2), 122–128.

Richardson, E. (2013). Developing critical hip hop feminist literacies: Centrality and subversion of sexuality in the lives of Black girls. *Equity & Excellence in Education, 46*(3), 327–341. https://doi.org/10.1080/1066568 4.2013.808095

Rogers, R. (2002). Between contexts: A critical discourse analysis of family literacy, discursive practices, and literate subjectivities. *Reading Research Quarterly, 37*(3), 248–277.

Rogers, R., & Mosley, M. (2006). Racial literacy in a second-grade classroom: Critical race theory, whiteness studies, and literacy research. *Reading Research Quarterly, 41*(4), 462–495.

Shannon, P., & Labbo, L. D. (2002). Critical literacy in everyday life. *Language Arts, 79*(5), 415–424.

Shor, I. (1999). What is critical literacy? *Journal of Pedagogy, Pluralism, and Practice, 1*(4). https://digitalcommons. lesley.edu/jppp/vol1/iss4/2

Stornaiuolo, A., Smith, A., & Phillips, N. (2017). Developing a transliteracies framework for a connected world. *Journal of Literacy Research, 49*(1), 68–91.

Thiel, J. J. (2015). "Bumblebee's in trouble!" Embodied literacies during imaginative superhero play. *Language Arts, 93*(1), 38–49.

Thiel, J. J. (2016). Shrinking in, spilling out, and living through: Affective energy as multimodal literacies. In G. Enriquez, E. Johnson, S. Kontovourki, & C. Mallozzi (Eds.), *Literacies, learning, and the body: Putting theory and research into pedagogical practice* (pp. 90–104). Routledge.

Thomas, E. E., & Stornaiuolo, A. (2016). Restorying the self: Bending toward textual justice. *Harvard Educational Review, 86*(3), 3.

Vander Zanden, S., & Wohlwend, K. E. (2011). Paying attention to procedural texts: Critically reading school routines as embodied achievement. *Language Arts, 88*(5), 337–345.

Vasquez, V. M., Janks, H., & Comber, B. (2019). Critical literacy as a way of being and doing. *Language Arts, 96*(5), 300–311.

Wager, A. C., & Perry, M. (2016). Resisting the script: Assuming embodiment in literacy education. In G. Enriquez, E. Johnson, S. Kontovourki, & C. Mallozzi (Eds.), *Literacies, learning, and the body: Putting theory and research into pedagogical practice* (pp. 252–267). Routledge.

Wargo, J. (2015). Spatial stories with nomadic narrators: Affect, Snapchat, and feeling embodiment in youth mobile composing. *Journal of Language and Literacy Education*, *11*(1), 47–64.

Wohlwend, K. E., & Lewis, C. (2011). Critical literacy, critical engagement, and digital technology: Convergence and embodiment in glocal spheres. In D. Lapp & D. Fisher (Eds.), *Handbook of research on teaching English language arts* (3rd ed., pp. 188–194). Lawrence Erlbaum Associates.

Woodard, R., Vaughan, A., & Coppola, R. (2020). Writing beyond "the four corners": Adolescent girls writing by, in, from, and for bodies in school. *Journal of Literacy Research*, *52*(1), 6–31. https://doi.org/10.1177/1086296X19896496

Zapata, A., Kuby, C. R., & Thiel, J. J. (2018). Encounters with writing: Becoming-with posthumanist ethics. *Journal of Literacy Research*, *50*(4), 478–501. https://doi.org/10.1177/1086296X18803707

1.8

QUEER CRITICAL LITERACIES

Navan Govender and Grant Andrews

Introduction

In this chapter, we argue for queer critical literacies (QCL) that engages with issues of power, access, diversity, and (re)design (Janks, 2010) in relation to both the big-P and little-p politics of (a)gender and (a)sexual diversity (Miller, 2015). Where a critical literacy approach to teaching and learning understands that language and literacy are socioculturally situated and bound to ideology, QCL foregrounds how issues of (a)gender and (a)sexual diversity are silenced, (mis)represented, and policed in educational contexts. We argue that language and literacy classrooms are well suited to engage in queer readings and writings of the word and the world (Freire, 1985).

Consider, for example, the introduction to Francis's (2017a) *Troubling the Teaching & Learning of Gender & Sexuality Diversity in South African Education*. Francis presents three striking narratives of LGBTIQ+ youth's schooling experiences that reveal the "heterosexist positions" (p. 5) that schools can (un)wittingly impose. The stories of violence, exclusion, and discrimination that learners report took place in South African schools which should uphold one of the world's most progressive constitutions, especially regarding the rights of gender and sexually diverse people. Similar policy-implementation gaps emerge globally: from the experiences of gender and sexually diverse people across Europe and Central Asia (ILGA, 2020), projects in South(east) Asia (Salzburg Global Seminar, 2019), the complexities of gender and sexual diversity in Latin America and the Caribbean (Corrales, 2015), the criminalisation or protection of LGBTIQ+ people across various African countries (Awondo, Geschiere, & Reid, 2012; Francis, 2017b), and media representation in the United States and Britain (GLAAD Media Institute, 2019; British LGBT Awards, 2020).

Both the personal stories and the larger international studies of LGBTIQ+ experiences highlight the need for teachers and learners to situate their literacy and language learning in both global issues of social justice and the local, (inter)personal politics of everyday life. This requires taking up a QCL position that engages with meaning-making as socioculturally situated, intrinsic to issues of identity, and that emerges from ideological systems of power and resistance (Street, 1985). Negotiating issues of (a)gender and (a)sexuality means confronting how (student) teachers, teacher educators, learners, institutions, curriculums, texts, media, academics, research, and even governments are implicated in those power relations that marginalise or actively oppress non-normative gender and sexual groups while serving the interests of heteronormativity and (hetero)patriarchy.

This chapter therefore has three aims: First, we conceptualise QCL by discussing what it means to be and do at the interface of queer and critical approaches to language and literacy education.

DOI: 10.4324/9781003023425-9

Second, a critical review of research is used to illustrate how academics and teachers have already worked within this interface. Finally, we consolidate the key pedagogical moves in the literature into a framework for doing QCL in the classroom.

Queer Critical Literacies: A Conceptual Framework

Queer critical literacies has implications for ways of being and doing in the language and literacy classroom (Vasquez, Janks & Comber, 2019) that takes seriously queer identities, perspectives, and experiences; ways of queering common-sense understandings of gender and sexuality; and ways of (re)constructing identities and more socially just representations. In this section, we define QCL by unpacking conceptualisations of queer literacy and then consolidating queer(ing) with the critical literacies project.

Queer(ing) Literacy

In its noun form, queer refers to an analytical framework and theoretical position that interrogates how heterosexuality, heterosexism, (hetero)patriarchy, and cisgender norms have become naturalised, and legitimised, in a range of ways across contexts (Britzman, 1995; Butler, 2004). As such, queer perspectives recognise how norms are (re)produced through discursive social and cultural practice. Language and literacy education is therefore well suited for teachers and learners to engage in the identification, (de)construction, disruption, and transformation of social norms (Miller, 2015).

Butler's (2004) work in *Undoing Gender* provides a useful analysis of norms: how they are read, measured, and regulated to uphold certain relations of power within heterosexual and gender-conforming matrices. (Hetero)norms are therefore achieved in two ways: (1.) through the common-sensical conflation of sex, gender, and sexuality and (2.) by recognising that norms govern intelligibility. First, conventional conflations of sex, gender, and sexuality maintain the male/female sex binary as natural and necessitate the respective masculine/feminine gender performances and identifications in many Western cultures (Butler, 1993). Furthermore, this logic prescribes heterosexuality. For example, when Canadian oilfield company, X-Site Energy Services, was called out for producing and distributing stickers depicting Greta Thunberg being sexually assaulted as child pornography, the general manager responded: "She's not a child, she's 17" (Beattie, 2020, np). The sticker constitutes symbolic violence (Bourdieu, 2004) that reproduces heteronormative notions of sexual assault and heteropatriarchal power through the objectification of women's bodies with intent to bring them into heterosexual order. While Alberta's Minister of Culture hailed the image as "deplorable, unacceptable and degrading" (cited in Beattie, 2020, np), these criticisms attended only to the symptoms of (hetero)sexism and heteronormativity rather than challenging the fundamental ideologies.

This moment exemplifies how norms govern intelligibility by framing the ways people read themselves and the world through common-sense (inter)actions and discourses (Sandretto, 2018). While this case is illuminating, it is but one example of a larger systemic issue that has become entrenched in everyday life in both visible and invisible ways. As such, "Norms may or may not be explicit, and when they operate as the normalizing principle in social practice, they usually remain implicit, difficult to read" (Butler, 2004, p. 41). What these effects look like, the nature of the norm at work, the subjectivities permitted, and the shapes that resistance takes are also bound to the cultural intelligibilities of time, place, and identity (Awondo et al., 2012). What it means to be regulated by gender and sexuality norms is therefore also deeply connected to the norms that regulate race, ethnicity, nationality or citizenship, (de)coloniality, the environment, indigeneity, and more. It becomes crucial to explore the image of Greta Thunberg, for example, in relation to a history of objectified bodies, discursive patterns of (hetero)patriarchy, and lived experience.

We therefore argue for a queer perspective in the classroom that recognises how issues of (a) gender and (a)sexual diversity emerge across texts (Govender, 2018), bodies, and spaces (Miller, 2015; Johnson, 2017), and to engage in *practices* of queering. In its verb form, queering has become synonymous with *interrupting heteronormativity* (Martino & Cumming-Potvin, 2016). Where heteronormativity constitutes "structures, institutions, relations and actions that promote and produce heterosexuality as natural, self-evident, desirable, privileged and necessary" (Cameron & Kulick, 2003, p. 55), interruptions involve: (1.) deconstructing established systems of power, (2.) exploring resistance, reconstructions of identity, and subversion, and (3.) turning the self into an object for analysis by locating it within prevailing ideologies.

First, queering literacy means developing a vocabulary and analytical prowess to see how heteronormativity, (hetero)sexism, and (hetero)patriarchy—powerful ideologies—are instantiated in and across texts and discourses (Govender, 2018) by making the common-sense strange. For instance, teachers and learners might take everyday (classroom) texts and interrogate how and to what extent they assume heterosexual and/or cis-gendered audiences, draw on a history of objectifying certain bodies, or whether certain characters play passive/active gendered roles.

Second, engaging with the long history of LGBTIQ+ activism, identities, culture, and scholarship is necessary for queering language and literacy curriculums. Over and above inclusion, it is necessary to interrogate LGBTIQ+ texts in the face of heteronormativity so as to unpack how resistance and nonconformity emerge. That is, doing the queer in queer literacies means actively accessing, questioning, deconstructing, and disrupting multimodal representations of (a)gender and (a)sexual diversity that do not place LGBTIQ+ people outside mainstream curriculums and pedagogies, nor engage with these representations by merely adding them to existing curriculums (Sandretto, 2018).

It is also necessary to explore how nonconforming identities and representations are shaped and to what extent they challenge and/or reproduce a range of norms. For instance, while an analysis of LGBTIQ+ pride flags might reveal the flag-designers' intention to unify those diverse (a)gender and (a)sexual identities, their use across place, person, and media reveals how white, middle-class, gay male identities are often privileged (Laskar, Johansson, & Mulinari, 2017; Andrews, 2018). Even within the LGBTIQ+ community new relations of power emerge that cannot be taken for granted.

The Critical Literacy Project Made Queer

From its Freirean roots, critical literacy as an orientation understands that power, access, diversity, and (re)design (Janks, 2010) are intrinsic to discursive (de)construction and a social justice agenda. Critical literacy draws on poststructuralist theories of power and sociocultural theories of meaning-making and applies these to the ever-changing communications landscape. Critical literacy teachers and learners thus take seriously how both meaning (texts) and ways of engaging with meaning (literacies) are imbued with issues of power. This resonates with queer objectives, where being literate "is at least in part being knowledgeable about what kinds of sexual scripts are acceptable and what are not acceptable" (Alexander, 2008, p. 46). By questioning why and how certain identities are privileged through educational and communicative practice, teachers and learners can begin to rethink how classrooms, ways of communicating, text selection, pedagogical decisions, institutional cultures, and government policies have significant material effects. Furthermore, QCL may also enable teachers and learners to recognise heteronormative power and to take conscious action to combat it in and beyond curriculum subjects.

But, how is this achieved? We argue that like all critical literacies, practice is shaped by the particular sociocultural, historical, and political contexts of the teachers, learners, and communities involved (Vasquez, Janks & Comber, 2019). There is no one way of doing QCL. This pays homage to the very diversity of (a)gender and (a)sexuality across the world: there is no one way of being and doing LGBTIQ+. Therefore, QCL teachers and learners must also develop a keen capacity for social semiotics (Kress, 2015) by learning how sign systems are used to (re)produce, challenge, and transform social relations of power (the interpersonal), ontology (the personal), and epistemology (knowledgeability and intelligibility).

A QCL Conceptual Framework

By consolidating queer and critical approaches to literacy, the following framework (Figure 1.8.1) maps out the various components of queer critical literacies (QCL):

[long description] Three interlocked circles with the words queer, literacies, and critical at the center of each. Below these are interlocked boxes that correspond with each circle so that queer is directly linked to the explanation "Foregrounding (a)gender and (a)sexual identities, cultures, perspectives, and representations", literacies is directly linked to the explanation "Literacies as socio-cultural practices of meaning making across modes and genres", and critical is directly linked to the explanation "Discursive meaning making as intrinsically related to issues of power, access, diversity, and (re)design". These are all then related to a final box which consolidates the interconnected circles and boxes with a definition: "Queer Critical Literacies as an approach to language and literacy education that troubles the discursive representation of (a)gender and (a)sexual diversity across modes and genres".

From this framework, it becomes clear that literacies are conceptualised as social practices (Cope & Kalantzis, 2000) which operationalise certain ideologies (Street, 1985; Fairclough, 2001). The "critical" foregrounds issues of access, power, diversity, and (re)design (Janks, 2010), while the queer dimension provides a specific lens and vocabulary (Alexander, 2008). Furthermore, both the critical and queer dimensions take seriously the intersectionality of (a)gender and (a)sexuality politics (Butler, 2004) with race, ethnicity, (de)coloniality, ableism, and so on.

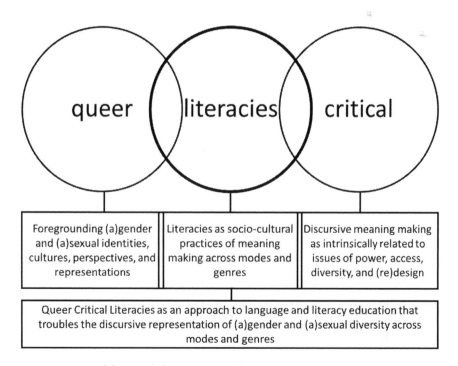

Figure 1.8.1 A conceptual framework for queer critical literacies

By taking a specifically queer lens to critical literacies, we hope that teachers and learners will be able to recognise the extent to which heteronormativity and heteropatriarchy permeate even the smallest spaces and (inter)actions of everyday life. Teachers and learners might then begin to (re)construct representations of (a)gender and (a)sexuality as well as their own identities in more socially just and affirming ways (Govender, 2019). This requires designing curriculums that offer learners opportunities to ask critical questions and access a diverse range of representations and perspectives. It also requires developing learners' capacity to use various sign systems to construct new and more socially just representations of themselves, each other, and the world.

QCL in Practice: A Review

As with other incarnations of critical literacies, there is no single way of doing QCL work in language and literacy education. However, the literature on the intersections between queer(ing) pedagogy and critical literacy highlight five important types of disruption or questioning that con-tribute to a pedagogy of QCL, which are aimed at challenging heterosexism and fostering critical engagement with the discourses of (a)gender and (a)sexual diversity. These five types of questioning are: (1.) questioning representation; (2.) questioning reading practices; (3.) questioning policing; (4.) questioning knowledge, assumptions and meaning-making; and (5.) questioning self.

Questioning Representation of Queer People and Experiences

Many working in the field of QCL emphasise the importance of representation of queer identities in texts across modes, and stress the need to meaningfully engage with these texts at all levels of education (DePalma, 2016; van Leent & Mills, 2017). DePalma (2016, p. 830) discusses including queer literature in primary school classrooms, stating that these texts have the "potential to produc-tively trouble the heteronormative spaces of schools by the mere presence of characters who do not conform to sex/gender/sexuality expectations". However, a critical stance is still necessary; teachers should be aware of the potential heterosexist underpinnings of some texts with queer elements or the dangers of choosing only queer texts that are deemed "safe" for primary school discussion (DePalma, 2016). The representations of queer people or experiences should also be subject to critique, as these might erase queer people of colour or identities other than those that fit an essentialised gay or les-bian mould, or the texts might be "sanitized" by, for example, using animals to represent same-sex sexualities or gender nonconforming behaviour in ways that distort human experiences.

Hartman (2018, p. 80) notes that there is a pressing need to represent LGBTIQ+ identities in elementary classrooms, as "[t]he exclusion of LGBTQ identities . . . sends the message that these identities do not exist or that they are wrong or strange". Hartman adds that incorporating literature discussions and using queer texts as the basis of classroom discussion can "affirm and sustain nondom-inant expressions of gender and sexual identities" (p. 81). Similarly, Ryan and Hermann-Wilmarth (2018) advocate for and outline in depth elementary-level literacy instruction for LGBTQ-inclusive pedagogies through the English language arts curriculum.

Alexander (2008, p. 73) describes his work with graduate students in reflecting on films about sex and sexuality and notes that the critical dialogue and reflection in the course "focuses students' atten-tion on the power of stories to shape our sense of self and our sense of potential agency". A QCL approach thus also includes critical engagement around why heteronormative media and texts are more readily available and more widely taught, as well as how these texts shape social understandings of gender and sexuality.

In practice, students could be asked to consider why gender and sexual minorities are excluded from texts that they encounter in various spaces, including in school. For example, van Leent and Mills (2017) discuss a queer critical media literacies strategy that asks students to construct montages of images of families that they source online. Students are then presented with a series of questions about who is represented in the images and what this says about gender, sexuality, and power in societies that produce these texts. Questions include: "What is depicted as normal in these images of families? . . . Which kinds of family structures are missing from these images?" (2017, p. 406). Students are prompted to question the dominance of heteronormative representations and how queer people are marginalised.

Questioning Reading Practices

The practices of reading, and how they are informed by ideology, are also brought into question in QCL. A QCL approach foregrounds queer reading practices and makes visible and readable the disruptive configurations of gender and sexuality already present in texts. Queer reading practices work to "[reposition] texts outside the borders of heteronormativity" (Dhaenens, Van Bauwel, & Biltereyst, 2008, p. 336), where moments that could be considered as queer, that is, representing same-sex desire or gender nonconformity, are not simply glossed over due to heterosexist blinders that might mark these moments as insignificant. Instead, these moments are read for their disruptive potential and are afforded significance in how the text is read. Sandretto (2018, p. 202) highlights that any text can be read with a queer lens and not only those texts that clearly represent (a)gender and (a)sexual diversity, and adds that "by creating the conditions for multiple, critical readings teachers can expose common-sense understandings of gender and sexuality".

Sandretto (2018, p. 204) offers questions when queering the reading of a text in the classroom setting, such as unpacking representations of heterosexual couples as parents: "Are parents always in a male/female pair?"; "What view of the world is the text presenting?" and "Who is missing from the text?". Students can also be prompted to recognise the types of omissions that heterosexist reading strategies exercise over texts by asking: "How would the story be different if one set of parents was two mums or two dads?" (Sandretto, 2018, p. 206). A final significant question offered by Sandretto (2018, p. 207) again looks at the way that texts are socially constructed from ideological positions: "Why do you think the author has constructed the text in this way?". This form of questioning *queers* the practice of reading and allows for the teacher and students to read with awareness of the social constructedness of texts.

Questioning the Policing of (A)Gender and (A)Sexuality

QCL directly discusses the dynamics in social and educational settings or texts that marginalise or disempower queer people and perspectives. This involves the continuous questioning of discourses of appropriateness surrounding gender and sexuality and the way learners engage in, witness, or respond to policing of gendered behaviour. Hartman (2018) asked students to weigh in on texts where characters with nonconforming gender expression suffer discrimination and bullying. Students therefore critically reflect on these explicit moments of gender policing to disentangle the assumptions of appropriate and normalised gender expression. Additionally, this challenges how queer topics are viewed as "inappropriate" in educational settings, and students could "disrupt the discourse of what is considered acceptable for young children to talk about in elementary school classrooms" (Hartman, 2018, pp. 87–88). DePalma (2016, p. 836) adds that queer literacies take a critical stance on the conditions of production of queer texts: "[r]ather than including new groups into the established order of social recognisability and respectability, the criteria defining recognisability and respectability are examined and questioned".

This type of questioning involves an ever-widening understanding of not only how gender, sexuality, and power are linked but also of how behaviours are policed discursively, institutionally, and socially. Ashcroft (2012) describes two activities to demonstrate the link between language and social effects: first, teenaged students think of slang words for sexual organs to notice the ways that language is linked to discomfort around sex and sexuality; second, students critically reflect on labels, such as "gay" not describing all men who have sex with men, or how particular terms like "homosexual" are laden with heterosexist connotations. These strategies demonstrate how language can be used as a form of policing and "how sexuality and identity are shaped and altered by the ways we talk about it" (Ashcroft, 2012, p. 610). Further questions for students could include who is allowed to show public affection, what words are used to reinforce "appropriate" behaviour or to suppress "inappropriate" behaviour, and what types of gendered language learners notice in texts that serve to control the behaviour or expression of other characters. This type of work leads to the critical capacity for these students to question "how language is used to shape particular kinds of stories, who benefits, and who is left out" (Ashcroft, 2012, p. 611).

Questioning Knowledge, Assumptions, and Meaning-Making

QCL also requires an epistemological disruption, as the practices expose how the suppression and marginalisation of diverse voices lead to significant epistemological shortcomings, impositions, and the devaluing of certain types of knowledges including experiential knowledges of gender and love. As Alexander (2008, p. 61) notes, "[f]ar from being a purely 'personal' or 'natural' phenomenon, what we know about sex/uality comes to us through a variety of discourses surrounding us and in which we frequently participate". Thus, by engaging in critical and dialogical reflection of discourses and texts, QCL seeks to challenge the "naturalness" of dominant gender and sexuality discourses and the types of "knowledges" constructed (or left unexplored) around gender and sexual minorities.

Gender and sexuality are often conceptualised as "difficult knowledge" in schools, since these are "topics that are often socially and politically constructed by adults as sensitive" (van Leent & Mills, 2017, p. 403). This means that knowledge about (a)gender and (a)sexuality are often inaccessible in schools or are taught in ways that reproduce dominant heterosexist ideologies, stifling critical thought (Francis, 2017b). In addition, Miller (2015) holds that one's ability to read, make meaning, and know oneself and others is mediated by discourse and ideology, and thus for queer people, marginalisation might lead to many parts of the self being "illegible" and unknowable. This chasm in meaning and knowing can be brought to light through QCL, which recognises, legitimises, and advocates for the rights of queer people and visibilises queer experiences and culture.

Hartman (2018, p. 87) explains that in his work with elementary school children reading queer texts, "the classroom operated as a space in which historically ignored identities were named, legitimized, and discussed". Hartman introduces a text about a transgender child and notes that this text "expanded the children's understanding of gender identity and expression and gave them a language that they did not seem to possess prior to this reading" (p. 88). Van Leent and Mills (2017, p. 404) note that the queer critical media literacies classroom should be one of dialogic reflection, where "all participants are engaged in constructing meaning with others and consider other meanings to create new understandings".

These strategies allow students to begin to see their own assumptions, and what is deemed as common sense about gender and sexuality, as socially constructed knowledges. This includes the assumed binary nature of gender and the socially constructed idea that diverse sexualities are "abnormal" (DePalma, 2016). It also allows them to recognise that (hetero)patriarchal systems necessarily produce knowledges and modes of learning that marginalise and exclude particular voices or knowledges.

As strategies within this theme, teachers could ask students to consider what knowledge they feel they already possess about sexual and gender minorities, and how they came to "know" this. Hermann-Wilmarth, Lannen, and Ryan (2017, pp. 19–20) describe a classroom activity in an upper elementary classroom where "male-identified students were asked to role play female-identified characters and vice versa to help students think about assumptions made about gender and how those assumptions situate our understandings of gender". Such activities destabilise gender norms and allow for critical engagement with social assumptions and knowledges. Additionally, students could question who the authorities of these knowledges are, whose voices matter and why, and what more they could know if gender and sexual minorities were not oppressed or marginalised. This reflects a commitment to engage in "classroom activities that actively push back against gender constructs and provide opportunities to explore, engage, and understand how gender is constructed" (Miller, 2015, p. 42).

Questioning Self

The final question type works to challenge students' ideas about themselves: first, in relation to how their own gender expressions are socially constructed; and second, to question how they can be active in challenging and dismantling systemic violence, marginalisation, and discrimination on the basis of gender and sexuality. This is a process of "desocialization" (Shor, 1992, p. 144), which involves "a demystifying of seemingly private topics so that students can understand their socio-cultural and political valences" (Alexander, 2008, p. 73). Sandretto (2018, p. 198) explains that "[u]nderstanding how heteronormativity can harm everyone generates an imperative for all of us to develop our skills of critique, including those who identify as heterosexual".

This calls for "daring conversations" (Ashcroft, 2012, p. 598) where students are given space to critically examine their identities and experiences. Hartman (2018, p. 89) adds that "the inclusion and discussion of LGBTIQ+ identities can provide students with expansive ways of not only conceptualizing gender, but also choosing to *do* gender". In this vein, van Leent and Mills (2017, p. 404) offer a framework for queer critical media literacies that is founded on the principle of recognising rights and explaining these rights to students. This approach can foster students' social consciousness and transform classrooms into safer spaces for queer, questioning or gender nonconforming students. When students are conscious of how understandings of gender and sexuality are socially constructed, they can begin to understand their own bodies, behaviours, and beliefs as *gendered* largely within heterosexist discourses.

The transformative potential extends beyond the classroom, where queer literacy educators "generate meaningful opportunities for students to become embodied change agents and to be proactive against, or to not engage in, bullying behaviour" (Miller, 2015, p. 42). Students can begin to see the links between power, knowledge, and the ability to effect social change. Hermann-Wilmarth et al. (2017) describe an activity where upper elementary school students were asked to consider the transphobic comments of a college student. Students were asked to inhabit the role of experts on transgender rights and present public service announcements on legislation to protect transgender people. These announcements were aimed at an "authentic audience" (p. 31), in this case college students with transphobic views. In activities like these, students can see how those in power can reframe public discourse and affect the lives of marginalised people through legislation, public announcements, or texts. In addition, they can begin to see themselves as participants and allies in transformative action to dismantle systemic violence, marginalisation, and discrimination.

Doing QCL: A Pedagogical Tool

Table 1.8.1 represents the moves necessary for doing QCL in the classroom, both as a way to *engage* with texts and *design* QCL curriculums. Each of the four moves (identification, deconstruction, disruption, and transformation) draws on queer and critical literacies, is non-linear, and interdependent (Janks, 2013). For instance, identification without deconstruction means that social norms are named but how they work remains obscured, while deconstruction and disruption without

Table 1.8.1 Doing Queer Critical Literacies

Identification: *Questioning Representation*	
What or who is represented? What identity categories are included/excluded in the text(s)? Are there any intersections with other identity categories like race, class, etc.?	Students discuss any identities of gender and sexuality present in the text and how these might be normative.
Can the norm be named? What language can be used to describe the content or identities represented in the text(s)? Where does this language come from, and are there different ways to describe the content or identities?	Students are asked to identify and describe norms and consider how these norms link to ideologies. They also see how language shapes understanding and meaning-making.
What are the conditions of production and reception? Where and when has the text been produced and found? What is the genre and social function of the text?	Students consider how texts serve social functions which link to power and might marginalise some identities.
Deconstruction: *Questioning Knowledge, Questioning Policing*	
What can be known about the text or topic? Whose knowledge/perspective is represented? What assumptions are made about the reader/ viewer? How is difference constructed? Whose interests are served? Can the privileged group be named?	Students confront how knowledge is socially constructed and how certain groups are privileged by certain forms of knowledges.
What is the grammar of power? What modes are used to represent the norm? What language features have been used to express the norm? What figurative devices have been used to express or reinforce the norm? What textual features are repeated across a range of texts?	Students confront how language and representation intersect with ideology and present a version of reality that aims to persuade an audience. They can recognise that norms are constructed across texts, genres, and modes. Additionally, they consider how language might police norms and behaviours.
What are the consequences? Can you describe how the norm has become naturalised? What do these representations say about who has power and who does not? How does the norm compare to lived experiences?	Students understand that texts have social effects. Norms of gender and sexuality can lead to stigma, prejudice, and violence against gender and sexual minorities or those who are gender nonconforming.
Disruption: *Questioning Knowledge, Questioning Representation*	
What is the grammar of subversion? What makes a text subversive? How is diversity represented through language and various modes of texts? What are the different forms that subversion can take? How do subversive texts differ from those that reproduce powerful norms? Why do these differences exist?	Students begin to see how language and forms of representation can be used to challenge hegemony and to represent diversity. They question what it means for (a)gender and (a)sexual diversity to occupy the centre rather than the margins. They are exposed to texts that challenge restrictive norms of gender and sexuality.

What subversive designs/representations of the norm are accessible? How easily available are they? Where can subversion be found? Why? Who produces subversive representations? Why? What is the genre (social function) of the text(s)?	Students consider how text production is linked to power, and the reasons disruptive texts may not be easily accessible. They confront the interrelationship between factors like social class, race, nationality, etc. and question these processes of production.
What are the consequences? What does the subversive form reveal about the norm itself? In what ways does subversion challenge normativity? In what ways does it reproduce or maintain normativity? What new relations of power emerge from this "alternative" representation?	Students maintain their critical stance in relation to disruptive texts and challenge these texts just like normative texts, rather than simply accepting them. They also consider how these texts might serve to challenge or reinforce power hierarchies in societies.
Transformation: *Questioning Self*	
What counts as social action and social transformation? What projects for design, redesign, or social participation/action can be constructed? How can norms be redefined or reconceptualised?	Students begin to see themselves as agents in confronting and (re)designing texts and creating disruptive texts of their own. Students also confront their roles in taking social action beyond texts in order to disrupt oppressive social configurations, to understand the constructed nature of their own gendered selves, and to advocate for social change.

identification removes the analysis and production of texts from real-world contexts. Deconstruction without disruption maintains the dominance of normative representations and excludes existing redesigns. And, transformation without deconstruction or disruption risks reducing social action to awareness without harnessing the productive power of diversity.

The left column presents the types of questions teachers should ask and could be adapted for various educational levels. The right column describes how students might engage with these questions.

Conclusion and Recommendations

The QCL approach allows for meaningful engagement with (a)gender and (a)sexual diversity in classrooms and higher education through texts and can disrupt heteronormativity to foster more inclusive and transformative spaces, societies, and approaches to literacy. This chapter has presented a theoretical framework for QCL founded on the disruption of heteronormativity through queer(ing) engagement with texts and literacies. A review of QCL pedagogy has shown how diverse the practice can be, and how (student) teachers and teacher educators have adapted QCL approaches in context to meet students' needs and to work for social change. As an *emerging* critical literacies approach, QCL can be an important intervention in light of the oppression of sexual and gender minorities and the ways that heteropatriarchal ideologies impact on violence, marginalisation, and the erasure of knowledges about queer lived experiences.

We developed the table presented in this chapter as a tool for doing QCL in a range of contexts. Future research could develop the table for particular settings or unpack its use in context. Research could also contribute to developing the field of QCL and to strengthening QCL practice by offering more tools and texts for teachers to use in classrooms. It would also be useful to see how (student) teachers use the table to structure critically reflexive accounts of curriculum design and pedagogical practice in primary, secondary, and higher education classrooms.

References

Alexander, J. (2008). *Literacy, sexuality, pedagogy: Theory and practice for composition studies.* Utah State University Press.

Andrews, G. (2018). The boundaries of desire and intimacy in post-apartheid South African queer film: Oliver Hermanus's *Skoonheid. Image & Text, 31*(1), 30–47.

Ashcroft, C. (2012). But how do we talk about it? Critical literacy practices for addressing sexuality with youth. *Curriculum Inquiry, 42*(5), 597–628. https://doi.org/10.1111/j.1467-873X.2012.00610.x

Awondo, P., Geschiere, P., & Reid, G. (2012). Homophobic Africa? Toward a more nuanced view. *African Studies Review, 55*(3), 145–168.

Beattie, S. (2020, February 27). Disgusting sticker of 'Greta Thunberg' linked to Alberta Oil Company shocks Canadians. *Huffington Post.* Retrieved from www.huffingtonpost.ca/entry/greta-thunberg-alberta-oil_ca_5e58175fc5b60102210e12ff

Bourdieu, P. (2004). Gender and symbolic violence. In N. Schepher-Hughes & P. Bougois (Eds.), *Violence in war and peace: An anthology* (pp. 339–47). Blackwell.

British LGBT Awards. (2020). *Top 10 media moments 2019.* Retrieved from www.britishlgbtawards.com/top-10-lgbt-media-moments-2019/

Britzman, D. P. (1995). Is there a queer pedagogy? Or, stop reading straight. *Educational Theory, 45*(2), 151–165.

Butler, J. (1993). Imitation & gender insubordination. In H. Abelove, M. Aina Barale, & D. M. Halperin (Eds.), *The lesbian & gay studies reader* (pp. 307–320). Routledge.

Butler, J. (2004). *Undoing gender.* Routledge.

Cameron, D., & Kulick, D. (2003). *Language & sexuality.* Cambridge University Press.

Cope, B., & Kalantzis, M. (2000). *Multiliteracies: Literacy learning & the design of social futures.* Routledge.

Corrales, J. (2015). The politics of LGBT rights in Latin America & the Caribbean: Research agendas. *European Review of Latin American & Caribbean Studies, 100,* 53–62. http://doi.org/10.18352/erlacs.10126

DePalma, R. (2016). Gay penguins, sissy ducklings . . . and beyond? Exploring gender and sexuality diversity through children's literature. *Discourse: Studies in the Cultural Politics of Education, 37*(6), 828–845. https://doi.org/10.1080/01596306.2014.936712

Dhaenens, F., Van Bauwel, S., & Biltereyst, D. (2008). Slashing the fiction of queer theory: Slash fiction, queer reading, and transgressing the boundaries of screen studies, representations, and audiences. *Journal of Communication Inquiry, 32*(4), 335–347. https://doi.org/10.1177/0196859908321508

Fairclough, N. (2001). *Language & power.* Longman.

Francis, D. A. (2017a). *Troubling the teaching & learning of gender & sexuality diversity in South African education.* Palgrave Macmillan.

Francis, D. A. (2017b). Homophobia & sexuality diversity in South African schools: A review. *Journal of LGBT Youth, 14*(4), 359–379. https://doi.org/10.1080/19361653.2017.1326868

Freire, P. (1985). Reading the world & reading the word: An interview with Paulo Freire. *Language Arts, 62*(1), 15–21.

GLAAD Media Institute. (2019). *Where we are on TV 2017–2018: GLAAD's annual report on LGBTQ inclusion.* GLAAD. Retrieved from http://glaad.org/files/WWAT/WWAT_GLAAD_2017-2018.pdf

Govender, N. (2018). Deconstructing heteronormativity & hegemonic gender orders through critical literacy & materials design. In E. Walton & R. Osman (Eds.), *Teacher education for diversity: Conversations from the Global South* (pp. 36–52). Routledge.

Govender, N. (2019). Critical literacy and critically reflective writing: Navigating gender and sexual diversity. *English Teaching: Practice & Critique, 18*(3), 351–364. https://doi.org/10.1108/ETPC-09-2018-0082

Hartman, P. (2018). A queer approach to addressing gender & sexuality through literature discussions with second graders. *Language Arts, 96*(2), 79–90.

Hermann-Wilmarth, J. M., Lannen, R., & Ryan, C. L. (2017). Critical literacy and transgender topics in an upper elementary classroom: A portrait of possibility. *Journal of Language and Literacy Education, 13*(1), 15–27.

ILGA Europe. (2020). *Annual review of the human rights situation of lesbian, gay, bisexual, trans & intersex people in Europe & Central Asia.* Belgium. Retrieved from www.ilga-europe.org/annualreview/2020

Janks, H. (2010). *Literacy & power.* Routledge.

Janks, H. (2013). Critical literacy in teaching & research. *Education Inquiry, 4*(2), 225–242. https://doi.org/10.3402/edui.v4i2.22071

Johnson, L. P. (2017). Writing the self: Black queer youth challenge heteronormative ways of being in an after-school writing club. *Research in the Teaching of English, 52*(1), 13–33.

Kress, G. (2015). Semiotic work: Applied linguistics & a social semiotic account of multimodality. *AILA Review, 28*(1), 49–71. https://doi.org/10.1075/aila.28.03kre

Laskar, P., Johansson, A., & Mulinari, D. (2017). Decolonising the rainbow flag. *Culture Unbound: Journal of Current Cultural Research, 8*(3), 192–217. http://dx.doi.org/10.25595/1454

Martino, W., & Cumming-Potvin, W. (2016). Teaching about sexual minorities & "princess boys": A queer & trans–infused approach to investigating LGBTQ-themed texts in the elementary school classroom. *Discourse: Studies in the Cultural Politics of Education, 37*(6), 807–827. https://doi.org/10.1080/01596306.2014.940239

Miller, sj. (2015). A queer literacy framework promoting (a)gender & (a)sexuality self-determination & justice. *English Journal, 104*(5), 37–44.

Ryan, C. L., & Hermann-Wilmarth, J. M. (2018). *Reading the rainbow: LBGTQ-inclusive literacy instruction in the elementary classroom*. Teachers College Press.

Salzburg Global Seminar. (2019). *Salzburg global LGBT forum: Advancing legal & social equality in South Asia*. Retrieved from www.salzburgglobal.org/fileadmin/user_upload/Documents/2010-2019/2018/Session_611/Salzburg Global_Report_611.pdf

Sandretto, S. (2018). A case for critical literacy with queer intent. *Journal of LGBT Youth, 15*(3), 197–211. https://doi.org/10.1080/19361653.2018.1466753

Shor, I. (1992). *Empowering education: Critical teaching for social change*. University of Chicago Press.

Street, B. (1985). *Literacy in theory & practice*. Cambridge University Press.

van Leent, L., & Mills, K. (2017). A queer critical media literacies framework in a digital age. *Journal of Adolescent & Adult Literacy, 61(4)*, 401–411. https://doi.org/10.1002/jaal.711

Vasquez, V. M., Janks, H., & Comber, B. (2019). Critical literacy as a way of being & doing. *Language Arts, 96*(5), 300–311.

1.9

CRITICAL LITERACY AND WRITING PEDAGOGY

Anwar Ahmed and Saskia Van Viegen

We begin the chapter with a mythological story. The Egyptian god Thoth, the mythical inventor of writing, was very excited about his invention and came to the king to seek royal blessings. Instead of being impressed, the king said to him:

You have invented an elixir not of memory, but of reminding; and you offer your pupils the appearance of wisdom, not true wisdom, for they will read many things without instruction and will therefore seem to know many things, when they are for the most part ignorant.

(Quoted in Robinson, 2009, p. 2)

This story, told by Socrates and recorded by Plato, has profound implications in our time of extraordinary speed of writing and the global spread of written texts.

For centuries, reading was the dominant form of literacy. However, in recent decades, there has been a sharp rise in writing as a literacy activity. In the contemporary knowledge economy, "writing has become a dominant form of labor as it transforms knowledge and news into usable, shareable form" (Brandt, 2015, p. 16). We write for various reasons, ranging from consoling ourselves to passing examinations, from engaging in discussion to involvement in civic activity. Alongside these diverse purposes, digital social media has expanded writing practice to new forms of multimodal composing, presenting opportunity to enrich communication and expand audiences for writing and also provoking concern relating to surveillance, security, and the influence of fake news and commercial interest on dialogue in the online sphere (Boler, 2010). Mediated by government and corporate influence, digital spaces can amplify dominant, hegemonic discourses and their intrusion in open public dialogue. Writing is but one way we participate and exercise agency in these social and institutional spaces, using communicative resources for action, engagement, or symbolic expression. For these reasons, cultivating "written acts of resistance" (Chun, 2019) that name injustice, inequality, and oppression remain important as ever to provide counter-narratives and contest the narrowing of public discourse. Engaging with these considerations, in this chapter we focus on writing in the educational context, making a case for why critical literacy is central to teaching and learning writing in schools. More specifically, we highlight questions about the nature of teaching and learning writing, asking what does a critical literacy approach to writing look like, and how can a critical writing pedagogy make visible oppressions that need to be challenged, to transform structures of inequality and privilege in schools and beyond?

In schools, writing is both a skill and mode of assessment in almost every subject area and across all levels of education. However, the sociopolitical context of schooling and increased testing and accountability measures can limit opportunities for critical engagement with and through writing pedagogy. At the same time, the affordances of digital social networks and use of new technologies in schools could give way to a new instrumentality if students are positioned as passive users and consumers of information rather than critical and active producers of knowledge and culture in the digital sphere (Coiro, Knobel, Lankshear, & Leu, 2014). As Morgan (2003) states, "writing could be both an act of conformity and an act of resistance" (p. 230). Therefore, we articulate a critical literacy approach to teaching writing that involves engaging students to make meaning, interpret and compose texts in emancipatory ways, supporting students to identify how social power relations are manifest in texts and assisting students to question the material and discursive construction of knowledge and power. These practices encompass both reading and writing, as students gain access to and participate in ever-broadening social discourse communities. Engaging students to learn, use, and negotiate rhetorical norms and conventions, meanings and identities, educators can teach students to contribute their own voices and values for *resistance from within* (Canagarajah, 2011; Seltzer, 2020).

Recent scholarship in writing pedagogy examines how written acts of resistance can be fostered in teaching and learning (see, for instance, a special issue by Chun, 2019). Whereas resistance is often seen in a negative light, some scholars in literacy, composition studies, and applied linguistics regard resistance as key to enacting liberatory pedagogy, promoting intellectual activism, and developing students' identities. Situating writing teaching within broader sociocultural, historical and political contexts, scholars have theorized ways to work critically with understandings of language, text, discourse, and subjectivity in writing. Drawing on Kamler's (2001) argument for the teaching of writing as a political project in schools, we suggest that critical perspectives can be fostered as educators teach students about audience, argument, and rhetorical situations, developing students' ability to question an author's claim, identify an author's reasoning, utilize linguistic and rhetorical tools, and mobilize creative, reflective capacities and their voice and identity as emergent writers (Kohls, 2019). Broadly, these pedagogic aims can be met with a critical literacy approach to writing.

Definitions of Key Concepts

What happens when we say/write the word "critical" before "writing" and "literacies"? Literacy is popularly understood as a person's ability to read and write; however, literacy practices are enmeshed within social, cultural, political, and economic conditions and circumstances. Post-colonial, post-structural, feminist, critical race theory, and cultural studies offer a theoretical basis for critical literacy and ideological critique of texts, reminding us that there is no singular critical literacy in theory or practice. Addressing literacy practices as situated and ideological in nature (Street, 1993), critical literacy asks us to reconceptualize literacy from perspectives that make visible practices of marginalization and oppression and to engage in collective effort to find democratic ways to counter and resist these practices. As Luke (2012) describes:

> Critical literacy has an explicit aim of the critique and transformation of dominant ideologies, cultures and economies, and institutions and political systems. As a practical approach to curriculum, it melds social, political, and cultural debate and discussion with the analysis of how texts and discourses work, where, with what consequences, and in whose interests.
>
> *(p. 5)*

Thus, teaching writing is more than preparing students for academic success at schools. It must involve a broader goal of political transformation and social justice.

As pedagogy, critical literacy focuses on teaching students to "read the word and the world" (Shor & Freire, 1987, p. 135). For the field of literacy studies, this conceptualization emphasizes the importance of teaching understanding of textual and material signs and meanings (Gee, 2015; Lankshear & Knobel, 2011). Making an explicit link to social theory, this approach to pedagogy locates literacy more broadly within sociopolitical realities, engaging with issues of race, social class, global location, and identity (Barton & Hamilton, 2000; Janks & Comber, 2006; Jimenez, Smith, & Teague, 2009; Jones & Enriquez, 2009; Kinloch, 2015; López-Gopar, 2007; Morrell, 2015; Vasudevan & Campano, 2009). Broadly, these changes lift educators' gaze beyond texts alone, to what students do with literacy, with whom, where, and how.

Writing, as a critical act, creates a space for writers to name, voice, and resist power. As Janks (2013) argued, critical literacy is not only about deconstructing texts, "it is also about *writing* and rewriting the world: it is about design and re-design" (p. 227, emphasis original). As social actors within their communities, students can develop empowered identities as they not only read and analyze texts but also as they create them. Critical literacy scholars have documented fieldwork involving children and youth in collaborative inquiry projects to understand and transform their lives and communities (see, for instance, Hull & Stornaiuolo, 2014; Jocson, 2008; Lau, 2015; López-Gopar et al., 2020; Seltzer, 2020; Vasudevan, Schultz, & Bateman, 2010). Enacting such a critical literacy pedagogy with youth in urban schools, Morrell (2015) articulates critical writing as both coming to a critical understanding of the world and playing a role in changing the world. Notably, such projects do not prescribe particular steps or techniques for teaching writing; rather, they are locally developed and situated in particular contexts and conditions. As such, agreeing with Kamler (2001), we see critical writing pedagogy

> not as a new method—but as a politicized frame which can help teachers think differently about teaching writing and reflect on what it is students are learning to write, what they do with that writing and what that writing does to them and their world.
>
> *(p. 173)*

Indeed, teaching writing through the lens of critical literacy invites a reflexive, dialogic approach and emphasizes relational aspects of pedagogy. Located within students' own lives and realities and inviting social-emotional and affective experiences to sit alongside critical engagement with social issues, critical literacy in writing pedagogy can address the material circumstances of students' experiences. We propose that a critical writing pedagogy takes this kind of explicit sociopolitical approach to power relations in the classroom and larger society, wherein writing becomes what Chun (2019) described as an act of resistance, which aims to overturn hegemonic discourses and holds the potential for cultural critique and social transformation.

Historical, Current, and/or Emerging Theory

Across multidisciplinary fields, including education, rhetoric and composition studies and applied linguistics, research highlights diverse theories of writing, drawing attention to how writing differs depending on its context and the people involved in the act of writing. In education, writing and knowledge about writing are critical to most aspects of curriculum, and approaches to teaching writing have undergone significant change in response to theories of writing and writing research. From an early focus on language and rhetoric, moving to expressiveness and writing as a social practice, current traditional approaches to teaching writing emphasized language usage and paragraph writing, later encompassing purposeful and meaningful composition writing and attention to the writing process (see overview of these developments in Grabe & Kaplan, 2014). The current moment calls attention to writing within the broader activity of multimodal communication and digital composition, as well as the multiplicity of voices in a networked, mobile, and digitized world (Andrews & Smith, 2011; Hull & Nelson, 2005; Horner, Selfe, & Lockridge, 2015; Pandya, 2019). Current theories of writing and literacies see this transformation from an individual, linguistic, or skills-based approach to community involvement, cultural production, and integration into cultural processes, recognizing writing as developed in and through social contexts and collaboration. Theorizing participatory composition, some scholars articulate the concept of "electracy," extending the conceptualization of digital literacy to include participation in the apparatus of a networked, mobile world (Arroyo, 2013; Ulmer, 2002). Further emerging scholarship has documented the material, embodied and digital ecology of writing as well as the reality of situated local and global contexts, highlighting the complexity of textual practices and socio-material relations across cultural and linguistic boundaries (Mills, Stornaiuolo, Smith, & Pandya, 2017; Mora, 2015).

Whereas there may be interest in articulating a coherent theory of writing to guide instruction, a singular approach runs counter to the aims of critical literacy. To understand writing's roles in personal and social spheres, we need to pay attention not only to how individuals write but also to what writing does to them. Prior and Lunsford (2008) discussed four factors that motivate deep reflections on writing, and we find these factors helpful for our purpose in this chapter. First, writing involves "the development of a script" as well as the development of "technologies of inscription (tools and media) and distribution" (p. 99). Second, reproduction of the literate practices of writing requires formalization, systematization, and institutionalization of various modes of transmission through education, apprenticeship, and socialization. Third, some written texts—not all—achieve a certain level of mobility and permanence. Finally, writing assumes "a key place in the production and critique of discourse and knowledge in political, social, scientific, philosophical, and religious spheres" because "written texts offer new means of representation" and afford "sustained and dispersed inspection of language and ideas" (p. 99). This final factor is particularly relevant for our conceptualization of critical writing pedagogy.

Theorizing the teaching of writing for social justice, scholars have articulated the importance of putting students at the centre of writing pedagogy, taking an inclusive and asset-oriented stance to the difference and multiplicity present in student writing. For instance, Lillis (2001) argues for dialogic approaches to giving feedback and turns the lens on educators, asking what forms of writing are valued in education and who benefits from the hierarchies that these values construct? Recognizing the import of white racial habitus in writing assessment and the disproportionately negative effects of writing assessment on students of colour, recent scholarship advocates for anti-racist work in the writing classroom, suggesting alternative assessment such as labour-based grading contracts (Inoue, 2015; Poe & Inoue, 2016). These theoretical and pedagogic issues and concerns relate to writing in English as a first and also as a second/additional language. Growing awareness of the needs of students from minoritized language backgrounds has drawn attention to further sociocultural and educational considerations in second language writing. Call for critical approaches to teaching writing has been a key theme in second language writing research, where scholars have raised questions concerning language and linguistic differences in teaching writing. Belcher (1995), for example, argued "critical writing will help students begin to see themselves as experts-in-training, to overcome their reluctance to challenge established authority, and to understand the social dynamics, or the ongoing dialectic, of their fields of study" (p. 135). More recent work in this area has brought attention to writing as translingual practice, recognizing the legitimacy of mixing and meshing languages in written communication (Canagarajah, 2012). This critical work is underscored by growing exploration of issues of class, gender, and ethnicity in second language writing (Kubota, 2003; Morgan & Ramanathan, 2005; Vandrick, 1995). Current discussions engage with language in writing studies to legitimize how writers make use of linguistic resources in flexible, strategic, and dynamic ways, countering the traditional focus on English writing and the monolingual bias in teaching writing (Horner, Lu, Royster, & Trimbur, 2011; Silva & Wang, 2020).

Broadly, this language of critique and hope provides a foundation for moving beyond a narrow conceptualization of writing instruction as a mechanical, skills-based approach to *learning to write*. Rather, educators can envisage *writing to learn* or *writing to engage* as a means to think, discover and deepen understanding, mobilizing the range of multidiscursive, multi-voiced practices involved in meaning-making and communication and encompassing intertextual, dialogic use of reading and writing to develop consciousness and thought (Bazerman, 2004). Drawing on these diverse perspectives and understandings, many educators spend their career teaching writing so passionately "as if the world depended on it" (Rothman, 2005, p. 43). Yet, others question whether or not writing is a teachable skill (Caplan & Johns, 2019; Elbow, 1998). Overall, the many theories of writing, as indicated earlier, suggest that defining writing, and therefore writing competence, comprises contested domains.

Implications for Pedagogy and Research

As Janks (2009) emphasized, "the move from critical reading to critical writing is important, because it enables us to think about where we might go after we have deconstructed a text" (p. 128). A critical literacy approach to writing can help us reflect on and understand how we position "ourselves and our readers by the choices we make as we write and to consider how the words we use to name the world may privilege some at the expense of others" (Janks, 2009, p. 128). Thus, writing should not be viewed as putting words on paper or screen, it is an act of empowerment and resistance—both for the writer and the reader. The writer starts with a commitment to social justice, chooses words and develops ideas and arguments that create, deconstruct, and re-create worlds. The writer should not be "dead" in the post-structuralist sense. Their voices are alive and powerful because readers enter the world created by the writer (Cremin & Myhill, 2013), and the writer bears responsibility for the kinds of worlds created in and through their texts.

What, then, does a critical literacy approach to writing look like? This question may be debated and engaged from a variety of perspectives. Our choice in this chapter is a pedagogical perspective because we teach writing, and we believe that learning to write benefits from some guidance and instruction either in or out of the classroom. When we use the phrase "the politics of writing" (Canagarajah, 2002; Clark & Ivanič, 1997), at least two distinct meanings come to mind. The first meaning is related to a negative connotation of the word "politics." Due to widespread corruption in the field of politics, the word has attracted distrust from people in all levels of society (a fair treatment of this topic requires a different paper). In this negative sense of the word, the politics of writing may suggest that the right to write is not equally distributed in contemporary social and academic structures. Discussing this concern, Clark and Ivanič (1997) wrote that "the political issues of which members of a society become transmitters of meanings . . . is an important starting point for thinking about any type of writing" (p. 4). They proposed a democratic pedagogy to fight the inequitable distribution of the right to write. On the other hand, a positive meaning of the phrase "the politics of writing" may suggest that writing is an effective tool to, in Rancière's words, redistribute the sensible. For Rancière (2015), what happens in the name of "politics" is actually "policing." Politics happens rarely, and when it does happen, all voices are heard and respected. But in hearing such voices, there must not be any hierarchy. As soon as one assumes the power and willingness to listen to others, it becomes charity—no longer politics. Emancipatory politics, as Rancière sees it, should not be reduced to consensual discourses and forms of action, as we see in the case of contemporary models of governance. It must be and remain on the principles of dissensus and contestation. With a vision of this kind of emancipatory politics, we now present four principles that we hope will constitute an overarching pedagogical framework for a critical literacy approach to writing.

Reclaiming the Experience of Writing

Writing is usually judged by the texts produced by a writer. Whether or not the text serves a purpose, for example, to send a message, to keep records, to pass an exam, and so on, determines the quality of writing. This text-based approach to evaluating writing undermines the writer's experience of writing. Traditional pedagogical models of teaching writing have focused predominantly on this text-based approach. Inspired by Yagelski (2009), we propose that writing instructors focus, whenever appropriate, on the experience of writing. Writers need to have an opportunity to feel the transformative power of writing, separate from texts they produce as an outcome of their act of writing. As Yagelski (2009) stated:

> When we write, we enact a sense of ourselves as beings in the world. In this regard, writing both shapes and reflects our sense of who we are in relation to each other and the world around us. Therein lies the transformative power of writing, for when writing is practiced as an act of being, it opens up possibilities for individual and collective change that are undermined by conventional writing instruction, which is often characterized by an obsession with textual form and adherence to convention.
>
> *(pp. 7–8)*

Thus, an ontological awareness of the act of writing, separate from the text produced, should be a first step towards understanding the writer's subjectivity and her/his position in a world where power is always differentially distributed.

Relocating the Personal

The second principle emerges from the many instances in our own classrooms when students asked if using "I" in their written assignments would be acceptable. Every time we said "yes" in response to this question, we surprised many of our students. We wonder whether students' hesitation to use "I" harkens back to a history of separating the student-writer from the text. For a long time, they were denied an authorial voice and were only judged by the text they produced as an "objective" artifact subjected to the teacher's evaluation. For a critical literacy approach to writing pedagogy, we cannot afford to ignore the writer's personal experience and positionality in the world. Doing so would ignore the conviction that the personal is the political. What a person experiences in everyday life is, in fact, symptomatic of larger social and political structures and effects. If the personal is discarded as "private" matters, then the realm of the public will be dominated by the few whose voices are already recognized as valid and meaningful and thus worthy of attention. As Friedan (1963) demonstrated many years ago, women's suffering was ignored by the larger society including physicians because their problems had no names. This understanding also relates to Freire's critical pedagogy when he emphasized the importance of naming the world, which he believed should be the first step toward changing the world. Therefore, the critical literacy perspective on writing pedagogy that we are proposing must view the writer as a person whose experiences are valid and worthy of attention. Educators must work to "relocate the personal for a more critical engagement with the writer's experience" in the world (Kamler, 2001, p. 14).

Rewriting Stories

Stories shape our understanding of the world. One reason why we love stories is because they have been a survival mechanism since the beginning of human's journey on earth. Stories are especially powerful for young children because in them they find seeming coherence about a complex world and conflictual relationships. Critical literacy does a good job in teaching how to decode traditional stories that perpetuate oppression and inequality of various kinds in society (e.g., Luke, 2018) and re-writing the stories that are harmful. If children are taught to change traditional stories, fairy tales, and modern capitalist narratives of such topics as consumption, beauty, individualism, etc., then they may recognize that they have a strong voice to counter the domination of stories that have created oppressive imaginations. For example, some exemplary work published by the Chalkface Press in Australia has provided instructional materials to teach students how to change the course of narrative in popular stories and thus develop awareness of race, gender inequality, social injustice, and unequal distribution of resources in society. This critical literacy approach to teaching how to rewrite popular stories can be an effective way of tackling what Adichie (2009) described as the danger of a single story. She argued that each human life is a collection of heterogeneous stories. However, if only one story is told over and over again about a person or a social or cultural group, then that person or group becomes reduced to the single narrative. The complexities of human experiences and conditions are erased in such single-storism.

Rethinking the Reader

The fourth pedagogical principle that we would like to propose is a rethinking of the reader. Any text can be read and interpreted in myriad ways, and the reader has a very active role in constructing meanings of the text. This has been sufficiently emphasized in a body of work known as reader-response criticism. As Rosenblatt (2005) showed, reading is a transaction between text and reader, and in such transactions, the reader's background and contexts exert important influence on the construction of meanings. In this light, a writer cannot predetermine the meaning of a text, which may sound like an extreme indeterminacy of meaning. A critical-literacy-oriented author should recognize the importance of readers' experiences and reactions, as suggested by reader-response theory. However, the writer maintains an ethical responsibility to remain active in the text and speak truth through written words. While this truth may be debated and disputed, the writer must take the side of the disadvantaged, the oppressed, and the weak. One of the ways a writer can demonstrate such positionality is to write in plain language (Greene, 2013). Thus, a rethinking of the reader involves respect for readers' cultural knowledge, diverse perspectives, and emotional reactions to texts, but it also compels readers to enter into a dialogue about issues that hinder the pursuit of social justice.

Recommendations and Forward Thinking

A critical literacy approach to writing can bring to the fore the nexus between writing and power in various social and political fields. It should strive to channel the processes and products of writing into creative and emancipatory forces that will develop an outlook and commitment to equity and justice. Thus, writing must serve as an act of resistance. Critical writers should not only "speak truth to power," but also "speak truths to those who are not in power" (Chun, 2019, p. 15). As we look into the future, we propose the following four points to emphasize our argument:

(1.) Greater emphasis needs to be placed on writing because it has the potential to enhance what Rothman (2005) called "our engagement with democracy" (p. 49). Writing provides an avenue to enter one's inner life as well as the public life. It can be an effective form of non-violent persuasion. Most importantly, writing "offers opportunities for people to counter alienation, isolation, and selfishness that undermine democracy" (Rothman, 2005, p. 43).

(2.) A critical literacy approach to writing must encompass the needs and potentials of those individuals who write in a second/additional language for academic and professional purposes.

Worldwide, the number of people who write in English as an additional language is increasing at a very high speed (Casanave, 2017).

(3.) Critical literacy's emphasis on writing (for both first-language and second/additional-language writers) should be deliberately included in the curriculum and pedagogy at all levels of education. Without a curricular mandate, some teachers may not be willing to adopt a critical literacy framework in their teaching. Luke's (2018) endeavour to include critical literacy in Australian curriculum is exemplary in this regard. Similar scholarly work and activism is needed all over the world.

(4.) Programmes of teacher education and training could be a good starting point for promoting critical literacy-oriented writing pedagogy. For instance, Kohls (2019) catalogues how, through tutor training in writing pedagogy, a more informed understanding of resistance and pedagogy is possible. Pre-service and in-service teachers need a theoretical ground to incorporate the principles of critical literacy into their curriculum. Thus, they will be able to justify their critical pedagogical practices which some detractors may challenge by putting a label of indoctrination.

Implications for Our Social Responsibility as Academics

The central argument in this chapter has been that the scholarship on critical literacies needs to focus more on writing pedagogy. We are born to speak (except for those with underlying physical conditions), but writing is something we learn. As Coulmas (2013) wrote, "If language is the most distinctive inborn trait of our species, writing is our most consequential invention. It is so ubiquitous in everyday life that one has to wonder what purposes it serves" (p. ix). Yet, writing can be both poison and remedy. Therefore, we have an ethical choice about the purposes of writing. As we have demonstrated throughout this chapter, one important consideration in making such ethical choices is how to teach writing to student-writers. We recognize that there are other important considerations about writing as a personal, social, and intellectual activity. However, we have focused on the teaching of writing because both of us teach academic writing at a large Canadian university that attracts students from diverse socio-economic and cultural contexts across the world. Regarding our social responsibility as academics, we concur with Baldwin's advice: "You write in order to change the world . . . if you alter, even by a millimeter, the way people look at reality, then you can change it" (as cited in Pipher, 2006). Our way of altering how our students look at reality is to create pedagogical spaces for paying attention to the world and for imagining just and equitable alternatives.

Because writing is inherently tied to power, we have suggested that we use writing as a tool to fight injustice and oppression in school and society. For such a stance, adopting a critical literacy approach will be helpful. We have also suggested that teacher educators and critical literacies scholars continue to develop innovative ways of preparing educators to teach writing from a critical literacy perspective. In their pedagogical work, they may weave the four broad principles that we have discussed as reclaiming the experience of writing, relocating the personal, rewriting stories, and rethinking the reader.

Critical literacy's increasing focus on writing pedagogy needs to be an important part of our intellectual work and social responsibility as educators. Our pedagogy must not "take for granted the status quo, but subjects it to critique, creates alternative forms of practice," and this should be done "on the basis of radical theories of language, the individual, and society that take seriously our hopes for improvement in the direction of goals such as liberty, equality, and justice for all" (Crookes, 2013, p. 1). Thus, we propose that, as teachers and researchers of critical writing pedagogy, we take the roles and responsibilities of the intellectual who must be "on the same side as the weak and the underrepresented" (Said, 2000, p. 368). With this intellectual and social responsibility, a critical literacy approach to teaching writing should be one of our ways to respond to the mythical

Egyptian king's concern about writing. We must utilize writing as a tool of critique, hope, action, and transformation.

References

Adichie, C. N. (2009). *The danger of a single story* [Video]. Retrieved from www.ted.com/talks/chimamanda_ngozi_adichie_the_danger_of_a_single_story?language=en

Andrews, R., & Smith, A. (2011). *Developing writers: Teaching and learning in the digital age*. McGraw-Hill Education.

Arroyo, S. J. (2013). *Participatory composition: Video culture, writing, and electracy*. SIU Press.

Barton, D., & Hamilton, M. (2000). Literacy practices. In D. Barton, M. Hamilton, & R. Ivanic (Eds.), *Situated literacies: Reading and writing in context* (pp. 7–15). Routledge.

Bazerman, C. (2004). Intertextualities: Volosinov, Bakhtin, literary theory, and literacy studies. In A. F. Ball & S. W. Freedman (Eds.), *Bakhtinian perspectives on language, literacy, and learning* (pp. 53–65). Cambridge University Press.

Belcher, D. (1995). Writing critically across the curriculum. In D. Belcher & G. Braine (Eds.), *Academic writing in a second language: Essays on research and pedagogy* (pp. 135–154). Ablex.

Boler, M. (Ed.). (2010). *Digital media and democracy: Tactics in hard times*. MIT Press.

Brandt, D. (2015). *The rise of writing: Redefining mass literacy*. Cambridge University Press.

Canagarajah, A. S. (2002). *A geopolitics of academic writing*. University of Pittsburgh Press.

Canagarajah, A. S. (2011). Translanguaging in the classroom: Emerging issues for research and pedagogy. *Applied Linguistics Review, 2*, 1–28.

Canagarajah, A. S. (2012). *Translingual practice*. Routledge.

Caplan, N. A., & Johns, A. M. (Eds.). (2019). *Changing practices for the L2 writing classroom: Moving beyond the five-paragraph essay*. University of Michigan Press.

Casanave, C. P. (2017). Epilogue. In J. Bitchener, N. Storch, & R. Wette (Eds.), *Teaching writing for academic purposes to multilingual students: Instructional approaches* (pp. 203–215). Routledge.

Chun, C. W. (2019). EAP students co-constructing alternative narratives: Classroom discursive representations of Islam and democracy. *TESOL Quarterly, 53*(1), 158–179.

Clark, R., & Ivanič, R. (1997). *The politics of writing*. Routledge.

Coiro, J., Knobel, M., Lankshear, C., & Leu, D. J. (Eds.). (2014). *Handbook of research on new literacies*. Routledge.

Coulmas, F. (2013). *Writing and society*. Cambridge University Press.

Cremin, T., & Myhill, D. (2013). *Writing voices: Creating communities of writers*. Routledge.

Crookes, G. (2013). *Critical ELT in action: Foundations, promises, and praxis*. Routledge.

Elbow, P. (1998). *Writing without teachers*. Oxford University Press.

Friedan, B. (1963). *The feminine mystique*. W. W. Norton & Company.

Gee, J. (2015). *Social linguistics and literacies: Ideology in discourses*. Routledge.

Grabe, W., & Kaplan, R. B. (2014). *Theory and practice of writing: An applied linguistic perspective*. Longman.

Greene, A. E. (2013). *Writing science in plain English*. University of Chicago Press.

Horner, B., Lu, M. Z., Royster, J. J., & Trimbur, J. (2011). Language difference in writing: Toward a translingual approach. *College English, 73*(3), 303–321.

Horner, B., Selfe, C., & Lockridge, T. (2015). *Translinguality, transmodality, and difference: Exploring dispositions and change in language and learning*. Retrieved from https://ir.library.louisville.edu/cgi/viewcontent.cgi?article=1083&context=faculty

Hull, G. A., & Nelson, M. E. (2005). Locating the semiotic power of multimodality. *Written Communication, 22*(2), 224–261.

Hull, G. A., & Stornaiuolo, A. (2014). Cosmopolitan literacies, social networks, and "proper distance": Striving to understand in a global world. *Curriculum Inquiry, 44*(1), 15–44.

Inoue, A. B. (2015). *Antiracist writing assessment ecologies: Teaching and assessing writing for a socially just future*. WAC Clearinghouse.

Janks, H. (2009). Writing: A critical literacy perspective. In *The Sage handbook of writing development* (pp. 126–136). Retrieved from http://sk.sagepub.com/reference/hdbk_writingdev/n9.xml

Janks, H. (2013). Critical literacy in teaching and research. *Education Inquiry, 4*(2), 225–242. https://doi.org/10.3402/edui.v4i2.22071

Janks, H., & Comber, B. (2006). Critical literacy across continents. In K. Pahl & J. Rowsell (Eds.), *Travel notes from the new literacy studies: Instances of practice* (pp. 95–117). Multilingual Matters.

Jimenez, R. T., Smith, P. H., & Teague, B. L. (2009). Transnational and community literacies for teachers. *Journal of Adolescent & Adult Literacy, 53*(1), 16–26.

Jocson, K. M. (2008). *Youth poets: Empowering literacies in and out of schools* (Vol. 304). Peter Lang.

Jones, S., & Enriquez, G. (2009). Engaging the intellectual and the moral in critical literacy education: The four-year journeys of two teachers from teacher education to classroom practice. *Reading Research Quarterly, 44*(2), 145–168.

Kamler, B. (2001). *Relocating the personal: A critical writing pedagogy.* SUNY Press.

Kinloch, V. (2015). *Harlem on our minds: Place, race, and the literacies of urban youth.* Teachers College Press.

Kohls, R. (2019). Making sense of resistance in an afterschool tutoring program: Learning from volunteer writing tutors. *Writing & Pedagogy, 11*(3), 351–375.

Kubota, R. (2003). New approaches to gender, class, and race in second language writing. *Journal of Second Language Writing, 12*(1), 31–47.

Lankshear, C., & Knobel, M. (2011). *New literacies.* McGraw-Hill Education.

Lau, S. M. C. (2015). Relationality and emotionality: Toward a reflexive ethic in critical teaching. *Critical Literacy: Theories & Practices, 9*(2), 85–102.

Lillis, T. M. (2001). *Student writing: Access, regulation, desire.* Psychology Press.

López-Gopar, M. E. (2007). Beyond the alienating alphabetic literacy: Multiliteracies in indigenous education in Mexico. *Diaspora, Indigenous, and Minority Education, 1*(3), 159–174.

López-Gopar, M. E., Sughrua, W. M., Córdova-Hernández, L., Torres, B. P. L., Aldaz, E. R., & Morales, V. V. (2020). A critical thematic unit in a teaching praxicum: Health issues and plurilingualism in the "English" classroom. In S. M. C. Lau & S. Van Viegen (Eds.), *Plurilingual pedagogies: Critical and creative endeavors for equitable language in education* (pp. 97–113). Springer.

Luke, A. (2012). Critical literacy: Foundational notes. *Theory into Practice, 51*(1), 4–11. https://doi.org/10.1080/00405841.2012.636324

Luke, A. (2018). *Critical literacy, schooling, and social justice: The selected works of Allan Luke.* Routledge.

Mills, K. A., Stornaiuolo, A., Smith, A., & Pandya, J. Z. (Eds.). (2017). *Handbook of writing, literacies, and education in digital cultures.* Routledge.

Mora, R. A. (2015). City literacies in second languages: New questions for policy and advocacy. *Journal of Adolescent & Adult Literacy, 59*(1), 21–24.

Morgan, B. (2003). Writing across the theory-practice divide: A longitudinal confession. In C. P. Casanave & S. Vandrick (Eds.), *Writing for scholarly publication: Behind the scenes in language education* (pp. 223–235). Lawrence Erlbaum Associates.

Morgan, B., & Ramanathan, V. (2005). Critical literacies and language education: Global and local perspectives. *Annual Review of Applied Linguistics, 25*, 151–169. https://doi.org/10.1017/S0267190505000085

Morrell, E. (2015). *Critical literacy and urban youth: Pedagogies of access, dissent, and liberation.* Routledge.

Pandya, J. Z. (2019). *Exploring critical digital literacy practices: Everyday video in a dual language context.* Routledge.

Pipher, M. (2006). *Writing to change the world.* Riverhead Books.

Poe, M., & Inoue, A. B. (2016). Toward writing as social justice: An idea whose time has come. *College English, 79*(2), 119–126.

Prior, P. A., & Lunsford, K. J. (2008). History of reflection, theory, and research on writing. In C. Bazerman (Ed.), *Handbook of research on writing: History, society, school, individual, text* (pp. 97–116). Lawrence Erlbaum Associates.

Rancière, J. (2015). *Dissensus: On politics and aesthetics* (S. Corcoran, Trans.). Bloomsbury.

Robinson, A. (2009). *Writing and script: A very short introduction.* Oxford University Press.

Rosenblatt, L. (2005). *Making meaning with texts: Selected essays.* Heinemann.

Rothman, D. (2005). The writing classroom as a laboratory for democracy: An interview with Don Rothman (Interviewed by D. Brown). *Higher Education Exchange*, 43–55. Retrieved from www.kettering.org/sites/default/files/product-downloads/HEX2005_0.pdf

Said, E. (2000). *The selected works of Edward Said* (M. Bayoumi & A. Rubin, Eds.). Vintage.

Seltzer, K. (2020). Translingual writers as mentors in a high school "English" classroom. In S. M. C. Lau & S. Van Viegen (Eds.), *Plurilingual pedagogies: Critical and creative endeavors for equitable language in education* (pp. 185–204). Springer.

Shor, I., & Freire, P. (1987). *A pedagogy for liberation: Dialogues on transforming education.* Bergin & Garvey.

Silva, T., & Wang, Z. (Eds.). (2020). *Reconciling translingualism and second language writing.* Routledge.

Street, B. V. (Ed.). (1993). *Cross-cultural approaches to literacy* (No. 23). Cambridge University Press.

Ulmer, G. L. (2002). *Internet invention: From literacy to electracy.* Pearson.

Vandrick, S. (1995). Teaching and practicing feminism in the university ESL class. *TESOL Journal, 4*(3), 4–6.

Vasudevan, L., & Campano, G. (2009). The social production of adolescent risk and the promise of adolescent literacies. *Review of Research in Education, 33*(1), 310–353.

Vasudevan, L., Schultz, K., & Bateman, J. (2010). Rethinking composing in a digital age: Authoring literate identities through multimodal storytelling. *Written Communication, 27*(4), 442–468.

Yagelski, R. P. (2009). A thousand writers writing: Seeking change through the radical practice of writing as a way of being. *English Education, 42*(1), 6–28.

1.10

CRITICAL MEDIA PRODUCTION

Olivia G. Stewart, Cassandra Scharber, Jeff Share, and Anne Crampton

Defining Critical Media Production

Critical media production is the process by which students create alternative media that question dominant narratives while learning the codes of representation of their social worlds. The process of media production can be highly creative, active, and meaningful, especially when students express their concerns about social and/or environmental issues. When youth create videos, music, social media, visual art, or video games, they empower themselves as they actively produce media that reflect their experiences and passions.

Perspectives on critical media *consumption* have roots in theories of mass and popular culture that establish the impossibility of escaping the "spectacle" of mass media (DeBord, 1994/1967) and remark upon the power of the vehicle itself, as in "the medium is the message" (McLuhan, 1964). Further critical theories have developed from Marxist, feminist, critical race, anti-colonial, eco-justice, queer, cyborg, and post-human paradigms, all of which support critical frameworks for consuming media, for reading "with and against" texts of all kinds (Janks, 2019). With the growth of information communication technologies and the requirements from Common Core State Standards for students to integrate, interpret, and analyze "diverse media and formats," literacy education has become increasingly comfortable with expanding the definition of what constitutes a text, to include popular media for both consumption and production, although this is seldom reflected in standardized tests, AP exams, and other recognized cultural signposts of literacy achievement.

Critical media *production*, on the other hand, recognizes critical approaches to texts but moves beyond critical responses toward the creation of critical arguments. It describes an act of composing to address social problems. Critical media production may not always result in compositions of professional quality, and in the context of critical literacy, these productions have been authored by people of all ages and levels of rhetorical and technical skill (Vasquez, 2014). While digital technologies make media production more available to all with some access to technology, "old" forms of media may also be considered as critical media productions.

As in print literacy, digital reading and writing are intimately connected. However, just creating media is not enough; it must be done with critical analysis that challenges hierarchies of power in order for the process to build what Freire (2010) calls conscientização, a revolutionary critical consciousness that involves perception as well as action against oppression. Even though early media education recognized the value of student-produced media (Masterman, 1985/2001), U.S. media education specifically has "not necessarily advocated a critical stance toward media production"

                    DOI: 10.4324/9781003023425-11

(Morrell, Dueñas, Garcia, & López, 2013, p. 4). Morrell and colleagues suggest educators need to enlighten "students about the potential they have, as media producers to shape the world they live in and to help to turn it into the world they imagine" (p. 3). In doing so, students can experience the power to influence public discourse and challenge the injustices that are often overwhelming and disempowering.

Freire (2010) promotes the power of praxis, the combination of theory and practice in action. Praxis is a core component of critical media literacy, as analysis and production are united by a theoretical framework with conceptual understandings and critical questions that guide students to analyze media representations they encounter, use, produce, and share (Kellner & Share, 2019). When students understand that media are never neutral and that somebody always benefits while others are harmed by all representations, they are more likely to reflect on the potential impact of the media they create.

Since 1984, youth from poor and marginalized communities at the Educational Video Center (EVC) in New York City have been learning to think critically about media by creating movies documenting the problems and assets of their communities. Founder of EVC, Goodman (2003) asserts that one of the best strategies for "teaching critical literacy is for students to create their own media" (p. 6). Goodman (2010) explains that the process of critical media production holds many promising practices, such as:

> ensuring that all students contribute to discussions and decision making; use the community as a source of knowledge and information; connect personal experiences to social concerns; use multiple modes of literacy in their daily work; develop critical questions to guide their inquiry; revise their work and reflect on their learning; and use their video to inspire community dialogue and action.
>
> *(p. 52)*

When youth create media, as opposed to merely reading and discussing it, they are involved in constructivist pedagogy that requires them to be active problem solvers (Vygotsky, 1978). Students learn best by doing and engaging their creative potential to construct meaning while also analyzing and critically reflecting on the messages they read and create (Dewey, 1963). Creating alternative media that challenge social injustice and dominant ideologies is also empowering because it provides students paths for taking action about problems they see and encounter. Students need to know how to use new tools to engage politically in their world in ways that can reach countless numbers of people, much as they do socially on their own with gaming, texting, Snapchat, Instagram, Twitter, and other practices.

Web 2.0 is about sharing, and social media provide platforms and potential for children and youth to engage with relevant issues that concern them (Prensky, 2010). Prensky asserts that real learning

> involves students immediately using what they learn to do something and/or change something in the world. It is crucial that students be made aware that using what they learn to effect positive change in the world, large or small, is one of their important roles in school.
>
> *(p. 20)*

He explains that digital technology provides useful tools for students to do this at any age. Students from elementary school to university level can create media that is shared globally as public service campaigns or alternative representations that challenge stereotypes and injustice "with output that both does good and supports their learning" (p. 66).

This type of social justice education using real-world digital projects is vital because most of the social problems in the world are supported by non-critical media that reproduce the status quo far more often than they challenge the inequalities and injustices. At the same time, new technologies are reshaping our environment and social relations, providing more opportunities for students to create media that can challenge problems, promote social justice, and enhance academics. Students and teachers can improve learning with production by using critical media literacy conceptual understandings and questions to analyze all media messages. By engaging with media as producers, students not only learn essential digital literacies, they also gain a sense of agency and empowerment to foster social justice. Like any good project-based learning, the *process* of creating a product is where most learning occurs (Dewey, 1963). Teachers should be cautious not to fall into the common trap of overvaluing the final product at the expense of the creation process. Critical media production emphasizes the application of critical inquiry and media production that can be used to address genuine concerns and promote a more democratic classroom (Goodman, 2003; Morrell et al., 2013).

Historical, Current, and Emerging Theory

Sociocultural Approaches to Literacy: Multiliteracies

Using a lens of critical literacy, critical media production takes the forms of talking back, redesigning, and presenting possible solutions. It has roots within sociocultural theories of the learning sciences, most especially multiliteracies and, by extension, participatory cultures and activist literacies.

Multiliteracies position literacy as a multiplicitous practice of interaction rather than a cognitive ability to read and write alphabetic text. Thus, multiliteracies recognize that people communicate via multiple and constantly evolving modes and through multiple layers of cultures and languages and that literacy practices exist across multiple, fluid contexts (Aguilera, Stewart, Mawasi, & Pérez Cortés, 2019). The New London Group (NLG) (1996) brought together disparate scholars in the then-emergent field of multiliteracies to present an urgent argument for the widespread adoption of a sociocultural approach to literacy education with the goal of global, social change. The group argued that an expanded view of literacy afforded more ways to *access* language used in work, school, and community for critique, design, and redesign rather than for passive decoding and comprehension of messages. The goal was for "full and equitable social participation" (p. 60) to address disparities in "life chances" (p. 61); in other words, the NLG sought a literacy education that could disrupt entrenched distributions of power through access to elements of design, always assuming a critical use and understanding of discourses as part of the meaning-making process.

The field of New Media Literacy Studies (NMLS) progressed along a parallel track to multiliteracies. With goals of strengthening the critical and reflective consumption of media coupled with the affordances of digital tools for the production of media, NMLS scholars also emphasized ways that amateurs (students) "transform society" (Gee, 2010, p. 14). Critical media production may therefore be traced to a cluster of theories surrounding and emerging from sociocultural perspectives on literacy.

Participatory Culture and Connected Learning

Critical media productions are the literacy practices imagined in theories of "participatory culture" in which members make meaningful contributions to improve their social worlds (Jenkins, Clinton, Purushotma, Robison, & Weigel, 2009). As with multiliteracies approaches, the goal of building participatory cultures assumes that greater involvement on the part of all members of society is a social good, championing diversity of thought and expression over conformity and silence(ing). This framework addresses, through critique, how literacy productions can reproduce oppressive social structures and envisions productions that promote significant emancipatory change. Similar to the stated desires of the NLG (1996), the possible impact of participatory approaches has been to "renegotiate relational and social power" (Garcia, Mirra, Morrell, Martinez, & Scorza, 2015, p. 155).

Another optimistic outcome envisioned through theories of participatory cultures is the potential for more robust social connections, which might be formed around like interests/backgrounds/affiliations, language use and expression, collaborative problem-solving through technology, and the ways that digital media make possible redesign and circulation of texts and projects (Jenkins et al., 2009). Adjacent to participatory cultures and extending the theme of social connection is connected learning, which relies on digital media and communications for increased engagement through popular modes of expression, increased access to information, increased social connectedness through social media, and increased diversity in terms of whose voices are allowed to contribute to conversations (Ito et al., 2013).

Activism and Mobility Fuel Developments in Critical Media Production

While the NLG's manifesto brought attention to possibilities for literacy's role in social change, inequities persist in education as with all public spaces and endeavors. In particular, researchers and practitioners with commitments to racial and educational justice continue to build the argument that social transformation must be the ultimate goal of a critical and digital literacy education (Garcia et al., 2015). Certainly, there is a growing understanding of the ways that literacy education systematically perpetuates racial/social inequities in the United States. Education that includes critical media production opens opportunities for students to discuss and participate in movements such as Black Lives Matter in meaningful, just protest.

Thus, from participatory literacy practices imagined by the NLG as doing literacy for social transformation, it requires only a short leap to view literacy acts as participatory *politics*, engagement in which might include youth participatory action research (YPAR) using digital tools and platforms to amplify critical arguments (Soep, 2014). The move toward a more youth-centered activism emphasizes what the NLG foretold: access to digital media has resulted in youth composing their own stories, creating counter stories, and demanding better futures. Youth in resistance movements (e.g., responses to anti-Blackness) are already creating critical messages; without co-opting their resistance, schools and teachers can conspire (Love, 2019) with youth and communities to make activist critical media production a culturally sustaining literacy practice that aims to change the world (Paris & Alim, 2014).

While activism through critical media production has made inroads toward acceptance in formal and informal learning environments, access to media tools coupled with legitimacy of critical arguments (e.g., schooling structures and racial injustice) remain challenging, depending upon the participants and the setting. For those historically marginalized from mainstream routes to literacy success (e.g., students who identify as Black/indigenous/people of color, English language learners, and special education students), these hurdles mean that critical media production, rather than becoming integral to literacy education as the NLG imagined, is still an add-on, perpetually outside of "real" literacy instruction. It is for this reason that powerful experiences in critical, connected learning and media production are often developed as out-of-school literacies, despite their relevance and power as academic literacy practices in classrooms around the world (Vasquez et al., 2019).

Emergent theories about critical media production include questions about citizenship amid increasing mobility and dislocation of students/producers, heightened fears, and distrust around social differences and surveillance, combined with the incredible sophistication and portability of tools of production, and the unending incoming messages from mass and dispersed media channels.

Review of and Implications for Future Research

With the exponential growth of new production tools and social network platforms that support the production and sharing of media, the possibilities for engaging in critical media production within education contexts have never been more accessible. However, critical media production has not been a dominant thread in published research during the past decade (2010–2020). While there were multitudes of journal articles that shared examples of the "what" of media production related to different tool use (e.g., PowerPoint, Final Cut Pro) as well as different media formats (e.g., music, podcasts), there was considerably less research that theorized, illustrated, and/or examined a critical orientation to media production itself. This smaller corpus of research reflects interpretive and critical research paradigms and methods and can be grouped into three categories: perspectives, places, and pedagogies, which are highlighted in this section. This review includes research published in journals and in books only and was explicitly focused on "critical media production," excluding research that focused more generally on critical literacies.

Perspectives. There are differing conceptual angles to critical media production despite common theoretical groundings including multiliteracies, sociocultural learning theory, and critical literacy. For example, Ávila and Pandya (2013) explore definitions and intersections within *critical digital literacies*, which are "skills and practices that lead to the creation of digital texts that interrogate the world; they also allow and foster the interrogation of digital, multimedia texts" (p. 3). They offer examples of varying forms of media used to engage students in critical digital literacies, illustrations of youth designing and producing media for praxis, and cautions for those engaged in this work.

Lee and Soep (2016) describe *critical computational literacy* (CCL) as a pedagogical and conceptual framework that uniquely fuses aspects of critical literacy and computational thinking. This framework grew out of the authors' work at Youth Radio (now YR Media) which is an outside-of-school youth-development organization and media production company. Through the use of computational thinking practices, young people "conceptualize, create, and disseminate digital projects that break silences, expose important truths, and challenge unjust systems, all the while building skills such as coding and design" (p. 480).

A final example is work by Mirra and colleagues (2018) who propose an updated and extended critical theory of multiliteracies that emphasizes student production and distribution of media. They argue for moving toward a *pedagogy of invention*, which is

> the re-envisioning of young people as not simply masterful and critical consumers, producers, and distributors of digital literacies, but as inventors with the competencies and dispositions needed to dream up digital forms of expressions that adults cannot yet image . . . this practice, by necessity, must focus on equity.
>
> *(p. 17)*

Places. Research that explores the types of settings that support critical media production was primarily drawn from outside of formal schooling contexts. Critical orientations within U.S. formal schooling can be in tension with common purposes/expectations of public schooling and/or educators' beliefs about learning. For example, Youth Radio is a noteworthy example of an outside-of-school setting that nurtures critical media production—the critical orientation is central to its organization's purpose (Soep & Chávez, 2010). Another example of settings that are positioned to support critical media production are makerspaces, which appear inside and outside of schools. In makerspaces, the emphasis is on "making," "doing," "creating," and "producing." Vossoughi and colleagues (2016) critique these spaces and

> examine the tensions and possibilities for equity-oriented education within the current maker movement and the ways we might reconceptualize making as a pedagogical practice that is grounded in the histories, needs, assets, and experiences of working-class students and students of color.
>
> *(p. 209–210)*

They offer a framework for equity-focused makerspace research and design comprising critical analyses of educational justice, historicized approaches to making as a cross-cultural activity, explicit attention to pedagogical philosophies and practices, and ongoing inquiry into the sociopolitical values and purposes of making.

One final highlight is a study that examined the features of a community-based learning program in order to highlight the synergy between its technology, literate practices, and social justice ethos that impact youth's learning and documentary filmmaking (Scharber, Isaacson, Pyscher, & Lewis, 2016). Using the lenses of activity theory and participatory culture, these findings illustrate the possibilities for youth's digital literacies and media production to facilitate, support, and extend engagement in social justice topics.

Pedagogies. A notable book on how to "do" critical media production in education is *Critical Media Pedagogy: Teaching for Achievement in City Schools* (Morrell et al., 2013). This book conceptualizes and illustrates critical media pedagogy and practices in schools and draws on sociocultural theories of learning as well as ideas from critical literacy and media studies. The authors are explicit about their philosophy of critical media production:

> Our project is interested in the act of media production, but we don't feel that producing media, in and of itself, necessarily constitutes critical activity. By contrast, we are explicitly interested in developing critical media pedagogies that result in the production of critical media . . . we feel that students can use media artifacts such as blogs and digital films as a way to encourage dialogue about inequities in education and society at large.
>
> *(p. 17)*

The critical media pedagogical practices used within three high school classrooms, multiple school clubs, and an outside-of-school summer program are described in chapters of the book by the teachers/directors themselves and serve as exemplars. There is also an appendix containing examples of lessons for different content areas.

Barron, Gomez, Pinkard, and Martin (2014) share the Digital Youth Network's unique model of an integrated inside/outside school program combined with digital spaces and mentors to support underserved urban youth's increased engagement with technology. The goal of the program is to cultivate middle-schoolers' digital media citizenship through becoming critical media producers. The book outlines the program design, research/evaluation findings, and implications for other youth media programs.

A final notable text that promotes critical digital and media literacies is *The Critical Media Literacy Guide* by Kellner and Share (2019), which offers a framework for teachers to use in the classroom. This framework outlines conceptual understandings and questions to use in order to deepen students' explorations into issues and to guide their media production responses that counter ideas and representations.

Suggestions for Research

This review points to the need for additional research that is grounded conceptually and theoretically in orientations to critical media production, including illustrations of critical media production in practice. These illustrations may be more apparent in outside-of-school and higher education settings, where the constraints with critical stances within K–12 settings are not as prevalent. This is often the case in schools, where the use of media is considered by teachers as objective technology, a distraction, or an opportunity for deviant behavior rather than powerful tools that can empower students.

An additional area in need of more inquiry is the connections and possibilities of using social media in critical media production. Often these avenues do not "count," are not valued, or are simply not accessible in K–12 schools (Aguilera et al., 2019). Social media platforms provide avenues for sharing and distribution of media productions with real audiences, which increases the potential for awareness, conversation, and impact (Stewart, 2015). A final area of need is alignment and connections with media consumption and distribution of "fake news." These directions for research are imperative to providing equity-centered learning for all students—especially young people of color and from lower socioeconomic backgrounds—that engage them in experiences that can change the communities around them.

Forward Thinking

Because media creators construct images and models of success, power, class, race, gender, sexuality, etc. for many people (Kellner, 2011), it is important to think about how critical digital media literacies/production can be iteratively reshaped moving forward as producers and their sites of production continue to change through physical and virtual mobility. As educators, we focus on the importance of educational systems in examining how critical digital media production can be revamped as media continue to pervade our lives, and as educational systems affect the ways in which students are enculturated to process much of the world. Kellner and Share (2005) argue that "education must meet the dual challenges of teaching media literacy in a multicultural society and sensitising students and the public to the inequities and injustices of a society based on gender, race, and class inequalities and discrimination" (p. 370). For students to critically examine and understand the ways in which media influence their lives, they must learn how to become sensitive to the ways in which media are produced and the ways in which they include/exclude voices and revoice inequalities and discrimination.

Therefore, as many others have argued for decades (e.g., Hammer, 2011; Mirra et al., 2018; NLG, 1996), it is essential that critical digital media practices be included not only in K–12 classrooms, but also at postsecondary levels. By including them, spaces can be opened for students to conceptualize novel counter-narratives through digital technologies, and students can better understand the sites of production as well as how to produce and reinvent media for their own purposes (Mirra et al., 2018). By creating contexts wherein students can become empowered to question, rethink, and reinvent digital media, teachers and students begin to co-create knowledge together rather than simply consuming media, viewing it as neutral, or maintaining current top-down educational structures (Hammer, 2011). According to Hammer:

> Teaching critical media literacy through production constitutes a new form of pedagogy in which students become more aware of how media is constructed, conveys dominant ideologies and is one of the most powerful, often unconscious, sources of education. And these critical skills not only make students aware of how their own views of the world are mediated by media, but also enable them to learn how to critically read, engage and decode media culture.
>
> *(p. 361)*

Students may therefore become more critical of the media around them, but also begin to understand where and how certain groups are (or are not) represented. Thus, it is important that both teachers and students examine the role of the creator of the media and the perspectives and voices that are included, and importantly, those that are excluded.

However, while many K–12 teachers may *want* to include critical media production in their classrooms, they may not know how to do so (Aguilera et al., 2020). By establishing critical digital

111

media courses at universities (particularly for preservice and current teachers) university students will have opportunities to practice and understand how to create spaces for their current/future students to critically read, and more importantly, *create* critical media in schools. In their research, Kellner and Share (2007) found that continual support and professional development for current teachers was essential to support/foster critical media literacy practices in classrooms. Thus, including courses designed specifically for preservice and current teachers can help to shift practices in K–12 contexts.

By opening space for future and current educators to include critical digital media projects in their classrooms wherein students can question, design, and create avenues for new media rather than simply consuming it, we can better prepare students at all levels to voice their experiences and the social issues that affect their lives (Mirra et al., 2018). This design can move beyond focusing on the technical aspects of media production to critically examining the relevant issues behind it and lead to positive literacy practices that go beyond the syntheses and analyses often seen in traditional classrooms (Hammer, 2011; Pangrazio, 2016). This shift, in turn, may lead to a more ideologically nuanced view of media for students and teachers alike.

However, revamping an educational system to include critical digital media practices and production can be slow and laborious given the institutional and practical constraints that many teachers and instructors face. Current and preservice teachers may be struggling with constraints typical of the educational systems writ large as well as the practicalities of digital media production in the classroom (e.g., classroom management, firewalls/fears about classroom technologies, institutional constraints, standardized curricula/testing). Teachers may face these barriers and have little recourse to change them without proper administrative support. Furthermore, instructors of preservice teachers often face the practicalities of larger institutional requirements such as programmatic and bureaucratic constraints that accompany many university programs (Stewart, Hseih, Smith, & Pandya, 2021).

Thus, we argue that it is essential that instructors create networks of support with other critical researchers and beyond to help establish global communities of support. Additionally, universities need to make critical digital media production a priority for students and for instructors and support them through courses specifically designed around critical digital literacies and critical media production. This support is vital, and by critically framing teacher education courses and teaching future teachers about critical media production, we can hope to engage and empower students as well as establish a more democratic system.

Implications for Our Social Responsibility as Academics

Throughout this chapter, we have asserted that critical media literacy and critical media production are vital requirements for understanding and engaging today's complex political, social, and economic systems wherein educational systems can sometimes be restrictive and outdated (Hammer, 2011). Without critical media-focused courses in our universities and classrooms as well as critical media production within informal learning settings, we run the risk of continuing a path toward neoliberal fascism from a previously much more democratic system. As Pangrazio (2016) argues, "if critical thinking is to remain within the digital literacy paradigm then an important question to consider is how digital design can use creativity to move beyond the personal to consider issues of a political and ethical nature" (p. 167). By creating critical digital media, one can push thinking forward in new ways to better represent a more democratic field of all of those who also "consume" it, rather than representing the few who typically create media.

Academics are uniquely positioned to impact a number of people through courses as well as research. Thus, we end this chapter with a discussion of our social responsibilities as academics concerned with critical media literacy and production. We do so through a discussion of the importance of critical media production, especially when current societal norms are often propagated through—and perhaps even determined by—media (Kellner, 2011), which can often be considered the most powerful and influential mediators of daily experiences and global perceptions (Hammer, 2011). We feel it is important to position ourselves, the authors, within the scope of digital media production to signal that we, like other academics writ large, have a social responsibility to criticality. However, we explore the responsibility of academics for critical media production in terms of the larger scope of academia rather than just our own experiences.

An important part of critical production is critique. Kellner and Share (2007) argue that critical media literacies and production must be a "critique of mainstream approaches to literacy and a political project for democratic social change" (p. 61). To accomplish this critique, one must critically examine "popular culture and the culture industries, that addresses issues of class, race, gender, sexuality, and power and also promotes the production of alternative counter-hegemonic media" (p. 61). This kind of critique is essential when people can explore the potential "structures of oppression" rather than simply voicing their opinions or experiences (Kellner & Share, 2005, p. 371). As academics, we are in unique positions to critique and create media productions, grounding our ideas within rich theoretical frameworks and through research designs that allow for more grounded, research-based critique over opinion. This grounded critique can be models for those in academia, the press, and for students. Additionally, there is another, perhaps more important, position for academics to recognize the voices of those *outside* of academia through jointly championing causes and opening spaces for new voices in courses, research, and social media.

Furthermore, as previously discussed, it is essential that we create and cultivate global networks of criticality that engage people in the academy and beyond. These networks can be created through media themselves (e.g., Twitter, listservs, hashtags) to continually reinvent and reimagine what media can be and how it can represent those who use it. They can also push conversations of criticality and media further by including voices beyond and outside of academia that may not otherwise be included. By opening spaces for those voices, we can continue to iteratively critique and question media to produce new representations that break down long-established hegemonic power structures of oppression.

We hope that through modeling our own production and creating diverse networks of criticality, we can also encourage students in our own courses to question, explore, and analyze the structures of oppression about which they may not have thought to previously question or critique. We assert that the role of the academic is not to explicitly direct students' critical media production or "unlock" these structures of oppression but rather to open spaces for and provoke critique of media as well as critical media production (Buckingham, 2003). Educators play an important role in critical media production as facilitators who can guide student exploration and production to question hierarchies of power and injustice. In doing so, students are more likely to come to their own conclusions and reinvent media in new critical ways.

However, we must remember that the social nature of most digital media production today can be overtly public, creating the need to be cautious when posting or encouraging students to share their work. As we enter the age of surveillance capitalism, more and more corporations are monitoring our activities online and off, collecting our data, and selling it to companies and governments interested in surveilling, predicting, and modifying behavior (Zuboff, 2019). It is ever more important for media producers to consider their audience and the potential positive and negative effects of sharing their content online, with increased visibility offering both protection and danger (Soep, 2014). Critical media production has its risks as productions are shared; however, these cautions need to be weighed against the powerful potential to positively affect audiences around the world, telling stories that are seldom told and empowering the media makers through the creation process.

References

Aguilera, E., Stewart, O. G., Mawasi, A., & Pérez Cortés, L. (2020). Seeing beyond the screen: A multidimensional framework for understanding digital-age literacies. In P. M. Sullivan, J. J. Lantz, B. Sullivan, & L. Tomei (Eds.), *Handbook of research on integrating digital technology with literacy pedagogies* (pp. 1–31). IGI Global. https://doi.org/10.4018/978-1-7998-0246-4.ch001

Ávila, J., & Pandya, J. Z. (2013). *Critical digital literacies as social praxis: Intersections and challenges.* Peter Lang.

Barron, B., Gomez, K., Pinkard, N., & Martin, C. K. (Eds.). (2014). *The digital youth network: Cultivating digital media citizenship in urban communities.* MIT Press.

Buckingham, D. (2003). Media education and the end of the critical consumer. *Harvard Educational Review, 73*(3), 309–327. https://doi.org/10.17763/haer.73.3.c149w3g81t381p67

Debord, G. (1994/1967). *The society of the spectacle.* Zone Books.

Dewey, J. (1938/1963). *Experience & education.* Collier Books.

Freire, P. (2010). *Pedagogy of the oppressed* (M. B. Ramos, Trans.). The Continuum International Publishing Group, Inc.

Garcia, A., Mirra, N., Morrell, E., Martinez, A., & Scorza, D. (2015). The council of youth research: Critical literacy and civic agency in the digital age. *Reading & Writing Quarterly, 31*(2), 151–167. https://doi.org/10.1080/10573569.2014.962203

Gee, J. P. (2010). A situated sociocultural approach to literacy. In E. A. Baker & D. J. Leu (Eds.), *The new literacies: Multiple perspectives on research and practice* (pp. 165–193). Guilford Press.

Goodman, S. (2003). *Teaching youth media: A critical guide to literacy, video production, and social change.* Teachers College Press.

Goodman, S. (2010). Toward 21st-century literacy and civic engagement: Facilitating student documentary projects. In J. G. Silin (Ed.), *High-needs schools: Preparing teachers for today's world* (pp. 44–54). Bank Street College of Education.

Hammer, R. (2011). Critical media literacy as engaged pedagogy. *E-Learning and Digital Media, 8*(4), 357–363. https://doi.org/10.2304/elea.2011.8.4.357

Ito, M., Gutierrez, K., Livingstone, S., Penuel, B., Rhodes, J., Salen, K., . . Watkins, S. C. (2013). *Connected learning: An agenda for research and design.* Digital Media and Learning Research Hub.

Janks, H. (2019). Critical literacy and the importance of reading with and against a text. *Journal of Adolescent & Adult Literacy, 62*(5), 561–564. https://doi.org/10.1002/jaal.941

Jenkins, H., Clinton, K., Purushotma, R., Robison, A. J., & Weigel, M. (2009). *Confronting the challenges of participatory culture: Media education for the 21st century.* MacArthur Foundation, MIT Press.

Kellner, D. (2011). Cultural studies, multiculturalism, and media culture. In G. Dines & J. M. Humez (Eds.), *Gender, race, and class in Media: A critical reader* (pp. 7–18). Sage.

Kellner, D., & Share, J. (2005). Toward critical media literacy: Core concepts, debates, organizations, and policy. *Discourse: Studies in the Cultural Politics of Education, 26*(3), 369–386. https://doi.org/10.1080/01596300500200169

Kellner, D., & Share, J. (2007). Critical media literacy: Crucial policy choices for a twenty-first-century democracy. *Policy Futures in Education, 5*(1), 59–69. https://doi.org/10.2304/pfie.2007.5.1.59

Kellner, D., & Share, J. (2019). *The critical media literacy guide: Engaging media and transforming education.* Brill/Sense Publishers.

Lee, C. H., & Soep, E. (2016). None but ourselves can free our minds: Critical computational literacy as a pedagogy of resistance. *Equity & Excellence in Education, 49*(4), 480–492. https://doi.org/10.1080/10665684.2016.1227157

Love, B. (2019). *We want to do more than survive: Abolitionist teaching and the pursuit of educational freedom.* Beacon Press.

Masterman, L. (1985/2001). *Teaching the media.* Routledge.

McLuhan, M. (1964). *Understanding media: The extensions of man.* McGraw Hill.

Mirra, N., Morrell, E., & Filipiak, D. (2018). From digital consumption to digital invention: Toward a new critical theory and practice of multiliteracies. *Theory into Practice, 57*(1), 12–19. http://doi.org/10.1080/00405841.2017.1390336

Morrell, E., Dueñas, R., Garcia, V., & López, J. (2013). *Critical media pedagogy: Teaching for achievement in city schools.* Teachers College Press.

New London Group. (1996). A pedagogy of multiliteracies: Designing social futures. *Harvard Educational Review, 66*(1), 60–92. https://doi.org/10.17763/haer.66.1.17370n67v22j160u

Pangrazio, L. (2016). Reconceptualising critical digital literacy. *Discourse: Studies in the Cultural Politics of Education, 37*(2), 163–174. https://doi.org/10.1080/01596306.2014.942836

Paris, D., & Alim, H. S. (2014). What are we seeking to sustain through culturally sustaining pedagogy? A loving critique forward. *Harvard Educational Review, 84*(1), 85–100.

Prensky, M. (2010). *Teaching digital natives: Partnering for real learning.* Corwin.

Scharber, C., Isaacson, K., Pyscher, T., & Lewis, C. (2016). Participatory culture meets critical practice: Documentary film production in a youth internship program. *English Teaching: Practice and Critique, 15*(3), 355–374. https://doi.org/10.1108/ETPC-01-2016-0021

Soep, E. (2014). *Participatory politics: Next-generation tactics to remake the public sphere.* MIT Press.

Soep, E., & Chávez, V. (2010). *Drop that knowledge: Youth Radio stories.* University of California Press.

Stewart, O. G. (2015). A critical review of the literature of social media's affordances in the classroom. *E-Learning and Digital Media, 12*(5–6), 481–501. https://doi.org/10.1177/2042753016672895

Stewart, O. G., Hseih, B., Smith, A., & Pandya, J. (2021). What more can we do? Examining critical digital literacies in teacher education across scales. *Pedagogies: An International Journal.*

Vasquez, V. M. (2014). Negotiating critical literacies with young children. Routledge.

Vasquez, V. M., Janks, H., & Comber, B. (2019). Critical literacy as a way of being and doing. *Language Arts, 96*(5), 300–311.

Vossoughi, S., Hooper, P. K., & Escudé, M. (2016). Making through the lens of culture and power: Toward transformative visions for educational equity. *Harvard Educational Review, 86*(2), 206–232. https://doi.org/10.17763/0017-8055.86.2.206

Vygotsky, L. S. (1978). *Mind in society: The development of higher psychological processes.* Harvard University Press.

Zuboff, S. (2019). *The age of surveillance capitalism: The fight for a human future at the new frontier of power.* Public Affairs Hachette Book Group.

Introduction to Area 2

Roberto Santiago de Roock and Raúl Alberto Mora

Area 2, framed as critical literacies across space, surveys critical literacy research from around the globe. The intent is to build on, decenter, and challenge the "foundational" theory and practice of the field, which is greatly concentrated in Anglophone countries. It is meant to be an initial foray into such transnational work, rather than exhaustive. The area is structured in two subsections: individual countries/colonies (2.1–2.15) followed by geographic regions or groups of countries (2.16–2.22), organized alphabetically within each to avoid any hierarchy, intended or unintended.

2.1 Aotearoa New Zealand
2.2 Australia
2.3 Brazil
2.4 Canada
2.5 Colombia
2.6 India
2.7 Indonesia
2.8 Iran
2.9 Japan
2.10 Mexico
2.11 Puerto Rico
2.12 Russia
2.13 Singapore
2.14 South Africa
2.15 United Kingdom
2.16 United States
2.17 Caribbean Isles (English and Dutch speaking)
2.18 Hong Kong and Mainland China
2.19 Nordic Countries
2.20 Norway and France
2.21 South Asia
2.22 Uganda and Congo

DOI: 10.4324/9781003023425-12

2.1

CRITICAL LITERACY PRAXIS IN AOTEAROA NEW ZEALAND

Susan Sandretto, Jane Tilson, and Derek Shafer

Introduction

Aotearoa New Zealand is a seafaring nation bordered by the Tasman Sea and the Pacific Ocean. Comprising approximately 600 islands, the majority of its 4.7 million inhabitants live on Te Ika-a-Māui (North Island), and Te Wai Pounamu (South Island). Aotearoa boasts 15,000 kilometres of coastline, the ninth longest in the world, and is the most isolated temperate landmass on the earth, with nearest neighbours about 1,600 kilometres away. Many people trace their whakapapa (genealogy) to one of the seven original canoes that arrived from Hawaiki (Taonui, 2005), while others can trace their arrival to tall ships from Europe or jumbo jets.

The metaphor of *kāpehu whetū* (star compass) as a guide resonates with our collective history and critical literacy. At its heart, critical literacy involves navigating the workings of power as captured in texts, critical consideration of the consequences of texts, and ultimately social action (Sandretto & Klenner, 2011). Texts can be any combination of linguistic, audio, gestural, spatial, and visual modes used to communicate; including but not limited to traditional paper texts and multimodal texts in online spaces (Kress, 2010). Action can be in the form of (re)constructing a new text to speak back to an unjust or inequitable text or challenging one's thinking. Ultimately, critical literacy is the compass that guides our research and pedagogical practice.

Social Landscape

Aotearoa's population is classified as "superdiverse," with more than 160 languages and predictions of multiethnic diversity to rise (Royal Society of New Zealand, 2013, p. 1). If we consider our population as a village of 100 people, 70 are European, 17 Māori, 15 Asian, eight Pacific, and two of other ethnicities[1] (Statistics New Zealand, 2019). Of the 70,000 teachers currently employed in the primary and secondary sectors, 69% are European, 11% Māori, 3.3% Pacific, 3.8% Asian, 0.3% other ethnicities, and 11% undisclosed (Education Counts, 2020). Problematically, all ethnic groups (apart from European) are underrepresented in the teaching workforce when students in Aotearoa are increasingly diverse.

Aotearoa's founding document Te Tiriti o Waitangi, the Treaty of Waitangi, was signed in 1840 by the British Crown and Māori. The Treaty ceded sovereignty of Aotearoa to Britain, giving the Crown exclusive rights to lands Māori might sell. In return, Māori were guaranteed ownership

DOI: 10.4324/9781003023425-13

of their lands, forests, fisheries, and other *taonga* (treasures), including language. Two versions of the Treaty exist, English and a Māori translation, with key concepts interpreted in different ways. For example, the Eurocentric concept of sovereignty had no direct translation in Māori. While Māori saw the Crown as a regulatory authority to protect *tino rangatiratanga* (self-determination) over their resources, the Crown sought sovereignty of all New Zealand at the expense of their Treaty partners (Fleras & Spoonley, 1999). Over time, the English version of the Treaty led to a raft of discriminative policies against Māori, particularly in education. These policies undermined *te reo* Māori to the point of near language death (Ka'ai-Mahuta, 2011). In response, Māori sought to revitalise *te reo* and *ngā tikanga* Māori (culture) through the establishment of *Kura Kaupapa* (Māori immersion schools). As New Zealand grew to include Pasifika voices and cultures, marginalisation and colonisation continued; resulting in persistant education inequalities for Māori, Pasifika, and students from low socio-economic status communities (McNaughton, 2020). More Māori (23.3%) and Pasifika (28.6%) young people live in low-income households with material hardships than the national average (13.4%) (Statistics New Zealand, 2019). A 1987 landmark High Court decision against the Crown conferred quasi-constitutional status to *Te Tiriti*, giving legal weight to the principle of partnership between Pākehā and Māori (Renwick, 1991). Today, *Te Tiriti* principles are embedded in the charters of many institutions, including schools and the national curriculum (Ministry of Education, 2007), providing a compass point for pedagogy and policy in Aotearoa.

Educational Policy

Briefly, educational policy changes in the late 1980s followed neoliberal ideologies common to many contexts internationally (Olssen, Codd, & O'Neill, 2004). The Ministry of Education's New Zealand Curriculum (2007) document, along with the policy frameworks of *Tātaiako* (2011), *Te Marautanga o Aotearoa* (2017), and Tapasā (2018), promote values and key competencies important to supporting Aotearoa's sociocultural identities and participation in national and international contexts. Together, a great deal of curriculum decision-making is devolved to the local school and community (Ministry of Education, 2007).

Mandate for Critical Literacy

There is no official mandate for critical literacy. At best, its principles can be promoted through charitable interpretations of the key competencies of *Thinking*, defined as: "using creative, critical, and metacognitive processes to make sense of information, experiences, and ideas"; and *Using language symbols and texts*, by recognising how thinking can "affect people's understanding and the ways in which they respond in communications" (Ministry of Education, 2007, p. 12). Consequently, these creative, critical, and metacognitive concepts are often conflated, and neither the curriculum nor accompanying literacy learning frameworks (Ministry of Education, 2002, 2010) define or guide critical literacy in classroom practice (Sandretto & Tilson, 2014).

Critical literacy is merely implied as part of the English curriculum (Ministry of Education, 2007), rather than explicitly named, suggesting students "deconstruct and critically interrogate texts in order to understand the power of language to enrich and shape their own and others' lives" (p. 18). Furthermore, the English subject strands of *Making meaning* and *Creating meaning* through texts offer little scope for critical literacy beyond developing processes and strategies to explore texts' "purposes and audiences, ideas, language features, and structures" (p. 18). Thus, critical literacy praxis in Aotearoa depends on individual teachers who can chart a course beyond the directives of official policy and support students to "listen and read critically, assessing the value of what they hear and read" (p. 16) across the curriculum.

Survey of Critical Literacy Praxis in Aotearoa

We reviewed publications, articles, and research reports dated between 1990 and 2020, concentrating database searches for critical literacy practice, research, and theory. Keyword searches for "critical literac*" and "critical pedagog*" were conducted across specific New Zealand databases such as "nzresearch.org," "NZCER Journals online," and "Index New Zealand," as well as international databases such as Proquest with support from the university subject librarian. We identified 61 articles and reports for analysis. Using Paulo Freire's (1999) description of praxis as "reflection and action upon the world in order to transform it" (p. 33), which informs a great deal of critical literacy pedagogy (e.g., Abbiss, 2016; Vea, 2010), we categorised the literature and structured our findings. Importantly, praxis does not operate outside of theory; rather praxis "requires theory to illuminate it" (Freire, 1999, p. 106), much like the *kāpehu whetū*. The search unearthed 38 articles/reports we categorised as action, 13 as reflection, four as theory, three as action/reflection, and three as reflection/theory. In the articles categorised as research, 26 were empirical, four policy analysis, six practice (in the form of teaching units), and two consisted of a research synthesis. We located four articles/reports in the early childhood sector, 14 in primary, 19 in secondary, eight in tertiary, and 15 in the compulsory sector (primary and secondary education). Next, we explore the work of researchers and practitioners (en)**acting**, **reflecting** on, and **theorising** critical literacy in Aotearoa, drawing attention to 35 articles/reports to illuminate the diversity and depth of this work in our space.

Action

McDowall (2015) synthesised 18 literacy research projects funded by the Teaching and Learning Research Initiative (TLRI) from 2003 to 2014 and observed the body of international research on critical literacy "has had surprisingly little effect" (p. 34) on policy, curriculum, or assessment in Aotearoa. This claim is supported by the policy analysis work of Bonnar (2017), who called for an urgent "re-evaluation of New Zealand's approach to literacy education" (p. 89) for the primary context. Carss's (2019) research illustrated that despite initial teacher education coursework on critical literacy, nine beginning primary teachers did not support their students to critically analyse texts; suggesting the continued influence of the narrow policy context on classroom practices.

Despite a slim education policy mandate, interesting and insightful work is being developed with a range of texts and across sectors. In early childhood education, for example, Kahuroa (2013) worked with children to analyse stickers as gendered texts, and Bishop and Jackson (2007) compared and contrasted the storybook with DVD representations of a popular story to conduct critical readings focused on the visual texts. During research on puberty education in the primary school context, Agnew and Sandretto (2016) identified how critical analysis of menstrual product advertisements could support students to deconstruct and possibly reconstruct negative discourses of menstruation.

Critical literacy research and practices are being developed across a range of curriculum areas. Researchers have used practitioner enquiry to explore critical literacy as a valuable pedagogy to enhance citizenship education in the social studies classroom (Abbiss, 2016). From research in secondary English classrooms, Matthewman, Rewi, and Britton (2017) argued for an eco-critical literacy focus supporting students to develop "critical and nuanced understanding of how texts shape environmental attitudes, values and identities" (p. 56). A number of English secondary teachers have contributed untheorised lessons (e.g., Munn, 2019) and theorised units (e.g., Latham, 2000) to support and encourage their colleagues through illustrations of practice.

Researchers and practitioners have drawn attention to the importance of including students who learn English as an additional language (EAL) in critical literacy lessons. Cooke (2004) provided an example of how to support adult EAL students to critically analyse a newspaper article, asking EAL teachers to resist assumptions that less developed skills in English means students are unable to critique texts. Harison (2008) conducted a critical ethnography in her teaching of a university EAL class. She emphasised the importance and ethics of text selection for vulnerable students, identifying that her students were able to deconstruct texts, recognise and express different perspectives, and disrupt ideas.

Two researchers illustrated the affordances of critical literacy to critique constructions of masculinity. Harrison (2010) conducted action research with two teachers and their classes of Year Seven/Eight (ages 11–13) and Year 12 (ages 16–17) students in English. She found the boys were able to challenge stereotypical representations of masculinity in some cases. Where they maintained a stereotype, such as an association between sporting and masculinity, the students were "prepared to have it challenged and in fact did much of the challenging themselves" (p. 58). Pringle (2008) constructed a collective story from interviews with eight men on their experiences of rugby union to explore the negotiation and formation of masculinities with secondary school students. He found the collective story acted as a critical pedagogical tool that supported some students to critically consider relationships between masculinities and rugby and wider issues of power.

In their case study from a larger TLRI-funded study, Locke and Cleary (2011) explored critical literacy teaching and learning with a group of culturally diverse Year 13 (ages 17–18) students who had been positioned as "non-achievers" (p. 136). The students found the critical literacy work challenging initially. Multiple readings across texts on the same topic, however, supported students to see that they had power to affirm *and* resist different messages identified during text analyses. Importantly, they observed that culture is an important resource that students bring to text analysis. In their research exploring the perceptions of Pasifika students on literacy learning, Taleni, Parkhill, Fa'afoi, and Fletcher (2007) acknowledge that teachers will need to support students to critically analyse texts, as some Pasifika students may find a critical stance incongruent with cultural norms at home.

Some Pasifika, Māori, and students attending low-to-mid socioeconomic schools (SES) may be missing out entirely on critical literacy teaching and learning, according to a group of Auckland researchers. Wilson, Jesson, Rosedale, and Cockle (2012) studied literacy and language teaching in 12 mathematics and science classrooms with students in upper primary and secondary classes and found no evidence of critical literacy instruction in any of their observations. Wilson, McNaughton, and Zhu (2017) reported findings from a study of literacy teaching in English, mathematics, and biology from 22 Auckland low-to-mid SES secondary schools. They also found a concerningly low frequency of critical literacy teaching and learning "given that students in low SES schools are more likely to experience social marginalisation and injustice" (p. 82). The work of these researchers highlights an urgent need to address these inequalities and provide opportunities for critical literacy praxis that *all* students deserve.

Reflection

Authors in Aotearoa have reflected on a number of affordances of critical literacy and argue for the inclusion of critical literacy pedagogy in every sector. From integration in the early childhood education context (Hamer, 2010), to reading aloud in primary classrooms (Villers, 2015), to empowering Pasifika secondary students (Robertson, 2013), to supporting tertiary students to enact in-depth, Freirian readings (Roberts, 1996); critical literacy is relevant for *every* student.

Recognised as particularly useful for digital spaces, McNaughton and Gluckman (2018) suggest critical literacy "can help optimise the benefits and reduce risks" (p. 8) when navigating the online world. Wilson (2018) suggests critical literacy is an important complement to information literacy. Havemann and Mackinnon (2002) concur and use it in their tertiary law course. McDowall (2017) promotes the use of critical literacy for the analysis and (re)construction of videogames, especially important given the success of the gaming experience lies in "immersing the player and making invisible the world view—or ideology—of the game" (p. 6).

One reflective insight for critical literacy comes from the powerful partnership between queer theory and critical literacy to deconstruct and transform texts to problematise taken-for-granted norms of sexuality and gender (see also Pringle, 2008). Fan (2019) illustrates the power of queering Disney films, while Sandretto (2015) uses texts of popular culture (TV, advertising) and a guided reading lesson (Sandretto, 2018) to demonstrate how queer theory can inform critical literacy and how teachers can use "critical literacy with queer intent" (Sandretto, 2018, p. 197). Such work fortifies the compass of critical literacy intent on developing agentic readers and writers who do not take texts at face value.

Theory

The compass, or theory, of critical literacy needs constant attention. We categorised articles/reports as "theory" if they brought insights to the theory of critical literacy itself. In the tertiary and initial teacher education context, Bertanees and Thornley (2005) raise important questions about the critical theory underpinnings of critical literacy and suggest it may not be able to critique representations of culture because "the kinds of questions usually posed are themselves framed within the colonial discourse and . . . incapable of challenging dominant ideologies" (p. 83). Similarly, Tuhiwai Smith (1994), reflecting on language and literacy in the primary school *Kura Kaupapa* Māori (Māori language immersion) setting, raises concerns about the use of critical literacy as a tool for "western academics to liberate the 'Other'" (p. 67). As a Māori academic, Tuhiwai Smith muses "What kind of imagination is needed to analyse the relationship between classroom pedagogic practice and the positioning of Māori learners and Māori ways of knowing?" (p. 173). Indeed, how can theories of critical literacy grounded in a Western world view critique colonial school practices?

Edwards (2010) argues for a synergistic combination of functional and critical literacy to develop "literacy for self-determination" (p. 4) (*tino rangatiratanga*) for Māori in the *Wānanga* (Māori tertiary institution) context. He suggests any form of literacy, however, "must be tested against indigenous paradigms and world views" (p. 36). The work of these authors emphasises the need to deconstruct the ideology and epistemology of critical literacy itself to ensure we are not reproducing colonial structures under the guise of emancipatory aims. This analysis may entail looking forward, or transforming theories of critical literacy, as much as it does looking backward or deconstructing critical literacy theories (McDowall, 2014).

Concluding Thoughts

Guided by *tino rangatiratanga*, our *kāpehu whetū* may be used to navigate within and across transnational borders. In Aotearoa, we are not immune to the impacts of globalisation, and so the ongoing work of our researchers and practitioners illustrates the importance of mediating "home-grown" versions of critical literacy alongside decontextualized orientations from elsewhere. An important aspect of this balancing act will be to find ways to address the silences in official policy and curriculum statements in order to enact critical literacy in every sector for every student beyond sanitised versions of critical thinking that omit the analysis of Aotearoa's power relations and equip students with the tools to navigate within and beyond them.

Additional, critical literacy praxis in Aotearoa is needed to recalibrate our compass. We can continue to explore and develop critical literacy praxis in partnership with our school communities for our *tūrangawaewae* (place to stand), Aotearoa, in terms of:

- different text types, curriculum, and knowledge areas;
- including environmental contexts as well as social and cultural;
- navigating online spaces;

- supporting EAL learners; and,
- expanding sexuality and gender norms.

Our compass can provide direction to further develop critical literacy pedagogy that respects and honours what students bring with them to school, while at the same time, supports their development as critical, agentic, and savvy text analysts and authors (Sandretto & Tilson, 2014). Importantly, we must ensure equitable access to critical literacy praxis, regardless of the socio-economic status of the student. Finally, in terms of our social responsibility as researchers, it is imperative that we take a critical literacy lens to our actions, reflections, and theories of critical literacy to avoid imposing our worldview onto our students and colleagues (Bertanees & Thornley, 2005). Without continual interrogation of our *kāpehu whetū*, we may find our students and ourselves lost at sea without the tools to voyage towards new horizons.

Note

1. Some respondents identified more than one ethnicity.

References

Abbiss, J. (2016). Critical literacy in support of critical-citizenship education in social studies. *SET: Research Information for Teachers, (3),* 29–35.

Agnew, S., & Sandretto, S. (2016). A case for critical literacy analysis of the advertising texts of menstruation: Responding to missed opportunities. *Gender and Education, 28*(4), 510–526. https://doi.org/10.1080/0954 0253.2015.1114073

Bertanees, C., & Thornley, C. (2005). Reading cultural representations: The limitations of critical literacy. *Pedagogy, Culture and Society, 13*(1), 75–85.

Bishop, J., & Jackson, W. (2007). Viewing beyond the narrative content: Young children discuss a popular DVD text. *New Zealand Journal of Teachers' Work, 4*(1), 11–31.

Bonnar, M. (2017). *Are New Zealand's literacy policies still relevant for the 21st century?* (Master of Education). University of Auckland, Auckland, NZ.

Carss, W. D. (2019). *Exploring the beliefs and practices of first year teachers of literacy in New Zealand primary schools* (Doctoral thesis). The University of Waikato, Hamilton, NZ. Retrieved from https://hdl.handle.net/10289/12421

Cooke, D. (2004). What can a text mean? *New Zealand Journal of Adult Learning, 32*(1), 52–65.

Education Counts. (2020). *Teacher workforce.* Retrieved January 10, 2020, from www.educationcounts.govt.nz/statistics/schooling/workforce/teacher-workforce

Edwards, S. (2010). Matauranga Māori literacies: Indigenous literacy as epistemological freedom v. Eurocentric imperialism. *WINHEC: International Journal of Indigenous Education Scholarship,* (1), 26–37.

Fan, J. (2019). Queering Disney animated films using a critical literacy lens. *Journal of LGBT Youth, 16*(2), 119–133. https://doi.org/10.1080/19361653.2018.1537871

Fleras, A., & Spoonley, P. (1999). *Recalling Aotearoa: Indigenous politics and ethnic relations.* Oxford University Press.

Freire, P. (1999). *Pedagogy of the oppressed* (M. B. Ramos, Trans.; revised ed.). Continuum.

Hamer, J. (2010). Should critical literacy be a part of early childhood education in New Zealand? *He Kupu, 2*(3), 16–27.

Harison, R. (2008). *"It's my think": Exploring critical literacy with low level EAL students* (Master of Arts). Auckland University of Technology, Auckland, NZ.

Harrison, B. (2010). Boys and literature: Challenging constructions of masculinity. *New Zealand Journal of Educational Studies, 45*(2), 47–60.

Havemann, P., & Mackinnon, J. (2002). Teaching note. Synergistic literacies: Fostering critical and technological literacies in teaching legal research methods at the University of Waikato. *Legal Education Review, 13*(1), 65–92.

Ka'ai-Mahuta, R. (2011). The impact of colonisation on te reo Māori: A critical review of the State education system. *Te Kaharoa, 4*(1), 195–225.

Kahuroa, R. (2013). Questions that matter, conversations that count: Implementing critical literacy with young children. *Early Childhood Folio, 17*(2), 9–14.

Kress, G. (2010). *Multimodality: A social semiotic approach to contemporary communication*. Routledge.

Latham, S. (2000). Resources: Mongrel Mob—group or gang? A critical literacy study. *English in Aotearoa, 42*, 39–46.

Locke, T., & Cleary, A. (2011). Critical literacy as an approach to literary study in the multicultural, high-school classroom. *English Teaching: Practice and Critique, 10*(1), 119–139.

Matthewman, S., Rewi, N., & Britton, R. (2017). Locating eco-critical literacy in secondary English. *SET: Research Information for Teachers,* (3), 51–57.

McDowall, S. (2014). Rethinking subject English for the knowledge age. *SET: Research Information for Teachers,* (1), 42–50.

McDowall, S. (2015). *Literacy research that matters: A review of the school sector and ECE literacy projects*. Retrieved from www.nzcer.org.nz/system/files/TLRI%2BLiteracyResearchMatters%28v5%29DIGITAL.pdf

McDowall, S. (2017). *Critical literacy and games in New Zealand classrooms: A working paper*. Retrieved from www.nzcer.org.nz/research/publications/critical-literacy-and-games-new-zealand-classrooms

McNaughton, S. (2020). *The literacy landscape in Aotearoa New Zealand: What we know, what needs fixing and what we should prioritise*. Retrieved from www.pmcsa.ac.nz/files/2020/01/The-Literacy-Landscape-in-Aotearoa-New-Zealand-Full-report-final.pdf

McNaughton, S., & Gluckman, P. (2018). *A commentary on digital futures and education*. Retrieved from www.pmcsa.org.nz/wp-content/uploads/18-04-06-Digital-Futures-and-Education.pdf

Ministry of Education. (2002). *Guided reading: Years 1–4*. Learning Media.

Ministry of Education. (2007). *The New Zealand curriculum for English-medium teaching and learning in years 1–13*. Learning Media.

Ministry of Education. (2010). *Literacy learning progressions: Meeting the reading and writing demands of the curriculum*. Learning Media.

Ministry of Education. (2011). *Tātaiako: Cultural competencies for teachers of Māori learners*. Ministry of Education.

Ministry of Education. (2017). *Te marautanga o Aotearoa*. Ministry of Education.

Ministry of Education. (2018). *Tapasā: Cultural competencies framework for teachers of Pacific learners*. Ministry of Education.

Munn, I. (2019). Exploring critical texts in the senior classroom: An example using two Janet Frame short stories. *English in Aotearoa,* (96), 14–18.

Olssen, M., Codd, J., & O'Neill, A.-M. (2004). *Education policy: Globalization, citizenship and democracy*. Sage.

Pringle, R. (2008). 'No rugby—no fear': Collective stories, masculinities and transformative possibilities in schools. *Sport, Education and Society, 13*(2), 215–237. https://doi.org/10.1080/13573320801957103

Renwick, W. (1991). The undermining of a National myth: The Treaty of Waitangi 1970–1990. *Stout Centre Review (VUW),* (1), 3–15.

Roberts, P. (1996). Critical literacy, breadth of perspective and universities: Applying insights from Freire. *Studies in Higher Education, 21*(2), 149–163. https://doi.org/10.1080/03075079612331381328

Robertson, K. (2013). Ensuring literacy acquisition for adolescent Pasifika learners. *Kairaranga, 14*(2), 40–46.

Royal Society of New Zealand. (2013). *Languages in Aotearoa New Zealand*. Retrieved from https://www.royalsociety.org.nz/assets/Uploads/Languages-in-Aotearoa-New-Zealand.pdf

Sandretto, S. (2015). 'I like my beer cold, my TV loud and my homosexuals f-laming': Using critical literacy to draw attention to heteronormative hegemony in texts of popular culture. In A. C. Gunn & L. Smith (Eds.), *Sexual cultures in Aotearoa/New Zealand education* (pp. 49–66). Otago University Press.

Sandretto, S. (2018). A case for critical literacy with queer intent. *Journal of LGBT Youth, 15*(3), 197–211. https://doi.org/10.1080/19361653.2018.1466753

Sandretto, S., & Klenner, S. (2011). *Planting seeds: Embedding critical literacy into your classroom programme*. NZCER Press.

Sandretto, S., & Tilson, J. (2014). "The problem with the future is that it keeps turning into the present": Preparing your students for their multiliterate future today *SET: Research Information for Teachers,* (1), 51–60.

Statistics New Zealand. (2019). *New Zealand as a village of 100 people: Our population*. Retrieved from www.stats.govt.nz/infographics/new-zealand-as-a-village-of-100-people-2018-census-data

Taleni, L. T., Parkhill, F., Fa'afoi, A., & Fletcher, J. (2007). Pasifika Students: What Supports them to become better readers?. *Pacific-Asian Education Journal, 19*(2), 56–71.

Taonui, R. (2005). *Canoe traditions*. Te Ara: The Encyclopedia of New Zealand. Retrieved from https://teara.govt.nz/en/canoe-traditions

Tuhiwai Smith, L. (1994). In search of a language and a shareable imaginative world/E kore taku moe e riro i a koe. *Hecate: An Interdisciplinary Journal of Women's Liberation, 20*(2), 162–174.

Vea, P. T. (2010). *Implementing critical literacy in a Tongan bilingual classroom* (Masters). University of Waikato, Hamilton, New Zealand. Retrieved from https://hdl.handle.net/10289/5021

Villers, H. (2015). Time out or a critical literacy approach: Is reading aloud still a valued approach in New Zealand classrooms? In D. Garbett & A. Ovens (Eds.), *Teaching for tomorrow today* (pp. 456–464). Edify Ltd.

Wilson, A. (2018). Teaching and learning critical literacy in a digital world. *Literacy Forum NZ Te Korero Panui Tuhituhi o Aotearoa, 33*(3), 13–17.

Wilson, A., Jesson, R., Rosedale, N., & Cockle, V. (2012). *Literacy and language pedagogy within subject areas in Years 7–11*. Ministry of Education.

Wilson, A., McNaughton, S., & Zhu, T. (2017). Subject area literacy instruction in low SES secondary schools in New Zealand. *The Australian Journal of Language and Literacy, 40*(1), 72–85.

2.2

CRITICAL LITERACIES IN AUSTRALIA

*Jennifer Alford, Lisa van Leent, Lynn Downes,
and Annette Woods*

Brief Overview of Australia in Its Sociopolitical Context

Australia is an island continent in the Asia Pacific region with just over 25 million people. Australia's First Nations Peoples—Aboriginal and Torres Strait Islander peoples—are recognised as the oldest surviving culture in the world and have been living in Australia for more than 65,000 years. Aboriginal and Torres Strait Islander peoples are diverse in languages and cultures. As a nation, Australia has continued to fail in recognising Aboriginal and Torres Strait Islander peoples adequately, stemming back to the time of invasion in 1788, when British migrants claimed Australia as a colony via Terra Nullius. The *Mabo Case* in 1992 established Australian lands were not Terra Nullius prior to 1788 and this led to the passing of a Native Title Act providing opportunities for claims to land rights and compensation. However, Australia's colonial history of racist policies continues to impact the cultural and sociopolitical contexts and discourses present in Australia today.

Successive policies have foregrounded representations of Australia as a society of Caucasian English speakers. However, Australia has a diverse population where trends in cultural background, language, and religion continue to shift. Between 3 and 4% of Australians are now Aboriginal and Torres Strait Islander people, and of the non-Indigenous population, approximately one in four were born overseas (Australian Bureau of Statistics (ABS), 2017). Migration has always featured in Australia's population growth. After World War II, the "populate or perish" immigration scheme welcomed more than two million migrants from Europe and Britain. In the late 1970s, refugees from Asia, mainly East Timor and Vietnam arrived, and since 1990 increasing numbers of asylum seekers and refugees from the Middle East and the Horn of Africa have made Australia their home (Australian Government, 2020a). More recently, mandatory detention of arrivals by sea and lengthy offshore processing have led to temporary visas being allocated to those seeking asylum. Whilst varied cultures and races are reflected in the present-day cultural practices (including literacies) in Australia, migration and diversity continue to be polarising public debates.

As a Federation, the country is now delineated into six states and two territories. It was not until 1948 that those born in Australia were registered as Australian citizens and not British citizens. Voting is compulsory for Australian citizens. Most women were given the vote for federal elections in Australia in 1902. There is a complicated history of voting rights for Aboriginal and Torres Strait Islander peoples at State and Commonwealth levels. However, the Commonwealth Electoral Act provided their right to vote in 1962 (Australian Electoral Commission, 2020). Aboriginal and Torres Strait Islander peoples were not counted as citizens within the Australian Census until 1967, and

       DOI: 10.4324/9781003023425-14

the Aborigines Protection Act, which had enabled Aboriginal and Torres Strait Islander people to be forcibly removed from their homes and lands to live on missions and reserves, was not repealed until 1969. In recent times, the rise of political parties based in racist rhetoric and increased power of a conservative media has seen right-wing politics take centre stage. This is somewhat of a shift from more centrist ideologies so successful to left-leaning political parties through the 1980s and 1990s. Having said this, many Australians continue to engage with global social movements such as climate change strikes and equality debates including the legalisation of same-sex marriage achieved in 2018.

Brief Overview of Australian Educational System

The overall goals for education in Australia are set out in ten-year intervals by ministers of education. The most recent, *The Alice Springs (Mparntwe) Education Declaration, 2019*, identifies two goals for Australia's education system. The first goal is focused on excellence and equity. The second focuses on encouraging confidence, creativity, lifelong learning, and opportunities to become active and informed citizens (Australian Government, 2020b). The federal government directly funds independent and faith-based schools. Public school education is funded and governed by state governments. As a result, curriculum and other policy decisions have historically been made by state governments, with varied levels of agreement across states and territories at different times.

Successive federal governments have claimed increasing control over curriculum and assessment within schools by tying funding available to the states for public education to a number of national mandates.[1] The staged implementation of a consistent Australian Curriculum from 2014 marks the first consistent national curriculum in Australia, although states still have control of implementation and delivery of the curriculum. After this introduction, related changes to the structure of schooling have occurred across states and territories—such as shifts in school starting age to bring systems into alignment and changes to the structure of year 12 assessment and calculation of tertiary entrance scores. School-starting age for most children is between 4.5 and 5.5 years and continues for 13 years (foundation to year 6 as primary education and year 7 to year 12 as secondary education).

Survey of Critical Literacy Work in Australia

Australia is recognised as a space where critical literacy has strong foundations in theory, curricula, and practice. Australian educators have continued to debate what critical literacy means and how to approach it within the mandated curriculum. Promoting both critique of textual worlds and enhanced access to them, critical literacy in Australia has drawn from a range of theoretical traditions including reader response, critical linguistics, post-structural critiques of normative gender, race and class understandings, and cultural studies.

There seems little doubt that political, policy, legal, moral, and relational conventions are shifting in local and global spaces. It is not within the purview of this chapter to discuss the reasons for this unprecedented shift in boundaries and responsibilities. However, in terms of literacies, it is relevant to note that new capacities for text production and consumption, including new conventions and practices, emerge each moment. These transitions provide "the staging grounds for a volatile ideological, geopolitical and social order" (Luke, 2018, p. vii). So, readers and writers "use a variety of modes of inscription—print, oral, and multimedia—to understand, analyse, critique and transform their social, cultural and political worlds" (Luke & Woods, 2009, p. 9), and yet, Australian policy and literacy curriculum continue to offer simple answers for complex problems seen in the recurrent push to basic skills, especially phonics, as the one best way to teach literacy. These debates and their solutions seem to be on rewind, and the responses of successive governments, policy makers, the media, and lobby groups are predictable. At a time when those pushing standardisation, highly defined curriculum to muzzle teacher professionalism, and the primacy of phonics seem to be winning the debates played out in the traditional and new media forms, a look back at the strong foundations of critical literacy in Australia is timely. To achieve this, we offer an almost chronological survey of critical literacy in Australia from the later parts of the twentieth century and the first two decades of the twenty-first. It is not exhaustive but highlights key contributions to what critical literacy has come to be known in this country.

Amidst widespread political reforms in the late 1970s in Australia, curriculum developers and educators were pushed to think deeply about how schools could provide greater equality of opportunity; less segregation in schools based on gender and class; and a more meaningful curriculum relevant to the lived experiences of students and their families. The document *Orientations to Curriculum and Transition: Towards the Socially-critical School* (Kemmis, Cole, & Suggett, 1983) ushered in the beginnings of a socially critical approach to literacy education in Australia. Kemmis et al. argued for the need to convert schools to "a socially critical orientation . . . involving the community, curriculum reflection and debate, in-service activities, school reviews, and monitoring progress" (p. 1). "Socially-critical" literacy, as a concept, was later mentioned by Luke (1988) in connection with the ideological, cultural, and political foundations of literacy that can be seen as reproduction of inequality. Luke and Walton (Luke & Walton, 1993) further distinguished critical social literacy from conventional literacy arguing that a critical social approach necessitated application of critique in the Freireian tradition and discourse analytic approaches.

Several key nodes of critical literacy work have been highly influential in developing critical literacy's presence in Australia and also in other international contexts where notable Australian critical literacy scholars networked and had influence. Critical literacy work developed in Queensland, Australia, for example, has been well networked into international contexts such as Ontario and South Africa, the United States and the UK. The most well-recognised of this work is by Peter Freebody and Allan Luke on the Four Resources Model of Reading (later literacy). Outlined in their initial contributions—Freebody and Luke (1990); Freebody (1992), and in an edited volume led by Muspratt (Luke & Freebody, 1997)—the model argues for four necessary and simultaneously occurring "roles" for readers (later expanded from reading to literacy) in a postmodern, text-based culture:

- Code breaker (coding competence)
- Meaning maker (semantic competence)
- Text user (pragmatic competence)
- Text critic (critical competence)

In adaptations of this work by the original authors and others (e.g., Luke & Freebody, 1999), the framing of roles developed to a more complex theorisation of literate beings having a repertoire of practices to call upon as required. Widely used by teachers and curriculum makers in Australia and beyond, the model has featured in curriculum policy in several Australian states. Readers of this handbook would not be strangers to this approach. As one example, the model was officially adopted in Queensland policy in 2000 in the *Literate Futures* materials (Luke, Freebody, & Land, 2000) and accompanying teacher resources. The four resources model also featured in innumerable textbooks, online resources, commercial packs, and reading resources from publishers and professional organisations.

Colin Lankshear's occasional paper *Critical Literacy* (1994) was instrumental in finessing Australian educator's understandings of critical literacy from a critical pedagogy perspective. It acknowledged that critical literacy was "a contested educational ideal" (p. 4) and addressed two important conceptual groundings at odds with each other: What does "critical" really mean? (or what characterises a "critical orientation"?), and second, how do we work with "critical" being a vague perennial ideal, constructed in different ways in different contexts? Grassroots work in this area was achieved by post-structural feminist researchers and teachers (e.g., Davies, 1989, 2003; Gilbert, 1989) encouraging teachers to consider the gendered assumptions of texts, schooling, and systems. As has been the case in other contexts, Indigenous, critical race theorists have taken this work forward in Australia as well (see, e.g., Nakata, 2000).

Critical literacy in Australia has also been influenced by a strong heritage in text analytic approaches founded in the linguistic theory of Michael Halliday and Ruqaiya Hasan (e.g., Halliday & Hasan, 1985) and subsequent work by genre theorists Fran Christie and Jim Martin. These approaches have still attended to ideological functions of texts but also provided resources to analyse texts (Luke & Woods, 2009). More recently, critical literacy foundations have been put forward in work related to bodies, time, place, and the environment and emotions such as those in work by Barbara Comber and colleagues (e.g., Comber, Nixon, & Reid, 2007), building on earlier work in South Australia by these researchers connected to leading critical literacy thinkers in the United States and South Africa such as Hilary Janks and in key work building on the traditions of multiliteracies (e.g., Cope & Kalantzis, 2000).

A particular feature of the Australian critical literacy work is that alongside these theoretical developments, the critical literacy agenda has always had an eye on policy and practice, and this has resulted in important texts written to both document the work of teachers and inform teaching colleagues. Supported by the National Language and Literacy Institute of Australia, Andrew Lohrey, (1998) prepared a foundational professional development package on critical literacy. The package did not engage with what Lohrey called "difficult matters" (p. 5), alluding to the problem of the contested ideal, and instead offered a hands-on resource for practical application.

Other textbooks and teacher professional development resources that emerged include Michelle Knobel and Annah Healy's *Critical Literacies in the Primary Classroom* (1998), a publication of teachers' classroom research which is still utilised in preservice and in-service teacher education and Wendy Morgan's *Critical Literacy in the Classroom: The Art of the Possible* (1997). Work by Barbara Comber, Helen Nixon, and Alison Simpson and others in South Australia highlighted the characteristic practitioner focus of much of this work in Australia with a basis in social justice, (e.g., Comber & Simpson, 2001; Comber, 2014). Teachers have also had access to resources, building on linguistic and ideological ways of thinking about texts that have encouraged the use of a range of everyday written and multimodal texts and classroom pedagogies (Exley & Kervin, 2013; Exley, Kervin, & Mantai, 2015) to encourage critical and analytic literacy practices in students from the early years of schooling (Exley, Woods, & Dooley, 2014; Ludwig, 2006; Woods, Comber, & Iyer, 2015) into secondary schooling (e.g., Alford, 2014; Alford & Jetnikoff, 2016).

In the late 1990s and early 2000s, critical literacy was gaining significant traction in secondary school English curriculum and in Queensland in primary curriculum as well, but not without resistance, mostly due to poor professional development of teachers. There was much debate, still lingering today, about how critical approaches would transform dearly held notions about teaching, especially of canonical literature. Attempts to reconcile this perceived disjunct were offered by Ray Misson and Wendy Morgan (2006), who argued that taking pleasure in texts while also critiquing was possible. Critical media work also encouraged engagement and access to digital ways of working while foregrounding critical literacies.

Current research contributions are continuing to emerge which consider new challenges and diverse cohorts of learners. For example, critical literacy has challenged how systems might work better with ideas related to diverse genders and sexualities. A foundational article by Misson, *Dangerous Lessons: Sexuality Issues in the English Classroom* (1995) disrupted the heteronormative status quo of critical literacy, and these ideas were expanded in *English in Australia* in a special issue published in 2018 (McGraw, van Leent, & Doecke). Queerying the state of critical literacy for English teachers in Australia, the publication focused on "love in English" pushing further the boundaries of critical literacy. van Leent and Mills (2017) refined a set of pedagogical approaches to equip teachers to critique heteronormative assumptions of texts in the context of adolescent multimodal and digital practices.

Another area emerging as a space for critical literacies to have influence challenges the notion that English learners should be provided predominantly with functional access to literacy and language instruction. While providing functional approaches to language and literacy is crucial for English learners, especially those with interrupted schooling, some have argued that given the right professional learning and agentive conditions, teachers can also provide English learners with access to critical literacies (Alford, 2014; Alford & Jetnikoff, 2016), although this is not without its challenges (Hammond & Macken-Horarik, 1999). Critical literacy theorists have also problematised the dominance of Standard Australian English over other migrant and Indigenous languages represented widely in schools (e.g., Alford & Kettle, 2017).

Moving Into More *Transnational* and Other Critical Work From the Perspective of Australia

In Australia, as in many other contexts, literacy education is currently being narrowly construed in public debate, media, and policy. An autonomous understanding of literacy as a set of defined skills, or as set content, challenges the spaces available for educators to engage children and young people in learning literacy as a social and material practice. Foregrounding the ideological base of all texts and teaching children ways to engage critically with texts is a difficult task in contexts where basics skills such as phonics are given priority. This is a recurring problem and literacy scholars have been drawn into these debates before. However, as world politics has been moved to Twitter; as social media is increasingly considered a space for fact rather than opinion; and in a context where world economies continue to structure policy on the myth of trickle-down economics, gaps between "knowers" and "the unknowing", rich and poor, left and right politics broaden, and expertise in procedural dimensions of literacy will increasingly fall short as a panacea for our youngest generations. As such, literacy researchers and educators must take a public and political stance on the place of critical literacies in education.

Engaging More Deeply With Indigenous Perspectives on Literacy and Language

Through reviewing the history of critical literacy in Australia it is notable that Aboriginal and Torres Strait Islander knowledges and ways of being are largely missing. Sandra Phillips (2015) argues Aboriginal and Torres Strait Islander people's engagement with writing is an imperial project. Critically, she highlights the complexities of "being ourselves and writing ourselves" in the twenty-first century, providing an insight into the dominant ideological positioning of literature, language, and literacy as published material. Melitta Hogarth (2019) also highlights the power of critical literacy to probe the dominance of the standard "Oostralin" English variety over local Indigenous languages. Exploring possibilities for engaging with Indigenous perspectives is an opportunity to reframe the critical locally and transnationally as other nation's Indigenous perspectives are privileged.

Critical Literacy and Intercultural Understanding

There is growing interest in developing intercultural capacity among school-age learners within increasingly plurilingual and diverse communities such as Australia. "Intercultural understanding involves students learning about and engaging with diverse cultures in ways that recognise commonalities and differences, create connections with others and cultivate mutual respect" (Australian

Curriculum and Assessment Authority (ACARA), 2020). Coupling critical literacy approaches with building intercultural understanding provides fertile ground for moving critical literacies forward transnationally. A guiding question for this kind of future project is: How do we embrace and fashion criticality from the point of view of diverse cultures, especially those of Indigenous peoples, as these cultures co-exist in complex ways and create shared history?

Critical Digital Literacy

As shown in Chapter 3.8 in this book, there is growing global interest in critical digital literacy. Australian researchers such as Lucy Pangrazio, Tanya Notley, and Michael Dezuanni (Notley & Dezuanni, 2019) call for the deliberate cultivation of a "critical digital disposition" (Pangrazio, 2019, p. 151) in all young people in Australia. From a transnational perspective, this sentiment is echoed by Juliet Hinrichsen and Antony Coombs (2013) in London, UK, who propose a model called "The five resources of critical digital literacy: A framework for curriculum integration". Similarly, Donna E. Alvermann (2017), in the United States, posits that critical literacy inquiry into social media is imperative when, amidst society's general tolerance of "fakeness", social media texts obscure the very facts young people need to critically reflect on issues and matters relating to life decisions. There is much work to be done in this regard, especially in relation to interpreting meaning critically from moving images such as videos and film clips (not static images), the staple diet of young people today. Transnational research of this nature would be highly beneficial to the future of the critical literacy project as the nature of the moving image continues to transform, and so does its demands on readers/viewers.

Conclusions/Suggestions for Further Research and Practice

The focus of Australian researchers has been "to remake the teaching of critical literacy in ways that both critiqued and reconstructed worlds, institutions and communities- while engaging directly with the need for enhanced access to mainstream cultural capital requisite for economic and civic participation" (Luke, 2018, p. 12). Further research and practice foci can build on this to ensure that perspectives from queer literacies, intercultural uses of languages and literacies are present, and by embedding Aboriginal and Torres Strait Islander ways of knowing, being, and doing within literacy practice and research.

Questions we take forward ourselves include:

- How might we question normative practices undertaken under the guise of critical literacy?
- How will we continue to engage with the critical literacies project globally while continuing to foreground the particular of the Australian critical literacy project?
- What will be the implications for critical literacy in Australia as researchers and educators answer the call for heightened environmental action?
- What will be the implications of super diversity in populations, language, religions, genders, and cultures, and how must critical literacy educators address these challenges?

Implications for Our Social Responsibility as Academics

With a long and rich history in critical literacy research and praxis, Australian academics are in a unique position to help shape new responses to oppressive discourses, institutions, and forces that are increasingly *transnational* in nature. One of our responsibilities is to continue to foster in preservice teachers a critical stance toward global forces of standardisation and measurability in education that run counter to critical literacy's interest in championing diversity and social justice. This is challenging in a higher education environment reverting to approaches to teacher *training* as opposed to providing a critical education.

At the same time, we are still responsible for engaging deeply with the growing socio-economic injustices and inequities in our own backyard, especially in relation to Aboriginal and Torres Strait Islander peoples and other marginalised groups. For these Australians, the criticality of literacy is underpinned by community responsibility, lifelong learning, and connectedness (Grant, 2016). Indigenous peoples' ways of knowing should be the bedrock of an education tradition that is learnt and understood by all. Academics and educators have a responsibility to engage with various ways of "knowing" critical literacy. It is the social responsibility of those who are in positions of power to walk with others, invite their expertise, and share knowledge respectfully. An increasingly diverse Australia means that intersections of identity, ways of being, ways of knowing are diverse and complex, providing a unique opportunity for critical literacies to flourish.

Note

1. For example, participation in the National Assessment Program for Literacy and Numeracy (NAPLAN) which was brokered across all States through the Ministerial Council on Education, Employment, Training and Youth Affairs (MCEETYA) in 2008.

References

Alford, J. (2014). "Well, hang on, they're actually much better than that!": Disrupting dominant discourses of deficit about English language learners in senior high school English. *English Teaching: Practice and Critique*, *13*(3), 71–88.

Alford, J., & Jetnikoff, A. (2016). Orientations to critical literacy for English as an additional language or dialect (EAL/D) learners: A case study of four teachers of senior English. *Australian Journal of Language and Literacy*, *39*(2), 111–123.

Alford, J., & Kettle, M. (2017). Teachers' reinterpretations of critical literacy policy: Prioritizing praxis. *Critical Inquiry in Language Studies*, *14*(2–3), 182–209. https://doi.org/10.1080/15427587.2017.1288067

Alvermann, D. E. (2017). Social media texts and critical inquiry in a post-factual era. *Journal of Adolescent & Adult Literacy*, *61*(3), 335–338. https://doi.org/10.1002/jaal.694

Australian Bureau of Statistics (ABS). (2017). *Cultural diversity—who are we now?*www.abs.gov.au/ausstats/abs@. nsf/Latestproducts/2024.0Main%20Features22016?opendocument&tabname=Summary&prodno=2024.0 &issue=2016&num=&view=

Australian Curriculum and Assessment Authority (ACARA). (2020). *Intercultural understanding*. Retrieved from www.australiancurriculum.edu.au/f-10-curriculum/general-capabilities/intercultural-understanding/

Australian Electoral Commission. (2020). *Electoral milestones for Indigenous Australians*. Retrieved from www.aec. gov.au/indigenous/milestones.htm

Australian Government. (2020a). *Australia's immigration history*. Retrieved from www.sea.museum/discover/ online-exhibitions/waves-of-migration/australia-immigration-history

Australian Government. (2020b). *Australian curriculum*. Retrieved from www.education.gov.au/australian-curriculum-0

Comber, B. (2014). Literacy, poverty and schooling: What matters in young people's education? *Literacy*, *48*(3), 115–123.

Comber, B., Nixon, H., & Reid, J. (2007). *Literacies in place: Teaching environmental communications*. Primary English Teachers' Association.

Comber, B., & Simpson, A. (2001). *Critical literacies in classrooms*. Lawrence Erlbaum Associates.

Cope, B., & Kalantzis, M. (2000). *Multiliteracies: Literacy learning and the design of social futures*. Routledge.

Davies, B. (1989). *Frogs and snails and feminist tails*. Allen & Unwin.

Davies, B. (2003). *Shards of glass: Children reading and writing beyond gendered identities* (2nd ed.). Hampton Press.

Exley, B., & Kervin, L. (2013). *Playing with grammar in the early years*. Australian Literacy Educators' Association.

Exley, B., Kervin, L., & Mantai, J. (2015). *Exploring with grammar in the primary years*. Australian Literacy Educators' Association.

Exley, B., Woods, A., & Dooley, K. (2014). Thinking critically in the land of princesses and giants: The affordances and challenges of critical approaches in the early years. In J. Avila & J. Zacher Pandya (Eds.), *Moving critical literacies forward: A new look at praxis across contexts* (pp. 59–70). Routledge.

Freebody, P. (1992). A socio-cultural approach: Resourcing four roles as a literacy learner. In A. Watson & A. Beadenhop (Eds.), *Prevention of reading failure* (pp. 48–80). Ashton–Scholastic.

Freebody, P., & Luke, A. (1990). 'Literacies' programs: Debates and demands in cultural context. *Prospect—an Australian Journal of TESOL, 5*(3), 7–16.

Gilbert, P. (1989). Personally (and passively) yours: Girls, literacy and education. *Oxford Review of Education, 15*(3), 257–265. https://doi.org/10.1080/0305498890150306

Grant, E. (2016). *Foundations for success.* Queensland Government.

Halliday, M. A. K., & Hasan, R. (1985). *Language, context, and text: Aspects of language in a social-semiotic perspective.* Deakin University Press.

Hammond, J., & Macken-Horarik, M. (1999). Critical literacy—Challenges and questions for ESL classrooms. *TESOL Quarterly, 33*(3), 528–544. https://doi.org/10.2307/3587678

Hinrichsen, J., & Coombs, A. (2013). The five resources of critical digital literacy: A framework for curriculum integration. *Research in Learning Technology, 21*(1), 1–16. https://doi.org/10.3402/rlt.v21.21334

Hogarth, M. (2019). Y is standard oostralin English da onlii meens of kommunikashun: Kountaring White man privileg in da kurrikulum. *English in Australia, 54*(1), 5–11.

Kemmis, S., Cole, P., & Suggett, D. (1983). *Orientations to curriculum and transition: Towards the socially-critical school.* Victorian Institute of Secondary Education.

Knobel, M., & Healy, A. (1998). *Critical literacies in the primary classroom.* Primary English Teaching Association.

Lankshear, C. (1994). *Critical literacy.* Australian Curriculum Studies Association.

Lohrey, A. (1998). *Critical literacy: A professional development resource.* Language Australia.

Ludwig, C. (2006). *Why wait? A way in to teaching critical literacies in the early years.* Curriculum Corporation.

Luke, A. (1988). *Literacy, textbooks, and ideology: Postwar literacy instruction and the mythology of Dick and Jane.* Falmer Press.

Luke, A. (2018). *Critical literacy, schooling and social justice: The selected works of Allan Luke.* Routledge.

Luke, A., & Freebody, P. (1997). Critical literacy and the question of normativity—An introduction. In S. Muspratt, A. Luke, & P. Freebody (Eds.), *Constructing critical literacies—Teaching and learning textual practice.* Allen & Unwin.

Luke, A., & Freebody, P. (1999). Further notes on the Four Resources Model. *Reading online [International Reading Association]*, 1–4.

Luke, A., Freebody, P., & Land, R. (2000). *Literate futures: Report on the literacy review for Queensland state schools.* Department of Education, Queensland, Australia.

Luke, A., & Walton, C. (1993). Teaching and assessing critical literacy. In T. Husen & N. Poselthwaite (Eds.), *The international encyclopaedia of education* (2nd ed.). Pergamon.

Luke, A., & Woods, A., F. (2009). Critical literacies in schools: A primer. *Voices from the Middle, 17*(2), 9–18.

McGraw, K., van Leent, L., & Doecke, B. (2018). Editorial [for English in Australia, 53(2), 2018]. *English in Australia, 53*(2), 2–3.

Misson, R. (1995). Dangerous lessons: Sexuality issues in the English classroom. *English in Australia, 112*, 25–32.

Misson, R., & Morgan, W. (2006). *Critical literacy and the aesthetic: Transforming English classrooms.* National Council of Teachers of English.

Morgan, W. (1997). *Critical literacy in the classroom: The art of the possible.* Routledge.

Nakata, M. (2000). History, cultural diversity and English language teaching. In B. Cope & M. Kalantzis (Eds.), *Multiliteracies: Literacy learning and the design of social futures* (pp. 106–120). Routledge.

Notley, T., & Dezuanni, M. (2019). Advancing children's news media literacy: Learning from the practices and experiences of young Australians. *Media, Culture and Society, 41*(5), 689–707. https://doi.org/10.1177/0163443718813470

Pangrazio, L. (2019). *Young people's literacies in the digital age: Continuities, conflicts and contradictions.* Routledge.

Phillips, S. (2015). Literature: Writing ourselves. In K. Price (Ed.), *Knowledge of life: Aboriginal and Torres Strait Islander Australia* (pp. 98–117). Cambridge University Press.

van Leent, L., & Mills, K. (2017). A queer critical media literacies framework in a digital age. *The Journal of Adolescent and Adult Literacy, 61*(4), 401–411. https://doi.org/10.1002/jaal.711

Woods, A., Comber, B., & Iyer, R. (2015). Literacy learning: Designing and enacting inclusive pedagogical practices in classrooms. In R. Smith, T. Loreman, L. Florian, & J. M. Deppeler (Eds.), *Inclusive pedagogy across the curriculum [International Perspectives on Inclusive Education, Volume 7]* (pp. 45–71). Emerald Group Publishing Limited.

2.3

CRITICAL LITERACIES *MADE IN BRAZIL*

Walkyria Monte Mór, Ana Paula Duboc, and Daniel Ferraz

Brief Overview of the Geographical Space in Its Sociopolitical Contexts

As the largest country in Latin America at 8.5 million square kilometers and with over 211 million people,[1] Brazil is formed by a rich multicultural and multilingual society as a result of its colonial past marked by the presence of indigenous peoples, enslaved Africans, and European settlers.

Inhabited by indigenous peoples prior to the landing of the Portuguese in 1500, Brazil remained a Portuguese colony until the nineteenth century, having declared its independence from Portugal in 1822. The country became a presidential republic in 1889. Later on, Brazilians experienced a harsh military dictatorship period between 1964 and 1985 followed by the formulation of the 1988 Constitution, which established democratic principles to the detriment of former authoritarian governance.

At the very present political moment, Brazil has built a very controversial image in the international scenario. From a global perspective, Brazil bears international significance as a prominent emerging economy along with the fact that it is home to one of the richest biodiversities in the world. However, this international recognition has been questioned provided that the current government has negatively shaken this image. From a local perspective, the country holds a leading position as the largest economy among South and Latin American countries. Again, the fact of holding a leading economic position in South and Latin America does not exempt the country from its well-known inequalities, such as the disenfranchisement of its poor population. With regard to public policies, Brazil still struggles in relation to formulating and implementing effective long-term actions in areas such as education, health care, housing, security, and infrastructure much as a result of the competing driving forces around politics and policy making.

Nonetheless, the country has witnessed significant advances in relation to democratic consolidation and human development. In the field of education, for instance, the report, *Brazil, 25 Years of Democracy—a Critical Survey: Public Policy, Institutions, Civil Society and Civic Culture—1988–2013*[2] asserts that despite undeniable differences concerning ideological and partisan positions among the governments ruling the country between 1995 and 2010, there is somehow a noticeable continuity in three different axes—access, financing, and assessment.

In addition, we find it wise that South–South relations have been built and given more attention by former presidencies due to which Brazil has emerged as an important player in discussions on local and global matters. Such relationships have allowed [or propelled] much academic and

DOI: 10.4324/9781003023425-15

knowledge exchange, strengthening ties between universities and colleagues who have the same or similar interests.

By acknowledging the intrinsic relationship between social quality education and democratic governance, this chapter outlines the importance of critical and sociocultural perspectives to literacy education against the dismantlement of socially just policies. The next section aims at briefly describing Brazilian educational system with an emphasis on shifting perspectives on language policies and literacy education.

Brief Overview of the Geographical Space's Educational System

The Brazilian educational system[3] is structured on two broad levels: basic education and higher education. Basic education comprises nursery school (0–3-year-old children), preschool (4–5-year-old children), elementary education (6–14-year-old students), and secondary education (15–17-year-old students). Education is compulsory from preschool to secondary and free in public schools. Higher education comprises undergraduate and graduate levels and is basically institutionalized by public and private sectors.[4]

The system consists of a complex web of institutional layers comprising federal, state, and municipal levels.[5] The Federal Union is responsible for coordinating national policies, along with the provision of technical and financial assistance to the states, the Federal District of Brasilia, and the municipalities as shown in the following flowchart (Figure 2.3.1).

As Brasil and Capella (2016) remind us, public policies are characterized by government priorities and competitive interactions among political parties and agents. For the purposes of this chapter, we will be illustrating how these competing driving forces have historically operated within the literacy debate.

Cope and Kalantzis (2000) explained that "schooling in general, and literacy teaching in particular, were a central part of the old order. The expanding, interventionary states of the nineteenth and twentieth centuries used schooling as a way of standardising national languages" (p. 14). As a matter of fact, Brazilian language policies echo this effective mechanism aimed at the formation of modern states as we witness a deeply rooted monolingual ethos in Brazil despite its multilingual character[6]

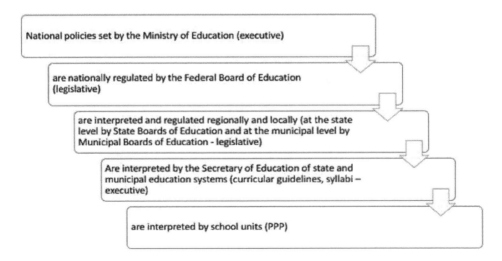

Figure 2.3.1 Policy flow in the Brazilian educational system.

Source: (Duboc, Garcia, & Rodrigues, 2018, p. 232)

(Morello, 2017). As a consequence, there is the reaffirmation of Portuguese as the national language.[7] This has reinforced the marginalization of minority languages, including nonstandard varieties of Portuguese, which, despite used among the majority of the population, are socially stigmatized and politically delegitimized (Faraco, 2002). Similarly, the teaching of foreign languages has been marked by constructs such as purity and standardization imbued in the notions of nativespeakerism and language imperialism (Blommaert, 2010; Makoni & Pennycook, 2007).

Efforts in breaking with hegemonic, monolingual language ideologies have been made in the last decades as recent language policies, curricular guidelines, and instruction materials have embraced the recent tenets discussed in Contemporary Sociolinguistics and Critical Applied Linguistics. As language, ideology, and politics are intertwined (Menezes de Souza, 2019), the next section discusses how the literacy debate has shifted in Brazil as it responds to different research trends and political agendas over time.

Survey of Critical Literacy Work by Researchers and Practitioners in Brazil

By providing an outline on the history of literacy instruction in Brazil, Mortatti (2006) refers to ongoing tensions around "old" and "new" literacy methods since the end of the nineteenth century in attempts to address the problem of illiteracy among Brazilian children, especially those enrolled in public schools. The author (2006) presents four main literacy instruction models that have permeated literacy instruction in Brazil:

(1.) *Phonics methodization* (1822–1890): A highly teacher-centered, part-to-whole model comprising dictation, copying, and rote memorization as the prevailing teaching techniques. Reading is an autonomous, decoding activity, while writing is limited to the mastery of handwriting and spelling. Concerns with language overlap pedagogical issues.

(2.) *Whole language institutionalization* (1890–1920): As a response to the Progressive Education Movement, this student-centered, whole-to-part approach claims that children would better learn how to read and write through contextual inference and language analysis. Psychological concerns overlap pedagogical ones.

(3.) *"Tailored" literacy instruction* (1920–1970): Ongoing tensions between "tradition" and "innovation" soon emerged, leading many Brazilian literacy teachers to the adoption of the so-called mixed or eclectic literacy methods. If on the one hand, this eclecticism opens up the terrain for breaking with any methodization toward a "tailored" approach to literacy, on the other hand, conventional teaching procedures still prevailed with drilling exercises aimed at the mastery of motor skill activities.

(4.) *Constructivist-based demethodization* (1970–?): Poor performance literacy levels among Brazilian children along with the emergence of new social and political demands made literacy teachers once again question the efficacy of the "eclectic literacy method". Constructivist perspectives became influential in which children's learning processes should prevail *vis-à-vis* any a priori literacy teaching method.

As one can see, the history of Brazilian literacy instruction somehow echoes the evolving literacy movement as addressed worldwide with the emergence of sociocultural and critical orientations to the detriment of strictly cognitive-based literacy models. In discussing this fundamental and conspicuous shift, Lankshear and Knobel (2007, p. 1) argue that "Understanding literacies from a sociocultural perspective means that reading and writing can only be understood in the contexts of social, cultural, political, economic, historical practices to which they are integral, of which they are a part". This perspective is rather different from the cognitivist traditional literacies for it reshapes and expands the notion of literacy as cognition and cracking the code: Meanings are not only in one's mind; instead, meanings are produced in the very encounter of one's mind and body, subjectivity, and the sociohistorical context in which a person belongs to.

This paradigm shift on literacy studies was highly influenced by the pioneering work of Brazilian intellectual Paulo Freire. As Monte Mór (2015) explains, Freire's ideas back in the 1960s began to attract wide acceptance along with some concern as the country was about to experience a harsh military dictatorship (1964–1985). As Freire's critical pedagogy aimed at empowering students to question reality and unveil the vested interests and unequal power relations within discourses in a process called *"conscientização"*, it clearly represented a threat, leading to Freire's exile. Presumably, back in the 1960s, Freire would already refer to critical perception, interpretation, and action in the reading activity. Under the premise that education is always a political practice (Freire, 1983, 2001), his well-known book *Pedagogy of the Oppressed* denounced the banking education, so to speak the educational/pedagogical practices in which students are supposed to memorize contents whereas the teacher is the one who determines what knowledge is. For his great influence on subsequent works, Monte Mór (2015) places Freire's ideas as the ***first generation*** on literacy studies in Brazil.

Years passed by and a group of scholars (Barton, 1994; Gee, 2000; Heath, 1983; Street, 1984, 1998 to name a few) reinvigorated the literacy debate in the 1980s by conceiving of literacy as a social and ideological practice, echoing Freire's conceptualizations. To Monte Mór (2015), this ***second generation*** of literacy studies was influential among Brazilian scholars as the country was entering a process of re-democratization. In this phase, one recognizes the first occurrences of the Portuguese-coined word *letramento* in Brazil (Soares, 2003, 2009). As we have emphasized elsewhere (Duboc & Ferraz, 2020), "The coined term 'New Literacy Studies' which questioned the autonomous notion of literacy in the beginning of 1980s was, later on, translated to *letramento* in Brazil". Thus, if New Literacy Studies would contrast with the conventional notion of literacy, in Brazil, the term *letramento* would contrast with the traditional term *"alfabetização"*.

As social transformations demand new epistemological orientations, a ***third generation*** of literacies in Brazil has been developed in more recent times. Along with discussions concerning multimodality in contemporary language uses, one of the most pioneering theoretical discussions now at stake in Brazil is the recently revisited concept of critical literacies, especially those addressed by scholars from the field of foreign language education (Monte Mór, 2009, 2015; Menezes de Souza, 2011; Jordão, 2013; Duboc, 2013, 2014; Duboc & Ferraz, 2018, 2020; Ferraz, 2015, 2019, to name a few). In fact, drawing from the work of Cervetti, Pardales, and Damico (2001), such debate takes critical literacies as necessarily grounded in historical and philosophical traditions. This implies that a certain notion of literacy will be attuned to certain notions of knowledge production and meaning-making processes (critique) and the subject positioning in the world (citizenship).

As no word exists in a vacuum, this chapter acknowledges tensions and overlaps in relation to how "literacy" has been conceived within and cross-nationally. In this respect, past contributions are not put aside; rather, they are constantly reframed as new social demands call for new theoretical assumptions. Table 2.3.1, which draws from Monte Mór's (2015) three literacy generations, is an attempt to show how these tensions and overlaps operate. More detailed information with regard to the third generation will be discussed in the subsequent section.

Visions for Moving Into More Transnational Work

In relation to transnational moves, one needs to acknowledge the robust transnational research and academic partnerships being carried out in the country, most of them related to Portuguese as a first language. According to a study conducted by Schwartz, Frade, and Macedo (2019), there are currently 95 indexed research groups on literacy in Brazil, whose diverse thematic approaches reveal

Table 2.3.1 Literacies Made in Brazil: Three Generations (Expanded from Monte Mór, 2015)

	First Generation *1960s*	*Second Generation* *1980s*	*Third Generation* *Late 1990s onwards*
Correlated terminologies	Critical Pedagogy = *Pedagogia Crítica*	New Literacy Studies = *Letramento*	Multiliteracies/New Literacies/Critical Literacy(ies) = *Letramentos [Multiletramentos/Novos letramentos/letramento(s) crítico(s)]*
Underlying concepts and theories (language, knowledge & critique)	Language as an expression of vested ideologies; emphasis on the critical and political knowledge dimensions; critique as unveiling unequal power relations and vested interests	Language as discourse; emphasis on the social and cultural knowledge dimensions; critique as discerning text functions and critically interrogating the participants' interests in communicative situations	Language as social practice; emphasis on the multiple modes of meaning; emphasis on critical and multimodal knowledge production; critique as unveiling, discerning, and problematizing under a self-reflection/self-implication process ("reading as we read ourselves" in Menezes de Souza's own understanding)
Reflections on Brazilian educational policies and literacy practices	Literacy education as precondition for social justice and empowerment of the oppressed; never adopted officially in dictatorship but somehow has come to inspire some of the hidden agenda of educators since that period.	Literacy education as precondition for sociocultural awareness and citizenship; highly influenced by Bakhtinian theory of genre in Portuguese textbooks and curricula in many Brazilian school systems.	Literacy and language education as precondition for agency and active citizenship; considers the complex, multimodal aspect in offline–online communicative situations; some Brazilian authors are now reframing critique under decolonial lenses. Mentioning of such ideas is now found in recent educational policies.

an interdisciplinary character.[8] For the purposes of this handbook, this chapter will describe the "National Project on Literacies: Language, Culture, Education and Technology" (henceforth PNL)[9] as an example of transnational work not only for its nationwide extension (Annex 1) but also for its pioneering nature in addressing critical perspectives to foreign language education as well as digital literacies in the classroom.

PNL is a collaborative network amongst more than 30 Brazilian public universities[10] engaged in research on teacher education, language education, and literacies. Along the two cycles (2009–2015 and 2016–2021), participants all over the country have developed actions aimed at: (i.) reflecting about language teaching policies; (ii.) designing language education programs in higher education; (iii.) offering courses to public school teachers; (iv.) establishing international agreements and exchanges with foreign universities with the participation of graduate students and postdoctoral students in internship programs.

The network seems to have brought about a lot of learning to all participants of the project, mainly in relation to: (i.) different understandings towards the concept of collaboration; (ii.) the importance of the *local* in mainstream global ideas (Mignolo, 2000); (iii.) agency and active citizenship through language education. What we mean by the first—a different view of collaboration— refers to the practice of a non-vertical hierarchy. Although the University of São Paulo enjoys greatest credibility in South America, the main purpose of the network has *not* been to make this university the leader or model to be followed but only one of the partners. In relation to the second aspect, all of the universities engaged in the nationwide project were expected to design and practice a languages literacy plan that reflected needs, values, cultures, and interests of their respective localities. For such, they could count on the partnership of network colleagues in the various Brazilian regions. Creative, besides critical, and mixed local–global languages literacy plans have been designed and practiced as well as teacher education programs. The exercise of reinterpreting the global–local relationship has greatly contributed to raise and enhance the feeling of agency and independence amidst some remains of—or interrogations toward—the role of the powerful and seductive global.

With regard to the third interest of this nationwide project, agency and active citizenship have been meaningful concepts relearned within a highly collaborative network. As a response to Freire's observation (1996 [1968]) about the strong coloniality manifested in the Brazilian oppressor–oppressed relationship—an unequal, closed, colonialist, proslavery relationship in the hierarchical Brazilian society of the 1960s that has not been overcome since old times—the reconceptualization of agency and citizenship has made a lot of sense, considering that these attitudes are seen as strategies and abilities that favor decoloniality. Contrary to the "one size fits all" projects, PNL reinforces social and educational purposes in order to enable the agonistic coexistence of plural identities.

Conclusions/Findings/Suggestions for Further Research and Practice

Analysis on the literacy conditions in Brazil in the last decades has undoubtedly shown that there has been considerable improvement with regard to literacy performance levels.[11] Among the factors that explain such improvement, Pietri (2018) mentions the growth in access to school among children who had historically been marginalized along with a renewal of the theoretical and methodological bases of language teaching in Brazil in the second half of the twentieth century. Concerning this latter aspect, Silva (2017) concludes that the theoretical–methodological foundations with regard to reading in Brazilian academic production between 2010 and 2015 are primarily founded on the Vygotskyan socio-interactionist perspective, the Bakhtinian's philosophy of language and the social perspectives to literacy.

Indeed, an overview on Brazilian curricular guidelines published in federal, state, and municipal levels in the past decades do acknowledge such epistemological orientations in which the notion of literacy as a social practice seems to be undeniable, leading to the perception that structuralist orientations to language and behaviorist perspective to language teaching are no longer advocated.[12]

Nonetheless, despite all these advances, current Brazilian illiteracy rate is 6.8%, which corresponds to 11 million people.[13] The scenario becomes ever more alarming when one zooms in on statistics and finds out that rate among blacks is double the rate among whites.[14] In view of these adversities, who is to blame and what can be done?

In times of neoconservative and neoliberal politics in Brazil and elsewhere, sociocultural-oriented literacy research and policies have been targeted as a great fallacy along with a growing "back to phonics" discourse in which evidence-based literacy instruction programs appear as a salvationist alternative[15] (Duboc & Ferraz, 2020).

Two greatest challenges for Brazilian literacy research are worth mentioning here. One refers to the ongoing battle between theory and practice. In his paper on directions for literacy research written nearly 20 years ago, Barton (2001) had stated that "issues of the elucidation of concepts and the development of methods and theoretical framing remain". More recently, Morgan (Ferraz & Morgan, 2019) somehow shows a similar concern as he questions to what extent certain theoretical priorities are truly beneficial to the practicalities in language education. Thus, we ponder: Would the remaining gaps in Brazilian literacy education be a result of such distance between theory and practice? The other challenge refers to the ongoing battle over literacy in which competing forces seem to get to the traps of a "part-as-a-whole" attitude. Along with Kern (2000), we assume that literacy is an elastic concept, marked by three imbricated dimensions: linguistic, cognitive, and sociocultural. In this respect, we ponder: To what extent haven't sociocultural perspectives to literacy been sidestepped in favor of linguistic and cognitive dimensions? Likewise, to what extent haven't cognitivist orientations to literacy been sidestepped in favor of the linguistic and sociocultural aspects to language? Future research and practice could highly benefit from questions such as these, paying justice to the very exercise of "reading ourselves as we read the word and the world" as literacy researchers and teachers.

Implications for Our Social Responsibility as Brazilian Academics

In his *Pedagogy of the Oppressed*, Freire (1996 [1968], p. 17) challenges us with questions that are preponderant for any critical literacies educator.

How can I dialogue if I always project ignorance onto others and never perceive my own? How can I dialogue if I regard myself as a case apart from others—mere "its" in whom I cannot recognize other "I's"?
Moreover, he (Freire, ibid., p. 17) asks
How can I dialogue if I start from the premise that naming the world is the task of the elite and that the presence of the people in history is a sign of deterioration, thus to be avoided? . . . Self-sufficiency is incompatible with dialogue.

Ethical responsibility. This is what lies behind Freire's notion of dialogue and what seems to be urgent for those involved with literacy research and practice, be them academic scholars or school teachers. While we still witness literacy wars in many parts of the globe founded on polarized theoretical differences, societies still face illiteracy levels that corroborate social injustice and inequality. Critical literacy studies have undoubtedly played a pivotal role in trying to respond to these issues. Critical literacies studies *made in Brazil*, in particular, have contributed to such debate, departing from Freire's pioneering ideas and expanding them vis-a-vis new social demands. As ethical responsibility implies the ability for one to speak and to listen, to ethically respond to the world, then this might be the missing element in the literacy battlefield.

Notes

1. According to statistics available at www.ibge.gov.br/pt/inicio.html Access 18 Feb 2020.
2. This ongoing project is being carried out by research members from the Center for Public Policy Research—NUPPS—at the University of Sao Paulo, Brazil. The full project might be found at http://nupps.usp.br/ Access 19 Feb 2020.
3. With regard to legislation, it is worth to mention that three main normative references regulate Brazilian formal education, that is, the 1988 National Constitution, the 1996 National Law of Education, and the 2014 National Plan of Education.
4. From the almost 8.5 million university students in 2017, 2.3 million registered in public universities whereas 6.3 million in private ones. Available at http://portal.mec.gov.br/docman/setembro-2018-pdf/97041-apre-sentac-a-o-censo-superior-u-ltimo/file Retrieved on 20 Feb 2020.
5. Further information is found at INEP website http://portal.inep.gov.br/web/guest/about-inep. Access 20 Feb 2020. See, for instance, the INEP report "Overview of the Brazilian Education System" (2016).

6. Today's Brazilian multilingual landscape is composed of 274 indigenous languages spoken by 305 different ethnicities, not to mention immigrant languages, sign languages, and Portuguese as the official language. Source: https://indigenas.ibge.gov.br/estudos-especiais-3/o-brasil-indigena/lingua-falada.

7. For the purposes of illustration, we mention two well-known language repression policies located in different historical times: one refers to the law issued in 1758 by Portuguese Secretary of State Marquis of Pombal, which established the prohibition of tupi indigenous languages and the adoption of Portuguese as the national language. Later on, ultra-nationalist president Getulio Vargas prohibited the use of immigrant languages in the 1930s, especially those from the World War II Axis Powers (German, Italian, Japanese).

8. Besides research groups, it is worth to recall the importance of associations in fostering knowledge production and distribution such as the *ABAlf—Associação Brasileira de Alfabetização* (Brazilian Association of Literacy). Further information available at http://abalf.org.br/.

9. From the original: *Projeto Nacional de Letramentos: Linguagem, Cultura, Educação e Tecnologia*. For further details, access http://letramentos.fflch.usp.br/sobre.

10. A map showing the university participants from all over Brazil is provided at the end of this chapter.

11. According to the UIS—UNESCO Institute for Statistics, Brazilian illiterate population aged 15–24 years has dropped drastically in the last 40 years. In 2018, Brazilian literacy population aged 15 years and older was 93.2%. Retrieved on http://uis.unesco.org/en/country/br. Access 21 Feb, 2020.

12. The "Reading & Writing Program" implemented in public schools all over the state of Sao Paulo in the past 12 years is an example. Under a strong genre-based approach, the program has been adopted in more than 300 state schools where 95% of children aged seven have become literate. Data available at www.educacao.sp.gov.br/ler-escrever. Access 23 Feb 2020.

13. The 2016 National Assessment of Child Literacy (Brazilian acronym ANA) results have demonstrated that around 54% of Brazilian children lack sufficient reading skills, which means they are not able to identify the text's main purpose or locate precise, explicit information within the text. On a global scale, Brazil's performance on the 2015 Programme for International Student Assessment (PISA) led the country below the OECD average and comparable with rates in Albania, Georgia, Jordan, Qatar and Thailand. Data available at www.oecd.org/pisa/PISA-2015-Brazil.pdf. Access May 1, 2019.

14. According to the Brazilian Institute of Geography and Statistics (IBGE), the rate among blacks or people of mixed race was 9.1%, more than twice the rate when compared to whites (3.9%).

15. We refer to the recently approved "National Literacy Policy" (2019), a phonic-based approach with a strong emphasis on systematic phonics and phonemic-awareness instruction that denies critical orientations to language (Windle & Batista, 2019; Duboc & Ferraz, 2020).

References

Barton, D. (1994). *An introduction to the ecology of written language*. Blackwell Publishers.

Barton, D. (2001). Directions for literacy research: Analysing language and social practices in a textually mediated world. *Language and Education, 15*(2&3), 92–104.

Blommaert, J. (2010). *The sociolinguistics of globalization*. Cambridge University Press.

Brasil, F. G., & Capella, A. C. N. (2016). Os Estudos das Políticas Públicas no Brasil: passado, presente e caminhos futuros da pesquisa sobre análise de políticas. *Revista Política Hoje, 25*(1), 71–90.

Cervetti, G., Pardales, M. J., & Damico, J. S. (2001). A Tale of differences: Comparing the traditions, perspectives and educational goals of critical reading and critical literacy. *Reading Online*. Retrieved from www.readingonline.org/articles/cervetti

Cope, B., & Kalantzis, M. (Eds.). (2000). *Multiliteracies: Literacy learning and the design of social futures*. Routledge.

Duboc, A. P. M. (2013). Teaching with an attitude: Finding ways to the conundrum of a postmodern curriculum. *Creative Education, Scientific Research, 4*(12B), 58–65.

Duboc, A. P. M. (2014). Letramento crítico nas brechas da sala de aula de línguas estrangeiras. In N. Takaki & R. F. Maciel (Orgs.), *Letramentos em terra de Paulo Freire* (pp. 209–229). Pontes.

Duboc, A. P. M., & Ferraz, D. M. (2018). Reading ourselves: Placing critical literacies in contemporary language education. *Revista Brasileira de Linguística Aplicada, 18*(2), 227–254.

Duboc, A. P. M., & Ferraz, D. M. (2020). What's behind a literacy war? A discursive and political analysis of the neoconservative Brazilian literacy policy, *Journal of Multicultural Discourses*. https://doi.org/10.1080/17447143.2020.1800714

Duboc, A. P. M., Garcia, B., & Rodrigues, L. (2018). Collaborative curriculum design under an ELF perspective: An innovative experience in Southern Brazil Municipal Schools. In X. Martin-Rubió (Ed.), *Contextualising English as a Lingua Franca: From data to insights* (pp. 229–250). Cambridge Scholars Publishing.

Faraco. (2002). Questões de política de língua no Brasil: problemas e implicações. *Educar*, (20), 13–22.

Ferraz, D. M. (2015). *Educação crítica em Língua Inglesa: neoliberalismo, globalização e novos letramentos*. Editora CRV.

Ferraz, D. M. (2019). English (mis)education as an alternative to challenge English hegemony: A geopolitical debate In M. Guilherme & L. M. T. Menezes de Souza (Eds.), *Glocal languages and critical intercultural awareness* (pp. 183–206). Routledge.

Ferraz, D. M., & Morgan, B. (2019). Transnational dialogue on language education in Canada and Brazil: How do we move forward in the face of neoconservative/neoliberal times? *Trabalhos em Linguística Aplicada*, (58), 196–218.

Freire, P. (1983). The importance of the act of reading. *Journal of Education*, *165*(1), 5–11.

Freire, P. (1996 [1968]). *Pedagogy of the oppressed*. Penguin Books.

Freire, P. (2001). *Política e educação*. Cortez.

Gee, J. P. (2000). The new literacy studies: From 'socially situated' to the work of the social. In D. Barton, M. Hamilton, & R. Ivanic (Eds.), *Situated literacies: Reading and writing in context* (pp. 180–196). Routledge.

Heath, S. B. (1983). *Ways with words: Language, life, and work in communities and classrooms*. Cambridge University Press.

Jordão, C. M. (2013). Abordagem comunicativa, pedagogia crítica e letramento crítico—farinhas do mesmo saco? In C. H. Rocha & R. F. Maciel (Orgs.), *Língua estrangeira e formação cidadã: por entre discursos e práticas* (pp. 69–90). Pontes Editores.

Kern, R. (2000). *Literacy and language teaching*. Oxford University Press.

Lankshear, C., & Knobel, M. (2007). *A new literacies sampler*. Peter Lang Publishing.

Makoni, S., & Pennycook, A. (Eds.). (2007). *Disinventing and reconstituting languages*. Multilingual Matters Ltd.

Menezes de Souza, L. M. T. (2011). O professor de inglês e os Letramentos no século XXI: métodos ou ética? In C. M. Jordão, J. Z. Martinez, & R. C. Halu (Orgs.), *Formação desformatada: práticas com professores de língua inglesa* (pp. 279–303). Pontes Editores.

Menezes de Souza, L. M. T. (2019). Glocal languages, coloniality and globalization from below. In M. Guilherme & L. M. T. Menezes de Souza (Eds.), *Glocal languages and critical intercultural awareness*. Routledge.

Mignolo, W. (2000). *Local histories/Global designs: Coloniality, subaltern knowledges, and border thinking*. Princeton University Press.

Monte Mór, W. (2009). Foreign language teaching, education and the new literacies studies: Expanding views. In G. R. Gonçalves et al. (Orgs.), *New challenges in language and literature*. FALE/UFMG.

Monte Mór, W. (2015). Learning by design: Reconstructing knowledge processes in teaching and learning practices. In B. Cope & M. Kalantzis (Eds.), *A pedagogy of multiliteracies* (pp. 186–209). Palgrave Macmillan.

Morello, R. (2017). The Languages on the Brazilian Borders: Documenting urban diversity, researching school and classroom practice, working towards change. In M. Cavalcanti & T. Maher (Eds.), *Multilingual Brazil: Language resources, identities and ideologies in a globalized world*. Routledge Critical Studies in Multilingualism.

Mortatti, M. R. (2006). *História dos métodos de alfabetização no Brasil*. Retrieved from http://portal.mec.gov.br/seb/arquivos/pdf/Ensfund/alf_mortattihisttextalfbbr.pdf

Pietri, E. (2018). A constituição dos discursos sobre ensino de língua portuguesa nas décadas de 1980 e 1990. *Trabalhos em Linguística Aplicada*, (57), 523–550.

Schwartz, C. M., Frade, I. C., & Macedo, M. S. A. N. (2019). Grupos de pesquisa em alfabetização no Brasil: diálogos com redes de pesquisa. *Roteiro*, *44*(3), 1–26.

Silva, G. S. O. (2017). Estado da arte da leitura no Brasil: 2010 a 2015 (Master Thesis). Universidade Federal de Goiás, Goiás.

Soares, M. (2003). A reinvenção da Alfabetização. *Revista Presença Pedagógica*, *9*(52), 1–21.

Soares, M. (2009). *Letramento—Um tema em três gêneros*. Autêntica.

Street, B. (1984). *Literacy in the theory and practice*. Cambridge University Press.

Street, B. (1998). Social literacies. In V. Edwards & D. Corson (Eds.), *Encyclopedia of Language and Education* (Vol 2, Literacy, pp. 133–141). Kluwer Academic Publishers.

Annex 1

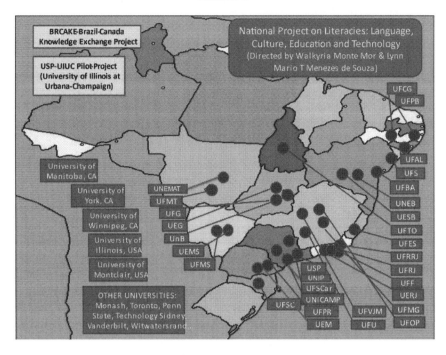

National Project on Literacies. Retrieved on: http://letramentos.fflch.usp.br/sobre

2.4

CRITICAL LITERACIES
IN CANADA

Past, Current, and Future Directions

Cassie J. Brownell, Ty Walkland, and Rob Simon

Long recognized as a leader in critical literacy research, Canada is perhaps unique because of how critical literacy remains entangled with the curriculum. Simultaneously, Canada continues to contend with ongoing issues related to systemic racism, settler colonialism, and the rise of populist nationalism, creating urgent sites for critical literacy curriculum and scholarship. In this chapter, we draw together the work of foundational critical literacy scholars alongside official curricular documents and illustrate how Canadian educators, students, researchers, and community organizers continue to address social and educational inequalities. Ultimately, we emphasize the tensions Canadians oriented toward critical literacies encounter and offer future directions for this work.

Overview of Canadian Geographical, Sociopolitical, and Educational Contexts

Canada prides itself as a uniquely pluralistic and cosmopolitical nation-state on the global stage (Sensoy & DiAngelo, 2017). The world's second largest country, Canada's geographic diversity is mirrored in the diversity of its populace. The most recent census indicates approximately 22% of Canada's 37.59 million citizens are foreign-born, with 1.2 million immigrants arriving between 2011 and 2016 alone (Statistics Canada, 2017). As Thurairajah (2017) described it, "[m]ulticulturalism in Canada has been branded as an ideology in which all Canadians are Canadians irrespective of difference; and, furthermore, these differences are meant to be a source of celebration" (p. 137). Such an ideology "values and encourages diversity and is usually associated with the liberal view that we be tolerant, nondiscriminatory, and respectful of others" (Perry, 2015, p. 1640). Multicultural discourses operate as formal policy and social good in the public imaginary.

While deeply entrenched in Canada's civic discourse, multiculturalism is not without its critics. Canada is a nation "built on the labor of peoples of Color" (Sensoy & DiAngelo, 2017, p. 130). Thurairajah (2017) highlights how the rhetoric of Canadian inclusiveness obfuscates the histories and persistence of racism, xenophobia, and anti-Semitism as well as the legacies of settler colonialism (Daigle, 2019). Multiculturalism also fails to account for diversities beyond ethnocultural difference, including, for example, gender identity and sexual orientation (Goldstein, Koecher, Baer, & hicks, 2018), paradoxically centering whiteness and Eurocentrism as the ontological and epistemological norms against which differences are defined and assimilated (Kubota, 2019).

DOI: 10.4324/9781003023425-16

Canada has a well-documented history of cultural genocide against Indigenous peoples—most visible, perhaps, in the Indian residential schooling system which operated for more than a century (Truth and Reconciliation Commission of Canada, 2015). Like many settler-colonial states, Canada has attempted to reconcile these historical injustices. The Truth and Reconciliation Commission (2015), for example, sought to "renew relationships on a basis of inclusion, mutual understanding, and respect" (p. 23) by including Indigenous histories and ways of knowing in the formal curriculum. While promising, Indigenous scholars remind us "the state's fetishization of Indigenous suffering tied to the history of residential schools mask[s] the ongoing truths of the colonial present" (Daigle, 2019, p. 704). Daigle (2019) therefore calls for "relations of responsibility and accountability based on Indigenous law that Indigenous peoples continue to embody, regenerate, and demand for radical and transformative change" (p. 715). As in the remainder of the chapter, these ideological tensions remain as sites of inquiry.

Education in Canada

Perhaps, owing to Canada's geopolitical diversity, ministries of education in the ten provinces and three territories fund public schools and establish provincial curriculum and assessment standards. Critical literacy—as a stance, set of skills, or curricular outcome—is embedded, both implicitly and explicitly, in most formal curricula across Canada. For example, the Ontario Deputy Minister of Education invited Allan Luke to integrate critical literacy into ministry documents and curriculum (Luke, personal communication, 2020). The Ministry distributed a series of policy briefs beginning in the late aughts, the first of which defined critical literacy and the imperative of including it within the curriculum (Literacy and Numeracy Secretariat, 2009). Additional briefs detailed how to infuse critical literacy across all content areas (including math, science, and social studies) and outlined specific instances of how critical literacy is used to "read the word and the world" (Freire, 1987) by offering a series of questions teachers, children, and families might consider in identifying gender stereotypes as portrayed in books (Roberge, 2013).

Our review of provincial curriculum documents revealed that, in some, critical literacy is explicitly named as a priority. For example, within our home province of Ontario, critical literacy has been formally recognized within the curriculum since 2007, and resources explicitly related to critical literacy were available to teachers beginning in 2003. Other provincial ministries of education encourage critical approaches to literacy without naming them critical literacy. In British Columbia, the term "critical literacy" is not used in official documents, yet the focus on critical issues—including a concern with diversity, access, power, and design (Janks, 2010)—is present (British Columbia Ministry of Education, 2018). Included among the "big ideas" in the grade 10 English Language Arts curriculum (2018) are the notions that "[t]exts are socially, culturally, geographically, and historically constructed" and "[q]uestioning what we hear, read, and view contributes to our ability to be educated and engaged citizens" (p. 2). In Manitoba, following the New Literacy Studies (e.g., Street, 1995) emphasis on a distinction between "skills" and "practices," the Ministry of Education cited critical literacy as a significant term in official documents under the broader umbrella of "English Language Arts Practices" (Manitoba Education and Training, 2019). The curriculum encourages teachers to investigate the work of well-known critical literacy scholars, including Barbara Comber, Hilary Janks, and Allan Luke (Manitoba Education and Training, 2019, p. 42). Although provinces and territories differ in how they name critical literacy tenets within the curriculum, in nearly all spaces, children and youth are asked to reflect on how language is connected to power, identity, and agency.

Despite calls from the Truth and Reconciliation Commission (2015), at the time of this writing, few provinces have adequately included or accounted for Indigenous histories, contributions, or ways of knowing within the formal curriculum. In part, this has to do with the will of provincial political leadership to both plan how to incorporate Indigenous knowledge and to scaffold such implementation. In Ontario, for example, plans were hatched to add Indigenous elements in a meaningful way across all subjects for early childhood learners through secondary students. Specifically, organizers intended to center Indigenous elders and work alongside knowledge keepers to ensure the curriculum was informed by Indigenous perspectives. However, following the 2018 election of Doug Ford as Premier of Ontario, these plans were scrapped. Since, few to no official changes have been made to curricular documents. This is but one example of how curriculum content remains a site of contestation within Canada.

Critical Literacy in Curriculum, Research, and Practice

Critical literacy has found a home in Canada's formal curriculum largely due to the efforts of foundational scholars in the field. One popular example of critical literacies research that likely informed curriculum in various provinces is the early work of Vivian Maria Vasquez. A Canadian native, Vasquez's (2014) research in a junior kindergarten class in the greater Toronto area not only emphasized young children as capable of discussing critical social issues but also the role children can play into their own learning. In her foundational text, Vasquez (2014) drew upon her teaching experiences—while grounding her scholarship in relevant theory—to negotiate the curriculum *with* young learners in her classroom. For instance, Vasquez (2014) detailed how she created an audit trail based on one child's inquiry about frogs and toads. Ultimately, Vasquez (2014) argued, the audit trail served as evidence of their shared curricular history and how students used particular incidents to negotiate critical literacies.

In addition to Vasquez's research in her own classroom, she has also worked alongside colleagues to help educators invoke critical literacies themselves. Albers, Vasquez, Harste, and Janks (2019) described an ongoing project in Canada wherein they worked alongside educators during a two-week summer institute focused on the integration of critical literacies and the arts, language, and technology. Albers et al. (2019) detail how over 80 Canadian teachers and administrators participated in arts-based practices as a means to craft new approaches for engaging learners in their schools while working toward social change.

In what follows, we detail different ways Canadian researchers have likewise invited teachers to embrace critical literacy as a pedagogical approach and engage with children (Beach & Cleovoulo, 2014; Cooper & White, 2006). While critical literacy is positioned in formal curriculum as a desired outcome, its presence does not dictate how power, language, and agency are taken up in real-time encounters in communities of students and teachers. We explore myriad ways students are encouraged to "live a critical curriculum" (Albers et al., 2019, p. 31) and mobilize critical literacy to address transnational equity issues.

Critical Media Literacy

In Ontario, ideas about critical literacy are used in professional development resources, often described interchangeably as "media literacy"—a stand-alone strand of study within the language expectations document. Media literacy is positioned alongside seemingly more traditional notions of language or literacy curriculum including oral communication, reading, and writing. Within the media literacy strand of Ontario's expectations, teachers are encouraged to provide children multiple opportunities to discuss a wide array of media (inclusive of print and digital texts). Children learn to "differentiate between fact and opinion; evaluate the credibility of sources; recognize bias; be attuned to discriminatory portrayals of individuals and groups, including women and minorities; and question depictions of violence and crime" (p. 13).

A number of leading scholars of critical media literacy, including Megan Boler, remain at the fore of conversations about the relationship of media and society. By taking an interdisciplinary approach to her scholarship, Boler (2004; Ratto & Boler, 2014) has long considered how democracy and (digital) media both intersect with and diverge from one another. For example, in her recent book, Boler and her colleague Elizabeth Davis (2021) discuss the role of modern information economies, the rise of "fake news," and the powerful role of emotion in politics in the "post-truth" era.

Bilingualism, Linguistic Diversity, and Multiliteracies

Canada's multicultural present includes official recognition of linguistic as well as cultural and ethnic diversity. The concept of "linguistic duality," including special protections in the *Constitution Act* of 1867 and the 1969 *Official Languages Act*, which granted French and English equal status, rights, and protections, "lies at the heart of the Canadian values of inclusiveness and diversity" (Office of the Commissioner of Official Languages, 2017, n.p.). Although, according to the 2016 census (Statistics Canada, 2017), nearly eight million Canadians reported speaking a home language other than English, Canada's language regime continues to be shaped by settler colonialism and pressure to include Indigenous languages alongside French and English.

As a result, one of the distinctive features of Canadian critical literacy scholarship is a commitment to addressing language diversity through the lens of concepts such as bilingualism or biliteracy (Cummins, 2000), transcultural multiliteracies (Ntelioglou, 2017; Zaidi & Rowsell, 2017), cosmopolitanism (Darvin & Norton, 2017), or translanguaging (Cummins, 2019). This concern for language diversity in critical literacy has informed school curriculum. For instance, in New Brunswick, language is framed as the "primary means by which people express their personal and cultural values" and, therefore, it is considered "critical that educators and students be sensitive to personal and cultural differences, respecting, understanding and appreciating differences in aspects of communication" (New Brunswick English Language Arts, p. 2).

Cummins's (2000) scholarship related to language acquisition and multiliteracies has been particularly influential, encouraging educators to consider language in relation to critical literacy. Cummins (2000) argued for promoting "critical biliteracy" in schools "as a necessary part of [the] empowerment process," without which, "[bilingual] students are unable to read either the word or the world in their two cultures" (p. 9). Kubota (2019), moreover, calls for "alternative conceptualizations and descriptions . . . regarding language use, acquisition, learning, teaching, and other topics within our field" (p. 15) as a means of confronting epistemological racisms embedded in language education and scholarship. Recent scholarship has taken up cosmopolitical (Simon, Nichols, Campano, & Edwards, 2019) or transcultural (Ntelioglou, 2017) perspectives on critical literacy. Ntelioglou (2017) coarticulated transcultural perspectives on language education with critical literacy and applied theatre research.

Reconciliation and Decolonization

A number of Canadian scholars have mobilized critical literacy pedagogies in their efforts to decolonize literacy education and account for the experiences of Indigenous youth (e.g. Brown & Begoray, 2017; Hare, 2012; Pirbhai-Illich, 2010/11; Wiltse, 2015). Their projects join others (e.g., Lopez, 2011; Low, 2010), which emphasize the necessity and challenge of developing culturally relevant pedagogies to meet the needs of a population as diverse as Canada's. Brown and Begoray (2017), for example, argued "[i]n order to decolonize language and literacy learning for Indigenous adolescents there is a need to shift educational pedagogy towards knowledge as embedded in place and experiences" (p. 35). The British Columbia youth participants drew on their lived experiences and funds of knowledge to write graphic novels that troubled deficit discourses about Indigenous youth and communities. Pirbhai-Illich (2010/11) likewise invited her students to explore "how language and literacy are used to construct their [own] identities and understandings of self" (p. 258), demonstrating both the possibilities and difficulties of engaging Indigenous youth in critical literacy work.

Beyond drawing on Indigenous young peoples' experiences and ways of knowing, Hare (2012), like Styres (2018) and others, reminds us "approaches to literacy need to include indigenous people's connection to the natural world as a legitimate 'text' from which to learn alongside the print traditions learned in educational settings" (p. 407). Increasingly, scholars in Canada are foregrounding land, space, and place as necessary sites of inquiry to explore the links between power and identity (e.g., Chambers & Radbourne, 2014; Douglas, Purton, & Bascuñán, 2020; Mendoza, 2018; Nxumalo, 2018). To that end, Michelle Honeyford (2017) invited a group of teachers to participate in a "Writing in Place" activity at one of Manitoba's most storied gathering places. Taking cues from Pahl and Rowsell's (2011) critical artifactual literacies framework and literary métissage (Hasebe-Ludt, Chambers, & Leggo, 2009), Honeyford's (2017) participants weaved together multimodal texts that "[remind] us of the significance of our relationships and responsibilities—to one another, the land, and our past, present, and future" (p. 281). Mendoza's (2018) field trips with teacher candidates to British Columbia's Museum of Anthropology likewise emphasized that teachers and students "can learn about the wider community through diverse and multimodal texts," including the spaces and places that make up those communities (p. 419).

Critical Literacy, Gender, and Sexual Diversity

Official policies related to gender and sexual diversity in Canada, like language policies, have been more progressive than other North American countries: in 2005, Canada officially recognized same-sex marriage; in 2017, the Canadian Human Rights Act prohibited discrimination on the basis of gender identity or expression. Simultaneously, many critical literacy scholars in Canada have explored gender, sexual diversity, and LGBTQ+ issues.

Martino and Cumming-Potvin (2011) brought queer theory into conversation with critical literacy perspectives in their examination of how elementary school teachers explore the "heteronormative limits of addressing critical literacy in the elementary English classroom" (p. 497), as part of "a queer-infused critical literacy framework" (p. 499). Sykes (2011) asked "why hetero-normative *and* homo-normative subjects rely on, yet so often disavow, the connections between whiteness, racisms and colonialisms" (p. 431), as the basis for an intersectional approach to engaging with gender and sexuality in critical literacy.

Other scholars have focused specifically on documenting and supporting the development of LGBTQ+ positive critical literacy curriculum in schools. A recent collection by Woolley and Airton (2020) includes gender diversity-affirming course materials for K–12 teachers. Simon, hicks, Walkland, Gallagher, Evis, and Baer (2018) documented their work in *Addressing Injustices*, a participatory project that brings youth and teachers together to address social injustices through reading, writing, and art-making. Youth and teachers' gender inquiries, in response to queer-in-content young adult literature, included photovoice projects to "directly [address] injustices to create different possible futures together" (Simon et al., 2018, p. 45).

While these projects suggest possibilities for queering critical literacy curriculum (hicks, 2017), progress toward gender equity in Canadian schools has required political activism. In her research with LGBTQ+ families in Ontario, Goldstein (2019) found that of all the schools attended by 37 families, only one school included LGBTQ+ positive curriculum. Iskander and Shabtay (2018) documented youth activists' responses to being denied their legal right to form a gay-straight alliance (GSA) at a public, Catholic school in Ontario. Their study echoed Goldstein's (2019) findings, which emphasized that "LGBTQ students and families don't want to be tolerated. They want to be expected, accepted, and supported for who they are" (p. 138).

Forwarding a Transnational Perspective

Allan Luke (2018) envisioned critical literacy as "an invitation to join an intergenerational, intercultural and peer conversation that is about imagining and building what could be" (p. xii). As we have documented in this brief chapter, in the spirit of Luke's invitation, Canadian critical literacy scholars have explored local manifestations of transnational issues. While there are aspects of this scholarship that are distinctive, critical literacy scholars in Canada do not view ourselves in isolation. By contrast, we regard borders as permeable; our work traversing international venues and organizations that connect us.

Increasingly, Canadian scholars are developing opportunities to cultivate research across borders, with the goal of cultivating transnational collaborations and perspectives on critical literacy. For example, Gallagher and colleagues (2017) developed a multisite, global ethnographic research project of drama classrooms in Greece, England, India, Taiwan, and Canada to explore "how concepts of hope and care function in the lives of today's youth, and how their creative and artistic engagement may provoke forms of engaged citizenship worth considering in times of increasing social, economic, and political instability" (pp. 114–115). This research is collaborative rather than comparative, supporting dialogue and a more intersectional approach to understanding the multiple political and identity issues facing youth in these and other contexts, with an acknowledgment of how "critical literacy work sits alongside affective non-relational work" (Gallagher, 2014, p. 210).

Suggestions for Future Research and Practice and Implications for Our Social Responsibility as Academics

The work surveyed in this chapter offers promising directions for current and future critical literacy scholarship and practice. While Canada has made positive steps in bringing critical literacy and social justice perspectives into the curriculum, progress—for example, the inclusion of First Nations, Métis and Inuit perspectives in the Ontario curriculum—is accompanied by impediments and challenges—Indigenous studies courses remain elective rather than required for all students. Perhaps, more than ever, we feel the need for Canadian critical literacy scholars, activists, and educators to link local projects with translocal social movements related to, among other concerns: health, poverty, and human rights; land, environment, and climate change; decolonization and reconciliation; and gender diversity and creativity.

We wrote the final sections of this chapter in isolation, as Toronto joined a global effort to combat the spread of COVID-19 and confronted issues of anti-Blackness. The current pandemic and forceful cries of redress for a legacy of white supremacy take place against the backdrop of intersecting global crises, including a rise in hate crimes, attacks on immigrants, and violence directed toward members of Indigenous and LGBTQ+ communities—all supported by populist nationalist politics in Canada and elsewhere. Following Sykes (2011), this moment calls for critical literacy scholars to adopt an intersectional approach in our research and teaching, since "[teaching] about gay or queer issues in critical literacy or citizenship education means engaging with interlocking issues of race and racism, patriarchy and sexism, indigeneity and colonialism" (p. 429).

What would an intersectional and transnational approach to critical literacy research look like? How might scholars and activist educators collectively reshape school curriculum to better account for the cosmopolitical (Stengers, 2010) perspectives of multilingual and multiethnic communities? And how can we continue to do this work in solidarity with #BlackLivesMatter, Indigenous solidarity, and other current and future social movements? For critical literacy scholars in Canada and globally, these and related questions may suggest future directions for working across geographic and political borders in pursuit of a more socially just future.

References

Albers, P. M., Vasquez, V. M., Harste, J., & Janks, H. (2019). Art as a critical response to social issues. *Journal of Literacy & Technology, 20*(1), 46–80.

Beach, P., & Cleovoulou, Y. (2014). An inquiry-based approach to critical literacy: Pedagogical nuances of a second-grade classroom. *Alberta Journal of Educational Research, 60*(1), 161–181.

Boler, M. (2004). *Democratic dialogue in education: Troubling speech, disturbing silence.* New York, NY: Peter Lang.

Boler, M., & Davis, E. (2021). *Affective politics of digital media: Propaganda by other means.* New York, NY: Routledge.

British Columbia Ministry of Education. (2018). *Literary studies 10* [Program of Studies]. Retrieved from https://curriculum.gov.bc.ca/sites/curriculum.gov.bc.ca/files/curriculum/english-language-arts/en_english-language-arts_10_literary-studies_elab.pdf

Brown, A., & Begoray, D. (2017). Using a graphic novel project to engage Indigenous youth in critical literacies. *Language and Literacy, 19*(3), 35–55.

Chambers, J. M., & Radbourne, C. (2014). Teaching critical literacy skills through the natural environment as text. *Applied Environmental Education & Communication, 13*(2), 120–127.

Cooper, K., & White, R. E. (2006). Action research in practice: Critical literacy in an urban grade 3 classroom. *Educational Action Research, 14*(01), 83–99.

Cummins, J. (2000). Biliteracy, empowerment, and transformative pedagogy. In J. V. Tinajero & R. A. DeVillar (Eds.), *The power of two languages 2000: Effective dual-language use across the curriculum.* New York, NY: McGraw Hill.

Cummins, J. (2019). The emergence of translanguaging pedagogy: A dialogue between theory and practice. *Journal of Multilingual Education Research, 9.* 19–36.

Daigle, M. (2019). The spectacle of reconciliation: On (the) unsettling responsibilities to Indigenous peoples in the academy. *Society and Space, 37*(4), 703–721.

Darvin, R., & Norton, B. (2017). Investing in new literacies for a cosmopolitan future. In R. Zaidi & J. Rowsell (Eds.), *Literacy lives in transcultural times* (pp. 89–101). New York, NY: Routledge.

Douglas, V., Purton, F., & Bascuñán, D. (2020). Possibility not difficulty: Difficult knowledge in K–12 classrooms as opportunities for renegotiating relationships with Indigenous perspectives and knowledges. *Alberta Journal of Education Research, 66*(3), 307–324.

Freire, P. (1987). The importance of the act of reading. In P. Freire & D. Macedo (Eds.), *Literacy: Reading the word and the world.* Westport, CT: Bergin and Garvey.

Gallagher, K. (2014). *Why theatre matters: Urban youth, engagement, and a pedagogy of the real.* University of Toronto.

Gallagher, K., & Rodricks, D. J. (2017). Hope despite hopelessness: Race, gender, and the pedagogies of drama/applied theatre as a relational ethic in neoliberal times. *Youth Theatre Journal, 31*(2), 114–128.

Goldstein, T. (2019). *Teaching gender and sexuality at school: Letters to teachers.* New York, NY: Routledge.

Goldstein, T., Koecher, A., Baer, P., & hicks, b. l. (2018). Transitioning in elementary school: Parent advocacy and teacher allyship. *Teaching Education, 29*(2), 165–177.

Hare, J. (2012). 'They tell a story and there's meaning behind that story': Indigenous knowledge and young indigenous children's literacy learning. *Journal of Early Childhood Literacy, 12*(4), 389–414.

Hasebe-Ludt, E., Chambers, C., & Leggo, C. (2009). *Life writing and literary métissage as an ethos for our times.* New York, NY: Peter Lang.

hicks, b. l. (2017). Gracefully unexpected, deeply present and positively disruptive: Love and queerness in classroom community. In D. Linville (Ed.), *Queering education: Pedagogy, curriculum, policy.* Occasional Paper Series 37. Bank Street College of Education.

Honeyford, M. (2017). Writing as teachers: The power of place. *Language Arts, 94*(4), 279–281.

Iskander, L., & Shabtay, A. (2018). Who runs the schools? LGBTQ youth activism and Ontario's Bill 13. *Journal of LGBT Youth, 15*(4), 339–352.

Janks, H. (2010). *Literacy and power.* New York, NY: Routledge.

Kubota, R. (2019). Confronting epistemological racism, decolonizing scholarly knowledge: Race and gender in applied linguistics. *Applied Linguistics,* 1–22.

Literacy and Numeracy Secretariat (Ontario Ministry of Education). (2009). Critical literacy. *Capacity Building Series.* Queen's Printer.

Lopez, A. E. (2011). Culturally relevant pedagogy and critical literacy in diverse English classrooms: A case study of a secondary English teacher's activism and agency. *English Teaching: Practice and Critique, 10*(4), 75–93.

Low, B. E. (2010). The tale of the talent night rap: Hip-hop culture in schools and the challenge of interpretation. *Urban Education, 4*(2), 194–220.

Luke, A. (Ed.). (2018). *Critical literacy, schooling and social justice: The selected works of Allan Luke.* New York, NY: Routledge.

Luke, A. (2020). Personal communication.

Manitoba Education and Training. (2019). *English language arts curriculum framework: A living document* [Program of Studies]. Retrieved March 2, 2020, from www.edu.gov.mb.ca/k12/cur/ela/framework/full_doc.pdf

Martino, W., & Cumming-Potvin, W. (2011). "They didn't have *out there* gay parents—they just looked like normal regular parents": Investigating teachers' approaches to addressing same-sex parenting and non-normative sexuality in the elementary school classroom. *Curriculum Inquiry, 41*(4), 480–501.

Mendoza, A. (2018). Preparing preservice educators to teach critical, place-based literacies. *Journal of Adolescent and Adult Literacy, 61*(4), 413–420.

Ntelioglou, B. Y. (2017). Examining the relational space of the self and other in the language–drama classroom: Transcultural multiliteracies, situated practice and the cosmopolitan imagination. In R. Zaidi & J. Rowsell (Eds.), *Literacy lives in transcultural times* (pp. 58–72). New York, NY: Routledge.

Nxumalo, F. (2018). Stories for living on a damaged planet: Environmental education in a preschool classroom. *Journal of Early Childhood Research, 16*(2), 148–159.

Office of the Commissioner of Official Languages. (2017). Canada's linguistic duality at the heart of inclusiveness and diversity. Retrieved March 2, 2020, from www.clo-ocol.gc.ca/en/newsletter/2017/canadas-linguistic-duality-heart-inclusiveness-diversity

Pahl, K., & Rowsell, J. (2011). Artifactual critical literacy: A new perspective for literacy education. *Berkeley Review of Education, 2*(2), 129–151.

Perry, B. (2015). Disrupting the mantra of multiculturalism: Hate crime in Canada. *The American Behavioral Scientist, 59*(13), 1637–1654.

Pirbhai-Illich, F. (2010/11). Aboriginal students engaging and struggling with critical multiliteracies. *Journal of Adolescent & Adult Literacy, 54*(4), 257–266.

Ratto, M., & Boler, M. (Eds.). (2014). *DIY citizenship: Critical making and social media.* Cambridge, MA: MIT Press.

Roberge, G. D. (2013). Promoting Critical literacy across the curriculum and fostering safer learning environments. Research Monograph #48, *What works? Research into practice*. Ontario Ministry of Education.

Sensoy, O., & DiAngelo, R. (2017). *Is everyone really equal?: An introduction to key concepts in social justice education.* New York, NY: Teachers College Press.

Simon, R., hicks, b. l., Walkland, T., Gallagher, B., Evis, S., & Baer, P. (2018). "But in the end, you are all beautiful": Exploring gender through digital composition. *English Journal, 107*(3), 39–46.

Simon, R., Nichols, P., & Campano, G., & Edwards, W. (2019). "There is really a lot going on here": Toward a cosmopolitics of reader-response. In S. Jagger & P. Trifonis (Eds.), *Handbook of cultural studies and education* (pp. 175–189). New York, NY: Routledge.

Statistics Canada. (2017). *Census profile, 2016 census.* Retrieved February 5, 2020, from https://www12.statcan.gc.ca/census-recensement/2016/dp-pd/prof/index.cfm?Lang=E

Stengers, I. (2010). *Cosmopolitics I.* Minneapolis, MN: University of Minnesota Press.

Street, B. V. (1995). *Social literacies: Critical approaches to literacy in development, ethnography, and education.* London, UK: Pearson.

Styres, S. (2018). Literacies of land: Decolonizing narratives, storying, and literature. In L. Tuhiwai Smith, E. Tuck, & K. W. Yang (Eds.), *Indigenous and decolonizing studies in education* (pp. 24–37). New York, NY: Routledge.

Sykes, H. (2011). Hetero- and homo-normativity: Critical literacy, citizenship education and queer theory. *Curriculum Inquiry, 41*(4), 419–432.

Thurairajah, K. (2017). The jagged edges of multiculturalism in Canada and the suspect Canadian. *Journal of Multicultural Discourses, 12*(2), 134–148.

Truth and Reconciliation Commission of Canada. (2015). Honouring the truth, reconciling for the future: Summary of the final report of the Truth and Reconciliation Commission of Canada. Retrieved from www.trc.ca/assets/pdf/Honouring_the_Truth_Reconciling_for_the_Future_July_23_2015.pdf

Vasquez, V. (2014). *Negotiating critical literacies with young children* (2nd ed). New York, NY: Routledge.

Wiltse, L. (2015). Not just 'sunny days': Aboriginal students connect out-of-school literacy resources with school literacy practices. *Literacy, 49*(2), 60–68.

Woolley, S., & Airton, L. (Eds.). (2020). *Teaching about gender diversity: Teacher-tested lesson plans for K–12 classrooms.* Toronto, ON: Canadian Scholars Press.

Zaidi, R., & Rowsell, J. (2017). *Literacy lives in transcultural times.* New York, NY: Routledge.

2.5

CRITICAL LITERACIES IN COLOMBIA

Social Transformation and Disruption Ingrained in our Local Realities

Raúl Alberto Mora, Claudia Cañas, Gloria Gutiérrez-Arismendy, Natalia Andrea Ramírez, Carlos Andrés Gaviria, and Polina Golovátina-Mora

Sociopolitical and Educational Context in Colombia

Sociopolitical Context

Colombia, like most of Latin America, is considered a developing country by current economic standards. Additionally, our recent admission in the Organization for Economic Co-operation and Development (OECD) and the political tensions after the 2016 peace accords with some of the guerrillas are posing a new set of challenges. Perhaps, the biggest challenge to date is the struggle against injustice and inequities, including how Colombian society will address the presence of different minority groups as part of their policies (Mora, Chiquito, & Zapata, 2019), as well as issues of gender and overall inclusion. Larger questions about the social and economic divides between the public and private institutions still abound, placing Colombia in a challenging yet interesting position as a potential political and economic player in the region for years to come.

Colombia has approximately 50 million inhabitants. Although Spanish is the official language in the country, the government recognizes 65 indigenous languages, two Afro-Colombian languages (Creole and Ri Palenque), and the Romani language as the native tongues of those ethnic and minoritized groups. Colombia is a multicultural country due to its ethnic and linguistic diversity: 10.6% is Afro-descendant, 3.4% indigenous, 0.01% Roma, and the remaining 85% is mixed-race (DANE, 2018). The overall poverty rate is 26.9%, with 7.4% of the country's population in extreme poverty (DANE, 2020).

Educational Context

The Colombian educational system is split into public and private education. Both are present in urban and rural areas, as well as at all levels of education. Schools in rural regions heavily affected by armed conflicts have had greater challenges than urban educational systems protected by the capital cities. These challenges were aggravated by the lack of government presence and control in some regions. Since the 1990s, the Colombian government has fueled educational reforms with the passing of the General Law of Education (Law 115; Congreso de la República de Colombia, 1994)

DOI: 10.4324/9781003023425-17

to improve teaching processes in schools, aimed at both enacting societal change and improving international test results.

In this landscape, the discourse of critical mindset appears in educational policies and practices. Law 115 introduced criticality from different perspectives and set "critical comprehension" and "critical capability" as two of the main goals for the educational system, linked to science and technology (Congreso de la República de Colombia, 1994, p. 2). For basic and middle school, "critical" refers to access to the scientific, technological, artistic, humanistic knowledge, as well as the relationship with others and nature (Congreso de la República de Colombia, 1994, p. 6). In recent years, the government has enacted policies to cover system needs in the different levels including higher education, sometimes devoid of clear guidelines to define criticality (Mora et al., 2019). In addition, it has become commonplace in national and local curricular initiatives to hear talk about developing critical students, fostering critical reading, boosting critical thinking, and creating critical consciousness. Although some administrative changes still seem mediatic, there is an ongoing mixture of real progress and pending work that surfaces when looking at classrooms.

Critical literacy (Esteban Nuñez, 2015; Gutierrez, 2015; Gómez Jiménez & Gutierrez, 2019; Mora, 2014a) fits within the larger scheme of Colombian education to help create a criticality blueprint with a perspective *from* and *in* our country and region (Mora, Cañas, Rosas Chávez, Rocha, & Maciel, 2020), thus setting the conditions for a critical praxis that can inspire students, teachers, and our communities to incorporate it as part of our educational and everyday lives.

Survey of Critical Literacy in Colombia

We searched for articles related to critical literacy, covering education in general and the specific area of Language Education (for an extended discussion on languages, see Handbook chapters by Chang-Bacon, Khote, Schell, & Crooks and Mattos, Pascoal, & Huh). We included 29 articles by Colombian and international scholars affiliated with local universities, published in national or international journals or book chapters. We used databases both in English (JSTOR, EBSCO, Google Scholar, Scopus) and Spanish (Scielo, Redalyc) for our searches, using terms in both languages: literacy, critical literacy, literacidad, literacidad crítica. Table 2.5.1 summarizes the context where the studies took place.

Salient Issues

We analyzed what authors in the studies did and how their work aligned with some of the underlying principles surrounding critical literacy, including the need to raise questions in our classroom practices about social justice and power dynamics in language use (Mora, 2014a), the use of languages to explore deeper societal issues, and the importance of equitable practices in classroom instruction. We profiled first the contexts of inquiry and then the major trends for critical literacy, once again returning to those principles we mentioned earlier. Although our analysis also kept track of whether the articles cited critical literacy authors, we were more interested in how the work aligned with those principles and ideas about what critical literacy should do rather than just focus on citations. This section shares two major patterns in the literature, which we connected to two main ideas present in critical literacy: the value of *social transformation* and the power of *disruption* to texts and curricular practices.

Critical Literacy as *Social Transformation*

The idea of how critical literacy can be a catalyst for social transformation appeared as a major theme that some of our scholars shared. Our local scholarship shows a firm belief in the potential for criticality to engage with the bigger questions that our country will need to address as we move

Table 2.5.1 Context for Inquiry in Surveyed Studies

Context	Studies
Policy Analysis	Calle Díaz, 2017
Critical Literature Review	Moncada Linares, 2016
Tertiary Education—Graduate	Mojica and Castañeda-Peña (2017); Mora (2014a)
Tertiary Education—General	Arce (2013), Giraldo (2018), Vargas Franco (2015)
Tertiary Education—Preservice Teacher Education	Aguirre Morales and Ramos Holguín (2011); Domiguez (2019); Echeverri Sucerquia and Pérez Restrepo (2014); Esteban Nuñez (2015); Gómez Jiménez and Gutierrez (2019); Granados-Beltrán (2018); Gutierrez (2015); Hernández Varona and Gutiérrez Álvarez (2020); Kern (2017); Piñeros Pedraza and Quintero Polo (2006); Samacá Bohórquez (2012)
Secondary Education	Benavides Buitrago (2017); Contreras León and Chapetón Castro (2016); Lara-Páez (2017); Ortega (2019); Rincón and Clavijo-Olarte (2016)
After-School Programs	Chaves and Chapetón (2019); Gómez Rodríguez (2017); Mojica (2007)
Elementary Education	Cañas, Ocampo, Rodríguez, López-Ladino, and Mora (2018)
Afro-Colombian Communities	Zárate, González Serrano, and Flórez Romero (2015)

forward in terms of equity, access, and social justice. In order to engage with those questions, the literature provides two initial considerations, *community involvement* and *interrogating practice*, detailed in the following.

Social Transformation Means Community Involvement. An important principle in critical literacy scholarship posits that we can only engage in criticality from the vantage point of our communities and those who are part of them. Local research stressed the importance of considering the outlook and needs of the communities we work with (Trigos-Carrillo, 2019b). Keeping our communities in mind, these studies argue, entails a careful revision of the social realities from the perspective and needs of those in the community (Rincón & Clavijo-Olarte, 2016) and those in charge of educational practices (Hernández Varona & Gutiérrez Álvarez, 2020). Without addressing these circumstances, a veritable engagement with critical literacies is not possible.

Social Transformation Means Interrogating Our Instructional Practices. Critical literacy is transformative by nature. One thing that all critical literacy scholars we surveyed agreed on is that education, both in schools and teacher education programs, should mobilize students to reflect on the bigger issues of social inequity and power dynamics in language. This must be a concurrent effort that congregates what happens in all the different scenarios where educational practices take place. That transformation includes weaving content and students' daily lives (Cañas et al., 2018; Rincón & Clavijo-Olarte, 2016) and raising questions about existing "dominant and dominated discourses in the classroom" (Benavides Buitrago, 2017, p. 16).

We are already seeing efforts taking place in schools (Samacá Bohórquez, 2012) inviting deeper reflexivity and larger societal questions as we read texts. In the context of teacher education, transformative efforts are already in motion in teacher education programs, both undergraduate and graduate alike, where teacher educators are infusing the conceptual and practical tenets of critical literacy (Aguirre Morales & Ramos Holguín, 2011; Echeverri Sucerquia & Pérez Restrepo, 2014; Gutierrez, 2015; Gómez Jiménez & Gutierrez, 2019; Kern, 2017) as starting points of reflexivity. We found other cases where the reflexivity is also moving into discussing instructional decisions related, for example, to the analysis of the literary texts (Chapetón, 2004; Chaves Barrera & Chapetón, 2019; Esteban Nuñez, 2015) and the textbooks (Mora, 2014a) that teachers choose as instructional materials on a daily basis.

Critical Literacy *as Disruption*

Critical literacy, drawing from the idea of "reading the word and the world" (Freire & Macedo, 1987), is an invitation to look at contents and texts more deeply, more carefully. Critical literacy invites us to provoke the curriculum (Calle Díaz, 2017) and the research we do (Granados-Beltrán, 2018; Piñeros Pedraza & Quintero Polo, 2006) as ways to raise questions that are not there (or some do not want to be there in the first place) and that way develop a real criticality that sees text engagement as disruption, as not going with the orthodoxy of the curriculum but proposing new ways to play with texts. Our exploration of the local literature highlighted two salient characteristics of such disruption, detailed in the following.

Disruption as Deeper Meaning–Making. Research that discussed meaning-making focused on what academic literacies (Trigos-Carrillo, 2019a) must consider to infuse criticality in instructional practices. Delving into deeper meaning-making means revisiting what we mean, for example, by *critical reading* (Arce, 2013; Vargas Franco, 2015) and how a true critical perspective moves beyond the traditional forms of text questioning that we regularly use (Gómez Jiménez & Gutierrez, 2019; Gutierrez, 2015). It also means transcending the usual causality relationships that link critical consciousness with language proficiency. Critical engagement with texts happens at different levels and students are all equally capable of deeper meaning-making, of course with textual creations tailored to their competence level (Giraldo, 2018).

Disruption as Larger Topics and Alternative Texts. Critical literacy is an invitation to question the canon, both in terms of topics and textual choices. From a critical literacy perspective, our instructional practices must always open possibilities to include content that enables more equitable learning and teaching practices.

Our survey showed two ways how local scholars are addressing that disruption. On the one hand, there is a growing interest in developing a *transmedial* perspective, understood as "the construction of narratives woven through multiple media platforms" (Mora, 2014b, Defining the Term, pa. 1). Alternative texts and genres are, in these cases, becoming entry points for larger sociopolitical issues. Advertisements (Lara-Páez, 2017), city signs (Dominguez, 2019), news outlets (Gómez Rodríguez, 2017), and films (Mojica, 2007) are some of the alternative textual forms that are inviting our students to question textual choices, motives, and the overall nature of text production.

On the other hand, a disrupting the curriculum through critical literacy means opening spaces for topics that we did not traditionally include in the classrooms, in part because of that belief we pointed out early that students with lower levels of competence were not able to critically interpret and create texts. Local research, ranging from examples in public schools (Contreras León & Chapetón Castro, 2016; Ortega, 2019), private schools (Cañas et al., 2018), and teacher education (Mojica & Castañeda-Peña, 2017), introduce examples for grounded pedagogical proposals (Moncada Linares, 2016) about the importance of tackling issues of social justice, gender, Othering, and socioeconomic status. All the studies showed that students benefit from these conversations, as they ground language in real life and our local contexts, as opposed to always seeing the target language as something that they cannot use as a conduit to talk about their everyday lives.

A Transnational View of Critical Literacy in Colombia: From Local to Glocal Scholarship

Colombian language and literacy scholars in recent years have become more interested in not just reproducing knowledge but contributing our knowledge base to the larger conversations about the meaning of critical literacy and the directions the field must move forward as a transnational affair (many of which are, in fact, informing this Handbook). We see that shift in positionality in our chronological analysis of the articles: Earlier articles (usually before 2015) usually framed critical literacy as a purely local phenomenon, citing very few international scholars (such as Paulo Freire and Ira Shor). More recent articles feature more robust frameworks that consider a more transnational author base that blend well-known Anglo scholars, growing numbers of international BIPOC scholars, and the work of local scholars delving into critical literacy.

The growth in the frameworks also shows evidence of the overall growth of the field of literacy studies in Colombia, even in relation to Latin America. In the past 20 years, we have witnessed the emergence of graduate programs that mention literacy as a field of inquiry. Our survey of the local literature showed a surge on critical literacy conversations in Colombian graduate programs. Discussions about literacies theory as a major topic of inquiry are already taking place in several Colombian universities, a reflection on the amount of master's theses that have emerged in recent years. Other universities have included criticality as a topic of interest and we expect our doctoral programs to follow suit, as issues of critical literacy are also appearing in their curricula. In addition, we have witnessed the growth in research groups and initiatives in higher education that explicitly mention literacy as either their main topic (Pandya, 2019) or within their research lines, and more scholars in the field (both locally and internationally trained) proposing new topics for exploration.

The transnational growth of critical literacy research is also evident in our local journals. They have moved from being an outlet just for local academics and practitioners to include literacy manuscripts from Brazil, Mexico, Iran, Saudi Arabia, Turkey, or Spain. This growing phenomenon is positioning our country as a potential knowledge center in literacy and language studies, with the questions and challenges that such a move would pose. The connection between local critical literacy studies in Colombia to larger social and historical backgrounds in other countries is a phenomenon that continues growing across Latin America (see Monte Mór, Duboc, & Ferraz, this Handbook; Hinton, this Handbook; Hernandez-Zamora, López Gopar, & Quesada-Mejía, this Handbook). In a transnational perspective, studies in critical literacy have emerged as the possibility to develop consciousness of social practices within countries which have inequity levels and share similar economic and political issues.

One of the major challenges that Colombian literacy scholarship will have to face this decade and beyond is how to decenter and decentralize (Mora, et al., 2020) our knowledge dissemination methods and conduits. By decentering and decentralizing, we mean "mov[ing] the conversation away from historically dominant groups (decenter) and geographical locales (decentralize)" (Mora, et al., 2020, p. 313) and what this means for who gets to publish, where, and in what languages. It does not escape our analysis that most articles we surveyed, despite being in Colombian journals, are in English and that there is still a great deal of scholarship that keeps emerging from the major knowledge centers in Colombia (i.e., higher education institutions in the largest metropolitan centers in Bogotá, Medellín, Cali, and Barranquilla).

As our scholars are gravitating to include more BIPOC scholarship from abroad to inform our frameworks, we also need to question what spaces we are creating for our local minority scholars to share their work. From a critical literacy perspective, the need to open spaces for the voices of marginalized groups in scholarship, including practitioners in some levels, minority scholars, grassroots organizations, to name a few, must remain a priority. Although we have made progress in developing a local critical literacy body of work, we cannot ignore how most of this scholarship still comes from higher education institutions and how we need more work that represents other sectors of society. This means that, as critical literacy in our country moves forward, we need to promote scholarship that reflects the diversity of theoretical perspectives present in our society, both in terms of cultural backgrounds and languages (Spanish, indigenous, Afro-Colombian, etc.). We also need to work with those minority scholars around the country and help them find ways for their stories to appear in English. This transnational, multilingual view of critical literacy research and advocacy dovetails with the challenges for Colombian critical literacy scholars in years to come, which we will discuss in the final section of this chapter.

Critical Literacy: The Social Responsibility of Our Academics

Critical literacy in Colombia provides an essential orientation in education that breaks age or educational level boundaries. There are studies of critical literacy practices across the P-20 system, both in public and private institutions. We know that there is still a lot of work to be done despite the political transitions and social changes that the country and its educational policies have experienced. Studies in Colombia have begun to develop the notion of "critical" beyond the traditional ideas. Teachers and teacher educators are advancing in the construction of practices that not only analyze critical thinking or reading but also promote social action in search of justice. There is a bigger push toward using language as a social practice that interrogates the role of texts in relation to discourses of power and domination.

These shifting views about critical literacy provide a set of challenges for Colombian literacy scholars. We need to continue our advocacy functions and start operating as mentor texts of our own. Our efforts to assist groups in the margins to tell their stories must grow stronger. Coauthoring and co-conducting research with students, practitioners, or community organizers must be the norm and not the exception. This also poses a challenge for our journals. They need to create and expand spaces for practitioners' voices so that their voices are not lost while more international submissions continue surfacing or having journals divided by levels. As we said in the review, there is a growing disparity between higher education and K-5 studies published in journals. Such disparities are dissipating when looking at graduate education, but they are yet to be fully translated into publications (however, our professional associations in language studies are moving forward with efforts to bridge that gap).

Coda: Critical Literacy in Colombia, an Ongoing Social Imperative

Every historical age has its own injustices and inequalities that deserve critical reflection and specific intervention. That is why critical literacy should not be understood as a transitory matter in education, but as a fundamental aspect and a social imperative for our country. A critical orientation to Colombian education will enable teachers, students, and their families to reflect and analyze the texts that build the policies and ideologies of daily life. Thus, they will not only read the word but also the world behind each textual construction.

Colombian education has begun to develop a critical consciousness of how we can collectively transform practices and, how communities would be able to undertake social actions which generate more justice, equality, and empowerment in daily life. Critical literacy affords people the possibility to rewrite their realities in order to transform injustices, thus improving their quality of life and having better chances of succeeding in the world. Critical literacy in Colombia becomes the reflective and analytical ability to read texts while understanding working ideologies to then promote social justice and transformation.

References

Aguirre Morales, J., & Ramos Holguín, B. (2011). Fostering skills to enhance critical educators: A pedagogical proposal for pre-service teachers. *HOW Journal, 18*(1), 169–197. Retrieved from www.howjournalcolom bia.org/index.php/how/article/view/58

Arce, L. C. (2013). La literacidad crítica en la universidad: análisis de una experiencia. *Zona Próxima, 18,* 93–102. https://dialnet.unirioja.es/servlet/articulo?codigo=6416662

Benavides Buitrago, C. (2017). EFL students' social identities construction through gender-based short stories. *Colombian Applied Linguistics Journal, 19*(1), 11–21. https://doi.org/10.14483/calj.v19n1.10641

Calle Díaz, L. (2017). Citizenship education and the EFL standards: A critical reflection. *Profile: Issues in Teachers' Professional Development, 19*(1), 155–168. https://doi.org/10.15446/profile.v19n1.55676

Cañas, C., Ocampo, A. P., Rodríguez, A. K., López-Ladino, M., & Mora, R. A. (2018). Toward a participatory view of early literacies in second language contexts: A reflection on research from Colombia. In G. Onchwari & J. Keengwe (Eds.), *Handbook of research on pedagogies and cultural considerations for young English language learners* (pp. 300–324). IGI Global. https://doi.org/10.4018/978-1-5225-3955-1.ch015

Chapetón, C. M. (2004). Reading the world as a literacy practice: A teacher's reflection. *Colombian Applied Linguistics Journal, 6*, 121–128. https://doi.org/10.14483/22487085.111

Chaves Barrera, C., & Chapetón, C. M. (2019). Creating a book club with a critical approach to foster literacy practices. *Folios, 50*, 111–125. https://doi.org/10.17227/Folios.50-10224

Congreso de la República de Colombia. (1994). *Ley 115 de 1994: Ley General de Educación.* www.funcionpublica.gov.co/eva/gestornormativo/norma_pdf.php?i=292

Contreras León, J. J., & Chapetón Castro, C. M. (2016). Cooperative learning with a focus on the social: A pedagogical proposal for the EFL classroom. *HOW Journal, 23*(2), 125–147. https://doi.org/10.19183/how.23.2.321

DANE. (2018). *Grupos étnicos en Colombia. Resultados del Censo Nacional de Población y Vivienda 2018.* Retrieved from www.dane.gov.co/index.php/estadisticas-por-tema/demografia-y-poblacion/grupos-etnicos

DANE. (2020). *Índice de Pobreza Multidimensional 2019.* Retrieved from www.dane.gov.co/index.php/estadisticas-por-tema/pobreza-y-condiciones-de-vida/pobreza-y-desigualdad/pobreza-monetaria-y-multidimensional-en-colombia-2019

Dominguez, C. (2019). Critical awareness of media and teacher education: An experience with Colombian ELT pre-service teachers. *Journal of Media Literacy Education, 11*(1), 32–51. https://doi.org/10.23860/JMLE-2019-11-1-2

Echeverri Sucerquia, P., & Pérez Restrepo, S. (2014). Making sense of critical pedagogy in L2 education through a collaborative study group. *Profile: Issues in Teachers' Professional Development, 16*(2), 171–184. https://doi.org/10.15446/profile.v16n2.38633

Esteban Nuñez, M. T. (2015). Exploring critical literacy skills in a literature and culture class. *Enletawa Journal, 7.* Retrieved from https://revistas.uptc.edu.co/revistas/index.php/enletawa_journal/article/view/3632

Freire, P., & Macedo, D. (1987). *Literacy: Reading the word and the world.* Bergin & Garvey.

Giraldo, F. (2018). Implementing critical literacy in A1 undergraduate students. *GIST—Education and Learning Research Journal, 16*, 100–116. https://doi.org/10.26817/16925777.399

Gómez Jiménez, M., & Gutierrez, C. (2019). Engaging English as a Foreign Language students in critical literacy practices: The case of a teacher at a private university. *Profile: Issues in Teachers' Professional Development, 21*(1), 91–105. https://doi.org/10.15446/profile.v21n1.7137

Gómez Rodríguez, L. F. (2017). Reading the world: Increasing English learners' global literacy through international news. *Lenguaje, 45*(2), 305–329. https://doi.org/10.25100/lenguaje.v45i2.5274

Granados-Beltrán, C. (2018). Revisiting the need for critical research in undergraduate Colombian English Language Teaching. *HOW Journal, 25*(1), 174–193. https://doi.org/10.19183/how.25.1.355

Gutierrez, C. P. (2015). beliefs, attitudes, and reflections of EFL pre-service teachers when exploring critical literacy theories to prepare and implement critical lessons. *Colombian Applied Linguistics Journal, 17*(2), 179–192. https://doi.org/10.14483/udistrital.jour.calj.2015.2.a01

Hernández Varona, W., & Gutiérrez Álvarez, D. (2020). English language student-teachers developing agency through community-based pedagogy projects. *Profile: Issues in Teachers' Professional Development, 22*(1), 109–122. https://doi.org/10.15446/profile.v22n1.76925

Kern, G. (2017). Opening a window to the world: Content-Based Instruction, cultural capital and critical pedagogy in an undergraduate EFL teaching program. *Matices en Lenguas Extranjeras, 11*, 154–172. https://doi.org/10.15446/male.n11.71858

Lara-Páez, M. (2017). Critical analysis of advertising: Enhancing identity construction in EFL classrooms. *Enletawa Journal, 10*(1), 27–42. Retrieved from https://revistas.uptc.edu.co/index.php/enletawa_journal/article/view/8668

Mojica, C. (2007). Exploring children's cultural perceptions through tasks based on films in an afterschool program. *Colombian Applied Linguistics Journal, 9*, 7–24. https://doi.org/10.14483/22487085.3143

Mojica, C., & Castañeda-Peña, H. (2017). A learning experience of the gender perspective in English teaching contexts. *Profile: Issues in Teachers' Professional Development, 19*(1), 139–153. https://doi.org/10.15446/profile.v19n1.56209

Moncada Linares, S. (2016). Othering: Towards a critical cultural awareness in the language classroom. *HOW Journal, 23*(1), 129–146. https://doi.org/10.19183/how.23.1.157

Mora, R. A. (2014a). Critical literacy as policy and advocacy: Lessons from Colombia. *Journal of Adolescent & Adult Literacy, 58*(1). 16–18. https://doi.org/10.1002/jaal.329

Mora, R. A. (2014b). Transmediality. *LSLP Micro-Papers, 14.* Retrieved from www.literaciesinl2project.org/uploads/3/8/9/7/38976989/lslp-micro-paper-14-transmediality.pdf

Mora, R. A., Campano, G., Thomas, E. E., Stornaiuolo, A., Monea, B., Thakurta, A., & Coleman, J. J. (2020). Decentering and decentralizing literacy studies: An urgent call for our field. *Research in the Teaching of English, 54*(4), 313–317.

Mora, R. A., Cañas, C., Rosas Chávez, P., Rocha, C. H., & Maciel, R. F. (2020). In Dialogue: Latin America. *Research in the Teaching of English, 54*(4), 439–451.

Mora, R. A., Chiquito, T., & Zapata, J. D. (2019). Bilingual education policies in Colombia: Seeking relevant and sustainable frameworks for meaningful minority inclusion. In B. G. G. Johannessen (Ed.), *Bilingual education: Politics, policies, and practices in a globalized society* (pp. 55–77). Springer. https://doi.org/10.1007/978-3-030-05496-0_4

Ortega, Y. (2019). "Teacher, ¿puedo hablar en español?" A reflection on plurilingualism and translanguaging practices in EFL. *Profile: Issues in Teachers' Professional Development, 21*(2), 155–170. https://doi.org/10.15446/profile.v21n2.74091

Pandya, J. Z. (2019). In the weeds: Critical literacy conversations with Allan Luke. *Curriculum Inquiry, 49*(2), 191–202. https://doi.org/10.1080/03626784.2019.1584732

Piñeros Pedraza, C., & Quintero Polo, Á. (2006). Conceptualizing as regards educational change and pedagogical knowledge: How novice teacher-researchers' proposals illustrate this relationship. *Profile: Issues in Teachers' Professional Development, 7*(1), 173–186. Retrieved from https://revistas.unal.edu.co/index.php/profile/article/view/11007

Rincón, J., & Clavijo-Olarte, A. (2016). Fostering EFL learners' literacies through local inquiry in a multimodal experience. *Colombian Applied Linguistics Journal, 18*(2), 67–82. https://doi.org/10.14483/calj.v18n2.10610

Samacá Bohórquez, Y. (2012). On rethinking our classrooms: A critical pedagogy view. *HOW Journal, 19*(1), 194–208. Retrieved from www.howjournalcolombia.org/index.php/how/article/view/46

Trigos-Carrillo, L. (2019a). A critical sociocultural perspective on academic literacies in Latin America. *Íkala, Revista de Lenguaje y Cultura, 24*(1), 13–26. https://doi.org/10.17533/udea.ikala.v24n01a10

Trigos-Carrillo, L. (2019b), Community cultural wealth and literacy capital in Latin American communities. *English Teaching: Practice & Critique, 19*(1), 3–19. https://doi.org/10.1108/ETPC-05-2019-0071

Vargas Franco, A. (2015). Literacidad crítica y literacidades digitales: ¿una relación necesaria? (Una aproximación a un marco teórico para la lectura crítica). *Revista Folios, 42*, 139–160. Retrieved from www.redalyc.org/articulo.oa?id=3459/345938959009

Zárate, G. C., González Serrano, A., & Flórez Romero, R. (2015). La literacidad en la comunidad afrocolombia de Tumaco. *Forma y Función, 28*(2), 155–182. https://doi.org/10.15446/fyf.v28n2.53548

2.6

CRITICAL LITERACY IN INDIA

A Case for Critical and Postcritical Education

Radha Iyer and Sneha Subramaniam

Historical Legacy of Criticality in India

The centrality of critical thinking that was an essential aspect of India's ancient system of education was overtaken by the mass, rote-focused education of the colonial period as it systematically wiped out critical elements from indigenous education. Vedic traditions that spanned centuries in the BCE and well into the modern period advocated *Nyaya*, which, as a school of classical Indian philosophy, brought developments in epistemology, metaphysics, and logic. *Nyaya* centered around arguments based on critical reasoning and *pramana,* or "knowledge-source" that drew on perception and inference (Dasti & Philips, 2017, p. 5). Indeed, the *Nyaya Sutra* was focused on testimony based on the meaning of words and sentences and broadly linguistic categories (p. 138). Nevertheless, even though the ancient system was holistic and focused on high-level critical thinking, such education was selectively offered only to higher caste men. Higher castes, mainly men, were provided education about the material and spiritual world, and character building, discipline, vocational development, grammar, philosophy, metrics, medicine, painting, and music (Bhatta, 2009), while the common person's education dealt with learning practical, hands-on skills.

With the arrival of Islam in India in the seventh century, there were Islamic influences on education. However, the major shift came with British colonization that introduced Western education. Schooling for "ordinary" (read lower caste) children changed from vernacular language village schools to mass public education, and missionary schools that focused on character building with English as the medium of instruction. English teaching meant moral instruction was the focus of literacy efforts. Through this quasi-Christian religious emphasis, children learned obedience, modesty, and the acceptance of their station in society. On the other hand, the upper classes received education around classical languages that promoted inquiry and reflection (Kumar, 1989). As a result of the divisive nature of education, the ideal, ordinary Indian colonial citizen was trained to be subservient, and their education eliminated the prospects of criticality.

To worsen this situation, MacCaulay's (1835) infamous *Minute on Indian Education* emphasized the importance of English and, although bilingual education continued in schools resulting in a multilingual education system, English, as superior, acquired linguistic capital over the 222 vernacular languages recorded by the 1921 census (Government of India, 1921, p. 193). Further, under British colonialism, as Kumar (2014, p. 5) and Topdar (2015) argue, textbooks were mandatory and restrained any questioning from students. Post-independence, the Indian education system has remained faithful to prescribed texts eventuating in a "textbook culture" (Kumar, 1988, p. 452) that

 DOI: 10.4324/9781003023425-18

has endured to the present day. As Syeed (2018) observes, in the current education system, where authors of textbooks have represented real-life contexts, NCERT officials have opposed these as a "distorted representation of Indian diversity, and the over-reliance on constructivist approaches to teaching content" (p. 554).

Although critical thinking was introduced to the curriculum by the National Curriculum Framework (NCF, 2005), the overreliance on textbooks and rote learning (Harrell, 2019) negates learners as meaningful text analysts and critical thinkers. Postcolonial education has engaged in hybridized mimicry by continuing the overall colonial education system framework while retaining the vernacular system. The colonial educational framework has meant that the moral focus and a transactional classroom with teachers explaining, interpreting, and imposing meaning on children persists. Much of what prevails in schools is an authoritarian system that follows control and teacher dominance. Student-centered classrooms are generally absent; the teacher does not take on the role of a "critical educator "(McLaren, 1992, p. 8) who can help students acquire a language of reflection and critique the dominant discourses. Subsequently, the education system positions children as passive receptacles taught to follow instead of as thinking individuals with a capacity to be meaning-makers, text participants, and text analysts.

Within this rather morbid landscape, Indian education, as the second-largest education system, attempts to provide uniform education across the country while attending to children's cultural and social needs Ministry of Human Resource Development (MHRD, 2017–2018). In 2009, the landmark bill of *The Right of Children to Free and Compulsory Education* Act (RTE) was passed, thereby granting free and compulsory education to all children between the ages of six and 14. Government schools now see unprecedented enrollment. All private schools have a 25% RTE quota, granting children of low socioeconomic status from the nearby vicinities access to primary schooling.

Nevertheless, 11 years into the systemic universalization of education, children from lower socioeconomic backgrounds continue year after year in the school system without gaining a sound education. The RTE Act and the *National Early Childhood Care and Education* (ECCE) Policy in 2013 raised awareness of the dire state of illiteracy among young children. Although school enrollment increased, many preschool children are not enrolled in schools, the dropout rate has been consistently high, and literacy rates in early primary years have remained below average National Council of Education, Research and Training (NCERT, 2019). The state of Kerala is at the top with 93.91% overall literacy and 91.98% female literacy, with such as Arunachal Pradesh, Jharkhand, and Bihar among states below the national average both in the overall rate and female literacy. Besides, although RTE enhanced enrolment, there has not been a comparable focus on high-quality education (Mehendale, 2014, p. 88). In addition, given the shortage of principals, teachers, and administrative staff, along with a scarcity of resources and necessary infrastructure, the goal of achieving full literacy is a distant aim. Standards for learning outcomes are demonstrably low. Of particular concern are the discriminatory approaches to educating children of Dalits (also known as Scheduled Caste; untouchables in the caste system) and indigenous children (Scheduled Tribes).

In India, the *Annual Status of Education Report* (ASER, 2019), a nationwide household survey that evaluates students' learning across India in its report on Early Years, assessed the foundational skills of a representative sample of 36,930 children in the age group of 4–8 years. It found that almost half of four-year-old and a quarter of five-year-old children from low socioeconomic backgrounds perform lower on cognitive ability and foundational ability assessments than children enrolled in private kindergartens (ASER, 2019, p. 48). ASER (2018) reported that of all children enrolled in Std. VIII about 73% can read a Std. II text and ASER (2019) reported that 50.8% children in Std.III can read a Std. I level text. These are the impoverished foundations on which the present-day Indian youth attempt to build their lives and livelihoods.

Within such a system, the opportunities for critical thinking and critical literacy are low or absent. Since the liberalization of the economy in 1991, the knowledge economy's neoliberal agenda has refined the commodification of education with elite schools focusing on market profitability through education. However, the discourse of (read customer-focused) education draws little on children's real-world experiences and primarily operates in the neocolonial mode of teacher-controlled pedagogies (Kumar, 2014). Although there are a sizeable number of private sector and elite schools that presumably apply critical thinking and critical literacy, it is otherwise generally absent from public schools.

Literacy and Critical Literacy

Although, as we have argued, critical reflection and critical debates had been an essential aspect of ancient Indian education, neocolonial mass education requires decolonization. The current neocolonial approach to literacy is noncritical acceptance of the textbook as the source of knowledge and exclusion of critical reflection that would enable meaningful text analysis.

Literacy as a meaning-making process is the ability to examine a text through a critical lens and question, appreciate, and make meaning with texts of all forms, whether written, oral, symbolic, or visual (Luke & Freebody, 1999; Luke, 2000/2018). As a social practice, critical literacy aims to provide contextual agency and power to the learner by being situated within the social and cultural contexts (see Luke & Freebody, 1999). Further, it is a constant iterative process with fluid, meaning potential (Iyer, 2007), that aims to unearth ideological positionings in texts and work toward a transformative politics (Iyer, 2007; see also McLaren & Lankshear, 1993). As Comber (2013) observes, critical literacy is "an evolving repertoire of practices of analysis and interrogation which move between the micro features of texts and the macro conditions of institutions, focusing on how relations of power work through these practices" (p. 589).

Morrell (2007) discusses critical literacy as a "pedagogy of access and dissent" (p. 237) that illustrates how language and power are interrelated and foregrounds people's interests in power and privilege. Morrell (2007) argues that by examining texts, there is a possibility of exposing and arriving at a socially just order. Lankshear (1994) observes that besides a critical perspective on texts, critical literacy provides "critical readings of wider *social practices, arrangements, relations, allocations, procedures*" (p. 10, emphasis in the original; see also Mulcahy, 2008). However, the current Indian education system, still primarily textbook-focused, has had little scope for examining broader social practices that inform texts.

A significant issue due to the overreliance on textbooks is students' unquestioned exposure to non-secular, inequitable, and ideological representations promoted by non-CBSE (Central Board of Secondary Education) schools. Further, textbooks constrain the students to basic understanding and deny them the opportunity to critically engage with the content, a tool kit that enables learners to unpack texts and social institutions where these texts are situated (Luke, 2000/2018). The textbook culture (Kumar, 1988, p. 452) results in dominant forms of literacy that "serve as a process of colonization," (McLaren, 1992, p. 12) which is especially salient in the problematic issue of local languages in schools that we now discuss.

The Systemic and Sociocultural Macrocosm

A typical scenario in public schools is of a six-year-old who enters Grade One with limited print exposure at home. More than 60% of the 30,000 children assessed across five states in Grades Two and Four come from families where no adult woman has ever been to school, and more than 50% of children have absolutely no print materials available at home (Bhattacharjea, Wadhwa, & Banerji, 2011). Therefore, it is worth concluding that the six-year-old's experience resonates with tens of millions of Indian children who depend on schools to introduce them to print literacy.

According to the *Language* paper by the Census of India (2011 p. 4), a raw count of mother-tongue languages resulted in 19569 languages. These languages are artificially "rationalised" (Jinghran, 2009,

p. 264) into 121 language groups. Of the 270 mother tongues across the country, only 17 are considered as a medium of instruction in primary schools (NCERT, 2002). Grouping and subsuming entire dialects, languages, and cultures under broader artificial categories, often defined in non-linguistic terms, leads to children's languages being rejected in the school. Regional languages are usually entirely different from the child's home language (Menon et al., 2017; Mohanty et al., 2009; Panda, 2004), leading to incomprehension and low literacy in children from low socioeconomic backgrounds.

The question is, then, whether this changes through the process of schooling. Studies that have examined teachers' beliefs about language hierarchy and the validity of students' cultural identities reveal that teachers consider the medium of instruction to be "correct" and "pure" (Menon et al., 2017). In contrast, children's languages are dismissed as "incorrect," "impure," and irrelevant (Menon et al., 2017, p. 96–101). Power dynamics and the need for "efficiency" in developing generalizable state education strategies and curricula further entrench the child in a quagmire of alienation and marginalization.

A Snapshot of the Classroom

The Literacy Research in Indian Languages (LiRIL, Menon et al., 2017) study sponsored by Tata trusts and collaborators QUEST, Kalikae, and Azim Premji University engaged in a five year longitudinal project in Wada in Maharashtra and Yadgir in Karnataka, to comprehend how primary school literacy is taught in two underprivileged regional sites in India, with two different regional languages: Marathi and Kannada. The study found that literacy within the early years of learning is almost entirely focused on rote and decoding practices. Children are taught alphabets and must write these individual letters in their notebooks repeatedly. The study concluded the urgent need to equip teachers with pedagogy that models comprehension, promotes oral communication, pedagogy that is "sensitized to the real-world context of learners", and promotes joyful learning (p. 132).

In the recently revamped curriculum adopted in three states, joyful learning (Sarva Skhiksha Abhiyan, Karnataka, 2014) and self-driven learning are promoted; therefore, children are taught symbols, or letters, in segmented groups. However, the first words children learn are more often words that are based on complex Sanskritized vocabulary. Subsequently, children's first written words are complex vocabulary that they do not understand. Children are found to be silently copying these words and symbols into their exercise books (Subramaniam et al., 2017b). Vowel sounds are taught almost one year later in the program which implies that children are unable to form words that have meaning for them until they reach Grade Two.

Sinha (2012) observes that comprehension is often disregarded in schools where the primary focus is decoding. Comprehension based on critical thinking is lost with oversimplification of texts based on explanation and paraphrasing of the text by the teacher that erodes the coherence, meaning, and interest in the content. The LiRIL study similarly found that teachers read the stories in textbooks to children and followed the *samjhana* [explanatory] method (Subramaniam et al., 2017a); as teachers read a story, they explained each sentence and its meaning to the child. Even with stories written in the medium of instruction, teachers had to simplify and explain because the children could not comprehend the content due to the highly Sanskritized and standardized language. The explanatory method is a common practice in present-day schools in India; there is no consideration that children may not be able to make their meaning of the language. Therefore, children are not equipped to develop critical comprehension. Stories are considered worthy of being in the curriculum because they are moralistic in content. Even when a story is intelligible to children, its relatability to the child's life and imagination is often negligible.

Children's lives as they know them are to be left outside the classroom door as they are compelled to submerge themselves in a language they do not understand, which makes them feel deficient. The

LiRiL study (Menon et al., 2017) provides case studies of three children and concludes that while these children were knowledgeable in their home environment and were responsible individuals who knew their communities, at school, they were considered incapable. In this way, within the classroom environment, children are robbed of their mode of thinking, expressing, sharing, communicating, knowing, and being. The school is linguistically, practically, and socioculturally devoid of the child's real world, just as the child, in school, is devoid of his/her identity.

Systemic Efforts in Literacy

Alarmed by the low literacy rates that continue to prevail post–RTE and the re-visioning of the system, including consideration of the enormous resources that it entailed, a series of systemic overhauls to address students' poor learning outcomes have been instituted. The NCERT (2017) provides the following learning outcomes: a child in Class One "identifies characters and sequence of a story and asks questions about the story" (page 25), in Grade Two "expresses verbally her or his opinion and asks questions about the characters, storyline, etc., in English or home language" (p. 26) or in Grade Five "connects ideas that he/she has inferred, through reading and interaction, with his/her personal experiences" (p. 30) and, in English, at the Upper Primary level a student is expected to "use his/her critical/thinking faculty to read between the lines and go beyond the text" (p. 33). However, the content in textbooks more often than not reflect dominant ideologies that do not cater to the needs of marginalized children (Bhattacharya, 2019; Syeed, 2018) and the development of thinking as promoted by the NCERT Learning Outcomes (2017). As the Central Advisory Board of Education (CABE) committee of MHRD (2005) reports, textbooks have an uneven focus where state and non-government school textbooks have "naturalized inequalities of caste, class, and gender" (p. i).

Early childhood language curricula across several states have been completely redesigned, favoring self-driven learning and learning-by-doing approaches (Nali Kali, 1995; see also Gowda et al., 2013). Teachers have subsequently been trained to learn how to use the new curricular materials or allow children to engage with the materials independently. While well-intentioned and massive in scale, these efforts have fallen short of their goals for the very reason that this top-down approach has instituted educational reform procedures without taking account of teachers and their pedagogical practices. Elite private schools are no better when it is a concern with literacy. As one school advertises on its website, the pedagogy is multidimensional and promotes flexibility, which gives the learner ample opportunities to explore and discover. Analytic skills are nurtured in such schools. However, critical literacy, as practiced in countries like Australia and Canada, is not followed.

Teacher preparation programs continue to be lacking in terms of language and literacy pedagogy. For example, establishing the importance of sociocultural contexts that informs every child's learning is still not covered in teacher training programs. Although teacher education has been overhauled, teacher training programs typically fail to build on ideas of literacy aims, in terms of *why* we teach language, and the study of multiple approaches to literacy pedagogy (Menon & Thirumalai, 2016).

Subsequently, critical thinking and criticality of the word and the world are unchartered territories in state-run teacher education programs in India. In an extensive empirical study on critical literacy for teacher trainees conducted in India in November 2009, the researcher (Iyer, 2010) found that the participants agreed that rote learning would not develop critical thinking. They acknowledged that a move beyond traditional modes of learning meant meaning-making and active participation with texts in a critical manner.

However, they reiterated the importance of textbook literacy and rote learning as advantages worth considering in the mass education system with a standardized examination system. The participants emphasized the importance of critical literacy yet were aware of the power dynamics involved in developing critical literacy. As some noted, critique does exist in the form of reflective thinking (Iyer, 2010; Zacher et al., 2014). Similar to research by Menon et al. (2017), this study indicates that teachers need to be trained to engage with critical literacy; curricular revisions and reform measures would not create a sustainable impact on the classroom unless situated in teacher professional development. In the recent National Policy on Education (2020), claims have been made on teaching languages through experiential pedagogies, through apps, and by weaving the cultural aspect through links to the theatre, films, poetry, and music. Much remains to be seen as to how these approaches will enable critical literacy.

Steps Toward Critical Literacy: In the Field and Academia

Academics and practitioners confronted with the vast and complex issues affecting children's literacy development in India have understood the irrelevance and potential harm of schooling when constructed as moral and vocational training ignoring the learner's intelligence and culture. Sinha (2019), for instance, advocates a fluid and collaborative literacy pedagogy where critical comprehension is considered to be central. Work toward critical literacy currently centers around pockets of pedagogical repositioning aimed at making schooling socioculturally relevant. Many researchers and organizations are working toward this. The *Organisation for Early Literacy Promotion* (OELP) https://www.oelp.org (OELP) has pioneered the *varna-samooha* method. It has a structure of teaching the 50+ alphasyllabaries of Indian languages based on children being able to use familiar, everyday language (Jayaram, 2008). Rather than learning the symbols in Indian languages all at once, this grouping of symbols is based on introducing children to the symbols found in emotionally charged, high-frequency words. Matras, or vowel symbols, are taught from the very beginning, so that word composition and meaning-making remain the focus of sound–symbol correspondence. With this introduction to print, children encounter decoding as meaning-makers from the outset of their schooling experience.

Researchers (Panda & Mohanty, 2009) undertook ethnographic studies of communities in order to structure educational programs around community funds of knowledge. These programs analyzed communities' histories, practices, and cultures to determine the development of curricular materials and ways to anchor pedagogy and concept formation in culture. Their study found that bilingual/multilingual education programs that focus on the child's language and culture in the classroom have their students showing significant gains in achievement compared to traditional school programs (See also Mohanty, 2010). Non profit organizations like *Language and Learning Foundation* (Languageandlearning foundation.org) partners with state governments to develop multilingual education (MLE) programs across six states. Instruction draws on additive bilingualism and is in the children's home language in the early grades. Instruction includes reading big books that the organization creates using community folklore and knowledge, which subsequently enriches the experiences of school-age children with cultural knowledge.

Academic institutions such as the Azim Premji University, a private university in Karnataka, have reoriented their institutional work in teacher education, with programs that focus explicitly on early years' literacy (APU, 2021). The Azim Premji Foundation works with state governments in teacher education with field institutes across 46 districts in six states, offering academic guidance to develop public school teachers' understanding of literacy and literacy pedagogy. The Tata Institute of Social Sciences began an Early Literacy Initiative that sought to use longitudinal literacy research to educate practitioners about why literacy development remains low and to advocate more effective pedagogies (TISS, 2017). Through resource material and courses, more teachers are enabled to be aware of children's sociocultural knowledge and create meaningful courses in literacy.

Work toward making classrooms culturally relevant by focusing on curriculum, pedagogy, and teacher education is happening in small pockets and vast NGO outputs across the country. An example of a micro interventionist practice in Haryana, a state in India, by Sahani (2001) illustrates how her work with two children led to them being able to form narratives, acquire symbolic power, and create symbolic worlds (p. 27). Sahani (2001) argues that redefining critical literacy as creative literacy is required to reconceptualize schooling for young children in India's poverty-ridden areas, as it would empower them.

A Way Forward

Although there is some level of critical thinking encouraged within language and literature classrooms, critical literacy as a means of uncovering power, comprehending sociopolitical context, and unpacking ideologies of gender and caste is largely absent. While private, international, IGCSE (International General Certificate of Secondary Education), University of Cambridge-affiliated elite schools develop critical thinking through English Language and English Literature, neocolonial approaches constrain public schools to develop essential reading and writing skills. There is little in terms of examining the issues of ideologies and power present in texts and discourses. NGO-supported schools and alternative schools focus their curricular and formal pedagogical efforts on establishing meaning, thereby making the language classroom and school experience relevant. Critical thinking discussions occur more through informal, reciprocal discussions in these spaces. Students are encouraged to discuss experiences, problems, and issues they face in "circle time" mediated by the teaching faculty. Issues of caste, religion, gender, experiences of discrimination are discussed through these conversations. Teachers ensure that this stems from children voicing their concerns, but such discussions draw on textbook-focused content. Therefore, these efforts typically preclude the activist principles that are advocated by critical literacy, and as Comber and Nixon (2009) observe, such literacy practices reaffirm the dominant ideologies and "bureaucratic demands" (p. 334). Literacy practices that reaffirm dominant ideologies can only be countered if there is a greater focus on meaning-making and text analysis of prescribed texts and as Sinha (2012) observes, adequate attention is paid to "critical education" as a means to promote equity in a democratic society.

Developing socio-cultural awareness in students as a means of critical engagement remains the next step toward critical literacy. At a systemic level, with curricula and pedagogy that emphasizes decoding the text, ensuring that students are equipped to construct meaning is now of national concern. In the recent National Education Policy (MHRD, 2020), higher-order cognitive capacities of critical thinking and problem-solving have been reiterated (p. 4). The policy affirms the importance of conceptual understanding and "to make space for critical thinking and more holistic, inquiry-based, discovery-based, discussion-based, and analysis-based learning" (p. 12).

Meaning-making and critical analysis appear to be almost lofty ideals to many practitioners countenanced with students' debilitating literacy scores. However, these resources must be developed in tandem with meaning-making, building on sociocultural awareness strongholds. As McLaren and Lankshear (1993) state, the contextual historical processes of becoming literate need to be considered if literacy is to shift into productive text analysis. Critical and postcritical perceptions that unpack social injustices of a prescriptive literacy system that privilege some texts and discourses in education are required. We need to question the "historical origins" of practices and "whose interests are served by them " (Anderson & Irvine, 1993, p. 94). The postcritical lens (Iyer, 2007) that is an iterative process is needed on how difference has been and continues to be subjected to marginalization in and through discourses.

Teacher training needs to take account of the subjectivities of students and comprehend the importance of social justice. Significantly, pedagogical practices need to decolonize from being textbook-oriented and teacher-controlled to teacher-facilitated discussions on real-world "texts" surrounding children. As Bhattacharya (2019) observes, textbooks need to be carefully examined to determine their suitability to all children and where it is not possible to use appropriate textbooks, teachers should "incorporate additional supplementary material for their students" (p. 676).

Alternative texts like the graphic novel, *Bhimayana*, promote discussion of socio-cultural and political issues such as caste and human rights (see Nayar, 2012) and need to be incorporated into teaching. As Majumdhar and Mooij (2011) observe, the current hierarchical control environment and a competitive meritocratic system needs to be dismantled. To achieve postcolonial, postcritical literacy (Iyer, 2007), as McLaren and Lankshear (1993, p. 415) insightfully state, "we need to make despair less salutary, and economic, social, racial, gender [and caste] equality politically conceivable and pedagogically possible."

References

Anderson, G. L., & Irvine, P. (1993). Informing critical literacy with ethnography. In C. Lankshear & P. L. McLaren (Eds.), *Critical literacy: Politics, praxis, and the postmodern* (pp. 81–104). SUNY Press.

APU. (2021). *Azim Premji foundation teacher education program.* Azim Premji University.

ASER. (2018). ASER 2018 (rural) findings. ASER Centre. Retrieved from http://img.asercentre.org/docs/ASER%202018/Release%20Material/aser2018nationalfindings.pdf

ASER. (2019). *Early years: National findings.* ASER Centre. Retrieved from https://img.asercentre.org/docs/ASER%202019/ASER2019%20report%20/nationalfindings.pdf

Bhatta, C. P. (2009). Holistic personality development through education: Ancient Indian cultural experiences. *Journal of Human Values, 15*(1), 49–59. https://doi.org/10.1177/097168580901500104

Bhattacharjea, S., Wadhwa, W., & Banerji, R. (2011). *Inside primary schools: A study of teaching and learning in rural India.* ASER.

Bhattacharya, U. (2019). My school is a big school: Imagined communities, inclusion, and ideology in Indian textbooks. *Journal of Curriculum Studies, 51* (5), 664–677, https://doi.org/10.1080/00220272.2019.1567822

Census of India (2011). *Language: India, states and union territories.* Office of the Registrar General, India. Retrieved from https://censusindia.gov.in/2011Census/C-16_25062018_NEW.pdf

Comber, B. (2013). Critical literacy in the early years: Emergence and sustenance in an age of accountability. In J. Larson & J. Marsh (Eds.), *The SAGE handbook of early childhood literacy* (pp. 587–601). Sage.

Comber, B., & Nixon, H. (2009). Teachers' work and pedagogy in an era of accountability, *Discourse: Studies in the Cultural Politics of Education, 30*(3), 333–345. https://doi.org/10.1080/01596300903037069

Dasti, M., & Philips, S. (2017). *The Nyaya- sutra: Selections with early commentaries.* Hackett Publishing Company.

Government of India. (1921). *Census of India, 1921: Volume 1. South Asia open archives.* Retrieved from https://www.jstor.org/stable/pdf/saoa.crl.25394120.pdf?refreqid=excelsior%3Aa81d6350b965191bd1eb1a5b72942554

Governement of India. (2009). *The Right of Children to Free and Compulsory Education Act.* Retrieved https://www.education.gov.in/sites/upload_files/mhrd/files/document-reports/RTEAct.pdf

Gowda, K., Kochar, A., Closepet, N., & Raghunathan, N. (2013). Curriculum Change and Early Learning: An Evaluation of an Activity Based Learning Program in Karnataka, India. Working papers no. 475. Stanford University. Retrieved from https://siepr.stanford.edu/sites/default/files/publications/475wp_0.pdf

Harrell, L. (2019). *Racing the legacies of the past: The development of student subjectivity in contemporary Indian secondary school education* (Doctoral thesis). Auckland University of Technology. Retrieved from http://openrepository.aut.ac.nz/bitstream/handle /10292/13494/Thesis- Final Version.pdf

Iyer, R. (2007). Negotiating critical, postcritical literacy: The problematic of text analysis. *Literacy, 41*(3), 161–168. https://doi.org/10.1111/j.1467-9345.2007.00451.x

Iyer, R. (2010). Literacy models across nations: Literacy and critical literacy in teacher training programs in India. *Procedia: Social and Behavioral Sciences, 2*(2), 4424–4428. https://doi.org/10.1016/j.sbspro.2010.03.705

Jayaram, K. (2008). Early literacy project—explorations and reflections, Part II: Interventions in Hindi classrooms. *Contemporary Education Dialogue, 5*(2), 175–212. https://doi.org/10.1177/0973184913411166

Jhingran, D. (2009). Hundreds of home languages in the country and many in most classrooms: Coping with diversity in education in India. In T. Skutnabb-Kangas, R. Phillipson, A. K. Mohanty, & M. Panda (Eds.), *Multilingual education for social justice: Globalising the local* (pp. 250–267). Orient Longman.

Kumar, K. (1988). Origins of India's "textbook culture. *Comparative Education Review, 32*(4), 452–464.

Kumar, K. (1989). Colonial citizen as an educational ideal. Economic ad Political Weekly, 24(4), PE45- PE51.https://www.jstor.org/stable/4394308

Kumar, K. (2014). *Politics of education in colonial India.* Routledge. Retrieved from https://doi-org.ezp01.library.qut.edu.au/10.4324/9781315656625

Language and Learning Foundation. Retrieved from https:// languageandlearningfoundation. org/

Lankshear, C. (1994). *Critical literacy*. Occasional paper No. 3. Belconnen, Act: Australian Curriculum Studies Association Inc.

Luke, A. (2000/2018). Critical literacy in Australia: A matter of context and standpoint. In A. Luke (Ed.), *Critical literacy schooling and social justice: Selected works of Allan Luke* (pp. 168–188). Routledge.

Luke, A., & Freebody, P. (1999). A map of possible practices: Further notes on the 'four resources' model. *Practically Primary, 4*(2), 5–8.

Macaulay, T. B. (1835). Minute on education. http:// www. columbia. edu/itc/ mealac/ pritchett/00generallinks/ macaulay/txt_minute_education_1835.html

Majumdar, M., & Mooij, J. (2011). *Education and inequality in India: A classroom view*. Routledge.

McLaren, P. (1992/1993). Critical literacy and postcolonial praxis: A Freirian perspective. *College Literature, 19*(3)/20 (1), 7-27.

McLaren, P. L., & Lankshear, C. (1993). Critical literacy and the postmodern turn. In C. Lankshear & P. L. Mclaren (Eds.), *Critical literacy: Politics, praxis, and the postmodern turn* (pp. 379–419). SUNY Press.

Mehendale, A. (2014). The question of "quality" in education: Does the RTE Act provide an answer? *Journal of International Cooperation in Education, 16* (2), pp.87 -103.

Menon, S., Krishnamurthy, R., Sajitha, S., Apte, N., Basargekar, A., Subramaniam, S., & Modugala, M. (2017). *Literacy research in Indian languages (LiRIL): Report of a three-year longitudinal study on early reading and writing in Marathi and Kannada*. Azim Premji University and Tata Trusts.

Menon, S., & Thirumalai, B. (2016). Curricular materials in early language and literacy classrooms in Karnataka and Maharashtra. In D. Nawani (Ed.), *Teaching- learning resources for school education* (pp. 394–404). Sage.

Ministry of Human Resource Development (MHRD). (2005). *Regulatory mechanisms for textbooks and parallel textbooks taught in schools outside the government system: A Report*. Central Advisory Board of Education, Government of India.

Ministry of Human Resource Development (MHRD). (2018). *Performance grading index (PGI) 2017–2018*. Retrieved from www.unicef.org/india/media/2596/file/Catalysing-transformational-change-in-school-education.pdf

Ministry of Human Resource Development (MHRD). (2020). National education policy. Ministry of Human Resource Development, Government of India. Retrieved from https://www.education.gov.in/sites/ upload_files/mhrd/files/NEP_Final_English_0.pdf

Ministry of Women and Child Development. (2013). National early childhood care and education (ECCE) policy. Retrieved from https://wcd.nic.in/sites/default/files/National%20Early%20Childhood%20Care%20 and%20Education-Resolution.pdf

Mohanty, A. K. (2010). Languages, inequality and marginalization: Implications of the double divide in Indian multilingualism. *International Journal of the Sociology of Language, 205*(2010), 131–154. https://doi. org/10.1515/IJSL.2010.042

Mohanty, A. K., Mishra, M. K., Reddy, N. U., & Gumidyala, R. (2009). Overcoming the language barrier for tribal children: MLE in Andhra Pradesh and Orissa, India. In A. K. Mohanty., M. Panda., R. Phillipson & T. Skutnabb-Kangas (Eds.), *Multilingual education for social justice: Globalising the local* (pp. 278–291). Orient Longman.

Morrell, E. (2007). Critical literacy and popular culture in urban education: Toward a pedagogy of access and dissent. In C. Clark & M. Blackburn (Eds.), *Working with/in the local: New directions in literacy research for political action*. Peter Lang.

Mulcahy, C. M. (2008). The tangled web we weave: Critical literacy and critical thinking. *Counterpoints, 326*, 15–27. Retrieved from www.jstor.com/stable/42980102

Nali Kali. (1995). *A changing revolution (Joyful learning)*. Retrieved from http://ssakarnataka.gov.in/pdfs/int_lep/ nk_report.pdf

National Council of Education, Research and Training. (2005). National curriculum framework. NCERT. Retrieved from https://ncert.nic.in/pdf/nc-framework/nf2005-english.pdf

National Council of Education Research and Training. (2002). *7th all India school education survey*. NCERT.

National Council of Education Research and Training. (2017). *Learning outcomes at the elementary stage*. NCERT.

National Council of Education Research and Training. (2019). *A report on the situational analysis of DM schools and designing of a model preschool (Phase II)*. NCERT. Retrieved from https://ncert.nic.in/dee/pdf/Phase-II_report.pdf

Nayar, P. (2012). Towards a postcolonial critical literacy: Bhimayana and the Indian graphic novel. *Studies in South Asian Film and Media, 3*(1), 3–21. https://doi.org.ezp01.library.qut.edu.au/10.1386/safm.3.1.3_1

Panda, M. (2004). Culture and mathematics: A case study of Saoras. In K. Chanana (Ed.), *Transformative links between higher education and basic education: Mapping the field* (pp. 119–132). Sage.

Panda, M., & Mohanty, A. K. (2009). Language matters, so does culture: Beyond the rhetoric of culture in multilingual education. In T. Skutnabb-Kangas, R. Phillipson, A. K. Mohanty, & M. Panda (Eds.), *Social justice through multilingual education* (pp. 301–319). Multilingual Matters.

Sahani, U. (2001). Children appropriating literacy. In B. Comber & A. Simpson (Eds.), *Negotiating critical literacies in classrooms* (pp. 19–36). Lawrence Erlbaum Associates.

Sarva Skhiksha Abhiyan Karnataka. (2014). *Annual report 2013–14.* Retrieved from http://ssakarnataka.gov.in/pdfs/media_doc/AREng1314.pdf

Sinha, S. (2012). Reading without meaning: The dilemma of Indian classrooms. *Language and Language Teaching, 1*(1), 22–26.

Sinha, S. (2019). Early literacy instruction in India. In N. Spaull & J. P. Comings (Eds.), *Improving literacy outcomes: Curriculum, teaching and assessment* (pp. 101–118). Brill. https://doi.org/10.1163/9789004402379

Subramaniam, S., Menon, S., & Sajitha, S. (2017a). *Comprehension. The teachers' guide to literacy research.* Azim Premji University.

Subramaniam, S., Menon, S., & Sajitha, S. (2017b). *Children's writing. The teachers' guide to literacy research.* Azim Premji University.

Syeed, E. (2018). Conflict between covers: Confronting official curriculum in Indian textbooks, *Curriculum Inquiry, 48*(5), 540–559. https://doi.org/10.1080/03626784.2018.1546099

Tata Institute of Social Sciences. (2017). *Early literacy initiative.* Retrieved from http://eli.tiss.edu/

Topdar, S. (2015). Duties of a 'good citizen': Colonial secondary school textbook policies in late nineteenth-century India. *South Asian History and Culture, 6*(3), 417–439. https://doi.org/10.1080/19472498.2015.1030877

Zacher Pandya, J., & Avila (Eds.). (2014). *Moving critical literacies forward: A new look at praxis across contexts.* Routledge.

2.7

CRITICAL LITERACIES IN INDONESIA

Zulfa Sakhiyya and Christianti Tri Hapsari

Landscape of Indonesia

Indonesia is the world's largest archipelagic country with more than 17,000 islands inhabited by more than 280 million people of 200 ethnicities and 500–700 spoken local languages (Sakhiyya & Martin-Anatias, 2020). The country's education system is immensely complex; it ranks the fourth in size after China, India, and the United States accommodating more than 50 million students, 2.6 million teachers in more than 250,000 schools, and more than 3,700 higher education institutions. This rich diversity and large educational infrastructure pose specific challenges regarding access to education. Indonesia's post-authoritarian condition magnifies this problem, where the excess of authoritarianism remains, actively shaping education in general even after the fall of the authoritarian New Order government in 1998 (Heryanto & Hadiz, 2005; Power, 2018). The terrible genius of the New Order administration lay not only in the use of bureaucratic control to undermine knowledge institutions (Guggenheim, 2012) but also the suppression of practices of critical literacies, that is, critical thinking and freedom of expression in educational institutions and public spaces (Heryanto, 2003).

This chapter focuses on the contested notion of "literacy" as defined by the government and as negotiated by grassroots literacy communities. The focus on the locus of literacy practices allows us to distinguish between "formal literacy" and "local literacies". The former assumes an autonomous model of literacy located in formal schooling and organized formally by the government, whereas the latter views literacy as social practices at the grassroots level. In the 1970s, the national literacy program was organized solely to improve literacy rates. "Literacy" as defined by the New Order government is the ability to read and write a particular script, in this case Bahasa Indonesia script. Despite the rise of the literacy rate which has reached up to 92.8% in 2011 (Tobias, Wales, Syamsulhakim, & Suharti, 2014), Indonesia remains the lowest among 61 countries surveyed on reading interests (Miller & McKenna, 2016). UNESCO further recorded that only 0.001% of the total population had reading interests (UNESCO, 2012). This gap means that formal literacy as indicated by the improvement in the literacy rate does not necessarily correspond with the advancement of reading interests and possession of critical thinking.

By reflecting on the case of Indonesia, this chapter offers insights about the importance of critical literacies in post-authoritarian Indonesia. This is done by highlighting the dynamic relationship between the state's formalized definition of literacy or 'formal literacy' and rising local literacies as enacted/practiced by grassroot communities. The questions central to this chapter are: How are

DOI: 10.4324/9781003023425-19

those literacies negotiated vis-à-vis the grassroot literacies in response to formal literacy? How does our academic engagement with those literacies move us toward more just outcomes for marginalized communities?

Historical Trajectories of Literacy in Indonesia

This section traces the historical trajectories of Indonesian educational policies and the impacts they have on the shifting state of literacy in Indonesia. Although the notion of literacy is conceptualized beyond schooling and pedagogy in this chapter, it is important to recognize that literacy practices are embedded within these educational institutions (Street, 1995) and that the notion of "literacy" is contested.

Early literacy practices in Indonesia, which can be categorized as mass literacy education, can be seen as beginning in about the sixteenth century in the form of local Islamic groups of learning called *pesantren* (Nakamura & Nishino, 1995; Pringle, 2010). Delivered in local languages (mostly Javanese), oral and informal in nature, *pesantren* provided basic religious knowledge about Islam and provided practice in reading sacred texts (Qur'an and Hadith), in the study of Islamic jurisprudence (*fikh*), and foreign language studies (Arabic). Although it is less structured as compared to the modern educational model introduced by the Dutch colonial government, *pesantren* is a literacy practice locally rooted in Indonesian soil long before the arrival of colonizers (Bruinessen, 1994).

During the nineteenth and twentieth centuries, Indonesia was colonized by some European countries (Portugal, Spain, France, England, and the Netherlands) and Japan. The modern secular education system was introduced by the Dutch colonial government as a consequence of the Ethical Policy in 1920s. However, it did not contribute to the literacy of the populace. Formal literacy, as conceptualized and taught by the Dutch colonial government as the ability to read and write, was designed only for the Eurasian and Indonesian urban elite (Lowenberg, 2000). It was aimed to produce *ambtenaars*, Indonesian elite whose jobs were to assist the colonial government in low-level administration and bureaucracy (Kell & Kell, 2014). Up to 1930, there were only 106 indigenous students enrolled in Dutch colonial schools (Yulaelawati, 2009). This formal literacy schooling was exclusive as compared to local literacies practiced by 1127 *pesantren* located in Java, Madura, and Sumatra (Penders, 1977). By the end of Dutch colonialism, most Indonesians remained illiterate (Lowenberg, 2000) as measured by their ability to read and write in any scripts or languages (only 6.4%).

In reconstructing the nation after independence in 1945, under Sukarno's leadership (1945–1965), Indonesia faced enormous problems related to illiteracy rates, the national language, textbooks, large population, financial resources, infrastructure, teachers, and educational administrators (Kell & Kell, 2014). Literacy in Indonesia gradually progressed from 9% in 1951 to 39% in 1961 (UNESCO, 1974).

During Soeharto's so-called New Order administration (1966–1998), literacy was synonymous with academic performance. The meaning of literacy was reduced to the ability to read and write as expected in formal education. During the New Order administration, the literacy rate improved from 56.6% in 1971, to 69.3% in 1980, and to 83.7% in 1990 (UNESCO, 1974, 1977, 1999). This achievement in literacy was mainly indicated by the rising enrollment rate in elementary schools. Nevertheless, enrollment rates were not in line with completion rates. Only 50% of pupils could attend first grade up to fourth grade, and only 35% completed six years of elementary school.

Despite improvements in the literacy rate as measured by standardized assessments, critical thinking and freedom of expression was suppressed by the authoritarian government. Leigh (1999) observes that schooling in Indonesia does not always mean learning, and in the same vein, reading does not mean understanding or thinking. The role of literacy in cultivating critical thinking to enable active participation in a democratic society was undermined. Education as an ideological state apparatus aimed to curb critical thinking. Texts and books deemed left wing were banned and burned (Anderson, 2006). Critical engagement with these texts as a form of critical literacy practices was forbidden and disbanded (Wiratraman, 2018). The authoritarian regime feared the continuation of such practices could destabilize their political power (Guggenheim, 2012; Hadiz & Dhakidae, 2005), as these activities could potentially identify social and political problems embedded in the government policies (Guggenheim, 2012; Street & Lefstein, 2007). Critical scholars and journalists had to face intimidation, death threats, (political) imprisonment, and even murder when challenging the authoritarian government (Budiarjo, 1974; Heryanto, 2003). The aftereffects of such suppression remain visible today.

Although the regime was overthrown in 1998, the narrow approach on education and bureaucratic structure developed by the New Order administration continues to impinge on the quality of Indonesian education system, generally and literacy, specifically. Indonesia's formal literacy performance, as recorded by the OECD's Program for International Student Assessment (PISA) remains staggeringly low as compared to the OECD-average countries. Indonesia was ranked amongst the lowest participating countries. This is despite efforts to improve the quality of education in general and literacy in particular by allocating education 20% of the national budget. The poor results in international literacy assessments such as the OECD's PISA have highlighted the importance of literacy as well as the inadequacy of the formal literacy approach. This has become a national concern and made the word "literacy" one of the most important in national education discourses in this decade (Dewayani & Retnaningdyah, 2017). The poor performance of Indonesia's youth on literacy assessments revealed that it is inadequate to associate literacy merely with formal schooling if we are to understand the more diverse and substantial meanings of literacy practices in contemporary society in Indonesia and beyond. This inadequacy highlights the urgency of using critical literacies as not only theoretical framework but also as "praxis" in reflecting and acting upon the field of education and literacy (Stromquist, 2014).

In the past four years (2016–2020), the Indonesian government has increasingly recognized the importance of community literacies to support formal literacy at schools. National movements on literacy since then have taken a more holistic approach into community movements (Agustino, 2019). As advocated by grassroots literacy communities, the government collaborated with provincial, municipal, and district administrators as well as the private sector, women's organizations, youth organizations, Non-Governmental Organizations (NGOs), and community organizations to promote more diverse local literacies in communities (UNESCO, 2015). Although scattered, NGOs and other local organizations and communities now have the space to establish their own literacy movements to support national goals of literacy. The forms of these new literacy communities are, to name a few, literacy through folk tales, local culture literacy, reading culture community, literacy for entrepreneurship, smart houses, and community learning hubs (Kusumadewi, 2017). According to Directorate of Community Education and Special Education, there are at least 4,348 community libraries (*Taman Bacaan Masyarakat*) across the archipelago and 83 literacy-base communities or selected communities which organize literacy programs to create and sustain literate communities (Directorate of Community Education and Special Education, 2021). The emergence of these diverse literacies in addition to basic literacy (reading and writing) has highlighted the need in Indonesia for literacies that are more aware of social and cultural practices in society.

As the historical recount has demonstrated, power and ideology influence the design of certain literacy programs and consequently influence social life. Critical literacies may reveal how literacy teaching and programs are not neutral, mechanistic processes of "civilizing" future generations. Instead, they are a battleground in which competing visions, ideologies, discourses, and political interests struggle for dominance in a given society. Literacy as a social practice accommodates values, cultural experiences, and ideologies that influence individual interactions with texts. This critical perspective enables us to embrace overlooked, devalued, and subjugated literacy practices, that is,

Indonesian local literacies, and to offer an alternative public discourse which highlights the role of literacy as "a communal resource contributing to the quality of local life" (Barton & Hamilton, 2012, p. xi). Critical literacies pinpointed the universal movement in supporting vulnerable young adults and disadvantaged groups as well as empowering gender equality, and so does in Indonesia. The emergence of this new orientation of literacy in Indonesia is under-researched, and it is the impetus of this chapter to capture this shift. The next section analyzes critical literacies work in Indonesia.

Critical Literacy Praxis in Indonesia

In surveying critical literacies in Indonesia, we adopt Paolo Freire's concept of praxis as "reflection and action upon the world in order to transform it" (Freire, 2000, p. 33). In undertaking this study, we reviewed not only the works of critical literacy researchers but also literacy activists (practitioners) at the community level. We also attempted to capture local literacies that have been working at the community level but are under-researched and overlooked. The interrelationship between the work of researchers and practitioners illuminates Freire's proposition that praxis does not actually operate outside theory; rather, praxis "requires theory to illuminate it" (Freire, 2000). Following this conceptual framework, we structure our analysis into action and reflection undertaken by critical literacies activists, practitioners, and researchers and categorize them into two groups: school settings and beyond formal schooling (local literacies).

School Settings

Although still relatively rare, critical literacy research and practices are being developed across a range of curriculum areas in Indonesia. English as a Foreign Language (EFL) is one area that started the inclusion of critical literacy pedagogy. In critical literacy perspectives, a language learner should be able to discover complex relationships between language and power (Janks, 2010), create their own critical standpoints, question the taken-for-granted facts (Luke & Dooley, 2011), and have the awareness to empower marginalized groups (Freire, 2000) (see also Chapters 1.4, 3.9, and 3.11 in this book). According to Gustine (2013), Indonesia's EFL curriculum generally has a limited space for critical literacy as it is dominated by rote learning and memorization. Gustine (2013) brought critical literacy into the classroom by adopting four dimensions of critical literacy proposed by Lewison, Leland, and Harste (2015). She provided four different popular topics for students to oppose taken-for-granted perspectives and develop their own critical viewpoints. Through critical literacy, Gustine succeeded in directing the students from having a passive perspective into developing critical viewpoints. White underarm skin on deodorant TV commercial adverts, homophobia, and catastrophes in some regions in Indonesia were among the popular topics introduced. Initially, students took the underlying assumptions of those ads for granted and did not question how social and cultural systems work. By helping students to question everyday issues from critical perspectives, consider different points of view, and relate their thoughts to sociopolitical systems, the teacher was able to direct the students to the heart of critical literacy. She managed to shift from using language as the practical use of skills into critical practices.

Such concerns led Gustine (2017) to undertake further study, especially on how teachers understand the notion of critical literacy and its practices. It seemed that four years of studying at preservice teacher education (a bachelor's degree) were not enough to lay the basic foundations for critical literacy. Although it was revealed that some EFL teachers who were also her graduate students had a little knowledge of critical literacy in the beginning of her study, there is a possibility that the other participants developed awareness of what a critical literacy classroom could be.

Mambu (2011) incorporated critical pedagogy into EFL practices by applying Freire's (2000) thematic investigation. He presented pictures of McDonald's burgers, a beauty pageant, a crowded city, and a beggar in front of a shrine to explore the concept of domination by discussing poverty and social class. He also proposed that writing an op-ed article could be a way to criticize the government. To demonstrate this concern to his students, he wrote an opinion piece in the *Jakarta Post* to criticize the ruling president as being too biased in selecting ministers based on political deals and calculations. In line with Janks's (2010) point of view, developing learners' understanding of the presence and importance of op-ed articles means providing them a gate to meaning-making processes that oppose the domination of political leaders. Mambu (2011) promoted English for advocacy purposes. It was done by encouraging ELT teachers to advocate and empower the marginalized, fight against oppression through English, and persistently question bias toward the notion of "the oppressed" to perceive diverse viewpoints that domination is not always about numbers. The use of English itself could potentially bring Indonesian local narratives to light and advocate for the rights of minoritized communities in Indonesia to wider international audiences.

Local Literacies

Critical literacy research has also started to move to areas beyond formal schooling, with a few notable researchers starting to document the local literacies of several communities. This shift in research focus has marked the global movement of critical literacies in Indonesia, showing that it does not focus only on literacy in formal schooling.

Dewayani (2013) investigated the identity construction of street children through their writing. The study depicted urban poverty and how it reproduced schooling discourses and marginalized those who did not have access to formal schooling. It unraveled the complex relationship between children, parents, society, and government through the discourse of formal schooling and argued that formal schooling as an important means of vertical mobility in society is not the only solution to eradicate poverty (Dewayani, 2013; Dewayani & Retnaningdyah, 2017). The stigma attached to street children as uneducated, working and living on the street, and prone to social deviance has created a vicious cycle of alienation contributing to children's construction of self. By exploring the critical literacy practices organized by local communities in cooperation with an NGO, they pursued equal literacy for street children in Bandung. They provided early childhood education programs for street children, such as play-based learning, reading, and writing to embed a learning mindset and motivate the youth to pursue further education. This project not only monitored children's learning progress, but it also introduced the notion of a "dream" to them—how they projected themselves as agents, positioned themselves in connection with others, and imagined future identities different from the ones constructed by mainstream Indonesian society.

Retnaningdyah (2013, 2015) studied one subordinate group of women in the global division of labor: Indonesian foreign domestic workers in Hong Kong. Arguing against the stigma of domestic workers as unintelligent, passive, and submissive, Retnaningdyah showed how the women were actively engaged in activities to negotiate the prevailing structures of power in transnational labor market, and that literacy practices were central to their activism. They reconstructed their identities and empowered their communities through blogging in which their identities underwent significant changes through meaning-making processes. Overtime working hours and never-ending house chores did not seem to make them give up on writing and digital activities. In challenging the dominant discourse, they used the term *Babu* (maid) to fight for the value of domestic workers. The juxtaposition of the notion of blogging and *Babu* gave an alternative interpretation as *Babu* had always been associated with passiveness, submissiveness, and low skills, whereas blogging was something smart and tech-savvy. This discursive reversal was intended to shift negative social constructions of domestic workers as unintelligent and passive to seeing them as smart, creative, strong-willed, and critical people. These literacy practices also empowered the community to speak their unspoken and unheard voices (Retnaningdyah, 2015). For example, Erwiana experienced domestic violence from her boss and was fired after eight months of working without receiving any salary. The social practice of literacy was proven to be able to move fellow international domestic workers to fight for legal justice for Erwiana. The literacy practices of these domestic workers have not only reconstructed their identities but also empowered their communities.

Agustino (2019) conducted a case study of one community library and argued that there was a relationship between local literacy movement and community empowerment. Community or local libraries in Indonesia are different from local libraries in the more developed countries that are government sponsored but locally run. In Indonesia, local libraries and their literacy movements are entirely voluntary and independent in nature. But according to Agustino's study, these libraries have been able to contribute to the socioeconomic life of their participants. The social literacy practices are visible in the form of a series of soft skill thematic activities to promote socioeconomic independence, along with providing books for reading.

In addition to this literature on grassroots literacies, we present two communities we have studied empirically, "Rumah Buku Cilegon" and "Adam and Sun" to paint more varieties of local literacies. The former community concerns one reading club, while the latter is a science club.

"*Rumah Buku Cilegon*" or Cilegon Book House was established in 2011 from a deep concern over the low reading interest and poor condition of city libraries in Cilegon, an industrial city in West Java, with rising economic inequality of its people. With the desire to bring together friends with shared passion about books, the community initially organized book picnics around Cilegon and surrounding cities to promote the culture of book reading through book picnics and an engaging mobile library. *Rumah Buku Cilegon* commutes from one place to another around Cilegon, familiarizing the locals with high-quality books to lay the foundation of literacy in the local community. They believe that critical literacy is important to fight against fake news and hoaxes (in-depth interview, February 2020). The book picnic was later dedicated to children since they were their most loyal participants. In addition, this community organized another program, "*Mencuri Ilmu dari Buku*" (Stealing Knowledge from Books). Unlike formal schooling in Indonesia, which is passive and makes children subservient to the learning process, this community encouraged freedom of speech and critical thinking. Everyone has the same opportunity to speak their mind. This approach resisted formal literacy as shaped and structured by the authoritarian government.

"Adam and the Sun" was also a community library initiated by the grassroots community in Banten in 2009 but then moved to Bandung in 2018. It focused on science and literacy, campaigning about the non-dichotomy of science and religion and using logic and critical thinking to deepen faith. When we interviewed the founder, he cited a verse in Al-Quran, especially *surah Al-Baqarah*, that the angel asked a question about why God created humans if they would do damage on earth. He explained, if "Angel, who is a submissive and passive creature, asked a question, why are people afraid to ask?" The social construction that those who question faith are labeled as nonbelievers discourages the questioning culture. Through science, one is able to contemplate why and how the universe was created. Thus, there is no dichotomy between religion and science. Adam and the Sun's literacy programs are, to name a few, Galileo Junior (visualizing astronomy through video), Dream Trigger (motivating children to dream high), Verse of Universe (doodle and rap music), local music (collaborating with local musicians to create minor notes of outer space sounds using Sundanese instruments), and Space for Space (urging Banten local government to build a planetarium). Adam and Sun also initiated Banten Science Day to promote science and astronomy to elementary school students.

The works of these literacy activists and practitioners at the community level embody local literacies (Barton & Hamilton, 2012) and show that vernacular literacies, although often subjugated by the discourse of formal literacy, play important roles in making sense of the world through words (Freire, 2000).

Concluding Thoughts

Indonesia's case, as demonstrated in this chapter, offers insights of how critical literacies could potentially liberate a range of important subjugated knowledge in any post-authoritarian context, irrespective of geographical location and local cultures. The historical trajectories of literacies in post-authoritarian Indonesia and the work of researchers and practitioners have highlighted the importance of linking literacy with social practices: literacy is ideologically and socially situated and it is mediated by texts and social networks. To make formal literacy more meaningful, it cannot be divorced from vernacular grassroot literacies (Barton & Hamilton, 2012). Unlike the more cognitive formal literacy imposed by the authoritarian administration, grassroots literacies have provided spaces in which people can truly engage in literacy acts as meaningful social practices and can potentially liberate Indonesia from its authoritarian shadow. As we have learned from the street children in Bandung, Indonesian foreign domestic workers in Hong Kong and local community libraries in Indonesia, critical literacy practices have the power not only to make the unheard voices heard but also to reconstruct one's identity and empower their respective community.

The current literacy praxis has demonstrated encouraging signs at community and grassroots levels. Future critical literacy praxis in Indonesia can expand existing work by exploring more in the areas of the impact of authoritarianism in ways of thinking and ways of doing literacy, the global pandemic, environmental issues (global warming), local languages, and gender equity. These four areas, while deserving top priority, are under-researched in the context of Indonesia. The global phenomena need to be contextualized locally in order to better address the problems through literacies. Critical literacies offer powerful ways to help navigate our post-authoritarian condition, while engaging with opportunities and inequalities accelerated by globalization.

References

Agustino, H. (2019). Pemberdayaan masyarakat berbasis gerakan literasi di Taman Baca Masyarakat Pondok Sinau Lentera Anak Nusantara. *Jurnal Sosial Politik, 5*(1), 142. https://doi.org/10.22219/sospol.v5i1.7890

Anderson, B. (2006). *Imagined communities: Reflections on the origin and spread of nationalism.* Verso. https://doi.org/10.1017/CBO9781107415324.004

Barton, D., & Hamilton, M. (2012). *Local literacies.* Routledge.

Bruinessen, M. Van. (1994). Pesantren and Kitab Kuning: Maintenance and continuation of a tradition of religious learning. In W. Marshall (Ed.), *Texts from the Islands: Oral and written traditions of Indonesia and the Malay world* (pp. 121–146). The University of Berne Institute of Ethnology.

Budiarjo, C. (1974). Political imprisonment in Indonesia. *Bulletin of Concerned Asian Scholars, 6*(2), 20–23.

Dewayani, S. (2013). What do you want to be when you grow up? Self-construction in Indonesian street children's writing. *Research in the Teaching of English, 47*(4), 365–390.

Dewayani, S., & Retnaningdyah, P. (2017). *Suara dari Marjin: Literasi sebagai praktik sosial.* Rosda.

Directorate of Community Education and Special Education (Ministry of Education and Culture). (2021, April 30). *Daftar TBM (List of community libraries).* Donasi Buku. https://donasibuku.kemdikbud.go.id/tbm

Directorate of Community Education and Special Education (Ministry of Education and Culture). (2021, April 30). *Membangun literasi masyarakat (Building community literacy).* Donasi Buku. https://donasibuku.kemdikbud.go.id/artikel/membangun-literasi-masyarakat

Freire, P. (2000). *Pedagogy of the oppressed.* Bloomsbury.

Guggenheim, S. (2012). Indonesia's quiet springtime: Knowledge, policy and reform. In A. J. S. Reid (Ed.), *Indonesia rising: The repositioning of Asia's third giant* (pp. 141–169). Institute of Southeast Asian Studies.

Gustine, G. G. (2013). Designing and implementing a critical literacy-based approach in an Indonesian EFL secondary school. *International Journal of Indonesian Studies, 1,* 2–21.

Gustine, G. G. (2017). A survey on critical literacy as a pedagogical approach to teaching English in Indonesia. *Indonesian Journal of Applied Linguistics, 7*(3), 531–537.

Hadiz, V. R., & Dhakidae, D. (2005). *Social science and power in Indonesia.* Equinox Publishing.

Heryanto, A. (2003). Public intellectuals, media and democratization: Cultural politics of the middle classes in Indonesia. In A. Heryanto & S. K. Mandal (Eds.), *Challenging authoritarianism in Southeast Asia: Comparing Indonesia and Malaysia* (pp. 24–59). Routledge Curzon.

Heryanto, A., & Hadiz, V. R. (2005). Post-authoritarian Indonesia: A comparative Southeast Asian perspective. *Critical Asian Studies, 37*(2), 251–275. https://doi.org/10.1080/146727

Janks, H. (2010). *Literacy and power.* Routledge.

Kebebasan akademik, non-feodalisme dan penindasan HAM. In A. Khanif & M. K. Wardaya (Eds.), *Hak asasi manusia: Politik, hukum dan agama di Indonesia* (pp. 53–67). LKI.

Kell, M., & Kell, P. (2014). *Literacy and language in East Asia: Shifting meanings, values and approaches.* Springer.

Kusumadewi, L. R. (2017, September 11). Model literasi yang bermanfaat untuk Indonesia: Bukan sekadar melek huruf. *The Conversation.*

Leigh, B. (1999). Learning and knowing boundaries: Schooling in new order Indonesia. *Journal of Social Issues in Southeast Asia, 14*(1), 34–56. https://doi.org/10.1355/sj14-1b

Lewison, M., Leland, C., & Harste, J. C. (2015). *Creating critical classrooms: K-8 Reading and writing with an edge.* Lawrence Erlbaum Associates.

Lowenberg, P. (2000). Writing and literacy in Indonesia. *Studies in the Linguistic Sciences, 30*(1), 135–148.

Luke, A., & Dooley, K. (2011). Critical literacy and second language learning. In E. Hinkel (Ed.), *Handbook of research in second language teaching and learning Volume 2* (pp. 1–15). Routledge.

Mambu, J. E. (2011). English for advocacy purposes: Critical pedagogy's contribution to Indonesia. *The Journal of ASIA TEFL, 8*(4), 135–173.

Miller, J., & McKenna, M. (2016). *World literacy: How countries rank and why it matters.* Routledge.

Nakamura, M., & Nishino, S. (1995). Development of Islamic higher education in Indonesia. In A. H. Yee (Ed.), *East Asian higher education: Traditions and transformations.* Pergamon.

Penders, C. (1977). *Indonesia, selected documents on colonialism and nationalism 1830–1942.* University of Queensland Press.

Power, T. P. (2018). Jokowi's authoritarian turn and Indonesia's democratic decline. *Bulletin of Indonesian Economic Studies, 54*(3), 307–338. https://doi.org/10.1080/00074918.2018.1549918

Pringle, R. (2010). *Understanding Islam in Indonesia: Politics and diversity.* Mainland Press Ltd.

Retnaningdyah, P. (2013). 'Kami juga punya suara': Dunia blogging buruh migran Indonesia di Hong Kong sebagai politik budaya. *Jurnal Komunikasi Indonesia, 2*(1), 23–30. https://doi.org/10.7454/jki.v2i1.7827

Retnaningdyah, P. (2015). *We have voices, too: Literacy, alternative modernities, and Indonesian domestic workers in Hong Kong* (PhD Thesis, University of Melbourne). Minerva Access.

Sakhiyya, Z., & Martin-Anatias, N. (2020). Reviving the language at risk: A social semiotic analysis of the linguistic landscape of three cities in Indonesia. *International Journal of Multilingualism*, 1–18. https://doi.org/10.1080/14790718.2020.1850737

Street, B., & Lefstein, A. (2007). *Literacy: An advanced resource book.* Routledge.

Street, B. V. (1995). *Social literacies: Critical approaches to literacy in development, ethnography and education.* Routledge.

Stromquist, N. P. (2014, June). Freire, literacy and emancipatory gender learning. *International Review Education, 60*, 545–558. https://doi.org/10.1007/s11159-014-9424-2

Tobias, J., Wales, J., Syamsulhakim, E., & Suharti. (2014). Towards better education quality: Indonesia's promising path. *Development Progress Case Study Report* (Issue July).

UNESCO. (1974). *Statistical Yearbook, 1973.* UNESCO.

UNESCO. (1977). *Statistical Yearbook, 1976.* UNESCO.

UNESCO. (1999). *Statistical Yearbook, 1999.* UNESCO.

UNESCO. (2012). *Education for all global monitoring report.* UNESCO.

UNESCO. (2015). *Promising EFA practices in the Asia-Pacific region: Indonesia literacy for life skills and entrepreneurship.* UNESCO.

Wiratraman, H. P. (2018).

Yulaelawati, E. (2009). *A new theory of education reform in Indonesia: Globalisation and recontextualisation in the postcolonial condition.* Nagara.

2.8

CRITICAL LITERACIES IN IRAN

A Tour D'horizon

Arman Abednia, Seyyed-Abdolhamid Mirhosseini, and Hossein Nazari

Sociopolitical Context

Iran is a unique context in a few respects which can be summarized as follows: the heart and remnant of the Persian empire shouldering a rich cultural heritage; a perennial strategic focus in the region occupying the center of several regional and international conflicts; and a site of struggles, some resulting in a revolution more than 40 years ago and some resulting from the post-revolution dynamics.

In September 1980, Iran, a post-revolutionary nation defined largely by ideas of independence from and resistance to foreign hegemony, faced Iraq's invasion of parts of its territory. All major Western powers, especially the United States, supported Iraq's aggression, supplying Saddam Hussein with financial assistance, battlefield intelligence, chemical weapons, and poison gas. Eight years later, in 1988, the war ended, with hundreds of thousands of Iranians killed or permanently injured. July 1988 in particular was etched on the Iranian collective consciousness when the United States shot down an Iran Air passenger plane, adding 290 deaths to its share of the nation's trauma.

The internal political conflicts between the right-wing principled and left-wing reformists in their battle for a share in the government have served as yet another intellectual stimulus for Iranians, for many of whom political and economic conversations are part and parcel of their daily life. Currently, strongly pushing ahead with its policies of challenging American global dominance, Iran is perhaps best known in the world for being subjected to the harshest US sanctions in history. However, Western dominance is not as forcefully challenged in the Iranian educational system, which is arguably largely copied from European/American models and run mostly based on imported conceptualizations of modern education.

Educational Context: From Perso-Islamic Teaching to Modern Schooling

Both Islam—the country's main religion—and the Persian/Iranian culture have historically placed great emphasis on learning and seeking knowledge. A famous narration by Prophet Muhammad, for instance, has it that "Seek knowledge even if it takes you to China"[1]—with China here serving as a metaphor for remoteness and inaccessibility. Also, one of the most famous lines of Persian poetry (itself a versified version of another narration attributed to the Prophet) reads "Seek knowledge from the cradle to the grave".[2] It is, therefore, little surprise that wo/men of learning have always enjoyed a prominent place in Perso-Islamic culture. The Shi'a branch of Islam, in particular, attaches great

DOI: 10.4324/9781003023425-20

value to reflection, debating, and discussion, even where the most sacred religious principles are in question. Islamic seminaries, for instance (contrary to the popular perception of them as intellectually conservative places), are characterized by polyphony and a multiplicity of voices, approaches, and views, which have given rise to different schools of thought and interpretation within Islamic scholarship (Reza'i-Esfehani, 2014).

The first public schools in their modern sense, which gradually replaced the traditional schools known as *maktab*, were established in Iran in the 1880s. The first modern Iranian University, the University of Tehran, was established in 1934. After the 1979 Islamic Revolution, the government continued (based on Article 30 of the Constitution of the Islamic Republic of Iran) to provide all citizens with free education up to the end of secondary school. After passing the University Entrance Exam, qualified high school graduates can proceed to study for free in state universities. To meet the ever-increasing demands of the very high number of applicants, the 1980s witnessed a proliferation of private universities in the country, which, since their establishment, have gone a long way toward providing those applicants who do not make it to state universities with an opportunity to further their education.

While at schools and universities both the predominantly imported Western curricula and the pedagogical approaches adopted to teach them have been mostly traditional and teacher-oriented, a review of the research literature on Farsi literacy education suggests that more attention has been paid in the last two decades to the notion of criticality, especially in the sense of cognitively oriented critical thinking. Apropos critical literacy, however, its teaching and practice have been mostly confined to academia, albeit in a limited sense. Critical Discourse Analysis, for instance, has been taught as part of Linguistics and Teaching English curricula at postgraduate levels. It is also worth mentioning that the convenience and accessibility afforded by online and digital modes of learning, teaching, and knowledge production seem to have contributed to students' (and teachers') awareness and practice of both critical thinking and critical literacy.

A Glimpse of the Critical Literacy Landscape in Iran

Our search for academic and otherwise accounts of critical literacy practices in Farsi literacy education yielded no published works. While tens of papers have been published with a focus on critical thinking (as a cognitive skill) in the context of schools and universities, none of these studies includes a critical literacy focus. This significant gap suggests a lack of investment in adopting a critical approach to teaching Farsi reading and writing to school children.

In teaching English as a foreign language (EFL), however, which to varying degrees defines the core of the present authors' professional and academic backgrounds, we can paint a more colorful picture. An internet search using terms such as "critical literacy", "critical pedagogy", and "Iran" yields tens of publications. Screening these works based on their rigor and whether they report on critical classroom practices leaves us mostly owing to the first criterion, with around a dozen reasonably rigorous published accounts of critical EFL literacy practices and another dozen similarly robust unpublished graduate theses. These works reflect more than two decades of rather sporadic, albeit worthwhile, critical literacy practices on the part of educators inspired by critical approaches to teaching EFL.

Perhaps, the oldest published account of critical literacy practice in EFL education in Iran is Ghahremani Ghajar and Mirhosseini's (2005) study of the second author's use of dialogue journal writing in a high school EFL class as part of his MA thesis. The students wrote journal entries every week, and Mirhosseini read and responded to them mainly focusing on the content by commenting on the points made, answering the questions raised, and asking questions to prompt critical thinking. The students were reported to engage with "expression-of-the-self" (p. 290) in their writing, become more self-confident in expressing their views, and move from a more descriptive mode of writing to a more critical and creative one. This article and Ghahremani Ghajar and Mirhosseini (2006), with the latter apparently being the only paper on critical literacy published in Farsi, each reported some of the findings in Mirhosseini's (2003) MA thesis.

Another master's level research project was conducted by Kafshgarsouteh, who adopted a reading the word/reading the world approach (Freire, 1991; Freire & Macedo, 1987) to critical analysis of texts, enabling students "to gain the power of critiquing, freeing their thoughts, finding and expressing their voice and position, discovering personal meanings in texts and contexts, cooperating and participating, and understanding learning for meaning" (Ghahremani Ghajar & Kafshgarsouteh, 2011, p. 26). The limited space does not allow for a discussion of several other valuable master's thesis projects, none apparently published in peer-reviewed journals, which explored critical literacy practices mostly in the context of EFL reading instruction (e.g., Gholamhossein, 2001; Khonamri, 1999; Khorshidi, 2002; Khodras, 2020; Parsaiyan, 2007).

In a series of critical literacy studies in undergraduate reading and writing courses taught by Abednia, adopting a dialogical and problem-posing approach to English instruction was reported to have contributed to a few aspects of students' development. In a writing course that involved peer and teacher critical feedback on content and language, students were reported to exercise agency through voicing their ideas in their writing, paying conscious attention to argumentation and reasoning, and developing a dynamic and authentic view of writing (Abednia & Karrabi, 2010). In a critical reading course, students were asked to write response journals which reflected examples of the students contextualizing reading topics, defining and redefining key concepts, drawing on one's own and others' experiences, and offering solutions and suggestions (Abednia & Izadinia, 2013). The students were also asked to write self-assessments and class assessments, where they described the experience as one that allowed them to have freedom of speech, enjoy a friendly classroom atmosphere, and improve critical thinking skills, self-confidence, self-awareness, and language skills (Izadinia & Abednia, 2010).

While all of the aforementioned studies were conducted in Tehran and in reading- or writing-based courses, Sadeghi (2008) incorporated critical pedagogy in an English-speaking class in a southern city, Bandar-Abbas, which focused on sociopolitical and cultural themes relevant to her students' indigenous community, such as gender discrimination, cultural invasion, and religion. Classroom discussions and dialogue journals were reported to help the students engage in critical examination of social issues that they had taken for granted and, therefore, grow more reflective about themselves and their surroundings. More recent studies such as Asakereh and Weisi (2018), Parsaiyan (2019), and Mirhosseini, Shirazizadeh, and Pakizehdel (2020) similarly report encouraging outcomes of EFL students' engagement with alternative literacy practices, including developing a deeper understanding of the complexities of linguistic structures and the ability to pose critical questions.

Another group of studies in Iran focused on equipping EFL teacher-learners with a critical literacy/pedagogy approach in the context of teacher education and development. Safari (2016), for example, conducted an online critical pedagogy teacher development intervention. The teachers were reported to have adopted a dialogical approach in their teaching, encouraged critical thinking, and helped their students develop a sense of belonging to the class. Abednia (2012) taught an undergraduate course of second language teaching methodology focused on critical pedagogy. He observed three major shifts in participants' views, namely from conformity to dominant ideologies to critical autonomy, from an instrumentalist orientation of teaching to a critical/transformative orientation, and from a linguistic and technical view of teaching EFL to an educational perspective. One more example is Abednia and Crookes (2019), who reported on how an online critical pedagogy course facilitated the participants' negotiation of a sense of community within and beyond the course, contribution to each other's engagement and learning, and refined teaching practice.

The critical literacy scholarship in Iran seems to reflect what we may call *typical* (i.e., (neo-)Marxist and Eurocentric) *critical theory*—ironic as it may sound. The credible published and unpublished studies on critical literacy practices in Iranian educational contexts tend to rely on the ideological foundations of critical theory and (neo)Marxist perspectives (Kellner, 1989; McLaren, 2014). Freirean "critical pedagogy" as a critical theory of education seems to shape the foundation of attempts at bringing critical literacy into the Iranian educational system (Freire, 1972, 1973; Giroux, 1997). Therefore, these educational endeavors and the research and writing activities that reflect them seem to mostly explore critical pedagogical conceptions like critical consciousness (Freire, 1973), problem posing (Freire & Faundez, 1989), and empowerment (Shor, 1992).

Iranian Visions, Transnational Perspectives

Our brief overview of the critical literacy scholarship in Iran indicates that questioning traditional positivist views of literacy has already started to be addressed. The broad view of relating words and worlds (Freire, 1991) embedded in such educational and research attempts is arguably relevant and promising in Iran, as in any other sociocultural context anywhere in the world. However, in the specific context of Iran, three major concerns may be raised about the overall possibilities for critical literacy practices: first, the limited scope of related practices and research; second, the absence of critical perspectives in Farsi language literacy education; and third, the need for developing a local conceptualization of the notion of critical.

Although about a dozen respectable publications have appeared about critical literacy education in Iran, and a further dozen unpublished graduate studies, the overall bulk of related research in our context is rather small. Given the population of the country, the sheer size of educational institutions at different levels, and the relatively large body of research and publication on issues of language and literacy education, our existing critical literacy scholarship is a tiny stream rather than a considerable trend. This, in turn, is an indication of the marginal status of critical literacy teaching practices in actual language and literacy teaching. Therefore, as a first concern, we may still need to echo a rather dated call for problematizing strictly cognitive views of education and literacy teaching and for embracing more critical attitudes.

More importantly, as seen in the previous section, almost all of the existing critical literacy practices and research activities in Iran appear to be shaped in the context of teaching English as a foreign language. There has been perhaps no significant attempt at bringing critical literacy perspectives into the realm of teaching and learning Farsi literacy in Iranian schools. It is true that English language teaching in Iran can be a major field of critical literacy contestation. Given the enormous American sway in the country's politics prior to the 1979 Islamic Revolution, English language and literature began to be hugely embraced at Iranian universities and schools alike. Most ironically, in the decades following the revolution there has been an unprecedented expansion of the English learning fever. Teaching English at private language centers around the country and the development of English Literature university programs have been the two crucial sides of this trend. Therefore, a critical attitude is indeed much needed in English language literacy education in Iran.

However, the major literacy education activity in the country is the teaching of Farsi literacy to school-age children, about one million of whom enter school each year. Within this primary literacy education arena, critical literacy appears to be nonexistent. For at least a century now, the modern schooling system has focused on teaching the alphabet and the so-called skills of reading and writing as decoding and encoding activities. Critical literacy of any persuasion or approach including a local one is yet to be introduced into the official educational system in which children usually start "their literacy with parroting the alphabet" and copying hardly meaningful *easy* sentences (Ghahremani Ghajar & Mirhosseini, 2011, p. 223).

Finally, beyond the call for the further embrace of critical attitudes, there lies a conceptual challenge. The expansion of critical literacy theory, practice, and research in the sociocultural context of Iran can hardly be envisaged based on theoretical standpoints like neo-Marxism, feminism, and postmodernism. Reproducing the ideological foundations of such standpoints does not necessarily contribute to locally relevant critical literacy if we take criticality as "a reflection on the relation between individual and society" (Miedema & Wardekker, 1999, p. 68). Taking cultural, social, economic, and political relevance and situatedness as the essence of critical attitudes, it may be argued that in our context, critical education in general, should be indispensably viewed against the backdrop of the local intellectual tradition, including the rich heritage of Persian literature.

Many figures of the world-famous Persian literature are known for their critical attitude toward the sociopolitical climate of their own time. The great thirteenth- and fourteenth-century poets, Mowlana (Rumi), Hafez, and Sa'di, three of the most famous Persian poets (if not the most famous ones), are quite well known for their critical perspectives, spanning issues of politics, economy, and religion. A significant consideration is that they were unquestionably religious not merely in the sense of being believers, but prominent religious figures of their own time. These scholars practiced critical literacy at its most radical level where they came to adopt a critical lens to the type of religious content they had been schooled into, transcended it, and explored their inner text in pursuit of liberation through divine love. In this spirit, Hafez concludes one of his sonnets with this couplet:

> *It is love that will redeem you even if, like Hafez,*
> *You know the fourteen readings of the Quran by heart.*[3]

Despite the widely held view of religion as related to individual spiritual experiences, Islam is importantly related to social and even political life. Therefore, the Persian cultural tradition combined with Islamic perspectives can shape the foundations of an alternative local approach to criticality that may problematize current conceptualizations of critical literacy, which has been widely treated as universal but is in fact a version of criticality handed down from certain sociocultural and political contexts and borrowed by others. Intriguingly, before modern schools started, literacy was strongly attached to Persian literature and Islam: "Traditionally, learning to read and write used to start with the Holy Quran and Sa'di's Golestan" (Ghahremani-Ghajar & Mirhosseini, 2011, p. 223).

It is beyond the scope of this chapter to provide a detailed image of such literacy practices, but within the existing literature of critical literacy in English language teaching in Iran, a few studies by Parsaiyan may provide a glimpse of such practices (Parsaiyan, 2014; Parsaiyan, Ghahremani Ghajar, Salahimoghaddam, & Janahmadi, 2014, 2016). Parsaiyan and her colleagues (2014) used simplified translations of masterpieces of Persian poetry in a number of undergraduate general English courses for non-English majors. Facilitating connections between the students' lived experiences in the modern world and the literary content, classroom discussions involved a focus on spiritual and moral concepts such as "shaking off the self", "cage of the body", enduring "difficulties", "abandoning mundane belongings", and "deception". Parsaiyan and her colleagues further reflect on this experience in a few other publications (e.g., Parsaiyan et al., 2016). Most recently, Parsaiyan and her colleagues (Parsaiyan, Ghahremani-Ghajar, & Sohrabi, forthcoming) conducted a study on her initial engagement with developing EFL reading materials using a Persian classic poet's anecdotes. These works may include clues as to the points of departure in developing locally rooted critical literacy practices, which, as we argue in the next section, is a prerequisite for moving toward transnational critical literacy work.

Toward More Local Criticalities for Future

The quest for locally rooted critical *literacies* referred to in the previous section may be the indispensable requirement for visions of transnational critical work with contributions from diverse sociocultural contexts. Critical literacy scholarship has had a persistent emphasis on conceptualizations and practices informed by contextual particulars, namely current dynamics and historical background as well as local and global aspirations and concerns. Regardless of how transnationally one wishes to approach critical literacy work, maintaining the local relevance and significance of such work is imperative. Relying on the example of a possibility for local critical literacy based on the heritage of Persian literature within the Iranian and Islamic sociocultural context, we would like to encourage a view which persistently maintains a local focus not only when it is most explicitly concerned with local issues but also when it considers global considerations of potential relevance and significance to its local concerns and aspirations.

We argue then that only a critical literacy which takes due account of the past, present, and future of the local and the global issues of its context can embark on the path of adopting a transnational approach. Reclaiming historicized and locally informed readings and practices of critical literacy is a definite prerequisite to and a catalyst for moving toward a transnational orientation. We would suggest that regaining a local critical literacy perspective already embedded within the sociocultural sphere of Iran not only shapes transformed literacy practices within Iran but may also contribute to such practices in similar cultural contexts and even to other places around the world. Similar contributions may also be envisaged from many rich but less-appreciated localities in Asia, Africa, South America, Oceania, and even marginalized cultures in Europe and North America.

Very importantly, it needs to be underlined here that the development of local—and by extension, transnational—conceptions of critical literacy necessitates a particular attitude of openness and tolerance within broad critical literacy work not necessarily experienced so far. Inviting diverse local worldviews and values into critical literacy theories and practices may highlight provocative ontological views of the human being and epistemological positions regarding language and learning. Therefore, some of the most fundamental concepts that tend to be taken for granted by *typical critical theory* may need to be revisited in light of alternative, locally informed ways of knowing. Within the climate of a true transnational critical literacy that is shaped by diverse localities, we should be prepared to problematize even the apparently axiomatic concepts like democracy, social justice, freedom, equality, equity, and diversity as they are currently defined in the critical scholarship.

Joining Voices and Shaping Praxis

In this chapter, which is focused on critical literacy *in Iran*, we have mainly discussed, quite ironically, critical approaches to EFL instruction rather than Persian literacy education, as we could not locate any relevant literature on the latter. In fact, we were approached to write this chapter because of our background in critical EFL literacy. Therefore, the further embrace of critical literacy in EFL teaching and the need for moving toward local conceptualizations of criticality in this regard has been highlighted by our discussions. However, our arguments also emphasize the indispensability of promoting a critical approach to theorizing and practicing critical Farsi literacy education as a major responsibility. Engaging in dialogue with researchers, practitioners, and policy makers in this area where all bring their intellectual, epistemological, cultural, and experiential resources to the proverbial table, and all values, beliefs, and insights are simultaneously acknowledged and critically examined in local and global terms would be a useful point of departure in conceptualizing critical Farsi literacy and incorporating it into the school curriculum. Such initiatives can be further facilitated by cultivating a culture of critical literacy research in undergraduate and postgraduate programs of teacher education, where practitioner-friendly types of research, such as teacher research, action research, and participatory action research, among other research designs, are encouraged.

Once a local sense of critical literacy starts to take shape in diverse local contexts around the world, and with the support of a research-informed approach, moving in transnational directions becomes increasingly viable. Practitioners everywhere, in collaboration with their academic colleagues and in an atmosphere of mutual support, will start to share their ideas and practices in local and international platforms such as teacher blogs, professional development events, conferences, practitioner journals, and research journals. Engaging in research as mentioned earlier would facilitate such sharing. Carving out their own space in the critical literacy scholarship will enable practitioners to actively contribute to international dialogue. For this dialogue to become transnational, practitioners should join in from different regions, especially those whose local ways of knowing and conceptualizing critical literacy are overshadowed by typical, mostly Western, versions of critical literacy and less acknowledged and appreciated around the world. Such dialogue should then involve, as mentioned in the previous section, a critical examination of concepts like democracy, social justice, equity, and diversity whose Western readings form basis of the current dominant perspective on critical literacy, a reading which the critical literacy scholarship appears to have accepted as universally and inherently valid and therefore not in need of revisiting.

Notes

1. اطلبوا العلم ولو في الصين
2. ز گهواره تا گور دانش بجوی
3. عشقت رسد به فریاد ار خود به سان حافظ، قرآن ز بر بخوانی در چارده روایت

References

Abednia, A. (2012). Teachers' professional identity: Contributions of a critical EFL teacher education course in Iran. *Teaching and Teacher Education, 28*(5), 706–717.

Abednia, A., & Crookes, G. V. (2019). On-line language teacher education for a challenging innovation: Towards critical language pedagogy for Iran. In H. Reinders, C. Coombe, D. Tafazoli, & A. Littlejohn (Eds.), *Innovation in language learning and teaching: The case of the Middle East & North Africa* (pp. 241–261). Palgrave Macmillan.

Abednia, A., & Izadinia, M. (2013). Critical pedagogy in ELT classroom: Exploring contributions of critical literacy to learners' critical consciousness. *Language Awareness, 22*(4), 338–352.

Abednia, A., & Karrabi, M. (2010, December 2–3). Freire and Bakhtin in EFL writing. Rethinking tertiary EFL writing in light of dialogic-critical pedagogy. In *Proceedings of writing the future: Tertiary writing network colloquium*, Victoria University of Wellington, Wellington.

Asakereh, A., & Weisi, H. (2018). Raising critical consciousness in teaching reading skills using critical pedagogy principles: A case of an Iranian school graduate. *Journal for Critical Education Policy Studies, 16*(1), 261–291.

Freire, P. (1972). *Pedagogy of the oppressed*. Penguin Books.

Freire, P. (1973). *Education for critical consciousness*. Seabury.

Freire, P. (1991). The importance of the act of reading. In C. Mitchell & K. Weiler (Eds.), *Rewriting literacy: Culture and the discourse of other* (pp. 139–146). Bergin & Garvey.

Freire, P., & Faundez, A. (1989). *Learning to question: A pedagogy of liberation*. Continuum.

Freire, P., & Macedo, D. (1987). *Literacy: Reading the word and the world*. Routledge.

Ghahremani Ghajar, S., & Kafshgarsouteh, M. (2011). Recovering the power inside: A qualitative study of critical reading in an Iranian university. *Turkish Online Journal of Qualitative Inquiry, 2*(3), 26–39.

Ghahremani Ghajar, S., & Mirhosseini, S. A. (2005). English class or speaking about everything class? dialogue journal writing as a critical EFL literacy practice in an Iranian high school. *Language, Culture and Curriculum, 18*(3), 286–299.

Ghahremani Ghajar, S., & Mirhosseini, S. A. (2006). Goftegoo va negaresh-e naghadaneh dar jaryan-e journal nevisi-ye goftegooei be zaban-e englisi dar yeki az dabirestanha-ye Tehran [Dialogue and critical literacy in English dialogue journal writing in a Tehran high school]. *Alzahra University Journal of Humanities (Special issue on foreign language education), 16*, 25–53.

Ghahremani Ghajar, S., & Mirhosseini, S. A. (2011). Whose knowledge? Whose language? Reeds crying tales of separation. In S. Ghahremani-Ghajar & S. A. Mirhosseini (Eds.), *Confronting academic knowledge* (pp. 217–233). Iran University Press.

Gholamhossein, F. (2001). *Reading from a critical pedagogical perspective: A microethnography of EFL reading practices for Iranian university students* (Unpublished MA thesis). Alzahra University, Tehran, Iran.

Giroux, H. A. (1997). *Pedagogy and politics of hope: Theory, culture and schooling*. Westview Press.

Izadinia, M., & Abednia, A. (2010). Dynamics of an EFL reading course with a critical literacy orientation. *Journal of Language & Literacy Education, 6*(2), 51–67.

Kellner, D. (1989). *Critical theory, Marxism, and modernity*. Polity Press.

Khodras, N. (2020). *Applying multiple literacies in English language teaching in Iran* (Unpublished MA thesis). Alzahra University, Tehran, Iran.

Khonamri, F. (1999). *A critical approach to literacy practices: On developing critical reading, thinking, and writing* (Unpublished MA thesis). University of Tehran, Tehran, Iran.

Khorshidi, S. (2002). *A whole language view of Iranian high school EFL learners' critical literacy practices* (Unpublished MA thesis). University of Tehran, Tehran, Iran.

McLaren, P. (2014). *Life in schools: An introduction to critical pedagogy in the foundations of education* (6th ed.). Routledge.

Miedema, S., & Wardekker, W. L. (1999). Emerging identity versus consistent identity: Possibilities for a postmodern repoliticization of critical pedagogy. In T. S. Popkewitz & L. Fendler (Eds.), *Critical theories in education: Changing the terrains of knowledge and politics* (pp. 67–83). Routledge.

Mirhosseini, S. A. (2003). *Critical Pedagogy and EFL Dialogue Journal Writing in an Iranian High School: A Microethnographic Inquiry* (Unpublished MA thesis). University of Tehran, Iran.

Mirhosseini, S. A., Shirazizadeh, M., & Pakizehdel, H. (2020). Bridging language education and 'New Literacy Studies': Reinvigorating courses of general English at an Iranian university. *Language, Identity and Education.* https://doi.org/10.1080/15348458.2020.1791713

Parsaiyan, S. F. (2007). *A study on language de-socialization: EFL learners' unlearning wor/l/ds through dialogics in critical English literacy classrooms* (Unpublished MA thesis). Alzahra University, Tehran, Iran.

Parsaiyan, S. F. (2014). *From roots to routes: Self-identity pedagogy in English language classrooms* (Unpublished doctoral dissertation). Alzahra University, Tehran, Iran.

Parsaiyan, S. F. (2019). "This is a food ad but it is presenting gender stereotypes!": Practicing critical language awareness in an Iranian EFL context. *Journal of English Language Teaching and Learning, 11*(24), 227–259.

Parsaiyan, S. F., Ghahremani Ghajar, S., Salahimoghaddam, S., & Janahmadi, F. (2014). Inquiring "tree of life" at home: Persian classic literature in English classes. *English Teaching: Practice and Critique, 13*(3), 89–109.

Parsaiyan, S. F., Ghahremani Ghajar, S., Salahimoghaddam, S., & Janahmadi, F. (2016). From spectator to composer: The roses and rocks in the life of a language teacher. *Language Teaching Research, 20*(2), 196–208.

Parsaiyan, S. F., Ghahremani-Ghajar, S., & Sohrabi, M. (forthcoming). Sculpting English language teaching materials: A practicing materials developer self-study narrative. *Journal of Language Horizons, 4*(1).

Reza'i-Esfehani, M. A. (2014). *Shiveha-ye tahsil va tadriss dar Howzeha-ye Elmieh* [Methods of learning and teaching in seminaries]. Bustan-e Ketab.

Sadeghi, S. (2008). Critical pedagogy in an EFL teaching context: An ignis fatuus or an alternative approach? *Journal for Critical Education Policy Studies, 6*(1), 276–295.

Safari, P. (2016). Proletarianization of English language teaching: Iranian EFL teachers and their alternative role as transformative intellectuals. *Policy Futures in Education, 15*(1), 74–99.

Shor, I. (1992). *Empowering education: Critical teaching for social change*. University of Chicago Press.

2.9

CRITICAL LITERACY IN JAPAN

Reclaiming Subjectivity in the Critical

Yuya Takeda and Shinya Takekawa

Sociopolitical Situation in Japan

Japan, located at the eastern edge of Asia, is an archipelagic nation, with 126 million people living on a total land surface area of approximately 378,000 km² (1/26 of the United States). Although it has been challenged and debunked in academic discourses, the myth of Japanese homogeneity is still prevalent in popular discourses, due not only to the nation's insularity but also to the promotion of a homogenous national identity by the government since modernization (Oguma, 1995).

In reality, Japan comprises diverse ethnic groups, such as the Indigenous communities of Ainu and Ryukyuan, migrants from China, Taiwan, and Korea during the Japanese Imperial era and their descendants, so-called Asian and Japanese-Brazilian newcomers, who migrated to Japan during the economic bubble in the 1980s, and recent migrants from countries like Vietnam, Philippines, and Indonesia. The myth of homogeneity continues to marginalize these communities today.

In addition, discrimination based on class and gender is also prevalent. The perdurable discrimination against *Buraku* (an "untouchable" caste within Japan's historical feudal system) people still remains. The post-war patriarchal system continues to be dominant and females and LGBTQ+ people are flagrantly under-represented in many spheres of society.

Since neoliberal reforms in the 2000s, the wealth gap between the rich and the poor has become ever more conspicuous. Today, the poverty rate of children is estimated to be 15% or higher, and the achievement gap associated with child poverty is also widening (MHLW, 2016). The shrinking middle class is not helping Japan stop its rapidly aging population, under which the economy suffers from a decrease in the working-age population. A negative spiral persists. Positioning itself as an advanced nation of issues (*kadai senshinkoku*), Japan is confronting social, political, and economic challenges.

School Education in Japan

If we were to describe the characteristic features of school education in Japan, we could point to the central control-based development and expansion of school education that took place during the rapid modernization of Japanese society. In 1872, the institutionalization of Japan's education took place, leading to a modern school education system (Inagaki & Sato, 1996). Upon establishing the elementary school system, the government started formulating the teaching content and pedagogy, modeled after classroom teaching in the United States (see Inagaki, 1966). Discourses of

185   DOI: 10.4324/9781003023425-21

teaching were constructed and distributed through writings of pedagogical approaches by teachers at normal schools, as well as reports of lesson studies using these materials (Inagaki & Sato, 1996). During this time, however, the purpose of the lesson studies was extremely restricted. This was because the fundamental elementary school teaching rules, "*Shogakko Kyosoku Taikō*," enacted in 1891, adopted nationalistic educational content, and the focus of lesson studies was restricted to how teachers might best implement the required curriculum. Consequently, each school had to record detailed and thorough teaching-related lessons. Teachers were requested not to utilize their expertise to autonomously make decisions but to execute the content stipulated by the national government.

In 1947, amidst the democratization of education after World War II, general curriculum guidelines (*gakushū shidō yōryō ippan-hen*), which gave schools and teachers more control over their own curricula, were published. However, the conclusion of the U.S.- Japan Security Treaty stimulated by the Korean War in 1950 led to Japan's rearmament and restrengthening of nationalistic controls over education. In 1958, moral education aiming for educating nationalistic values were added to government course guidelines and were defined as legally binding. Moreover, in Japan, it is required for textbooks to receive official government approval for school use. These many structures allowed the national government to directly intervene in the content of school education.

In the post-war period, however, the system was consolidated from above and below: that is, both the government and teachers and educational scholars promoted the idea of "politically neutral education." On the one hand, the conservative government forbade teachers and high school students from taking part in political social activities, under the concept of neutrality, and attempted to restrict teachers from bringing up political controversies in their curricula, and on the other hand, in the educational research activities of teachers and scholars, the importance of neutrality was emphasized as a way to distance their work from the governmental interventions in education.

The emphasis on "neutrality" did not lead to politically balanced approaches to education; instead, it treated politics within education as "colorless and transparent," making them seem natural and invisible. Acts of making the political visible were seen as deviations from neutrality and therefore tabooed. The discourse of child development, in which children were seen as pre-political beings who needed to be sheltered from politics, and a view of education as a system of meritocracy, where the main task of students was considered to be attaining high scores on high school and university entrance examinations, both supported the myth of neutrality (Kodama, 2016). Against such a background, citizenship education was marginalized in discourses of education in Japan.

Kodama (2016) argues that there have been theoretical and social changes that prompted a re-politicization of education since the 1990s. On the theoretical side, sociocultural theorists illustrated teaching and learning as participatory actions in communities (Sato, 1997). In addition, globalization and lowering of the voting age from 20 to 18 catalyzed the recognition of the importance of citizenship education.

The effects of the Programme for International Student Assessment (PISA), which symbolizes education under globalization, have been an impediment for the re-politicization of education. Japan's 2003 and 2006 PISA results showed a trend wherein the country was falling in the overall rankings. As a reaction to the resulting so-called PISA shock, decontextualized notions of literacy and abstract thinking skills were promoted by the Ministry of Education, Culture, Sports, Science and Technology (MEXT) (Matsushita, 2014). For example, current textbooks for all subject areas include content regarding language skills, such as logical writing and speech construction, as well as the selection and utilization of practical information. Many local boards of education now treat such decontextualized and abstract models as the "curriculum standard." Under these conditions, teachers are required to teach the same standardized content through the same methods. Such a situation, we claim, precipitates the "de-skilling" of teachers (Apple, 1982).

Two Modes of Criticality in Japan's Literacy Education

In what follows, we illustrate two modes of criticality in literacy education in Japan: (1.) critical reading based on a critical thinking approach and (2) critical literacy that resonates with the Freirean school of thought. Despite the similarity in appearance, these two models have fundamental differences in terms of their orientations. While the critical reading model is oriented toward objectivity, critical literacy emphasizes the centrality of subjectivity in the reading of the objective world.

To discuss this point, it is important to note that in Japanese, the word "subjectivity" can be translated into two different but interrelated words: *shutaisei* (主体性) and *shukansei* (主観性). The word *shu* in both words denotes centrality and ownership, and *tai* in the former means a body, while *kan* in the latter means a perspective. Thus, *shutai* recognizes a subject as a person, and *shukan* means the subjective perspective. In educational discourses, *shutaisei* is often used synonymously with *jishusei* [voluntariness], whereas *shukansei* is often used pejoratively as a form of bias contrasted to unbiased *kyakkansei* [objectivity]. The conflation of *shutaisei* with voluntariness and the denigration of *shukansei* play into the neoliberalization and depoliticization of education in Japan. As we elaborate next, while the promotion of *shutaisei* renders individuals responsible for their survival and prosperity, discrediting *shukansei* neuters subjective voices and bleaches out what is political from personal.

Critical Reading Based on Critical Thinking

Much of the work in critical reading draws on the critical thinking model developed mainly in educational psychology. One of the prominent scholars in this field, Kusumi (2018), defines critical thinking as "a logical, neutral, and reflexive thought based on evidence" (p. 130). Similarly, Michita (2001) defines critical thinking as logical and rational thinking that utilizes a skeptical attitude toward deceptive appearances. While they complexify this understanding of critical thinking by listing up other elements like dispositions, sympathy toward relativism, recognition of uncertainty, and so forth (Kusumi, 2013; Michita, 2003), their model of critical thinking undeniably demonstrates the characteristics of logicism, rationalism, and positivism. In fact, the literature on critical thinking in Japan shows a significant influence from Robert H. Ennis, whose logicism has been criticized by Walters (1994).

The criticality in this school of thought is oriented toward objectivity (*kyakkansei*). As we discussed earlier, "subjectivity" is expressed in two different words in Japanese—*shutaisei* and *shukansei*—and the latter tends to be seen as something akin to "bias." The exercise of critical thinking in reading, therefore, demands a reader to get out of one's own limited perspective through use of logic and rationality. Critical reading, according to Tsuzuki and Aragaki (2012), is "an act of reading texts while exercising critical thinking, thereby scrutinizing the validity of the authors' logic and conclusion and deepening one's understanding through identification of problems by oneself" (p. 41). This definition suggests that criticality is mobilized to identify inconsistencies and incoherence in an author's arguments, and the underlying assumption is that by doing so, the reader can gain a deeper understanding of the given topic.

Based on this understanding of critical reading, Tsuzuki and Aragaki (2012) report on a research project in which they had university students read two texts: (1.) an article that discussed the relationship between *yutori kyōiku* (Japan's educational policy that reduced the content of the curriculum) and Japan's decline in the PISA literacy ranking and (2.) a sample PISA test question. The topic of *yutori kyōiku* was chosen because the researchers thought their participants could find it relatable as they are the generation who went through compulsory education under that policy. In other words, Tsuzuki and Aragaki deliberately selected a topic about which participants are likely to have strong opinions, so that participants' subjective involvement in reading would be more visible.

Echoing the popular discourse around *yutori kyōiku*, the article participants read argued that abolishing *yutori kyōiku* and returning to the previous curriculum would improve Japan's position in the PISA literacy rankings. Yet, according to Tsuzuki and Aragaki, the types of literacy measured by PISA are quite different from the traditional reading skills Japan's education was aiming to cultivate. Therefore, in order to evaluate participants' demonstrations of critical reading, Tsuzuki and Aragaki used the following criterion: whether the participants pointed out the gaps between the reading skills Japan's older curriculum aimed to cultivate and the types of literacy PISA demands students demonstrate. They conducted two rounds of data collection with different groups of students: one with a written questionnaire and another through a recording of their thought process, in which participants were guided to vocalize what they were thinking as they responded to the written questionnaire.

As they evaluated participants' performance based on the aforementioned criterion, Tsuzuki and Aragaki categorized participants into three types. The first type is the "objective and deliberate" participants who were able to withhold their subjective opinion on the topic and point out the contradictions. They were considered to have critical reading skills. The second type of participants expressed their opinions regarding the topic in the early phase of the task and juxtaposed their opinions with the article and the PISA question. Although this type of participant reflexively questioned their opinions in the process, they did not end up pointing out the contradictions. The third type of participants also expressed their opinion during the early phase of the task and picked up some elements from the article and the PISA question in order to support their opinion. Tsuzuki and Aragaki considered the last two types of participants as showing confirmation bias, and these participants were evaluated as uncritical readers.

The critical reading model delineated in Tsuzuki and Aragaki's (2012) research is exemplary as an application of critical thinking in the act of reading. What is considered as "critical" in this model is the elimination of subjectivity (*shukansei*) and judging texts based on their objective aspects such as internal logical coherence and consistency of argument.

Critique of Critical Reading

While the orientation toward objectivity is an important critical posture in order to scrutinize one's own limited perspective and approach truthfulness, this mode of criticality has certain limitations. Here, we discuss two interrelated factors: (1.) de-valuation of subjectivity and (2.) depoliticization of texts.

As we discussed earlier, the model of critical reading informed by critical thinking tends to treat subjectivity as a form of bias. In fact, Tsuzuki and Aragaki's (2012) evaluation of the participants' critical reading ability depended on whether the participants could withhold their own opinions and make objective judgment on the logical coherence of the texts. They stated,

> The topic of "*yutori kyōiku*" in this research was highly relevant to the participants who are regarded as the "*yutori generation.*" Because this theme was related to their own identity, they were strongly motivated to bring their arguments to a certain direction, and/or as a person who belongs to this generation (*tōjisha*), they might have thought that their own experience has a certain persuasiveness.
>
> *(Tsuzuki & Aragaki, 2012, p. 51)*

Through this, they speculated that even those who were evaluated as "uncritical" might be able to read other texts critically. While this argument appears to have a certain persuasiveness, since there are many cases where an uninterested third person is well suited to make a judgment on a dispute (e.g., in the judicial system), they also seem to suggest that people's direct involvement is an obstacle for them to understand the issue concerned. In order for the participants in Tsuzuki and Aragaki's research to demonstrate their criticality, they had to detach themselves from the issue and solve the logical puzzle within the preset parameter. This model of criticality does not permit people to challenge the very question to which they are asked to respond.

When criticality treats subjectivity as something illegitimate, it also excludes its potential to account for power. What is purely objective, if we ever succeed in grasping such a thing, does not depend on politics. However, once we start investigating our subjective involvements in the construction of reality, and how our subjectivities are in turn constructed by it, the question of power becomes inevitable. This is because subjectivity is inherently inseparable from power. Judith Butler (1997) states:

> "Subjection" signifies the process of becoming subordinated by power as well as the process of becoming a subject. Whether by interpellation, in Althusser's sense, or by discursive productivity, in Foucault's, the subject is initiated through a primary submission to power.
>
> *(p. 2)*

For English speakers, this recognition of subjectivity as something subjugated and subjected to (state) power is embedded in its very vocabulary. However, as we discussed earlier, the Japanese equivalents to subjectivity, *shutaisei*, and *shukansei*, foreground individual ownership of body and perspective. This might be one of the theoretical reasons why questions of subjectivity are often not linked to questions of power in discourses in Japan.

This depoliticization of criticality is quite evident in the literature around critical thinking. This can be seen most vividly in Kusumi's (2018) discussion of "civic literacy," which he defines as citizens' "communication competence to read information that is necessary for a civil life, take appropriate actions, and express themselves" (p. 133). He also states that civic literacy is a sum of different literacies such as "law, risks, health, and finances," and "is supported by critical thinking" (p. 133). This rather peculiar elimination of politics from civic literacy is not accidental.

Critical Literacy and Seikatsu-tsuzurikata

In comparison to the critical thinking model, critical literacy has not gained much popularity in either academic or popular discourse in Japan. It is plausible to think that this is largely due to critical literacy's overtly political orientation to education. As we discussed earlier, the myth of neutrality has been somewhat uncritically accepted in education discourses since the 1950s (Kodama, 2016), and the maintenance of neutrality has led to the depoliticization of education, rather than a balanced examination of different political perspectives.

Yet, even though they are not operating under the label of critical literacy, there have been numerous educational practices that highly resonate with the tenets of critical literacy. There have been Japanese scholars who engage with the work of Paulo Freire, Henry Giroux, and other critical theorists of education. Thus, our task here is to connect the theoretical and pedagogical work and delineate forms of critical literacy that are already there, unlabeled as such.

One of the most significant philosophical insights Freire proposes is that he views literacy as a dialectical movement between subjectivity and objectivity, and a consciousness emerges out of the act of reading the word and the world. Freire (1970) states:

> Humankind *emerge* from their *submersion* and acquire the ability to *intervene* in reality as it is unveiled. Intervention in reality—historical awareness itself—thus represents a step forward

from emergence, and results from the *conscientização* of the situation. Conscientização is the deepening of the attitude of awareness characteristic of all emergence.

(p. 109)

Through conscientização, roughly translated here as critical awareness-raising, people come to become cognizant of "the very condition of [their] existence" (p. 109), and become able to intervene in the reality. This intervention dissolves the dichotomy between subjectivity and objectivity.

> If social transformation was once understood in a simplistic form (that is, forming itself with a change in conscience, as if the conscience were, in fact, the transformer of what is real), now the social transformation is perceived as a historic process in which subjectivity and objectivity are united dialectically. There is no longer a way to make either objectivity or subjectivity absolute.
>
> *(Freire & Macedo, 1987, p. 28)*

This ontology is at the core of Freirean pedagogy—a pedagogy that invites learners to be more [*ser mais*] (Rocha, 2018).

Reflecting on the current situation of Japanese education, where schools demand learners to uncritically adapt to the world as is, which lacks love, humility, and trust for those who do not demonstrate the outcome of learning in a quantifiable manner, Sato (2016) calls for education that takes Freire's idea of liberation seriously and invites the emergence of subjectivity.

One such approach is "*seikatsu-tsuzurikata*" [life-writing], "a writing education movement designed to help students develop a strong sense of self by having them write descriptive, detailed compositions about their daily life and the world around them" (Kitagawa & Kitagawa, 2007, p. 52). The history of *seikatsu-tsuzurikata* can be traced back to the 1920s, where teachers at the time of the Great Depression struggled over the mismatch between the national curriculum and the desperate poverty of their students. As a response to this mismatch, some teachers started to have their students write about their everyday lives. Hence, *seikatsu-tsuzurikata* was born as an attempt to "unify actual lives and education" (Sakota, 1981, p. 16). In other words, what *seikatsu-tsuzurikata* confronts is the type of education that is decontextualizing and alienating. Kuroyabu (1981) states:

> [C]hildren's acquisition of language/words should neither be cramming of knowledge nor it be fluffy and hollow. Each word is deeply and solidly connected to their lives. Words must be acquired through picking and tying them to children's senses, emotions, desires, and through that process, language acquisition stimulates development of children's sensibility, establishment of their lives, and ability to think through words.
>
> *(p. 34)*

Suggested here is the deep resonance with Freirean conception of literacy where reading and (re) writing of words start from learners' immediate worlds and through which consciousness emerges. For the emergence of consciousness, it is not enough to just let students write about their lives, but it requires teachers' skillful intervention in their writing practices and invitation of students' subjectivity.

For instance, Kawaji (2013) introduces a teaching practice demonstrated by Jiro Shiraki, an elementary school teacher in Fukushima. Just before the one-year anniversary of the triple disaster in 2011, people in Fukushima received messages from all over the world showing support and cheering those who were devastated. In Shiraki's class, students read those messages and wrote reflective essays in Japanese. One of the fifth graders, Ami, wrote the following: "Listening to those messages, I thought we have to look forward as we live. I thought we have to be cheerful and energetic.

I thought there are many people who support us. They made me happy" (Ami's writing in Kawaji, 2013, p. 13).

Rather than simply echoing and praising the positivity of Ami's writing, Shiraki asked Ami "does this mean you have not been able to feel energetic?" In response, Ami said,

[A]lthough I have been able to sing together in the choir and gradually move on with life, those friends who left are yet to be able to come back, and the radiation makes me feel anxious. So to be honest, I cannot feel energetic.

(Shiraki, 2012, pp. 212–214)

In this instance, Shiraki intuited deeper layers of emotional expression in Ami's use of words like "have to" (*shinakutewa ikenai*) and adeptly asked questions to invite Ami to elaborate on her ambivalent emotional experience.

Shiraki's practice demonstrates the care *seikatsu-tsuzurikata* teachers take with students' subjective experiences. However, if the act of reading and writing is oriented only toward subjectivity, it risks falling into superficial relativism where everything becomes a matter of one's interpretation. The following example shows a literacy teacher's attempt to go beyond this.

An elementary school teacher, Yuichi Honya, tries to deconstruct the traditional style of teaching literature in Japan that emphasizes reading for the "right" and "objective" interpretation (Honya, 2011). Instead of such an approach, he focuses on how students responded to the text and what they found in their reading. In the teaching process, Honya prepared reading cards for students to describe their questions and what they wanted to share with other students about the text. Using those cards, students engaged in discussions and negotiated interpretations of the texts. They were thereby encouraged to participate in the class based on their reading and responses.

As Honya points out, in Japanese language reading class, teachers tend to elicit students' interpretations of the texts to match what teachers think is right. In other words, the goal of the class is for students' readings to converge with the "right" and "authorized" reading. Honya's practice tries to reverse this. Starting from the subjective reading of each student, consensus and confirmation are built through negotiations and discussions. Rather than stopping at the private level of subjective reading, by creating a space for dialogue and negotiation, Honya encourages students to construct meanings at the level of the public. Whereas the teaching of a "correct" reading is prone to serve specific interests and ideological stances, Honya's approach highlights how a plurality of meanings is produced based on readers' perspectives. Moreover, through this approach, students learn to anchor the plurality of meanings through participating in dialogues and negotiations.

Conclusion

We reviewed two different modes of criticality in Japan's literacy education. Critical reading and critical literacy are juxtaposed based on their orientations to objectivity and subjectivity.

Because of its sociopolitical contexts, discourses of education in Japan have long embraced the idea of neutrality, which has led to the depoliticization of education. In such a situation, a mode of criticality that is oriented toward objectivity enjoys its popularity. However, as we pointed out earlier, such a reading cannot account for power and it risks alienating learners.

In contrast, critical literacy starts from learners' subjectivity. Through the tradition of *seikatsu-tsuzurikata*, Japanese literacy teachers have been weaving a pedagogy that connects learners to their words. Yet, if acts of reading were to be only a matter of subjective interpretation, it forecloses the possibility for us to construct a common world. Following Freire, we posit that central to literacy is the dialectic between subjectivity and objectivity. Honya's collaborative reading approach provides great insight into how educators occasion such dialectics in their classrooms.

In addition, there have been rich discussions around media literacy and political literacy education in Japan (e.g., Sekiguchi, 2019; Yamauchi, 2003), and we see great potential in the dialogical appreciation developed in art education (Hirano, 2010). Future projects may shed light on the resonances and dissonances between critical literacy and these bodies of literature. Especially in countries like Japan, where the body of literature under the label of critical literacy is not sizable, part of our responsibility as critical literacy scholars is to find notes from diverse literature and teaching practices that resonate with our work and augment the harmony.

We are painfully aware that some of the issues and challenges we discussed here are recursive: the myth of neutrality, the depoliticization of education, and the devaluation of subjectivity have already been problematized by proponents of critical literacy. We are pessimistic enough to think that we will once again have to point out these issues down the road; however, at the same time, we are optimistic enough to think that the transnational network of critical literacy advocates can evoke a much larger movement against their recurrence.

References

Apple, M. (1982). *Education and power*. Routledge.

Butler, J. (1997). *The psychic life of power: Theories in subjection*. Stanford University Press.

Freire, P. (1970). *Pedagogy of the oppressed* (M. B. Ramos, Trans.). Continuum.

Freire, P., & Macedo, D. (1987). *Literacy: Reading the word & the world* (pp. 32–41). Routledge.

Hirano, T. (2010). Mirukoto ni yoru manabi: Shichokaku kyoiku riron to hihanteki riterashii no shiten kara [Learning through viewing: From the perspectives of visual education theory and critical literacy]. *Reports on Art Communication Project*, 23–33.

Honya, Y. (2011). *Kodomo ga "hatsumon" suru manabi no kyoshitsu: "gakusyuzai" de kawaru kokugo no jyugyo* [Students' questioning and classroom teaching]. Ikkosya.

Inagaki, T. (1966). *Meiji kyōjyu rironshi kenkyu: Kokyōiku kyōjyu teikei no keisei* [The history of teaching theory in Meiji era]. Hyōronsya.

Inagaki, T., & Sato, M. (1996). *Jyugyo kenkyu nyumon* [Introduction to lesson studies]. Iwanami Shoten.

Kawaji, A. (2013). Seikatsu-tsuzurikata jissen ni okeru riarizumu to kyōiku mokuhyō [Realism and the goals of education in the praxis of seikatsu-tsuzurikata]. *Shinrikagaku* [Psychological Science], *34*(1), 11–22.

Kitagawa, M. M., & Kitagawa, C. (2007). Core values of progressive education: Seikatsu tsuzurikata and whole language. *International Journal of Progressive Education*, *3*(2), 52–67.

Kodama, S. (2016). *Kyouiku seijigaku wo hiraku: 18-sai senkyoken no jidai wo misuete* [Creating educational politics: Looking ahead to the lowering of voting age to 18]. Keiso shobo.

Kuroyabu, T. (1981). Kodomo no ikiru chikara o hagemasu seikatsu-tsuzurikata [Seikatsu-tsuzurikata that stimulates children's ability to live]. In S. Murayama (Ed.), *Seikatsu-tsuzurikata Zissen no Sōzō* [Creation of seikatsu-tsuzurikata praxis] (pp. 21–46). Minshūsha.

Kusumi, T. (2013). Hihanteki shikōryoku o mini tsukeru, hagukumu [Acquiring and cultivating critical thinking skills]. *Kodomogaku* [Child Studies], *15*, 75–102.

Kusumi, T. (2018). Riterasii o sasaeru hihanteki shikō: Dokusho kagaku heno shisa [Critical thinking that supports literacy: Suggestions for the science of reading]. *The Science of Reading*, *60*(3), 129–137.

Matsushita, K. (2014). PISA riterasii o kainarasu: Gurōbaru na kinouteki riterashii to nashonaru na kyōiku naiyō [The taming of PISA literacy: Global functional literacy and national educational content], *Kyōikugaku Kenkyū* [Educational Research], *81*(2), 150–163.

Michita, Y. (2001). Hihanteki shikō: Yori yoi shikō o motomete [Critical thinking: The pursuit of better thinking]. In T. Mori (Ed.), *Omoshiro shikō no raboratorii* [Laboratory of amusing thinking] (pp. 99–120). Kitaōji Shobō.

Michita, Y. (2003). Diversity and a fundamental image of the major concepts of critical thinking. *Japanese Psychological Review*, *46*(4), 617–639.

Ministry of Health, Labour and Welfare (MHLW). (2016). *Heisei 28 nen kokumin seikatsu kiso chōsa no gaikyō* [Overview of the basic survey on national life]. Retrieved from www.mhlw.go.jp/toukei/saikin/hw/k-tyosa/k-tyosa16/.

Oguma, E. (1995). *Tanitsu minzoku shinwa no kigen: "Nihonjin" no jigazō no keifu* [The origin of the myth of the homogeneity: Genealogy of the self-portrait of Japanese]. Shinyosha.

Rocha, S. (2018). "Ser mais": The personalism of Paulo Freire. *Philosophy of Education*, *1*(1), 371–384.

Sakota, K. (1981). Seikatsu-tsuzurikata no kokoro [The heart of seikatsu-tsuzurikata]. In S. Murayama (Ed.), *Seikatsu-tsuzurikata Zissen no Sōzō* [Creation of seikatsu-tsuzurikata praxis] (pp. 7–20). Minshūsha.

Sato, M. (1997). *Karikyuramu no hihyō: Koukyōsei no saikōuchiku he* [Critiquing curriculum: Toward reconstruction of the public]. Seori Shobo.

Sato, Y. (2016). Contemporary significance of Paulo Freire's educational thoughts of "liberation" and "problem-posing education": Focus on "generative words"/"generative themes" mediating "dialogue" and "conscientization". Kyōiku *Hōhōgaku Kenkyū* [Pedagogical Research], *41*(1), 49–59.

Sekiguchi, M. (Ed.). (2019). *Seiji riterashii o kangaeru: Shimin kyōiku no seiji shisō* [Thinking about political literacy: Political thoughts on citizenship education]. Fuko Sha.

Shiraki, J. (2012). *Soredemo watashitachi wa kyōshi da: Kodomotachi to tomo ni kibō o tsumugu* [Yet, we are teachers: Weaving hope with children]. Hon no Izumi Sha.

Tsuzuki, Y., & Aragaki, N. (2012). Sanpi no wakareru mijika na shakai mondai ni taisuru daigakusei no shikō purosesu no bunseki [Analysis of thinking process by university students on controversial social issues that are relevant to them]. *Cognitive Studies*, *19*(1), 39–55.

Walters, K. (1994). Introduction: Beyond logicism in critical thinking. In K. Walters (Ed.), Re-thinking reason: *New perspectives on critical thinking* (pp. 1–22). SUNY Press.

Yamauchi, Y. (2003). *Dejitaru shakai no riterashii: "Manabi no komyunitii" o dezain suru* [Literacy in the digital society: Designing "community of learning"]. Iwanami Shoten.

2.10

CRITICAL LITERACIES
IN MÉXICO

*Gregorio Hernandez-Zamora, Mario López-Gopar, and Rosa María
Quesada-Mejía*

Sociopolitical Context

The purpose of this chapter is to shed light on the critical literacy practices in Mexico, which
have been neglected or invisibilized. Along with the rest of Latin America, Mexico suffered the
Spanish rule for three centuries (1521–1821), resulting in exploitation, despair, and the hier-
archization of both people and knowledge, including language and literacy (López-Gopar, 2007;
Hernandez-Zamora, 2009, 2010). The remaining state of coloniality—the colonial domination
through the imposition of Eurocentric models of subjectivity, authority, economy, and knowledge
(Quijano, 2007)— and Mexico's current troublesome relation with the United States and Canada
and their inherent multinational corporations (e.g., Walmart, Canadian mining companies) have
brought perennial poverty, social inequalities, and injustice (López-Gopar & Sughrua, 2014). By
2020, Mexico has the widest gap between rich and poor people among the OECD countries
(OECD, 2020), with at least 52 million people, 42% of the country's population, living in poverty
(CONEVAL, 2020).

In contrast, some of the richest men in the world are Mexicans, and 43% of the country's wealth
is controlled by 0.02% of the population (López-Gopar & Sughrua, 2014). This reality impacts
workers and Indigenous groups the hardest, who survive on minimum wage of 7 USD for eight
hours of work (CNSM, 2020). Along with coloniality and socioeconomic inequality, in the last two
decades the deeply entrenched government corruption, and its connection to firms and drug cartels,
resulted in widespread criminal violence and feminicides (Morris, 2018; Wright, 2011). Despite
this adverse historical scenario, Mexican people have resisted for centuries and continue to do so as
evident in their critical literacy practices described in this chapter.

Educational System

With a population of 135 million in 2020, Mexico endures perennial education issues. It systematically ranks the lowest of the OECD nations in PISA tests of reading (from 2000 to 2020), and
it has enormous disparities in access, graduation, and learning across lines of class, ethnicity, and
region. To understand the roots of our current situation, let us sketch a historical picture. Before the
Spanish conquest in 1521, many cultures in today's Mexican and Central American territory were
already subjugated by the Aztec Empire, who imposed its language (Nahuatl), cultural ways, and a
segregated school system: one serving the children of nobility and other for the common people.

The *Calmecac* educated future leaders through literacy, higher war techniques, and arts; while *Tel-pochcalli* prepared the lower castes to feed the labor force and common soldiery. Afterwards, during the three centuries of colonial Spanish rule, schools, including the Royal and Pontifical University of Mexico (founded 1551) were reserved to educate the upper caste of Spaniards, while Mestizos and Indigenous were submitted by force, cultural substitution, and religious indoctrination intended to instill obedience.

The nineteenth century (post-independence) was a period of construction of a nation-state in the middle of violent civil disputes between "liberals" and "conservatives". To create a minimum sense of unity and nationhood, schools and churches were used to forge cultural homogenization through Christianization, and the imposition of Spanish as the "national language". The twentieth century began with a revolutionary uprising that promulgated a new Constitution and established the new Ministry of Education in 1929, whose mission was to continue instilling a sense of national identity among a population still hierarchized and divided by ethnicity and class. In the post–World War II era (1945–2020) Mexico experienced an explosive demographic growth that tripled the population (from 40 to 130 million), which in turn forced the expansion of the school system to supply schooling to the now urbanized and industrialized "modern" country. Nonetheless, during this period, Mexico achieved some social justice in terms of education, by closing social gaps not only among Mexicans but also among citizens of Central and South America hosted by Mexican institutions in times of military dictatorships and revolutionary movements in Latin America. However, since the 1980s, neoliberal economic policies significantly widened the socioeconomic and educational inequalities. As a result, sharp inequalities in the quality of teaching and learning still remain across the Mexican territory.

Survey of Critical Literacy Work

As literacy educators, researchers, and activists ourselves, the authors of this chapter have enacted and witnessed diverse critical literacy endeavors taking place officially and unofficially, inside and outside of schools. We are thus aware of the pervading invisibility of most of this work that challenges hegemonic discourses and practices. Our goal is to visualize actions and actors usually neglected in government accounts about Mexican education. Because of space limits, we will survey only a sample of experiences embodied by educators who have learned to think outside the system, as Horton and Freire put it in their spoken book *We make the road by walking* (1990).

We identify work carried within and outside of the school system. Within the system, while public education is heavily controlled by political bureaucracies committed to short-term goals linked to the party in power, pockets of individual and networked educators engage in critical literacy projects, often at a high price. This work takes place in public and private schools from elementary to college level. And outside the system, we distinguish two types of critical education work:

(i.) Work done by grassroots educators, cultural activists, and NGOs that promote literacy education in marginalized communities (e.g., reading "mediators" working at homes, plazas, or in public libraries; and

(ii.) Work done by organizations and individuals whose primary goal is not education itself, but their actions have significant impact on the (critical) education of poor communities (e.g., grassroots activists engaged in health, religious, art projects).

In Teacher's Training at Elementary Level

Different initiatives across the Mexican territory have sought to introduce critical approaches in the literacy education of teachers (in service and in training). Drawing from literacy theorists and local developments, much of this work aims at developing teacher's agency, voice, and reading–writing skills to enable them to teach those same traits to their students. These are two examples.

The *Red de Lenguaje por la transformación de la escuela y la comunidad*, a collective led by academics at *Universidad Pedagógica Nacional* (Ruíz & Rosales, 2018; Ruíz, Correa, & Chona, 2010; Chona, 2016) has developed for decades an important work of networking hundreds of basic education teachers in Mexico City and Oaxaca, and training them in project-based pedagogy (as theorized by French scholar Josette Jolibert), and narrative documentation of teacher's experiences (as theorized by Argentinian scholars Daniel Suárez, Gabriel Roizman, and others).

In the State of Mexico, teachers at *Escuela Normal de Zumpango* have undertaken initiatives to teach critical literacy and critical research methods to both students (teachers-to-be) and their professors at this and other Normal schools across the country. Their aim is to move them from traditionalist ways of teaching language and literature into critical pedagogies. Estela Ramírez, head of teachers' development, has sought to explore new ways of being a teacher by rethinking and re-experiencing the links between the personal, the social, the literary, and the pedagogic. To do so, she engages their students in critical reading, creative writing, class dialogue, and hands-on activities. She uses children's literature to develop "non-parametric" didactic methods (Ramírez, 2019) that enable student-teachers to use reality as a teaching device, to articulate varied knowledges, and to develop a historical consciousness, all linked to children's literature. Also, in the State of Mexico, Víctor Espinoza (2014) and Mercado and Espinoza (2013) have developed critical writing pedagogies to empower teachers-to-be through first-person academic writing experiences that link their teaching and life worlds by engaging their feelings, thoughts, and actions. The goal is to create stronger identities as teachers.

It might take a whole book to expose the stories of many other teachers committed to critical literacy education. There is also a long list of historically influential critical educators who shaped the ideas and practices of hundreds of Mexican teachers, such as Patricio Redondo (✝), José de Tapia (✝), Chela González, Ramiro Reyes (✝), Tere Garduño, and many others. The YouTube channel *Ser Maestro*, hosted by another remarkable teacher, Marco Esteban Mendoza (Mendoza, n/d), showcases interviews with dozens of influential Mexican educators. Also, we should include the names of pedagogic collectives such as *Movimiento Mexicano de la Escuela Moderna* (MMEM), *Red LEO Oaxaca*, *Red Estatal para la Transformación Educativa de Michoacán*, as much as historically critical *escuelas normales*, such as *Normal de Ayotzinapa*, *Normal del Mexe*, and *Benemérita Escuela Nacional de Maestros*.

In Higher Education

Two examples of critical literacy work occur at public universities serving low-income students. The first is *Universidad Autónoma de la Ciudad de México* (UACM), founded in 2001. This university seeks to counter the tendency of reserving higher education for the elites, while offering a scientific, humanistic, and critical education. Here, professor Claudia Bernaldez and colleagues drew on critical academic literacy theorists, such as Freire (Brazil), Hernandez-Zamora (Mexico), Carlino (Argentina), and Lomas and Castelló (Spain), in order to create a Department of Language and Thought and design the syllabi of Language and Argumentation courses. Her work focuses on teaching critical reading and argumentative writing, with the aim of developing the voice of students unaccustomed to speaking their minds. The second example is at *Universidad Autónoma Metropolitana* (UAM), which also serves students coming from low SES at the outskirts of Mexico City. Here, professor Alejandra García Franco (in press) teaches Academic Literacy to freshmen students. She has sought to develop students' sense of authorship and capability as writers and thinkers, by building links between subject knowledge and their literacy biographies. They interview each other and write coherent and interesting pieces that make them feel capable of thinking and expressing themselves freely and critically, even if their grammar is far from perfect.

In Private Schools

While critical literacy has been often seen as education for and with the poor, diverse private schools in Mexico (from K to Graduate) embrace also the goal of raising critical consciousness among children of affluent families. This is the case of the so-called active schools, which have not only served upper social strata but have also triggered true pedagogical movements embracing critical literacy as key to their models, pedagogies, and goals. Examples of these are preschool and elementary schools inspired by Celestine Freinet and Maria Montessori (French and Italian educators) such as the elementary school *Manuel Bartolomé Cossío*, founded and headed by a couple of socially committed teachers (José de Tapia, ✝, and Graciela González). This small school in southern Mexico City has inspired the creation of many other "active schools" across the country and formed generations of kinder and elementary teachers in both private and public schools. They have learned to teach critical literacy through the class journal, free text, school assembly, student conferences, the dialogued class, and other reading, writing, thinking, and speaking practices (González, 1970; Jiménez, 1990). As explained by Graciela González, the key goal of this pedagogy is "to give the children the word".

Individual initiatives by commited teachers have also taken place, such as these:

(1.) In Mexico City, Gilda Cervantes creates projects that depart from questions posed by the children and involve library and field research, surveys, art creations, and class discussions about the topic at hand and reflections on their own feelings and thoughts.

(2.) In the state of Morelos, to develop the literacy skills of students at a K–12 school, Claudia Gaete engaged the students in critical reflection, examination, and learning of Indigenous languages still spoken in Mexico. By organizing activities around Nahuatl vocabulary, stories, and literature, she moved the students from reflecting on their ancestry and cultural legacies to their own beliefs, practices, and identities.

(3.) Working with senior high school students, Claudia Zendejas has created the social and intellectual space capable of encouraging students to write thoughtful and critical commentaries on cultural images (photography, movies, Netflix series) in which they trace connections between the social issues involved (criminal and gender violence, poverty, despair, etc.), and the intertextual relations with real social phenomena. The resulting textual productions are true exercises of thoughtful and fluid verbal articulation and literacy-mediated critical thinking.

In the Formal Curriculum

Over the last two decades, educational reforms have begun to include *critical reading* and *critical thinking* as official learning goals in public education, even though they do so with watered-down and narrow conceptions of "critical literacy" (Hernandez-Zamora, 2008). In practice, critical literacy has remained a written intention rather than actual (trans)formation of students. In contrast, committed educators and researchers have worked to materialize these goals through more substantial programs, syllabi, and instructional materials. We share two examples here.

Between 2004 and 2007, Hernandez-Zamora and his colleagues, working for the Ministry of Education, developed a series of foundational documents and teaching materials to teach critical literacy in Telesecundaria schools, the middle school system attended by the poorest rural and urban youth. Drawing on the ideas of educators like Paulo Freire, Jim Cummins, Alma Flor Ada, and Shirley Heath, these materials sought to develop *literate behaviors* through critical approaches to reading and writing. They were used in schools for nearly a decade, despite the censorship they suffered from top education officials (Hernandez-Zamora, 2008).

In the northern state of Baja California, Karla Canett worried that while Mexico champions in low reading skills and high gender violence, critical literacy and thinking courses were nonexistent in the formal curriculum at high school, university, and teacher training programs. She took action and developed syllabi to teach critical reading with a gender approach, based on field research with students and theoretical ideas from New Literacy scholars such as Gee, Shor, Luke, and Cassany (Cannet, 2020).

In Social Movements

One of the goals of critical literacy is the transformation of people's lives in their own terms (Cummins, 2000; Ada & Campoy, 2004). In order to achieve this, the creation/authorship of multimodal and multilingual texts and their dissemination is essential. There is a long history of social movements in Mexico involving such practices. Let us see two examples.

In Chiapas, Mexico, the Zapatista Movement in 1994 gained national and international recognition by using the incipient internet to manifest to the world the social inequities and discrimination against Indigenous peoples in Mexico. Through thousands of multimodal texts created and shared through the internet, they spoke back to the government rhetoric that labeled them as illegal rebels. In addition, in their territories they constructed a system of autonomous schools where they decide contents, methods, languages of use, and reading materials (Baronnet, 2009).

The second example is the teachers' movement in Oaxaca. For decades, Indigenous and mestizo teachers have challenged educational policies and reforms, publicly denounced neoliberal educational agendas and engaged both children and parents in their struggle (Meyer & Maldonado Alvarado, 2004, 2010). Critical literacy has been "taught" not as much inside classrooms but displayed and modeled through political and educational resistance. Due to this praxis (reflection plus activism), they have been portrayed as "revoltosos" (unruly, overly rebellious) by both government and media, which has often turned the public's opinion against their strikes and demonstrations. To counter these derogating representations, often used to justify episodes of brutal police repression, a literary circle invited activist teachers to write their intimate and personal accounts of the struggle from inside. These were published in the book *Escribir para resistir* (Writing to resist) (González & Salazar, 2013).

In Streets and Communities

Outside the school system, there is plenty but unacknowledged critical literacy work carried out by people engaged in practices that challenge hegemonic institutions and discourses. Through self-authoring practices of diverse kinds (art, health care, unschooled reading, etc.) they are, to a large extent, a territory to be explored by formal research and acknowledged by official institutions.

Street musicians are but an example. Countless and talented musicians, especially young people, use their artistic talents to "talk back" and create powerful multimodal texts to address issues of gender, poverty, and social (in)justices. In southern Mexico, *Mare Advertencia Lirika* is a young Oaxacan Indigenous female rapper, who majored in language teaching at a public university in Oaxaca, the most culturally and linguistically diverse state of Mexico, where women, especially Indigenous, have historically struggled socially and economically (Stephen, 2005). In Mare's song, *What are you waiting for?*, she denounces the social inequities she faced as soon as she arrived in the world,

> I was born a woman in times of breast cancer,
> When sexism killed many sisters,
> When lesbians were hunted as witches,
> Among secret abortions, AIDS and sex slavery.
> I am one among so many, and the few.

(Mare, 2013)

Regarding Mare's reality, Motta (2014) adds, "Indigenous women of color like Mare are subject to multiple oppressions, including political and epistemological invisibilization . . . yet . . . [Mare] articulate[s] a voice from the margins" (p. 21). Young people's articulation in different modes is testament to the presence of critical literacy practices in the homes, communities, and possibly the schools, where they resist daily oppression. In similar lines, Aranda (in press) argues that rap should be understood as a vernacular and potentially critical literacy practice, which should be used working with the youth.

Critical literacy practices emerge also in community library projects. Since 2002, a community multilingual library, *BIBLOCA*, has operated in Oaxaca, Mexico, with the collaboration of students who major in teaching languages at the Oaxacan public university. BIBLOCA has four objectives: (i.) to develop critical literacy; (ii.) to foster Indigenous languages; (iii.) to teach English critically; and (iv.) to offer future language teachers the opportunity to work with children (López-Gopar et al., 2020). At this library, children do not only read books critically, but they also work on critical thematic units about important issues in their lives (e.g., water shortage in their community, health, and nutrition) and create videos that are shared with children in other countries (López-Gopar, Huerta Cordova, Sughrua, & León Jiménez, in press).

In Iztapalapa, the most overpopulated area of Mexico City, the Movement of Naturist Health engages hundreds of people in critical education encounters under the guidance of local leaders such as Liliana Vazquez, Jesús Ramírez, and Guadalupe Corona. They engage humble people in critical dialogues, reflective reading of texts, writing of personal experiences, book recommendations, and exercises of alternative therapeutics (Hernandez-Zamora, 2003).

Finally, cultural work with books and reading across the country has exploded in recent years. An example is María Esther Pérez-Feria´s project called *Palabras para darte vuelo* (Words to make you fly) (Pérez-Feria, 2018a, 2018b). Challenging dominant visions of book reading as "educated entertainment", she uses poetry and children's literature to empower young and adult people, especially women, to raise their awareness as writers and push their sense of agency, voice, creativity, and imagination. Working at schools, book fairs, public libraries, and community spaces across the country, as well as through internet workshops, she uses poetry to encourage the creative power of every woman to resist inequality and injustice.

Toward More Transnational Critical Work

No critical literacy project in today's world is viable in isolation. Mexican active schools and *Red de Lenguaje*, for instance, have always networked with educators and scholars from Europe and Latin America. Likewise, in our own research, we have networked with colleagues from Canada and the United States in order to study young Mexicans in and out of school settings, as they move back and forth between transnational borders (Cummins, López-Gopar, & Sughrua, 2019; Hernandez-Zamora, Sanchez, & Ramírez, 2016; López-Gopar, 2011; Sánchez, Hernandez-Zamora, & Ramírez, in press). Yet, altogether much work is done in solitary and against the odds of powerful national and transnational policies and forces, fostered by international agencies such as the World Bank or the OECD. Critical literacy educators and scholars should also network at local, national, and transnational levels and engage with existing transnational and transdisciplinary projects and movements committed to social change. As shown in the previous section, countless groups and individuals engage in critical literacy practices not as an end-goal, but as a mediating process in projects focused on gender issues, environment, economic and human rights, self-determination, health care, among others. We should *learn* from these transnational and transdisciplinary organizations as they have been able to self-author their place in the world.

Suggestions for Research and Practice

We have provided but a quick glance at critical literacy work in Mexico, a window to a world still to be explored and furthered. More collaboration between scholars and practitioners is needed to get this type of work out of the shadows, and this requires: (i.) Attention to actors and actions invisibilized by educational policies and institutions; (ii.) Counter hegemonic policies within scientific circles, which despise and devalue uncanonical contributions; and (iii.) A commitment to show what cannot be found by searching the keywords "education" and "literacy" in academic searching engines and databases. It is grassroots literacy at work, visible only through actual actions, texts, and people, often shadowed by mainstream institutions and discourses engaged in a political practice called *production of inexistence* by Portuguese thinker Boaventura De Sousa Santos (2009).

Implications for Our Social Responsibility as Academics

As academics, we believe that we must develop sensibility and capacity to communicate through more inclusive and horizontal ways with practitioners and educators. This very Handbook is an example of a text hardly accessible to most educators presented in this chapter because of issues of language (English), register and purposes (academic), and cost (expensive). Since most grassroots teachers and educators in Mexico are monolingual Spanish speakers, we anticipate a minimum audience among them. It is valuable, though, that at least summaries of their actions and names are legitimized through a prestigious international publishing house. It remains, thus, as a task for us to expand the information barely sketched here and find appropriate venues to be communicated. It is our challenge to reconcile educational scholarship and practice, which seem to exist so far as separate worlds.

References

Ada, A. F., & Campoy, I. (2004). *Authors in the classroom: A transformative education process.* Allyn and Bacon.

Aranda, J. A. (in press). El rap: Literacidad vernácula, académica y crítica. *Sinéctica: Revista Electrónica de Educación.*

Baronnet, B. (2009). *Autonomía y educación indígena: Las escuelas zapatistas de las cañadas de la selva lacandona de Chiapas* (PhD thesis). El Colegio de Mexico.

Cannet, K. (2020). *Formación de docentes de bachillerato en literacidad crítica con enfoque de género* (Master's thesis). UABC.

Chona, J. (2016). La investigación narrativa, un dispositivo para destejer la complejidad en el aula. En F. Monroy (Ed.), *Temas de formación docente.* CAPUB.

CNSM. (2020). Incremento al salario mínimo para 2021. Gobierno de México: Comisión Nacional de los Salarios Mínimos. Retrieved from https://www.gob.mx/conasami/es/articulos/incremento-al-salario-minimo-para-2021?idiom=es

CONEVAL. (2020). *Medición de pobreza, México 2008–2018.* Retrieved from www.coneval.org.mx/Medicion/MP/PublishingImages/Pobreza_2018/Cuadro_1_2008-2018.PNG

Cummins, J. (2000). *Language, power and pedagogy.* Multilingual Matters.

Cummins, J., López-Gopar, M. E., & Sughrua, W. M. (2019). English language teaching in North American schools. In X. Gao (Ed.), *Second handbook of English language teaching* (pp. 1–21). Springer. https://doi.org/10.1007/978-3-319-58542-0_1-1.

De Sousa Santos, B. (2009). *Una epistemología del Sur.* CLACSO-Siglo XXI.

Espinoza, V. A. (2014). Dispositivos de escritura académica para el empoderamiento de la formación docente. *Temachtiani, 9*(19), 4–18.

Freire, P., & Macedo, D. (1987). *Literacy: Reading the word and the world.* Routledge.

García, F. A. (in press). Un ensayo narrativo en la universidad: Reconociendo la voz de los estudiantes. *Sinéctica: Revista Electrónica de Educación.*

González, G. (1970). *Cómo dar la palabra al niño.* SEP-Caballito.

González, N., & Salazar, D. (2013). *Escribir para resistir.* Lele ediciones.

Hernandez-Zamora, G. (2003). Comunidades de lectores: Puerta de entrada a la cultura escrita. *Decisio: Saberes para la Acción en Educación de Adultos*. México: CREFAL, No. 6.

Hernandez-Zamora, G. (2008). Alfabetización: teoría y práctica. *Decisio*. México: CREFAL, No. 21, 18–24.

Hernandez-Zamora, G. (2009). Neocolonialimso y políticas de representación: La creación histórica y presente del anafalbetismo en México y Estados Unidos. *Lectura y Vida*, *30*(1), 30–43.

Hernandez-Zamora, G. (2010). *Decolonizing literacy: Mexican lives in the era of global capitalism*. Multilingual Matters.

Hernandez-Zamora, G., Sanchez, P., & Ramírez, G. (Eds.). (2016). *20 Años después: Jóvenes migrantes en Norte América*. PIERAN-UAM-ITESO-UNAM.

Horton, M., & Freire, P. (1990). *We make the road by walking: Conversations on education and social change*. Temple University Press.

Jiménez, F. (1990). *Vida, obra y pensamiento de José de Tapia: Un maestro singular*. Robin.

López-Gopar, M. E. (2007). Beyond the alienating alphabetic literacy: Multiliteracies in Indigenous education in Mexico. *Diaspora, Indigenous and Minority Education: An International Journal*, *1*(3), 159–174.

López-Gopar, M. E. (2011). Cross-cultural connections: Developing teaching principles through stories. In P. R. Schmidt & A. Lazar (Eds.), *We can teach and we can learn: Achievement in culturally responsive literacy classrooms* (pp. 168–181). Teachers College Press.

López-Gopar, M. E., Huerta Cordova, V., Sughrua, W., & León Jiménez, E. N. (in press). Developing decolonizing pedagogies with Mexican pre-service "English" teachers. In M. Hawkins (Ed.), *Transmodal communications: Transpositioning semiotics and relations*. Multilingual Matters.

López-Gopar, M. E., Sughrua, M., Córdova-Hernández, L., López Torres, B. P., Ruiz Aldaz, E., & Vásquez Morales, V. (2020). A critical thematic unit in a teaching praxicum: Health issues and plurilingualism in the "English" classroom. In S. M. C. Lau & S. Van Viegen (Eds.), *Plurilingual pedagogies: Critical and creative endeavors for equitable language in Education* (pp. 97–114). Springer.

López-Gopar, M. E., & Sughrua, W. (2014). Social class in English language education in Oaxaca, Mexico. *Journal of Language, Identity and Education*, *13*, 104–110.

Mare Advertencia Lirika. (2013). *¿Y tú qué esperas?* [Video]. YouTube. Retrieved from https://youtu.be/aEs7Okf0SPc

Martínez-Torres, M. E. (2001). Civil society, the internet, and the Zapatistas. *Peace Review*, *13*(3), 347–355. https://doi.org/10.1080/13668800120079045

Mendoza, M. E. (n.d.). *Playlists* [Ser Maestro]. YouTube. Retrieved from www.youtube.com/playlist?list=PL0lTQwrrPbHlnIe4VH_nSxUgh0cS0ed6g

Mercado, E., & Espinoza, V. A. (2013). *Escritura y empoderamiento en la formación inicial de los docentes: problemas y tensiones*. Paper presented at XII CNIE, Guanajuato, Mexico.

Meyer, L. & Maldonado Alvarado, B. (Eds.). (2004). *Entre la normatividad y la comunalidad: Experiencias educativas innovadoras del Oaxaca indígena actual*. IEEPO.

Meyer, L., & Maldonado Alvarado, B. (Eds.). (2010). *New world of Indigenous resistance: Noam Chomsky and voices from North, South and Central America*. City Lights books.

Morris, S. (2018). Corruption in Mexico: Continuity and change. In B. Warf (Ed.), *Handbook on the geographies of corruption* (pp. 132–153). Edward Elgar Pub.

Motta, S. C. (2014). Latin America: Reinventing revolutions, an "Other" politics in practice and theory. In R. Stahler-Sholk, H. E. Vanden, & M. Becker (Eds.), *Rethinking Latin American social movements: Radical action from below* (pp. 21–44). Rowman & Littlefield.

OECD. (2020). *Income inequality (indicator)*. Retrieved November 29, 2020, from https://doi.org/10.1787/459aa7f1-en

Pérez-Feria, M. E. (2018a). Leer, Leer-nos, Leer el Mundo. In *Leer para la Vida*. SEP-Secretarí;a de Cultura.

Pérez-Feria, M. E. (2018b). *¿Para qué sirve la poesía?* UVEJOTA. Retrieved from https://uvejota.com/articles/4828/para-que-sirve-la-poesia-invitada-maria-esther-perez-feria/

Quijano, A. (2007). Coloniality and modernity/rationality. *Cultural Studies*, *21*(2–3), 168–178. https://doi.org/10.1080/09502380601164353.

Ramírez, R. E. (2019). *Formación de maestros desde una didáctica no parametral*. Paper presented at CONLES, Lima, Perú.

Ruíz, C., Correa, G., & Chona, J. (2010). Transformar el aula, la escuela y la comunidad. *Revista Entre maestr@s*, *10*(33), 8–18.

Ruíz, C., & Rosales, L. (2018). Formarnos para transformarnos. Experiencias en la formación de profesores desde la Pedagogía por Proyectos. *Revista Nodos y Nudos*, 37–56.

Sánchez, P., Hernández-Zamora, G., & Ramírez, G. (Eds.). (in press). *In search of hope and home: Mexican immigrants in the trinational NAFTA context*. Peter Lang Publishing.

Stephen, L. (2005). *Zapotec women: Gender, class and ethnicity in globalized Oaxaca* (2nd ed.). Duke University Press.

Stewart, Y. (2000). *Dressing the tarot* (Master's thesis). Auckland University of Technology.

Wright, M. W. (2011). Necropolitics, narcopolitics, and femicide: Gendered violence on the Mexico-U.S. Border. *Signs: Journal of Women in Culture and Society, 36*(3), 707–731.

2.11

CRITICAL LITERACY IN PUERTO RICO

Mapping Trajectories of Anticolonial Reaffirmations and Resistance

Carmen Liliana Medina and Sandra L. Soto-Santiago

Puerto Rico's Sociopolitical Contexts

Puerto Rico, an archipelago located in the Caribbean, was inhabited by Taíno indigenous communities who named it Borikén, land of the great lords. In 1493, Borikén became a possession of Spain. Upon the genocide of its indigenous people, a colonial society was built grounded in enslaved models of European empire (Quijano, 2000). With these unequal relationships, Puerto Rico evolved as a diverse nation with hierarchies of power that still have an impact in the present (Duany, 2017; Godreau, 2015).

In 1898, through a military invasion, and as a result of the Hispanic American war, Puerto Rico became a colonial possession of the United States. The settling of the United States in this archipelago has historically been manifested in multiple ways, such as through military occupations and removal of people from their land, economic exploitation and unfair regulatory policies that do not allow for a sovereign economic system (Ayala & Bernabe, 2011). These in addition to modern colonialities that reaffirm hierarchies of oppression at the intersection of language, race, gender, sexuality and spirituality. An example of this is the US federal imposition of the Fiscal Oversight and Management Board whose members make all financial decisions for Puerto Rico that have severely hurt institutions like the University of Puerto Rico, (UPR), K–12 public education and put at risk essential services and retirement pension funds (Cabán, 2018). These impositions have made Puerto Rico a site of constant resistance (see https://puertoricosyllabus.com) that centers our analysis on this chapter.

Puerto Rico's Educational System

After the US invasion in 1898, a military government imposed an educational system through the *Departamento de Instrucción Pública*. As part of the larger agenda of "americanization" for Puerto Rico, instruction was mandated and modeled after the US school system (Torres González, 2002). As in other instances, teachers and community members resisted these changes, arguing these were not in the best interests of students (Del Moral, 2013). More than a century later teachers, parents and students continue protesting policies that have been detrimental to the schools and students (López Alicea, 2018).

Public schools in Puerto Rico are part of the US Department of Education (DOE), resulting in the schools' forced compliance with federal educational laws. Attempts to make English the

 DOI: 10.4324/9781003023425-23

official language and to shift Puerto Rico from a dominant Spanish speaking to an English speaking nation have historically marked multiple educational policies and initiatives (Schmidt, 2014). The issue of the officiality of language in Puerto Rico has always been highly politicized and contested. Despite several decades of exploratory changes in language policies, all subjects in public schools in Puerto Rico are currently taught in Spanish except for English class. However, Puerto Ricans often engage in translingual practices in Spanish and English in their day-to-day communication (Carroll & Mazak, 2017).

Within that historical context, it is worth highlighting some implications of the recent sequence of events around environmental, humanitarian, political and pandemic catastrophes (Maldonado-Torres, 2019). In September 2017, the damages caused by Hurricanes Irma and María had major consequences for children and the local educational system (Brusi & Goudreau, 2019). As people were left without support and an immediate effective response from both local and federal governments, issues with safe housing, lack of essential resources such as electricity, in many cases for over a year, had a major impact on the local communities' well-being (Bonilla & LeBrón, 2019; Enchautegui-Román, Segarra-Alméstica, Cordero-Nieves, & Rivera-Rodríguez, 2018). Schools closed for months and a corruption scheme that involved the top stakeholders in the DOE resulted in the permanent closing of over 250 schools.

January 2020 began with an earthquake where citizens, particularly in the south side of the island, were again left homeless and without an adequate support system. All schools closed for at least a month, many suffered severe damage and around 68 schools never opened, creating an overlap in school closure and children's educational experiences with the COVID-19 pandemic. The effects of these catastrophic events are complex and challenging to overcome. Close to 60% of students in Puerto Rico live in poverty (Enchautegui-Román et al., 2018) with a larger number of Puerto Ricans (5 million) now in the United States. A sense of a major *desconfianza* (distrust) has put into question the governments' capabilities to foreground people's well-being over corruption and neoliberal policies and actions. The resistance developments that led to the resignation of governor Ricky Roselló, in July 2019, emerged from these activist spaces that aim to visibilize and act upon social injustice (Atiles-Osoria, 2020).

The DOE, particularly children and teachers, are among those who have suffered the most (Education Week, 2020). The local DOE has not been able to develop an effective recovery plan for any of these crises. Currently, access to technology for economically disadvantaged students adds to these issues and the development of mechanisms that allow for vulnerable parents and caregivers to manage the educational shifts during the pandemic such as support for children attending school virtually.

Influential Perspectives in the Development of Critical Literacy Initiatives in Puerto Rico

The methodological design of our scholarship has been grounded in decolonial research traditions (Patel, 2015). For the purpose of this chapter, this translated to a review of works combined with elements of cultural intuition that relies on local expert knowledges. In order to develop the inquiry core of this chapter, we identified publications related to critical literacy, mostly focusing on work foregrounding the reality of the archipelago and that suggested a critical literacy perspective in their writing. Initially, our searches included critical practices in education that might remain at the outset of more situated scholarship in critical literacy. Through online searches and informal conversations with activist-experts, we were able to identify and examine approximately 14 publications and developed a set of consolidated themes across works that frame the structure and focus of the rest of this chapter.

Mapping Histories of Anticolonial Literacy Education

To understand CL work in Puerto Rico it is imperative to visibilize and disrupt colonial logic and impositions. In Hostos's influential works on education for democracy from the late nineteenth century (Hostos, 1991), we can identify a trajectory of texts that speak of liberatory and *concientización* pedagogies that cover Puerto Rico, the Caribbean and Latin America. As Rojas Osorio (2012) described it: "For Hostos, the goal for Latin American educators should be to develop an awareness of our collective identity, an identity that is historical; a nation is not a fixed essence, but a shared history" (p. 17). Foregrounding arts and language as fundamental aspects in a liberatory education, in Hostos's philosophical works, he perceived arts as forms and spaces to reflect on sociopolitical aspects of the world and: "saw in language not only the intellectual functions of the human mind, but also its emotional expression, sensitivity, necessity and action" (p. 26).

As we just described through Hostos's work, one aspect that mobilizes the emergence of CL work in Puerto Rico is the relationship between literacy and coloniality. These forms of colonial literacy are manifested in both the imposition of English as an official and dominant language, in addition to how literacy has been used to systematically control and manipulate local knowledges through US policies, practices and curricular reforms (González-Robles, 2011; Torres González, 2002). Foregrounding Puerto Rican students' voices, Walsh (1987, 1991) explores a critical literacy pedagogy where Puerto Rican children wrestle with tensions they live across literacies and languages and also how they strategically navigate across as forms of agency and empowerment.

Drawing from her own experiences, Medina (2003) looks into the material consequences of a colonial approach to literacy through a literacy narrative of her school years in Puerto Rico. Medina argues that autobiographical literacy narratives, in the context of Puerto Rico, can serve as tools to locate, make visible and disrupt the normalized ways in which the americanization of schools materializes and impacts people's lives and also the decolonial tactics that are afforded as a storying resistance project.

Critical Literacy as Sites for Social and Activist Knowledge Production in Schools

Dominant approaches to literacy tend to be more grounded on an autonomous model of literacy (Street, 2006) with the development of phonetic knowledge, skills drills and grammar as the main focus. Although many schools and teachers still believe and work from these autonomous views to literacy, locally, teacher preparation and professional development has gone through significant changes to create more expansive processes to literacy teaching and learning through *lenguaje integral* situated in sociocultural and Whole Language perspectives (Sáez Vega et al., 1999; Sáez Vega & González-Robles, 2015).

Efforts to develop school-based CL curricula and initiatives in Spanish, Puerto Rico's dominant language, have been present in Puerto Rico. An analysis of those studies points to a number of relevant aspects such as (1.) The construction of literature-based reading and writing pedagogies for CL engagement, foregrounding children "understandings about how power, ideology and identity are interwoven in society" (González-Robles, 2020, p. 1; González-Robles et al., 2016). (2.) CL, literacy as social practices and multiliteracies—play, popular media literacies, reading, writing—to center children's ways of knowing in literacy work and to examine the relationship between out-of-school every day experiences, children's voices, agency and the deconstruction of power across literacies (Costa, Medina & Soto, 2011; Medina & Costa, 2013). (3.) CL in relation to local schools activism—children, parents, teachers and librarians—within recent catastrophic times (Lugo, 2018; Martínez-Roldán, 2019). These works provide examples of locally Spanish-based socially engaged and culturally sustaining pedagogies that aim to move a historically imposed curricula out of its neutral space and that proposes humanizing and activist forms of doing literacy. Of significance to this section are works that explicitly document socially engaged efforts that emerge after the catastrophic events that began with Hurricanes Maria and Irma. A study worth examining is Martinez-Roldán's (2019) case study of one local school activism and organization to preserve the school open and how these actions simultaneously serve to construct critically engaged curricula with the children. Also relevant is Lugo's (2018) and Medina (2020) research documenting the role of librarians, literature and literacy educators in supporting children in the aftermath of multiple catastrophic events.

Critical Literacy as Transformative Spaces in Teacher Education

Teacher education programs go through the same institutional accreditation processes than those in the United States and are also aligned to local curricular standards for teacher education that, as we stated earlier, are regulated by federal mandates. A few studies have documented what CL engagement looks like in language arts and literacy, teacher preparation courses and professional development. Grounded on a sociocultural, sociopolitical and culturally sustaining approach to literacy, the works of Medina and Costa (2010) and Zambrana-Ortiz (2011) in teacher education gathered fundamental experiences that attempt to develop socially transformative pedagogies with teacher candidates. Using an asset approach to out-of-school literacies and knowledges, Medina and Costa constructed a language arts methods course where the Puerto Rican preservice teachers' out-of-school literacies became the invitation for inquiries into how local and situated literacies are constructed, used and mobilized. The focus of the process was grounded on investigating, questioning and redesigning multiliteracy invitations such as reggaeton, bumper stickers, local gossip magazines and the examination of a local public service media campaign among others. Teacher candidates then produced critical invitations to work in their school placements field experiences with children. This work points to the importance of reclaiming local literacies as entangled in complex global/local relationships that are ideologically constructed. It also resituates situated local literacies as productive tools for literacy instruction to foreground a view of literacy as a social and critical practice.

A pedagogy in (e)motion that is critical and transformative is an added perspective through the work of Zambrana-Ortiz (2011). Her research works across cognition, pedagogy and social transformation. Among the different inquiries into emotions presented in her book, one of her particular interests is the work with teachers and teacher candidates. Emerging from culturally situated traditions and foregrounding the historical and affective memory through curricular projects that she describes as "ideas in motion for a sensible learning", she creates experiences that foreground how to work with the whole being—body, mind, creativity—to reflect and reconfigure different political realities.

Critical Literacy as Anti-Racist Sites to Disrupt Systemic Forms of Erasure and Prejudice

Racial dynamics in Puerto Rico relate to complex legacies of racism and oppression grounded on the archipelago's colonial history with both Spain and the United States (Godreau, 2015). Research on anti-racism and Afro-Puerto Ricanness points out to significant aspects in which individual, institutionalized and systemic forms of racism are produced and circulated in society and its implications to perpetuating discourses and practices of discrimination and oppression toward Afro-Puerto Rican communities (Rivera-Rideau, 2013). Two problematic perspectives seem to dominate discourses in relation to blackness and Afro-Puertorican communities in Puerto Rico (Godreau, 2002). First, the notion of *folklorismo* through the objectification and romanticizing of "how blackness is accounted for" (p. 283) by the state, elites and ideas around *mestizaje*. This issue gets complicated with ideologies around *blanqueamiento* or the " 'gradual purging' of black features from the general population" (p. 283). Godreau explains that scholarship and activism have demonstrated "how notions of whitening often go hand in hand with discourses of mestizaje or race mixture that tend to exclude blacks, deny racism, and also de-legitimize indigenous claims and demands" (pp. 281–282).

Research on CL curricular efforts to challenge myths, discriminatory racist practices and that produce new anti-racist visions and actions can be locally found (Godreau, 2015; Godreau et al. 2013; Godreau, Reyes Cruz, Franco Ortiz, & Cuadrado, 2008). The research framing the book *Arrancando mitos de raíz: Guía para una enseñanza antiracista de la herencia africana en Puerto Rico* (Godreau et al., 2013) is perhaps the most comprehensive research example of work locally produced in this area. Here we paraphrase, translate and share the key objectives of this work. Through a multiplicity of resources, strategies and approaches, this research and curricular work aims to: (1.) foster pride for African heritage in school grade children; (2.) encourage children to create identifications with traits, contributions and practices related to their blackness and their histories as Afro-descendants; (3.) question racial hierarchies that relate blackness and the African to inferiority and whiteness and the European with superiority and (4.) mitigate the effects of racial discrimination in school children. In summary, the curricular framework produced as a result of this study is an effort to support teachers in the process of countering dominant myths and fallacies about Puerto Ricans' African roots that have been accepted and perpetuated as normative "truths".

Activism and Critical Literacies in Educational Projects and Grassroots Initiatives

Countless initiatives in Puerto Rico produce intersectional work seeking social, political and educational justice. These spaces engage children and youth in activities that foster CL (in arts and literature, see Carbonell et al., 2019; Fullana-Acosta, 2019; Medina, 2020, 2021). In the past years, this population has endured a financial crisis, hurricanes, earthquakes, a global pandemic, school closures and a corrupt government (Brusi & Goudreau, 2019) and thus, it is crucial to ensure that children and youth understand the inequities that exist in Puerto Rico and feel empowered to change them. An example of such initiatives is *La Gran Victoria* (De la Cruz, 2020), a book that narrates the events of the Summer of 2019 through the eyes of two brave sisters who help defeat a snake that governs their city. Another noteworthy example is the Centro Universitario para el Acceso (Center for University Access), an educational justice project for underserved youth that supports them during their school years and in their journey as first-generation college students. Years of research (Centro Universitario para el Acceso, 2017) and service demonstrate the need for such spaces of reflection and action, where children and youth can understand the social issues that affect them and their families.

Role of the Puerto Rican Diaspora and Other Transnational Possibilities

There is a trajectory of contributions from the Puerto Rican diaspora to CL. These scholars and activists have committed their work to investigating the relationship between transnational language and literacy practices, access and power. Although we believe this section deserves its own entry to make justice to this work, we want to acknowledge educational scholars like Sonia Nieto, Antonia Darder, Maria Franquiz, Lourdes Díaz-Soto, Sandra Quiñones-Rosado, Ana Celia Zentella, Luis Moll, Carmen Mercado, María Torres-Guzmán, Carmen Martínez-Roldán, Enid Rosario-Ramos and Maria Acevedo-Aquino, among others. Their research documents existent challenges and most importantly, provide a reaffirmation of the value of asset-based discourses and pedagogies for Puerto Ricans and the larger Latinx communities in the United States, Latin America and the Caribbean.

These works have impacted the education of immigrant communities in the United States with significant implications for schooling issues related to voice, advocacy and the development of culturally sustaining pedagogies across cultures, languages and identities. Emerging research has also put an emphasis in studying the impact of recent catastrophic events for new Puerto Rican immigrant/ transnational communities (Hamm-Rodríguez & Sambolín-Morales, 2021; Rosario-Ramos, Rodriguez, Sawada, & Diaz De La Guardia, 2020). The overwhelming migration (150,000–200,000), and the consequences for those who moved, require urgent attention, specifically in education, language and literacy.

Critical transnational projects, particularly with the Global South, have historically been present in relation to Puerto Rico. From Hostos to Freire to the educational focus on social sciences and justice in the work of CLACSO (Consejo Latinoamericano de Ciencias Sociales), these all represent forms of interconnections that touch upon Puerto Rico. A recent example that focuses on critical literacy within the parameters of how this handbook defines it, is Hamm-Rodríguez & Medina (under review), a multi-site research project on critical transnational literacies to investigate the role of language and social semiotics in activism via social media across the Dominican Republic and Puerto Rico. Through this work it is possible to understand the "chain of historical and sociocultural events that transcend utterances and geographic locations" (p. 2). Nevertheless, it is indeed an area that holds much promise for more research.

Conclusions, Findings and Suggestions for Further Research and Practice

The emergence of countless grassroots and community-based projects within the island and the diaspora that materialize as CL education makes it crucial to continue expanding on the research conducted in Puerto Rico, both in and out of school and in the transnational spaces for Puerto Rican communities in the diaspora and other transnational solidarities. Locally, the weak political and economic infrastructure added to the neoliberal attempts to deliberately dismantle the research and scholarship of institutions such as the University of Puerto Rico, makes it extremely challenging for many well-prepared and established scholars to conduct research in these areas. Reclaiming and reaffirming the university's right to scholarship, teaching and research is a top priority in order to further develop CL research that supports and emerges from local social justice and anticolonial work.

Two areas we feel need further research are intersectional identities for gender and race. Several initiatives work with youth to question and reflect upon queer identities and gender binaries, but more studies that examine gender, particularly in school literacy curricula, are needed. Puerto Rican scholars have made significant contributions to work on race, Afro Puerto Rican identities and racism, but more research on CL with regard to race in Puerto Rico is also needed. This topic is re-emerging as an area of interest in social and educational justice.

Given the diverse initiatives that materialize as everyday CL practices (artistic, health, food access, environmental, anti-racist, etc.) Puerto Rico provides a thriving context to understand the connections between literacy, empowerment and resistance in people's engagement with texts and literacies in their everyday lives. The contribution in this chapter is for and with its people but could also serve as examples of powerful research on anticolonial counter-narratives for others around the world. Participatory Action Research (PAR) is one methodological design that holds much potential. Although used in other areas within social science research in Puerto Rico, we were unable to identify studies focusing on CL that fully use PAR as a methodology that foregrounds students, community and educators' voices. There is also a need to document how localized and culturally sustaining research methods (Patel, 2015; Paris & Winn, 2013) surface within the inquiry practices that are put forth in different local contexts.

References

Atiles-Osoria, J. (2020). *Profanaciones del Verano del 2019: Corrupción, frentes comunes y justicia decolonial*. Editora Educación Emergente.

Ayala, C., & Bernabe, R. (2011). *Puerto Rico en el siglo americano: Su historia desde 1898*. Ediciones Callejón.

Bonilla, Y., & LeBrón, M. (Eds.). (2019). *Aftershocks of disaster: Puerto Rico before and after the storm*. Haymarket Books.

Brusi, R., & Goudreau, I. (2019). Dismantling public education in Puerto Rico. In Y. Bonilla & M. LeBrón (Eds.), *Aftershocks of disaster: Puerto Rico before and after the storm*. (pp. 234–249). Haymarket Press.

Cabán, P. (2018). PROMESA, Puerto Rico and the American empire. *Latino Studies, 16*(2), 161–184. https://doi.org/10.1057/s41276-018-0125-z

Carbonell, M., Gómez-Cuevas, M., Gutierrez, J. L., Hernández, J. E., Negrón, M., Pérez-Otero, M., & Villarini, B. (2019). ¡Ay María! In Y. Bonilla & M. LeBrón (Eds.), *Aftershocks of disaster: Puerto Rico before and after the storm*. Haymarket Books.

Carroll, K. S., & Mazak, C. M. (2017). Language policy in Puerto Rico's higher education: Opening the door for translanguaging practices. *Anthropology & Education Quarterly, 48*(1), 4–22. https://doi.org/10.1111/aeq.12180

Centro Universitario para el Acceso. (2017, December 30). *Investigación*. Retrieved from https://cuauprm.wordpress.com/investigacion/

Costa, M. del R., Medina, C. L., & Soto, N. (2011). Abrir la puerta: La escritura a través de un lente diferente. *Cuaderno de Investigación en la Educación, 22*, 34–53. Retrieved from https://revistas.upr.edu/index.php/educacion/article/view/13316

De La Cruz, V. (2020). *La gran victoria*. n.p.

Del Moral, S. (2013). *Negotiating empire: The cultural politics of schools in Puerto Rico, 1898–1952*. University of Wisconsin Press.

Duany, J. (2017). *Puerto Rico: What everyone needs to know*. Oxford University Press.

Education Week. (2020, February 25). Putting Puerto Rican schools back on track. *Education Week*. Retrieved from www.edweek.org/ew/collections/puerto-rico-hurricane-maria-aftermath/index.html

Enchautegui-Román, M. E., Segarra-Améstica, E. V., Cordero-Nieves, Y., & Rivera-Rodríguez, H. P. (2018). *Los efectos del huracán Maria en la niñez en Puerto Rico* (Vol. 3: Impactos del huracán María en niños y adolescentes y la respuesta público privada). Instituto Desarrollo Juventud. Rio Piedras, P.R.

Fullana-Acosta, M. (2019). Y no había luz presenta su primer cuento para niños y niñas. *El Nuevo Día*. Retrieved from www.elnuevodia.com

Godreau, I. P. (2002). Changing space, making race: Distance, nostalgia, and the folklorization of blackness in Puerto Rico. *Identities: Global Studies in Culture and Power, 9*(3), 281–304. https://doi.org/10.1080/10702890213969

Godreau, I. P. (2015). *Scripts of blackness: Race, cultural nationalism, and US colonialism in Puerto Rico*. University of Illinois Press.

Godreau, I. P., Ortiz, M. F., Lloréns, H., Pumarejo, M. R., Torres, I. C., & Concepción, J. A. G. (2013). *Arrancando mitos de raíz: guía para una enseñanza antirracista de la herencia africana en Puerto Rico*. Editora Educación Emergente.

Godreau, I. P., Reyes Cruz, M., Franco Ortiz, M., & Cuadrado, S. (2008). The lessons of slavery: Discourses of slavery, mestizaje, and blanqueamiento in an elementary school in Puerto Rico. *American Ethnologist, 35*(1), 115–135. https://doi.org/10.1111/j.1548-1425.2008.00009.x

González-Robles, A. E. (2011). *Creating spaces for critical literacy within a Puerto Rican elementary classroom: An ideological model of literature discussions* (Unpublished doctoral dissertation). University of Arizona, Tucson, AZ.

González-Robles, A. E. (2020). Equidad de género: La construcción del concepto mediante tertulias literarias. *Revista Leer, Escribir y Descubrir, 1*(6), 29–43. Retrieved from https://digitalcommons.fiu.edu/led/vol1/iss6/4

González-Robles, A. E., Figarella García, F., & Soto Sonera, J. (2016). Aprendizaje basado en problemas para desarrollar alfabetización crítica y competencias ciudadanas en el nivel elemental. *Actualidades Investigativas en Educación, 16*(3), 217–251. http://dx.doi.org/10.15517/aie.v16i3.26063

Hamm-Rodriguez, M., & Medina, C. L. (under review). Intra-Caribbean solidarities and the language of social protest. *Applied Linguistics* (Special issue on social justice)

Hamm-Rodríguez, M., & Sambolín Morales, A. (2021). (Re)producing insecurity for Puerto Rican students in Florida schools: Raciolinguistic perspectives on English-only policies. *CENTRO: Journal of the Center for Puerto Rican Studies, 32*(1).

Hostos, E. M. de (1991). *Ciencia de la pedagogía: Nociones e historia* (Vol. 1). La Editorial, UPR.

López Alicea, K. (2018, April 18). *Maestros y padres se expresan en contra del cierre de escuelas.* El Nuevo Día. Retrieved from www.elnuevodia.com

Lugo, S. (2018). Local educators lead relief efforts in Puerto Rico. *School Library Journal* www.slj.com/?detailStory=local-educators-lead-relief-efforts-puerto-rico

Maldonado-Torres, N. (2019). Afterword: Critique and decoloniality in the face of crisis, disaster, and catastrophe. In Y. Bonilla & M. LeBrón (Eds.), *Aftershocks of disaster: Puerto Rico before and after the storm* (pp. 332–342). Haymarket Books.

Martínez-Roldán, C. (2019). Prácticas pedagógicas después del huracán María: Colaboración de familias y maestros como agentes de cambio en una escuela elemental en Puerto Rico. *Sargasso, 1&2,* 71–95.

Medina, C. L. (2003). Puerto Rican subjective locations: Definitions and perceptions of literacy. *Journal of Hispanic Higher Education, 2*(4), 392–405. https://doi.org/10.1177/1538192703256046

Medina, C. L. (2020, February). *Re-existir en las grietas de la colonialidad: Storying and improvising in the ruptures of community resistance acts in Puerto Rico* [Keynote presentation]. 2020 National Council for Teachers of English Assembly of Research, Nashville, TN, United States.

Medina, C. L. (2021). *Barruntos:* Youth improvisational work as anticolonial literacy actionings in Puerto Rico. *Research in the teaching of English, 56(2).*

Medina, C. L., & Costa, M. del R. (2010). Collaborative voices exploring culturally and socially responsive pedagogy in teacher preparation. *Language Arts, 87*(4), 263–276. Retrieved from www.jstor.org/stable/41804191

Medina, C. L., & Costa, M. del R. (2013). Latino media and critical literacy pedagogies: Children's scripting *telenovelas* discourses. *Journal of Language and Literacy Education, 9*(1). Retrieved from http://jolle.coe.uga.edu/wp-content/uploads/2013/05/Latino-Media.pdf

Paris, D., & Winn, M. (2013). *Humanizing research: Decolonizing qualitative inquiry with youth and communities.* Sage.

Patel, L. (2015). *Decolonizing educational research: From ownership to answerability.* Routledge.

Quijano, A. (2000). Coloniality of power, eurocentrism, and Latin America. *Neplanta: Views from the South, 1*(3), 533–580. https://doi.org/10.1177/0268580900015002005

Rivera-Rideau, P. R. (2013). From Carolina to Loíza: Race, place and Puerto Rican racial democracy. *Identities, 20*(5), 616–632. https://doi.org/10.1080/1070289X.2013.842476

Rojas Osorio, C. (2012). Eugenio María de Hostos and his pedagogical thought. *Curriculum Inquiry, 42*(1), 12–32. https://doi.org/10.1111/j.1467-873X.2011.00576.x

Rosario-Ramos, E. M., Rodriguez, A., Sawada, J. L., & Diaz De La Guardia, A. M. (2020). Backpacks and hoodies: Puerto Rican Families' experiences of displacement in the aftermath of hurricane Maria and their receiving district's enactment of care. *Teachers College Record, 122*(11). Retrieved from www.tcrecord.org ID Number: 23472

Sáez Vega, R. J., Cintrón de Esteves, Carmen, C., Rivera Viera, D., Guerra, C., & Ojeda, M. (1999). *Al son de los tiempos: Procesos y prácticas de la lectoescritura.* Editora Centenario.

Sáez Vega, R. J. y González Robles, A. (2015). (Eds.) *En voces de maestras: La transformación de prácticas pedagógicas hacia la pedagogía del lenguaje integral.* CELELI.

Schmidt, J. (2014). *The politics of English in Puerto Rico's public schools.* First Forum.

Street, B. (2006). Autonomous and ideological models of literacy: Approaches from new literacy studies. *Media Anthropology Network, 17,* 1–15. Corpus ID: 16534223

Torres González, R. (2002). *Idioma, bilingüismo y nacionalidad: La presencia del inglés en Puerto Rico.* Editorial de la Universidad de Puerto Rico.

Walsh, C. E. (1987). Language, meaning, and voice: Puerto Rican students' struggle for a speaking consciousness. *Language Arts, 64*(2), 196–206. Retrieved from www.jstor.org/stable/41961592

Walsh, C. E. (1991). *Pedagogy and the struggle for voice: Issues of language, power, and schooling for Puerto Ricans.* Praeger Pub Text.

Zambrana-Ortiz, N. J. (2011). *Pedagogy in (e) motion: Rethinking spaces and relations* (Vol. 16). Springer Science & Business Media.

2.12

CRITICAL LITERACY IN RUSSIA

Margarita Gudova, Maria Guzikova, and Rafael Filiberto Forteza
Fernández

Introduction to the Current Sociopolitical Context and Educational System of Russia

In 1917, with the introduction of general education for all, the Soviet system tried to solve the illiteracy problem in the country where 80% of the population could not read and write. This general literacy policy was a must for the industrialization of an essentially agricultural society and was marked by ideological indoctrination. It is undeniable that despite its ups and downs (war, repression, famines) in 76 years, the Soviet system was one of the best educational systems in the world, as its achievements in science and industrialization attested. Nevertheless, the ideological straitjacket implied that going outside the system to criticize the state of affairs (censure, poor working conditions, low salaries, shortages, and arbitrary arrest) was utterly impossible.

Nearing the three decades of the Soviet dream demise, Russia is still trying to reassert its place as one of the world-leading countries. With a very strong presidential power, the Russian economy is still largely dependent on its vast natural resources, especially oil and gas, the main source of export and income for the country. Although the economy has significantly grown since 2000 and its human capital per capita increased, they are still much lower than in the OECD countries. Today, its hydrocarbon wealth is largely exposed to risks due to uncertain global prices and Western hostility. As a result, to continue its stable development, Russia needs to reorient its portfolio of assets in the direction of a knowledge-based economy, a model entirely dependent on education.

Russian Educational System

As part of the transformations undergone in all spheres of life in Russia, the early 1990s witnessed educational reforms (see Kuzminov & Frumin, 2019) aimed at dismantling the Soviet ghost and subsequent humanization, democratization, and decentralization of the school system. In 2003, Russia transformed all the educational levels along with Western practices when the country joined the Bologna process in 2003, though "centralized control, curricular rigidity, and political—ideological functions" (Karpov & Lisovskaya, 2005, p. 23) seemed to be returning as a reflection that the Soviet educational mentality was still much alive. This move coincided with the reorganization of the country that had fallen into a deep social, economic, and political crisis as a result of the shock caused by the neoliberal policies implemented after 1992 (see Klein, 2007 for its aftermath). Furthermore, though the education-related social, health, and demographic issues expounded by Kerr (2005) have

DOI: 10.4324/9781003023425-24

been acknowledged and addressed by the state, the poorly paid and work overloaded teacher at all levels of the educational system usually holds two or more jobs and has little power and/or energy to fight against the bureaucratic system, including the educational one. Besides, the unequal development within and between regions and cities not only affects the quality of the educational processes but also the prospects of future development in each place and the country as whole. Finally, while the mostly "technocratic" (Kirylo, 2020, p. 17) focus only serves the reproduction of the current political and economic status, higher education seems to be driving toward elitism and the subsequent exacerbation of social problems (Lozovskaya, Menshikov, & Purgina, 2020).

This depressing panorama means that preparing students for a critical outlook of the present modeling the future is not the main focus of the vast majority educators in Russia. The subordination of education to the goals of the economy and the state remains, as in the Soviet past, the main goal of contemporary educational policy. However, the growing social divide, now accentuated by the COVID-19 pandemic, provides the fertile ground for critical literacy (CL), for there is an understanding that all social progress goes through education.

Critical Literacy in Russia—Analytical Review

The driving forces of definitions of CL are found within the elite higher education (HE) institutions, top-level officials, and economic executives who, conscious of their socioeconomic and political status, advocate and exercise their power of voice and representation to focus education solely on preparation for the digital economy. For instance, the expert status in HE of the Higher School of Economics (HSE) allows the institution to elaborate the government vision of educational processes, as well as key points of educational policy in Russia. These include the need for restructuring education as a result of the digital revolution and the transition from the German didactic system to e-learning, lifelong learning, and new literacies (Kuzminov & Frumin, 2015; Kuzminov, 2018). Kuzminov's team interprets CL as numerous competencies in various areas of life, such as information technology, medicine, law, and finance, paying special attention to multimodal and multilingual literacies with the goal of improving general communicative and creative skills (Kuzminov & Frumin, 2019). The HSE concept of multiple literacy is economically biased where numerous social issues affecting the country—justice, equality, poverty, and access to education are absent.

In close collaboration with the HSE group, the Sberbank CEO Herman Gref and his charitable foundation, The Contribution to the Future, work

> to support Russian education in light of the challenges of the 21st century . . . to promote an inclusive environment [with the introduction of] new technology, knowhow and solutions for giving trainees knowledge, skills and abilities crucial to our volatile world.
>
> *(Gref, n.d.)*

The foundation's development of competitions,[1] the urge to develop creativity,[2] and contact with HE institutions[3] all seem that this interpretation of CL is based on the Russian Educational System's inability to create the *Homo economicus*. That is, "an intelligent, single-minded, . . . and automated creature who, being fully aware of economic conditions, acts rationally solely on the basis of his or her personal interest" (Papadogiannis, 2014, p. 51). The *Homo economicus* consistently makes self-profiting individual choices regardless of the consequences to his social environment, and Russia does not need more of them.

Following the same technocratic line, the mission of the State Pedagogical University in Saint-Petersburg is to prepare the new generation of teachers to work in the era of information society and digital economy. In their study of text pedagogy, researchers from this university explore the texts of new media to develop educational technologies that facilitate the individualization and democratization of educational processes (Galaktionova, 2016). Multimodal texts and multimodal literacies, the author claims, provide forms of inclusive education in all subjects of secondary and professional education. However, multimodality by/in itself does not mean critical literacy.

In sum, the aforementioned perspectives in appropriating the term *critical* usurp the true connotations of CL and its sociopolitical underpinnings and project their own vision of the future: a neoliberal Russia. True, Russia needs to move beyond the economic issues, but the existing social problems are excruciating and demand urgent attention.

The second force seeking to have a say in CL is that of HE educators working separately without any coordination in the vast Russian geography. The Russian Science Citation Index contains only nine research papers on CL and multimodality. Some consider CL as a fashionable term (Maslov, 2013); others, as a research method (Gudova, Guzikova, & Rubtsova, 2018; Gudova & Guzikova, 2019), and one in the broad context of educational research (Gorbova & Kindirov, 2012). These are notably poor, in quantity and sometimes quality; research outcomes indicate the urgent need to engage with the conceptualizations of what *critical* means in/for Russian education where the work of Freire, Macedo, and Bourdieu, among others is largely unknown.

Nevertheless, presumably based on Freire's ideas, Chigisheva (2018) studies the close connection of phenomena such as power, pedagogic technology, discrimination, and freedom in the context of modern researchers' training. This author points out two development directions of critical literacy ideas in the contemporary Russian educational system: Critical Pedagogy and Critical Reading and Writing. However, the author assumes that critical pedagogy is learning in collaboration, when the content of knowledge is decided by the student and not the teacher; she notes that "the student has the right to freely choose an educational program, courses and educational technologies" (p. 367). This thesis is overly optimistic because the control exercised by the system and the overwhelming hierarchical domination at the school make it practically impossible to go outside the lines established. At the same time, the fear to attempt any changes may endanger the teacher's job and possibility to continue his practice in any public institution. However, the conception of the CL movement pioneered by Paulo Freire's educational theory to increase social well-being in the Russian context (Savostyanov, 2017) envisions the impossibility to deal with educational problems from a neutral class position in questioning the system's appropriation of educational discourse and current state of power relations and a fearless stance on social issues.

At the institutional level, the research group *Multilingualism and Inter-culturalism in the Era of Post-Literacy* at the Ural Federal University (UrFU) in Ekaterinburg has been engaged in the discussion and application of ideas coming from the New London Group, namely Gunther Kress, Mary Kalantzis, and Bill Cope. These have yielded studies in such phenomena as modern reading (Gudova, 2014; Goodova, Rubtsova, & Fernández, 2015), pedagogical communication (Fedorova, Rasskazova, & Muzafarova, 2018), values (Vershinina, Guzikova, & Kocheva, 2019), e-learning technologies (Sukhov, 2015, 2018), ecologies of education (Kocheva & Guzikova, 2017), the distortion of history and neoliberal ideology (Forteza Fernández, 2019), and ideological issues in English language teaching (Forteza Fernández, Rubtsova, & Forteza, 2020).

From a practical perspective, CL practice is the action research carried out by Forteza with an international group of master's students at Ural Federal University, where the program Language and Region Studies and the Advanced Practical Course in English have been articulated to serve the social needs of future graduate-teachers. The main objective in both cases has been to "read the word and the world" (Freire & Macedo, 1987) so as to glocalize events on the basis of their rich cultural heritage. As a result, Language and Region Studies focuses on the historical production and reproduction of inequality from a social class perspective and its connection with racism, antisemitism, and all forms of discrimination, historically determined by colonialism, neocolonialism, and neoliberalism. The practical course, aimed at the development of integrated language skills, has been based on materials denouncing neoliberal ideology in ELT textbooks (Gray, 2000, 2010a, 2010b, 2012; Block, 2006, 2014, 2017, 2018; Block, Gray, & Holborow, 2012).

In sum, critical literacy in Russia is still in its infancy. At the moment, the diversity of research interests does not allow for a concerted effort to use education as a tool to challenge the existing order and empower the future generations to do so. The individual effort of most educators is plagued with ignorance of what CL means. Besides, research in HE institutions does not usually reach the school where most praxis takes place. If to these considerations the generalized rejection to everything related to *ideology, ethics, oppressed, social class*, and all the like is added, considerable resistance to changes in pedagogical outlook are expected not only from the population and educators in general, but from the elites, in particular.

Utilitarian Perspective of CL in Russia

The specific concept of CL in most other articles written by Russian researchers approaches the idea of CL from a utilitarian point of view, very often without direct reference or knowledge of Freirean concepts (see Freire & Macedo, 1987; Freire, 1998). Freire's books and articles in Russian, on the one hand, and the presence of the concept of CL in the educational discourse, advocated by the elites, on the other, blur the significance of the conceptual apparatus used. Furthermore, the need to solve these issues from the ontological and epistemological points of view is pressing. The transit from the Soviet to the capitalist economy simply meant a change of masters; while the former's proclaimed equality never arrived, inequality has increased with the latter. The common denominator of both has been the control over the ideas of emancipation.

Though not neoliberal in nature but plagued with neoliberals who bathe in money swimming pools, decision-makers in Russian politics, economics, social policies have to understand that any advancement entails a redistribution of the country's wealth. This understanding encompasses the formation of an ethical and moral stance at all levels of society: institutions, schools, and the family and attainable only through education where CL acquires universal significance for it means pressing for changes from below. This is a time-taking endeavor that will meet with resistance. Therefore, it is paramount to join the educational community in producing the counter-discourse necessary to change the actual state of affairs with the very technological weapons people are oppressed.

Perspectives of the Comparative Analysis of CL Ideas

The term *critical* is ubiquitous in Russian pedagogical research. However, a social connection with literacy, social class, means of production, and productive forces is missing. In other words, Freire's view of education as a way to achieve social justice is ignored, though it deserves a place in Russian claims for liberation. Today, the growing interest in Freire's theory has its underpinnings in a world undergoing a cultural and civilizational revolution associated with transition to the next stage of development: the creation of a fifth economic platform based on a synthesis of information, biological and physical technologies. The de-westernization of education is essential for, if seen from a Western perspective, it will fall in the same neoliberal trap.

International cooperation in Freirean CL began with Raúl Alberto Mora in 2018 when he paved the way for a different understanding of the topic, exchange, and possibilities of application in the Russian context. In 2019, the exchange with Mary Kalantzis and Bill Cope helped gain a different clarifying perspective on CL. Their visit to UrFU and return visit to Illinois initiated a period of collaboration, exchange of experience coming mostly from the Australian colleagues, and the possibility of unlimited use of their platform *Scholar*. Hitherto, the full application of their conceptual apparatus: education by design, pedagogy of multiliteracies, practices, empowered and collaborative learning (Kalantzis & Cope, 2012, 2015), applied by Forteza Fernández in the discipline Language and Regional Studies, demonstrated its feasibility in the Russian educational context[4] while their validity[5] was signaled by the positive responses of almost all the class. The annual conference *Communicative Trends* at the university in 2019 hosted scholars from Central and Eastern Europe who also brought their work on social issues while exchange pointed out areas still virgin in Russian education research (see Gudova & Guzikova, 2020).

Social Responsibility of Russian Academics

Despite the strict control through the state educational standards, the recommendations of methods, teaching materials, and pedagogical approaches, especially at the school level, and the fact that majority of children study at state schools and colleges, academics must become active practitioners of CL in their everyday work as well as promote their research output. This ethical and moral position recommends establishing communication channels between the university and the school where the word and exchange between academics and the schoolteacher rather than imposition and relations of power unveils their common goal. At the same time, the university is to become responsible for introducing schools to technology and showing their use for the empowerment of the disposed. It is, at the same time, the one who should exercise control over the digitalization of education by establishing the ethical and moral grounds of its social implications and effects.

The popularization of CL pedagogy in Russia should be connected to the strong tradition of Russian pedagogical humanism; not everything done in the past must be discarded, for Russians are not newcomers to education. The wealth of Russian thought must be appraised and foreign experiences carefully assessed and contextually applied, if feasible. Russian CL practitioners have to be facilitators of the spread and domestication of CL ideas in the Russian context. This entails the organization, funding, and articulation of interests in only one direction, may it be by the creation of a circle of CL practitioners and researchers or scientific activities.

This research was supported by the Russian Foundation for Basic Research (RFBR), project № 17–29–09136/20.

Notes

1. http://en.kremlin.ru/events/president/transcripts/615000
2. http://sberbank.ai/en/news/german-gref-na-vtorom-uroke-tsifry-prizval-shkolnikov-byt-creativnymi/#
3. https://news.itmo.ru/en/news/7335/
4. https://cgscholar.com/community/community_profiles/a-cultural-history-of-the-other/community_activity_streams
5. https://docs.google.com/forms/d/1VUXDCzLsuJkfNQbmA1CrJq7rgSJXD-t1YZgjV-dwze4/edit#responses

References

Block, D. (2006). *Multilingual identities in a global city. London Stories*. Palgrave Macmillan.

Block, D. (2014). *Social class in applied linguistics*. Routledge.

Block, D. (2017). Neoliberalism, the neoliberal citizen and English language teaching materials: A critical analysis. *Ruta Maestra, 21*, 4–15.

Block, D. (2018). *Political economy in sociolinguistics: Neoliberalism, inequality and social class*. Bloomsbury.

Block, D., Gray, J., & Holborow, M. (2012). *Neoliberalism and applied linguistics*. Routledge.

Chigisheva, O. P. (2018). U istokov "kriticheskoy gramotnosti": teoreticheskie vozzreniya Paulu Freyre v kontekste podgotovki sovremennyih issledovateley [At the origins of critical literacy: Theoretical views of paolo freire in the context of the training of contemporary researchers]. *Gumanitarnyie i sotsialnyie nauki [Humanities and Social Sciences], 6*, 359–368. In Russian. https://doi.org/10.18522/2070-1403-2018-71-6-359-368

Fedorova, E., Rasskazova, T., & Muzafarova, A. (2018). Teaching English via Skype: Challenges and opportunities. In L. G. Chova, A. L. Martinez, & I. C. Torres (Eds.), *12th international technology, education and development conference* (pp. 663–667). International Academy of Technology, Education and Development.

Forteza Fernández, R. F. (2019, May). *Historical lies and distortions in ELT. A case study.* Keynote speech at the International Conference on Multilingualism, Multiculturalism and Literacy, Ural Federal University, Ekaterinburg, Russia.

Forteza Fernández, R. F., Rubtsova, E. V., & Forteza Rojas, S. (2020). Content edulcoration as ideology visualization in an English language coursebook. *Praxema. Problems of Visual Semiotics, 4*, 172–193. https://doi.org/10.23951/2312-7899-2020-4-172-193

Freire, P. (1998). *Pedagogy of freedom. Ethics, democracy, and civic courage.* Rowman & Littlefield.

Freire, P., & Macedo, D. (1987). *Literacy: Reading the word and the world.* Bergin & Garvey.

Galaktionova, T. G. (2016). Tekstyi "novoy prirodyi" i novaya gramotnost ["New nature" texts and new literacy]. In T. G. Galaktionovoy & E. I. Kazakovoy (Eds.), *Sbornik materialov VIII mezhdunarodnoy nauchno-prakticheskoy konferentsiya "Pedagogika teksta"* [Collection of Materials of the 8th International Scientific and Practical Conference "Pedagogy of Text"] (pp. 13–17). In Russian. SpB.: Herzen University.

Goodova, M., Rubtsova, E., & Fernández, R. F. F. (2015). Multimedia resources as examples of polymorphic educational hypertexts in the post-literacy era. *Procedia—Social and Behavioral Sciences, 214*, 952–957. https://doi.org/10.1016/j.sbspro.2015.11.679

Gorbova, T. M., & Kindirov, A. A. (2012). Kulturnaya transformatsiya, vliyayuschaya na organizatsionnuyu effektivnostь korporatsii, posredstvom obladaniya individami kriticheskoy gramotnostyu [Cultural transformation affecting corporate organizational performance through individuals' possession of critical literacy]. *Vestnik Bryanskogo gosudarstvennogo universiteta [The Bryansk State University Herald], 3–1*, 62–65. In Russian. Retrieved from http://vestnik-brgu.ru/wp-content/numbers/v2012_31.pdf

Gray, J. (2000). The ELT coursebook as cultural artifact: How teachers censor and adapt. *ELT Journal, 54*(3), 274–283. https://doi.org/10.1093/elt/54.3.274

Gray, J. (2010a). *The construction of English: Culture, consumerism and promotion in the ELT global coursebook.* Palgrave Macmillan.

Gray, J. (2010b). The branding of English and the culture of the new capitalism: Representations of the world of work in English Language Textbooks. *Applied Linguistics, 31*(5), 714–733. https://doi.org/10.1093/applin/amq034

Gray, J. (2012). English the industry. In A. Hewings & C. Tagg (Eds.), *The politics of English: Conflict, competition, and co-existence* (pp. 137–163). The Open University, Routledge.

Gref, H. (n.d.). *Sberbank president and CEO in a TASS special project top officials.* A conversation with Herman Gref [Interview by A. Vadenko]. Retrieved from https://tass.com/top-officials/1043741

Gudova, M. Yu. (2014). The women's reading in social network. In F. Uslu (Ed.), *International conference on education and social sciences (INTCESS-14)* (Vols. I and II, pp. 1009–1011). Organization Center of Academic Research.

Gudova, M. Yu., & Guzikova, M. O. (2019). Model poliyazyichnogo obrazovaniya v universitete: kriticheskaya teoriya gramotnosti i opyit Kitaya [The multilingual education model at the university: A critical theory of literacy and the experience of China]. *Otechestvennaya i zarubezhnaya pedagogika [Russian and Foreign Pedagogy], 2*(64), 186–199. In Russian. Retrieved from http://ozp.instrao.ru/images/nomera/OZP_2.2.64.2019.pdf

Gudova, M. Yu., & Guzikova, M. O. (Eds.). (2020). *Proceedings of the fourth international scientific conference communication trends in the post-literacy era: Multilingualism, multimodality, multiculturalism.* Retrieved from https://knepublishing.com/index.php/KnE-Social/issue/view/199

Gudova, M. Yu., Guzikova, M. O., & Rubtsova, E. V. (2018). Polilingvalnoe i polikulturnoe obrazovanie v universitete: kriticheskiy diskurs gramotnosti [Multilingual and multicultural education at the university: A critical discourse of literacy]. *Izvestiya Uralskogo Federalnogo Universiteta. Seriya 3: Obschestvennyie nauki [Journal of Ural Federal University. Series 3. Social Sciences].* V. 13, 4(182), 221–228. In Russian. Retrieved from https://journals.urfu.ru/index.php/Izvestia3/article/view/3625

Kalantzis, M., & Cope, B. (2012). *New learning. Elements of a science of education* (2nd ed.). Cambridge University Press.

Kalantzis, M., & Cope, B. (2015). *A pedagogy of multiliteracies. Learning by design.* Palgrave Macmillan.

Karpov, V., & Lisovskaya, E. (2005). Educational change in time of social revolution: The case of post-Communist Russia in comparative perspective. In L. E. Ben Eklof & V. Kaplan (Eds.), *Educational reform in post-Soviet Russia. Legacies and prospects* (pp. 23–55). Frank Cass.

Kerr, S. T. (2005). Demographic change and the fate of Russia's schools: The impact of population shifts on educational practice and policy. In L. E. Ben Eklof & V. Kaplan (Eds.), *Educational reform in post-Soviet Russia. Legacies and prospects* (pp. 153–175). Frank Cass.

Kirylo, J. D. (Ed.). (2020). *Reinventing pedagogy of the oppressed: Contemporary critical perspectives*. Bloomsbury Academic. https:/doi.org/10.5040/9781350117211

Klein, N. (2007). *The shock doctrine. The rise of disaster capitalism*. Metropolitan Books.

Kocheva, O., & Guzikova, M. (2017). In quest of the third learning space. In Z. Bekirogullari, M. Y. Minas, & R. X. Thambusamy (Eds.), European Proceedings of Social and Behavioural Sciences EpSBS, *8th International Conference on Education and Educational Psychology (ICEEPSY 2017)* (pp. 701–708). Future Academy. https://doi.org/10.15405/epsbs.2017.10.67

Kuzminov, Y. I. (2018). Vyzovy i perspektivy razvitiya universitetov v Rossii [Prospective development of universities in Russia]. *Universitetskoe upravlenie: praktika i analiz [University Management: Practice and Analysis]*, V. 22, 4(116), 5–8. In Russian. Retrieved from www.umj.ru/jour/article/view/179

Kuzminov, Y. I., & Frumin, I. D. (2015). On- lajn-obuchenie: kak ono menyaet strukturu obrazovaniya i ekonomiku universiteta: otkrytaya diskussiya Ya. I. Kuz'minov—M. Karnoj [Online learning: How it changes the structure of education and university economics: open discussion Ya. I. Kuzminov—M. Karnoy]. *Voprosy obrazovaniya [Educational Studies Moscow]*, 3, 8–43. In Russian. https://doi.org/10.17323/1814-9545-2015-3-8-43

Kuzminov, Y. I., & Frumin, I. D. (Eds.). (2019). *Kak sdelat obrazovanie dvigatelem sotsialno-ekonomicheskogo razvitiya? [How to turn education into an engine of social and economic development?]*. Moskva: Natsionalnyiy Issledovatelskiy Universitet "Vyisshaya Shkola Ekonomiki". In Russian.

Lozovskaya, K. B., Menshikov, A. B., & Purgina, E. S. (2020). "Horizons of the future": Realities and aspirations of top-ranking BRICS universities (Analysis of Mission Statements). *Vestnik Tomskogo gosudarstvennogo universiteta. Filosofiya. Sociologia. Politologia [Tomsk State University Journal of Philosophy, Sociology and Political Science]*, (55), 163–174. https://doi.org/10.17223/1998863X/55/17

Maslov, M. P. (2013). K voprosu o kriticheskoy gramotnosti. Aktivnyie i interaktivnyie formyi obucheniya [On the issue of critical literacy. Active and interactive forms of education]. In G. M. Mandrikova (Ed.), *Mezhvuzovskiy sbornik nauchnyih trudov [Interuniversity collection of scientific papers]* (pp. 41–44.). In Russian. NSTU.

Papadogiannis, Y. (2014). *The rise and fall of homo economicus. The myth of the rational human and chaotic reality*. CreateSpace Independent Platform.

Savostyanov, V. O. (2017). Kriticheskiy podhod k obrazovaniyu v rabotah brazilskogo filosofa i pedagoga Paulu Freyre [A critical approach to education in the works of the Brazilian philosopher and educator Paolo Freire]. *Pedagogicheskiy zhurnal [Pedagogical Journal]*, 7(2A), 213–221. In Russian. Retrieved from http://publishing-vak.ru/file/archive-pedagogy-2017-2/21-savostyanov.pdf

Sukhov, A. (2015). Computer games and education. In F. Uslu (Ed.), *ADVED 15: International conference on advances in education and social sciences* (pp. 138–142). International Organization Center of Academic Research.

Sukhov, A. (2018). Educational dimension of "Total War: Medieval II". In M. Ciussi (Ed.), *Proceedings of the 12th European conference on game-based learning, ECGBL 2018* (pp. 669–676). Academic Conferences and Publishing International Limited.

Vershinina, T. S., Guzikova, M. O., & Kocheva, O. L. (2019). Development of foreign language learners' value system in multilingual urban environment. In Bataev Dena Karim-Sultanovich (Ed.), European Proceedings of Social and Behavioural Sciences, *Social and cultural transformations in the context of modern globalism (SCTCGM 2018)* (Vol. 58, pp. 2461–2468). Future Academy. https://doi.org/10.15405/epsbs.2019.03.02.284

2.13

A SURVEY OF CRITICAL LITERACY EDUCATION IN SINGAPORE

Challenges and Potentialities

Mardiana Abu Bakar and Siao See Teng

Introduction

According to Luke (2012), critical literacy "refers to the use of the technologies of print and other media of communication to analyze, critique, and transform the norms, rule systems, and practices governing the social fields of everyday life" (p. 5). Literacy education is always situated in local contexts of culture, economy and politics (Gee, 1990; Street, 1984), and the objective of critical literacy includes "the critique and transformation of dominant ideologies, cultures and economies, and institutions and political systems" (Luke, 2012, p. 5). Thus, we begin this chapter with an examination of the political economic environment of Singapore, which provides the context for critical literacy possibilities in the island Republic.

Spanning over 720 square kilometres of land with few natural resources and little primary industry, Singapore has defined its future as a service/information/digital economy driven by educational development and investment. A former British colony, it has transformed rapidly into a developed, largely middle-class society that punches above its weight in the global economy (Obama, quoted in Chuang, 2015). The unbroken governance of the same ruling party over 50 years meant Singapore's political, economic and sociocultural landscapes are largely shaped by the ideology of the People's Action Party (PAP). The notion of Singapore's size and vulnerability in relation to its larger neighbours is an overarching discourse of the first generation of the PAP leaders utilizing an ideology of pragmatism (Chua, 1983; Hill & Lian, 1995; Tan, 2012). With economic development prioritized in its agenda, English, the language of its colonial masters, was retained as the language of administration, business and education to stay plugged into the global capitalist economy. The government built an education system modelled after the British. This has had implications on knowledge consumption and production in Singapore. One key manifestation of this is the shift in language usage and the elevated status of English literacy at the expense of ethnic tongues (Pennycook, 2017), which has had repercussions on its historiography (Teng, 2006) and social memory (Ibrahim, 2012). Recently, scholars and writers described a 2020 translated volume of Singapore's Sinophone literature as an "overdue tribute", and one which revealed a world "hiding in plain sight" (Quah & Hee, 2020). This points to the marginalization of Sinophone literature and its writers from mainstream knowledge production. Similarly, Ibrahim (2012) pointed to the Malay community's historical experiences and voices written in the Malay language being marginalized and not captured in the dominant, mainstream historical narratives of the country.

DOI: 10.4324/9781003023425-25

The Singapore state may be described as an interventionist one (Hill & Lian, 1995; Rodan, 2016) that makes no apology for its authoritarian governance. Lee Kuan Yew, its first Prime Minister, justified the need for a strong interfering government "who decides what is right" for economic progress (National Day Rally Speech 1986, cited from Lim, 2018, p. 142). The State positioned itself as the arbitrator of the national narrative. According to Loh (1998), the chapter of the Singapore story dealing with its founding years was authorized "primarily by the primary experiences of the PAP Old Guard" (p. 1) who were mostly English-educated. This has disallowed "alternative interpretations" (p. 1) of the era. In this narrative, race and religion are seen as fault lines to be carefully managed. Through the years, the Singapore state has come down hard on individuals or online media construed to have overstepped the acceptable boundaries of discourse (e.g., Lim, 2018; George, 2000). Opposition politicians, academics and activists have learnt that Singapore has "an authoritarian system in which any real resistance to them would not find legitimate platforms" (Tan, 2008, p. 19).

Prioritizing responsibilities rather than rights of citizenry is paramount. The recent Protection from Online Falsehoods and Manipulation Act 2019 (POFMA) is described as the "wider Whole-of Government effort to address online falsehoods that affect public interest" (POFMA, n.d.) and may be seen as further reinforcement. The government is exempt from POFMA. Limited public access to official data also curtails the ability to partake in public discussions (Cheng, 2019). This narrow discursive space provides limited scope for the nurturing of critical literacy in schools as we will discuss in the following sections.

Singapore School Structure and System: Narrow Spaces for Critical Literacy

Education is seen as both a public and a merit good in Singapore and is heavily subsidized (Goh & Gopinathan, 2008). The country has a much-admired public education system globally, garnering top spots in international tests such as Programme for International Student Assessment (PISA), Progress in International Reading Literacy Study (PIRLS) and Trends in International Mathematics and Science Study (TIMMS) since 1995. Education is the driving factor in Singapore's development and since independence in 1965, an intimate link between education and economic development was strongly emphasized (Goh & Gopinathan, 2008, p. 14). The ideological and cultural discourse on education was instituted around a rigorous, competitive, meritocratic education system. Tan (2008) spoke of Singapore's meritocracy as "the main ideological resource for justifying authoritarian government" (p. 7) which has an unshakeable *confidence in its own correctness* (p. 19).

Its founding prime minister foresaw the setting up of education in "elite schools", the "middle strata" and the "broad base" (Lee, 1966, pp. 10–11). Not surprisingly, the divide between "elite" and the non-elite ones remains (Lim, 2014; Mardiana, 2012; Gopinathan & Mardiana, 2013) despite the "every school a good school" slogan put out since 2014. Streaming had been a controversial issue and until recently, a stoutly defended policy feature of Singapore's school structure. This will be replaced by Full Subject-based Banding in secondary schools in 2024. Singapore primary schools were de-tracked in 2009.

Since the Thinking School Learning Nation (TSLN) initiative in 1997, the education system has begun emphasizing innovation and creativity and set out to recognize and reward a plurality of talents, not just performance in high-stakes assessment. Critical thinking became a central feature of TSLN. In his TSLN speech, then Prime Minister Goh called for a response to the knowledge economy by using, creating, critiquing and applying knowledge (Goh, 1997). But as Lim (2014) and Koh (2002, 2019) pointed out, what has taken place since then has been the de-location of critical thinking from its liberal underpinnings and relocating it as instrumental knowledge. Koh (2019) said critical thinking in Singapore schools was to produce a generation of workers with the "ability to problem-solve for the Singaporean economy" (p. 206). It is to this "pedagogic recontextualization" (Lim, 2014, p. 692) of critical literacy teaching and learning in Singapore classrooms that we now turn.

Critical Literacy in and Beyond Singapore Classrooms

Critical literacy is not an established term in the official and academic discourses in Singapore. However, there is a small but significant body of research around "critical thinking" analyzing its concept within the hope of TSLN. These studies pointed out that critical thinking is conceived mostly as a set of skills to be imparted. Yeo and Zhu (2005) found little indication of higher order thinking in Singapore classrooms, and few opportunities for students to question, verify arguments or self-explore. Studies on the use of Information and Communication Technology (ICT) in facilitating higher order thinking also revealed that little critical thinking is found in the use of ICT platforms (Cheung & Hew, 2005; Cheong & Cheung, 2008). Churchill (2006) situated the Singaporean approach as one that merges the paradigms of logical-philosophical and psychological-cognitive problem-solving models with emphasis on specific skill-related critical thinking strategies influenced by Edward de Bono. Curdt-Christiansen (2010) found that Singapore English language teachers have difficulty justifying the use of class time to teach critical literacy, privileging instead time to prepare students to pass their language examination.

Koh (2002), noting that the strong social justice orientation requisite within the teaching and learning of critical literacy may not agree with the state, attempted to construct a bridge between "critical thinking" and "critical literacy". He tried positioning critical literacy as a set of "thinking tools" that may arrive at a more effective critical pedagogy to achieve the intended outcomes of critical thinking but found many structural challenges. High-stake assessments in particular narrowed skills training to a specific genre of writing (Koh, 2019).

The body of literature relating to critical literacy in Singapore may be found within English language and Social Studies. Singapore's bilingualism policy upholds English as the first language and three other official languages—Malay, Mandarin and Tamil—as second languages. In existing literature, Social Studies is described as the perfect forum for nurturing critical literacy as it questions power and makes moral judgements about how to act and what to believe (Wolk, 2003). It is the best forum to help students become critical consumers of information (Soarse & Wood, 2010). We will now examine the critical literacy within the Singapore curriculum of these two subjects and the implicit national education messages therein.

A pragmatic approach to literacy and the choice of English literacy have resulted in a functional view of literacy acquisition since the early days of education (Cheah, 2001). The conceptions of literacy education in English language have oscillated between the epistemology of skill-based instruction and meaning-based communicative approach (Curdt-Christiansen, 2010). In the 1980s and 1990s, literacy instruction in Singapore focused on the correct mastery of the linguistic code. Learning English was for functional literacy—reading and writing were taught for examination purposes (Cheah, 2001). The 2001 syllabus, however, emphasized a text-based approach and prioritized the use of language for social functions. It proclaims to nurture "independent lifelong learners, creative thinkers and problem solvers who can communicate effectively". Its key concern was to develop higher levels of literacy through resource-based "self-access learning", through "evaluative" and "critical reading" of materials from multimedia sources and the understanding and production of a range of complex texts and genres. A significant component of the syllabus was the focus placed on language use for "literacy response and expression", aiming to prepare students to respond critically to literary texts, relate them to personal experiences and prior knowledge, culture and society and use language to express selves and identities (Albright & Kramer-Dahl, 2009).

However, classroom research evidenced "a long-standing instrumentalist logic" (Albright & Kramer-Dahl, 2009, p. 201) prevailing. Albright and Kramer-Dahl observed "a palimpsest of often overlapping and contradictory discourses that had sedimented in teachers' pedagogy" (2009, p. 201). Weninger (2020) pointed to classroom interaction based on "heavily procedural frame that prompted surface responses at the expense of deeper exploration through personal, emotive or experiential talk" (p. 123). The habituated, embodied pedagogic practice of Singapore teachers is rooted in "an ideology of subject pedagogy that prioritizes 'delivering and covering content' above understanding" (p. 123).

Ho (2010) found that the Singapore Social Studies curriculum constructed "a narrow and limited discourse of harmony and use it to legitimize policies that privilege particular groups, limit politi-cal freedoms, marginalize groups with less power or status, and circumscribe the kinds of actions a citizen can legitimately take" (p. 476). Citizen political participation is relegated to a secondary role in this curriculum: "As citizens participate more actively in shaping outcomes in society, they become more conscious of how they complement government actions" (MOE, 2016, p. 83). In addition, fear of risky talk pervades the enacted curriculum (Churchill, 2006; Ho, 2010, 2017; Sim, 2011). Social Studies lessons simplify complex events into bite-sized "lessons" (Sim & Ho, 2010) adhering to state discourse. Events such as those involving ethnic conflicts in other countries like Sri Lanka and Northern Ireland are narrated without the full range of complexities with the intention of placing Singapore at the centre of normative possibilities as a success story of ethnic and religious harmony. The importance of good governance, economic development, social cohesion is empha-sized. These serve to justify the state-defined vision and objectives for the nation and undermine participatory citizenship (Sim, 2011).

Studies examining teachers' and students' responses to the curriculum reflected uncritical adher-ence to the official narrative (Ho, 2010). In this narrative, Singapore is a vulnerable society with no natural resources surrounded by larger, at times hostile, neighbours. Harmony is emphasized (Ho, 2017) alongside a focus on progress and consensus, the subscription to race as stable and unchang-ing. There was a paucity of alternative views in the conceptions of citizenship understood by stu-dents (Ho, 2010, pp. 228–230). The idea of conflict-avoidance is also prevalent (Ho, 2010, 2017) with "little or no discussion of sensitive and controversial issues" (Ho, 2010, p. 240). The avoidance of contentious topics in classroom discussions meant missed opportunities of meaningful learning through discussion of issues such as discrimination. A surface culture approach has emerged in Social Studies classrooms (Bokhorst-Heng & Wee, 2007; Tan, 2012; Tan &Tan, 2014; Ismail, 2014), and emphasis is placed instead on the 3 Fs—fashion, food and festivals of cultural understandings.

Teachers' belief and knowledge on critical literacy too adhered to the state's narrative (Curdt-Christiansen, 2010). Researchers have observed how teachers felt constrained when discussing topics like race, in case they overstep the OB markers (Sim, Chua, & Krishnasamy, 2017; Ho, Alviar-Martin, & Leviste, 2014; Alviar-Martin & Ho, 2011). Educators in these studies do not feel empow-ered to engage students in deeper learning (Sim & Print, 2009). Existing studies also suggest that teachers do not discuss structural inequalities (Ho, 2010, 2017). Students, regardless of background, therefore demonstrated little awareness of institutional or structural inequalities having internalized the national narrative (Sim, Chua, & Krishnasamy, 2017).

Scholars also observed that the differentiated Social Studies curriculum for various academic streams positioned students differently, resulting in differentiated transmission of citizenships. Although there have been changes to the curriculum over the years, the Social Studies curriculum for the lowest academic stream of Normal Technical (NT) contains less higher order thinking. Sim and Krishnasamy (2016) found that students from the high academic ability tracks of Express and Normal Academic demonstrated higher levels of civic knowledge and more nuanced understandings of democratic principles while NT students demonstrated less awareness about democratic processes.

In addition, students in elite schools have school-based curriculums that hone their critical abilities with targeted inquiry approaches (Lim & Apple, 2015; Koh, 2019).

Media literacy has been receiving greater attention over the years in and beyond Singapore classrooms. Critical media literacy may be defined as the notion of literacy which encompasses different forms of media and communication technologies, including new media, as well as the ability to analyze relationships between media and audiences, information and power (Kellner & Share, 2007). Singapore's media landscape is highly "influenced" by the state's discourse. Major newspapers in Singapore's official languages are owned by the Singapore Press Holdings (SPH), which is closely associated with the government. Chairmanship of SPH is often assumed by former politicians or civil servants. One academic has likened reading newspapers in Singapore to a ritual of "mass tutorial" on the government's ideology, policies and actions (Bokhorst-Heng, 2002, p. 562). Within this hegemonic media environment, not surprisingly a study on newspaper literacy among students suggests that they tend to see newspapers as uncritical sources of knowledge and not information that needs to be critically assessed (Koh, 2004).

There is no single guideline for media literacy education in Singapore although media literacy is mentioned as one of the literacy skills to enhance the teaching of various language competences in the 2010 English Language Syllabus for Primary & Secondary (MOE, 2008). However, there was a recent attempt at an infusion of critical media literacy into the teaching of English at the secondary level (Weninger, 2020). However, findings around media education in Singapore echoes the situation analyzed in the teaching and learning of English language and Social Studies. Media education is framed by the Media Literacy Council (MLC), a government public education and community engagement initiative to foster "discerning Singaporeans who are able to evaluate media content effectively, and to use, create and share content safely and responsibly" (MLC, n.d.). However, Weninger (2017) pointed out that information communicated by MLC has "protectionist and paternalistic overtones and dispenses advice" (p. 406). Much less attention is paid to innovative and active media use that does not revolve around imperatives. She sees little hope for critical media literacy, given the instrumental nature of language teaching and learning.

Implications for Future Research and Practice

We have painted a rather grey image of Critical Literacy Education in Singapore here referencing the available body of research. The reality may not be as bleak. About 16 years ago, Kramer-Dahl (2004) surveyed four classes of 10–12-year-olds in three primary schools and concluded that Singaporean youngsters engage with and talk about out-of-school texts in ways that may "immensely complicate previously held conceptions of them as docile, non-critical and inarticulate literacy learners within the school" (p. 237). Her study found Singapore youths to be "'worldkids', whose experiences, especially with popular culture texts, produced mostly through multinational corporations and disseminated across the globe, are more likely to resemble those of young teenagers in London, San Francisco or Tokyo" (p. 237).

We also note that Singapore university students are engaging in meaningful public discussions. Students at Yale-NUS College and the Faculty of Law of the National University of Singapore (NUS) established the Community for Advocacy and Political Education (CAPE) in 2017. CAPE has since been active in organizing public forums on topics relating to racism and political literacy.

There are positive signs too from the Ministry of Education (MOE). Its National Education Forte (NE Forte) has called for more spaces for educators and students to have more critical conversations on citizenship, social mobility and racism issues especially in the light of the COVID-19 situation. NE Forte is the fortnightly e-newsletter produced by the National Education, Character and Citizenship Education Branch emailed to all schools and education officers. There is also promise that the 2021 Citizenship and Character Education (CCE) curriculum will provide teachers with more resources for critical discussions of contemporary issues using questioning strategies and dialogic pedagogies. However, how such spaces would be translated into the enacted curriculum in schools depend on the readiness of school leaders and teachers. Just recently, a leading school, the Hwa Chong Institution, issued a directive to students discouraging them from engaging in exchanges over social media and messaging platforms on Singapore's General Elections. The new CCE2021 curriculum may provide the necessary affordances, but, as we argued earlier, critical literacy is yet to be prevalent in Singapore's English language lessons despite a rich and contextualized national curriculum (Kramer-Dahl, 2001).

If there are overwhelming ideological constraints in practising critical literacy in Singapore English language and Social Studies classrooms, how do we explain Kramer-Dahl's 2004 findings and the CAPE phenomenon? Do Singapore universities offer more spaces for critical literacy? Do digital natives find their own ways of exploring issues they are interested in as they mature? Research on the multiple literacies of youth in Singapore across different phases of their lives could offer a picture on how various literacies evolve as the young grow up, as well as meaningful points for educational affordances and interventions. The term multiliteracies takes into account how literacy is recognized as being influenced by "social, cultural, and technological change" (Anstey & Bull, 2006, p. 23). As a consequence, a "pedagogy of multiliteracies" (Cope & Kalantzis, 2000, p. 5) should encompass the ability to critically analyze relationships between media and citizens, sources of information and power. Perhaps, it is time for Singapore to work on a blueprint for a multiliteracy education which will undergird the critical literacy teaching and learning in its English language and Social Studies classrooms amongst others, which would also go beyond the current purview of the MLC's messages of imperatives.

As the authors write this chapter, opposition parties had just made further inroads into the PAP-dominant parliament. Observers have attributed this outcome to young voters wanting greater diversity in representations and a different style of engagement (Hong, 2020; George & Low, 2020). Some also credited the opposition for the successful use of social media. It would be worth conducting comparative research on how digital natives in different societies use social media in their lived experiences as citizens, as well as the role of schools in facilitating social media leverages to develop critical literacies.

Last but not least, the instrumental assigning of a "functional" role to the English language in Singapore should be interrogated. English has long been positioned as a "neutral" language that serves to unify Singapore's multiethnic citizenry and a means to plug into the global economy. Luke (2004) argued for a reframing of English-language education under a political economic lens where there are important implications of its neocolonial role as a global capital when embraced by populations who might not traditionally have claimed English as their first language. A more critical assessment of knowledge representation and production through the English language is necessary when Singapore has dramatically transformed from a pre-independent society with less than 10% of its population speaking English, to one where English is the working language of its entire population. How does Singapore develop a critical literacy education with a postcolonial perspective that also takes into consideration linguistic diversity? How might the language situation then shape the understanding of other non-English-speaking history-making subalterns (e.g., Kwok & Teng, 2018, pp. 73–77; Kwok & Chia, 2012) who are silenced or feel handicapped to represent themselves in the English language? A critical approach to literacy in Singapore will require further research entailing a postcolonial perspective investigating power relations and knowledge production involving language. A comparative research with other former colonies where the colonial language still has much currency could shed light on how it shapes discursive spaces for critical literacy education.

Conclusion

Willinsky (2007) cites critical literary education as the "the supremely educational event" for individuals and communities to "work out critiques that can seize hold of the most basic contradictions, broken promises, seeming conundrums, and necessary compromises" (p. 17). Perhaps in recognition of this, Singapore academics and educators have begun enlarging discursive spaces by engaging the wider civil society in deconstructing the notion of differentiated deservedness amongst citizens (see, e.g., Teo, 2018; Tan, 2018, and the work of Academia.sg), writing in an accessible manner for the public and/or organizing and speaking at forums that involve a range of societal actors. There is hope for societal critical literacies development within this ground-up widened discursive space.

Current public discussion as long-standing perceptions of racial injustice may yet come to a boiling point (Tharman, 2020) in Singapore. Teachers therefore need to step up to the plate and grapple with literacy as a "risky" social and political process. Exposing students to dialectic conversations, inviting them to consider alternative arguments and the perspectives and positionalities these hold, have now become crucial. Teachers could do more to provide agency and voice to students, in particular those from minority groups. Curriculums, especially the enacted and the hidden, are the narrative construction and contestation of learner identities and citizen ontologies and possible life projects and social trajectories. Teachers must realize that what is at the moment high-stakes for their students in the "new normal" is not performing well in competitive, summative examinations but how to negotiate the riskier economic and social ecologies, in both virtual and real worlds, locally and globally as competent, critically literate persons. Teacher education, in turn, needs to support teachers in the intellectual labour central to teaching and learning of critical literacy.

References

Albright, J., & Kramer-Dahl, A. (2009). The legacy of instrumentality in policy and pedagogy in the teaching of English: The case of Singapore. *Research Papers in Education, 24*(2), 201–222.
Alviar-Martin, T., & Ho, L.-C. (2011). "So, where do they fit in?" Teachers' perspectives of multi-cultural education and diversity in Singapore. *Teaching and Teacher Education, 27*(1), 127–135.
Anstey, M., & Bull, G. (2006). *Teaching and learning multiliteracies: Changing times, changing literacies.* International Reading Association.
Bokhorst-Heng, W. (2002). Newspapers in Singapore: A mass ceremony in the imagining of the nation. *Media, Culture & Society, 24*, 559–568.
Bokhorst-Heng, W., & Wee, L. (2007). Language planning in Singapore: On pragmatism, communitarianism and personal names. *Current Issues in Language Planning, 8*(3), 324–343.
Cheah, Y. M. (2001). From prescription to participation: Moving from functional to critical literacy in Singapore. In B. Comber & A. Simpson (Eds.), *Negotiating critical literacies in classrooms* (pp. 75–89). Routledge.
Cheng, K. (2019, July 13). The big read: Strides made, but some way to go for government to quench thirst for data. *Today.*
Cheong, C. M., & Cheung, W. S. (2008). Online discussion and critical thinking skills: A case study in a Singapore secondary school. *Australasian Journal of Educational Technology, 24*(5), 556–573.
Cheung, W. S., & Hew, K. F. (2005). How can we facilitate students' in-depth thinking and interaction in an asynchronous online discussion environment? A case study. *Proceedings of the AECT International Convention*, 114–121.
Chua, B. H. (1983). Reopening ideological discussion in Singapore: A new theoretical direction. *Southeast Asian Journal of Social Science, 11*, 31–45.
Chuang, P. M. (2015, November 25). Leaders' wise policies allow Singapore to 'punch above its weight': Obama. *The Business Times.*
Churchill, K. (2006, April). *Critical literacy in Singapore social studies: 'Weaving the fabric of a nation'.* Paper presented at the annual meeting of the American Educational Research Association, San Francisco.
Cope, B., & Kalantzis, M. (2000). *Multiliteracies: Literacy learning and the Design of Social Futures.* Palgrave Macmillan.
Curdt-Christiansen, X. L. (2010). Competing priorities: Singaporean teachers' perspectives on critical literacy. *International Journal of Educational Research, 49*, 184–194.

Gee, J. P. (1990). *Social linguistics and literacies: Ideology in discourses, critical perspectives on literacy and education.* Falmer Press.

George, C. (2000). OB markers and the rules of political engagement. In *Singapore: The air-conditioned nation—essays on the politics of comfort and control 1990–2000.* Landmark Books.

George, C., & Low, D. (2020, July 7). GE2020: Why Singapore may lose, whatever the final score. *Academic Views, GE 2020.* Retrieved from www.academia.sg/academic-views/ge2020-why-singapore-may-lose/.

Goh, C. B., & Gopinathan, S. (2008). The development of education in Singapore since 1965. In S. K. Lee, C. B. Goh, B. Fredriksen, & J. P. Tan (Eds.), *Toward a better future: Education and training for economic development in Singapore since 1965* (pp. 12–38). The World Bank and the National Institute of Education.

Goh, C. T. (1997, June 2). *Speech by Prime Minister Goh Chok Tong at the opening of the 7th International Conference on Thinking.* Retrieved from http://ncee.org/wp-content/uploads/2017/01/Sgp-non-AV-2-PM-Goh-1997-Shaping-Our-Future-Thinking-Schools-Learning-Nation-speech.pdf

Gopinathan, S., & Mardiana, A. B. (2013). Globalization, the state and curriculum reform. In Z. Y. Deng, S. Gopinathan, & C. Lee (Eds.), *Globalization and the Singapore curriculum: From policy to classroom* (pp. 100–123). Springer.

Hill, M., & Lian, K. F. (1995). *The politics of nation building and citizenship in Singapore.* Routledge.

Ho, L.-C. (2010). "Don't worry, I'm not going to report you": Education for citizenship in Singapore. *Theory and Social Research in Education, 38*(2), 217–247.

Ho, L.-C. (2017). 'Freedom can only exist in an ordered state': Harmony and civic education in Singapore. *Journal of Curriculum Studies, 49*(4), 476–496.

Ho, L.-C., Alviar-Martin, T., & Leviste, E. N. (2014). "There is space, and there are limits": The challenge of teaching controversial topics in an illiberal democracy. *Teachers' College Record, 116*(5), 1–28.

Hong, H. (2020, July 14). Stern political realities call for shift in PAP governance. *The Straits Times.*

Ibrahim, A. (2012). Literature and social memory: The case of suratman markasan. *Commentary, 21,* 72–84.

Ismail, R. (2014). The "new" multiculturalism: National and educational perspectives. *HSSE Online.* National Institute of Education, *3*(2).

Kellner, D., & Share, J. (2007). Critical media literacy is not an option. *Learning Inquiry, 1*(1), 59–69.

Koh, A. (2002). Towards a critical pedagogy: Creating 'thinking schools' in Singapore. *Journal of Curriculum Studies, 34*(3), 255–264.

Koh, A. (2004). Newspaper literacy: An investigation of how Singaporean students read the Straits Times. *English Teaching: Practice and Critique, 3*(3), 43–60.

Koh, A. (2019). Travelling with and teaching critical literacy in Singapore, Australia, and Hong Kong: A call for postcritique. *Curriculum Inquiry, 49*(2), 203–216.

Kramer-Dahl, A. (2001). Importing critical literacy pedagogy: Does it have to fail? *Language and Education, 15*(1), 14–32.

Kramer-Dahl, A. (2004). Constructing adolescents differently: On the value of listening to Singapore youngsters talking popular culture texts. *Linguistics and Education, 15*(3), 217–241.

Kwok, K.-W., & Chia, K. (2012). Memories at the margins: Chinese-educated intellectuals in Singapore. In R. Waterson & K.-W. Kwok (Eds.), *Contestations of memory in southeast Asia* (pp. 230–269). National University of Singapore Press.

Kwok, K.-W., & Teng, S. S. (2018). *Chinese.* Singapore Chronicles. Straits Times Press & Institute of Policy Studies.

Lee, K. Y. (1966, August 29). *New bearings in our education system: An address to principals of schools in Singapore.* Ministry of Culture.

Lim, L. (2014). Critical thinking and the anti-liberal state: The politics of pedagogic recontextualization in Singapore. *Discourse: Studies in the Cultural Politics of Education, 35*(5), 692–704.

Lim, L., & Apple, M. W. (2015). Elite rationalities and curricular form: "Meritorious" class reproduction in the elite thinking curriculum in Singapore. *Curriculum Inquiry, 45*(5), 472–490.

Lim, L. Y. C. (2018). *Business, government and labor: Essays on economic development in Singapore and southeast Asia.* World Scientific.

Loh, K. S. (1998). Within the Singapore story: The use and narrative of history in Singapore. *Crossroads: An Interdisciplinary Journal of Southeast Asian Studies, 12*(2), 1–21.

Luke, A. (2004). The trouble with English. *Research in the Teaching of English, 39*(1), 85–95.

Luke, A. (2012). Critical literacy: Foundational notes. *Theory into Practice, 51*(1), 4–11.

Mardiana, A. B. (2012). *Of perspectives and policy: A case study of the implementation of the subject-based banding policy in one Singapore primary school* (Unpublished thesis). National Institute of Education.

Media Literacy Council (MLC) website. (n.d.). Retrieved from www.imda.gov.sg/for-community/digital-readiness/Media-Literacy-and-Cyber-Wellness

Ministry of Education. (2016). *Upper secondary social studies -express course normal (academic) textbook.* Curriculum Planning and Development Division.

Ministry of Education. (2008). *English language syllabus 2010 primary & secondary (Express/ Normal [Academic]).* Curriculum Planning and Development Division.

Pennycook, A. (2017). *The cultural politics of English as an international language.* Routledge.

POFMA. (n.d.). Retrieved from www.pofmaoffice.gov.sg/about-us/#:~:text=The%20POFMA%20 Office%2C%20situated%20within,that%20affect%20the%20public%20interest

Quah, S. R., & Hee, W. S. (2020). *Memorandum: A Sinophone Singaporean short story reader* (D. F. Tan, Trans.). Ethos Books.

Rodan, G. (2016). Capitalism, inequality and ideology in Singapore: New challenges for the ruling party. *Asian Studies Review, 40*(2), 211–230.

Sim, J. B.-Y. (2011). Social studies and citizenship for participation in Singapore: How one state seeks to influence its citizens. *Oxford Review of Education, 37*(6), 743–761.

Sim, J. B.-Y., Chua, S., & Krishnasamy, M. (2017). "Riding the citizenship wagon": Citizenship conceptions of social studies teachers in Singapore *Teaching and Teacher Education, 63*, 92–102.

Sim, J. B.-Y., & Ho, L.-C. (2010). Transmitting social and national values through education in Singapore: Tensions in a globalized era. In T. Lovat, R. Toomey, & N. Clement (Eds.), *International research handbook on values education and student wellbeing.* Springer,

Sim, J. B.-Y., & Krishnasamy, M. (2016). Building a democratic society: Exploring Singapore students' understandings of democracy. *Asian Education and Development Studies, 5*(1), 37–58.

Sim, J. B.-Y., & Print, M. (2009). Citizenship education in Singapore: Controlling or empowering teacher understanding and practice? *Oxford Review of Education, 35*(6), 705–723.

Soarse, L. B., & Wood, K. D. (2010). A Critical literacy perspective for teaching and learning social studies. *The Reading Teacher, 63*(6), 486–494.

Street, B. (1984). *Literacy in theory and practice.* Cambridge University Press.

Tan, C. (2012). Deep culture matters' multiracialism in Singapore schools. *International Journal of Educational Reform, 21*(1), 24–38.

Tan, C., & Tan, C. S. (2014). Fostering social cohesion and cultural sustainability: Character and citizenship education in Singapore. *Diaspora, Indigenous and Minority Education, 8*(4), 191–206.

Tan, K. P. (2008). Meritocracy and elitism in a global city: Ideological shifts in Singapore. *International Political Science Review, 29*(1), 7–27.

Tan, K. P. (2012). The ideology of pragmatism in Singapore: Neoliberal globalization and political authoritarianism. *Journal of Contemporary Asia, 42*(1), 67–92.

Tan, K. P. (2018). *Singapore: Identity, brand and power.* Cambridge University Press.

Teng, S. S. (2006). *The cultural politics of History-writing in Singapore: A postcolonial critique* (Unpublished PhD thesis). University of Essex.

Teo, Y. Y. (2018). *This is what inequality looks like.* Ethos Books.

Tharman, S. (2020, June 17). A stronger and more cohesive society: Full text of Senior Minister Tharman Shanmugaratnam's national broadcast. *The Straits Times.* Retrieved from www.straitstimes.com/ politics/a-stronger-and-more-cohesive-society-full-text-of-senior-minister-tharman-shanmugaratnams.

Weninger, C. (2017). Media literacy education in Singapore: Connecting theory, policy and practice. In K. Chan, K. Zhang, & A. Lee (Eds.), *Multidisciplinary approaches to media literacy: Research and practices* (pp. 399–416). Communication University of China Press.

Weninger, W. (2020). Investigating ideology through framing: A critical discourse analysis of a critical literacy lesson. *Classroom Discourse, 11*(2), 107–128.

Willinsky, J. (2007). *Of critical theory and critical literacy.* Retrieved from https://pkp.sfu.ca/files/Critical%20 Literacy.pdf.

Wolk, S. (2003). Teaching for critical literacy in social studies. *The Social Studies, 94*(3), 101–106.

Yeo, S. M., & Zhu, Y. (2005). *Higher-order thinking in Singapore Mathematics classrooms.* Paper presented at conference: Redesigning Pedagogy: Research, Policy, Practice. Singapore Centre for Research in Pedagogy and Practice, National Institute of Education.

2.14

CRITICAL LITERACIES IN POST-APARTHEID SOUTH AFRICA

Hilary Janks and Carolyn McKinney

History

The Hector Pietersen Museum located in the heart of Soweto, Johannesburg records for posterity the role played by youth in the struggle against apartheid. It is named for Pietersen, the first child who was shot during the 1976 civil uprising. Sparked by children marching to protest the imposition of Afrikaans as a medium of instruction in primary schools, the protest led to nation-wide riots and prolonged school boycotts. The student rebellion focused on Bantu Education which under apartheid had been deliberately designed to confine black people to "certain forms of labour" and to exclude them "from the green pastures of European society where they were still not allowed to graze" (Verwoerd, Minister of Native Affairs, 1954). When, towards the end of 1985, students were calling for 1986 to be the year of no schooling, Soweto parents called for a national consultative conference within the resistance movement. At this conference the National Education Crisis Committee (NECC) was formed and People's Education for People's Power was conceived. People's Education aimed to encourage students not to withdraw from the system but rather to identify and fight for their educational priorities. Three commissions were established at the outset: People's Maths, People's History and People's English. Janks was invited to join the commission on People's English because of her research on language and power under apartheid (Janks, 1988) and its application to education. This commission produced the *Draft proposals for People's English* (Butler, 1993) which described language competence as the ability to:

- hear what is said and what is hidden;
- explore relationships: personal, structural, political;
- make one's voice heard;
- read print and to resist it where necessary;
- understand the relationship between language and power;

amongst other things. When the NECC became a banned organisation, Janks was advised to spend her time working on critical language awareness materials. *The Critical Language Awareness Series* (Janks, 1993) gave birth to critical literacies in the South African context. This was developed further by the work of her early graduate students Clarence (1994), Granville (1996), Shariff (1998), Prinsloo (2002) and that of McKinney and van Pletzen (2004) in the Western Cape.

DOI: 10.4324/9781003023425-26

Education has been an ongoing site of struggle in South Africa which continues to this day, with language as a flashpoint. As a consequence of how language in education policy is currently implemented, the languages spoken by black South Africans stop being used as language/s of instruction after Grade 3. Furthermore, translanguaging is not seen as a valued pedagogy. These languages are also not a requirement as a subject for matriculation despite being spoken by most South Africans. Curriculum policy is prescriptive and mandates standardised testing. The move to decolonising education which is the focus of current struggles in Higher Education has not yet resulted in a challenge to the knowledge that is privileged in the national Curriculum and Assessment Standards (CAPS) for Grades 1–12. Currently, bua-lit (http://bua-lit.org.za), a national collective, is leading the fight against the narrow, technicist, skills-based orientation to language and literacy education in early literacy education policies. These effectively sideline sociocultural approaches to literacy, including critical literacies.

South Africa's Educational System

South Africa has compulsory schooling for children aged 7–15 years (Grades 1–9) with the official school leaving or matriculation examination taking place at the end of Grade 12. While there is near universal access to primary schooling, the reality is that 40% of children who begin Grade 1 drop out of the system before completing Grade 12 and achieving the school leaving certificate. Of the 60% who matriculate, less than half of these students meet minimum entrance requirements for higher education institutions (Van Broekhuizen, Van der Berg, & Hofmeyr, 2016).

Of even more concern is the racialised, classed and gendered nature of access to quality schooling. In the annual matriculation results as well as standardised assessments, there is a clear bi-modal distribution where a small minority of students (mostly white and black middle class) perform well, while the vast majority of black students underachieve. There are two schooling systems, one highly resourced, fee paying and catering to a minority of elite students, white and black, and one catering for the majority of students in no-fee schools (Fleisch, 2008). For the most part though, all schools follow the same national curriculum. The low throughput and poor quality of South Africa's education system is widely recognised as a national priority. Most recently, the statistic regularly reproduced is that 78% of children in Grade 4 "cannot read for meaning in any language" according to the results of the latest international standardised test Progress in Reading Literacy or PIRLS 2016. The conclusions drawn are that teachers do not know how to teach literacy and that teacher education programmes are not doing their job. Systemic inequalities such as infrastructure, class size and access to literacy resources are seen as contributing factors, but the failure of education to build on existing community literacy and language practices is ignored.

In response to results on standardised literacy tests, policy makers and the national Department of Basic Education double-down on implementing a skills-focused, "back to basics" approach where the goal of becoming literate is decoding and the comprehension of texts. Teachers are encouraged to follow a sequential process beginning with the "building blocks" of sounds and words moving on to sentences. Success is measured by an adapted form of the Early Grade Reading Assessment (EGRA) and Oral Reading Fluency (ORF). The government is currently supporting initiatives to develop normative standards for different levels of ORF in the nine indigenous languages through which most children learn for the first three years of schooling before they transition to English as the medium of instruction in Grade 4. In the recently produced drafts of Primary Teacher Education Standards, critical literacy and sociocultural approaches were completely absent and it took deliberate intervention by black academics at national consultative workshops to force limited inclusion. The current approach to standardised testing using imported tests such as the EGRA and PIRLS is aligned with psycholinguistic and cognitive approaches to literacy pedagogy and deficit constructions of childhood (Compton-Lily, Dixon, Janks, & Woods, 2020) that negate opportunities for sociocultural and critical approaches to literacy interventions to improve literacy outcomes for children.

Critical literacy approaches were embedded in the high school language curriculum in the first post-apartheid outcomes-based curriculum, Curriculum 2005, which made a radical break from the apartheid ideologies that informed education. Outcomes-based education which relied on teacher autonomy that had been eroded under apartheid (Jansen & Christie, 1999; Chisholm, 2005) led to Curriculum 2005 and its revised version being replaced by a highly prescriptive, "knowledge focused" curriculum, in 2012, CAPS (the national *Curriculum and Assessment Policy Statement*). In this current policy response and intervention, the notion that teachers and students might be alienated from the schooling system itself and from exclusively Western and monolingual approaches to knowledge and pedagogy continues to be ignored. In this regard, the need for critical literacies is ongoing and could contribute to decolonising the curriculum.

Survey of Critical Literacies Work in South Africa

This survey is based on critical literacies research since 2005 published as books and electronic dissertations and theses (ETD) (www.netd.ac.za). Owing to constraints of space, we have limited our survey of journal articles to four key South African journals, *Reading and Writing*, *South African Journal of Linguistics and Applied Language Studies*, *Perspectives in Education* and the *Journal of Education* as these are less well known than international journals. Ferreira's (2019) survey of critical literacies work in South Africa is worth reading, in addition.

Critical Literacies: Book Reviews

Because there are so few books on critical literacies published in South Africa, it has been possible to give a sense of each. *Language and Power* (Janks, 2010) and *Doing Critical Literacy* (Janks, Dixon, Ferreira, Granville, & Newfield, 2014) explain Janks's interdependent model of critical literacy and provide related classroom activities that can be used or adapted by teachers. Janks argues that issues of power, access, diversity (identity and difference) and design and redesign need to work together in critical literacies education and that any one without the others creates a problematic imbalance. This is important in the South African context where access to education often ignores diversity and expects assimilation to white middle-class norms and colonising practices. Othering on the basis of race, gender, sexuality and nationality continue in South Africa and are manifest in violence against women, xenophobic and homophobic attacks, and in systemic barriers—institutional, spatial and economic—that continue to privilege whiteness (Steyn, 2001). These barriers reproduce conditions of exclusion and poverty for the black majority in South Africa. What the post-apartheid period has shown is how difficult it is to change systemically entrenched inequality and the stark horror of failing to do so.

Literacy Power and the Schooled Body (Dixon, 2011) is a critical analysis of early childhood literacy education from Grade 0 to Grade 3 at the intersection of time–space and children's bodies. This ethnographic study shows that the literate subject of schooling is one who has a good vocabulary, writes neatly, spells correctly and reads fluently with expression and comprehension. The emphasis on skills such as decoding and encoding texts, rather than meaning-making, constructs limited literate subjects who are increasingly individualised, surveilled and confined to their desks. A more agentive vision of childhood is evident in the work of Murris (2016), who uses picture books to engage both children and teachers in Philosophy for Children enquiries, underpinned by a post-humanist onto-epistemology.

McKinney's (2017) work refocuses attention on language. Her study of language ideologies in practice in *Language and Power in Post-Colonial Schooling* shows the effects of anglonormativity and the persistence of the ideological construction of languages as bounded entities. Given that multilingualism is the norm in South Africa, she argues for the importance of the use of multiple languages in education, including translanguaging pedagogies and for teaching about language ideologies. She concludes her book with examples of transformative educational initiatives that promote the use of students' full linguistic repertoires and critique the normativity of monolingual English. These include a multiliteracies poetry project in Soweto (Newfield & Maungedzo, 2006; Newfield, 2011) and the Phemba Mfundi (fire learners) writing project (McKinney, 2017) with 10–12-year-old children taking part in 2–3 days' multilingual writing camps in rural Eastern Cape. To this could be added the work of Sibanda (2007), a high school English teacher, who engaged his students in researching the stickers found in taxis which are the main source of transport for black South Africans. The stickers, written in many of South Africa's 11 official languages, were then analysed to uncover prevailing discourses and their underlying power relations.

Work in the area of multimodality is not always critical as is discussed by Newfield (2011). Stein's book *Multimodal Pedagogies in Diverse Classrooms* does attend to "representation, rights and resources" and is founded on a respect for the languages, funds of knowledge, voice and agency of children living in poverty. She pays attention to the ways in which different modes offer differing perspectives and different uses of rhetoric. *Multimodal Approaches to Research and Pedagogy: Recognition, Resources and Access*, an edited collection, (Archer & Newfield, 2014) looks at the ideological nature of discourses with a view to understanding transformative multimodal pedagogies in South Africa that contribute to greater equity and social justice.

Critical Literacies Review Beyond Books

The remainder of this overview provides a synthesis of the findings from the review of dissertations, theses and articles. Chetty (2015) argues that CAPS is too prescriptive, provides too little space for critical literacies and runs counter to the emancipatory aims of post 1994 educational policy. This is supported by Cahl's (2016) analysis of the textbooks approved for CAPS and Govender's (2011) research evaluating whether SA textbooks demonstrate critical literacy activities. He found that these often perpetuate conservative ideologies and the exercises preclude critical engagement. In a similar vein, Silverthorne's (2011) research finds that set literary texts remain predominantly anglocentric with the inclusion of some South African and African poets as a form of tokenism in a curriculum that is at its core Eurocentric. Research that focuses on current practice in education has found little evidence of critical literacies practices in state schools and classrooms at all levels (Dixon, 2007; Petersen, 2014; Lloyd, 2016) as well as the difficulties experienced by teachers in the context of CAPS (Enslin, 2017).

Teacher-Taught Interventions. Research on teacher-taught interventions show these have had mixed success. Nonkwelo (2012) found that teachers were ill-prepared to teach critical literacies even with materials that invited them to do so. However, in research where teachers were selected because they had some knowledge of critical literacies, they were able to work productively with the materials designed by the researcher (Ferreira, 2013). Working with teachers to transform practices in relation to reconciliation (Ferreira & Janks, 2009) or diversity in schools (Dornbrack, 2008) heightened teachers' understanding of power relations both within and outside of their classrooms and effected some change.

Practitioner-researchers. Researchers with an understanding of critical literacies who examine their own interventions have had some measure of success. The research in early childhood education (Grades 0–3) are cases in point, but most of it has been conducted in privileged schools (Hearn, 2018; Anastassopoulos, 2015; Dixon & Janks, 2019). Treffrey-Goatly's (2017) analysis of folk tales in the African Storybook corpus shows affordances in relation to critical literacies and transformative design in the representation of girls. Our literature search found no evidence of research undertaken in Grades 4–9.

From Secondary to Tertiary Education. Ndlangamandla's (2006) research shows that many high school students were able to engage critically with the subject positions on offer in advertisements for denim jeans, and Kur (2009) was able to disrupt adolescent girls' acceptance of racialised notions of beauty. Perhaps, the most important finding by Enslin (2017) is that the teacher in her study who had an overall critical orientation was more able to sustain ongoing critical literacies pedagogy in relation to the content and texts prescribed by CAPS than the other two teachers she investigated. These teachers saw critical literacy as outside of, separated from, and in opposition to, the curriculum rather than a part of ongoing ways of doing and being (Vasquez, Janks, & Comber, 2019).

At the tertiary level, researchers have also been able to construct meaningful critical literacies interventions. Researching his undergraduate course on gender, Govender (2016) shows positive changes in students' understanding of and attitude to heteronormativity and gender diversity; Walton (2016) undertook a critical analysis of the language and practices of inclusive education, and Reed (2010) analysed the ways in which distance teacher education materials construct teacher–students' subjectivities.

Multilingualism and Translanguaging. The return to the focus on language as central to critical literacies is evident in more recent research on multilingualism and translanguaging pedagogies that recognise the importance of students' African languages and that challenge the dominance of colonial languages in South African education (Makalela, 2018; McKinney, 2017). Nal'ibali (https://nalibali.org), African Storybook (www.africanstorybook.org) and Molteno (www.molteno.co.za) have been developing stories in African languages for primary school children and researching their use. Maduna (2010) investigated South African rap music to understand the representations of language creoles and hybrid identities with a view to their inclusion in English poetry lessons at the secondary level.

Petersen's (2014) research on critical literacies with Afrikaans teachers found that teacher's age and consequent apartheid histories affected their selection of texts and their approach to meaning in these texts, which differed from that of their younger students consequently affecting their critical engagement. Mendelowitz and Davies (2011) show how the sharing of language narratives in classrooms produced more positive attitudes to linguistic diversity and an appreciation of multilingualism. By way of contrast (Wentzel, 2013) research with immigrant girls in an inner city secondary school found that the inclusion of language and literacy practices is tied to the ways in which the different school communities are valued or marginalised. Given wa Thiongo's (1986) work on the centrality of language in colonising minds, work in this area is likely to assume greater importance as the demand for the decolonisation of education in South Africa grows.

Visions for Moving Into More Transnational and Critical Work From the Perspective of South Africa

According to Ngũgĩ wa Thiongo (1986)

> The biggest weapon wielded and actually daily unleashed by imperialism against that collective defiance is the cultural bomb. The effect of a cultural bomb is to annihilate a people's belief in their names, in their languages, in their environment, in their heritage of struggle, in their unity, in their capacities and ultimately in themselves. . . . It makes them want to identify with that which is furthest removed from themselves; for instance, with other people's languages rather than their own.
>
> *(p. 3)*

A focus on the stratification and the exclusion of languages, rooted in racialised colonial ideologies has always been a central concern of critical literacies in South Africa (Janks, 1990; Orlek, 1993). This connects with more recent work on raciolinguistic ideologies (Flores & Rosa, 2015; Baker-Bell, 2020) and provides many opportunities for transnational collaboration in challenging the normativity of monolingualism and the hegemony of standard varieties of the dominant language. (See McKinney's, 2017 work on anglonormativity). The alignment of linguistic hegemony with whiteness in post-colonial anglophone countries (e.g., Uganda, Kenya, the USA) also manifests in education as the language of teaching and learning, exclusionary curricula and national/international standardised assessments of literacy, providing further opportunities for transnational research and advocacy. Challenges to this hegemony can be seen in Alim's (2010) examples of critical literacies pedagogy working with African American English and Baker-Bell's (2020) work on linguistic justice. Alim and Smitherman's (2012) writing that meshes African American Language with Mainstream United States English (MUSE) is inspirational in challenging norms and expanding the repertoire of "academic" English.

What counts as powerful literacies and language use is deeply shaped by coloniality, defined by Maldonado Torres (2007) as that which "survives colonialism" (243). Mignolo explains how the colonial matrix of power (Grosfoguel, 2007) includes control of the economy, authority, gender and sexuality and subjectivity and knowledge (Mignolo, 2009, p. 19). Critical applied linguistics scholars have challenged the construction of knowledge with the demonstration of the colonial "invention" (Makoni, 1999) of bounded, standard African languages through missionary intervention (Makoni & Pennycook, 2007; Makalela, 2015, 2018); the construction of the myth of monolingualism as the norm (Phillipson, 1994; Garcia & Lin, 2018) and multilingualism in languages other than European languages as a deficient "linguistic jumble" (Garcia & Lin, 2018, p. 81). De/colonial theory produced by Latin American (e.g., Grosfoguel, 2007; Mignolo, 2009; Maldonado Torres, 2007) and African scholars (Ndlovu-Gatsheni, 2013) thus provides a significant further point of transnational connection for critical literacies activists and educators in South Africa.

Tools of decolonial theory such as "delinking" and "pluriversality" as well as knowledge construction from the perspective and position of the excluded are crucial to an expanded critical literacy. This requires collaboration between scholars in countries that share histories of colonial oppression. Such collaboration will move South African scholars beyond their existing history of transnational critical literacies network with scholars in Australia, the UK, Sweden, Canada, and the United States.

Conclusions and Suggestions for Further Research and Practice

To the extent to which critical literacies work itself is entangled with Western epistemologies and the consequences thereof, it is implicated in universalist ideas, which Mignolo (2013) argues are a fiction of Western modernity. Further work in critical literacies needs to open itself to pluriversal epistemologies, cosmologies and imaginaries. This includes, amongst others, new materialist perspectives that focus on the entanglement of all living and non-living entities and our culpability with regard to the destruction of the planet and the extinction of other species. In this regard, countries in the Global South are more vulnerable to climate change as a result of the historical legacy and continuing profligacy of capitalism in the Global North.

Human beings' inability to value other human beings whom they construct as Other can be seen in the growing power of right-wing nationalist and white supremacist groups across the globe and a surge in the number of populist leaders. Black lives are constantly devalued and under the threat of attack, while a global pandemic has posed a greater threat to people living in precarity without access to employment, healthcare and food security. Lack of access to the internet and online platforms has also affected the schooling of millions of children. Countries close their borders to desperate migrants, separate children from parents and confine migrants to crowded inhumane refugee camps.

South Africa faces many of these challenges along with other parts of the world. Here, in addition, rampant corruption has led to money being stolen that could have been used to provide basic social services such as running water, sanitation, healthcare, safe transport and food. Gender-based violence, homophobic and xenophobic attacks and police killings are regular occurrences. Systemic inequality introduced by colonialism and exacerbated by apartheid remains, and unequal access to quality education along lines of race and class continues to perpetuate structural divides that perpetuate white privilege. The economic, social, linguistic, spatial and racial justice that the transition to democracy promised has yet to be realised across all institutions that make up the social fabric. There is still an urgent need for education committed to critique and social action based on an ethics of care for all living and non-living entities.

Implications for Our Social Responsibility as Academics

Since the pioneering work of Paulo Freire, critical literacy has been aligned with social action. Currently, young people around the world are taking the lead and mounting social action campaigns to address issues that threaten their futures. Students at Marjory Stoneman Douglas High organised a nationwide demonstration, March for our Lives, for greater gun control in the United States. Greta Thunberg, a Swedish student, generated a youth climate movement involving over a million students in school strikes across 125 countries. In South Africa, tertiary students mounted the #Rhodes Must Fall and #FeesMustFall campaigns. Our responsibility as academics is fourfold: First, we have to educate critically literate teachers with a sense of ethical responsibility to strive for equity and social justice. Teachers, and we include ourselves, need to *prepare* students to care about injustice and develop the skills needed to meet the challenges of their time. Second, as teachers we need to *support* students in their struggles to achieve justice as was the case in the teacher education programme at McKinney's university, where lecturers and students created banners and marched together in recent #FeesMustFall and Gender Based Violence activism. Third, we have a responsibility to conduct *research* that contributes to better educational outcomes for all young people. Finally, we have a significant role to play in *advocacy* work that puts the typical African language-speaking child at the centre. The launch of the bua-lit collective in South Africa is an example of the use of social media to raise awareness about the current limitations in literacy education and to advocate for change.

References

Alim, H. S. (2010). Critical language awareness. In N. Hornberger & S. McKay (Eds.), *Sociolinguistics and language education* (pp. 205–231). Multilingual Matters.

Alim, H. S., & Smitherman, G. (2012). *Articulate while black: Barack Obama, language and race in the U.S.* Oxford University Press.

Anastassopoulos, N. (2015). *Transforming literacy teaching: A teacher's experience of implementing critical literacy and philosophy for children in a grade three South African classroom* (Masters dissertation). University of the Witwatersrand, Johannesburg. Retrieved from http://hdl.handle.net/10539/17844

Archer, A., & Newfield, D. (Eds.). (2014). *Multimodal approaches to research and pedagogy: Recognition, resources, and access.* Routledge.

Baker-Bell, A. (2020). *Linguistic justice: Black language, literacy, identity, and pedagogy.* Routledge & National Council of Teachers of English.

Butler, I. (1993). *'People's English' in South Africa theory and practice* (Masters dissertation). Rhodes University, Grahamstown. Retrieved from https://core.ac.uk/download/ pdf/145045716.pdf

Cahl, G. (2016). *An analysis of dominant discourse in Grade 8 English home language textbooks* (Masters dissertation). University of Cape Town, Cape Town. htto://hdl.handle.net/11427/23458

Chetty, R. (2015). Freirean principles and *critical literacy* to counter retrograde impulses in the curriculum and assessment policy statement. *Reading & Writing, 6,* 1–7.

Chisholm, L. (2005). The politics of curriculum review and revision in South Africa in regional context. *Compare, 35*(1), 79–100.

Clarence, J. A. (1994). *Black students in an open university: A critical exploration of student responses to a selection of texts which form part of the discourse of the University of Natal* (Masters dissertation). University of Natal, Pietermaritzburg.

Compton-Lily, C., Dixon, K., Janks, H., & Woods, A. (2020). Summative assessments and how they imagine children. In C. Martin et al. (Eds.), *Handbook of research on formative assessment in Pre-K through Elementary Classrooms*. IGI Global.

Dixon, K. (2007) *Literacy, power and the embodied subject* (Doctoral thesis). University of the Witwatersrand, Johannesburg. Retrieved from http://hdl.handle.net/10539/4998

Dixon, K. (2011). *Literacy power, and the schooled body*. Routledge.

Dixon, K., & Janks, H. (2019). Researching a child's embodied textual play. In N. Kucirkova, J. Rowsell, & G. Falloon (Eds.), *The Routledge international handbook of learning with technology in early childhood*. Routledge.

Dornbrack, J. (2008). *Reflection as a tool for managing difference in the post-apartheid classroom* (Doctoral thesis). University of the Witwatersrand, Johannesburg. Retrieved from http://hdl.handle.net/10539/6872

Enslin, E. (2017). *The uptake of critical literacy in the classrooms of PGCE graduates: An auto-ethnographic inquiry of teacher identities* (Honours research report). University of the Witwatersrand, Johannesburg.

Ferreira, A. (2013). *Subjectivity and pedagogy in a context of social change* (Doctoral thesis). University of the Witwatersrand, Johannesburg. Retrieved from http://hdk,handle.net10539/13489

Ferreira, A. (2019). Critical literacy in South Africa: Tracking the chameleon. In J. Lacina & R. Griffith (Eds.), *Preparing globally minded literacy teachers: Knowledge, practices and case studies* (pp. 99–126). Routledge.

Ferreira, A., & Janks, H. (2009). Doves, rainbows and an uneasy peace: Student images of reconciliation in a post-conflict society. *Perspectives in Education, 27*(2), 133–146.

Fleisch, B. (2008). *Primary education in crisis: Why South African school children underachieve in reading and mathematics*. Juta.

Flores, N., & Rosa, J. (2015). Undoing appropriateness: Raciolinguistics and language diversity in education. *Harvard Educational Review, 85*(2), 149–171.

Garcia, O., & Lin, A. (2018). English and multilingualism: A contested history. In P. Sergeant, A. Hewings, & S. Pihlaja (Eds.), *Routledge handbook of English language studies* (pp. 77–92). Routledge.

Govender, N. (2011). Do textbooks practice what they preach? *English Quarterly, 42*(3–4), 57–83.

Govender, N. (2016). *Negotiating the gendered representations of sexualities through critical literacy* (Doctoral thesis). University of the Witwatersrand, Johannesburg. Retrieved from http://hdl.handle.net/10539/20001

Granville, S. (1996). *Reading beyond the text: Exploring the possibilities in critical language awareness for reshaping student teachers' ideas about reading comprehension* (Unpublished Masters dissertation). University of the Witwatersrand.

Grosfoguel, R. (2007). The epistemic decolonial turn. *Cultural Studies, 21*(2–3), 211–223.

Hearn, K. (2018). *Critical literacy and children's "out-of-school" spaces* (Masters dissertation). University of the Witwatersrand, Johannesburg. Retrieved from https://hdl.handle.net/10539/27172

Janks, H. (1988). *To catch a wake-up: Language awareness in the South African context* (Masters thesis). University of the Witwatersrand, Johannesburg.

Janks, H. (1990). English education in South Africa. In I. Goodson, & P. Medway (Eds.), *Bringing English to order: The history and politics of a school subject* (pp. 242–261). Falmer Press.

Janks, H. (Ed.). (1993). *Critical language awareness series*. Wits University Press and Hodder and Stoughton.

Janks, H. (2010). *Literacy and power*. Routledge.

Janks, H. with Dixon, K., Ferreira, A., Granville, S., & Newfield, D. (2014). *Doing critical literacy*. Routledge.

Jansen, J., & Christie, P. (Eds.). (1999). *Changing curriculum: Studies on outcomes based education in South Africa*. Juta.

Kur, S. (2009). *Examining constructs of beauty through literature* (Masters dissertation). University of the Witwatersrand, Johannesburg. Retrieved from http://hdl.handle.net/10539/7220

Lloyd, G. (2016). Are we teaching *critical literacy*? Reading practices in a township classroom: Original research. *Reading & Writing, 7*, 1–6.

Maduna, M. (2010). *Elastic vernac: The(in)significance of indigenous languages in South African rap music* (Masters dissertation). University of the Witwatersrand, Johannesburg. Retrieved from http://hdl.handle.net/10539/7668

Makalela, L. (2015). Moving out of linguistic boxes: The effects of translanguaging strategies for multilingual classrooms, *Language and Education*. https://doi.org/10.1080/09500782.2014.994524

Makalela, L. (2018). Community elders' narrative accounts of *ubuntu* translanguaging: Learning and teaching in African education. *International Review of Education, 64*, 823–843.

Makoni, S. (1999). African languages as colonial scripts. In C. Coetzee & S. Nuttall (Eds.), *Negotiating the past: The making of memory in South Africa* (pp. 242–248). Oxford University Press.

Makoni, S., & Pennycook, A. (2007). Disinventing and reconstituting languages. In S. Makoni & A. Pennycook (Eds.), *Disinventing and reconstituting languages* (pp. 1–41). Multilingual Matters.

Maldonado Torres, N. (2007). On the coloniality of being: Contributions to the development of a concept. *Cultural Studies, 21*(2–3), 240–270.

McKinney, C. (2017). *Language and power in post-colonial contexts: Ideologies in practice.* Routledge.

McKinney, C., & van Pletzen, E. (2004). 'this apartheid story . . . we've decided it's gone we've finished with it': Student responses to 'politics' in a South African English Studies course, *Teaching in Higher Education, 9*(2), 159–170.

Mendelowitz, B., & Davies, H. (2011). A circle of learning: The impact of a narrative multilingualism approach on in-service teachers' literacy. *Reading & Writing, 2*(1), 41–61.

Mignolo, W. (2009). Epistemic disobedience, independent thought and de-colonial freedom. *Theory, Culture and Society, 26*(7–6), 1–23.

Mignolo, W. (2013). *On pluriversality.* Retrieved from http://waltermignolo.com/on-pluriversality/

Murris, K. (2016). *The posthuman child: Educational transformation through philosophy with picturebooks.* Routledge.

Ndlangamandla, C. (2006). *Sex sells—or does it? Responses to the construction of youth identities in print advertisements* (Masters dissertation). University of the Witwatersrand, Johannesburg. Retrieved from http://hdl.handle.net/10539/1587

Ndlovu-Gatsheni, S. J. (2013). *Empire, global coloniality and African subjectivity.* Berghahn Books.

Newfield, D. (2011). From visual literacy to critical visual literacy: An analysis of educational materials. *English Teaching Practice and Critique,* (1), 81–94.

Newfield, D., & Maungedzo, R. (2006). Mobilising and modalising poetry in a Soweto Classroom. *English Studies in Africa, 49*(1), 71–93.

Nonkwelo, N. (2012). *From the page to the classroom: Responses of some rural teachers and learners to textbook material on sensitive topics* (Masters dissertation). University of the Witwatersrand, Johannesburg. Retrieved from http://hdl.handle.net/10539/11582

Orlek, J. (1993). *Languages in South Africa.* Wits University Press & Hodder and Stoughton.

Petersen, L. (2014). *Teachers' understanding of critical language awareness and their enactment of this understanding in the classroom* (Masters dissertation). University of Cape Town, Cape Town. Retrieved from http://hdl.handle.net/11427/6865

Phillipson, R. (1994). English language spread policy. *International Journal of the Sociology of Language, 107,* 7–24.

Prinsloo, J. (2002). *Possibilities for critical literacy and exploration of schooled literacies in the province of Kwazulu-Natal* (Doctoral thesis). University of the Witwatersrand, Johannesburg.

Reed, Y. (2010). *Mediating knowledge and constituting subjectivities in distance education materials for language teachers in South Africa* (Doctoral thesis). University of the Witwatersrand, Johannesburg. Retrieved from http://hdl.handle.net/q0539/8584

Shariff, P. (1998). *Dialogue gender and performance: Producing a rural South African comic beyond the learner paradox* (Doctoral thesis). University of the Witwatersrand, Johannesburg.

Sibanda, R. (2007). *Reading bumper stickers critically: A teaching and research project with Grade 12 students at Randfontein secondary school* (Masters dissertation). University of the Witwatersrand, Johannesburg. Retrieved from http://hdl.handle.net/10539/6731

Silverthorne, R. (2011). *Tradition and transformation: A critique of English setwork selection 2009–2011* (Masters dissertation). University of the Witwatersrand, Johannesburg. Retrieved from http://hdl.handle.net/10539/7670

Stein, P. (2008). *Multimodal pedagogies in diverse classrooms.* Routledge.

Steyn, M. (2001). *'Whiteness just ain't what it used to be'. White identity in a changing South Africa.* SUNY Press.

Treffrey-Goatly, T. A. (2017). *A critical literacy and narrative analysis of African Storybook folktales for early reading* (Masters dissertation). University of the Witwatersrand, Johannesburg. Retrieved from http://hdl.handle.net/10539/23002

Van Broekhuizen, H., Van der Berg, S., & Hofmeyr, H. (2016). Higher education access and outcomes for the 2008 national matric cohort. *Economic Working Paper, 16*(16). Bureau for Economic Research: University of Stellenbosch. Retrieved from https://resep.sun.ac.za/wp-content/uploads/2016/10/Van-Broekhuizen-et-al.pd

Vasquez, V., Janks, H., & Comber, B. (2019). Research and policy: Critical literacy as a way of being and doing. *Language Arts, 96*(5), 300–311.

Verwoerd, H. (1954, June). *Speech as minister of native affairs*. Retrieved from www.sahistory.org.za/archive/ hendrik-verwoerd-10-quotes-hendrik-verwoerd-politics-web-20-september-2016

Wa Thiongo, N. (1986). *Decolonising the mind: The language of African literature*. James Currey.

Walton, E. (2016). *The language of inclusive education*. Routledge.

Wentzel, K. (2013). *Literacy journeys: The language and literacy experiences of a group of immigrant girls in an inner city school* (Masters dissertation). University of the Witwatersrand, Johannesburg. Retrieved from http://hdl. handle.net/10539/12452

2.15

CRITICAL LITERACIES WORK IN THE UNITED KINGDOM

Jennifer Farrar, Kelly Stone, and Donna Hazzard

This chapter offers a survey of critical literacies work in the United Kingdom of Great Britain and Northern Ireland, known as the UK. Comprising four constituent countries, Scotland, Northern Ireland, Wales and England, the UK is a unitary parliamentary democracy that is centrally governed from London. Certain legislative powers, including education, were ceded to the devolved administrations of Wales and Northern Ireland that were established in 1998 following sustained campaigns for the decentring of power from London. While the devolved Scottish Parliament was also established in 1998, Scotland's education system had been retained as a "pillar of cultural identity" (Arnott & Menter, 2007, p. 253) by eighteenth-century lawmakers when England and Scotland unified their parliaments in 1707. As this overview indicates—and as current political debates continue to illustrate—tensions related to questions of power, autonomy and national identity have dogged the unification of these nations for centuries and show no signs of abating.

Our research for this chapter has highlighted that a paucity of research explicitly addresses critical literacies within a UK setting. Consequently, this review encompasses scholastic educational policy to consider the ways in which it constructs teachers and learners in relation to the *possibility of being critically literate* in classrooms and beyond. This admittedly narrow focus reflects our roles as academics whose work in higher education centres around initial teacher education (ITE) and our parallel interests in equipping primary and secondary student teachers with understandings of critical literacies for possible use in their future classrooms. We overview each constituent country's educational system, consider the status of critical literacies within each policy setting and conclude with a brief vision for increased critical literacies work across national and international borders. We begin with Scotland because its curriculum is the only one of four "home" nations to make explicit reference to critical literacy in its documentation.

Scotland: Context and Curriculum

Educational policy making in Scotland has long been influenced by a belief in Scottish education's "peculiarly democratic" nature, a pervasive perspective often referred to as the "Scottish myth" (Arnott & Menter, 2007, p. 253). Over the decades, this attitude has led to Scotland's educators and policy makers resisting moves that have seemed ideologically at odds with Scottish cultural traditions of education, especially those regarded as overtly "anglicized" (Arnott & Menter, 2007, p. 253), a reference to Scotland's centuries-old historical and political differences with neighbouring England.

 DOI: 10.4324/9781003023425-27

This foregrounded discourse of democracy and citizenship can be traced to Scotland's current national educational framework for 3–18-year olds, *The Curriculum for Excellence* (CfE), which has been recognised by the OECD as an "ambitious and important departure" (2015, p. 37). Organised around capacities and areas of learning rather than school subjects, the stated aims of the CfE are to develop young people as successful learners, confident individuals, responsible citizens and effective contributors (Scottish Government, 2009). In addition, "the important skills of critical literacy" are highlighted as being of central significance to all, with critical literacy linked to the following, "Children and young people need to be able to work out what trust they should place on information and to identify when and how people are aiming to persuade or influence them" (Scottish Government, 2009, p. 2).

As Farrar and Stone (2019) have argued, the version of critical literacy presented in the CfE can be problematised for its conflation of skills-based and psychological constructions of literacy with socio-political perspectives, largely through the intermingling of the terms "critical literacy", "critical reading" and "critical thinking". Added to this is the CfE's "ahistorical and atheoretical" design (Priestley & Humes, 2010, p. 358), which means that key terms such as critical literacy remain untheorised within the documentation. In turn, this makes it harder for teachers to get to grips with critical literacies as a concept, although the problems associated with any possible standardisation of critical literacy must also be resisted (Farrar & Stone, 2019).

Critical Literacy in Scotland: Research

Critical literacy may be undefined within the pages of the Scottish school curriculum, yet it is a familiar concept in parts of the wider education community. Scotland's capital, Edinburgh, is home to the Adult Learning Project, established in 1979 to deliver adult and community education using Freirean-inspired methods (Kirkwood & Kirkwood, 2011). Crowther and Tett (2011) have argued that Scotland's adult education curriculum is unusual for its conceptualisation of literacy as a social practice; a positioning that enables a move away from deficit approaches to adult literacy.

Researchers have explored how critical literacies have been enacted in Scottish primary and secondary schools in one local authority (Stone, 2017; Sangster, Stone, & Anderson, 2013); and within an English as an Additional Language context (Foley, 2015). Pratt and Foley (2019) have also explored the role of critical literacy when teaching and developing issues of gender and identity with learners in Scottish secondary schools. The potential of children's literature as a vehicle for critical literacy practices has been explored within an early years classroom and with young children and their parents (Farrar, 2017), with findings indicating that a productive relationship exists between readers' responses to the effects of metafiction in picture books and key critical literacy moves.

Emerging research from scholars working in Scotland also includes an exploration of Glasgow's monuments through an anti-racist lens (Govender, 2019) and a discussion of critical literacy as a theoretical framework for teaching LGBTI issues (Stone & Farrar, 2020; Govender & Andrews, this Handbook). Indeed, as teacher educators in Scotland, we have observed an increased take-up of critical literacies as a focus for dissertations and practice-based enquiry at both undergraduate and master's level.

Northern Ireland: Context and Curriculum

With a population of 1.8 million people, Northern Ireland's specific sociocultural and political context is marked by a period of political violence and social unrest known as The Troubles (1968–1998). The signing of the Good Friday Agreement in 1998 resulted in a devolved, power-sharing government called the Assembly. Since devolution, the Assembly has operated intermittently, with operations suspended following policy disagreements. In a society transitioning from conflict and uncertainty, education is widely seen as a vehicle of social change and hope.

The Department of Education for Northern Ireland's (2007) curriculum for primary and secondary schools resembles Scotland's CfE in that its core learning objectives are tied to the development of learners' capacities, in this case, as individuals, as contributors to society and as contributors to the economy and the environment (CCEA, 2007, p. 4). The potential for the development of a critical literacy attitude in teachers and learners (Luke, 2012) is clear under the "contributors to society" heading, where teachers are to support learners as they develop ethical awareness, cultural understandings, a sense of environmental responsibility and media awareness, by, for example, learning how to respect the different lifestyles of others; by becoming aware of the media's impact and influence on themselves and others; and by recognising the impact of local and global imbalances. The curriculum is also used as a space in which to encourage specific characteristics, including community spirit, moral courage, tolerance and, for the oldest learners in secondary, optimism (CCEA, 2019). While "critical thinking" is mentioned and prominence is given to digital media skills (including "digital citizenship"), great emphasis is placed on the development of shared cultural understandings through the medium of Irish Gaelic and Ulster Scots and through whole-school approaches to engaging with controversial issues linked to religion, culture and identity.

Critical Literacy in Northern Ireland: Research

As this summary suggests, there is curricular scope for teachers to enact critical literacies, but, similarly to Scotland, this relies on practitioners' awareness of what critical literacies are and how such enactment might occur. Recent studies have indicated that more work is required in this area, with implications for ITE.

Writing in 2013, Greenwood observed that while the Northern Ireland Curriculum might support the exploration of different places, cultures and environments, it risked the stereotyping and superficial treatment of other countries and cultures, particularly if such work was grounded in commercially produced workbooks as opposed to authentic children's texts. Hazzard's (2020) exploration of student-teachers' orientation towards the development of a critical literacy perspective found that participants' capacity to develop such sensibilities was restricted by pre-existing mindsets of relative privilege (Swalwell, 2013).

Research by Jarman and McClune (2002) and Alexander, Jarman, McClune, and Walsh (2008) used media texts in the secondary science classrooms across Northern Ireland to build teachers' and learners' cross-curricular understandings with a focus on the role of scientific and critical literacies. However, as Alexander et al. note, the inclusion of critical literacies into the existing curriculum requires recognition and "conscious forethought" from teachers (2008, p. 26), as well as the realisation that critical literacy is a "longer-term goal and not [an] objective that can be realised by a one-off task" (2008, p. 34). The authors conclude that current curricular pressures and the non-compulsory nature of critical literacy makes it a "likely casualty" (2008, p. 34). To help foreground critical literacies in the minds of school students, a project launched between Northern Ireland schools, a national newspaper and a Belfast-based higher education institution has also grounded explicit instruction about critical literacies within a practical journalism context (Hazzard, 2015).

Wales: Context and Curriculum

According to Power (2016, p. 285), "Education in Wales has long been the site of political struggle," a reference to the centuries-long governance of Wales from London that often failed to account for their differences. Following devolution in 1998, when Wales gained legislative responsibility for education, the newly formed Welsh government's rhetoric emphasised the significance of citizens over consumers and prioritised issues of social justice going forwards (Power, 2016, p. 286).

Following the recommendations of the Donaldson review of Welsh Education (Welsh Government, 2015), a new Curriculum for Wales was launched at the start of 2020 for implementation in 2022. In common with those of Scotland and Northern Ireland, the new Curriculum for Wales is organised around four core educational purposes to develop children and young people as: (1.) ambitious, capable learners; (2). healthy, confident individuals; (3.) enterprising, creative contributors; (4). ethical, informed citizens; six areas of learning and experience and 27 "statements of what matters" that are to be linked to curriculum content. Using this framework, individual schools are to design their own curriculum to suit the needs of learners and contexts. While references to "critical thinking" and "critical evaluation" exist within the documentation, the outcomes described seem to have more in common with the "liberal-humanist" approaches to criticality (Luke, 2012, p. 6) that can also be found in Scotland's CfE (Farrar & Stone, 2019).

Of interest to critical literacy scholars is the Curriculum's privileging of mulitilingualism and its linked focus on the significance of place and space in relation to the learners' self-development. With a stated focus on *cynefin*, a Welsh word that refers to the "historic, cultural and social place which has shaped and continues to shape the community that inhabits it" (Welsh Government, 2020), it is possible to see how this could enable rich discussions that draw from critical artefactual literacies (Rowsell & Pahl, 2015) and spatial literacies (Comber & Nixon, 2009).

Critical Literacy in Wales: Research

While there is currently limited critical literacies research from Wales, the work that does exist centres around questions of language, power and identity. Martin-Jones, Hughes, and Williams (2009) explored the ways in which the literacy practices of young bilingual Welsh–English agricultural workers were connected to the land they farmed; Coupland (2012) considered how the framing of bilingual Welsh/English displays contributed to readers' responses to each text; while Selleck (2015) examined how teenagers negotiate their bilingual identities in recreational spaces that lie both outside of home and the school.

England: Context and Curriculum

The most populous country within the UK, England does not have a devolved administration, with governance coming directly from the UK-wide Westminster government in London. England's National Curriculum was most recently revised in 2013 to widespread critique from academic and professional communities for its "endless lists of spellings, facts and rules [that] will not develop children's ability to think, including problem-solving, critical understanding and creativity" (Bassey, 2013).

Similar criticisms have been levied at the National Curriculum's current approach to literacy that privileges synthetic phonics (Davis, 2017) for placing "greater emphasis on the acquisition and application of knowledge and concepts than on the skills of critiquing the underpinning values and power structures and socially constructed concepts" (Jones, 2016, p. 105).

Unlike the approaches taken by policy makers in Scotland, Northern Ireland and Wales, the authors of England's National Curriculum have resisted the shift towards organising the curriculum into broader areas of learning by preserving traditional subject boundaries and specifying the content to be covered by teachers (DfE, 2014). Arnott and Reay argue that an effect of such "strong external frames of pedagogy by the state" is the likely "aggravation of social disadvantage" (2013, p. 22).

Critical Literacy in England: Research

Against this backdrop, recent critical literacies work in England has focused largely on the development of critical digital literacies. Burnett and Merchant's Practices, Identities and Networks Model attends to the socio-material aspects of digital literacies (2019) by prompting questions about the ethics of production; whose interests are served and how different layers of meaning-making interface. Working with dyslexic 18-year-olds, Barden (2012) found that using social media as a catalyst for learning enabled them to reframe themselves as able learners and dyslexia experts. McNichol (2016) has argued for the use of critical digital literacies rather than internet filtering in schools to ensure that young people have the critical tools to understand and confront controversial issues. Polizzi's (2020) exploration of digital literacies within secondary education in England highlights the importance of media literacy as a cross-curricular subject.

This work takes place within a rich tradition of critical literacies work from England that dates back to Fairclough's seminal works on language, power and critical discourse analysis (1989, 1995); includes David Wray's work on critical literacy as a twenty-first-century priority (2004) and Searle's practice of critical literacies as cultural action (Lankshear & Knobel, 2009).

More recently, growing interest in critical literacies was evidenced by the launch of a Parliamentary Commission on Fake News and the Teaching of Critical Literacy Skills in Schools (NLT, 2018). The Commission found that only 2% of children surveyed could tell if a news story was real or fake (NLT, 2018). The final report called for "an updated framing of literacy skills . . . that reflects the changing digital landscape" (2018, p. 16), with reference to literacy frameworks such as Luke and Freebody's Four Resources Model and Hinrichsen and Coombs's Five Resources Model as underpinning approaches.

Transnational Connections and Further Recommendations

As this review suggests, there is much that could be done to develop connections between the critical literacies work taking place within the UK. From the research that exists emerge themes of language, culture, identity and power; all of which would provide rich material for the pursuit of connections internally within the UK and externally, on a global scale. Yet, the literature that exists is disparate, with each country pursuing its own critical literacies agenda, implicitly or explicitly, in quite separate directions. For future transnational work to take place within the UK, we need robust conversations about what critical literacy is, what it may look like in the UK's different (but also related) sociopolitical contexts and why this matters now.

To emphasise this further, we take up a point raised in a textual analysis of the education policy documents produced in Scotland, England and Wales shortly after devolution (Laugharne & Baird, 2009) that noted:

> Each nation's policy document refers almost exclusively to its own agenda. There are hardly any cross-references one to another and, in this regard, our analysis could be said to reveal national monologues: England, Wales and Scotland are speaking to themselves, but not to each other.
>
> *(2009, p. 238)*

Building on this, we make several recommendations:

- To turn such monologues into dialogues by connecting existing research in ways that account for prevailing national contexts. We argue for research that explores teachers' engagement with critical literacies across educational contexts, including higher and adult education, so that such practices become more widely known.

- To create practical opportunities for engagement with critical literacies via school and community-based experiences that build on the seminal work of the ALP in Scotland and media-based initiatives in Northern Ireland (Hazzard, 2015).
- To increase policy makers' theoretical understandings of critical literacies to ensure that developments in curricula are research-informed and connected to work already being done within ITE.
- To strengthen transnational connections outside the UK with a view to developing shared work along themes of language, culture, identity, as well as critical literacies pedagogies.

Social Responsibility as Academics

As stated earlier, this chapter's focus reflects our shared and quite specific perspectives as UK academics and teacher educators who are committed to critical literacies. While our survey of the literature reveals that critical literacies work in the UK is limited and fragmented, it also reveals the potential for collaboration across national and international boundaries. Given that student-teachers—and, of course teacher-educators—can unwittingly act as ideological mirrors of systems that can marginalise the disadvantaged (Cieslik & Simpson, 2015), our social responsibility as academics lies in supporting future educators as they develop critically literate attitudes. This will require new paradigms of thinking about teacher education that not only meet student needs in learning to teach but also provide experiences that are purposeful, emancipatory and which move teachers, learners and learning beyond superficial approaches to literacy pedagogies.

References

Alexander, J., Jarman, R., McClune, B., & Walsh, P. (2008). From rhetoric to reality: Advancing literacy by cross-curricular means. *The Curriculum Journal, 19*(1), 23–35. https://doi.org/10.1080/09585170801903225

Arnot, M., & Reay, D. (2013). The framing of performance pedagogies: Pupil perspectives on the control of school knowledge and its acquisition. In J. Soler, C. Walsh, A. Craft, J. Rix, & K. Simmons (Eds.), *Transforming practice: Critical issues in equity, diversity and education* (pp. 19–32). Trentham Books.

Arnott, M., & Menter, I. (2007). The same but different? Post-devolution regulation and control in education in Scotland and England. *European Educational Research Journal, 6*(3), 250–265. https://doi.org/10.2304/eerj.2007.6.3.250

Barden, O. (2012). If we were cavemen we'd be fine: Facebook as a catalyst for critical literacy learning by dyslexic sixth-form students. *Literacy, 46*(3), 123–132. https://doi.org/10.1111/j.1741-4369.2012.00662.x

Bassey, M. (2013). Gove will bury pupils in facts and rules. *The Independent.* Retrieved from www.independent.co.uk/voices/letters/letters-gove-will-bury-pupils-in-facts-and-rules-8540741.html

Burnett, C., & Merchant, G. (2019). Revisiting critical literacy in the digital age. *The Reading Teacher, 73*(3), 263–266. https://doi.org/10.1002/trtr.1858

CCEA. (2007). *The Northern Ireland curriculum primary.* Retrieved from https://ccea.org.uk/learning-resources/northern-ireland-curriculum-primary

CCEA. (2019). *The "big" picture of the curriculum at key stage 4.* Retrieved from https://ccea.org.uk/learning-resources/big-picture-curriculum-key-stage-4

Cieslik, M., & Simpson, D. (2015). Basic skills, literacy practices and the hidden injuries of class. *British Sociological Association, 20*(1), 1–12. https://doi.org/10.5153/sro.3569

Comber, B., & Nixon, H. (2009). Spatial literacies, design texts, and emergent pedagogies in purposeful literacy curriculum. *Pedagogies: An International Journal, 3*(4), 221–240. https://doi.org/10.1080/15544800802026637

Coupland, N. (2012). Bilingualism on display: The framing of Welsh and English in Welsh public spaces. *Language in Society, 41*(1), 1–27. https://doi.org/10.1017/S0047404511000893

Crowther, J., & Tett, L. (2011). Critical and social literacy practices from the Scottish adult literacy experience: Resisting deficit approaches to learning. *Literacy, 45*(3), 134–140. https://doi.org/10.1111/j.1741-4369.2011.00599.x

Critical Literacies Work in the UK

Davis, A. (2017). *A critique of pure teaching methods and the case of synthetic phonics.* Bloomsbury Academic.

Department for Education. (2014). *National curriculum in England.* Retrieved from https://gov.uk/government/collections/national-curriculum

Fairclough, N. (1989). *Language and power.* Longman.

Fairclough, N. (1995). *Critical discourse analysis.* Addison Wesley.

Farrar, J. (2017). *I didn't know they did books like this! An inquiry into the literacy practices of young children and their parents using metafictive picturebooks* (Unpublished doctoral dissertation). University of Glasgow.

Farrar, J., & Stone, K. (2019). Silenced by the gaps? The status of critical literacy in Scotland's Curriculum for Excellence. *English Teaching: Practice and Critique, 18*(3), 335–350. https://doi.org/10.1108/ETPC-03-2019-0041

Foley, Y. (2015). Critical literacy. In B. Street & S. May (Eds.), *Literacies and language education. Encyclopaedia of language and education* (3rd ed., pp. 109–120). Springer.

Govender, N. (2019, October). *Can you see a social issue? (Re)Looking at everyday texts.* The Anti-Racist Educator. Retrieved from www.theantiracisteducator.com/post/can-you-see-a-social-issue-re-looking-at-everyday-texts

Greenwood, R. (2013). Teaching student teachers about development issues—Is it possible to avoid stereotype and prejudice? In F. Waldron (Ed.), *Proceedings of the Irish association for social, scientific and environmental education annual conference 2013* (pp. 40–44). Retrieved from www.tara.tcd.ie/bitstream/handle/2262/69112/IASSEE%20Final%20Report-2.pdf?sequence=1

Hazzard, D. (2015). *Creating young newsreaders: The Irish News critical literacy project.* Retrieved from https://youngnewsreaders.irishnews.com/

Hazzard, D. (2020). *Developing student teachers' critical literacy perspectives: A Bourdieusian analysis* (Unpublished doctoral thesis). University of Glasgow.

Jarman, R., & McClune, B. (2002). A survey of the use of newspapers in science instruction by secondary teachers in Northern Ireland. *International Journal of Science Education, 24*(10), 997–1020. https://doi.org/10.1080/09500690210095311

Jones, R. (2016). Curricular and extra-curricular opportunities to engage school students in critical literacy in England. In S. McNichol (Ed.), *Critical literacy for information professionals* (pp. 105–114). Facet Publishing.

Kirkwood, G., & Kirkwood, C. (2011). *Living adult education: Freire in Scotland.* Sense Publishers.

Lankshear, C., & Knobel, M. (2009). More than words: Chris Searle's approach to critical literacy as cultural action. *Race & Class, 51*(2), 59–78. https://doi.org/10.1177/0306396809345577

Laugharne, J., & Baird, A. (2009). National conversations in the UK: Using a language-based approach to interpret three key education policy documents (2001–2007) from England, Scotland and Wales. *Cambridge Journal of Education, 39*(2), 223–240. https://doi.org/10.1080/03057640902902278

Luke, A. (2012). Critical literacy: Foundational notes. *Theory into Practice, 51*(1), 4–11. https://doi.org/10.1080/00405841.2012.636324

Martin-Jones, M., Hughes, B., & Williams, A. (2009). Bilingual literacy in and for working lives on the land: Case studies of young Welsh speakers in North Wales. *International Journal of the Sociology of Language,* (195), 39–62. https://doi.org/10.1515/IJSL.2009.005

McNichol, S. (2016). Responding to concerns about online radicalization in U.K. schools through a radicalization critical digital literacy approach. *Interdisciplinary Journal of Practice, Theory and Applied Research, 33*(4), 227–238. https://doi.org/10.1080/07380569.2016.1246883

National Literacy Trust. (2018). *Fake news and critical literacy: The final report of the Commission on Fake News and the Teaching of Critical Literacy in Schools.* National Literacy Trust.

OECD. (2015). *Improving schools in Scotland: An OECD perspective.* OECD Directorate for Education and Skills.

Polizzi, G. (2020). Digital literacy and the national curriculum for England: Learning how the experts engage with and evaluate online content. *Computers & Education.* https://doi.org/10.1016/j.compedu.2020.103859.

Power, S. (2016). The politics of education and the misrecognition of Wales. *Oxford Review of Education, 42*(3), 285–298. https://doi.org/10.1080/03054985.2016.1184871

Pratt, L., & Foley, Y. (2019). Using critical literacy to 'do' identity and gender. In R. Arshad, T. Wrigley, & L. Pratt (Eds.), *Social justice re-examined: Dilemmas and solutions for the classroom teacher* (2nd ed., pp. 65–82). Trentham Books.

Priestley, M., & Humes, W. (2010). The development of Scotland's curriculum for excellence: amnesia and déjà vu. *Oxford Review of Education, 36*(3), 345–361. https://doi.org/10.1080/03054980903518951

Rowsell, J., & Pahl, K. (2015). Introduction. In J. Rowsell & K. Pahl (Eds.), *The Routledge handbook of literacy studies* (pp. 1–14). Routledge.

243

Sangster, P., Stone, K., & Anderson, C. (2013). Transformative professional learning: Embedding critical literacies in the classroom. *Professional Development in Education, 39*(5), 615–637. https://doi.org/10.1080/1941 5257.2012.751617

Scottish Government. (2009). *Curriculum for excellence literacy across learning principles and practice.* Scottish Government.

Selleck, C. (2016). Re-negotiating ideologies of bilingualism on the margins of education. *Journal of Multilingual and Multicultural Development, 37*(6), 551–556. https://doi.org/10.1080/01434632.2015.1093494

Stone, K. (2017). *Reconsidering primary literacy: Enabling children to become critically literate.* Routledge.

Stone, K., & Farrar, J. (2020). Advancing an LGBTI-inclusive curriculum in Scotland through critical literacy. *Improving Schools.* https://doi.org/10.1177%2F1365480220943322

Swalwell, K. (2013). With great power comes great responsibility: Privileged students' conceptions of justice-oriented citizenship. *Democracy and Education, 21*(1), 1–11.

Welsh Government. (2015). *Successful Futures: Independent Review of Curriculum and Assessment Arrangements in Wales.* Welsh Government.

Welsh Government. (2020). *Humanities.* Retrieved from https://hwb.gov.wales/curriculum-for wales/ humanities/statements-of-what-matters/

Wray, D. (2004). *Developing critical literacy: A priority for the 21st century.* National Centre for Language and Literacy.

2.16

CRITICAL LITERACY IN THE UNITED STATES OF AMERICA

Provocations for an Anti-Racist Education

Cheryl McLean, Cynthia Lewis, and Jessica Zacher Pandya

The United States of America and Its Sociopolitical Contexts

The United States of America (U.S.) is geographically located in the middle of the continent of North America, bordered by Mexico to the south and Canada to the north. Officially founded/colonized in 1776 by white Christian European settlers, it is a representative, constitutional democracy built on the precepts of manifest destiny via the extensive enslavement of Africans since 1619 and the colonization of land of Native American peoples. In the first two decades of the 21st century, the political landscape continues to be uneasy and heavily polarized; decolonizing movements like #BlackLivesMatter and #metoo press for racial and social justice and empowerment for African Americans and women respectively, while the political right wing deny the fundamentals of such movements, pushing for anti-immigrant laws and more restrictive policies limiting rights related to gender, race, and other protected categories. This period has also seen the rise of white[1] nationalism and white supremacist groups and ideologies within mainstream political and cultural discourse (Southern Poverty Law Center, 2019). Yet, even within this polarizing socio-political landscape where calls for justice and inclusion are increasingly championed, American academics continue to rely on the dominance of a nativized or Global English (Canagarajah, 2000; Pennycook, 2016)—in itself a form of cultural and ideological hegemony—to produce and share their work, even as they write about the negative impact of English-only politics in U.S. K–12 schools. These historical and contemporary issues have shaped the public school system described in the next section.

The United States' Educational Systems

The U.S. public school system seeks to prepare responsible citizens for the workforce through 4 levels of K–12 formal compulsory schooling: Early Childhood (infant to Pre-K); Elementary (grades 1–5); Middle School (6–8); and High School (9–12). While schooling is mandatory to age 16, there are three main formal school choices: public, private, and charter. Public schools rely on federal, state, and local funding, and follow state curriculum and assessment guidelines. Charter schools are free to the public, receive government funding, and are independently run, although local educational authorities hold them accountable for maintaining high test scores. Generally funded by tuition and donations, private schools have independent control over curriculum and administration.

A series of standards-based reform initiatives have concretized the U.S. system's focus on accountability and achievement. Such reforms are often guided by the belief in a neutral body of

DOI: 10.4324/9781003023425-28

academic knowledge, skills, texts, and assessments. The assumption behind this ideology is that normative standardization of knowledge and testing raises achievement. Yet, the movement towards standardized achievement limits attention to cultural, linguistic, and learning differences. In the last decade, national standards have been implemented by 42 of 50 states and 4 territories. However, they are another one-size-fits-all set of curriculum and testing standards that reflect dominant, normative value systems. Consequently, they foster opportunity gaps along racial and social class lines. Instead of viewing these gaps as the result of an "education debt" (Ladson-Billings, 2006), the response to these "gaps" has been the continuous adoption of deficit approaches to solving the "problem" of failing students through remediation. There are some movements by teachers (e.g., Teachers for Social Justice), teacher educators, and researchers focused on changes for culturally sustaining pedagogy (Paris & Alim, 2017) as antidotes to these standardized approaches with deficit underpinnings.

While white teachers comprise 84% of the national teaching force (Swanson & Welton, 2019), data place the traditionally white student majority at 47% compared with 27% Latinx, 15% Black, and 10% Asian, Indigenous, or multiracial students (U.S. Department of Education, 2018). Critical literacy researchers and educators have attributed these gaps to the normalized Eurocentric literacy and sociocultural practices, experiences and ideologies that define the U.S. educational system and its structures. As historically marginalized student populations grow and significant education debts remain, more calls to action by critical literacy educators and researchers have emerged. However, as we discuss in the rest of the chapter, critical literacy in the U.S. is an historically and predominantly white field that has overlooked Black and Indigenous traditions of criticality.

Approaches to Critical Literacy in the United States

The broad theoretical approaches associated with critical literacy in the U.S. address questions of how and what texts and discourses count as literacy and result in social and cultural capital, which, when deployed, afford individual and collective power. U.S. approaches are often grounded in Freire's (1970) philosophy that critical consciousness increases individuals' and groups' power to analyze, critique, and transform their sociocultural and political contexts and texts. Research in the U.S. has offered useful critical literacy approaches in the areas of: inquiry and problem-posing approaches in classrooms (Lewison, Seely Flint, & Van Sluys, 2002); the analysis of everyday cultural forms; and the disruption of normative texts.

Inquiry and Problem-Posing Classroom-Based Approaches

Critical literacy in the U.S. is deeply rooted in schooling as a site of social transformation; it views teachers and students as social actors whose praxis effects change. It promotes awareness of and actions against discriminatory structures embedded in curricular texts and pedagogical practices, particularly as they are visible in normative discourses and linguistic categorizations and hierarchies. In schools, it is focused on inquiry and problem-posing curriculum (Heffernan & Lewison, 2009) through critical text analysis and critical pedagogy (Lankshear & McLaren, 1993). Teacher education has served as a path to engaging with critical literacy practices (Hsieh, 2017). For example, preservice and inservice teachers learn how to frame their teaching and use pedagogical resources from a critical literacy perspective (Vasquez, Tate, & Harste, 2013). Through teacher narratives and research stories, researchers have explored ways to create critical classrooms (Lewison, Leland, & Harste, 2007). However, as we discuss in the following, this work has not managed to substantively reshape the educational landscape in the U.S., where whiteness is perpetuated and enforced by regimes of standardized curriculum and assessments.

Critical Literacy as Analysis of Everyday Cultural Forms

One dense strand of American scholarship in critical literacy focuses on critiquing the everyday cultural forms children and youth bring from home and those they encounter at school, and on producing new texts that critically interrogate popular culture texts and students' lifeworlds (Shor & Freire, 1987). Paralleling British cultural theorists, American scholars like Giroux and Simon (1989) and Grossberg (1997) argued that we must attend to the messages youth receive through cultural forms that they consume, produce, and enjoy. Roman, Christian-Smith, and Ellsworth (1988) and others focus their work in the field of feminist cultural studies, contributing to examinations of popular culture texts that children, youth, and teachers produce to interrogate their worlds, examining issues of race, class, gender, and language variation, often with a focus on civic action.

At the high school/secondary level, Morrell (2008) has written explicitly about the role of popular culture in engaging youth of color in critical literacy practices, often using a Youth Participatory Action Research (YPAR) framework (Mirra, Garcia, & Morrel, 2015) while Sanchez's (2010) work highlights urban Latina youth producing countertexts with participatory action research. Garcia, Mirra, Morrell, Martinez, and Scorza (2015) ask how digital media can foster civic agency in critical, digital contexts. Examining media production and consumption, Lewis, Doerr-Stevens, Tierney, and Scharber (2013) argue that the interrelationship of the global market economy and local consumption practices is under-examined in critical literacy research. Other scholars write about how mainstream media reinforces white supremacy (McArthur, 2016) and how students become more critical consumers of everyday media (Alvermann & Hagood, 2000; Share, 2015). Research on productive critical literacies—practices in which people critically read, analyze and produce texts—in elementary school contexts has focused to some extent on immigrant and bilingual students who are learning English (Kim, 2016; Peterson & Chamberlain, 2015). Pandya's (2018) research offers examples of the pedagogical complexity of English learners producing critical, digital texts in elementary school. Enciso (2011) reports on the critical storytelling of middle-school immigrant youth in a project in which she purposefully helped youth speak across in-school boundaries, "so that students' voices and purposes for telling stories are recognised within school settings" (p. 23). Similarly, Medina and Campano (2006) argue that drama and *teatro* productions can open critical spaces for youth learning English as a second language. Flint and Laman (2012) show how poems as "forms of social action" can "invite resistance" (p. 17). Next, we turn to another major body of U.S. work: teaching children and youth to disrupt normative texts.

Disrupting Normative Texts

Whereas much U.S.-based critical literacy scholarship focuses on using texts to ask questions about dominant assumptions, oppression, and social change, several traditions in critical theory have influenced critical approaches to literacy that examine normative texts as they produce human subjects. Such critical text analysis occurs through the examination of mainstream curriculum, from the literary canon (Appleman, 2015; #disrupttexts) to children's texts for teaching reading (Aukerman, Grovet, & Belfatti, 2019) as well as multicultural young adult literature as a form of counter-storytelling (Hughes-Hassell, 2013; Thomas & Stornaiuolo, 2016), and graphic novels to foster critical conversations (Chun, 2009). These school-based and societal texts contribute to the neoliberal construction of the "child," the "nation," and "citizenship," and the production of desirable subjects. Critical examination of these texts as well as acts of counter-narration and restorying challenge-dominant storylines and enact more humanizing subjectivities (Campano, Ghiso, & Sánchez, 2013). We highlight two prominent traditions for critiquing normative texts: critical sociolinguistics and critical sociocultural theory.

Critical Sociolinguistics and Raciolinguistics

Drawing on Foucault and Fairclough (Fairclough, 1992), the work of critical sociolinguists shows, as Janks (2012) aptly notes, "that discourses produce us, speak through us, and can nevertheless be challenged and changed" (p. 159). Janks has close ties with U.S. scholars who have developed a critical sociolinguistic strand in the U.S. that examines how institutional and structural power is sustained through language, texts, and signs. This work has involved critical readings of institutional discourses such as policies and processes. Examples include special education placements (Rogers, 2002), public policy and reading (Woodside-Jiron, 2011), whiteness stances in book talk (Lewis & Ketter, 2011), and racial and linguistic diversity in preservice literacy teacher education (Haddix, 2016). Alim (2007) used critical sociolinguistic frameworks to study the language awareness of Black youth who understand the language politics and take up myriad styles to suss out the complex expectations of interlocutors. Alim and other linguists (Alim, Rickford, & Ball, 2016; Flores & Rosa, 2015; Rosa & Flores, 2017) showed how language and race are co-naturalized, and contest linguistic injustice (Baker-Bell, 2020) and power formations (Reyes, 2016) through studies that highlight dynamic linguistic repertoires among non-dominant youth (de los Rios & Seltzer, 2017; Smith, 2019). Critical sociolinguistics and raciolinguistics provide theories and tools for disrupting normative texts/ signs in ways that are central to the goals of critical literacy, so that we can all better understand how texts work to marginalize some and privilege others, as well as how they can support transformative relationships and liberatory practices.

Critical Sociocultural Theory and Sociocritical Literacy

An influential strand that disrupts normative critical frameworks is critical sociocultural theory and sociocritical literacy. Lewis, Enciso, and Moje (2007) used the term "critical sociocultural theory" to retain constructs from sociocultural theory while pushing for more direct attention to issues of power, identity, and agency that are central to critical literacy practice. Sociocritical literacy work (Gutierréz, 2008) draws on theories of activity and expansive learning to reframe everyday, institutional literacies among non-dominant youth as "powerful tools oriented toward critical social thought" (p. 129). Both draw on empirical data to show how criticality is deeply embedded in youth, family, and community literacies that have not been recognized as legitimate forms of literacy in schools and other dominant institutions. This work demonstrates non-dominant youth's learning strengths and the environments that work best to sustain and extend their learning.

Black Girls' Literacies

White scholars have generally centered white theorists in their work on critical literacy. In recent years, Black scholars in the U.S. have offered a much-needed intervention by surfacing the deep and extensive work Black feminists, sociologists, and educators have contributed to the long history and tradition of Black criticality in the U.S. context. The "Black Girls' Literacies" framework is an especially prominent intervention (Price-Dennis & Muhammad, forthcoming). It is important to note that although these scholars directly discuss criticality in their work, they do not identify with the primarily white tradition of U.S. critical literacy. Rather, this framework draws on Black feminist (Collins, 1999) and "endarkened feminist" (Dillard, 2000) epistemologies as well as the rich histories of Black women's literary societies (McHenry, 2002; Muhammad, 2020; Muhammad & Haddix, 2016) to analyze and support the literacies of Black girls and women. It is important not to co-opt this work, and yet it must be included to fully understand the current limits of critical literacy in the U.S. and to recognize the historical legacy and contributions of criticality in the work of Black activists, community organizers, abolitionists, and scholars. To relegate it to a section on the future of critical literacy ignores the long history and legacy of this work. These traditions disrupt normative critical frameworks and serve as testament to the historical, collaborative, intellectual, identity-connected, and political/critical components of Black Girls' Literacies. Similar movements have emerged related to decolonizing, transnational literacies as challenges to U.S. and Western-centric traditions in critical literacy (Cushman, Juzwik, Macaluso, & Milu, 2015; Morrell, 2017), as explained in the next section.

Visions for Moving Into More Transnational Work

The challenge of writing this section revealed to us the ways that scholars of critical literacy in the U.S. have been oriented towards and frequently cite research by white, English-speaking colleagues from Australia, the UK, Canada, and South Africa. In most cases, these scholars may work with children and youth of color, while explicitly acknowledging the racial, ethnic, and linguistic differences between themselves and their research subjects. Our vision for moving into more truly transnational work is that we break away from these predominantly white, English-oriented perspectives, that we cite and disseminate the work of colleagues from around the world, and that we in the U.S. take up the humbling challenge of learning from others instead of trying to export our knowledge to others, or, even worse, ignoring the perspectives of non-white scholars. Freire's work is the exception; U.S. progressive scholars have adopted and adapted his work since the 1970s, perhaps because Freire's vision for learner-centered, liberation-focused, experiential education aligns with progressive traditions in the U.S. However, since then, we have not sufficiently looked to our Brazilian Latinx colleagues, or to others around the globe, to learn more, despite robust critical traditions informed by critical sociolinguistics and critical sociocultural theory in Brazil. In many ways this collection is part of that effort—a calling out of the perpetuation of Eurocentric, hegemonic perspectives by white scholars, and a call to action for a field that looks through and thinks from many lenses.

Conclusions and Suggestions for Further Research: Engaging Critical Race Theory and Critical Indigenous/Decolonial Studies

In the U.S. two theoretical frameworks informing recent work in critical literacy are critical race theory (CRT) and critical Indigenous/decolonial studies. For example, Lamar Johnson recounts how his all-white class of preservice English teachers were largely unaware of the police killing of Michael Brown (Baker-Bell, Butler, & Johnson, 2017). Mourning Brown's death and that of other victims of police brutality, Johnson explained to his students: "Not only does white supremacy protect you from seeing the humanity in Black and Brown people, it also protects you from seeing the humanity within yourself" (p. 123). CRT also informs research with preservice teachers of color. Haddix (2012) examined Black female preservice teachers' perspectives on their linguistic and racial identities as they are positioned within teacher education and make agentive decisions about their levels of engagement. In both cases, CRT leverages socio-political understandings of language and literacy to call for racial and linguistic justice for communities of color. San Pedro (2015) draws on decolonial theory to show how Indigenous students used silence as a form of critical literacy to contest assumptions of settler colonialism that devalue Indigenous knowledge. de los Rios et al. (2019) argue that in order to repair the harm of English education in the U.S., scholars and educators need to critically trace the colonial roots of the subject of English and center their work in ethnic studies, linguistic justice, and critical translingualism. Finally, in a book on qualitative methods, Paris and Winn (2013) urge us as critical literacy scholars to decolonize our theories and humanize our methods as we look to use critical literacy for greater social justice—not *for* others but *with* others. We turn next to the implications for our social responsibility as academics.

Implications for Our Social Responsibility as Academics

In this moment, when we see the ravages of capitalism, and the continued oppression of Black, Indigenous, and people of color (BIPOC) by our educational systems, we ask how can critical literacy in the U.S. be a relevant body of research and practice that makes real, systemic differences in peoples' lives and experiences? Perhaps the U.S.' shifting and downtrending place in the global order provides the space to go beyond inquiring into inequities, posing problems, critiquing everyday cultural forms, and disrupting normative texts. Perhaps this is the moment we can turn our collective literacies gazes to—the most insidious and relevant texts of all: those that uphold the white supremacist ideologies that keep structures of oppression in place, not just in the U.S. What might this look like? We should not only cite the work of scholars of color and decolonize our citations, actions we have taken seriously in this entry, but also should recognize the leadership of BIPOC scholars who are remediating the field by showing us the histories of criticality that have existed for centuries in communities in which public institutions could not be trusted not to do violence to their children's minds and bodies. As a field constituted in whiteness, we must hold ourselves accountable to the BIPOC youth, communities, and educators with whom we should be partnering.

One way to collaborate more deeply and directly with youth, communities, and educators is to fully acknowledge that we do not have the last word on what it means to be critical. As critical literacy scholars and educators, we have all had experiences that have challenged our limited perspectives on criticality. Being accountable means learning from the communities who place their children in our hands (Larson & Moses, 2017). It also means learning about criticality from youth, whose activism and leadership can teach us about the complexity of critical literacy and how to advance critical perspectives (Rombalski, 2020; Watson & Marciano, 2015). Finally, it means attending to the superb work of educator-scholars who have developed websites, units, and syllabi to help educators enact critical literacy through a focus on the most pressing issues of our time such as linguistic justice for speakers of Black language (Baker-Bell, 2020; see also www.blacklanguagesyllabus.com/) and critical analyses of much used and canonized novels taught in high school (#disrupttexts). These are just a few examples of the work that can and should guide our scholarship and practice in critical literacy so we hold ourselves accountable, and take up the reconstructive critical literacies championed by Luke (2018) and others. The future of critical literacy in the U.S. is in our collective desire for dynamic and aspirational approaches, alongside traditions grounded in the communities to which we are accountable.

Note

1. We capitalize Black to represent people of the African diaspora. We use lowercase for "white" because white Christians were not involuntarily dispersed as were other diasporic groups and because we do not wish to align with white nationalists who capitalize white as a form of dominance.

References

Alim, H. S. (2007). Critical hip-hop language pedagogies: Combat, consciousness, and the cultural politics of communication. *Journal of Language, Identity, and Education, 6*(2), 161–176.

Alim, H. S., Rickford, J., & Ball, A. F. (Eds.). (2016). *Raciolinguistics: How language shapes our ideas about race.* Oxford University Press.

Alvermann, D., & Hagood, M. (2000). Fandom and critical media literacy. *Journal of Adolescent & Adult Literacy, 43*(5), 436–446.

Appleman, D. (2015). *Critical encounters in secondary English: Teaching literary theory to adolescents* (3rd ed.). Teachers College Press.

Aukerman, M., Grovet, K., & Belfatti, M. (2019). Race, ideology, and cultural representation in Raz-Kids. *Journal of Adolescent and Adult Literature, 96*(5), 286–299.

Baker-Bell, A. (2020). *Linguistic justice: Black language, literacy, identity, and pedagogy*. National Council of Teachers of English-Routledge Research Series. Routledge.

Baker-Bell, A., Butler, T., & Johnson, L. (2017). The pain and the wounds: A call for critical race English education in the wake of racial violence. *English Education, 49*(2), 116–128.

Campano, G. Ghiso, M. P., & Sánchez, L. (2013). "Nobody one knows the . . . amount of a person": Elementary students critiquing dehumanization through organic critical literacies. *Research in the Teaching of English, 48*(1), 97–124.

Canagarajah, S. (2000). *A geopolitics of academic writing*. University of Pittsburgh Press.

Chun, C. W. (2009). Critical literacies and graphic novels for English-language learners: Teaching Maus. *Journal of Adolescent & Adult Literacy, 53*, 144–153.

Collins, P. H. (1999). *Black feminist thought: Knowledge, consciousness, and the politics of empowerment* (Revised 10th Anniv 2nd ed.). Routledge.

Cushman, E., Juzwik, M., Macaluso, K., & Milu, E. (2015). Decolonizing research in the teaching of English(es). *Research in the Teaching of English, 49*(4), 333–339.

Darling-Hammond, L. (2014). What can PISA tell us about U.S. education policy? *New England Journal of Public Policy, 26*(1), Special Issue on Education, 1–14.

de los Rios, C. V., Martinez, D., Musser, A., Canady, A., Camangian, P., & Quijada Cerecer, P. G. (2019). Upending colonial practices: Towards repairing harm in English Education. *Theory Into Practice*, 1–9.

de los Rios, C. V., & Seltzer, K. (2017). Translanguaging, coloniality, and English classrooms: An exploration of two bicoastal urban classrooms. *Research in the Teaching of English, 52*(1), 55–76.

Dillard, C. B. (2000). The substance of things hoped for, the evidence of things not seen: Examining an endarkened feminist epistemology in educational research and leadership. *International Journal of Qualitative Research in Education, 13*(6), 661–681.

#disrupttexts. Retrieved from https://disrupttexts.org/

Enciso, P. (2011). Storytelling in critical literacy pedagogy: Removing the walls between immigrant and non-immigrant youth. *English Teaching, 10*(1), 21–40.

Fairclough, N. (1992). *Discourse and social change*. Polity Press.

Flint, A. S., & Laman, T. T. (2012). Where poems hide: Finding reflective, critical spaces inside writing workshop. *Theory Into Practice, 51*(1), 12–19. https://doi.org/10.1080/00405841.2012.636328

Flores, N., & Rosa, J. (2015). Undoing appropriateness: Raciolinguistic ideologies and language diversity in education. *Harvard Educational Review, 85*(2), 149–171.

Freire, P. (1970). *Pedagogy of the oppressed* (M. Ramos, Trans.). Continuum.

Garcia, A., Mirra, N., Morrell, E., Martinez, A., & Scorza, D. (2015). The council of youth research: Critical literacy and civic agency in the digital age. *Reading and Writing Quarterly, 31*(2), 151–167. https://doi.org/10.1080/10573569.2014.962203

Giroux, H., & Simon, A. (Eds.). (1989). *Popular culture: Schooling and everyday life*. Bergin & Garvey.

Grossberg, L. (1997). *Bringing it all back home: Essays on cultural studies*. Duke University Press.

Gutierréz, K. D. (2008). Developing a sociocritical literacy in the third space. *Reading Research Quarterly, 43*(2), 148–164.

Haddix, M. (2012). Talkin' in the company of my sistas: The counterlanguages and deliberate silences of Black female students in teacher education. *Linguistics and Education, 23*(2), 169–181.

Haddix, M. (2016). *Cultivating racial and linguistic diversity in literacy teacher education: Teachers like me*. NCTE/Routledge.

Heffernan, L., & Lewison, M. (2009). Keep your eyes on the prize: Critical stance in the middle school classroom. *Voices from the Middle, 17*(2), 19–27.

Hsieh, B. (2017). Making room for discomfort: Exploring critical literacy and practice in a teacher education classroom. *English Teaching: Practice and Critique, 16*(3), 290–302.

Hughes-Hassell, S. (2013). Multicultural young adult literature as a form of counter-storytelling. *The Library Quarterly, 83*(3), 211–228.

Janks, H. (2012). The importance of critical literacy. *English Teaching: Practice and Critique, 11*(1), 150–163.

Kim, S. J. (2016). Expanding the horizons for critical literacy in a bilingual preschool class- room: Children's responses in discussions with gender-themed picture books. *International Journal of Early Childhood, 48*, 311–327.

Ladson-Billings, G. (2006). From the Achievement Gap to the Education Debt: Understanding Achievement in U.S. *Educational Researcher, 35*(7), 3–12.

Lankshear, C., & McLaren, P. (Eds.). (1993). *Critical literacy: Politics, praxis and the postmodern*. SUNY Press.

Larson, J., & Moses, G. (2017). Community literacies as shared resources for transformation. Routledge.

Lewis, C., Doerr-Stevens, C., Tierney, J. D., & Scharber, C. (2013). Relocalization in the market economy: Critical literacies and media production in an urban English classroom. In J. Ávila & J. Zacher Pandya (Eds.), *Critical digital literacies as social praxis: Intersections and challenges* (pp. 179–196). Peter Lang.

Lewis, C., Enciso, P., & Moje, E. (Eds.). (2007). *Reframing sociocultural research on literacy: Identity, agency, and power*. Routledge.

Lewis, C., & Ketter, J. (2011). Learning as social interaction: Interdiscursivity in a teacher and researcher study group. In R. Rogers (Ed.), *An introduction to critical discourse analysis in education* (2nd ed., pp. 128–153). Routledge.

Lewison, M., Leland, C., & Harste, J. C. (2007). *Creating critical classrooms: K-8 reading and writing with an edge*. Lawrence Erlbaum Associates.

Lewison, M., Seely Flint, A., & Van Sluys, K. (2002). Taking on critical literacy: The journey of newcomers and novices. *Language Arts, 79*(5), 382–392.

Luke, A. (2018). No grand narrative in sight: On double consciousness and critical literacy. In A. Luke (Ed.), *Critical literacy, schooling, and social justice: The selected works of Allan Luke* (pp. 1–27). Routledge.

McArthur, S. (2016). Black girls and critical media literacy for social activism. *English Education, 48*(4), SPECIAL ISSUE: Black Girls' Literacies, 362–379.

McHenry, E. (2002). *Forgotten readers: Recovering the lost history of African-American literary societies*. Duke University Press.

Medina, C. L., & Campano, G. (2006). Performing identities through drama and Teatro practices in multilingual classrooms. *Language Arts, 83*, 332–342.

Mirra, N., Garcia, A., & Morrell, E. (2015). *Doing youth participatory action research: Transforming inquiry with researchers, educators, and students*. Routledge.

Morgan, W. (1997). *Critical literacy in the classroom: The art of the possible*. Routledge.

Morrell, E. (2008). *Critical literacy and urban youth: Pedagogies of access, dissent, and liberation*. Routledge.

Morrell, E. (2017). Toward equity and diversity in literacy research, policy, and practice: A critical global approach. *Journal of Literacy Research, 49*(3), 454–463.

Muhammad, G. E. (2020). *Cultivating genius: An equity framework for culturally and historically responsive literacy*. Scholastic.

Muhammad, G. E., & Haddix, M. (2016). Centering black girls' literacies: A review of literature on the multiple ways of knowing of black girls. *English Education, 48*(4), 299–336.

Pandya, J. Z. (2018). *Exploring critical digital literacy practices: Everyday video in a dual language context*. Routledge.

Paris, D., & Alim, S. (Eds.). (2017). *Culturally sustaining pedagogies: Teaching and learning for justice in a changing world*. Teachers College Press.

Paris, D., & Winn, M. (2013). *Humanizing research: Decolonizing qualitative inquiry with youth and communities*. Sage.

Pennycook, A. (2016). *The cultural politics of English as an international language*. Routledge.

Peterson, K. E., & Chamberlain, K. (2015). "Everybody treated him like he was from another world": Bilingual fourth graders develop social awareness through interactive read-alouds focused on critical literacies. *Literacy Research and Instruction, 54*, 231–255.

Price-Dennis, D., & Muhammad, G. E. (Eds.). (forthcoming). *Black girls' literacies: Transforming lives and literacy practices*. Routledge.

Reyes, A. (2016). The voicing of Asian American figures: Korean linguistic styles at an Asian American cram school. In H. S. Alim, J. Rickford, & A. F. Ball (Eds.), *Raciolinguistics: How language shapes our ideas about race* (pp. 309–326). Oxford University Press.

Rogers, R. (2002). Through the eyes of the institution: A critical discourse analysis of decision making in two special education meetings. *Anthropology and Education, 33*(2), 213–237.

Roman, L., Christian-Smith, L., & Ellsworth, E. (1988). *Becoming feminine: The politics of popular culture*. Falmer Press.

Rombalski, A. (2020). I believe that we will win! Learning from youth activist pedagogies. *Curriculum Inquiry, 50*(1), 28–53.

Rosa, J., & Flores, N. (2017). Unsettling race and language: Toward a raciolinguistic perspective. *Language in Society, 46*, 621–647.

Sánchez, P. (2010). "In between Oprah and Cristina": Urban Latina youth producing a countertext with participatory action research. *Social Justice: A Journal of Crime, Conflict, and World Order, 36*(4), 54–68.

San Pedro, T. (2015). Silence as shields: Agency and resistances among native American students in the urban Southwest. *Research in the Teaching of English, 50*(2), 132–153.

Share, J. (2015). *Media literacy is elementary*. Peter Lang.

Shor, I., & Freire, P. (1987). *A pedagogy of liberation*. Bergin and Garvey.

Smith, P. (2019). (Re)positioning in the Englishes and (English) literacies of a Black immigrant youth: Towards a 'transraciolinguistic' approach. *Theory into Practice, 58*(3), 292–303.

Southern Poverty Law Center. (2019). *A year of hate and extremism 2019: A report from the Southern Poverty Law Center.* Retrieved from www.splcenter.org/sites/default/files/yih_2020_final.pdf.

Swanson, J., & Welton, A. (2019). When good intentions only go so far: White principals leading discussions about race. *Urban Education, 54*(5), 732–759.

Thomas, E., & Stornaiuolo, A. (2016). Restorying the self: Bending toward textual justice. *Harvard Educational Review, 86*(3), 313–338.

U.S. Department of Education. (2018) Institute of Education Sciences, National Center for Education Statistics.

Vasquez, V., Tate, S., & Harste, J. (2013). *Negotiating critical literacy with teachers: Theoretical foundations and pedagogical resources for pre-service and in-service contexts.* Routledge.

Watson, V. W. M., & Marciano, J. E. (2015). Examining a social-participatory youth co-researcher methodology: A cross-case analysis extending possibilities of literacy and research. *Literacy, 49*(1), 37–44.

Woodside-Jiron, H. (2011). Language, power, & participation: Using critical discourse analysis to make sense of public policy. In R. Rogers (Ed.), *An introduction to critical discourse analysis in education* (2nd ed., pp. 173–204). Routledge.

2.17

CRITICAL LITERACY IN THE CARIBBEAN ISLES (ENGLISH- AND DUTCH-SPEAKING)

Lavern Byfield

The focus of this chapter is engagement with critical literacy (CL) in educational settings in the English-speaking islands and Dutch Isles of the Caribbean. It must be noted that the countries in this region vary in terms of size, geography, history, demographics, levels of literacy, economic development, political stability, etc. Although most islands have gained independence, vestiges of their colonial past are still evident in society, at large, and particularly within the educational systems.

Traditionally, a banking model of education (Freire, 1972) has been prevalent within these educational systems, where the teacher is the authority figure, whose knowledge is unchallenged. Mayne (2012) argues that "historically, Caribbean education has adopted Western approaches for over 350 years" (p. 4) and she explains that the predominantly British model is a legacy of colonialism. A common thread across the social fabric of both the English-speaking islands and Dutch Isles, is a Eurocentric model of education that scholars, native to the region, argue further marginalizes the poor (Mayne, 2012; Mijts, Kester, & Faraclas, 2014). According to Mijts et al. (2014), while most citizens speak the local vernaculars within the context of the Dutch Isles, Dutch is the language of instruction in schools, similar to the usage of English in the Anglophone Caribbean. Nonetheless, although a European model is dominant, Middlehurst and Woodfield (2003) contend that, currently, the United States is increasingly influencing policies and practices in the Caribbean.

Critical Literacy

Luke (2012) delineates the history of CL and highlights the dilemma of governments as they provide access to different forms and modes of technology to their citizens in the 21st century. With the changing definition of what it means to be literate, the onus is on educators to take new trajectories as they make content accessible to diverse populations (Byfield, Shelby-Caffey, Bacon, & Shen, 2015; Vasquez, Janks, & Comber, 2019). "The premise of critical literacy is that language and literacy are not neutral acts" (Towell & Marinaccio, 2020, p. 15), but are contextualized socioculturally within personal, social, historical, and political milieus (Flint, 2008).

Within the last two decades, contemporary Caribbean scholars have been advocating for the usage of native languages in a region where, whether Dutch or English, the majority of the general population are vernacular speakers (Devonish & Carpenter, 2007). Aligned with the tenets of CL, scholarship within the Caribbean academy has shifted to follow the principles of CL although not explicitly named as such. For example, the work of Devonish, Craig, and others, implicitly subscribe to Freire and seek to deconstruct the effects of colonialism and the power dynamics at play that

DOI: 10.4324/9781003023425-29

render the population in need of a European language/culture to be deemed educated and success-ful. CL has appeared in educational policies in which there is now an additive approach to bilingual instruction to add English to students' language registers while recognizing their mother tongues as well as formalization of the local vernaculars (Devonish and Carpenter).

Geographical Space/Sociopolitical Contexts: English-Speaking Islands

The West Indies, used synonymously with the Caribbean, is a large group of islands that separate the Caribbean Sea from the Atlantic Ocean: three main physiographic areas comprise this region. They consist of three main island groups: The Bahamas (north), Greater Antilles (central), and the Lesser Antilles (southeast). While English is the most common language in the Caribbean, several languages are also dominant including Spanish, French, Creole French, Dutch, etc. English remains the dominant language in Anguilla, the Bahamas, Bermuda, Cayman Islands, British Virgin Islands, Antigua and Barbuda, Dominica, Barbados, Grenada, Trinidad and Tobago, Jamaica, St. Kitts and Nevis, St. Vincent and the Grenadines, Montserrat, St. Lucia, and Turks and Caicos. There is even some debate regarding islands and countries that are traditionally considered Carib-bean which are actually situated within the Atlantic Ocean (the Bahamas, Turks and Caicos, and Bermuda) and Guyana, which sits on top of South America, but has political and social connections with the Caribbean (Moen, 2020).

Greater and Lesser Antilles

Jamaica is the only English-speaking island in the Greater Antilles and is the third largest island in the Caribbean. Three smaller island groups make up the Lesser Antilles: The Windward Islands, Leeward Islands, and Leeward Antilles. The Windward Islands, also called Islands of Barlovento, are southern islands which are larger than the others in the Lesser Antilles and include Saint Lucia, Saint Vincent, the Grenadines, and Grenada. Also included in the Lesser Antilles are Barbados and Trinidad and Tobago, which is the southernmost country in the Caribbean. The northern islands of the Lesser Antilles called the Leeward Islands include the U.S. Virgin Islands, British Virgin Islands, Anguilla, Saint Kitts and Nevis, Barbuda, Antigua, and Montserrat (Moen, 2020).

Sociopolitical Contexts

According to Davids (2013):

> Many contemporary Anglophone Caribbean nations with a colonial past have evolved over time to represent a source of social divide where the legacy of the hegemonic rela-tionship between the language of conquest and the languages of contact established on the sugar plantations and in the plantation houses is now mirrored in the social fabric of these societies [. . .] Standard English [is] the perceived language of prestige linked to wealth, power and or level of education.
>
> *(p. 1)*

Davids argues that folks who are perceived superior based on previously listed markers are often jostled against the understood Creole.

Within the Anglophone Caribbean, the official language and language of instruction (LOI) is English due to the historical ties with the British. However, the majority of the population speak Patois or Creole, which was once viewed as broken English, and is still viewed as such by many.

However, after careful examination, linguists from the region lobbied with heads of government to teach the native tongue alongside English in schools, using a bilingual approach to instruction (Devonish & Carpenter, 2007).

Educational Systems

The educational system starts at the Basic School/Pre-Primary level where students are enrolled at age 3 and graduate by the time they are 6 years old. This is sometimes called infant school if it is affiliated with a Primary or Junior High School/All Age School. The primary level offers education to students 6 years through age 12, and the Junior High/All Age, if it houses the infant department prepares students 3 through 15 years. The Junior High/All Age overlaps with secondary/high which offers education to students 12–17. Students can spend an additional 2 years in secondary/high school for Advanced Studies, which is said to better prepare them for university. There is some variation across islands with regard to age of entry to Primary school as well as public versus private. For example, in the Bahamas, students enter Primary school at age 5.

The University of the West Indies is the premiere university serving 17 English-speaking countries in the region. Having five campuses including Mona, Jamaica; Cave Hill, Barbados; St. Augustine, Trinidad and Tobago; Five Islands, Antigua and Barbuda; and Open Campus, these campuses offer a myriad of degree options. It is widely known in the region that the Mona (Jamaica) campus houses the region's flagship medical school, Cave Hill (Barbados) is known for law, and engineering is the focus at the St. Augustine campus (Trinidad and Tobago). Also scattered throughout these islands are other local and off-shore universities and colleges as well as teacher training institutions.

According to Lewis (2010), "by the mid-1960s when numerous African and Caribbean nations became independent of colonial powers, issues regarding the relationship between literacy and language surfaced" (p. 24). Coulmas (2005) argues that a significant issue that became prominent was associated with the language of instruction in educational settings or via a specific literacy program. Similar to other former British colonies around the globe, the English-speaking Caribbean struggled with legitimizing the localized language and in the context of Jamaica and other English-speaking islands, even attempted to eradicate the native tongue. For decades, many of the governments disregarded the local vernaculars spoken by the natives (Craig, 1976; Simmons-McDonald, 2004). "Similar to the U.S., many Anglophone Caribbean islands defined themselves as English monolingual speaking countries partly owing to their British colonial heritage" (Lewis, 2010, p. 26). Some including Barbados even deride other countries for their "lack of English-speaking capabilities."

Bilingual Framework Within Schools

Currently, there is a push for a bilingual framework in addressing the language needs of students in this region. Several Caribbean scholars have lobbied for a bilingual approach:

> Within the Caribbean, educators/linguists such as Bryan (2001), Craig (2006), and Pollard (1993) have suggested transitional forms of bilingual education, while others like Devonish (1986; Devonish & Carpenter, 2007) have proposed full bilingualism and changing the status quo to make both Standard Jamaican English (SJE) and Jamaican Creole (JC) the official languages of Jamaica.
>
> *(Lewis, 2010, p. 12)*

Caribbean linguists contend that if children are taught English within some form of bilingual framework, then English literacy scores would improve (Craig, 2001; Devonish & Carpenter, 2007).

Within schools, a transitional bilingual approach is implemented in which the native language is promoted and used as a vehicle to promote English language acquisition. This push, for a transitional approach to bilingual education, started in the early 2000s when many teachers were trained to facilitate the language development process by capitalizing on students' home language and culture. Although there is/was some backlash, teachers were trained to use local realia, music, and cultural practices in their teaching methodologies in order to improve students' language proficiency.

As discussed by Hewitt-Bradshaw (2014), it is imperative that a structure be implemented to facilitate a dual language approach. She argues the need for a "Linguistic landscape (LL) as a language learning and literacy resource in Caribbean Creole contexts" (p. 157). LL as an educational tool is highly recommended in contexts such as the English-speaking Caribbean where "two different language systems operate inside and outside of schools" (p. 158). Hewitt-Bradshaw uses LL to explore Caribbean Creole language settings and highlights a variety of materials/resources that has implications for language and literacy pedagogy. She focuses on "critical literacy and language awareness of language learners in a region where a variety of Creole language is the vernacular of the majority of speakers and Standard English is the official language of instruction (LOI)" (p. 157).

Given the dichotomy between the language spoken by the majority and the LOI, several challenges are noticeable. As school performance is tied to proficiency in the LOI, there is a call to employ strategies that will promote English language acquisition while affirming the native tongue. With this call, Middlehurst and Woodfield (2003) argue that within the Caribbean context, education has become progressively centralized as a result of governmental mandates that attempt to expand access to equitable instruction.

Caribbean Center of Excellence in Teacher Training

Several calls in the Caribbean to use an instructional approach to improve literacy levels were heralded in numerous countries with the establishment of the Caribbean Centre of Excellence for Teacher Training (Caribbean CETT), which was sponsored by USAID (there are Andean CETT and CETT for Central America and Dominican Republic). A major goal of CETT is the improvement of literacy skills and its major goal has been the improvement of literacy in the Commonwealth Caribbean, especially in the first three grades of primary school. Countries that participate in research on strategies to increase literacy levels include Trinidad and Tobago, Barbados, and Jamaica. A major aim of CETT is "Teaching language skills in the Commonwealth Caribbean" (p. 3, Welcome Address CETT).

Touting improvement in the teaching of reading with the intention of ensuring that all students are literate by grade 3, CETT sponsors and facilitates workshops with classroom teachers to gather data about their practice. As discussed in the *CETT White Paper Series*, the "program was a Presidential Initiative to improve the pedagogical skills of teachers in the first, second, and third grades in economically disadvantaged communities" (Valverde, Wolfe, & Roncagliolo, 2012, p. 1). Researchers in the CETT program found that a lack of technological infrastructure was a major hurdle in preparing students for the realities of the 21st century. With that said, the promotion of information and communications technologies (ICTs) were included "to broaden access to the program" (p. 1).

Warrican (2015) argues "great potential exists for developing true literacy in the Commonwealth Caribbean" (p. 384). The author contends with "Governmental awareness, dissatisfaction with the social landscape, and other enabling conditions" (p. 384) the islands are on track towards developing a truly literate citizenry. In facilitating true literacy, Warrican posits Commonwealth Caribbean countries should examine the historical legacy of the area and its impact on current literacy practices and rates of literacy.

Furthermore, Warrican (2015) maintains literacy practices that further marginalize citizens should be evaluated and strategic actions taken to remedy such. He argues it is imperative that there is a critique of institutions in which literacy is developed and sustained: the home and school. There are further calls for interrogation of the ideology that the native tongue is a substandard dialect of a superior European language. This requires a new definition of what it means to be literate, within the Caribbean context, with an affirmation of the mother tongue.

Geographical Space/Sociopolitical Contexts: Dutch Isles

Dutch is spoken in the ABC islands of Aruba, Bonaire, and Curacao as well as Saaba, Sint Eustatius, and Sint Maarteen. While these islands were once all considered islands a part of the Kingdom of the Netherlands, Bonaire, Sint Eustatius, and Saaba are now municipalities of the Netherlands upon dissolution of the Netherlands Antilles in 2010 (Veenendaal, 2015). Aruba, Curacao, and Sint Maarten are considered autonomous countries within the Kingdom of the Netherlands, and the Netherlands is the fourth and largest in the Kingdom. Sint Maarten shares half of the eastern island of Sint Maarten/ Saint Martin while Bonaire and Curacao are in the southern Caribbean. Saba and Sint Eustatius are the "smallest non-sovereign jurisdictions in the Caribbean" (Veenendaal, p. 15). In 1986, Aruba became a separate country within the Kingdom while Bonaire, Sint Eustatius, and Saba are considered "public bodies" of the Netherlands.

Sociopolitical Context

The United Kingdom and the Netherlands tried to grant independence up until the end of the 1980s to enduring colonies in the Caribbean and the Pacific (Veenendaal, 2015), even though lawmakers were cognizant of the former colonies' rights to still be affiliated with the metropolitan country. In stark contrast to the British and Dutch methods of governance/rule, France and the U.S. have endeavored to maintain overseas territories in the Caribbean and other parts of the world, "primarily on the basis of geostrategic arguments" (Miles, 2001, p. 48).

What is significant in understanding how former and current colonies operate is the conflicting views of their populations with regard to independence. For example, Veenendaal (2015) postulates that within the context of "contemporary non-independent island jurisdictions in the Caribbean and elsewhere, broad majorities of the population oppose political independence" (pp. 16–17). Stuart (2009) argues even though there are more than 100 sub-national islands jurisdictions there are major differences in the way regions function with regard to independence (Watts, 2009). Within the Caribbean context, "the French Departements d'Outre Mer (DOMs) have since 1946 been fully constitutionally integrated in the French Republic, whereas The Netherlands in 1954 agreed to grant its islands in the Caribbean the status of an autonomous country within the Kingdom" (p. 17).

Dissolution of the Netherlands Antilles

The country of the Netherlands Antilles was formally dissolved in October 2010. This was precipitated by impassioned deliberations between the five islands comprising the Netherlands Antilles and the Dutch government in The Hague, which resulted in the two largest islands of the country (Curacao and Sint Maarten) attaining a status similar to Aruba's obtained in 1986, as its own country in the Kingdom. Prior to this reconfiguration, the Dutch empire included Indonesia (the Dutch East Indies) and Suriname. Both became independent in the 1940s and 1970s, respectively. According to Oostindie and Verton (1998), the Dutch Caribbean islands, unlike Indonesia and Suriname, did not seek independence.

Educational Systems

The educational system comprises primary school for students 4 through 12, secondary school for 12 through 16 years, or pre-university for 12 through 18. The secondary strand constitutes a general secondary area or a technical and vocational area. It is estimated that 94% of the population is literate, with 38% of the populace having graduated from secondary school and 32% finished primary school (Edens, 2020). In the Netherlands Antilles, there is one university, the Universiteit van de Nederlandse Antilles. In this university, degree options include law, social sciences and economics, and engineering comprising architecture, civil, mechanical, and electrical. Teachers at the primary level study in Curacao at the teachers' college.

There are structural reconfigurations in the Netherlands Antilles since 2000, which are still in progress. Some include: more alignment with technology and theories related to education from the Netherlands and around the world; integrating foundation-based education in the first two years of secondary education; merging kindergarten with primary education; and categorizing students into three major groups: 4–8, 8–12, and 12–15.

International Comparison

The indigenous populations experienced similar atrocities in the U.S. where attempts were made to eliminate Native Americans' languages. May (2005) brings to the forefront the U.S. Commissioner of Indian Affairs, in which he recommends "schools should be established, which [Native American] children should be required to attend [and where] their barbarous dialects should be blotted out and English substituted" (p. 324). These attitudes parallel those of British inspectors' views of the usage of the native tongue in the former colonies in the Caribbean.

Additionally, Pike (2014) highlights the struggles of Anglophone Caribbean students in the New York Metropolitan area. According to Pike "some . . . immigrant students struggle with oral and written Standard English" (p. 30). Similar to calls in the English-speaking Caribbean to use a bilingual approach to teach students, immigrants of African and Anglophone Caribbean descent are in need of bilingual education to help them transition in an English-speaking medium in the U.S. Essentially, it has become more prevalent for scholars to advocate for an instructional approach that capitalizes on students' home cultures and languages.

Discussion/Implications

According to Mijts et al. (2014), "The language situation in the Dutch Caribbean is complex and often considered problematic" (p. 2). Most of the populace in the Leeward Islands of Aruba, Bonaire, and Curacao speak a native tongue called Papiamento and in the Windward Islands of Saba, Sint Eustatius, and Sint Maarten, citizens speak a dialect of Caribbean English (Mijts et al.). Although natives of these islands speak a language other than Dutch, the official language, up until the start of the 21st century has been Dutch. Dutch was the language used by educational institutions and administration. Similar to the English-speaking Caribbean islands, there have been arguments about the language of instruction in these Dutch isles for decades.

Mijts et al. (2014) argue:

> Most of the students in Sint Eustatius (and in most of the rest of the Dutch Caribbean) find themselves in a situation at school where Dutch is used as the language of instruction, even though the overwhelming majority of them almost never encounter written or spoken Dutch outside of the classroom.
>
> *(p. 2)*

It is claimed that success in school is limited for these students and the few who actually manage to succeed, more often than not, come from families who speak Dutch, pay for Dutch tutoring, and have exceptional learning motivation. However, the vast majority are left behind (Mijts et al., 2014).

A similar fate is meted out in the English-speaking Caribbean, where the majority are speakers of Creole or some variety. Teachers and parents, alike, express frustration in an education system that does not meet the needs of the locals. To improve the literacy levels of students, the CETT was established to curtail the reading difficulty that students encounter in a system where English is the language of instruction, but for most students, school is the only place where this is practiced.

In the Dutch isles, in Mijts et al.'s (2014) study, one of the teachers interviewed by the research team described her despondency by stating:

> When we teach in Dutch at the secondary school, we are teaching to the walls. Nine out of every 10 students who go on to Holland for studies each year fail and have to come back and their families have to reimburse their scholarships.
>
> *(p. 2)*

To further highlight the despair, the researchers shared a parent's concern of her son's thoughts about attending secondary school. The parent stated:

> My son is terrified of going to the secondary school. He is shutting down. He is begging to get out of Statia (Sint Eustatius). His biggest fear is going to secondary school and not being able to express himself in Dutch.
>
> *(Mijts et al., 2014, p. 3)*

Dutch was never the first language for most of the locals in the Dutch Caribbean isles and several factors created this scenario, but the major variable was the hesitation of the Dutch to teach their language and way of life to non-Dutch colonial subjects for the first two centuries of monarchical rule. The result is a series of interactions with traders, plantation owners, and Catholic missionaries, which saw the development of Papiamentu (Mijts et al. (2014).

While it is evident in the literature that a concerted effort is underway in the Anglophone Caribbean to challenge the status quo and interrogate the ideology that the native tongue is substandard (Warrican, 2015), it is not readily apparent in the Dutch Isles. Within the English-speaking context, scholarship and government policies are geared towards promoting the usage of the native tongue and capitalizing on the lived experiences of students' in school practices. In countries, for example, Jamaica, there is now a formalization of the mother tongue with books including the Bible written in Jamaican. In schools, policies have been implemented where standard English is taught using an additive approach while recognizing the mother tongue.

In summary, many citizens of these territories continue to struggle to gain proficiency in the language of colonizers although these European languages are considered the official languages of the region. There is also a push by many local linguists and scholars to employ an additive bilingual approach and capitalize on an understanding of the mother tongue in order for citizens to gain proficiency in the languages that are used for official business.

References

Bryan, B. (2001). *Language education policy*. Retrieved from www.moec.gov.jm/policies/languagepolicy.pdf.

Byfield, L. G., Shelby-Caffey, C. V., Bacon, H. R., & Shen, X. (2015). Digital literacy and identity formation in 21st century classrooms: Implications for second language development. *International Journal of Applied Linguistics and English Literature, 5*(1), 39–45.

Coulmas, F. (2005). *Sociolinguistics: The study of speakers' choices*. Cambridge University Press.

Craig, D. (1976). Bidialectal education: Creole and Standard in the West Indies. *International Journal for the Sociology of Language, 8*, 93–134.

Craig, D. (2001). Language education revisited in the Commonwealth Caribbean. In P. Christie (Ed.), *Due respect: Papers on English and English-related Creoles in the Caribbean in Honour of Professor Robert Le Page*. UWI Press.

Craig, D. (2006). *Teaching language & literacy to Caribbean students: From vernacular to Standard English*. Ian Randle Publishers.

Davids, M. P. (2013). Languages in contemporary Anglophone Caribbean Societies. Retrieved from https://files.eric.ed.gov/fulltext/ED539135.pdf

Devonish, H. (1986). *Language and liberation: Creole language politics in the Caribbean*. Karia Press.

Devonish, H., & Carpenter, K. (2007). Full bilingual education in Creole language situation: The Jamaican Bilingual Primary Education Project. *Society for Caribbean Linguistics, (35)*.

Edens, D. (2020). *Netherlands Antilles*. Retrieved from https://education.stateuniversity.com/pages/1076/Netherlands-Antilles.html

Flint, A. S. (2008). *Literate lives: Teaching, reading, and writing in elementary classrooms*. John Wiley & Sons.

Freire, P. (1972). *Pedagogy of the oppressed*. Herder and Herder.

Hewitt-Bradshaw, I. (2014). Linguistic landscape as a language learning and literacy resource in Caribbean Creole Contexts. *Caribbean Curriculum, 22*, 157–173.

Lewis, Y. E. (2010). *Literacy in Elementary School in Jamaica: The Case of the Grade Four Literacy Test* (Unpublished doctoral dissertation). The University of Iowa, The University of Iowa's Institutional Repository.

Luke, A. (2012). The future of critical literacies in U.S. schools. *Theory into Practice, 51*(1), 4–11.

May, S. (2005). Language rights: Moving the debate forward. *Journal of Sociolinguistics, 9*(3), 319–347.

Mayne, H. (2012). *From roots to blossoms: A description of the shared teaching experiences of Jamaican teacher educators* (Unpublished doctoral dissertation). University of Illinois at Urbana-Champaign, IDEALS Theses and Dissertations.

Middlehurst, R., & Woodfield, S. (2003). *The role of transnational, private, and for-profit provision in meeting global demand for tertiary education: Mapping, regulation and impact. Case Study: Jamaica*. Commonwealth of Learning.

Mijts, E., Kester, E., & Faraclas, N. (2014). *Multilingualism and education in the Caribbean Netherlands. A community based approach to a sustainable language education policy. The case of St. Eustatius*. Retrieved from www.core.ac.uk/reader/154952932

Miles, W. F. S. (2001). Fifty years of assimilation: Assessing France's experience of Caribbean decolonization through administrative reform. In A. G. Ramos & A. I. Rivera (Eds.), *Islands at the crossroads: Politics in the non-independent Caribbean* (pp. 45–60). Ian Randle Publishers.

Moen, J. (2020). *What countries are in the West Indies?* www.worldatlas.com/webimage/countrys/namerica/caribb/special/westind.htm

Oostindie, G., & Verton, P. (1998). *Ki sorto di Reino/What sort of Kingdom? Visies en verwachtingen van Antillianen en Arubanen omtrent het Koninkrijk*. KITLV.

Pike, E. W. (2014). *School leaders' perceptions of Caribbean students' English language needs*. (Unpublished doctoral dissertation). Walden University, Walden Dissertations and Doctoral Studies.

Pollard, V. (1993). *From Jamaican Creole to Standard English: A handbook for teachers*. Caribbean Research Center.

Simmons-McDonald, H. (2004). Trends in teaching standard varieties to Creole and Vernacular speakers. *Annual Review of Applied Linguistics, 24*, 187–208.

Stuart, K. (2009). The world's populated sub-national island jurisdictions. In G. Baldacchino & D. Milne (Eds.), *The case for non-sovereignty* (pp. 11–20). Routledge.

Towell, J. L., & Marinaccio, P. S. (2020). *Hooked on books: Language Arts and Literature in elementary classrooms, PreK—Grade 8* (3rd ed.). Kendall Hunt.

Valverde, G., Wolfe, R., & Roncagliolo, R. (2012). *CETT white paper series: Testing and assessment*. Retrieved from https://pdf.usaid.gov/pdf_docs/PA00JG2Z.pdf

Vasquez, V. M., Janks, H., & Comber, B. (2019). Critical literacy as a way of being and doing. *Language Arts, 96*(5), 300–311.

Veenendaal, W. (2015). The Dutch Caribbean municipalities in comparative perspective. *Island Studies, 10*(1), 15–30.

Warrican, S. J. (2015). Fostering true literacy in the Commonwealth in the Caribbean: Bridging the cultures of home and school. In P. Smith & A. Kumi-Yeboah (Eds.), *Handbook of research on crosscultural approaches to literacy development* (pp. 367–392). IGI Global.

Watts, R. L. (2009). Island jurisdictions in comparative constitutional perspective. In G. Baldacchino & D. Milne (Eds.), *The case for non-sovereignty* (pp: 21–39). Routledge.

2.18

CRITICAL LITERACY IN HONG KONG AND MAINLAND CHINA

Benjamin "Benji" Chang

Sociopolitical Context Overview

This chapter concerns the development of critical literacy within the Hong Kong Special Administrative Region (HKSAR) of the People's Republic of China (PRC, or mainland China). When aligning it with this Handbook's structure, this chapter was first discussed as one that might focus on Hong Kong and the PRC. This was challenging given the very different histories of Hong Kong versus mainland China, and their disparities in critical literacy (CL) scholarship. While there has been a significant body of critical education research done in Hong Kong (some of which includes CL), there has been relatively little 'critical' education scholarship in the PRC (Hu, 2019; Yan & Chang, 2011), and even less on CL. This absence can be partly attributed to research paradigms that mainland professors often have to operate under, and the restricted bandwidth they have to critique PRC educational and political systems. Given mainland China's global prominence in recent decades we could not simply omit any mention of it, but to discuss the two entities' separate political and educational systems would already exceed our word limit. Thus, our approach here is to foreground Hong Kong, while making connections to mainland China and key intersections that may be of interest to CL scholarship.

Hong Kong is a city-state of 7.5 million that is strategically located on the southern tip of China at intersections of Southeast and East Asia. Acquired in the 1840s through the imperialist Opium Wars, Hong Kong was one of the British Empire's prized territories until it returned control to the PRC in the 1997 Handover. Despite being officially under the rule of mainland China, Hong Kong was given the status of '*1 nation, 2 systems*' until 2047 and allowed to maintain a separate political, economic, and educational system, carrying over much of its previous infrastructure. Along with independent Taiwan, Macau (also an SAR), and mainland China itself, Hong Kong is often categorised as part of Greater China. Emerging from the Cold War, Hong Kong became known as a global metropolis with massive high-rises, a large multiracial population, one of the world's most efficient and profitable mass transportation systems, and a highly tech-savvy society that was bi- and then tri-lingual (English and Cantonese, and then Mandarin Chinese as well). During the 20th century, Hong Kong was host to many dissident artists, intellectuals, political figures and others who fled civil war, the Cultural Revolution, and martial law in Greater China. For several decades, Hong Kong was the pop culture mecca of Chinese people (e.g., kung fu, Cantopop music, TVB, HK cinema) and the portal city to China and much of Asia. It continues to be a global financial centre after New York and London, while consistently garnering Top Five rankings on international education exams

DOI: 10.4324/9781003023425-30

like the TIMSS and PISA (Chang & McLaren, 2018; Ip, 2017). Post-Handover, the HKSAR's shiny cosmopolitan image has been diminished by its increasing dependence on the mainland China juggernaut. This relationship has kept its economy afloat in many ways while also decreasing elements that made Hong Kong attractive to locals and migrants, including a relatively stable society, and home ownership as a path to the middle class.

Hong Kong has endured numerous societal problems from British rule to the present. Some of the more prominent issues have included extensive corruption and white supremacist policies (especially during British colonisation), as well as environmental degradation, gender inequities, and systemic racism towards non-Chinese Southeast and South Asians (e.g., Pakistani, Nepalese, 'mixed race') in a society that is over 90% people of Chinese heritage. The SAR has struggled to recognise and connect its diversity, and is fraught with divisions along oversimplified binaries of '*Mainlander*' versus '*Hongkonger*,' '*Chinese*' versus '*Westerner*,' and '*Local*' versus '*Ethnic Minority*' (which typically refers to darker-skinned Asians, regardless of how many generations they have resided in Hong Kong). An example of Hong Kong's inequities is the second-class treatment of its 390,000 domestic workers (mostly Pilipina and Indonesian women sojourners), who are typically required to live with their host, denied many rights that other residents have, and subject to abuse by their host families (Constable, 2009; Leung, 2019). Despite its image as a haven of cosmopolitan capitalism, Hong Kong is no stranger to mass dissent. Major protest movements have included the 'Pro-Communist' 1967 Riots, annual demonstrations of the PRC's 1989 Tiananmen Square Massacre, 2003 resistance to national security law agreements with the PRC, and challenges to the 2012 Moral & National Education revisionist school curriculum promoted by the PRC (Leung & Chiu, 1991; Morris & Vickers, 2015). In 2013 and 2018, Hong Kong had one of the greatest rich/poor gaps of any developed state (Oxfam, 2018). Subsequently in 2014 and 2019, massive long-term protests erupted for democratic elections and socioeconomic reforms while under de facto rule by mainland China. The 2014 protests are commonly referred to as the *Umbrella Movement*, and the 2019–present protests are often labelled the *Anti-ELAB Movement* in reference to the pending extradition law amendment bill with the PRC. Following both protest periods which included demonstrations in the thousands to the millions, increased sociopolitical repression was enforced upon students, professors, elected officials, other activists, and much of mainstream society. This repression occurred in numerous forms, including police brutality, retaliation in courts of law, and conservatism and censorship in the news media, schooling system, and academia (Lee, 2019). At the time this chapter was submitted, the mass protests were ongoing. While Hong Kong's government has not made any substantial ELAB decisions, the PRC has moved to pass a national security law that imposes extradition on Hong Kong.

Schooling System Overview

Hong Kong's schooling system spread significantly during industrialisation and urbanisation in the mid-late 1900s and followed some models similar to Commonwealth nations. However, there are also distinct characteristics of the system, many of which relate to the SAR's tensions with the British Empire and communist China. Here we mostly focus on developments that began in the 1990s as it is the period that most current primary to university students in Hong Kong have experienced.

The Education Bureau of Hong Kong (EDB) runs free compulsory schooling from primary to junior secondary years, with several options for senior secondary (Forms 4–6). In 2019, there were about 372,000 students and 27,000 teachers in 587 primary schools, and 325,000 students and 29,000 teachers in 506 secondary schools. Government spending on education was 20.4% of its budget. Aside from publicly funded government-run schools, the EDB also permits various bodies (including religious institutions) to be publicly funded should they follow the curriculum and assessment system. In addition to these 'aided' schools, there are also private campuses which generally run their own curriculum and generate their own funding, and the hybrid DSS (Direct Subsidy

Scheme) schools which receive significant public funding but also have significant freedom to run their own curriculum, similar to US charter schools. Hong Kong schools have a unique trio of instructional languages, given its history of Cantonese as lingua franca, English as prestige language, and Putonghua Mandarin as both somewhat, given developments with mainland China in recent decades. With students of Chinese heritage making up over 90% of the population, Cantonese is commonly used in public schools as the mode of instruction (MOI) for most subjects. Post-1997 there has been an increased use of, and resistance to, the 'patriotic' dialect of Putonghua as the general MOI. Putonghua is a PRC-developed variety of Mandarin using simplified written characters, and was commonly dismissed in previous decades by Hongkongers and Chinese-fluent communities around the world who were taught, and communicated in, traditional characters for centuries. Aside from Chinese MOI issues, in many of the more prestigious private, DSS, or publicly funded schools, English has been the MOI for subjects other than language courses. MOI issues also include '*Non-Chinese Speaking*' (NCS) pupils. These students are typically racialised as South and Southeast Asian students whose needs in learning academic Chinese language are glossed over via 'social promotion' (i.e., very low benchmarks to pass in order to move students to the next grade), or they were segregated into NCS-designated schools which are often in subpar facilities at the outskirts of Hong Kong (Gube & Gao, 2019).

In the 1990s, all Hong Kong schools were instructed to follow the same schooling years arrangement (5 + 2 years), and the policy of School-Based Curriculum (SBC). In theory, SBC promoted a more customised curriculum at the campus level, in response to longstanding critiques of the EDB being too top-down and disconnected with local contexts. In 2000, the EDB began a series of reforms to develop 21st-century skills to help students address the needs of the digital information society and globalised economy. These reforms were influenced by constructivist and cognitivist learning research which emphasised process, experience, and learner-centred pedagogy including formative assessments (Berry, 2011). The EDB's reforms have commonly been linked together under the banner of 'Learning To Learn' (LTL), which promoted creativity, critical thinking, collaboration, and project-based learning (Hui & Chan, 2006). During this period, some schools did explore elements of CL-related pedagogies (Firkins & Forey, 2006; Pérez-Milans & Soto, 2014), but these were more on an individual campus basis through studies with university researchers, which had relatively low influence on the general schooling system. Aside from LTL, another major reform occurred in 2012 when the Diploma of Secondary Education (DSE) became the only public exam used to evaluate students' applications for universities. For the DSE's score calculation, some local teacher-administered School-Based Assessments (SBA) are included to provide a more holistic assessment of students' skills. But despite over two decades of SBA, SBC, and LTL, the HKSAR seems to still largely operate within paradigms of teacher-centred direct instruction and high-stakes exams (Koh, 2015; Lin, 2004).

Because of its top PISA and TIMSS rankings, Hong Kong's didactic system is often highlighted by overseas conservative policymakers as something to be emulated, in opposition to the more 'liberal' curricula of 'The West' (Forestier & Crossley, 2015; Takayama, 2016). This research is commonly interweaved with notions of 'The Chinese Learner' or 'Confucian Heritage Culture' in praising the seemingly innate test-taking aptitude of pupils in the HKSAR, Singapore, South Korea, and Shanghai (Watkins, Ho, & Butler, 2017), which has striking similarities to problematic research on 'Model Minority' Chinese in North America (Chang, 2019). In contrast, local and international scholarship has critiqued Hong Kong schooling for several decades. Studies have found that since British rule, Hong Kong has had limited effectiveness in promoting innovation, critical analysis, and democratic civic engagement (Leung & Yuen, 2009; Walker, 2004). These results were influenced by practices of censoring politics in the colonial curriculum, especially those that addressed revolutionary China and its themes of anti-imperialism and proletariat solidarity, and Post-1997 attempts to foster pro-PRC ideologies (Fairbrother, 2008; Morris & Vickers, 2015). Despite the introduction of Liberal Studies as a subject in 1992 and its inclusion within the DSE, EDB curricula, assessments, administrators, and teaching practices still highly revolve around the high-stakes DSE. This entails a teaching-to-the-test paradigm (i.e., teachers often just do test prep for the last two high school years), where shadow education (private tutoring) becomes a necessary norm for students of all socioeconomic backgrounds. This normalisation of privatised and out-of-school education tends to mask systemic problems, and those who cannot afford a private or international education find themselves in a fiercely elitist and neoliberalised ranking system of schools with few pathways to higher education (Wang & Bray, 2016; Woo, 2013).

Survey of Critical Literacy Scholarship

The HKSAR government tends to strongly favour and fund research that falls under quantitative and positivist paradigms. In a city-state with nine publicly funded universities, this has a restrictive effect on the types of research conducted, especially when coupled with dominant views of literacy as traditional reading, writing, speaking, and listening. Thus, despite using CL theories and methodologies, scholars may opt to not 'advertise' critical literacy in their titles, key terms, or abstracts in order to maintain a visage of positivist objectivity: this all has the effect of hiding critical work in the region. In this section addressing the 15-plus years of Hong Kong CL scholarship, the first section addresses broader schooling critiques, and the second focuses on classroom teaching.

Schooling Inequity Issues

Much of Hong Kong's CL scholarship is informed by critical pedagogy, post-structural feminism, sociocultural learning, New Literacy Studies, and the works of Bakhtin and Bourdieu. Subsequently, common CL methodologies include ethnography, case studies, and discourse analysis. Utilising such approaches, HKSAR research has extensively critiqued its high-stakes exam system which privileges rankings and elite schooling, and exacerbates schooling inequities, class privilege, and social reproduction (Tsoi, 2015; Wang & Bray, 2016). Within works addressing the broader system, CL scholarship has critiqued how the EDB, government officials, and corporate interests have tended to follow policy trends in the UK and US, without appropriate modifications for Hong Kong's context. This scholarship has examined roots of inequity in colonisation and Orientalist ideologies (Lee & Law, 2016; Morrison & Lui, 2000). Researchers have also interrogated schooling massification via globalisation and neoliberalism's perpetual auditing of student 'performance,' its belief in technology and market ideology as saviour, and the ubiquity of private corporate interests in the commodification of childhood and public schools (Choi, 2005; Woo, 2013). These ideologies and practices are carried out through curriculum, pedagogy, and assessment, which are further perpetuated when Hong Kong's PISA and TIMSS rankings are lauded by government and corporate interests in promoting the SAR as a 'go-to-hub' for commerce, higher education, and educational tourism (Chang & McLaren, 2018; Kell & Kell, 2010). Outcomes that do not get publicised include widespread student individualism and apathy, debilitated school and community relationships, and intense stress levels of youth and teachers which can be indexed by recent suicide rates (Cheung & Chiu, 2016).

Aside from broader critiques, CL scholarship has examined specific contexts such as gender, migration, race, and ethnicity. While there are many HKSAR-based studies of schooling and gender, few utilise critical approaches. This small body of works has addressed issues of sexism and patriarchy in contexts like teacher education and textbooks, but more research has focused on administration and leadership which includes interrogating institutionalised practices tied to European and/or 'Confucian' ideologies (Chan, 2011; Chiu, 2008; Lin, 2004; Luke, 1998). While there has been some high-profile research on the marginalisation of cisgender females in education, it is difficult to find CL research on LGBTQI+ communities. Similarly, Special Education Needs (SEN) students have not received much study despite EDB policies of inclusive education and 'mainstreaming' SEN pupils for full or partial school days. The existing critical research discusses ways to address inequities for SEN students, and explores problematic criticisms by students, parents, and teachers on how SEN training, staff, and materials are under-resourced and detrimental to 'mainstream' pupils (Chan & Lo, 2016; Poon-McBrayer, 2004).

Some critical scholarship has addressed issues of race and ethnicity in the HKSAR. This work has looked at the legacies of colonisation, whiteness, and Han Chinese supremacy, and the continued presence of racial hierarchies with whites, Chinese, and 'ethnic minorities' from textbooks to school rankings (Chang et al., 2021; Jackson, 2016; Lee & Law, 2016). One context is the Native English Teacher (NET) scheme begun in 1998 (Boyle, 1997; Pérez-Milans, 2017), which controversially affords better employment packages and often lighter teaching loads to one teacher per school who is designated to have 'native-fluency,' although they might have less training and experience. It has been observed that schools hiring NETs may discriminate against hiring 'ethnic minority' (EM) educators, despite them having native-fluency. In addition to who gets to be considered fluent and effective educators, the racialisation of 'EMs' as low-achieving students has also been problematised. While there have been longstanding critiques of discrimination and segregation in public schools, 'EM' research has just recently become a funding priority due to the shrinking population of Chinese-heritage students, and the EDB's strategy of recruiting 'EMs' to fill up seats as the population has increased some 30% since the late 2000s (Bhowmik, 2014). Also of concern are 'Newly Arrived Students' from mainland China (NAS) and 'Cross-Border Students' (CBS) who live in the mainland but travel across the border to go to Hong Kong schools. Students of either group may have relatively low English or Cantonese skills, and sociocultural understandings of Hong Kong. NASs and CBSs come from diverse class and family backgrounds, but it is clear that the EDB has been insufficient in attending to the needs of non-Cantonese fluent or non-elite students, and that educators often harbour deficit views of these pupils (Gu, 2011).

Classroom Pedagogies Towards Equity

Studies of CL pedagogy implementation in Hong Kong are not common due in part to the aforementioned restrictive paradigms for researchers and teachers which do not applaud or fund critical work. Publications that do study classrooms promoting CL practices typically concern university-based scholars providing training and support for diverse groups of teachers, including pre-service, early career, NET, and veteran (Chang et al., 2021; Firkins & Forey, 2006; Luk & Lin, 2015). While CL projects tend to be conducted with youth from working-class or 'EM' backgrounds in secondary settings (Luk & Lin, 2015; Soto, 2019), there have been some studies in primary/elementary schools (Chan & Lo, 2016; Moorhouse, 2014). Unlike CL research in other regions that may include STEM subjects, CL pedagogies in Hong Kong are often developed within English and Liberal Studies (LS) which are seen to have more curricular leeway (Hui & Chan, 2006; Koh, 2015). English in particular is a more common subject assignment for teachers who have grown up or been at least partly trained in Anglophone countries outside of Hong Kong. In some media outlets LS has been blamed for 'radicalizing' students to be pro-democracy, anti-PRC, and an instigator for mass student protests, although research has not necessarily shown this to be so (Fung & Su, 2016; Wu, 2020).

In terms of pedagogies promoted by HKSAR CL scholarship, perhaps the most common emphasis has been on variations of the '4-Resources' model with critical consciousness (Freebody & Luke, 1990; Luk & Lin, 2015). These pedagogies have often constructed CL as going beyond just 'critical thinking,' to student and teacher worldviews, various forms of individual agency (e.g., academic, political), and connecting one's education to community and social justice. One rich context for this work has been the engagement of popular culture, especially those of high student interest like

Bollywood films, advertisements, and music (Luk & Hui, 2017; Soto, 2019). Not merely a trick to get students to pay attention, pop culture has been used as a more accessible platform to engage with traditional academics and critically understand and build upon youth perspectives. An arena that has been examined extensively is hip-hop and how its practices of style, mixing, and performativity can be transformative for schooling and act as a voice for youth and working-class resistance. Implications of hip-hop within translanguaging, literacy, and culture research, its utility for Chinese and English language education, and collaborations between artists, teachers, and researchers have been among the topics explored (Lin, 2007, 2012a). While hip-hop and pop culture engagement varies considerably across divisions like gender, race, language, class, and sexual orientation, digital media engages most Hong Kong students. Thus many CL researchers have built in digital media to their studies (e.g., YouTube, forums) for developing and studying multiple literacies (Lo & Clarke, 2010; Pérez-Milans & Soto, 2014). Digital venues have been used to engage students who have historically been left behind in official schooling, facilitate classes in connecting with each other and the world, and create real-time artefacts of their learning.

Hong Kong CL pedagogy has also emphasised collaborations, mentorship, and community development. CL collaboration has been operationalised as action research and as more equitable identities and relationships of power between schools/teachers, university programs/researchers, and sometimes parents (Forey, Firkins, & Sengupta, 2013; Mok, 1997). Collaboration has also been examined on a smaller scale between students and teachers, including dialogical forms of mentorship (Chan, 2019; Lin, 2012b), which can challenge teacher-centred hierarchies that are routinely justified as being part of 'Confucian Heritage Culture' (CHC) (Yuen, 2017). The research on collaboration can be viewed as part of two oft-discussed components of effective CL pedagogy, which are identity/positionality negotiation and the often simultaneous negotiation of community. This chapter has previously discussed the HKSAR's social fractures which include essentialised identities of *CHC*, '*Han Chinese*,' '*The Chinese Learner*,' '*Local Hongkonger*,' and '*Mainlander*' for Chinese-heritage students, and essentialised identities of '*Ethnic Minority*,' '*Non-Chinese Speaking*,' '*South Asian*,' and '*non-Local*' for Othered communities (Gube & Gao, 2019; Thapa, 2017). Some CL researchers have worked with students and teachers to interrogate these false binaries, and how they have been used to pit groups against each other and exacerbate inequities. Beyond just suggesting communicative language teaching, CL scholarship has explored communities of practice, community organising, and higher education pipelines for teacher-researchers (Chan, 2019; Chang, 2017; Soto, 2019; Zhang, Li, Liu, & Miao, 2016). Amongst these studies, focus has been placed on critical dialogue, identity negotiation, and community-building. The Umbrella Movement of 2014 provided generative spaces to further explore social justice-oriented pedagogies (Fung & Su, 2016). However, in the years that followed, government retaliation against pro-democracy advocates was clear. Keeping in mind the black-listings and imprisonments of dissenting students and academics, some CL colleagues were still open to presenting on these issues, yet far fewer were willing to publish on them, with some resorting to writing under pseudonyms (Partaken, 2017).

Further Research and Practice

As of June 2020, the powers that be in the PRC and Hong Kong continue to cast a shadow over educational equity and social justice. Although 2047 was the official year for government transition, the rights of HKSAR residents have been increasingly curtailed in recent years. Examples include PRC law enforcement jurisdiction on public transportation, People's Liberation Army (PLA) 'exercises' in protest areas, and 'disappeared' activist booksellers somehow ending up in the mainland with video confessions of 'past' crimes. While nation-states (e.g., UK, Sweden) and transnational corporations (e.g., Apple, NBA) waffle at making lukewarm rhetorical rebukes of the PRC for human rights abuses of their employees and citizens, HKSAR residents increasingly find themselves politically isolated despite a sea of social media sympathy and solidarity, and blustering by the US Presidential administration. In addition to increased surveillance and economic recession brought on by the COVID-19 epidemic, the anti-ELAB protests, unprecedented police state, and shuttering of schools and services have rocked Hong Kong to its core. During such desperate mass movements, how are we to develop research and practice towards a more transnational and transformative future? How can we reinvent our roles as critical literacy proponents, especially when our praxes were primarily developed in Global North societies with histories of indigenous genocide, white supremacy, and 'democratic' governance that are quite different from Hong Kong/China?

Given the PRC's position as the world's second largest economy with the military, natural resources, and people power to challenge the US over the next few decades, Hong Kong can be seen as a potential foothold and springboard for social movements and related scholarship in the Asia-Pacific and the globe. Over its relatively brief history on the world stage, at times Hong Kong has been seen as a beacon of hope and resistance to white imperialism, Asian fascism, and the devastations of capitalism. These moments have included the 2005 World Trade Organization (WTO) protests, and the explosion of Bruce Lee and kung fu cinema as inspirations and praxis for hip-hop and decolonising Power Movements of the 1970–1980s (Chang, 2020). Through the Umbrella and Anti-ELAB protest movements, Hong Kong has again provided inspiration and hope for resistance. Occurring during a more optimistic time, The Umbrella Movement featured peaceful protests and coalitions that came together in three *Occupy*-like encampments in Hong Kong's busiest and most prominent spaces for shopping and governance. Learning from the government's strategy of prosecuting publicised Umbrella leaders after the encampments were peacefully disassembled, Anti-ELAB protests have largely been made to appear faceless and leaderless, which has similarities to the indigenous Zapatista movement in Mexico (Marcos, 2004), and modern protest movements which use guerrilla tactics to disrupt and confuse government surveillance and policing, including via dark web applications (Ting, 2020). While international media has tended to focus on mass police brutality, (looting-less) vandalism, and sieges of Hong Kong's three most famous universities, the Anti-ELAB protests have also been widely supported by school and university communities (Lee, 2019). Picketing, walkouts, and other actions have been supported by masses of administrators, teachers, and students as young as primary ages, despite the government warning that teachers can be prosecuted for online comments alone, and that principals can be fired for supporting teachers that are being investigated (Cheng, 2019).

For their part, critical scholars have been publishing about the Umbrella Movement and literacy-related studies that promote forms of civic engagement, critical consciousness, and citizenship via formal and informal educational spaces (Lau, 2017; Leung, 2020). As can be expected there has been little Anti-ELAB scholarship, with the existing few being mostly commentary. Yet if we are to advance the CL literature, these protests should be addressed to a greater degree. In addition to the more transformative elements of the movement(s), an intersectional analysis of Hong Kong's interlocking systems leading to the protests and their implications for education, would help provide dynamic insights and ways forward (Chang, 2019). For one, protest movements in Hong Kong have continued to be dominated by men and those of Chinese ethnic heritage in visible leadership and media coverage. While there has been participation by minoritised communities (e.g., women, ethnic minority, LGBTQI+), and calls for changes in inclusion and decision-making by Han Chinese leadership (Convery, 2019; Walsh, 2017), these have not been widely implemented.

Another issue has been the lack of historical knowledge and use of racist and xenophobic binaries by various bodies of protesters. These problems partly originate with aforementioned British-colonial curricula which sought to divide and disconnect Chinese peoples through omission of revolutionary efforts in Greater China over the past century (Wong, 2012). The problems are also tied to previously addressed paradigms of high-stakes exams/audit culture and anesthetised LTL reforms. While there are structural inequities generated by mainland Chinese investments and pro-Beijing corporate elites in elected office, there is also notable ignorance and scapegoating towards working-class peoples 'racialised' as Mainlanders (Lowe & Tsang, 2018; Wong, 2020). Some unfortunate displays have ranged from professors and student societies bullying mainland students on campus, to protest groups aligning themselves with Trump and US Republicans in bizarre pleas for human rights and liberation. Word of these problematic activities, fanned by the fires of fake news, has helped instigate sensationalised tensions between '*Hong Kongers*' and '*Mainlanders*' around the world.

If Hong Kong is to heal its deep social fractures and sustain its social movement(s), emerging CL-related pedagogies of dialogue, restorative justice, and critical healing can prove important in constructing a more humanising and effective social movement (Sosa-Provencio, Sheahan, Desai, & Secatero, 2018; Winn, 2017). Despite romanticisations of fighting the police state with sidewalk bricks and Molotov cocktails, the effectiveness of social justice movements have not been decided by civil disobedience alone, but also with multi-level community organising, leadership development, and infrastructure building which can be better sustained via ongoing popular education (Horton & Freire, 1990; Kelley, 2002; Mohanty, 2003). It is through these historical and ongoing spaces that CL scholarship can also learn a great deal from Hong Kong's unique hybridities and positionalities with '*East*' and '*West*,' with China, and implications for how we teach literacies for all. At this historical moment, its protest movement(s) may perhaps be its most dynamic site for critical scholarship, and one that beckons greater engagement, critique, and support.

Acknowledgements

Special thanks to Sunny Man Chu Lau (Bishop's University) and the Hong Kong students, educators, and researchers who helped review this chapter but prefer to remain anonymous due to the SAR's current political climate.

References

Berry, R. (2011). Assessment trends in Hong Kong: Seeking to establish formative assessment in an examination culture. *Assessment in Education: Principles, Policy & Practice, 18*(2), 199–211. https://doi.org/10.1080/0969 594x.2010.527701

Bhowmik, M. K. (2014). *'Out of school' ethnic minority young people in Hong Kong*. Hong Kong Institute of Education.

Boyle, J. (1997). Native-speaker teachers of English in Hong Kong. *Language and Education, 11*(3), 163–181. https://doi.org/10.1080/09500789708666726

Chan, A. K.-w. (2011). Feminising and masculinising primary teaching: A critical examination of the interpretive frameworks of male primary school principals in Hong Kong. *Gender and Education, 23*(6), 745–759. https://doi.org/10.1080/09540253.2011.611041

Chan, C. (2019). Crossing institutional borders: Exploring pre-service teacher education partnerships through the lens of border theory. *Teaching and Teacher Education, 86*, 102893. https://doi.org/10.1016/j.tate.2019.102893

Chan, C., & Lo, M. (2016). Exploring inclusive pedagogical practices in Hong Kong primary EFL classrooms. *International Journal of Inclusive Education, 21*(7), 714–729. https://doi.org/10.1080/13603116.2016.1252798

Chang, B. (2017). Building a higher education pipeline: Sociocultural and critical approaches to 'internationalisation' in teaching and research. *The Hong Kong Teachers' Centre Journal, 16*(1), 1–25.

Chang, B. (2019). Two more takes on the critical: Intersectional and interdisciplinary scholarship grounded in family histories and the Asia-Pacific. *Curriculum Inquiry, 49*(2), 156–172. https://doi.org/10.1080/036267 84.2019.1595537

Chang, B. (2020). From 'Illmatic' to 'Kung Flu': Black and Asian solidarity, activism, and pedagogies in the Covid-19 era. *Postdigital Science and Education, 2*(2), 741–756. https://doi.org/10.1007/s42438-020-00183-8

Chang, B., Baimaganbetova, S., Yang, M., Cheung, I., Pun, C., & Yip, B. (2021). The Project for Critical Research, Pedagogy & Praxis: An educational pipeline model for social justice teacher education in times of division and authoritarianism. In B. S. Faircloth, L. M. Gonzalez, & K. Ramos (Eds.), *Belonging: Conceptual critique, critical applications* (pp. xx–xx). Rowman & Littlefield.

Chang, B., & McLaren, P. (2018). Emerging issues of teaching and social justice in Greater China: Neo-liberalism and critical pedagogy in Hong Kong. *Policy Futures in Education, 16*(6), 781–803. https://doi. org/10.1177/1478210318767735

Cheng, K. (2019, December 30). Hong Kong education chief warns principals may be fired if they support teachers under investigation over protests. *Hong Kong Free Press*. Retrieved from https://hongkongfp.com/2019/12/30/hong-kong-education-chief-warns-principals-may-fired-support-teachers-investigation-protests/

Cheung, E., & Chiu, P. (2016, March 12). Students at breaking point: Hong Kong announces emergency measures after 22 suicides since the start of the academic year. *South China Morning Post*. Retrieved from www.scmp.com/news/hong-kong/health-environment/article/1923465/students-breaking-point-hong-kong-announces

Chiu, P. P.-k. (2008). 'A position of usefulness': Gendering history of girls' education in colonial Hong Kong (1850s–1890s). *History of Education, 37*(6), 789–805. https://doi.org/10.1080/00467600802368715

Choi, P.-K. (2005). A critical evaluation of education reforms in Hong Kong: Counting our losses to economic globalisation. *International Studies in Sociology of Education, 15*(3), 237–256. https://doi. org/10.1080/09620210500200142

Constable, N. (2009). Migrant workers and the many states of protest in Hong Kong. *Critical Asian Studies, 41*(1), 143–164. https://doi.org/10.1080/14672710802631202

Convery, S. (2019, September 1). Denise Ho: Hong Kong has reached 'a point of no turning back' *The Guardian*. Retrieved from www.theguardian.com/world/2019/sep/02/denise-ho-hong-kong-has-reached-a-point-of-no-turning-back

Fairbrother, Gregory P. (2008). Rethinking hegemony and resistance to political education in Mainland China and Hong Kong. *Comparative Education Review, 52*(3), 381–412. https://doi.org/10.1086/588760

Firkins, A., & Forey, G. (2006). Changing the literacy habitus of a Hong Kong secondary school. In W. D. Bokhorst-Heng, M. D. Osborne, & K. Lee (Eds.), *Redesigning pedagogy: Reflections on theory and praxis* (pp. 33–45). Sense. https://doi.org/10.1163/9789087900977_004

Forestier, K., & Crossley, M. (2015). International education policy transfer—borrowing both ways: The Hong Kong and England experience. *Compare: A Journal of Comparative and International Education, 45*(5), 664–685. https://doi.org/10.1080/03057925.2014.928508

Forey, G., Firkins, A. S., & Sengupta, S. (2013). Full circle: Stakeholders' evaluation of a collaborative enquiry action research literacy project. *English Teaching: Practice and Critique, 11*(4), 70–87.

Freebody, P., & Luke, A. (1990). Literacies programs: Debates and demands in cultural context. *Prospect: An Australian Journal of TESOL, 5*(3), 7–16.

Fung, D., & Su, A. (2016). The influence of liberal studies on students' participation in socio-political activities: The case of the Umbrella Movement in Hong Kong. *Oxford Review of Education, 42*(1), 89–107. https://doi. org/10.1080/03054985.2016.1140635

Gu, M. M. (2011). 'I am not qualified to be a Honkongese because of my accented Cantonese': Mainland Chinese immigrant students in Hong Kong. *Journal of Multilingual and Multicultural Development, 32*(6), 515–529. https://doi.org/10.1080/01434632.2011.614350

Gube, J., & Gao, F. (2019). *Education, ethnicity and equity in the multilingual Asian context*. Springer.

Horton, M., & Freire, P. (Eds.). (1990). *We make the road by walking: Conversations on education and social change*. Temple University.

Hu, Z. (2019, November 16). *Proceedings of the 3rd international conference on critical pedagogy*. The 3rd International Conference on Critical Pedagogy, Guangzhou, China.

Hui, P.-K., & Chan, S. C. (2006). Contextual utility and practicality: Cultural research for the school community in Hong Kong. *Cultural Studies Review, 12*(2), 165–182.

Ip, I.-c. (2017). State, class and capital: Gentrification and new urban developmentalism in Hong Kong. *Critical Sociology, 0*(0), 0896920517719487. https://doi.org/10.1177/0896920517719487

Jackson, L. (2016). Learning about diversity in Hong Kong: Multiculturalism in liberal studies textbooks. *The Asia-Pacific Education Researcher, 26*(1), 21–29. https://doi.org/10.1007/s40299-016-0323-0

Kell, M., & Kell, P. (2010). International testing: Measuring global standards or reinforcing inequalities. *International Journal of Learning, 17*(9), 485–501.

Kelley, R. D. G. (2002). Roaring from the east: Third world dreaming. In R. D. G. Kelley (Ed.), *Freedom dreams: The Black radical imagination* (pp. 60–109). Beacon.

Koh, A. (2015). Popular culture goes to school in Hong Kong: A language arts curriculum on revolutionary road? *Oxford Review of Education, 41*(6), 691–710. https://doi.org/10.1080/03054985.2015.1110130

Lau, J. Y.-F. (2017). Reflections on the umbrella movement: Implications for civic education and critical thinking. *Educational Philosophy and Theory*, 1–12. https://doi.org/10.1080/00131857.2017.1310014

Lee, F. (2019). Solidarity in the anti-extradition bill movement in Hong Kong. *Critical Asian Studies*, 1–15. https://doi.org/10.1080/14672715.2020.1700629

Lee, K.-M., & Law, K.-Y. (2016). Hong Kong Chinese "orientalism": Discourse reflections on studying ethnic minorities in Hong Kong. In A. Pratt (Ed.), *Ethnic minorities: Perceptions, cultural barriers and health inequalities* (pp. 81–116). Nova Science.

Leung, H. (2019, March 6). Here's how much migrant domestic workers contribute to Hong Kong's economy. *Time*. Retrieved from https://time.com/5543633/migrant-domestic-workers-hong-kong-economy/

Leung, K.-P., & Chiu, W.-K. (1991). *A social history of industrial strikes and the labour movement in Hong Kong, 1946–1989.* Social Sciences Research Centre Occasional Paper, Issue 3. University of Hong Kong.

Leung, W.-T. (2020). *Applying critical pedagogy in the senior secondary Liberal Studies curriculum: An action research study in Hong Kong.* The Education University of Hong Kong.

Leung, Y.-W., & Yuen, W.-W. (2009). A critical reflection of the evolution of civic education in Hong Kong schools. *Pacific-Asian Education Journal, 21*(1), 35–50.

Lin, A. M.-Y. (2004). Introducing a critical pedagogical curriculum: A feminist reflexive account. In B. Norton & K. Toohey (Eds.), *Critical pedagogies and language learning* (pp. 271–290). Cambridge University Press.

Lin, A. M.-Y. (2007). Independent hip-hop artists in Hong Kong: Youth sub-cultural resistance and alternative modes of cultural production. *Journal of Communication Arts, 25*(4), 47–62.

Lin, A. M.-Y. (2012a). Critical practice in English language education in Hong Kong: Challenges and possibilities. In K. Sung & R. Pederson (Eds.), *Critical ELT practices in Asia: Key issues, practices, and possibilities* (pp. 71–83). Sense.

Lin, A. M.-Y. (2012b). Multilingual and multimodal resources in L2 English content classrooms. In C. Leung & B. V. Street (Eds.), *"English" in education* (pp. 79–103). Multilingual Matters.

Lo, M., & Clarke, M. (2010). Practicing or preaching? Teacher educators and student teachers appropriating new literacies. In P. Darren Lee & R. C. David (Eds.), *Multiliteracies and technology enhanced education: Social practice and the global classroom* (pp. 147–166). IGI Global.

Lowe, J., & Tsang, E. Y.-H. (2018). Securing Hong Kong's identity in the colonial past: Strategic essentialism and the Umbrella Movement. *Critical Asian Studies*, 1–16. https://doi.org/10.1080/14672715.2018.1503550

Luk, J., & Hui, D. (2017). Examining multiple readings of popular culture by ESL students in Hong Kong. *Language, Culture and Curriculum, 30*(2), 212–230. https://doi.org/10.1080/07908318.2016.1241258

Luk, J., & Lin, A. (2015). Voices without words: Doing critical literate talk in English as a Second Language. *TESOL Quarterly, 49*(1), 67–91. https://doi.org/10.1002/tesq.161

Luke, C. (1998). "I got to where I am by my own strength": Women in Hong Kong higher education management. *Education Journal, 26*(1), 31–58.

Marcos, S. I. (2004). *Ya basta!: Ten years of the Zapatista uprising.* AK Press.

Mohanty, Chandra T. (2003). "Under Western Eyes" Revisited: Feminist solidarity through anticapitalist struggles. *Signs, 28*(2), 499–535. https://doi.org/10.1086/342914

Mok, A. (1997). Student empowerment in an English language enrichment programme: An action research project in Hong Kong. *Educational Action Research, 5*(2), 305–320. https://doi.org/10.1080/09650799700200024

Moorhouse, B. L. (2014). Using critical pedagogies with young EFL learners in a Hong Kong primary school. *International Journal of Bilingual & Multilingual Teachers of English, 2*(2), 79–90.

Morris, P., & Vickers, E. (2015). Schooling, politics and the construction of identity in Hong Kong: The 2012 'Moral and National Education' crisis in historical context. *Comparative Education, 51*(3), 305–326. https://doi.org/10.1080/03050068.2015.1033169

Morrison, K., & Lui, I. (2000). Ideology, linguistic capital and the medium of instruction in Hong Kong. *Journal of Multilingual and Multicultural Development, 21*(6), 471–486. https://doi.org/10.1080/01434630008666418

Oxfam. (2018). *Hong Kong inequality report.* Oxfam. Retrieved from www.oxfam.org.hk/tc/f/news_and_publication/16372/Oxfam_inequality%20report_Eng_FINAL.pdf

Partaken, J. (2017). Listening to students about the Umbrella Movement of Hong Kong. *Educational Philosophy and Theory*, 1–11. https://doi.org/10.1080/00131857.2017.1318045

Pérez-Milans, M. (2017). Bilingual education in Hong Kong. In O. García, A. M. Y. Lin, & S. May (Eds.), *Bilingual and multilingual education* (pp. 207–218). Springer. https://doi.org/10.1007/978-3-319-02258-1_17

Pérez-Milans, M., & Soto, C. (2014). Everyday practices, everyday pedagogies: A dialogue on critical transformations in a multilingual Hong Kong school. In J. S. Byrd Clark & F. Dervin (Eds.), *Reflexivity in language and intercultural education rethinking multilingualism and interculturality* (pp. 213–233). Routledge.

Poon-McBrayer, K. F. (2004). Equity, elitism, marketisation: Inclusive education in Hong Kong. *Asia Pacific Journal of Education, 24*(2), 157–172. https://doi.org/10.1080/02188791.2004.10600207

Sosa-Provencio, M. A., Sheahan, A., Desai, S., & Secatero, S. (2018). Tenets of body-soul rooted pedagogy: Teaching for critical consciousness, nourished resistance, and healing. *Critical Studies in Education*, 1–18. https://doi.org/10.1080/17508487.2018.1445653

Soto, C. (2019). *Critical pedagogy in Hong Kong: Classroom stories of struggle and hope*. Routledge.

Takayama, K. (2016). Deploying the post-colonial predicaments of researching on/with 'Asia' in education: A standpoint from a rich peripheral country. *Discourse: Studies in the Cultural Politics of Education*, *37*(1), 70–88. https://doi.org/10.1080/01596306.2014.927114

Thapa, C. B. (2017, February 1). Who, really, are Hong Kong's ethnic minorities? No policy can work without understanding. *South China Morning Post*. Retrieved from http://www.scmp.com/comment/insight-opinion/article/2084614/who-really-are-hong-kongs-ethnic-minorities-no-policy-can

Ting, T.-y. (2020). From 'be water' to 'be fire': Nascent smart mob and networked protests in Hong Kong. *Social Movement Studies*, *19*(3), 362–368. https://doi.org/10.1080/14742837.2020.1727736

Tsoi, I. S.-P. (2015). Post-secondary educational pathways of young people in Hong Kong: The influence of cultural capital. *International Journal of Continuing Education & Lifelong Learning*, 7(2), 121–147.

Walker, A. (2004). Constitution and culture: Exploring the deep leadership structures of Hong Kong schools. *Discourse: Studies in the Cultural Politics of Education*, *25*(1), 75–94. https://doi.org/10.1080/0159630042000178491

Walsh, S. (2017). Under the Umbrella: Pedagogy, knowledge production, and video from the margins of the movement. *Educational Philosophy and Theory*, 1–12. https://doi.org/10.1080/00131857.2017.1310018

Wang, D., & Bray, M. (2016). When whole-person development encounters social stratification: Teachers' ambivalent attitudes towards private supplementary tutoring in Hong Kong. *The Asia-Pacific Education Researcher*, *25*(5), 873–881. https://doi.org/10.1007/s40299-016-0307-0

Watkins, M., Ho, C., & Butler, R. (2017). Asian migration and education cultures in the Anglo-sphere. *Journal of Ethnic and Migration Studies*, *43*(14), 2283–2299. https://doi.org/10.1080/1369183X.2017.1315849

Winn, M. T. (2017). Building a "lifetime circle": English education in the age of #BlackLivesMatter. *Urban Education*, *53*(2), 248–264. https://doi.org/10.1177/0042085917747114

Wong, A. C.-K. (2020). On racial hatred: How the coronavirus has uncovered the dark side of Hong Kong's movement. *Lausan*. Retrieved June 19, from https://lausan.hk/2020/on-racial-hatred-how-the-coronavirus-has-uncovered-the-dark-side-of-hong-kongs-movement/

Wong, T.-H. (2012). The unintended hegemonic effects of a limited concession: Institutional incorporation of Chinese schools in post-war Hong Kong. *British Journal of Sociology of Education*, *33*(4), 587–606. https://doi.org/10.1080/01425692.2012.674789

Woo, D. (2013). Neoliberalism in two Hong Kong school categories. *Current Issues in Comparative Education*, *16*(1), 37–48.

Wu, W. (2020). Politics, textbooks, and the boundary of 'official knowledge': The case of Liberal Studies in Hong Kong. *Pedagogy, Culture & Society*, 1–18. https://doi.org/10.1080/14681366.2020.1765846

Yan, G.-c., & Chang, Y. (2011). The circumstances and the possibilities of critical educational studies in China. In M. W. Apple, W. Au, & L. A. Gandin (Eds.), *The Routledge international handbook of critical education* (pp. 368–385). Routledge.

Yuen, G. (2017). Ready for ethical and critically reflective practice in supercomplex times? Discourses, knowledge and values in the postmodern society of Hong Kong. In M. Li, J. Fox, & S. Grieshaber (Eds.), *Contemporary issues and challenge in early childhood education in the Asia-Pacific region* (pp. 293–308). Springer.

Zhang, Z., Li, J., Liu, F., & Miao, Z. (2016). Hong Kong and Canadian students experiencing a new participatory culture: A teacher professional training project undergirded by new media literacies. *Teaching and Teacher Education*, *59*, 146–158. https://doi.org/10.1016/j.tate.2016.05.017

2.19

CRITICAL LITERACY IN THE NORDIC EDUCATION CONTEXT

Insights From Finland and Norway

*Aslaug Veum, Heidi Layne, Kristiina Kumpulainen
and Marianna Vivitsou*

Nordic Socio-Political Context

The Nordic Region consists of Denmark, Norway, Sweden, Finland and Iceland as well as the Faroe Islands, Greenland and Åland. The Nordic countries are rather small, with a total population of 26.8 million. About 4 million people in the Nordic countries have an immigrant background (Østby & Aalandslid, 2020). Finland, Sweden and Norway also have a Sámi population who have the status of indigenous people. All Nordic countries are members of the Organisation for Economic Co-operation and Development (OECD), while three countries are members of the European Union (EU) (Nordic Co-operation, 2020). The Nordic welfare model rests on the values of democracy and equality, including universally available public services.

The Nordic social model combines tripartite cooperation amongst employers' organisations, trade unions and the state, and provides universal health, social protection, labour market support and education.

In the Nordic countries, free education is available to all citizens irrespective of their ethnic origin, age, wealth or where they live (Miettinen, 2013). The Nordic countries are often regarded as leaders on gender equality at home, at work and in public life in general. The countries have also established comprehensive early childhood education and care services, and these family policies have contributed considerably to economic growth in the Nordic countries (OECD Nordic Council of Ministers, 2018). The educational systems in the Nordic countries have much in common. Public schools dominate in all Nordic countries, but the proportion of private schools varies. There are differences amongst the countries in terms of organisation and traditions, for instance, in how much autonomy local authorities have in organising schooling, controlling the school curriculum and allocating resources (Gustafsson & Blömeke, 2018). Next, we will give brief introductions to the Finnish and Norwegian systems.

Finland

Since the birth of the current Finnish basic education system in 1970, the fundamental idea has been to provide free access to quality education for all. The Basic Education Act (628/1998, Chapter 7, §25) defines the concept of *oppivelvollisuus*, which translates literally as the 'responsibility to learn', known in the English-speaking world as compulsory education. Basic education starts in Finland when the children turn seven years old. Curriculum reforms have taken place every ten years. The

DOI: 10.4324/9781003023425-31

recent reform of the Finnish national curriculum for basic education came into effect in August 2016 and it resonates with the international trend of competence-based curricula. In the new curriculum, transversal competence is defined as a set of knowledge, skills, values, attitudes and will, which are to be promoted across the curriculum for all age groups. In Finland, each municipality or education provider is responsible for developing a more specific local curriculum (EDUFI, 2016).

Norway

The Norwegian elementary school was established in 1889, and included children from all social classes. In 1952, the Common Educational Act included all Norwegian children, regardless of where in the country they lived. During the last 50 years, the Norwegian government implemented several educational reforms. Compulsory school now includes all children from the ages of 6–16. In 1994, all young people from the ages of 16–19 gained the legally established right to three years of upper secondary education and training after completing compulsory school (Thune, 2020). In 2006, the National Curriculum for Knowledge Promotion in Primary and Secondary Education and Training was introduced. This reform sanctioned a competence-based curriculum, national tests and the establishment of a national quality assessment system for primary and secondary education and training. The curriculum was characterised as a literacy reform (Berge, 2005). The recent reform for the Norwegian national curriculum was introduced in 2020.

Nordic Research on Critical Literacy

An international overview in Routledge Handbook of Literacy Research (Rowsell & Pahl, 2015) reveals that the number of empirical articles on critical literacy has increased during the last years, especially during 2010–2012. However, very few of these studies were located in Europe (Rogers & O'Daniels, 2015). Our own review on Nordic research on critical literacy that took account of research published in Nordic languages echoes these findings. Using the search term *critical literacy* (including the Scandinavian term '*kritisk* [critical] literacy'), we made a search in two Nordic/Scandinavian journals: *Nordic Journal of Literacy Research* and *Scandinavian Journal of Educational Research*, covering the years from 2015 to 2021. Within this period, ten articles that explicitly referred to critical literacy were published. Five of these studies were located in Norway (Blikstad-Balas, 2016, 2018; Magnusson, 2021; Krulatz & Iversen, 2020; Veum, Siljan, & Maagerø, 2020), four in Sweden (Liberg & Nordlund, 2019; Sturk, Randahl, & Olin-Scheller, 2020; Tjernberg, Forsling, & Roos, 2020; Walldén, 2021) and one in Finland (Tainio & Slotte, 2017). The studies covered education from lower as well as upper secondary schools. Our analysis of the Nordic research literature in the field reveals that critical literacy was part of investigating literacy (i.e. writing and reading) education as well as multilingual literacy. None of the identified studies investigated critical literacy as their key focus.

Godhe (2019) analysed all four Nordic countries as to how digital competence as a part of critical literacies is applied to the national curriculum. Godhe concluded that different terms are used in the national curricula of these countries when addressing how compulsory education can prepare students for living and working in a digitalised society. The Norwegian curriculum uses digital skills (*ferdigheter*), whereas in Finland, multiliteracy and information and communications technology (ICT) skills are listed as transversal competence areas in the curricula for pre-primary and basic education. For early childhood education and care, ICT skills are part of multiliteracy. The diversity of approaches and labelling in the documents reflects a complex reality within the education system in the Nordic countries, where efforts are being made to respond to a rapidly changing population and the diverse needs of students. This indicates that, while critical literacy research calls for harnessing different types of media to learn to live together in diversity, have mutual respect and tolerate differences, the policy documents still do not adequately address complex social issues. Building convivial, welcoming, just and life-sustaining communities and societies is the key educational challenge facing this generation of young people and their teachers (Luke & Sefton-Green, 2018). In addition, the review of the literature showed that the way critical literacy is implemented is rather obscure, which can be associated with the ways the term is represented in the curriculum. Unclear representations and interpretations can lead to educational practices that are not synchronised with or are disengaged from political-economic developments and changes, and are not directly related to societal needs.

Some research studies have identified that the understanding of critical literacy, as well how to develop critical literacy skills, is broad and unclear in Nordic educational settings (Johansson & Limberg, 2017; Molin, Godhe, & Lantz-Andersson, 2018). Teachers tend to understand critical literacy in a restricted way, referring to a set of criteria for evaluating the reliability and sustainability of sources. The work on issues regarding the relation between power and language and scaffolding students in how to deconstruct and discuss texts appears limited (Brante & Lund, 2017). Few Norwegian studies have focused specifically on critical literacy. However, national Norwegian reading tests as well as results from the Programme for International Student Assessment (PISA) 2018 indicate that lower secondary school students do not perform evaluations of the trustworthiness of texts. Less than half of the Norwegian students reported that they had learnt about critical literacy at school (Weyergang & Frønes, 2020). Some small-scale studies from Norwegian upper secondary schools have also suggested that older students read texts in a naïve way, treating informative texts as objective representations, and do not have sufficient metalanguage for discussing linguistic and semiotic choices in various kinds of texts (Blikstad-Balas & Foldvik, 2017; Undrum & Veum, 2018). Other studies have found that Norwegian teaching practices tend to rely heavily on available textbooks and that textbook exercises guide the students to search for 'correct' meaning and answers instead of encouraging multiple critical readings and analysis of underlying value-laden assumptions in text (Skjelbred, 2009). Similar observations on the teaching methods relying on textbook orientation have been made in the Finnish context (Kumpulainen, Kajamaa, & Rajala, 2018); furthermore, teachers' preparedness and ability to tackle critical issues and promote critical literacy is still dependent on the teacher's individual interest and level of understanding (Zacheus et al., 2019).

Critical Perspectives in Two Nordic Curricula

Next, we discuss our analysis of the national curricula in Finland and Norway and consider how critical literacy is understood in these documents. The curriculum analysis focuses on how critical literacy is presented in the curriculum and under what terminology, using thematic analysis (Braun & Clarke, 2012).

Critical Literacies in the Finnish Curriculum

The Finnish National Curriculum for Basic Education (EDUFI, 2016) emphasises transversal competences, one of them being multiliteracies. The National Curriculum serves as a framework for municipalities and schools to design their own local curricula. The National Curriculum consists of objectives and core contents for all the subjects and it describes the mission, values and structure of education with special needs support.

Core Values and the Role of Basic Education. The core values for Finnish basic education are framed by the principles of equality, equity and justice. Education is intended to promote the learning and development of each individual and their understanding of and responsibility towards society, other people and cultures and the environment (EDUFI, 2016). The most recent curriculum introduced six transversal competence areas: *Thinking and learning to learn; Cultural literacy,* *communication and expression*; *Managing daily life, taking care of oneself and others*; *Multiliteracy*; *Entrepreneurial and working life skills*; *Participation and building a sustainable future*; and *ICT skills*. Following the Nordic welfare model, the goal of Finnish education is to foster every individual's active participation, a sustainable lifestyle and growth towards democratic membership in society (EDUFI, 2016). This can be linked to Freire's (1970) idea of curriculum building in communities.

The Finnish National Curriculum recognises increasing language diversity in the Finnish society, in addition to Finland being a bilingual country with both Finnish and Swedish as official languages. Bilingual and multilingual children are referred to in the curriculum documents as 'children with a different mother tongue' (Utbildningsstyrelsen, 2016) or as 'other plurilingual students', together with Sámi and Sámi-speaking students, Roma students and sign language users (Utbildningsstyrelsen, 2016; Kulbrandstad, Layne, Paavola, Hellman, & Ragnarsdóttir, 2018). The recognition of language hierarchy between the languages spoken at home and taught at school is not specifically addressed in the Finnish National Curriculum (Daryai-Hansen, Layne, & Lefever, 2018).

Focus on Critical Thinking. Critical literacy (*kriitinen lukutaito*, in Finnish) is not a key term in the Finnish National Curriculum. However, the use of the term 'critical' is mentioned in connection to the values of basic education that emphasise supporting students' critical thinking. Also, the description of transversal competences addresses supporting students' development of thinking and learning to learn. The curriculum states that students should be guided to use information independently, engage in problem-solving and discuss topics critically from different viewpoints (EDUFI, 2016).

Multiliteracies has been defined in the Finnish National Curriculum as a transversal competence to produce and make value judgements from various cultural representations and texts, developed through learning experiences allowing these texts to be produced in written, spoken, printed, audio-visual or digital formats (EDUFI, 2016). Although multiliteracies include the critical dimension, earlier studies have revealed that the cultural and critical dimensions of literacies are more vaguely represented in the curriculum documents compared with operational dimensions that emphasise skills (Kumpulainen, 2018; Kumpulainen & Sefton-Green, 2019; Palsa & Mertala, 2019). Hence, the Finnish curriculum places a lot of trust in the teachers' professional expertise to promote critical literacy in their teaching.

Critical Literacies in the Norwegian Curriculum

The implementation of the current Norwegian national curriculum started in 2020 and consists of a core curriculum and several subject-specific parts. This curriculum applies to primary and secondary education and training, including education for children from the age of six through university-preparatory education and vocational training. The curriculum elaborates on the Norwegian Education Act and comprises three main chapters: (1) Core values of the education and training, (2) Principles for education and all-round development (*Bildung*) and (3) Principles for the school's practice (Norwegian Directorate for Education and Training, 2020a).

Core Values and the Role of Basic Education. In the curriculum, 'Critical thinking and ethical awareness' is listed as one of a total of six core values of education and training. The other core values are 'Identity and cultural diversity', 'Democracy and participation', 'Human dignity', 'The joy of creating, engagement and the urge to explore' and 'Respect for nature and environmental awareness' (Norwegian Directorate for Education and Training, 2020a). According to the curriculum, students should be given the opportunity to be inquisitive and to question. The curriculum underlines very explicitly that students must be prepared to critically reflect on knowledge, and 'what is the truth' (Luke, 2012).

If new insight is to emerge, established ideas must be scrutinised and criticised by using theories, methods, arguments, experiences and evidence. The pupils must be able to assess different sources of knowledge and think critically about how knowledge is developed (The Norwegian Directorate for Education and Training, 2020a, p. 6).

Critical literacy works at the interface of language, literacy and power, and discourses are linked to social identities (Janks, 2010). The Norwegian core curriculum is not very explicit about how democracy is linked to literacy. However, the formal status of some languages is emphasised, referring to the fact that Norwegian and the Sámi languages have equal standing in Norway, that the Norwegian language comprises two assimilated standards of written Norwegian ('*Bokmål*', developed from Danish and Danish-Norwegian] and '*Nynorsk*', developed from Norwegian dialects]) and that Norwegian sign language is acknowledged as language in its own right. According to the curriculum, 'The teaching and training shall ensure that the pupils are confident in their language proficiency, that they develop their language identity and that they are able to use language to think, create meaning, communicate and connect with others' (The Norwegian Directorate for Education and Training, 2020a).

Focus on Critical Thinking. While the terms 'critical thinking' and 'think critically' appear frequently and in the first two parts of the Norwegian core curriculum, we do not find any explicit use of the term 'critical literacy'. Instead, the curriculum defines five basic skills: reading, writing, numeracy, oral skills and digital skills. Critical thinking is defined as a competence the students need to acquire in order to navigate in a complex and knowledge-based society: 'The competence concept also includes understanding and the ability to reflect and think critically in subjects, which is vital for understanding theoretical reasoning and for carrying out practical tasks' (Norwegian Directorate for Education and Training, 2020a, p. 11). While the core curriculum is rather general when it comes to how critical thinking should be included in teaching practices, the subject-specific parts of the curriculum are more specific in that respect. For the academic subject of Norwegian, 'critical approaches to text' is one out of six core elements, referring to how students at the end of lower secondary school should be able to critically evaluate the power of influence and the trustworthiness of texts and explore how digital media influences language and communication (Norwegian Directorate for Education and Training, 2020b). However, the curriculum is not very specific in terms of how the teacher should work with critical approaches to text.

Recommendations and Future Directions

When comparing the analysis of the Finnish and the Norwegian curricula, we found that the concept of 'critical thinking' was referred to in both curricula. The concept was explained both as a core value and as a competence aiming for developing 21st-century skills, and defined as critically reflecting on assessing knowledge, as well as evaluating sources. Emphasis on critical thinking derives from and is linked to European pedagogic theory and the German *Bildung* tradition typical of the Nordic education system and its underlying pedagogy. The notion of *Bildung* is historically both an educational and a philosophical concept (Nordenbo, Hirsjärvi, Frímannsson, Lovlie, & Safstrom, 1997). *Bildung* could be translated to 'formation' or 'all-around development', describing the formation of the human personality, behaviour and morality. An important philosopher within this tradition, Georg Wilhelm Friedrich Hegel, emphasised that individuals develop through a critical and explorative process that takes place in the relationship between the individual and language, culture and history (Hogstad, 2020).

Our curriculum analysis revealed that critical literacy did not appear as a key term in either the Finnish or the Norwegian curriculum. Perspectives of the mutual influence between language and society (Fairclough, 1992) and Freire's (1974) ideas of how language and literacy are linked to human agency, transformation and change are not really acknowledged in either of the curricula. A possible explanation for this finding could be the fact that either Freire's critical pedagogy or perspectives from recent international critical literacy theory (see overview in Rogers & O'Daniels, 2015) are prominent within Nordic education. The limited number of Nordic research studies on critical literacy identified in the preceding review does support this impression.

Critical literacy education is characterised by a multiplicity of conceptual positions (Behrman, 2006). However, some traditions have been established internationally during the last decades. Rogers and O'Daniels (2015) have described two twin pillars of critical literacy education: one is to develop students' voice and ability to critique, and the other is to teach students some technical resources for understanding how texts work. The first pillar is present within the German *Bildung* tradition on which the Nordic philosophy of education is based. Critical thinking refers to the ability to question, evaluate and criticise knowledge of various kinds, which needs to be developed. Thus, critical thinking is linked to democracy, individuality and inclusiveness. However, in the two Nordic curricula we have analysed, the link to the second pillar of critical literacy, referring to the development of students' awareness of texts and how agency through language and texts is connected to power, justice and democratic citizenship (Janks, 2010; Pandya & Ávila, 2014; Vasquez, Tate, & Harste, 2013), seems to be weaker.

Rogers and O'Daniels (2015) found that the majority of studies on critical literacy education have been carried out in the United States, Australia and Canada, and called for more research from other parts of the world. Our review of Nordic research and the analysis of how critical literacy is integrated in two current Nordic curricula are far from sufficient. However, it seems evident that there is a need for more research on and development of critical literacy education within the Nordic Region. Since the Nordic countries have much in common when it comes to socio-political development, and are, to a certain extent, based upon similar educational philosophies, it would be interesting to have similar studies from all the Nordic countries. Moreover, we believe the future development and implementation of Nordic critical literacy will profit from connecting more closely with the research of critical literacy that has been done in the international field of education.

References

Behrman, E. H. (2006). Teaching about language, power, and text: A review of classroom practices that support critical literacy. *Journal of Adolescent and Adult Literacy, 49*(6), 481–486. https://doi.org/10.1598/JAAL.49.6.4

Berge, K. L. (2005). Skriving som grunnleggende ferdighet og som nasjonal prøve –Ideologi og strategier. [Writing as a main competence and as national assesment]. In A. J. Aasen & S. Nome (Eds.), *Det nye norskfaget* (pp. 161–189). Fagbokforlaget.

Blikstad-Balas, M. (2016). "You get what you need": A study of students' attitudes towards using Wikipedia when doing school assignments, *Scandinavian Journal of Educational Research, 60*(6), 594–608, https://doi.org/10.1080/00313831.2015.1066428

Blikstad-Balas, M. (2018). Skrivediskurser i norskfaget—en analyse av hvordan norsklærere snakker om skriving på åttende trinn. *Nordic Journal of Literacy Research, 4*(1). https://doi.org/10.23865/njlr.v4.1020

Blikstad-Balas, M., & Foldvik, M. C. (2017). Kritisk literacy i norskfaget—Hva legger elever vekt på når de vurderer tekster fra internett? [Critical literacy in the subject Norwegian—What do the students emphasise when evaluating sources from Internet?]. *Norsklæreren, 4*, 28–39.http://urn.nb.no/URN:NBN:no-62425

Brante, E. W., & Lund, E. S. (2017). Undervisning i en sammansatt textvärld: En intervjustudie med svenska och norska gymnasielärare om undervisning i kritisk läsning och kritisk värdering av källinformation [Reading in a complex textual world. An interview study with Swedish and Norwegian upper secondary school teachers regarding critical reading and evaluation of sources]. *Nordic Journal of Literacy Research, 3*(2), 1–18. http://dx.doi.org/10.23865/njlr.v3.671

Braun, V., & Clarke, V. (2012). Thematic analysis. In H. Cooper, P. M. Camic, D. L. Long, A. T. Panter, D. Rindskopf, & K. J. Sher (Eds.), *APA handbook of research methods in psychology, Vol. 2: Research designs: Quantitative, qualitative, neuropsychological, and biological* (pp. 57–71). American Psychological Association.

Daryai-Hansen, P., Layne, H., & Lefever, S. (2018). Language hierarchisations and dehierarchisations: Nordic parents' views towards language awareness activities. *International Journal of Bias, Identity and Diversities in Education (IJBIDE), 3*(2). http://doi.org/10.4018/IJBIDE.2018070105

EDUFI. (2016). *National core curriculum for basic education 2014.* Publications 2016:5. Finnish National Board of Education.

Fairclough, N. (1992). *Discourse and social change.* Polity Press.

Freire, P. (1970). *Pedagogy of the oppressed.* Herder and Herder.

Freire, P. (1974). *Education for critical consciousness.* Seabury Press.

Godhe, A.-L. (2019). Digital literacies or digital competence: Conceptualizations in Nordic curricula. *Media and Communication, 7*(2), 25–35. http://dx.doi.org/10.17645/mac.v7i2.1888

Gustafsson, J. E., & Blömeke, S. (2018). Development of school achievement in the Nordic countries during half a century. *Scandinavian Journal of Educational Research, 62*(3), 386–406. https://doi.org/10.1080/00313 831.2018.1434829

Hogstad, H. K. (2020, December 29). *Dannelse* {formation]. Store norske leksikon. Retrieved from https:// snl.no/dannelse

Janks, H. (2010). *Literacy and power.* Routledge.

Johansson, V., & Limberg, L. (2017). Seeking critical literacies in information practices: Reconceptualising critical literacy as situated and tool-mediated enactments of meaning. *Information Research, 22*(1), 1–16. Retrieved from http://informationr.net/ir/22-1/colis/colis1611.html

Krulatz, A., & Iversen, J. (2020). Building inclusive language classroom spaces through multilingual writing practices for newly-arrived students in Norway. *Scandinavian Journal of Educational Research, 64*(3), 372–388. https://doi.org/10.1080/00313831.2018.1557741

Kulbrandstad, L. A., Layne, H., Paavola, H., Hellman, A., & Ragnarsdóttir, H. (2018). Immigrant students in Nordic educational policy documents. In H. Ragnarsdóttir & L. A. Kulbrandstad (Eds.), *Learning spaces for inclusion and social justice* (pp. 32–68). Cambridge Scholars Publishing.

Kumpulainen, K. (2018). A principled, personalised, trusting and child-centric ECEC system in Finland. In S. L. Kagan (Ed.), *The early advantage 1: Early childhood systems that lead by example* (pp. 72–98). Teachers College Press.

Kumpulainen, K., Kajamaa, A., & Rajala, A. (2018). Understanding educational change: Agency-structure dynamics in a novel design and making environment. *Digital Education Review, 33*, 26–38. Retrieved from https://revistes.ub.edu/index.php/der/article/view/21633/pdf

Kumpulainen, K., & Sefton-Green, J. (2019). *Multiliteracies and early years innovation: Perspectives from Finland and beyond.* Routledge.

Liberg, C., & Nordlund, A. (2019). Lärares samtal om elevers skrivande av berättande texter i tidiga skolår. *Nordic Journal of Literacy Research, 5*(2). https://doi.org/10.23865/njlr.v5.1666

Luke, A. (2012). Critical literacy: Foundational notes. *Theory into Practice, 51*(1), 4–11.

Luke, A., & Sefton-Green, J. (2018, November 11). *Critical media literacy and digital ethics.* The World Association for Christian Communication. Retrieved from www.waccglobal.org/articles/critical-media-literacy-and-digital-ethics

Magnusson, C.G. (2021). Reading Literacy Practices in Norwegian Lower-Secondary Classrooms: Examining the Patterns of Teacher Questions, *Scandinavian Journal of Educational Research*, DOI: 10.1080/00313831.2020.1869078

Miettinen, R. (2013). *Innovation, human capabilities and democracy: Towards an enabling welfare state.* Oxford University Press.

Molin, L., Godhe, A.-L., & Lantz-Andersson, A. (2018). Instructional challenges of incorporating aspects of critical literacy work in digitalised classroom. *Cogent Education, 5*(1516499), 1–17. https://doi.org/10.1080/2331186X.2018.1516499

Nordenbo, S. E., Hirsjärvi, S., Frímannsson, G. H., Lovlie, L., &. Safstrom, C.-A. (1997). Forty years of the philosophy of education in the Nordic countries. *Scandinavian Journal of Educational Research, 41*(3–4), 365–396. https://doi.org/10.1080/0031383970410313

Nordic Co-operation. (2020). *Facts about the Nordic countries.* Retrieved from www.norden.org/en/information/facts-about-nordic-countries

Norwegian Directorate for Education and Training. (2020a). *Core curriculum—values and principles for primary and secondary education.* Retrieved from www.udir.no/lk20/overordnet-del/?lang=eng

Norwegian Directorate for Education and Training. (2020b). *Curriculum in Norwegian* www.udir.no/lk20/nor01-06?lang=eng

OECD Nordic Council of Ministers. (2018). *Is the last mile the longest? Economic gains from gender equality in Nordic countries.* Retrieved from www.oecd.org/publications/is-the-last-mile-the-longest-economic-gains-from-gender-equality-in-nordic-countries-9789264300040-en.htm

Østby, L., & Aalandslid, V. (2020). *Immigration and immigrants in the Nordic countries.* Statistics Norway Reports 2020/40. Retrieved from www.ssb.no/befolkning/artikler-og-publikasjoner/innvandring-og-innvandrere-i-norden

Palsa, L., & Mertala, P. (2019). Multiliteracies in local curricula: Conceptual contextualizations of transversal competence in the Finnish curricular framework. *Nordic Journal of Studies in Educational Policy, 5*(2), 114–126. https://doi.org/10.1080/20020317.2019.1635845

Pandya, J. Z., & Ávila, J. (2014). *Moving critical literacies forward: A new look at praxis across contexts.* Routledge.

Rogers, R., & O'Daniels, K. (2015). Critical literary education: A kaleidoscopic view of the field. In J. Rowsell & K. Pahl (Eds.), *The Routledge handbook of literacy studies* (pp. 62–78). Routledge.

Rowsell, J., & Pahl, K. (Eds.). (2015). *The Routledge handbook of literacy studies.* Routledge.

Skjelbred, D. (2009). Lesing og oppgaver i lærebøker [Reading and exercises in textbooks]. In S. V. Knudsen, D. Skjelbred, & B. Aamotsbakken (Eds.), *Lys på lesing. lesing av fagtekster i skolen* (pp. 271–289). Novus Forlag.

Sturk, E., Randahl, A.-C., & Olin-Scheller, C. (2020). Back to basics? Discourses of writing in Facebook groups for teachers. *Nordic Journal of Literacy Research, 6*(2). https://doi.org/10.23865/njlr.v6.2005

Tainio, L., & Slotte, A. (2017). Interactional organization and pedagogic aims of reading aloud practices in L1 education. *Nordic Journal of Literacy Research, 3*(1). https://doi.org/10.23865/njlr.v3.469

Thune, T. (2020, March 21). *Norsk utdanningshistorie* [Norwegian history of education]. Store norske leksikon. Retrieved from https://snl.no/norsk_utdanningshistorie

Tjernberg, C., Forsling, K., & Roos, C. (2020). Design för multimodal och kreativ skrivundervisning i tidiga skolår—Lärare reflekterar i fokusgruppsamtal. *Nordic Journal of Literacy Research, 6*(1). https://doi.org/10.23865/njlr.v6.2044

Undrum, L. V. M., & Veum, A. (2018). Kritisk literacy i den digitale tekstkulturen. Unges selvfremstilling i og selvrefleksjon over kommunikasjon på sosiale medier. [Kritical literacy i the digital textual culture. Teenagers self-presentation in and self-reflection on communication in social media]. In K. Kverndokken (Ed.), *101 litteraturdidaktiske grep—om å arbeide med skjønnlitteratur og sakprosa* (pp. 132–151). Fagbokforlaget.

Utbildningsstyrelsen. (2016). Retrieved from www.finlex.fi/sv/laki/ajantasa/2016/20160564

Vasquez, V. M., Tate, S. L., & Harste, J. C. (2013). *Negotiating critical literacies with teachers.* Routledge.

Veum, A. Siljan, H. H., & Maagerø, E. (2020). Who am I? How newly arrived immigrant students construct themselves through multimodal texts. *Scandinavian Journal of Educational Research.* https://doi.org/10.1080/00313831.2020.1788147

Walldén, R. (2021). "You know, the world is pretty unfair"—Meaning perspectives in teaching social studies to migrant language learners. *Scandinavian Journal of Educational Research.* https://doi.org/10.1080/00313831.2020.1869073

Weyergang, C., & Frønes, T. S. (2020). Å lese kritisk: Elevers vurderinger av teksters troverdighet og pålitelighet. [Critical reading. How students evaluate trustworthiness and reliability of texts. In T. S. Frønes & F. Jensen (Eds.), *Like muligheter til god leseforståelse. 20 år med lesing i PISA* (pp. 166–195). Universitetsforlaget. https://doi.org/10.18261/9788215040066-2020-07

Zacheus, T., Kalalahti, M., Varjo, J., Saarinen, M., Jahnukainen, M., Mäkelä, M.-L., & Kivirauma, J. (2019). Discrimination, harassment and racism in Finnish lower secondary schools. *Nordic Journal of Migration Research, 9*(1), 81–98. http://doi.org/10.2478/njmr-2019-0004

2.20

CRITICAL LITERACIES PRAXIS IN NORWAY AND FRANCE

Silje Normand, Alexandre Dessingué and David-Alexandre Wagner

Introduction

The following chapter explores critical literacies praxis in Norway and France. Following a brief overview of the socio-political and educational contexts in the respective countries, the chapter considers national critical literacy perspectives and examines critical literacy work in three subject disciplines, drawing on an ongoing Erasmus+ funded strategic partnership project, *Critical Literacies and Awareness in Education* (CLAE). CLAE was designed as a transnational and collaborative project focused on developing critical literacies praxis in sixth and seventh grade in four Norwegian schools and three French schools with participants from different disciplinary and national backgrounds. The authors of the present chapter all share a transnational background, influenced by Norwegian and French contexts, and the project aimed to encourage critical literacies with younger learners while fostering collaboration between educational sectors and across national boundaries.

Researchers, teachers and school leaders formed a transnational, cross-professional and pluri-disciplinary "community of inquiry" (Lipman, 2003) and "community of practice" (Wenger & Wenger-Trayner, 2015) that met regularly to observe, reflect on and develop their critical literacies praxis. Drawing on tenets from critical text analysis (Janks, 2010; Luke, 2012) and critical pedagogy (Freire, 1970; Freire & Macedo, 1987), participants collectively developed an understanding of critical literacies as comprising skills, values and attitudes, developed through critical dialogic exchanges, that emphasise learner voice and agency, active citizenship and the addressing of social injustices. Through exchanges of teaching practice and the collaborative design of lessons, Norwegian and French teachers worked on developing their own critical literacy practices and those of their learners, and the chapter argues for the benefits of further transnational critical literacy work.

Socio-Political Contexts

In 2020, Norway and France share comparable sociodemographic characteristics, while also having clear historical, political and cultural differences. Norway is a relatively young country that values its independence gained in 1905 and enjoys a high level of trust in its institutions. It has historically been sparsely and homogeneously populated, with little immigration until recently. Although Norway was among the poorest countries in Europe 100 years ago, it has since developed a strong welfare model, based on social dialogue, relatively low social and wage differences, low unemployment rates, high labour market participation, and high levels of gender equality. This welfare model

 DOI: 10.4324/9781003023425-32

has produced a substantial and stable economic growth, largely sustained by the discovery of oil in the late 1960s. In contrast, France is a much older country that has long held a prominent role in Europe. It is densely and heterogeneously populated following multiple periods of migration. Following World War II, France developed a strong welfare model and enjoyed significant economic growth until the mid-1970s. Since then, the country has suffered lower economic growth and higher unemployment rates. While the values inherited from the French Revolution are actively used to promote the ideals of liberty, social justice and equality of opportunity, France also has a long tradition of political tensions, social inequalities and centralisation.

Since the 1980s, both countries have experienced an increase in political and social tensions, with issues of immigration and rapidly changing economic conditions fuelling the rise of extreme-right and populist political parties. In Norway, the oil-based economic growth has been accompanied by an increase in socio–economic and geographic inequalities, particularly affecting immigrant families, as well as an increase in relative poverty. Recently, ethical questions have been raised regarding the responsibility of Norway in the global climate challenges the world is facing. Critical light has also been shed on the idealised representation Norway and Norwegians have had of their own past, including the treatment of national minorities, the role of its institutions during and following World War II, and the country's image as a peace nation (Aas & Vestgården, 2014). In France, different issues related to the country's colonial past, especially in Africa, remain sensitive and unsettled (Bancel et al., 2010), and social, geographic and economic inequalities have led to recurrent tensions in urban outskirts since the 1970s (Wacquant, 2008), as well as to the more recent "Yellow Vests" protests.

Educational Contexts

In both countries, education is considered key to meeting present and future economic and societal challenges. Both educational systems aspire to promote democratic values and culture and to function as inclusive arenas that ensure equal opportunities for all children. Education, including at higher levels, is mainly public and free of charge and the state provides educational guidelines and curricula for primary and secondary education. However, while in Norway, schools have experienced a higher level of early school leavers and growing differences between genders and between children of immigrant or non-immigrant backgrounds; in France, increasing social tensions and decreasing social mobility in recent years have placed additional pressure on the school's mandate to counteract societal inequalities.

A main educational difference relates to the specialisation, recruitment and supervision of teaching staff. In France, recruitment is centralised, and teachers are assigned to schools following a national competitive exam. In Norway, recruitment is decentralised, and school principals hire their own staff through a public process. From lower secondary level onwards, French teachers are specialists, usually only teaching the subject they studied at university, while Norwegian teachers teach at least two or three different subjects. French teachers usually work individually and are not required to stay at school outside of their teaching hours, but their curricula are set in detail for each class and discipline, and they must report and respect strict norms of progression and curricular content. In contrast, Norwegian teachers usually work in subject or grade-level teams, are expected to remain at school during mandatory hours, and while national curricula regulate learning outcomes after certain grades, schools are granted the autonomy to establish their own annual plans.

Critical Literacy Perspectives in Norway and France

Critical literacy perspectives are apparent in the official educational documents of both countries. In France, the Common Core highlights critical awareness through citizen engagement, distancing from prejudice and stereotypes, respect and empathy for others, historical and geographical consciousness, an awareness of inequalities and environmental issues, and interpreting texts to understand the contemporary world. Different subject curricula emphasise the importance of critical thinking: as responsible attitudes and values in Moral and Civic Education; as part of the scientific process in Science and Technology; as text-analytical skills in French, Art Education, or Media and Information Education. In Norway, the new Core Curriculum positions critical thinking and ethical awareness among its main goals and values. Critical thinking is identified as a specific core element in Norwegian, social studies, history and geography subject curricula and components of critical literacy are apparent in several language learning curricula, where critical thinking, multiperspectivity and awareness of minority perspectives are emphasised.

However, while the concept of literacy has been widely accepted in Norway, drawing on Anglo-Saxon research and terminology, in France, the term has proved difficult to translate (Fraenkel & Mbodj-Pouye, 2010) and French researchers have relied on the francophone Canadian neologisms "littératie" and "littératie critique" (Dagenais, 2012; Painchaud, d'Anglejan, Armand, & Jezak, 1993). The term "lettrisme" has been used for literacy in French educational contexts, but is seldom associated with criticality, and the terms "pensée critique" or "esprit critique" (critical thinking), both as skill and attitude, are far more prevalent. Nevertheless, critical reflections related to issues of power and empowerment have been well-integrated in French educational programmes since the 1950s through critical theories and critical discourse analysis by a long tradition of thinkers as diverse as Althusser, Bourdieu, Foucault, Derrida, De Certeau, Ricoeur or Barthes. In Norway, work on critical literacy has been embedded in experiential, socio-cultural and critical teaching approaches, emphasising learner voice and agency, and drawing on the work of Dewey, Vygotsky and Freire.

Critical Literacy Research Across Subject Disciplines in Norway and France

Research on critical literacies in the first language (L1) in Norway and France has been relatively limited. Critical approaches to texts in the Norwegian and French L1 subjects have traditionally focused on questioning of perspective, voice, context and agency within fictional work, although scholars have also pointed to the potential of promoting learner voice and critical literacies through the production and performance of reflective texts (Grossmann, 1999; Skaftun, 2020; Smidt, 2011). Recent publications in both countries have shown an increasing interest in critical literacy issues, especially in relation to media education (Blikstad-Balas, 2016; Blikstad-Balas & Foldvik, 2017; Corroy & Jehel, 2016; Ihadjadene, Saemmer, & Baltz, 2015; Kiyindou, Barbey, & Corroy-Labardens, 2016) and the analysis of factual and multimodal texts (Blikstad-Balas & Tønnesson, 2020; Eilertsen & Veum, 2019; Martel, Sala, Boutin, & Villagordo, 2018; Veum & Skovholt, 2020).

Similarly, research on critical literacies related to history or social studies education in both national contexts is relatively scarce. Much of the research written in French stems from Canada (as illustrated by Éthier, Lefrançois, & Audigier, 2018), although recent publications in France have also addressed critical historical consciousness, critical pedagogy and critical thinking (e.g. De Cock & Perreira, 2019; Falaize, 2014; Pereira et al., 2016). In Norway, the interest is recent and mainly related to democracy and citizenship (Lorentzen & Røthing, 2017), notions of critical cultural heritage and critical historical consciousness (Dessingué, 2016, 2020), visual literacy (Wagner, 2019), the representation of migrants and national minorities in the curriculum (Ekeland, 2017; Normand, 2020), or recommendations for teaching practice (Ferrer & Wetlesen, 2019).

Critical literacy work within the fields of second language (SL) and foreign language (FL) learning has been influenced by perspectives from critical pedagogy (Freire, 1970; Giroux, 2011; Norton & Toohey, 2004), multimodal literacies (Jewitt & Kress, 2003) and multiliteracies frameworks (The New London Group, 1996), as well as an increasing recognition of multilingualism as a resource

(Krulatz, Dahl, & Flognfeldt, 2018). In Norway, teacher educators have promoted the use of picture books, graphic novels, digital media and film (e.g. Bland, 2018; Habegger-Conti, 2015), highlighting the need for language learners to develop critical visual literacy (Brown, 2019) and to question representations of indigenous and minority populations (Brown & Habegger-Conti, 2017). Critical literacy work is often linked to developing intercultural competence, and the awareness of English as a lingua franca, the multiplicity of global Englishes, and the potential of language learning to support the development of multiperspectivity serve to underline that "exercising intercultural understanding and empathy must go hand in hand with critical literacy" (Bland & Mourão, 2017, p. ii). This is particularly apparent within literature didactics research where the potential of children's literature and young adult literature to raise critical awareness in language learners has been emphasised (Bland, 2018). Work with developing learners' multiperspectivity and ability to problematise power hierarchies within language learning has also drawn on the field of drama pedagogy, notably Boal's *Theatre of the Oppressed*, with drama's potential to engage learners in critical literacy practices closely linked to citizenship education and engagement (e.g. Greenwood & Sæbø, 2015; Normand & Savić, 2018; Sæbø, Eriksson, & Allern, 2017). In France, similar critical literacy concerns are observed within the fields of second and foreign language didactics (e.g. Molinié & Moore, 2012; Marquilló-Larruy, 2012), building on the work of francophone Canadian scholars (Dagenais, 2012; Hébert & Lépine, 2013).

Critical Literacy Practices in Norway and France

National and subject-specific perspectives were also apparent in the teacher logs, interviews, lesson plans and observations of teaching practice within the CLAE project. French and Norwegian L1 teachers identified similar learning aims and outcomes in the critical literacy lessons they designed but differed in their material and methodological choices. While the French teachers often drew on canonical literary texts, which they supplemented with contemporary resources such as comics and popular music, the Norwegian teachers centred their teaching on a larger variety of different genres and resources, ranging from newspaper articles to YouTube videos. In French L1 lessons, the literary text was often central, with individual reflections starting from the text in the form of textual analysis and ethical or philosophical questioning of textual content. This was connected to the learners' context in a second step. In Norwegian L1 lessons, the texts and topics selected were more closely related to the learners' everyday context, with the focus less on the interpretation of the text or on literary devices, but rather on a broader societal topic that the text illuminated. Despite such differences, the L1 teachers all emphasised the importance of creating a safe and motivating learning environment, developing dialogic classroom practices to encourage independent thinking and promote learner voice and agency, and regarded critical literacies as a means to active citizenship.

French and Norwegian social studies teachers also identified the same overarching goal for critical literacies in their reflections—developing their learners' intellectual autonomy and agency as future citizens—but differed in their approaches to working with critical literacies in their classrooms. Activities tended to be more disciplinary and content-centred in France, with teachers drawing on their subject expertise, while Norwegian teachers focused on developing critical literacy skills and attitudes related to broader and less subject-specific topics. As an example, Norwegian teachers focused on current topics (environment/global warming, political ideologies and democracy, refugees, digital awareness) while French teachers emphasised topics directly related to their curriculum (e.g. studying antiquity through Asterix, assessing the Bible as a historical source, or identifying power relations in propaganda posters). Despite such differences, the teachers reported similar developments in their critical literacy beliefs and practices. Firstly, they all moved from critical literacy as a self-centred logical skill (evaluating and defending own opinions) to a more empathic attitude (being open to dialogue and the perspectives of others, including the disadvantaged), which was seen an integral part of everyday life, and not only a practice reserved for classroom contexts. Secondly, the teachers' practices moved towards more interaction and dialogism in class, especially in the French context, traditionally more hierarchical and teacher-centred.

While L1 and social studies teachers in the CLAE project differed in their initial approaches to working with critical literacies, the EFL teachers shared largely similar focuses and concerns. In line with the multimodal focus in the field, French and Norwegian EFL teachers conceptualised critical literacy work in the EFL classroom as comprising a strong visual literacy element. On the one hand, visuals (pictures, newspaper images, videos, films, graphic novels) were used to aid comprehension. On the other hand, visuals were employed to promote critical visual literacies and critical thinking, that is, to foster multiperspectivity, to facilitate discussions about the ways in which visual images position the viewer and invite certain textual interpretations, and to stimulate discussions about social responsibility. The English teachers shared common concerns regarding critical literacy work in their subject, finding it particularly challenging due to the learners' relatively low EFL proficiency levels and agreeing that to work in-depth with critical literacy required a great degree of both language and visual scaffolding, which they did not always have enough time to provide due to curricular requirements. Nevertheless, the teachers all underlined the relevance of critical literacies for raising language learners' awareness of representations and cultural stereotypes, as well as the importance of enacting critical literacies themselves by taking learner concerns as starting points, encouraging multiple perspectives, legitimising learners' viewpoints and promoting learner agency.

Across subjects, French teachers often maintained an emphasis on disciplinary skill development and text analysis in their initial critical literacy lessons, while Norwegian teachers tended to focus on larger social issues and learners' active participation. Such differences align with critical literacy perspectives in the respective countries, but may also be the result of different teacher education systems and school cultures; indeed, French teachers in the project often expressed stronger disciplinary identities than the Norwegian teachers, who instead tended to emphasise their roles as educators, rather than subject teachers, as well as their responsibility for developing their learners' *Bildung*.

CLAE teachers also pointed to the importance of external factors affecting their critical literacy practices. While Norwegian critical literacy lesson sequences often lasted several hours or even weeks, French lesson sequences usually consisted of 1- to 2-hour sessions and French teachers indicated experiencing time-pressure when working with critical literacies. They also noted having less methodological and pedagogical flexibility than their Norwegian colleagues, a factor they considered a barrier to implementing critical literacies and which they related to the complexity, level of detail, and the large number of learning outcomes they were required to document. Due to the frequent grading requirements in lower secondary school for their 12- to 13-year-old learners, French teachers also faced the additional challenge of whether and how to formally assess critical literacy; Norwegian teachers, on the other hand, had 12- to 13-year-old learners who were still in primary school, and as such, had no formal grading.

Transnational Reflections on Critical Literacy Praxis

One of the most enriching aspects of the CLAE project was the extent to which French and Norwegian participants drew on classroom observations and discussions with their international colleagues to envision new ways of approaching their own critical literacies praxis. Transnational collaboration was encouraged in the form of collaborative seminars and workshops, joint observations of teaching practice, and digital exchanges through online platforms such as Facebook groups and a common project website (www.clae.no). Through common workshops in the second year of the project, the French and Norwegian teachers collaboratively designed critical literacy lesson sequences within their subject-disciplines, which they subsequently taught in their respective countries. The topics covered ranged from gender stereotypes to environmental awareness and critical media literacy.

Reflecting on the workshop sessions, the teachers underlined the extent to which the teacher exchanges and co-design of critical literacy lessons had been enriching for their own development as critical literacy educators. Their joint lesson sequences drew on strengths from both national contexts and addressed shared concerns of how to develop learners' critical awareness of societal issues, how to encourage dialogic practices in the critical literacy classroom, and how to assess critical literacy development. Despite differences in national curricula and school contexts, teachers noted that the best ideas had emerged from the interaction between the French and Norwegian teachers. For the French teachers, used to working independently, the collaborative design of lessons was a new and enriching experience, which they hoped to implement within their own national contexts, while Norwegian teachers highlighted the theoretical and subject expertise of their French colleagues.

Through the meeting of different teaching cultures, teachers were able to better reflect on the opportunities and barriers for enacting critical literacy within their own educational frameworks. Discussions moved from an initial emphasis on differences in educational contexts and practices to a consideration and understanding of the other's perspectives, viewed as key elements in the development of the teachers' critical awareness and critical literacies praxis. Engaging in a transnational community of inquiry and practice centred on critical literacies led teachers to critically reflect on their social responsibility as teachers, as well as to efforts to encourage critical literacy work within their greater school communities. In the reflections following the teaching of their common lesson plans, teachers emphasised the importance of dialogic practices for fostering critical literacies, conceptualised both as the ability to discuss and problematise established values and structures in texts and societies, and as a means of socially and critically engaging with others and with the world (Hébert & Lépine, 2013). Several teachers reported that the professional development towards more critically literate and dialogic practices within their classrooms had led to a renewed sense of motivation and a reflection on their role as teachers, as well as to increased engagement from their learners.

For the authors, partaking in CLAE opened for reflections on the power relationships inherent in educational research, a consideration of research as a collaborative process rather than a product, and to renewed efforts to negotiate spaces for critical literacies in their teacher education classrooms (Vasquez, Tate, & Harste, 2013). The CLAE community of practice extended beyond the initial school contexts to include the development of critical literacy practices within teacher education, with CLAE teachers invited to contribute to university courses, the integration of critical literacy perspectives into existing history education courses and the design of a new EFL course focused exclusively on critical literacies pedagogy.

Engaging in transnational reflections on critical literacies praxis, through an increased awareness of the educational perspectives and practices of others, had an impact on the social and educational engagement of researchers, teachers and learners alike. The authors argue that the development of transnational critical literacies praxis is fostered through the establishment of strong transnational communities of inquiry and practice, especially within the field of educational research where national boundaries and priorities are deeply integrated into teachers' practices, understandings and policies. The second phase of the CLAE project (2019–2022) therefore includes additional English and Spanish researchers and teachers in an extended transnational community of inquiry and practice, which continues to focus on collaboratively developing dialogic critical literacy practices across national boundaries to encourage the integration of social justice perspectives within and beyond the critical literacies classroom.

References

Aas, S., & Vestgården, T. (2014). *Skammens historie. Den norske stats mørke sider*. Cappelen-Damm.

Bancel, N., Bernault, F., Blanchard, P., Boubeker, A., Mbembe, A., & Vergès, F. (2010). *Ruptures postcoloniales: Les nouveaux visages de la société française*. La Découverte.

Bland, J. (Ed.). (2018). *Using literature in English language education: Challenging reading for 8–18-year olds.* Bloomsbury.

Bland, J., & Mourão, S. (2017). Editorial: Intercultural learning and critical literacy—There is no single story, *CLELEjournal, 5*(2), ii–iv.

Blikstad-Balas, M. (2016). "You get what you need": A study of students' attitudes towards using Wikipedia when doing school assignments, *Scandinavian Journal of Educational Research, 60*(6), 594–608. https://doi.org /10.1080/00313831.2015.1066428

Blikstad-Balas, M., & Foldvik, M. C. (2017). Kritisk literacy i norskfaget—hva legger elever vekt på når de vurderer tekster fra internett? *Norsklæreren, 4,* 28–39.

Blikstad-Balas, M., & Tønnesson, J. L. (2020). *Inn i sakens prosa.* Universitetsforlaget.

Brown, C. W. (2019). "I don't want to be stereotypical, but . . .": Norwegian EFL learners' awareness of and willingness to challenge visual stereotypes. *Intercultural Communication Education, 2*(3), 120–141. https:// dx.doi.org/10.29140/ice.v2n3.194

Brown, C. W., & Habegger-Conti, J. (2017). Visual representations of indigenous cultures in Norwegian EFL textbooks. *Nordic Journal of Modern Language Methodology, 5*(1), 16–34. https://doi.org/10.46364/njmlm. v5i1.369

Corroy, L., & Jehel, S. (2016). *Stéréotypes, discriminations et éducation aux médias.* L'Harmattan.

Dagenais, D. (2012). Littératies multimodales et perspectives critiques. *Recherches en Didactique des Langues et des Cultures. Les Cahiers de l'Acedle, 9*(2), 15–46. https://doi.org/10.4000/rdlc.2338

De Cock, L., & Perreira, I. (Eds.) (2019). *Les Pédagogies critiques.* Agone.

Dessingué, A. (2016). Dynamisk kulturarv, kritisk literacy og (fler)kulturforståelse i norsk grunnskole? *Nordidactica, 2,* 22–46.

Dessingué, A. (2020). Developing critical historical consciousness: Re-thinking the dynamics between history and memory in history education, *Nordidactica, 1,* 1–17.

Eilertsen, A., & Veum, A. (2019). Kritisk lesing av historiske sakstekster. *Norsklæreren, 1,* 1–14.

Ekeland, T. G. (2017). Enactment of Sámi past in school textbooks: Towards multiple pasts for future making. *Scandinavian Journal of Educational Research, 61*(3), 319–332. https://doi.org/10.1080/00313831.2016.1147 067

Éthier, M. A., Lefrançois, D., & Audigier, F. (2018). *Pensée critique, enseignement de l'histoire et de la citoyenneté.* De Boeck Superieur.

Falaize, B. (2014). L'enseignement des sujets controversés dans l'école française: Les nouveaux fondements de l'histoire scolaire en France? *Revista Tempo e Argumento, 6*(11), 193–223. https://doi. org/10.5965/2175180306112014193

Ferrer, M., & Wetlesen, A. (Eds.). (2019). *Kritisk tenkning i samfunnsfag.* Universitetsforlaget.

Fraenkel, B., & Mbodj-Pouye, A. (2010). Introduction: *Les New Literacy studies,* jalons historiques et perspectives actuelles. *Langage et Société, 133*(3), 7–24. https://doi.org/10.3917/ls.133.0007

Freire, P. (1970). *Pedagogy of the oppressed.* Penguin.

Freire, P., & Macedo, D. (1987). *Literacy: Reading the word and the world.* Routledge.

Giroux, H. (2011). *On critical pedagogy.* Bloomsbury.

Greenwood, J., & Sæbø, A. B. (2015). Literacy, creativity and democracy: Creative strategies for teaching critical literacy & implications for teacher education e-article, *20*(1). https://doi.org/10.15663/wje.v20i1.182

Grossmann, F. (1999). Littératie, compréhension et interprétation des textes. *Repères, recherches en didactique du français langue maternelle, 19,* 139–166. https://doi.org/10.3406/reper.1999.2294

Habegger-Conti, J. (2015). Critical literacy in the ESL classroom: Bridging the gap between old and new media. *Nordic Journal of Modern Language Methodology, 3*(2), 106–127. https://doi.org/10.46364/njmlm.v3i2.170

Hébert, M., & Lépine, M. (2013). De l'intérêt de la notion de littératie en francophonie: Un état des lieux en sciences de l'éducation. *Globe, 16*(1), 25–43, https://doi.org/10.7202/1018176ar

Ihadjadene, M., Saemmer, A., & Baltz, C. (Eds.). (2015). *Culture informationnelle: vers une propédeutique du numérique.* Hermann.

Janks, H. (2010). *Literacy and power.* Routledge.

Jewitt, C., & Kress, G. (Eds.). (2003). *Multimodal literacy.* Peter Lang.

Kiyindou, A., Barbey, F., & Corroy-Labardens, L. (Eds.). (2016). *De l'éducation par les médias à l'éducation aux médias.* L'Harmattan.

Krulatz, A., Dahl, A., & Flognfeldt, M. E. (2018). *Enacting multilingualism: From research to teaching practice in the English classroom.* Cappelen Damm.

Lipman, M. (2003). *Thinking in education* (2nd ed.). Cambridge University Press.

Lorentzen, G., & Røthing, Å. (2017). Demokrati og kritisk tenkning i lærebøker. *Norsk Pedagogisk Tidsskrift, 101*(2), 119–130. https://doi.org/10.18261/issn.1504-2987-2017-02-02

Luke, A. (2012). Critical literacy: Foundational notes. *Theory Into Practice, 51*(1), 4–11. https://doi.org/10.108 0/00405841.2012.636324

Marquilló-Larruy, M. (2012). Littératie et multimodalité ici & là-bas . . . En réponse à Diane Dagenais. *Recherches en Didactique des Langues et des Cultures. Les Cahiers de l'Acedle, 9*(2), 47–84. https://doi.org/10.4000/ rdlc.2350

Martel, V., Sala, C., Boutin, J. F., & Villagordo, É. (2018). Développer des compétences en littératie visuelle et multimodal par le croisement des disciplines histoire/français/arts: l'enquête culturelle. *Revue de recherches en littératie médiatique multimodale, 7.* https://doi.org/10.7202/1048357ar

Molinié, M., & Moore, D. (2012). Les littératies: une notion en questions en didactique des langues (NeQ). *Recherches en didactique des langues et des cultures, 9*(2), 1–10. https://doi.org/10.4000/rdlc.2757

Normand, L. (2020). From blind spot to hotspot: Representations of the 'immigrant others' in Norwegian curriculum/schoolbooks (1905–2013). *Journal of Curriculum Studies.* https://doi.org/10.1080/00220272.2 020.1734665

Normand, S., & Savić, M. (2018). Fostering intercultural competence through process drama in EFL teacher education. In N. Lazarević, T. Paunović, & L. Marković (Eds.), *Teaching languages and cultures: Developing competencies, re-thinking practices* (pp. 163–186). Cambridge Scholars Publishing.

Norton, B., & Toohey, K. (2004). *Critical pedagogies and language learning.* Cambridge University Press.

Painchaud, G., d'Anglejan, A., Armand, F., & Jezak, M. (1993). Diversité culturelle et littératie. *Repères, essais en éducation,* (15), 77–94.

Pereira, I., Séverac, P., De Aranjo Mameda, M., Joigneaux, C., Chaar, N., Pettier, J.-C., & Le Roux, R. (2016). Un exemple de recherche sur l'esprit critique à l'Université. *Diotime, 70*(10).

Sæbø, A. B., Eriksson, S. A., & Allern, T. H. (2017). *Drama, teater og demokrati. Antologi I: I barnehage, skole, museum og høyere utdanning.* Fagbokforlaget.

Skaftun, A. (2020). Rom for muntlighet? Språklig tenkning og tekstsamtaler i norskfagets literacy. *Nordic Journal of Literacy Research, 6*(1), 238–258. https://doi.org/10.23865/njlr.v6.2022

Smidt, J. (2011). Finding voices in a changing world: Standard language education as a site for developing critical literacies. *Scandinavian Journal of Educational Research, 55*(6), 655–669. https://doi.org/10.1080/003138 31.2011.594608

The New London Group. (1996). A pedagogy of multiliteracies: Designing social futures. *Harvard Educational Review, 66*(1), 60–92. https://doi.org/10.17763/haer.66.1.17370n67v22j160u

Vasquez, V. M., Tate, S. L., & Harste, J. C. (2013). *Negotiating critical literacies with teachers: Theoretical foundations and pedagogical resources for pre-service and in-service contexts.* Routledge.

Veum, A., & Skovholt, K. (2020). *Kritisk literacy i klasserommet.* Universitetsforlaget.

Wacquant, L. (2008). *Urban outcasts. A comparative sociology of advanced marginality.* Polity Press.

Wagner, D. A. (2019). Critical thinking and use of film in Norwegian lower secondary history classrooms. *History Education Research Journal, 16*(2), 274–290. https://doi.org/10.18546/HERJ.16.2.08

Wenger, E., & Wenger-Trayner, B. (2015). *Communities of practice. A brief introduction.* Retrieved from http:// wenger-trayner.com/introduction-to-communities-of-practice

2.21

CRITICAL LITERACIES IN SOUTH ASIA

Pramod K. Sah and Prem Phyak

Introduction: Sociopolitical Context of South Asia

South Asia comprises eight contiguous countries (Afghanistan, Bangladesh, Bhutan, India, Maldives, Nepal, Pakistan, and Sri Lanka), with diverse linguistic, cultural, and religious practices. The region has unique geographical features and diverse ethnic, indigenous, and caste groups. All these countries, except for Nepal, have a long history of British colonization. Coloniality has had a strong impact on shaping socio-historical changes, including literacy and education, in the region. Scholars have often shown a connection between the colonial processes and social divisions based on class, castes, religions, and hence relations of power along the lines of such social categories (Bose & Jalal, 1998). This was particularly the case when the associates of the British colonizers (during the colonial era), who were generally from higher social class and caste backgrounds, in the Indian subcontinent received higher social and educational privileges. The legacy of such privileges still perpetuates unequal power in South Asian societies. The hierarchical caste and class system continues to shape various communities' access to literacy, education, and public services in the region.

Given that all literacy practices are situated within sociocultural, political, and ideological contexts, the understanding and practices of critical literacy within the South Asian context inevitably differ from how they are understood in Western contexts. For example, as Canagarajah (2000) argues, while there are serious concerns for food, clothing, shelter, and safety in South Asia, education and literacy learning make a close connection with material realities of the communities. Literacy programs accordingly focus on addressing issues such as poverty, food deficiency, gender, and health. While some practices may overlap with those practiced in Western societies, the major distinctions are there in terms of unique South Asian political economy, ideological constructs (e.g., authoritarian and populist politics), life struggles, and colonial legacies, which have defined literacy education in the region.

The colonial regimes that shaped the language ecology and policies in the past are still alive, especially in the selection and promotion of the media of literacy instruction. English was established as a dominant medium of literacy instruction during the colonial regime and was made available to an exclusive group of elites, who associated themselves with the colonizers or those with sufficient capital (social, political, and economic) needed for elite education. Currently, the use of English medium in education has become a *cultural paradigm* (Sah, 2020a) for people from all socioeconomic backgrounds, and those who cannot afford an English-medium education face both material and social discriminations (Canagarajah & Ashraf, 2013). Although such social and cultural relations in

    DOI: 10.4324/9781003023425-33

the region are a product of processes of constant (re)negotiation and reformation during the colonial era, especially since the last decades of the last century, it has also been shaped by the global capitalist world and its associated social, economic, and cultural forces (Boss & Jalal, 1998; Sah, 2020b). For example, South Asian nation-states' adaptation of neoliberal developmental policies has justified public–private partnerships for providing educational services, which in turn has motivated a commodified education system, and human capital rational for individual and collective socioeconomic development (Regmi, 2016).

Although India is the fastest growing economy, the South Asian region, in general, is significantly lagging in terms of its economic, social, and educational development. For example, the United Nation's (2020) report describes all South Asian countries as developing economies with an average GDP per capita of $2,100, in comparison to the world average of $11,300. Most South Asian countries are still struggling to address poverty and other issues tied with social and environmental conditions like climate change, labor productivity, conservatism, and inequalities, which can have an important meaning for literacy education in the region. The young labor force is the greater capital of the region, with a high potential for economic development, although the unemployment crisis is acute (United Nation, 2020). Because of such crises in the region, at least 40 percent of youth in India do not have access to schools/universities, employment, or training; and 30 percent of such deprived youth are each in Afghanistan, Bangladesh, Pakistan, and Sri Lanka. These data show the lack of opportunities for literacy education for the poor. The region has become one of the epicenters for various supranational organizations (e.g., UNESCO, UNICEF) and aid agencies (e.g., USAID, Australian Aid), including the World Bank, which have invested a significant amount of aid for literacy education in the region.

Many children need to work with their family members for their livelihood, thus they normally wish for a short-term education with quick employment placement. Schools themselves do not constitute equally quality learning environments, often due to linguistic and cultural gaps between community and school. Hence, what actually constitutes literacy education in the hierarchical South Asian social structures is a crucial subject of analysis to provide insights for educators, policymakers, and funding agencies.

Educational Contexts of South Asia

South Asia has embraced the importance of education for social, political, and economic development (Unterhalter, 2006). Since the beginning of the century, there has been a greater focus on access and equity, with an emphasis on gender and marginalized communities. The nation-states in the region have shown their commitment to implement global education programs by participating in landmark global initiatives and declarations. Such programs have emphasized the need for connecting education with human development, such as the literacy and education initiative of organizations such as UNESCO. According to UNESCO's (2015) report on the achievement of the Education for All program in South Asia, the gross enrollment rate in primary education has increased by 78 percent between 1999 and 2013 in Afghanistan, 41 percent in Bhutan, 23 percent in Pakistan, 7 percent in India (1999–2014), and 13 percent in Nepal (1999–2014). Similarly, there have been positive achievements in gender parity indexes (except for Pakistan): between 2010 and 2013, the gender parity index for primary education was 1.05, 1.03, 1.0, and 0.99, respectively, in Bangladesh, Bhutan, Sri Lanka, and Nepal. The percentage of primary age out-of-school children, in the region, has also declined by 73 percent, from 37.7 million to 9.8 million during 2000–2015. Similarly, as seen in Table 2.21.1, adult literacy (age 15 and above) has also increased by 18 percent between 2001 and 2015. Regarding gender disparities, however, an average of 15 percent of the male populations are more literate than females in the region.

Table 2.21.1 Per capita income and literacy rate (15 + years) in South Asia

Countries	Per Capita Income (US$)	15+ Year Literacy Rate (%)		
		Male	Female	Total
Afghanistan	520.9	55	30	43
Bangladesh	1,698.3	77	71	74
Bhutan	3,243.2	75	57	67
India	2,010.0	82	66	74
Maldives	10,330.6	97	98	98
Nepal	1,033.9	79	60	68
Pakistan	1,482.4	71	46	59
Sri Lanka	4,102.5	93	91	92

Source: World Bank (2018)

Despite such positive achievements, there are still some critical concerns in terms of access, equity, and quality in education, often stemming from issues like child labor, unequal social structures (Based on class, castes, ethnicity, and religious hierarchies), linguistic challenges, poverty, armed conflicts, and disasters. Other macro social structural and ideological problems such as nationalist ideology (based on religion, language, and ethnicity), patriarchy, social beliefs, and superstitions are creating unfavorable situations for minoritized (e.g., religious, language, and ethnic), transgender, and female students to access quality literacy education. The data show that 11.3 million primary level children and 20.6 million lower secondary level children are still out of school in the region, which makes up the most out-of-the school children in the world (UNICEF, 2020). Most of such children are girls, religious and ethnolinguistic minorities, special needs children, and the economically impoverished. Similarly, millions of children attending primary schools graduate without mastering the fundamental skills of basic numeracy and literacy. For example, as the report of Nepal's Early Grade Reading Assessment (EGRA) shows 37 percent of second graders and 19 percent of third graders could not read a single word of Nepali (a dominant national medium of literacy instruction). Furthermore, EGRA, a US-funded literacy project, is itself an example of ways dominant monolingual ideologies of literacy learning are perpetuated—the funding is focused on teaching Nepali rather than focusing on minoritized languages and multilingual literacy learning.

There is also a gender disparity in education. According to UNICEF (2020), more girls (82%) than boys (41%) are likely to never go to school, and the girls who attend school are not necessarily receiving quality learning in the region. This issue is coupled with other forms of discrimination like class, caste, ethnicity, and religion. For example, girls from poor families and Muslim backgrounds are more likely to never attend school or drop out early. This issue stems from the ideology of patriarchy at both house-hold and societal levels, constructing assumptions that girls do not need education (Upadhaya & Sah, 2019). In a society like Sri Lanka, with a greater gender parity in education, there is lack of equal employment opportunities for young men and women (Kamat, 2014). Similarly, gender parity is observed in terms of enrollment in higher education (sometimes women's numbers surpassing that of men) and preference of disciplines. Women are concentrated in Social Sciences and Humanities majors, while boys have much more access to pure sciences and professional education, which shapes future opportunities in the job market (Kamat, 2014).

Finally, there are more general and significant gaps between the attainment of education and access to the labor market. As Dewan and Sarkar (2017) report, education in South Asia provides fundamental literacy and numeracy, often falling short of equipping young people with the skills needed in the job market and, therefore, they argue that school education should align with the job market and prioritize life and soft skills for employment. Doing so will decrease drop-out rates in schools and sustain the labor market with relevant skills, importantly addressing the concerns of inequalities and economic insecurity (Erling, 2014).

Critical Literacies in South Asia: Theory and Pedagogy

Theoretical Developments

Although there is lack of academic works on critical literacies in South Asia, there are some interesting practices of critical literacies in the grassroots communities and organizations, often based on a traditional apprenticeship approach (e.g., carpentry, pottery, bamboo works). Regarding academic works on critical literacies in the region, the existing studies have drawn on postcolonial theory (e.g., Nayar, 2011), Freirean critical pedagogy (e.g., Canagarajah, 2000; Liyanage, 2012), gross national happiness approach (Young, 2012), and New Literacy Studies (e.g., Azza, 2007; Maddox, 2005; Rao & Hossain, 2011; Robinson-Pant, 2000). Most studies on critical literacies have defined literacy education from somewhat different perspectives than those discussed in the Western scholarship. In South Asia, literacy education is dominantly framed within a *livelihood approach*, which is to develop the skills and capabilities to sustain daily lives. Therefore, literacy education is focused on (a) alleviating poverty; (b) developing health and financial literacy skills; and (c) ensuring socio-political and economic participation of different social groups—mostly women and marginalized communities—in the mainstream social structure. This approach is grounded on global education campaigns such as Education for All, Millennium Development Goals, and Sustainable Development Goals which are funded mostly by international aid agencies.

Empowerment, livelihood, and development are major ideas shaping critical literacy education in the region. In Bhola's (2009) words, literacy in the region is perceived "as a human invention that redefined its human inventors and then humanity itself," which makes people "empowered, livelihoods improve, their children join (and stay longer in) school, family health improves, and childbirths are spaced" along with reduced gender violence and improved spiritual life (p. 373). Drawing on the context of Bangladesh, Bhola (2009) argues that literacy creates a possibility for a decent life for the poor and minorities, which can be achieved through *innovations* and *partnerships* of the state, civil society, private sector, international donors, and individual philanthropists. The notion of *partnership* is, for example, visible in Afghanistan's National Literacy Action Plan (2012–2015) that, in addition to partnering with international organizations, local communities would be mobilized to provide "house, land, and/or contribute in cash or kind to build a venue for conducting literacy courses" (p. 10). Both local communities and international organizations are invested in providing resources for conducting literacy programs. In Nepal, UNESCO's (2017) meta-analysis of the studies on literacy education shows that the ongoing literacy programs have contributed to strengthening "enablement, enfranchisement and empowerment" of the women and marginalized communities (p. 8). The study claims that Nepal's literacy programs, for example, have contributed to the social transformation of illiterate women by helping them to become aware of the value of education and take leadership positions in society. In addition, the study shows that literacy programs have also developed women's financial literacy which eventually has supported their livelihood. Similarly, in Pakistan, Denuwara and Gunawardena (2017) focus on the importance of health literacy in the mainstream literacy curricula to help students develop an awareness of health issues for a good life.

Critical literacy functions as a counter-hegemony to both empower the minoritized groups and challenge the dominant literacy practices. In South Asia, critical literacy initiatives are designed in a project model that includes a series of participatory actions, particularly with women groups and minoritized communities. This model may not always draw on Freire's concepts but on locally situated needs and actions. Literacy programs in South Asia have built on subaltern literacy practices, especially for religious, regional, class, gender, and linguistic minority groups. For example, Rao and Hossain's (2011) study in rural Bangladesh recognizes learning in Madrasas (an affordable education system for the poor) as a strategy to resist a dominant literacy approach of formal secular schooling. Learning in Madrasas focuses "on character and morality as represented through an Islamic identity, alongside communitarian values, is seen as important for maintaining a degree of social cohesion" (Rao & Hossain, 2011, p. 623). For them, morality and public ethics are "essential features of literacy learning," which are important in the time of insecurities stemming from a global capitalist production system (p. 631).

In the context of Bhutan, Young (2012) discusses the role of critical literacy in enhancing the values and principles of gross national happiness, emphasizing the holistic development of children through literacy learning. Studies have also analyzed literacy as a political tool to transform discriminatory social structures and practices in South Asia. As Maddox (2005) deliberates, subaltern literacy learning emphasizes "the processes of negotiating and resisting over new gender roles and identities," arguing for the empowerment of girls through literacy education (p. 125). For example, Latif (2009) discusses how critical literacy has given voice to Pakistani girls and contributed to developing their critical awareness about gender inequalities in their own country. Robinson-Pant (2000) takes an ethnographic approach to analyze the role of literacy to empower women and transform gender-based inequalities in Nepal. Considering literacy as an ideological approach, she argues that the literacy programs in Nepal have contributed to developing critical agency of women to resist the patriarchal ideologies of Nepal.

Further, Nayar (2011) builds on postcolonial critical literacy to analyze how *Bhimayana*, a graphic novel, has been used as a tool to resist the cultural and political oppression of Dalits in India. While analyzing the images and narratives used in the novel, he argues that the reading of such novels helps Dalits and other groups understand and challenge the oppressive caste system in India and fosters "an anterior moment to a larger formatting of the public space through the production, dissemination and consumption of such stories" (p. 19). Holland and Skinner (2008) analyze literacy within social movements in Nepal. They consider songbooks written and performed during social movements as *literacy events* that empower women to resist patriarchy and the exclusion of women in society. For them, women's songs in social movements have potential to "effect social, cultural and political change" and "evoke liberator worlds" (p. 850). Similarly, as Canagarajah (2000) argues, in the context of Sri Lanka, critical literacy enables teachers and students to resist Western epistemologies and methodologies in education while promoting local knowledge in postcolonial contexts. Liyanage (2012) also claims that critical literacy provides opportunities to bring local ideas and cultural practices in learning literacy, especially in second/foreign languages.

Pedagogical Developments

Critical literacy in South Asian countries has adopted a wide range of pedagogical approaches. In Nepal, for example, Parajuli and Enslin (1990) discuss *storytelling, songs*, and *drama* as pedagogical approaches to raising critical awareness of women through literacy activities. In these activities, women are engaged in telling stories about their own life struggles and express them in different modes such as songs and dramas. Barton (1991) uses *oral history, language experiences approach*, and *photography* as methods to develop alternative perspectives about social values, knowledge, and identities through literacy in Nepal. In these activities, minoritized people are engaged in sharing their past and tell their lived experiences related to language difficulties. They are also engaged in photo-taking and description activities to collectively raise their critical awareness and resist dominant discourses. Tuladhar's (1994) adoption of *participatory video making* is an example of raising critical awareness of

Nepali women about social issues that impact their livelihood. In this activity, women make videos to capture social issues that they have observed and discuss how these issues could be addressed.

Chitrakar and Maddox (2008) discuss a community literacy approach that focuses on the development of localized literacy practices to empower communities. Keeping community participation at the center, they used the publication of wall newspapers and engaged villagers in the documentation of daily activities such as the process of vegetable production and distribution. Sharma and Phyak (2017) use *dialogue* and *workshops* to prepare in-service teachers to use critical pedagogy in English language teaching. Wijetunge and Alahakoon (2005), in the context of Sri Lanka, discuss how a *workshop approach* to literacy learning can be effective to help students develop their critical skills to assess information, which contributes to their empowerment while engaging in the process of learning (through) literacy texts. This approach requires teachers to be trained in creating resources and engaging students in identifying, exploring, creating, assessing, and applying information in the learning process with attention to power dynamics.

ICT-integration is another approach in critical literacy instruction in South Asia. In Bangladesh, Anwaruddin (2015), for example, makes a case of how ICT tools can promote multiliteracies in language and literacy curricula. He argues that ICT helps teachers understand the complex relationship among *content*, *pedagogy*, and *technology* and their critical consciousness about oppressive social and cultural practices. In Afghanistan and Maldives, UNESCO (2008) has proposed a competency-based ICT literacy with (a) fundamental knowledge approach (awareness of technologies and appreciation of their relevance), (b) technical skills approach (use of technology to encompass information and knowledge), and (c) critical assessment approach (understanding that ICT acquisition and use impacts on personal and social development). In the Maldives, Azza (2007) adds that it is crucial to have a sustained (e.g., ten years of schooling) instruction for technological literacy to ensure equity and access in education. Similarly, Singha (2009), in the context of Bhutan, also explores access to digital literacy among girls and argues that literacy has played a crucial role for girls in terms of their increased opportunities with higher levels of education and access to digital literacy.

In some countries, literacy programs are designed to develop spirituality. Young (2012), in the context of Bhutan, discusses the pedagogy to enhance the values and principles of spirituality. Young argues that building strong human interrelationships strengthens a holistic ecological environment in the classroom that leads to the development of critical pedagogy. Such pedagogy eventually contributes to strengthening happiness which "gives rise to both an inner and outer transformation that can move toward social and ecological harmony" (p. 20).

Learner-autonomy is another approach in critical literacy education in South Asia. Iyer (2010) explores preservice teachers' beliefs about the adaptation of critical literacy in the context of India. The study shows that critical literacy pedagogy can be implemented by creating student-centered classrooms and providing learners with autonomy in the learning process. Iyer argues that this approach disrupts the long-standing domination of teacher-centered and textbook-based approaches to literacy instruction. Iyer's (2010) claims are in line with Azza's (2007) findings that critical literacy should be student-centered and culturally relevant to produce diverse learning opportunities.

Conclusion and Future Directions

We draw three major conclusions from the review of the status of critical literacy in South Asia. First, most critical literacy programs and activities are designed and implemented as part of global educational campaigns and supported by supranational organizations and aid agencies. Although such initiatives do not explicitly mention critical literacy is their goal, the activities they do with communities and individuals have a transformative role and political implications. Considered as part of developmental programs, literacy programs in the region focus mostly on women, minoritized groups, and rural populations. Literacy programs are taken as part of social and economic develop-ment through income generation. However, critical literacy has not yet been an integral part of formal education which still promotes exclusionary knowledge through teacher-centric and text-book-based pedagogies.

Second, the efforts to integrate critical literacy in the formal education system face structural and ideological challenges. As Iyer's (2010) study in India shows that teachers find it challenging to implement critical literacy because of the deep-rooted teacher-centered teaching and lack of learner autonomy. Third, critical literacy activities, in the region, do not explicitly take a political stance to resist and transform structural inequalities. Rather they take literacy as one of the major tools for social empowerment and better livelihood of the poor and marginalized communities. This kind of implicit critical literacy takes a participatory approach to engage communities in a series of actions through which they transform themselves and communities. This approach does not put ideological analysis at the forefront.

With these conclusions, we suggest two major ideas for future research and policy discourse. First, there is a strong need for integrating critical literacy in the mainstream education and engaging students in exploring and analyzing critical sociopolitical issues. One of the major issues, which has not been much discussed in the literature, is the oppressive history and impact of caste-based social structure in the region. Future researchers could focus on how teachers and schools can develop and integrate critical literacy activities in the formal education system. Second, future studies could focus on teachers' agency in negotiating the existing structures and policies to create space for critical literacy in formal education.

Finally, we argue that academics can play a critical role in educating teachers and policymakers to create space for critical literacy. As academics, we need to engage ourselves with the broader community of teachers and teacher educators to understand, analyze, and transform sociopolitical inequalities through a range of activities such as workshops, critical ethnography, and a community-based participatory approach. In South Asian context, it is important to focus on collaborative approaches, building on local contexts and complexities, to develop the actions that address local needs. Since the region has diverse sociopolitical issues (linguistic, ethnic/caste, class, gender, etc.), a one-size-fits-all approach to critical literacy may not work. This approach involves collaboration between scholars from within and outside of the country.

References

Anwaruddin, S. M. (2015). ICTs in language and literacy education in Bangladesh: A Critical Review. *Critical Issues in Education, 18*(1), 1–11.

Azza, F. (2007). *EFA Mid decade assessment.* Ministry of Education.

Barton, D. (1991). Photographing literacy practice in Kathmandu. *Center for Language in Social Life, Working Paper Series 27,* Lancaster, UK.

Bhola, H. S. (2009). Reconstructing literacy as an innovation for sustainable development: A policy advocacy for Bangladesh. *International Journal of Lifelong Education, 28*(3), 371–382.

Bose, S., & Jalal, A. (1998). *Modern South Asia: History, culture, political economy.* Routledge.

Canagarajah, A. S. (2000). The fortunate traveler: Shuttling between communities and literacies by economy class. In D. Belcher & U. Connor (Eds.), *Reflections on multiliterate lives* (pp. 23–37). Multilingual Matters.

Canagarajah, A. S., & Ashraf, H. (2013). Multilingual and education in South Asia: Resolving policy/practice dilemmas. *Annual Review of Applied Linguistics, 33,* 258–285.

Chitrakar, R., & Maddox, B. (2008). A community literacy project: Nepal. In B. V. Street & N. H. Hornberger (Eds.), *Encyclopedia of language and education* (2nd ed., pp. 191–205). Springer.

Denuwara, H. M. B. H., & Gunawardena, N. S. (2017). Level of health literacy and factors associated with it among school teachers in an education zone in Colombo, Sri Lanka. *BMC Public Health, 17,* 631.

Dewan, S., & Sarkar, U. (2017). *From education to employment: Preparing South Asian youth for the world of work.* UNICEF. Retrieved from www.unicef.org/rosa/media/1326/file/Preparing%20South%20Asian%20Youth%20for%20the%20World%20of%20Work.pdf

Erling, E. J. (2014). *The role of English in skills development in South Asia: Policies, interventions, and existing evidence.* British Council.

Holland, D., & Skinner, D. (2008). Literacies of distinction: (Dis)empowerment in social movements. *The Journal of Development Studies, 44*(6), 849–862.

Iyer, R. (2010). Literacy models across nations: Literacy and critical literacy in teacher training programs in India. *Procedia Social and Behavioral Sciences, 2,* 4424–4428.

Kamat, S. (2014). Gender and education in South Asia. In L. Fernandes (Ed.), *Routledge handbook of gender in South Asia* (pp. 277–290). Routledge.

Latif, A. (2009). A critical analysis of school enrollment and literacy rates of girls and women in Pakistan. *Educational Studies, 45*(5), 424–439.

Liyanage, I. (2012). Critical pedagogy in ESL/EFL teaching in South-east Asia: Practices and challenges with examples from Sri Lanka. In K. Sung & R. Pederson (Eds.), *Critical ELT practices in Asia: Key issues, practices, and possibilities* (pp. 137–151). Sense Publishers.

Maddox, B. (2005). *Real options for policy and practice in Bangladesh.* Background paper prepared for the Education for All Global Monitoring Report 2006 Literacy for Life.

Nayar, P. K. (2011). Towards a postcolonial critical literacy: *Bhimayana* and the Indian graphic novel. *Studies in South Asian Film and Media, 3*(1), 3–21.

Parajuli, P., & Enslin, E. (1990). From learning literacy to regenerating women's space: A story of women's empowerment in Nepal. *Convergence, 23*(1), 44–56.

Rao, N., & Hossain, M. I. (2011). Confronting poverty and educational inequalities: Madrasas as a strategy for contesting dominant literacy in rural Bangladesh. *International Journal of Educational Development, 31,* 623–633.

Regmi, K. D. (2016). World Bank in Nepal's education: Three decades of neoliberal reform. *Globalisation, Societies and Education, 15*(2), 188–201.

Robinson-Pant, A. (2000). Women and literacy: A Nepal perspective. *International Journal of Educational Development, 20*(4), 349–364.

Sah, P. K. (2020a). English-medium instruction in South Asian's multilingual schools: Unpacking the dynamics of ideological orientations, policy/practices, and democratic questions. *International Journal of Bilingual Education and Bilingualism.* https://doi.org/10.1080/13670050.2020.1718591.

Sah, P. K. (2020b). Reproduction of nationalist and neoliberal ideologies in Nepal's language and literacy policies. *Asia Pacific Journal of Education.* https://doi.org/10.1080/02188791.2020.1751063.

Sharma, B. K., & Phyak, P. (2017). Criticality as ideological becoming: Developing English teachers for critical pedagogy in Nepal. *Critical Inquiry in Language Studies, 14*(2–3), 210–238.

Singha, C. (2009). Effects of education and ICT use on gender relations in Bhutan. *Information Technologies and International Development, 5*(3), 21–34.

Tuladhar, S. (1994). Participatory video as a post-literacy activity for women in rural Nepal. *Convergence, 27*(2–3).

UNESCO. (2008). *Strategy framework for promoting ICT literacy in the Asia-Pacific region.* UNESCO Bangkok.

UNESCO. (2015). *Status, trends, and challenges of Education for All in South Asia (2000–2015): A summary report.* UNESCO Office.

UNESCO. (2017). *Reading the past, writing the future: A report on National Literacy Campaign and Literate Nepal Mission.* UNESCO Office.

UNICEF. (2020). *South Asia: Education.* Retrieved from www.unicef.org/rosa/what-we-do/education

United Nations. (2020). *World economic situation and prospects 2020.* Retrieved from www.un.org/development/desa/dpad/wpcontent/uploads/sites/45/WESP2020_FullReport.pdf

Unterhalter, E. (2006). *Measuring gender inequality in education in South Asia.* United Nations Children's Fund, Regional Office for South Asia.

Upadhaya, A., & Sah, P. K. (2019). Education, English language, and girls' development: Exploring gender-responsive policies and practices in Nepal. In S. Douglas, P. Kennett, R. Ingram, P. Dexter, & Y. Hutchinson (Eds.), *Creating an inclusive school environment* (pp. 105–114). British Council.

Wijetunge, P., & Alahakoon, U. P. (2005). Empowering 8: The information literacy model developed in Sri Lanka to underpin changing education paradigms of Sri Lanka. *Sri Lanka Journal of Librarianship & Information Management, 1*(1), 31–41.

World Bank. (2018). *South Asia.* Retrieved from https://data.worldbank.org/country/8S

Young, D. G. (2012). The role of critical pedagogy in enhancing the values and principles of Gross National Happiness in the Royal University of Bhutan. *Bhutan Journal of Research & Development, 1*(1), 13–22.

2.22

CRITICAL LITERACY IN UGANDA AND CONGO

The Urgency of Decolonizing Curricula

Jean Kaya and Amoni Kitooke

The East and Central African regions comprise, respectively, six and nine countries that are not politically, socio-culturally, and economically uniform. This chapter points to the influence of neo-colonialism on the current sociopolitical and educational contexts in two countries: Uganda in East Africa and Congo[1] in Central Africa. It draws on critical theories to suggest that a democratic and critical literacy education that provides "all students the opportunity to question, discover, and trans-form their futures" (Wallowitz, 2008, p. 1) be instituted in the two countries. We argue that educa-tion in Uganda and Congo will remain a tool for the denigration, distraction, and destruction of Ugandan and Congolese languages, cultures, and ways of knowing and being until citizens of these countries have attained an emancipatory criticality rooted in self-consciousness and implemented Afro-centric curricula informed by their own languages and epistemologies.

Sociopolitical Contexts in Congo and Uganda

Located astride the equator, Congo is bordered to the north by Cameroon and Central African Republic, the south and the east by the Democratic Republic of Congo (DRC), the south-west by Angola, and the west by Gabon. Seventy-five years after Europeans carved and claimed most of Africa at the Berlin Conference of 1884–1885, Congo gained independence from France, in 1960. Even so, the post-colonial Congo has known sociopolitical instability. Attempts to establish democracy are slow to yield (Balencie & De La Grange, 2001) and a long-lasting socio-economic crisis continues to impact the country. Congo is, ironically, rich with 90% of its economy based on oil exportation, but poor considering its socio-economic inequalities and the poverty level of the majority of the population. Relatedly, although the need to fight against established injustices and inequalities exists, Western-imposed supremacy maintains its colonial practices in different sectors, including education.

Uganda is a landlocked East African country bordered by Kenya to the east, South Sudan to the north, the DRC to the west, Rwanda to the south-west, and Tanzania to the south. The aftermath of 68 years of British Protectorate status (1894–1962) saw a Republican government and a way of life with indigenous and Western-leaning social, political, and economic aspects lying side by side: traditional with republican leadership, indigenous versus popular cultural values, indigenous languages versus English as the "official" language, and formal versus informal education, among others. Navigating these binaries requires a critical mind, which necessitates an education with effec-tive ways of facilitating the development of the abilities to critique knowledge presented in various

 DOI: 10.4324/9781003023425-34

forms and fora. As the country grapples with economic empowerment agenda, especially focusing on industrialization, science education is prioritized over the humanities (cf. Nakkazi, 2015). Even within the humanities, euro-centric views dominate (Adyanga, 2014) and indigenous knowledges, although relevant to local contexts, are sidelined.

Educational Systems in Uganda and Congo

Many African countries gained independence in the 1960s. Yet, neocolonialism persists in most ex-colonies, including Uganda and Congo. Prior to the arrival of colonizers, African communities employed their local ways of educating members on the knowledge, skills, and values regarding social behavior, environment, spirituality, health and healing, among others (Wane, 2000).

In Uganda, the beginnings of "formal" education can be traced to 1877, following the invitation by King Muteesa I of Buganda for Christian missionaries to preach religion and teach literacy and numeracy in his kingdom (Khadidja, 2014). The current system comprises nursery and kindergarten (age 3–5), primary school (7 years), secondary school (4 years), high school (2 years), and college and university. Education financing and widespread access today is partly rooted in the National Resistance Movement government's early efforts towards democratization (Stasavage, 2005) and the recommendations made by the 1987–1989 William Senteza Kajubi Education Policy Review Commission (Oketch & Rolleston, 2007; Ward, Penny, & Read, 2006). Free Universal Primary Education, which has been implemented since 1997 in government-aided schools, and the Universal Secondary Education and Universal Post-Secondary Level Training which followed have increased enrollment and completion rates. Individuals opting for privately sponsored schools still pay tuition. A limited number of scholarships are awarded to college and university students based on academic excellence and/or physical disability.

Primary and secondary schools choose either, or a blend, of the national and international curricula, both of which are characterized by an overwhelming emphasis on examinations as a measure of learning and basis of transition to further levels of education. The National Curriculum Development Centre (NCDC) drafts the teaching curriculum which, in practice, is seldom followed as teachers prefer teaching in accordance with the examination curricula issued by the Uganda National Examinations Board (UNEB). The higher-class and preferred, but less socio-economically accessible, international schools follow a myriad of curricula, including Cambridge, the National Curriculum for England, Montessori, and International Baccalaureate.

In Congo, the education system has been questioned since the country's accession to independence on the grounds of not being harmonious with the realities of the country, an issue that results in high school and college/university graduates joining a large pool of unemployed individuals. Attempts to reform and restructure an education system that reflects local realities and capitalizes on students' *funds of knowledge*—their "households, family practices, and cultural resources" (Moll, 2019, p. 137)—seem to be unsuccessful. As a result, despite its 60-plus indigenous languages and two national languages (Kituba and Lingala), Congo continues to use French as the country's official and instructional language from Pre-K through tertiary education. Its education institutions are housed in three government ministries; the Ministry of Elementary and Secondary Education, the Ministry of Technical Education and Vocational Training, and the Ministry of Higher Education.

Regardless of the education sector, public or private, Congolese schools are reflective of France's design (Ndouna-Nsonde, 2005). Students are required to complete 13 years of schooling to graduate high school: pre-school (optional), elementary (grades 1–6), middle school (grades 7–10), and high school (grades 11–13). Transitions from elementary to middle and then to high school are dependent on students' success on national standardized examinations. Regrettably, the Congolese education reform of 1990 (Réorganisation du Système Éducatif, 1990) that aimed to reorganize the education system was not implemented as civil wars dominated the country between 1993 and 2003.

Therefore, Mbemba (2010) writes that the beginning of school for the Congolese youth is in fact an imposed separation from their local practices. It is common to see young Congolese townspeople who have never left their town/country provide detailed accounts of neighborhoods of Paris while finding it difficult to locate their parents' native villages and discuss their cultures.

The anomalies described in the Ugandan and Congolese education systems can be mediated by reclaiming and redesigning their curricula, which explains the necessity of critical theories.

Colonialism, Neocolonialism, and Critical Theories

Colonialism outlasts its tenure under temporally appropriate and politically correct terms such as development and globalization where the west denigrates ex-colonies' ways of knowing, being, and doing and continues to decide, think, and speak for them. Freire (2000) views this notion of thinking for others as an oppressive action: "I cannot think *for others* or *without others*, nor can others think *for me*" (p. 108). Yet, Europe continues to use different approaches to control Africa in different areas. Rodney (2018) describes Europe's "structural blockades to economic . . . political, and social progress on the [African] continent" (p. x) and discusses how Europe underdeveloped Africa with supposedly development agendas. Development, as Abdi (2007) cautions, "cannot be imposed, despite any good intentions, from outside; it must take place within the *consciousness* [emphasis added] of people" (p. 54). The awakening of *consciousness* allows people to reject yes-manism and engage in social justice actions. It "enrolls them in the search for self-affirmation and thus avoids fanaticism" (Freire, 2000, p. 3).

Ex-colonies like Uganda and Congo need to critically analyze concepts such as globalization and development because they embody agendas of neocolonialism. Moving towards this consciousness requires that ex-colonies deconstruct the western self-affirmed supremacy and repudiate the long-internalized belief that positions their cultures as shameful and worthless. Although Africans traditionally believed their wisdom and knowledge came with aging, their internalization of the western modernism resulted in self-mistrust to favor western-styled or "formal" schooling. Wane (2000) shares an example of a Kenyan woman underestimating her indigenous wisdom and knowledge despite her being a senior citizen and her role as a respected elder in her community. During an interview with Wane, the woman responded:

> What could you learn from me, an old woman like me with no education? I cannot speak English . . . What do I know except to hold my hoe? . . . I am sure you have not come all this way to learn [from me]
>
> (p. 54).

This case demonstrates how neocolonialism forces Africans to delegitimize their indigenous languages and ways of knowing. It illustrates how colonization was an epistemological, socio-cultural, and socio-linguistic exploitation in addition to its territorial aspect, which all contribute to the disconnect between African education systems and African realities. wa Thiong'o (1993) writes about this language-culture-world/reality disconnect: "Our Language gave us a view of the world . . . Then I went to primary school and the bond was broken. The language of my education was no longer the language of my culture" (p. 11). Clearly, in formerly colonized African countries, the incongruence between euro-centric curricula and local realities makes students victims of text rather than its agents or producers. Freire's (1970) notion of reading the world by reading the word suggests that "the cognitive dimensions of the literacy process must include the relationships between men with their world" (p. 212). Integrating the worlds of ex-colonies in the words they read, from this perspective, connotes an emphasis on critical literacies and the socio-linguistic and socio-cultural capital of these ex-colonies.

Luke (2014) writes that "critical literacy approaches view language, texts, and their discourse structures as principal means for representing and reshaping possible worlds" (p. 27), a view that makes clear how ex-colonies must deconstruct colonial practices before or while also stimulating their critical literacy consciousness. If texts in the Ugandan and Congolese curricula are not reflective of people's lived worlds and experiences, they cannot advance notions of liberation. Text as language and word that Ugandan and Congolese students encounter must reflect their worlds. Freire (1983) explains how reading a text is mediated through our everyday experiences. He elucidates the intertwinement between language and world/reality, arguing that "Reading the world always precedes reading the word, and reading the word implies continually reading the world" (p. 10).

Critical literacy in ex-colonies must start—or continue—with reclaiming epistemologies and cultural practices. For example, rather than teach the western individualistic philosophy that praises the famous Cartesian "I think, hence I am" (Descartes, 1916, p. 27), African educators need to instill how they conceptualize their own sense of self rooted in the *Ubuntu* and Mbitian "I am because we are" (Mbiti, 1990, p. 106) philosophy that defines the individual by collectivism or his/her place in and relationships with the community.

Critical Self-Consciousness and Critical Literacy in Uganda and Congo

Critical literacy concerns the awakening of people's critical self-consciousness that can lead to self-empowerment and activism for social change. One goal of a critical approach to literacy is to educate youth who are capable of reading and analyzing information critically in ways to identify potential bias and power relations (Freire, 2000; Janks, 2013; Luke, 2018). As an approach that views language, texts, and discourse structures as means for representing and transforming the world (Luke, 2014), critical literacy is about "*writing* and rewriting the world: it is about design and re-design" (Janks, 2013, p. 227) or deconstructing and reconstructing societies (Janks, 2014). Since critical literacy is tasked, in part, with providing avenues for reflection and expression of positions on social (in)justice (Wilkey, 2009) and such expressions and reflections use language and literature as media, it is important to emphasize self-consciousness as its bedrock.

Uganda has long used English—the language of the ex-colonizer (Britain)—as language of instruction from nursery school. The Ugandan National Curriculum Development Centre (NCDC, 2014; see also Altinyelken, 2010) has argued that literacy development is fast achieved in mother tongues and when the themes explored relate to one's immediate environment and experiences. Relatedly, a recently promulgated "thematic curriculum" has established instruction in mother tongues from primary 1–3, making English one of the disciplines. Although positive results have been reported (Ahimbisibwe & Wasai, 2018; NCDC, 2014), the thematic curriculum poses strategic challenges. Uganda is a country with over 48 languages and the cosmopolitan nature of most areas dictates that the thematic curriculum be implemented in the dominant language of the area, a practice that creates disparities in understanding and critical reflection and affects speakers of non-dominant languages.

The reintroduction of English as the medium of instruction from primary 4 breeds further challenges, especially in secondary and tertiary education where most of the literature is Western-type and paints worlds unfamiliar to the students, despite the prevalence of Ugandan and other African texts. Literary texts by the likes of Shakespeare, Charles Dickens, and Emily Dickinson dominate school reading lists despite substantial efforts to integrate more local texts in the Ugandan curriculum. Images of snow and winter, and festivals like midsummer (as in Shakespeare's *A Midsummer Night's Dream*) and the like hardly speak to the indigenous in Uganda, Congo, and other ex-colonies. Even indigenous texts are consumed with borrowed interpretive praxis. In Congo, the predominance of literary texts in secondary and tertiary education is shared between the works of Shakespeare and French writers such as Voltaire, René Descartes, Jean de La Fontaine, and Jules Romains.

The works of Congolese writers such as Emmanuel Dongala, Alain Mabanckou, and Dominique Ngoïe-Ngalla are often discovered outside of the school curriculum.

Critical literacy continues to take root globally in various ways and at different pace. Vasquez (2017) observes that in the African continent, critical literacy is mostly documented in South Africa with predominantly the work of Hilary Janks (see Janks, 2013, 2014, 2020; Janks & McKinney, this Handbook). In pointing to this perceived gap in the literature on critical literacy in Africa, we remind scholars in and from Congo, Uganda, and other ex-colonies of their role in bringing critical literacy to the forefront given that "as a practical approach to curriculum, it melds social, political, and cultural debate and discussion with the analysis of how texts and discourses work, where, with what consequences, and in whose interests" (Luke, 2014, p. 22).

Globalization and Indigenous Funds of Knowledge

This chapter has provided insight into how the West maintains Euro-centric discourses in ex-colonies while holding deficit perspectives of their funds of knowledge. It has pointed to the urgency for ex-colonies to reclaim their epistemologies and curricula. Here, we note how ex-colonies can decide to function in a third space—independent of the "either indigenous or western" reasoning—where they can benefit from globalization and their own funds of knowledge. Afro-centric curricula have the potential to help bridge the schooling-realities gap and therefore lay the groundwork for preparing youth activists who can then use the technologies and languages of ex-colonizers to write/talk back to ex-colonizers, share their own ways of knowing, doing, and being, and address inequities as initial stages to contribute to globalization. We contend that critical literacy relies on the critique of dominant discourses and "the interdependence of power, diversity, access, and design/redesign" (Janks, 2020, p. 569). As such, African institutions of higher learning should not undervalue their role and responsibility to educate teachers who can prepare students to become critically literate producers of text and activists for social justice.

Critical Literacy in Action: Spaces, Places, and Voice

Critical pedagogy scholars (e.g. Freire, 2000) and critical literacy scholars (e.g., Janks, 2020; Luke, 2014) emphasize the importance of critical self-consciousness and activism. While these have played an important role in efforts to halt social injustices in democratic societies, ex-colonies are rather confronted with dissimilar realities. Uganda, for example, has experienced difficulties in critical creative and performative arts due to the political environment. Byron Kawadwa was murdered in 1977 for staging a play that was critical of extrajudicial killings during the Idi Amin regime (Lubega, 2015). Several other literary and creative artists such as Wyciff Kiyingi, Lubwa p'Chong, and Robert Serumaga were either jailed or forced to exile (Mulekwa, 2011). Today, writers have been imprisoned and cases include Stella Nyanzi for "insulting the president" in her rather expressive poetry (Anena, 2020; McCool, 2020; Nyanzi, 2020) and Vincent Nzaramba for his "book that called for President Yoweri Museveni to relinquish power" (Human Rights Network for Journalists—Uganda, 2011, para. 2).

Congo has known similar scenarios with arbitrary arrests and torture of activists: "Dozens of activists and opposition members are languishing in prisons in Congo Brazzaville, some for almost three years, simply for exercising their right to freedom of expression" (Amnesty International, 2018, para. 1). Critical literacy approaches also take into consideration the spaces and places that we occupy. Vasquez (2017) reiterates the role of educators to find ways to engage students with spatiality and place-based pedagogies. Spatiality and place-based pedagogies emphasize geographical and geopolitical dimensions to implement culturally responsive practices. They recognize and value local ways of knowing, being, and doing and help students form "relationships with places, both in terms of belonging and responsibility" (Comber, 2016, p. 96).

Radical efforts which lay the foundation for valorizing African funds of knowledge and revolutionizing African curricula and interpretive lenses (Sicherman, 1998) were exerted after the wave of independence around the 1960s–1990s in the works of African writers such as Ngugi wa Thiong'o (1986, 1993). Ngugi wa Thiong'o has long discussed the role of African languages and epistemologies as tools and social forces necessary to decolonize the minds of Africans and reclaim the economy, politics, and cultures of Africa. He takes issues with the practice of non-Africans making decisions about and for Africa: "It seems it is the fate of Africa to have her destiny always decided around conference tables in the metropolises of the western world" (wa Thiong'o, 1986, p. 4). From a Freirean perspective, this is an oppressive practice of westerners thinking *for* and *without* Africans. Furthermore, works like *Home and Exile* (Achebe, 2001) and *The Education of a British-Protected Child* (Achebe, 2009) reverse the otherwise denigrated African ideals, thereby providing an alternative critical lens. Conceptual contributions have also featured: for example, "orature" was coined and preferred to "oral literature" as it was deemed more contextually appropriate to African indigenous literatures (Moolla, 2012, p. 434).

Efforts made by earlier generations of African scholars to decolonize western-centered curricula and claim African interpretive lenses are less visible in today's literary and literacy practices. This leaves externally determined standards as the only interpretive lenses, thereby depriving Africans of their voice in their own affairs. Because ex-colonizers can only seek to maintain the status quo given that the current educational contexts work in their favor, it is the responsibility of educators and scholars in ex-colonies to start integrating critical literacies into their practice.

Concluding Thoughts and Recommendations

The emancipatory effect of critical literacies cannot be overstated (Stromquist, 2014), and context plays an indispensable part. The continued presence of overly euro-centric curricula in Ugandan, Congolese, and other former colonial systems of education scores against this ideal and undermines efforts to strengthen the capacity of critical literacies on the African continent. Rather, it continues the trends of reorienting the African mind and personality to Western modes of knowing, being, and doing (Sicherman, 1995). Therefore, reiterating the need to decolonize curricula by focusing on interpretive lenses that salvage the sovereignty of critical literacies in Uganda, Congo, and other former colonies will remain an important pathway until the call is heeded. We suggest that critical self-consciousness, as we have discussed, plays an important role in this endeavor.

Noting that colonialism and neo-colonialism are political, intellectual, cultural, spiritual, and educational, it is essential for higher education institutions to prepare critically literate teachers using emancipatory curricula and instruction that allow ex-colonies like Uganda and Congo to imagine possibilities and continually problematize, deconstruct, and reconstruct their imagined selves and communities. This practice, or the "redesign cycle" as Janks (2014) calls it, is "an iterative process in which a design is deconstructed and then reconstructed" (p. 354). We highlight social activism, socio-cultural environment, and pedagogical strategies as valuable elements of critical literacy while acknowledging how space, place and voice play a crucial role in critical literacy actual practices.

In this chapter, we described the influence of neocolonialism on the present-day Ugandan and Congolese sociopolitical and educational contexts and argued for the need to decolonize eurocentric curricula and implement Afro-centric curricula that reflect African realities and promote Africans' ways of knowing, being, and doing. We noted that critical literacy scholarship is highly needed in Africa and overarchingly recommend a consortium of critical literacy scholars' efforts as emerging work (e.g. Hilary Janks in South Africa) seems uncoordinated. Although the bulk of critical literacies is typically placed in literature and linguistics studies, the interpretive praxis pervades the humanities and often spreads to the social sciences; and, therefore, demands multidisciplinary integration. Current efforts like the African Humanities Program are a good springboard, but with a focus aside from the specifics of critical literacies. In this vein, we propose the creation of a Critical Literacies African Network (CLAN) which will serve as an African scholars' macro-level community of practice where context-specific meanings, identities, and practices will be negotiated and operationalized. It is preferred and anticipated that the CLAN will lend African specific critical literacies a shape that can be showcased in broader platforms, especially the Transnational Critical Literacies Network (TCLN) which has a global reach. Further, we hope that the CLAN can inspire the institution of other regional or continental platforms which will then commune at uniting platforms for an enriched spectrum of viewpoints from multiple worldviews and pose a truly transnational critical stance.

Note

1. Also called the Republic of Congo or Congo-Brazzaville.

References

Abdi, A. A. (2007). Oral societies and colonial experiences: Sub-Saharan Africa and the de-facto power of the written word. *International Education*, *37*(1), 41–59.

Achebe, C. (2001). *Home and exile*. Penguin Books.

Achebe, C. (2009). *The education of a British-protected child: Essays*. Penguin Books.

Adyanga, F. A. (2014). *African indigenous science in higher education in Uganda* (Publication No 3630407) (Doctoral dissertation). University of Toronto. ProQuest Dissertations and Theses.

Ahimbisibwe, P., & Wasai, H. (2018, June 7). Pupils excel in local languages, fail English. *Daily Monitor*. Retrieved from www.monitor.co.ug/News/National/Pupils-excel-local-languages-fail-English/688334-4599314-bjaqnq/index.html

Altinyelken, H. K. (2010). Curriculum change in Uganda: Teacher perspectives on the new thematic curriculum. *International Journal of Educational Development*, *30*(2), 151–161. https://doi.org/10.1016/j.ijedudev.2009.03.004

Amnesty International. (2018, March 21). *Congo-Brazzaville: Torture and arbitrary detentions of dozens of people put freedom of expression under severe strain*. Author. Retrieved from www.amnesty.org/en/latest/news/2018/03/congobrazzaville-torture-and-arbitrary-detentions-of-dozens-of-people-put-freedom-of-expression-under-severe-strain/

Anena, H. (2020, February 25). Review: No roses from my mouth by Dr. Stella Nyanzi. *Columbia Journal*. Retrieved from http://columbiajournal.org/review-no-roses-from-my-mouth-by-dr-stella-nyanzi/

Balencie, J.-M., & De La Grange, A. (2001). *Mondes rebelles*. Éditions Michalon.

Comber, B. (2016). *Literacy, place, and pedagogies of possibility*. Routledge.

Descartes, R. (1916). *A discourse on method* (J. Veitch, Trans.). E. P. Dutton & Co.

Freire, P. (1970). The adult literacy process as cultural action for freedom. *Harvard Educational Review*, *40*(2), 205–226.

Freire, P. (1983). The importance of the act of reading (L. Slover, Trans.). *The Journal of Education*, *165*(1), 5–11. Retrieved from www.jstor.com/stable/42772842

Freire, P. (2000). *Pedagogy of the oppressed*. Continuum.

Human Rights Network for Journalists—Uganda. (2011, September 21). *Author arrested for publishing book that called for president to step down*. IFEX. Retrieved from https://ifex.org/author-arrested-for-publishing-book-that-called-for-president-to-step-down/

Janks, H. (2013). Critical literacy in teaching and research. *Education Inquiry*, *4*(2), 225–242. https://doi.org/10.3402/edui.v4i2.22071

Janks, H. (2014). Critical literacy's ongoing importance for education. *Journal of Adolescent and Adult Literacy*, *57*(5), 349–356. https://doi.org/10.1002/jaal.260

Janks, H. (2020). Critical literacy in action: Difference as a force for positive change. *Journal of Adolescent and Adult Literacy*, *63*(5), 569–572.

Khadidja, D. (2014). *Western education in Uganda (1878–1939)* (Magister thesis). University of Oran. Retrieved from https://theses.univ-oran1.dz/document/TH4326.pdf

Lubega, H. (2015, June 6). How playwright Byron Kawadwa met his death. *Daily Monitor*. Retrieved from www.monitor.co.ug/News/Insight/playwright-Byron-Kawadwa-death/688338-2741512-xxggolz/index. html

Luke, A. (2014). Defining critical literacy. In J. Z. Pandya & J. Avila (Eds.), *Moving critical literacies forward: A new look at praxis across contexts* (pp. 19–31). Routledge.

Luke, A. (2018). *Critical literacy, schooling, and social justice: The selected works of Allan Luke*. Routledge.

Mbemba, G. (2010). Pratiques culturelles et réforme des curricula en Afrique centrale. *La Recherche en Éducation*, *4*, 3–15.

Mbiti, J. S. (1990). *African religions and philosophy*. Heinemann.

McCool, A. (2020, March 19). "After prison, I'm stronger, more vulgar!": The irrepressible Stella Nyanzi. *The Guardian*. Retrieved from www.theguardian.com/books/2020/mar/19/prison-irrepressible-stella-nyanzi-uganda-poet

Moll, L. C. (2019). Elaborating funds of knowledge: Community-oriented practices in international contexts. *Literacy Research: Theory, Method, and Practice*, *68*, 130–138.

Moolla, F. F. (2012). When orature becomes literature: Somali oral poetry and folktales in Somali novels. *Comparative Literature Studies*, *49*(3), 434–462. https://doi.org/10.5325/complitstudies.49.3.0434

Mulekwa, C. (2011). Theatre, war, and peace in Uganda. In C. E. Cohen, R. G. Varea, & P. O. Walker (Eds.), *Acting together I: Performance and the creative transformation of conflict* (pp. 45–71). New Village Press.

Nakkazi, E. (2015, May 8). 'Humanities useless' debate sparks science teacher boost. *University World News*. Retrieved from www.universityworldnews.com/post.php?story=20150507124615874

National Curriculum Development Centre. (2014). *Effectiveness of the primary four curriculum (The transition class)*. Author.

Ndouna-Nsonde, Y. M. (2005). *Les représentations de trois enseignantes de première année de Brazzaville par rapport à l'enseignement de la lecture* (Doctoral dissertation). Université de Montréal.

Nyanzi, S. (2020). *No roses from my mouth: Poems from prison*. Ubuntu Reading Group.

Oketch, M., & Rolleston, C. (2007). Policies on free primary and secondary education in East Africa: Retrospect and prospect. *Review of Research in Education*, *31*, 131–158. https://doi.org/10.3102/0091732X07300046131

Réorganisation du Système Éducatif en République Populaire du Congo, Titre II: De la Structure du Système Éducatif. (1990). Retrieved from www.sgg.cg/JO/1990/congo-jo-1990-09.pdf

Rodney, W. (2018). *How Europe underdeveloped Africa*. Verso.

Sicherman, C. (1995). Ngugi's colonial education: The subversion . . . of the African mind. *African Studies Review*, *38*(3), 11–41. https://doi.org/10.2307/524791

Sicherman, C. (1998). Revolutionizing the literature curriculum at the University of East Africa: Literature and the soul of the nation. *Research in African Literatures*, *29*(3), 129–148.

Stasavage, D. (2005). The role of democracy in Uganda's move to universal primary education. *The Journal of Modern African Studies*, *43*(1), 53–73. https://doi.org/10.1017/S0022278X04000618

Stromquist, N. P. (2014). Freire, literacy and emancipatory gender learning. *International Review of Education*, *60*(4), 545–558.

Vasquez, V. M. (2017). Critical literacy. *Oxford Research Encyclopedias*, 1–16. https://doi.org/10.1093/acrefore/9780190264093.013.20

Wallowitz, L. (Ed.). (2008). *Critical literacy as resistance: Teaching for social justice across the secondary curriculum*. Peter Lang.

Wane, N. N. (2000). Indigenous knowledge: Lessons from the elders—A Kenyan case study. In G. J. S. Dei, B. L. Hall, & D. G. Rosenberg (Eds.), *Indigenous knowledges in global contexts: Multiple readings of our world* (pp. 54–69). University of Toronto Press.

Ward, M., Penny, A., & Read, T. (2006). *Education reform in Uganda—1997 to 2004: Reflections on policy, partnership, strategy and implementation*. Department for International Development.

wa Thiong'o, N. (1986). *Decolonising the mind: The politics of language in African literature*. James Currey.

wa Thiong'o, N. (1993). *Moving the centre: The struggle for cultural freedoms*. East African Education Publishers.

Wilkey, C. (2009). Engaging community literacy through the rhetorical work of a social movement. *Reflections: A Journal of Community-Engaged Writing and Rhetoric, Archive 9.1*. Retrieved from https://reflectionsjournal.net/2019/09/engaging-community-literacy-through-the-rhetorical-work-of-a-social-movement-by-christopher-wilkey/

INTRODUCTION TO AREA 3

Noah Asher Golden and Jennifer Helen Alford

The chapters in this area each tackle a unique watershed opportunity for critical literacy to extend beyond present boundaries and catalyse the field further into the 21st century. As our colleagues Nicole Mirra and Antero Garcia note, what constitutes the necessary literacies for the 21st century is very much contested. We are now living well into the 21st century and, to date, the idealised notion of this century offering the people of the globe bursts of creativity, innovation, and interconnectedness has given way to increasing xenophobia, rising nationalisms, and ever-expanding inequality. The COVID-19 pandemic, continuing to spread with new variants of the virus discovered recently as of this writing, has only intensified these conditions. In our field, "21st-century literacies" is often used to signify the use of digital tools and platforms, but current research indicates these tools and platforms are rarely used in the service of equity, democratic engagement, and connectedness with broad, beyond-formal education publics (for more on this, see Mirra & Garcia, 2020). The critical literacy practices, platforms, and directions profiled in Area 3 of our Handbook, though, offer us pathways forward as we collectively re-think how critical analyses and production might engender more equitable conditions through multiple forms of civic engagement. Specifically, these chapters call our attention to three domains which are central to 21st-century critical literacies: the practical affordances of contemporary texts types and associated shifts in the technologies that shape literacies, critical literacies as emergent processes, and interruptions of the social production of hierarchies that privilege some people at the expense of others.

Three chapters challenge educators practically to consider the affordances of different text types, including contemporary and experimental types of literature, and those of multimodal arts-literacies practices. The chapters probe how teachers' choices in these aspects shape what critical work is possible. In Chapter 3.1, **Critical Literacy and Contemporary Literatures**, David E. Low, Anna Lyngfelt, Angela Thomas, and Vivian Maria Vasquez explore the contemporaneous nature of literature genres and formats (e.g., augmented reality stories) that give rise to new forms of participation and networking and promote transmediality across formats. It addresses the debates around the use of contemporary literatures in schools, and invites teachers and scholars to reflect on the possibilities of utilising such literatures using a critical lens to investigate: what counts as literature, the sociopolitical systems that give rise to contemporary literature, and the transformative affordances of such literatures. James S. Chisholm and Kathryn F. Whitmore, in Chapter 3.2, **Critical Arts-Literacies in Classrooms: Moving with Abduction, Imagination, and Emotion Across Modalities**, examine empirical work into critical arts-literacies, and establish a research agenda that augments this body of work through three conceptual lenses: abduction, imagination, and emotion. They

 DOI: 10.4324/9781003023425-35

foreground the affordances of multimodal tools for arts-based critique, especially activism and artfulness. In Chapter 3.3, **Critical Literacy Out of the Comfort Zone: Productive Ttextual Tantrums**, George Lovell Boggs, Nerida Spina, Barbara Comber, and Donna E. Alvermann present an inquiry-driven examination of the consequences of textual choice for critical literacy classrooms. Drawing on Smith's (2005) understanding of how texts organise and regulate people's work, this authors explore how the selection of a children's book on climate change lead them to interrogate standpoint, the influence of time and place, and what work "gets done" with texts. In Chapter 3.5, **Critical Literacy, Digital Platforms, and Datafication**, T. Philip Nichols, Anna Smith, Scott Bulfin, and Amy Stornaiuolo push the boundaries of critical literacy praxis to encourage analysis of shifting media environments shaped by new platforms and processes of datafication.

The next thread across this area of the Handbook is one of emergence. As Casey Philip Wong and Tanja Burkhard write in Chapter 3.14, **Supporting Critical Literacies Through Culturally Sustaining Pedagogy**, criticality is not a position that one can occupy; instead, it is an ongoing process. This framing of critical literacies work emerges across chapters: Alexander Bacalja, Earl Aguilera, and Edison Ferney Castrillón-Ángel argue in Chapter 3.8, **Critical Digital Literacy**, that digital literacies must be, like all literacies, understood as social practices, and that critical digital literacies are an ongoing interrogation of digital media themselves as well as the production or consumption of texts using these technologies. In Chapter 3.12, **Proposing a Politics of Immediation for Literacy Studies, or What Is Possible for Literacy Studies Beyond Critical Theory's Mediations?**, Christian Ehret, Jennifer Rowsell, and Kelly C. Johnston call on our research communities to open our work to "everything, everyone, every moment" as they explore concepts that further our ability to enact critiques of power. Catarina Schmidt, Ninni Wahlström, and Amy Vetter offer examples grounded in such openness as they describe emergent situated moments of critical literacy enactment in classroom discourse in Chapter 3.13, **The Situational in Critical Literacy**. Pushing the historical limitations on the emergent processes we engage in critical literacy praxis, in Chapter 3.4, **Planetary Literacies for the Anthropocene** authors Karin Murris and Margaret Somerville draw on posthuman and new materialist methodologies to encourage planetary literacies that offer new understandings of subjectivity—understandings that can help us to address the urgency of the unfolding climate crisis.

Finally, these chapters return to a mainstay of critical literacies praxis—a focus on the social production of hierarchies that privilege some people at the expense of others, but offer fresh perspectives and new directions for this work. These chapters both document contemporary ways linguistic and other forms of cultural capital are used to produce and further social dominance, and offer us glimpses of approaches that can interrupt this social production. In Chapter 3.9, **Critical Literacy and Additional Language Learning: An Expansive View of Translanguaging for Change-Enhancing Possibilities**, Sunny Man Chu Lau, Zhongfeng Tian, and Angel M. Y. Lin discuss recent work on translanguaging that engenders "diverse cognitive, affective, social and material affordances" for learners of additional languages. Seonmin Huh, Lílian Vimieiro Pascoal, and Andréa Machado de Almeida Mattos explore critical literacies in the context of English language teaching in Chapter 3.11, **Critical Literacy and English Language Teaching**, offering analysis of the tensions between critical literacy praxis and language skills with examples from South Korean and Brasilian contexts. In Chapter 3.10, **Indigenous Youth Digital Language Activism**, Kristian Adi Putra and Lusia Marliana Nurani detail the specific ways Indonesian youth are leveraging digital tools to engage in language activism as they encourage revitalization of indigenous languages via social media. In Chapter 3.15, **Critical Community Literacies in Teacher Education,** Pooja Dharamshi, Laura Ruth Johnson, and Judy Sharkey encourage us to rethink relationships in schooling and teacher education, inviting us to resist deficit framings by partnering with community members and offering new notions of community in teacher education programs. In Chapter 3.6, **Connecting Critical Literacy and Dis/Ability Studies: Opportunities and Implications**,

David I. Hernández-Saca encourages the cross-fertilization of critical literacies and dis/ability studies as a means to disrupt global, ableist hegemonies, inviting researchers and practitioners to center on the experiences of minoritised youth given special education disability labels. We are invited to grow new pedagogies, ones that can interrupt xenophobia and colonial legacies in Chapter 3.16, **Disrupting Xenophobia Through Cosmopolitan Critical Literacy in Education**, and Chapter 3.17, **Border Literacies: A Critical Literacy Framework from Nepantla.** In Chapter 3.16, Rahat Zaidi and Suzanne S. Choo call for a cosmopolitan critical literacy that can disrupt current manifestations of Islamophobia. In Chapter 3.17, Enrique David Degollado, Idalia Nuñez, and Minea Armijo Romero invite us to draw on border literacies to ground lived experience in ways that interrupt eurocentrism and continuing imperialism in schooling. Chapter 3.8, **Critical Literacy and Abolition**, extends these framings, with authors Justin A. Coles, Roberto S. de Roock, Hui-Ling Sunshine Malone, and Adam D. Musser offering a critique that critical literacy must move beyond the liberal imagination and engage radical, humanizing possibilities to counter ongoing and intensifying anti-Blackness and systems of domination.

As editors of Area 3, we offer these as the 21st-century literacies needed as we shift from neoliberal academic production to collectively engage in the dismantling, disrupting, and re-building that these transnational concerns—the rising nationalisms, xenophobia, the unfolding climate crisis, continuing and intensifying systems of domination—demand of us.

References

Mirra, N., & Garcia, A. (2020). In search of the meaning and purpose of 21st century literacy learning: A critical review of research and practice. *Reading Research Quarterly, 0*(0), 1–34. https://doi.org/10.1002/rrq.313

Smith, D. E. (2005). *Institutional ethnography: A sociology for people.* Rowman Altamira.

3.1

CRITICAL LITERACY AND CONTEMPORARY LITERATURES

David E. Low, Anna Lyngfelt, Angela Thomas,
and Vivian Maria Vasquez

Introduction

In this chapter, we define literature to include prose texts of various genres and formats, including illustrated and multimodal print texts, filmic and musical story texts, digital stories, virtual and augmented reality stories, and game/play objects. Additionally, we consider the discourses and situated practices within which contemporary literatures are debated, subverted, and revisioned, such as online fanfiction and role-playing spaces centred on literary universes. For us, what makes literature "contemporary" is its often participatory and interactive nature, its networkability, the proximity among its authors, fans, and other readers, and its transmediality across forms and formats. These features make it ripe for boundary-pushing critical literacy work.

Classroom Vignette

In a classroom for 3–5-year-old children, in an ethnically and economically diverse neighbourhood in Ontario, Canada, Bryan Woods read the book *Froodle* (Portis, 2014) to his students. He had been working with Vivian on creating spaces for his students to engage with critical literacies by reading with and against texts to make visible and disrupt problematic notions. After working with various fiction and non-fiction texts, the children became accustomed to reading diverse texts critically. *Froodle*'s publisher described the book as taking place on a typical day, where birds chirp, dogs bark, and cats meow, until one of the birds decides she wants to sing a different song and begins to invent sounds. All the other birds follow suit except crow, who spends most of the book resisting the idea of making up sounds until the end of the story. Reviews of the book note *Froodle* is about disrupting monotony and predictability with an underlying message that it's good to try something new.

When Bryan read the book with his students, rather than picking up on the message that it's good to try something new, the children talked about how they felt crow was pushed into making other sounds when he really did not want to. Whereas adult reviewers of *Froodle* read *with* the text, Bryan's students' experiences with reading texts critically afforded them the skills to read *against* the text. Bryan invited the children to sketch a time when they felt pressured to do something they weren't comfortable doing. In Figure 3.1.1, Kushi, whose parents are from India, represents a time when her mom wanted her to help cook Indian food. Kushi didn't want to help because

DOI: 10.4324/9781003023425-36

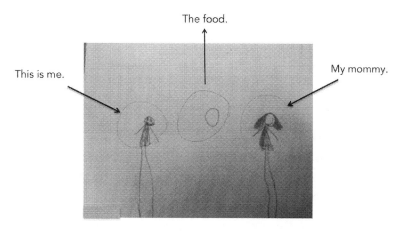

The food.

This is me.

My mommy.

Figure 3.1.1 Kushi's drawing

she worried if she brought this food to school, her classmates might laugh at her because of its different smell. She likened herself to the crow who was also being forced to do something he didn't want to do.

Kushi was conflicted because she knew how much her mom wanted her to help. She experienced a struggle over her identity being caught between the politics of home and school. This was evident in her drawing, in which she positioned the food as a wedge between herself and her parent.

Continuing to explore issues of identity, Bryan had his students read advertisement flyers and catalogues from a familiar toy store. As with *Froodle*, children read with and against the text and discussed how they felt the ads led them to desire certain kinds of toys. Three-to-five-year-old children asked questions like: "Who would want these toys?," "Do I see myself in these toys?," "What kind of play is encouraged?," and "What kinds of toys would I want to see in a toy catalogue?" Kushi questioned the lack of dolls with which to personally identify. Amending the flyer, she added various dolls wearing different Indian saree, inserting herself into the flyer to correct its cultural omission. Kushi had come a long way, from wanting to hide her cultural identity (i.e., not wanting to bring Indian food to school) to making that identity visible in the form of dolls she included in her revision of a toy advertisement.

Using a variety of texts, Bryan created a space for his students to identify, name, and take up issues of importance in their lives. Reading contemporary literature from a critical literacy perspective afforded a different discourse that was more culturally relevant. Such discourses were part of developing skills to critically read texts, which resulted in opening up space for Kushi to make visible her home values.

Key Concepts

Vasquez, Janks, and Comber (2019) note "critical literacy should be viewed as a lens, frame, or perspective" (p. 306) for reading and producing texts, including contemporary literature. Because it would be difficult to pin down an all-encompassing definition for what it means to work with contemporary literature from a critical literacy perspective, we offer key tenets drawn from the opening vignette, beginning with the notion that texts used in school settings should reflect students' lives, and support meaningful discussions of topics that matter to them. Following are key concepts to consider when working with contemporary literature from a critical literacy perspective.

- Contemporary literature is always constructed from particular perspectives and is therefore never neutral. Readers need to question the perspectives on offer.
- Readers' readings of contemporary literature are never neutral. Each time we read, write, or create, we draw from past experiences and understandings about how the world works and should work. We therefore must also analyse our own readings of texts and unpack the position(s) from which we engage in literacy work.
- The world is a socially constructed text that can be read. The earlier students are introduced to this idea, the sooner they are able to understand what it means to be researchers of language, image, gesture, spaces, and objects, critically exploring such issues as what counts as literature, whose stories matter and who gets to decide, and how texts can be revised, rewritten, or reconstructed to shift or reframe the message(s) conveyed.
- Critical literacy involves making sense of the sociopolitical systems through which we live our lives and questioning those systems. Critical literacy work using contemporary literature must focus on social issues, including inequities of race, class, gender, sexuality, and disability, and the ways in which text producers use language and other semiotic resources to shape readers' understanding of these issues.
- Critical literacy practices can be transformative, changing inequitable ways of being and problematic social practices. Children who engage in critical literacy are equipped to make informed decisions regarding issues of power and control, to engage in democratic citizenship, and to think and act ethically. As such, students who enact critical literacies are better able to contribute to making the world a more just place.
- "Critical literacy is about imagining thoughtful ways of reconstructing and redesigning texts, images, and practices to convey different and more socially just and equitable messages and ways of being that have real-life effects and real-world impact" (Vasquez, 2017, para. 19).

Critiques of Critical Literacy in This DOMAIN

Luke (2014) describes critical literacy as "the object of a half-century of theoretical debate and practical innovation in the field of education" (p. 21). Subsequently, different theoretical paradigms and traditions of scholarship have influenced its practice starting with feminist poststructuralist theories (Davies, 1993), critical discourse analysis (Fairclough, 1995), critical race theory (Ladson-Billings, 1999), postcolonialist traditions (Meacham, 2003), critical sociolinguistics (Makoni & Pennycook, 2007), critical media literacy (Share, 2009), cultural studies (Pahl & Rowsell, 2011), queer theory (Vicars, 2013), and place-conscious pedagogy (Comber, 2006). Given these different orientations to critical literacy, a more generative way to talk about "critiques" would involve approaching contemporary literature from a broadly critical perspective. Regardless of one's orientation to critical literacy, its focus should be on "understanding the relationship between texts, meaning-making, and power to undertake transformative social action that contributes to the achievement of a more equitable social order" (Janks & Vasquez, 2011, p. 1). Following are other items to attend to.

Cultural Resources Should Be Mobilised Rather Than Misrepresented

Vasquez (2014) describes critical literacy as a perspective and way of being that should be constructed organically, building from the inquiry questions of learners, beginning from children's first day of school. Critical literacy can therefore be described as "an evolving repertoire of practices of analysis and interrogation which move between the micro features of texts and the macro conditions of institutions, focusing on how relations of power work through these practices" (Comber, 2013, p. 589). This means work done with contemporary literature from a critical literacy perspective will and should look different in different places. In keeping with this thinking, Campano, Ghiso, and Sánchez (2013) argue critical literacy is not a framework developed by academics and transmitted to teachers and students, but arises "organically in local contexts" when readers "mobilise cultural and epistemic resources in their transactions with texts and with their worlds" (p. 119). However, it is difficult to mobilise one's cultural resources when working with contemporary literature that misrepresents or minimally represents one's culture.

Distortions of Culture and Identities Should Be Disrupted

Rudine Sims Bishop (1990) posits that books can serve as windows into other people's lives as well as mirrors of our own. What happens when some readers are provided with an endless hall of mirrors to peruse while others find few or no mirrors of their own lives in literature? The Cooperative Children's Book Center (CCBC) reviews thousands of children's books published each year in the United States. In their 2018 report they noted small shifts in publishing to make inroads in response to the need for books that accurately reflect diverse cultures and identities (Horning, Lindgren, Schliesman, & Tyner, 2019). The CCBC reports that in 2018, 50% of children's books published in the United States focused on white characters, 27% focused on animals, 10% had Black characters, 7% had Asian Pacific Islanders and Asian Pacific Americans, 5% had Latinx characters, and 1% had American Indian and First Nations characters. The report also shows a slow increase in the number of books that do not default to white protagonists. In spite of these gains, the report notes there continue to be many books featuring brown-skinned protagonists with no specific cultural or ethnic identifiers. According to Thomas (2019), such books distort and misrepresent cultures and become distorted funhouse mirrors of the self. Thomas adapts Bishop's (1990) windows and mirrors analogy to perform critical work around literary misrepresentations.

Problematic representations can be unpacked and disrupted using critical literacies to help readers understand the problematic positioning put on offer by such texts and the effect they have on individuals and groups, so in their own writing they can focus on more powerful representations of diverse cultures and identities. The same distortion and misrepresentation of cultures and identities exist across other contemporary literature, including digital texts, pop culture texts, gaming narratives, and fanfiction, making it even more important to imagine ways of using critical literacy as a framework or perspective rather than as a unit of study. In the next section we discuss responses to such critiques.

Responses to Any Critiques and Current Research in the Area

Responses to the distortions and misrepresentations of cultures and identities in contemporary literature includes the #ownvoices hashtag movement which makes use of Twitter to recommend books with diverse characters written by authors from the group represented in the books. Other responses take the form of blogs and coalitions, such as Debbie Reese's *American Indians in Children's Literature* (AICL) blog which provides critical analysis of Indigenous peoples in children's and young adult books, and the Pop Culture Hero Coalition, a non-profit organization that uses TV, film, and comics to take a stand against bullying, racism, and other forms of hate.

In their 2018 report, The Cooperative Children's Book Center (CCBC) noted a small but important increase in the number of books published that focus on issues of diversity, including the publication of what they referred to as groundbreaking books for young children that move away from binary gender norms to expand LGBTQ+ offerings. One such book, *Julián is a Mermaid* (Love, 2018), centres on a Latinx gender non-conforming character. The CCBC debated over whether to include the book in their recommended books list because the author is neither Latinx nor LGBTQ+, which flies against the intent of the #ownvoices movement. Their reason for including the book speaks to some of the critiques of the movement, namely, that some books are too important not to include, especially where there are wide gaps in representations of certain identities in contemporary literature.

Implications for Pedagogy: Adult- and Youth-Led Enactments of Literary Critique

In classrooms, libraries, and youth affinity spaces, we see numerous instantiations of critical literacy in relation to contemporary literatures, some adult-driven and some initiated by children and youth. All carry deep pedagogical implications because selecting, reading, and teaching texts is inherently political—a "contested domain fostering debates about the social and cultural functions of literature" (Low & Campano, 2013, p. 26). As questions surge around which texts, authors, genres, modes, and media should be elevated at the expense of others, educators must make decisions. Is literature meant to reproduce a literate citizenry through a shared canon or should a critical literary pedagogy centre diverse perspectives and multimodal formats? Who gets to decide? In this section, we explore implications for teaching contemporary literature, first by examining critical work initiated by educators, then youth-driven enactments of literary critique.

One common feature of educator-led critical discussions of literature is a set of questions, such as:

- Who is included and omitted? Who appears at the centre and who at the margins? Who is the hero? Whose languages, experiences, histories, and perspectives are elevated and whose are minimised?
- Are characters authentically and multidimensionally depicted? Are stereotypes or generalisations used? Has the author appropriated or misrepresented cultural traditions or histories?
- What is the author's background and how might it contribute to our understanding of the text? What is the author's view of success, justice, and "normal"? What assumptions are made about readers of the text?

Such questions (e.g., World of Words, 2020) invite readers to apply critical lenses to deconstruct texts in age-appropriate ways.

In the opening vignette, an early childhood educator created space for 3–5-year-olds to explore a variety of social issues using a picture book and toy store advertisements. In middle school classrooms, we have observed educators prompting students to perform feminist critiques of superhero films for their representation of women (Dallacqua & Low, 2019). In high school settings, students apply critical lenses toward canonical novels (Borsheim-Black, Macaluso, & Petrone, 2014). Because texts are "a product of culture as well as evidence of power relationships" (Botelho & Rudman, 2009, p. 72), educators may encourage students of all ages to read all texts critically, for their implicit and explicit messages and for the stories and identities they feature, conceal, or distort. As the literary and media landscape continues to shift in the 21st century, critical educators should prioritise texts that represent through many modes the mirrors, windows, and doors of human experience; grapple with major sociopolitical issues such as the climate crisis, systemic racism, populist authoritarianism, wealth and health disparities, and gender/sex/ual discrimination; and invite readers to experience a range of critical and emotional responses, including joy.

While educators play an undeniable role in inviting students to participate in critical readings, we are drawn to youth-led enactments of literary critique, and to the lessons educators can learn from them. For examples of youth-initiated critical literacies, we turn to fandoms, where readers organise, face-to-face and online, around shared literary affinities. Whether dedicated to *Naruto* manga,

Harry Potter novels, or *Pokémon* games, many fandoms take on a critical nature as members both joyfully consume pop culture and produce counter-texts. Fan art and fanfiction (Thomas, 2006) are examples of communal literary critique in which readers expand and alter official storyscapes by "restorying" them, making meanings "that are not just independent of authorial intent but that can deliberately contradict it" (Thomas, 2019, p. 156). We have witnessed children critiquing the racial and gender politics of fictive universes by creating new characters (Low, 2017). Some readers race- and gender-bend existing characters to create more inclusive narratives (Thomas & Stornaiuolo, 2016). Others "ship" characters, putting them in relationships that expand the sexual parameters of the source material (i.e., slash fiction). Restorying race, gender, and sexual representations across literary forms is a powerful example of critical literacy. Enactments of "interpretive agency" (Thomas, 2019, p. 154) are active, procreative, social, and organically youth-driven.

Using literature that addresses the topics, social issues, and questions young people raise is central to creating an inclusive critical curriculum. We argue educators should also incorporate the critical literacy practices of youth as fans of various media-texts. This means both validating the texts students are passionate about and including within the literary curriculum agentive critical practices that arise in affinity spaces, incorporating students' fandom practices and modal/genre preferences into a critical literacy pedagogy.

Implications for Research

As researchers in the space of contemporary literature, we are aware there is an urgent need for more critical work. We have identified three challenges for researchers of contemporary literature: the need to interrogate our own positions from which we conduct research; the need to always be critically "switched on" and wary of selective data collection which tells a single narrative; and the need to seek out, research, and illustrate examples of practice with contemporary literature where participants are subverting power, whether it be power written into the literary text or power from beyond, found in local and global contexts.

The ways we read text, including contemporary literature, are never neutral. Each time we read, write, or create, we draw from our past experiences and understandings of how the world works (Vasquez, 2014). We therefore should also analyse our own readings of text and unpack the position(s) from which we engage in research into contemporary literacies by asking questions such as:

- How am I positioning the participant practices and responses within my own frame of reference?
- What alternate readings of participant practices and responses are possible?

A cautionary tale comes from our own work, recasting an eye over research on fanfiction practices that was published over a decade ago (Thomas, 2007). Angela had a distinct feeling of discomfort that there were critical issues with the data that hadn't been identified at the time. For example, in discussing opportunities and notions for alterity in fanfiction practices, Angela explored how adolescent girls were adopting masculine roles in their role-playing, and described the practice as a way for girls to place themselves in unknown subject positions, and to explore alternative ways of being. Angela argued the context of community provided a unique opportunity to reconfigure and transform identities, so much so that all the usual markers of identity (age, gender, race, class) were disrupted. Whilst there was truth in this reading of the participant practices, it was not the *whole* truth. In a retrospective analysis, Angela discovered there were instances of practice that could be held up for critique. For example, the girls would write storylines in which their male character "selves" were idealised versions of males playing romantic fantasy storylines. It's easy *not to see* data that doesn't fit the narrative we have developed, or to ignore aspects of the data which could offer alternative insights into a context when selecting what gets written about and published (e.g., Low & Pandya, 2019).

A growing trend with researchers in this space is to do *positive discourse analysis* (Hughes, 2018), seeking out those instances of practice with contemporary literatures that subvert power in some form with the aim of energising social change. Martin (2004) argues "we need a complementary focus on community, taking into account how people get together and make room for themselves in the world—in ways that redistribute power" (p. 184). The very nature of the spaces of contemporary literatures is that some have emerged as agents of social change, creating safe places for hitherto disenfranchised voices to be heard.

In some fanfiction spaces, a challenge some participants have is moderators enforcing rules about writing "in canon." This means that if the canonical literature has problematic storylines with respect to gender, class, ethnicity, etc., the participant cannot move beyond them. As researchers, it is imperative to seek out and analyse the success of *alternate* spaces: spaces in which participants resist canon, and find creative and critical ways to subvert power. By researching instances of resistance, researchers have the power to shed light on possible spaces where social critique is happening.

Critical Literacy and Contemporary Literature: Implications for Our Social Responsibility as Academics

Making sense of the sociopolitical systems through which we live our lives, and questioning these systems, means focusing on social issues such as inequities of race, class, gender, or disability, and considering and interrogating the ways we use language and other semiotic resources to shape our understanding of these issues. Here our work as academics is crucial. We must keep in mind that enacting critical literacy through contemporary literature could benefit from making use of the *fictionality* of fictional texts, since knowledge about literature (genres, formats, conventions, etc.) may increase learning through literature (social issues, identity construction, etc.).

Frederking et al. (2012) stress that the use of literary texts involves both semantic and idiolectical literacy, and also contextual literacy. Semantic literacy means understanding the content of a literary text through the ability to read between the lines and take in its semantic plurality, so a variety of interpretations is possible and can be evaluated. To possess the ability of idiolectic literacy, on the other hand, means being able to see structural patterns in fiction and through them distinguish what is specific in the aesthetic expression of a literary text. However, idiolectic literacy can also include the ability to reflect on how the form and content of a literary text affect each other, that is, the ability to link semantic literacy with idiolectic literacy, and draw conclusions from this connection when interpreting a literary text. Finally, contextual literacy means the ability to interpret literary text based on its historical, social, and cultural contexts.

Academics must ensure in their various teaching contexts that attention is given to unpacking all aspects of fictionality, so that critical literacy has space to be enacted meaningfully. Researchers within the field of children's literature have argued that reading fiction for specific purposes at school is problematic, since young people's literature is historically linked to didactic impulses, but has nevertheless evolved into a literary form with artistic legitimacy (Lyngfelt, 2017). However, since contemporary literatures have characteristics such as genre blending, postmodernist features, paratextual practices, and complex plots and characters, literature is an art form that opens the way for new approaches to critical literacy. This would include work with semantic, idiolectical, and contextual literacy, along with work on reader positioning, and the investigation of social and discursive practices around and related to the contemporary literature of focus.

For this work, the academic's social responsibility is crucial, since not only theoretical knowledge about fiction and interpretation is needed, but also knowledge about intersectionality and the social conditions implied by various educational settings. As Arendt stresses, there is a risk that teachers' professional lives are increasingly taken over by "labour" and "work," at the expense of "activity," making the teachers define themselves as bureaucrats rather than "civic professionals" (Arendt, 1958). In line with this, there is a risk that *knowing* democracy, that is, critical thinking as a competence developed by reading, and *doing* democracy, that is, critical literacy as a practice in which fiction is used, become fused to teachers—especially if teachers regard themselves to be a cog in a bureaucratic machine. Hence, critical thinking could be characterised as "labour" rather than "activity," meaning critical literacy as an activity could be made to prioritise decontextualised interpretations of textual meaning. Our responsibility as academics is to discourage such neutral stances by pointing out the relation between issues such as race, gender, and climate change, and showing how the ways we contribute to interpretations of texts ourselves is linked to interpretations of the surrounding world.

Recommendations for Future Research and Praxis

We end this chapter with some recommendations. We first ask teachers to consider how they might make use of contemporary forms of literature to develop critical literacy, and suggest that new directions in working with such texts and practices from a critical literacy perspective should include multimodal pedagogies (Albers, Vasquez, & Harste, 2008), much like Bryan was able to do with Kushi in the classroom vignette presented earlier.

As a pedagogical call to action, we urge educators to move beyond the idea of applying individual critical lenses (i.e., reading a literary text through the lens of race or dis/ability) and toward critical intersectional inquiries of race, culture, class, ability, age, religion, and sexuality. By focusing on the ways in which power, privilege, and oppression are enacted in contemporary society, educators invite students to respond to literary representations in nuanced, critical ways. Coupled with this, we urge educators to consider the ways in which social action can be embedded into local practices with contemporary literatures.

As a call to action for future research, we suggest there is a need for longitudinal studies on students' development of critical literacy with contemporary literatures, individually as well as collectively, and within various socio-economic groups. We urge researchers to seek out, research and shed light on young people's subversive work with literature, and to illustrate positive instances where critical work with contemporary literatures has offered opportunities for restorying one's own identity and place in the world. Finally, we end with a call to creators of contemporary literature to embrace diversity of representation, engage with and integrate ways of storytelling that reflect a wide scope of cultural inheritances, and open spaces for all peoples to imagine and speculate on new possibilities for both present and future selves.

References

Albers, P., Vasquez V. M., & Harste, J. C. (2008). A classroom with a view: Teachers, multimodality, and new literacies. *Talking Points, 19*(2), 3–13.

Arendt, H. (1958). *The human condition*. University of Chicago Press.

Bishop, R. S. (1990). Mirrors, windows, and sliding glass doors. *Perspectives: Choosing and Using Books for the Classroom, 6*(3), ix–xi.

Borsheim-Black, C., Macaluso, M., & Petrone, R. (2014). Critical literature pedagogy. *Journal of Adolescent & Adult Literacy, 58*(2), 123–133. http://dx.doi.org/10.1002/jaal.323

Botelho, M. J., & Rudman, M. K. (2009). *Critical multicultural analysis of children's literature: Mirrors, windows, and doors*. Routledge.

Campano, G., Ghiso, M. P., & Sánchez, L. (2013). "Nobody one knows the . . . amount of a person": Elementary students critiquing dehumanization through organic critical literacies. *Research in the Teaching of English, 48*, 97–124.

Comber, B. (2006). Pedagogy as work: Educating the next generation of literacy teachers. *Pedagogies: An International Journal, 1*(1), 59–67. https://doi.org/10.1207/s15544818ped0101_9

Comber, B. (2013). Critical literacy in the early years: Emergence and sustenance in an age of accountability. In J. Larson & J. Marsh (Eds.), *The SAGE handbook of early childhood literacy* (pp. 587–601). Sage.

Dallacqua, A. K, & Low, D. E. (2019). "I never think of the girls": Critical gender inquiry with superheroes. *English Journal, 108*(5), 76–84.

Davies, B. (1993). *Shards of glass: Children reading and writing beyond gendered identity.* Allen & Unwin.

Fairclough, N. (1995). *Critical discourse analysis: The critical study of language.* Longman.

Frederking, V., Henschel, S., Meier, C., Roick, T., Stanat, P., & Dickhäuser, O. (2012). Beyond functional aspects of reading literacy: Theoretical structure and empirical validity of literary literacy. *L1-Educational Studies in Language and Literature, 12,* 1–24. https://doi.org/10.17239/L1ESLL-2012.01.02

Horning, K. T., Lindgren, M. V., Schliesman, M., & Tyner, M. (2019). A few observations: Literature in 2018. *Cooperative Children's Book Center.* Retrieved from http://ccbc.education.wisc.edu/books/choiceintro19.asp

Hughes, J. M. F. (2018). Progressing positive discourse analysis and/in critical discourse studies: Reconstructing resistance through progressive discourse analysis. *Review of Communication, 18*(3), 193–211. http://dx.doi.org/10.1080/15358593.2018.1479880

Janks, H., & Vasquez, V. (2011). Editorial: Critical literacy revisited: Writing as critique. *English Teaching: Practice and Critique, 10*(1), 1–6. https://edlinked.soe.waikato.ac.nz/journal/files/etpc/files/2011v10n1ed.pdf

Ladson-Billings, G. (1999). Just what is critical race theory and what's it doing in a nice field like education? In L. Parker, D. Deyhle, & S. Villenas (Eds.), *Race is . . . race isn't: Critical race theory and qualitative studies in education* (pp. 7–30). Press.

Love, J. (2018). *Julián is a mermaid.* Candlewick.

Low, D. E. (2017). Students contesting "colormuteness" through critical inquiries into comics. *English Journal, 106*(4), 19–28.

Low, D. E., & Campano, G. (2013). The image becomes the weapon: New literacies and canonical legacies. *Voices from the Middle, 21*(1), 26–31.

Low, D. E., & Pandya, J. Z. (2019). Issues of validity, subjectivity, and reflexivity in multimodal literacy research and analysis. *Journal of Language and Literacy Education, 15*(1), 1–22.

Luke, A. (2014). Defining critical literacy. In J. Z. Pandya & J. Avila (Eds.), *Moving critical literacies forward: A new look at praxis across contexts* (pp. 19–31). Routledge.

Lyngfelt, A. (2017). Fiction at school for educational purposes. What possibilities do students get to act as moral subjects? In O. Franck & C. Osbeck (Eds.), *Ethical literacies and sustainability education: Young people, subjectivity and democratic participation* (pp. 73–84). Palgrave Macmillan.

Makoni, S., & Pennycook, A. (Eds.). (2007). *Disinventing and reconstituting languages.* Multilingual Matters.

Martin, J. R. (2004). Positive discourse analysis: Solidarity and change. *Revista Canaria de Estudios Ingleses, 49,* 179–202.

Meacham, S. J. (2003, March 20). *Literacy and "street credibility": Plantations, prisons, and African American literacy from Frederick Douglass to 50 Cent* [Conference presentation]. ESRC Seminar Series Conference, Sheffield, UK.

Pahl, K., & Rowsell, J. (2011). Artifactual critical literacy: A new perspective for literacy education. *Berkeley Review of Education, 2*(2), 129–151. https://doi.org/10.5070/B82110050

Portis, A. (2014). *Froodle.* Roaring Brook Press.

Share, J. (2009). *Media literacy is elementary: Teaching youth to critically read and create media.* Peter Lang.

Thomas, A. (2006). Fan fiction online: Engagement, critical response and affective play through writing. *Australian Journal of Language and Literacy, 29*(3), 226–239.

Thomas, A. (2007). *Youth online: Identity and literacy in the digital age.* Peter Lang.

Thomas, E. E. (2019). *The dark fantastic: Race and the imagination from Harry Potter to the Hunger Games.* New York University Press.

Thomas, E. E., & Stornaiuolo, A. (2016). Restorying the self: Bending toward textual justice. *Harvard Educational Review, 86*(3), 313–338. https://doi.org/10.17763/1943-5045-86.3.313

Vasquez, V. M. (2014). *Negotiating critical literacies with young children* (10th anniversary ed.). Routledge.

Vasquez, V. M. (2017). Critical literacy. In *Oxford research encyclopedia of education.* https://doi.org/10.1093/acrefore/9780190264093.013.20

Vasquez, V. M., Janks, H., & Comber, B. (2019). Critical literacy as a way of being and doing. *Language Arts, 96,* 300–311.

Vicars, M. (2013). Queerer than queer. In J. N. Lester & R. Gabriel (Eds.), *Performances of research critical issues in K–12 education* (pp. 245–272). Peter Lang.

World of Words. (2020). 10 quick ways to analyze children's books for racism and sexism. *The Council on Interracial Books for Children.* Retrieved from https://wowlit.org/links/evaluating-global-literature/10-quick-ways-to-analyze-childrens-books-for-racism-and-sexism/

3.2

CRITICAL ARTS-LITERACIES IN CLASSROOMS

Moving With Abduction, Imagination, and Emotion Across Modalities

James S. Chisholm and Kathryn F. Whitmore

Introduction

In this chapter we review trends in recent research and practice in critical literacies and classroom engagement with the arts, which we characterize as a sociopolitical stance researchers and teachers take either implicitly or explicitly to disrupt hegemonic thinking in education. Although there exists a rich body of exemplary empirical work on both critical literacies and arts-based classroom engagement, we focus on studies that leverage the power in both of these pedagogical stances—the critical and the arts-based—to examine literacies learning in classrooms. To set up a research agenda that leverages "critical arts-literacies," we situate our argument by describing prerequisite theoretical concepts: abduction, imagination, and emotion. We then characterize critical literacies and engagement with the arts by briefly reviewing broad recent trends in the field, highlighting specifically quintessential critical arts-literacies studies and their affordances. We close by recognizing generative classroom practices in critical arts-literacies research, and articulating implications for future pedagogy and research.

Abduction, Imagination, and Emotion

Central to our conceptualization of critical arts-literacies are the connected, interwoven, and foundational concepts of abduction, imagination, and emotion. Recognizing and leveraging these integral concepts can transform classroom learning. We emphasize that these are not just theoretical notions, but directives for teachers and researchers who desire to use the arts to confront social injustice with action and change.

Abduction

In his argument for the arts for critical literacies learning, Harste (2014) highlighted the role of abductive thinking:

> First, art encourages learners to see more differently, more aesthetically, more emotionally, more parsimoniously . . . Second, art affords critical expression . . . Third, art affords

 DOI: 10.4324/9781003023425-37

abduction—the exploration of possibility, creativity, and imagination . . . Fourth, art affords agency—the ability to impose a different order on experience.

(pp. 96–97)

Abduction, as a distinct mode of thinking based on intuition and insight rather than induction or deduction (Batchelor, 2018), accounts for ideas that simply occur to learners as they "explore possibilities, their creativity, and their imagination" (Albers, Vasquez, Harste, & Janks, 2019, p. 61). It is a concept that grounds and rationalizes research and practice in critical literacies and the arts. Abduction "means the focus in art is on insight whereas in induction and deduction the focus is on the logical conclusion of facts, data, and information" (Harste, 2014, p. 97). Abduction is a foundational concept for critical arts-literacies since it creates space in education for new modes of "thinking/being/becoming" (Shields, Guyotte, & Weedo, 2016, p. 45).

Imagination

Imagination also sits at the intersection of critical literacies and the arts; theorists and philosophers have long argued that imagination opens spaces for recognizing, empathizing, and acting in ways that disrupt the status quo—that transform (Boal, 1979; Dewey, 1934/2008; Greene, 1995). For, as argued by Greene (1995), "To tap into imagination is to become able to break with what is supposedly fixed and finished . . . to see beyond . . . to form notions of what should be and what is not yet" (p. 19). Enacting critical arts-literacies in classrooms is not possible without imagination. English (2016) described:

As Dewey helps us see, imagination connects to empathy; it is a form of "empathetic projection", giving us "access" to a view of the world as others may see it. With this connection to empathy, imagination facilitates transformative learning processes that happen through our interactions with others, and thereby it makes possible our ability to learn with and from others.

(p. 1055)

The arts are a means through which imagination may be accessed and exploited for such a transformation. "The arts," said Dewey, "allow us to 'enter, through imagination and the emotions they evoke, into other forms of relationships and participation than our own' (1934/2008, p. 336)" (quoted in English, 2016). And as Greene (1995) argued, "encounters with the arts have a unique power to release imagination" (p. 27).

Emotion

Emotion is central to meaning making and the "reification and transformation of signs" (Lewis, 2020, p. 275), and perhaps requisite to critical arts-literacies. "Understanding what emotion *does* to signs is central to teachers and researchers of critical literacy and literary response" (p. 275). Conceptualizing emotion as an action allows researchers to investigate the ways in which "mediating signs or tools such as language, texts, bodies (gestures), objects, and space" (Lewis & Crampton, 2016, p. 105) act to transform signs. This transformation is a goal of critical arts-literacies work and it "comes when the circulation of emotion challenges dominant readings and practices" (Lewis, 2020, p. 277). As Johnson and Enriquez (2016) emphasized, "transformation of signs is emotional work . . . and critical engagements are impossible when emotion is invisible, erased in disciplinary practices that seek to mediate or mitigate its presence" (pp. 272–273).

Critiques of Critical Literacies in the Arts

We promote the potential transformative impact of these foundational concepts in classrooms across diverse contexts beyond what researchers and teachers have already been able to accomplish. To that end, we identify some critiques of critical literacies in the arts and some recent powerful work that has responded to those critiques to support our call for a critical arts-literacies agenda.

Critique 1: Concept Dilution

As other authors have noted in this volume, the term critical literacies suffers from concept dilution. Specifically, the descriptor "critical" has been applied to a wide range of studies that to varying degrees examine "literate practices individuals need in order to survive and thrive in the world" (p. 3, this volume). With a classical focus on interrogating texts and contexts, some researchers and teachers have described as critical what are actually studies of "critical thinking" (Paul & Elder, 2013) or studies about learning related to "critical reflection" (Mezirow, 1998).

Arts integration suffers from a similar type of concept dilution. Instead of characterizing a "way of knowing" (Eisner, 2002, p. 10) or a mode of "thinking/being/becoming" in the world (Shields et al., 2016, p. 45), arts-integration has been mischaracterized to "decorate" traditional literacies learning or in service of more "rigorous" literacies learning. Two examples may be useful here. First, the arts have been used in classrooms as a way to demonstrate, in another mode, learning that has already been completed in the linguistic mode. Students might read a short play, discuss its meaning and importance, and create a diorama of the play's setting to culminate the study. As Harste (2014) noted, "[d]rawing, sculpting, or putting together a collage are more than tools for rendering and capturing likenesses. These processes transform perception and thought into images and teach us how both to see and to think with our eyes" (p. 96).

Second, the arts have been marginalized to function in service of a more powerful autonomous literacies model (Street, 1995). For example, children's picture books studied only for the language contained across the pages and not for the images (Whitelaw, 2017)—or more importantly the interaction between the image and the language—communicates a modal bias. Albers (2006) argued, "meaning is not located within any one mode, but in how the modes are interpreted in relation to each other" (p. 77) and Kress (1997) asserted that learners' multiple literacy resources could be productively used to leverage more conventional linguistic literacy skills if educators valued the multimodal nature of all signs equally. Given the diverse multimodality of many texts in the 21st century, a modal hierarchy seems short-sighted, if not dangerous inside or outside of a critical literacies framework.

Critique 2: Lacking Academic "Rigor"

The arts and the multiple modes across which the arts move—visual, linguistic, dramatic/gestural, sculptural, musical, kineikonic—are often perceived to be appropriate for younger learners, but not for older learners. Not unrelated to the modal preference for the linguistic mode cultivated in verbocentric schools, painting, sketching, or performing meaning is perceived to be less rigorous or academic than writing that meaning (see Foertsch, 2006). Perhaps given the connection (albeit dwindling) the arts have with early childhood and elementary classrooms, they have also been perceived inaccurately as apolitical, requiring aesthetic prowess, and with a singular purpose toward beauty, a standard that seems out of reach for some learners and teachers alike.

Critique 3: "Literal" Transmediation

This last critique might be the most controversial critique we offer. While we highly value the multimodal projects and the activist stances that have been promoted in classrooms, given the dilution of the terms and the modal biases described previously, we believe the power of multimodal research and practice could be dramatically improved by emphasizing the movement learners make across modes—and the thinking that such movement generates—over the products created as a result of combining multiple modes. Decades of work by literacy researchers have developed the concept of transmediation—recasting meanings across sign systems (Siegel, 1995), and the generative power such movement has. In fact, some researchers in the field have *equated* transmediation with literacy (Albers, 2006; Berghoff, Egawa, Harste, & Hoonan, 2000).

Importantly, Suhor (1984) identified the distinction between "generative" transmediation and "literal" transmediation when he conceptualized an extra-linguistic curriculum. The latter might be said to focus too much on the product of multimodal instruction over the process, venerated in the former. Harste noted, for example, one teacher's directive, "Draw your favorite scene from the text" as an unfortunate attempt at transmediation through the "sketch-to-stretch" activity. The invitation to "draw a picture symbolizing what the story means to you" would have required students to generate new understanding rather than merely reproduce ideas already available in the text. "While talk mediates experience, taking what you talked about and drawing a sketch 'transmediates' it" (Berghoff et al., 2000, p. 2).

And although we hesitate to critique critical literacies projects enacted with learners to address injustices locally in a globalized world, as teachers carve out spaces in which to support students' political stances, neoliberal policies that construct teachers as neutral and apolitical often block the connection of these projects with the very audiences and practices toward which they are directed—an injustice in its own right.

Critical Arts-Literacies in Classrooms

Many researchers have documented the myriad ways in which engagement with the arts mediates learning. Growing interest in fusing the arts into literacies classrooms is evidenced by special issues in *Harvard Educational Review* (Clapp & Edwards, 2013) and *English Journal* (Emert, Macro, & Schmidt, 2016), and volumes such as *Arts-based Teaching and Learning in the Literacy Classroom* (Whitelaw, 2019); *Literacies, the Arts, and Multimodality* (Albers & Sanders, 2010); *Literacies, Learning, and the Body* (Enriquez, Johnson, Kontovourki, & Mallozzi, 2015); and *A Symphony of Possibilities* (Macro & Zoss, 2019).

In this section, we demonstrate the power of combining methods and purposes in a critical arts-literacies agenda that draws on the affordances of abduction, imagination, and emotion. By extending Shields et al.'s (2016) notion of artful pedagogy—"an approach to the process of teaching and learning that situates artful ways of thinking, moving, and being at the center of how we teach" (p. 45)—to critical literacies, we characterize a literature in which moving with abduction, imagination, and emotion across modalities results not only in complex, layered understandings, but also interrogates social injustices by engaging significantly in calls to social action.

Brazilian educator Soares, whose work we learned about in *A Reason to Read: Linking Literacy and the Arts* (Landay & Wootton, 2012), enacted a critical arts-literacies educational experience with his high school students and the cordel—a clothesline on which texts of various sorts and for different purposes can be hung to introduce learners to content, display artwork, or engage in critical literacies learning (see Whitmore, Chisholm, & Fletcher, 2020; Wootton, 2010). In response to drug-related violence in their communities, Soares, his students, and other students from the city created a cordel that included more than 6,000 artful texts (e.g., poems, paintings, etc.) to surround the perimeter of the local lake. Soares' artful description of the march for peace that ensued demonstrates the unique power of the arts to pair with critical literacies learning to promote social justice:

> And the cordel was there for two days so people could see it, and many people saw it, many people talked about it. Visually it was beautiful. The sun was setting. It reflected on the water, really something to see.
>
> *(Wootton, 2010, p. 5)*

Artists have always provided critical perspectives on society (Darts, 2004). Because the arts often combine multiple modes in one textual space, they encourage readers to engage abductively and emotionally and to imagine new ways of thinking.

Simon and colleagues mobilized the arts to promote critical literacies learning about, among other topics, Holocaust literature (Simon et al., 2014). Simon, Evis, Walkland, Kalan, and Baer (2016) described how middle school students created paintings and artist statements in response to personally meaningful panels from Spiegelman's (1986) *Maus: A Survivor's Tale*. Simon et al. (2016) dedicated most of their manuscript to reproducing students' artworks and artist statements to demonstrate how the arts are essential for human experience (Eisner, 2002; Greene, 1995) and especially for humanizing pedagogical experiences. In these stunning visual works, students reproduced central panels from *Maus* that moved them, around which they created their own panels to convey their responses to the text, choosing to maintain Spiegelman's style or break from his conventions. Some students connected to their family histories to investigate contemporary racism and anti-Semitism. One student juxtaposed images of her African American grandparents with panels that featured mice who were hanged by cats (symbolizing Jews and Nazis, respectively, in the graphic novel). She noted in her artist's statement:

> Because my family were black, they experienced a lot of racism not unlike the Jews experienced in Nazi Germany. My family history made it easier for me to relate to and understand the discrimination that Jewish people experienced. This made the history more real for me, and it made the project more meaningful.
>
> *(p. 448)*

Moving from the visual to the musical arts, Goering and Mathews (2019) described how they engaged secondary students in social action while they learned about the history, structure, and techniques involved in writing protest songs. Students examined with Goering and Mathews the songs "Ohio" (Young, 1970) and "Hurricane" (Dylan & Levy, 1976). They listened closely to the melodies and rhythms of these songs and examined their structures before researching contemporary protest songs, identifying issues of importance in their lives, and trying their hand at protest songwriting. Throughout the unit, students heard from songwriters about their writing process and analyzed lyrics and structure, which they could lean on (or not) to draft their own protest songs. The results produced seven collaborative protest songs that addressed topics including LGBTQ rights, the environment, and "government incompetence," and transformed how students thought about writing. This classroom story demonstrated the capacity of critical approaches to bring learning to life for students who are "thinking, moving, and being" (Shields et al., 2016, p. 45) with the arts.

Studies of informal classroom drama emphasize how "[i]mprovisations in classrooms also bring words to life, lifting language off the one-dimensional page and reinvesting it with the three-dimensional features of voice, movement, gesture, and timing that are present in every human conversation" (Landay & Wootton, 2012, p. 99). Because learning is not just acquiring information and committing it to memory, "[l]earners must *do* something with what they are finding out from teachers or peers, not merely listen or speak" (Edmiston, 2014, p. 201). Edmiston and others (Whitmore, 2015; Wohlwend & Medina, 2014) have demonstrated how the dramatic and performing arts provide exceptional opportunities to demonstrate literacies learning. Importantly, through such classroom performances, students compose another text to be interpreted by their classmates.

Miller, Tanner, and Murray (2018) designed a pedagogy rooted in improvisational theatre to understand how fourth graders imagined whiteness in relationship to texts or signs relevant to social hierarchy—namely, castles and walls—and to imagine ways to disrupt implied power in such symbols.

> We were particularly interested in the fact that so many of the children imagined themselves with power, getting the things they wanted and bossing other people around. To them, the imaginary was a place in which they could feel powerful.
>
> *(p. 11)*

As children improvised, they often saw themselves as inside the castle, where power was inherent in status and place. When debriefing, the children began to think about themselves in terms of power; how did their positions as royals, for example, relate to those in positions as servants inside or others outside the castle?

> These children . . . were beginning to imagine that people outside the castle have to think about the world differently . . . the improvisational theater work and the dialogic reflection on that work facilitated the critical literacy of the workshop.
>
> *(pp. 18–19)*

Ninth grade social studies students also experienced process drama that blurred boundaries of historical and contemporary discrimination (Schroeter & Wager, 2017). Their teacher, Rose, co-facilitated with Schroeter a process drama interaction designed to engage students in an imagined, role-played social hierarchy reflective of witch hunts in 17th-century England. Group debriefing and individual interviews revealed students' emotional connections to discrimination in their current lives. "Working in the embodied medium of drama enabled students to physically and visually perceive exclusion. As the students' comments reflect, drama facilitated making critical links between discrimination in the process drama and contemporary forms of sexism and racism" (p. 411).

In an example of our own work with process drama (Chisholm & Whitmore, 2018), eighth graders engaged in layered drama- and movement-infused strategies to deepen meaning making about challenging Holocaust texts, including Anne Frank's diary. As students experienced drama strategies such as tableau, pantomime, and sculpture garden, they imagined and authored new embodied texts and their performances were celebrated and interrogated like other texts under study. The students' thinking and creations became more specifically critical when they chose to perform for outside audiences historical excerpts alongside contemporary illustrations of power dynamics in their lives: students choreographed a modern dance illustrating the effects of body image for women and girls, scripted and dramatized a skit about domestic abuse, and performed Ernestine Johnson Morrison's spoken word poem "The Average Black Girl," among others.

Across these studies, the arts were integrated in classrooms where social injustices were interrogated with learners of all ages and in ways that generated new meaning making across semiotic systems (rather than ornamenting linguistic meanings). We recognize in them evidence of foundational critical arts-literacies concepts. Abduction encouraged students and teachers to take risks and construct meanings in new ways. Students released their imaginations and engaged their emotions to empathize with experiences and positions different from their own. Implications from these studies guide teachers and researchers, as we suggest next.

Toward Critical Arts-Literacies Classroom-Based Research and Pedagogy

Much of the research in the intersection of critical literacies and the arts—which we name critical arts-literacies—is designed from critical ethnographic, teacher-research, and/or action research methodological perspectives, and therefore includes pedagogical as well as research implications. Readers can find in the rich descriptions of classroom interactions the teaching practices that can support and extend a critical arts-literacies pedagogy. Illustrations include:

- stringing visual, numeric, and verbal texts on cordels to support students' entry to literature such as the picture book *Knock Knock* (Beaty, 2013) which invites exploration of incarceration inequities (Whitmore et al., 2020);
- studying and writing protest songs (Johnson & Goering, 2016), for example, in the context of Black Lives Matter;
- creating editorial cartoons to persuade someone to agree with students' opinions on current social issues (Baize & Chisholm, 2020);
- collaborating with teaching artists (musicians, visual artists, drama artists) to deepen students' experiences (Chisholm, Jamner, & Whitmore, 2021).

We advocate for arts-based research methods which, like the arts themselves, offer "ways to tap into what would otherwise be inaccessible" (Leavy, 2015a, p. 21) and generate insights that can be "emotionally and politically evocative, captivating, aesthetically powerful, and moving" (p. 23). Arts-based research designs include artmaking as data or artmaking as a form of presentation. Albers et al. (2019) provide an example of artmaking as data in their analysis of teacher learning in a professional development institute in which critical literacy and the arts are explored via "critical making" (p. 51). Both the process and product of teachers' artworks became rendered as data in the authors' study, where the materiality and multimodality of the artifacts were analyzed in relationship to the teachers' linguistic artist statements. Examples of artmaking as presentation include Leavy's (e.g. 2015b) use of fiction-based research in which analysis of interview data is presented as a novel; ethnodrama and ethnotheater, in which qualitative data analysis is written in play form (e.g. Goldstein, 2013); and graphica, in which traditional empirical research narratives are told using the visual-linguistic conventions of a graphic novel (Jones & Woglom, 2013; Sousanis, 2015).

Multimodal tools for arts-based analysis hold particular promise given that, as Sousanis (2015) argues, "[t]he medium we think in defines what we can see" (p. 52). Examples of productive methods include:

- Visual Learning Analysis, in which photography is used to understand emotion and embodiment (Chisholm & Whitmore, 2018);
- Mapping, to understand where learning is emotionally resonant (Fleet & Britt, 2011);
- Visual Discourse Analysis, which analyzes how visual texts work from the perspectives of semiotics and critical literacy (Albers, 2013); and
- Software-supported embodied multimodality (Ntelioglou, 2015) that hyperlinks coded moments represented in transcripts, videos, documents, etc.

When researchers center critical arts-literacies in research design and research questions, and develop tools and methods for interpreting data, they push against logical, mathematical, and verbal privilege to emphasize abductive, imaginative, and emotional ways of understanding literacies learning and teaching.

Such practices will catalyze a research agenda that builds on the generative traditions of critical literacies research and practice and arts integration. A critical arts-literacies agenda comes, however, with social responsibilities. Schroeter and Wager (2017) advise "strong ethics and good communication with students, teachers, and counselors" and recognize "the disquieting difficulty of protecting students during in-depth explorations of discrimination" (p. 412). Such work will support learners in moving with abduction, imagination, and emotion across modalities to develop activist stances and artful pedagogies.

References

Albers, P. (2006). Imagining the possibilities in multimodal curriculum design. *English Education, 38*(2), 75–101.

Albers, P. (2013). Visual discourse analysis. In P. Albers, T. Holbrook, & A. Flint (Eds.), *New methods of literacy research* (pp. 101–114). Routledge.

Albers, P., & Sanders, J. (Eds.). (2010). *Literacies, the arts, and multimodality*. National Council of Teachers of English.

Albers, P., Vasquez, V. M., Harste, J. C., & Janks, H. (2019). Art as a critical response to social issues. *Journal of Literacy and Technology, 20*(1), 46–80.

Baize, J., & Chisholm, J. S. (2020). "It's important for people to see these types of issues on their own": Soundings during multimodal composing. In K. F. Whitmore & R. J. Meyer (Eds.), *Reclaiming literacies as meaning-making: Manifestations of values, identities, relationships, and knowledge* (pp. 208–211). Routledge.

Batchelor, K. E. (2018). Middle school writers' attitudes and beliefs on revision paired with transmediation during a flash fiction unit. *English Education, 50*(4), 337–364.

Beaty, D. (2013). *Knock knock: My dad's dream for me* (B. Collier, Illus.) New York: Hachette.

Berghoff, B., Egawa, K. A., Harste, J. C., & Hoonan, B. T. (2000). *Beyond reading and writing: Inquiry, curriculum, and multiple ways of knowing*. National Council of Teachers of English.

Boal, A. (1979). *Theater of the oppressed* (A. Charles & Maria-Odilia Leal McBride, Trans.). Theater Communication Group.

Chisholm, J. S., Jamner, J., & Whitmore, K. F. (2021). Amplifying students' musical identities, meanings, and memories. *English Journal, 110*(4), 45–52.

Chisholm, J. S., & Whitmore, K. F. (2018). *Reading challenging texts: Layering literacies through the arts*. Routledge and National Council of Teachers of English.

Clapp, E. P., & Edwards, L. A. (Eds.). (2013). Expanding our vision for the arts in education. *Harvard Educational Review, 83*(1).

Darts, D. (2004). Visual culture jam: Art, pedagogy, and creative resistance. *Studies in Art Education, 45*, 313–327.

Dewey, J. (1934/2008). Art as experience. In J. A. Boydston (Ed.), *The collected works of John Dewey: The later works* (Vol. 1). Southern Illinois University Press.

Dylan, B., & Levy, J. (1976). Hurricane. [Recorded by B. Dylan]. On *Desire*. New York: Columbia.

Edmiston, B. (2014). *Transforming teaching and learning with active and dramatic approaches: Engaging students across the curriculum*. Routledge.

Eisner, E. W. (2002). *The arts and the creation of mind*. Yale University Press.

Emert, T., Macro, K., & Schmidt, P. S. (Eds.). (2016). Imagination, creativity, and innovation: Showcasing the "A" in English language arts. *English Journal, 105*(5).

English, A. R. (2016). John Dewey and the role of the teacher in a globalized world: Imagination, empathy, and 'third voice'. *Educational Philosophy and Theory, 48*(10), 1046–1064.

Enriquez, G., Johnson, E., Kontovourki, S., & Mallozzi, C. A. (Eds.). (2015). *Literacies, learning, and the body: Putting theory and research into pedagogical practice*. Routledge.

Fleet, A., & Britt, C. (2011). Seeing spaces, inhabiting places. In D. Harcourt, B. Perry, & T. Waller (Eds.), *Researching young children's perspectives: Debating the ethics and dilemmas of educational research with children.* (pp. 143–162). Routledge.

Foertsch, J. (2006). Books as broccoli? Images as ice cream? Providing a healthy menu in a college English classroom. *Pedagogy: Critical Approaches to Teaching Literature, Language, Composition, and Culture, 6*(2), 209–230.

Goering, C., & Mathews, A. (2019). "I am Arkansas": Social activism through protest songwriting in a high school classroom. In K. Macro & M. Zoss (Eds.), *A symphony of possibilities: A handbook for arts integration in secondary English language arts* (pp. 19–35). National Council of Teachers of English.

Goldstein, T. (2013). *Zero tolerance and other plays: Disrupting xenophobia, racism and homophobia in school*. Brill Sense.

Greene, M. (1995). *Releasing the imagination: Essays on education, the arts, and social change*. Jossey-Bass.

Harste, J. C. (2014). The art of learning to be critically literate. *Language Arts, 92*(2), 90–102.

Johnson, E., & Enriquez, G. (2016). On literacies, learning, and bodies. In G. Enriquez, E. Johnson, S. Kontovourki, & C. A. Mallozzi (Eds.). (2015), *Literacies, learning, and the body: Putting theory and research into pedagogical practice* (pp. 272–277). Routledge.

Johnson, L., & Goering, C. Z. (Eds.). (2016). *Recontextualized: A framework for teaching English with music*. Sense Publishers.

Jones, S., & Woglom, J. F. (2013). Graphica: Comics arts-based educational research. *Harvard Educational Review, 83*(1), 168–189.

Kress, G. (1997). *Before writing: Rethinking the paths to literacy*. Routledge.

Landay, E., & Wootton, K. (2012). *A reason to read: Linking literacy and the arts*. Harvard Education Press.

Leavy, P. (2015a). *Method meets art: Arts-based research practice*. Guilford Publications.

Leavy, P. (2015b). *Low-fat love: Expanded anniversary edition*. Brill Sense.

Lewis, C. (2020). Emotion, critical response, and the transformation of signs: The fundamentals of language arts. *Language Arts, 97*(4), 274–278.

Lewis, C., & Crampton, A. (2016). Literacy, emotion, and the teaching/learning body. In G. Enriquez, E. Johnson, S. Kontovourki, & C. Mallozi (Eds.), *Literacies, learning, and the body* (pp. 105–121). Routledge.

Macro, K., & Zoss, M. (Eds.). (2019). *A symphony of possibilities: A handbook for arts integration in secondary English language arts*. National Council of Teachers of English.

Mezirow, J. (1998). On critical reflection. *Adult Education Quarterly, 48*(3), 185–198.

Miller, E. T., Tanner, S. J., & Murray, T. E. (2018). Castle"ing" whiteness: White youth and the racial imagination. *Journal of Language and Literacy Education, 14*(2), 1–23.

Ntelioglou, B. Y. (2015). Embodied multimodality framework: Examining language and literacy practices of English language learners in drama classrooms. In M. Perry & C. L. Medina (Eds.), *Methodologies of embodiment* (pp. 86–101). Routledge.

Paul, R., & Elder, L. (2013). *Critical thinking: Tools for taking charge of your professional and personal life*. Pearson Education.

Schroeter, S., & Wager, A. C. (2017). Blurring boundaries: Drama as a critical multimodal literacy for examining 17th-century witch hunts. *Journal of Adolescent & Adult Literacy, 60*(4), 405–413.

Shields, S. S., Guyotte, K. W., & Weedo, N. (2016). Artful pedagogy: (En)visioning the unfinished whole. *Journal of Curriculum and Pedagogy, 13*(1), 44–66.

Siegel, M. (1995). More than words: The generative power of transmediation for learning. *Canadian Journal of Education, 20*(4), 455–475.

Simon, R., Evis, S., Walkland, T., Kalan, A., & Baer, P. (2016). Navigating the "delicate relationship between empathy and critical distance": Youth literacies, social justice and arts-based inquiry. *English Teaching: Practice & Critique, 15*(3), 430–449.

Simon, R., and The Teaching to Learn Project: Bailey, A., Brennan, J., Calarco, A., Clarke, K., Edwards, W., Fujiwara, C., Kalan, A., Kruja, J., McInnes-Greenberg, E., & Pisecny, A. (2014). "In the swell of wandering words": The arts as a vehicle for adolescents' and educators' inquiries into the Holocaust memoir *Night*. *Perspectives on Urban Education, 11*(2), 90–106.

Sousanis, N. (2015). *Unflattening*. Harvard University Press.

Spiegelman, A. (1986). *Maus: A survivor's tale*. Random House.

Street, B. V. (1995). *Social literacies: Critical approaches to literacy in development, ethnography and education*. Longman.

Suhor, C. (1984). Toward a semiotics-based curriculum. *Journal of Curriculum Studies, 16*(3), 247–257.

Whitelaw, J. (2017). Beyond the bedtime story: In search of epistemic possibilities and the innovative potential of disquieting picturebooks. *Bookbird: A Journal of International Children's Literature, 55*(1), 33–41.

Whitelaw, J. (2019). *Arts-based teaching and learning in the literacy classroom: Cultivating a critical aesthetic practice*. Routledge.

Whitmore, K. F. (2015). Becoming the story in the joyful world of "Jack and the Beanstalk". *Language Arts, 93*(1), 25–37.

Whitmore, K. F., Chisholm, J. S., & Fletcher, L. (2020). Fostering, activating, and curating: Approaching books about social injustices with the arts. *Language Arts, 98*(1), 7–19.

Wohlwend, K., & Medina, C. L. (2014). Producing cultural imaginaries in the playshop. In R. J. Meyer & K. F. Whitmore (Eds.), *Reclaiming writing: Composing spaces for identities, relationships, and action* (pp. 198–209). Routledge.

Wootton, K. (2010). The cordel: Stories on a string. *Habla best practice handbook* (pp. 1–6). Retrieved from https://media-openideo-rwd.oiengine.com/attachments/ceb26787-7f86-4130-8703-bb38a0226104.pdf

Young, N. (1970). Ohio. [Recorded by D. Crosby, S. Stills, G. Nash, & N. Young]. In *So far*. Atlantic.

3.3

CRITICAL LITERACY OUT OF THE COMFORT ZONE

Productive Textual Tantrums

George L. Boggs, Nerida Spina, Donna E. Alvermann,
and Barbara Comber

Introduction

This chapter opens up a discussion around missed opportunities for moving critical literacy out of its comfort zone. Wisdom literature often invites readers on a "going-down" path, a *katabasis*, a path that involves a stage of self-destruction in order to reach greater fulfillment. As we consider our role in this volume, we affirm that *the way up and the way down are one and the same* (Heraclitus). Curiosity often drives these stories, and for us, it's about the role of texts in the creation and maintenance of human relations. We use a work of transnational children's literature about climate change as a place to start our journey. Our goal is to challenge and help move beyond an old cliché of critical literacy scholarship that weakens—we go along to get along. Our journey invites researchers to embrace critical awareness of their role in and consequences of research-based knowledge production.

To begin, four teacher educators and literacy researchers set out, at different times, in different time zones, and by different methods—all with sufficient resources—to find a children's book about climate change that they would use to investigate critical literacy itself. We'll foreground Barbara Comber's story. Barbara ventured to a bookshop on her way to her university to try to buy the children's book, *The Tantrum that Saved the World* [hereafter, *The Tantrum*] (Herbert & Mann, 2017), her interest having been piqued by Donna E. Alvermann's (2019) discussion of this text. Barbara's journey to the bookshop followed her morning re-reading a chapter in Dorothy Smith's *Institutional Ethnography: A Sociology for People* (2005) on text-reader relations and the notion of activating the text. In brief, Smith contends that texts can be considered as active and occurring, rather than as units of analysis in their own right. Revealing how readers interpret and act on texts is important for understanding their accomplishments. It is when real people in real places read and make sense of a text, and then do something with it, that it has the capacity to connect people in different locations. Smith's approach as an institutional ethnographer is to consider how people activate texts in order to get things done. Her research is primarily concerned with how texts organize and regulate people's work, which necessitates an interrogation of the assumed "innocent" and "sacred" nature of *all* texts, including those which might promote themselves as already "critical." Smith (2005) writes: "The power of the sacred text to remain across seas and generations is a condition of its holiness and its capacity to be read again, rediscovered, reinterpreted in the ever-changing local actualities of people's lives and doings" (p. 102).

DOI: 10.4324/9781003023425-38

Barbara discovered she would need to order a copy and wait for its arrival from the USA, or go against her usual preference and order it as a digital text. When she investigated further, she discovered that one of the book's authors is in fact an Australian writer and illustrator, Meagan Herbert, who teamed up with Michael Mann, "an award-winning American climate scientist" to produce the text. It interested her that the book was not readily available in Australia. Perhaps it was because she had tried to buy it from an independent bookseller. She tried a larger Australian book retailer. Using their online search for the title produced several children's picture books including *The Worms that Saved the World* (Doyle & Deeley, 2017) and *The Fart that Saved the World* (Gill, 2017), but not *The Tantrum that Saved the World*. Having made a note of these two books for her grandchildren, the second book in particular, she decided to go ahead and order this "world saving," "carbon-free" book. After several fraught attempts where she was directed to go to either Amazon or Paypal accounts, she managed to purchase the online book, for some reason in Euros rather than Australian dollars.

At this point, our story turns downward. The trouble of finding a necessary tool for conducting literacy scholarship accompanies awareness that our financial and technological resources, mobility, social networks, and native language are interlocking features of privilege inextricably tied to the forces of domination and control we aspire to alter. In one moment, we are wondering how another person might go about finding this book without a computer; simultaneously we are aware that the physical, political, and economic infrastructures that make possible the habits of mind by which we know ourselves are fundamentally unsustainable and incompatible with taken-for-granted aspects of life. But first, some key concepts, as we proceed.

Definitions

Climate Change: the human-caused warming of the planet, and the changes in wind and air currents, rainfall patterns, droughts, storms, melting of ice, and rise in sea level that come with it (Herbert & Mann, 2017, n.p.).

Critical Literacy: refers to the "use of technologies of print and other media of communication to analyze, critique and transform the norms, rule systems and practices governing the social fields of everyday life" (Luke, 2012, p. 5).

Foucauldian Analysis: invokes "a method of writing critical history: a way of using historical materials to bring about a 'revaluing of values' in the present day. Genealogical analysis traces how contemporary practices and institutions emerged out of specific struggles, conflicts, alliances, and exercises of power, many of which are nowadays forgotten" (Garland, 2014, p. 372).

Institutional Ethnography: a method of inquiry developed by Marxist feminist scholar Dorothy E. Smith to study the everyday social networking relations among women but later extended to people in general (Carroll, 2010). Smith has advocated for inquiry that begins from the standpoint of people, rather than from objectified, discursively constructed positions. One of Smith's key contributions in revealing the operation of power in contemporary times is her focus on the significant role texts play in mediating social-relations and lives.

Power Relations: a concept French philosopher Michel Foucault views as not something that is acquired, seized, or shared, something that one holds on to or allows to slip away; power is exercised from innumerable points, in the interplay of non-egalitarian and mobile relations (Foucault, 1976/1990, p. 94).

Textual Analysis: a method for analyzing "an institutionally-located text comes with a kind of analytical frame which provides or implies instructions for reading, establishes sources of authorization, self-constitutes as factual, indicates differences with contrary viewpoints, and adds up to a micro politics" (Stanley, 2018, p. 33).

Critiques of Critical Literacy

Back to *The Tantrum*, Barbara's search for the book reminds us of the importance of taking into account these kinds of everyday actualities of people as they engage with texts. As the account of getting one's hands on the book illustrates, local particularities matter. Smith's attention to standpoint provides an analytic approach that accesses tacit, embodied knowledge that might otherwise remain invisible because it is "not yet discursively appropriated" (Smith, 1997, p. 395). Even in an activity as seemingly unproblematic as accessing a picture book, time, and place are important, although they often disappear in objectified accounts. As Smith (2005) writes, "texts perform at the key juncture between the local settings of people's everyday worlds" and the operation of power that organizes social relations, which Smith calls "ruling relations" (p. 101). These organizing forces might be noted in analysis of picture books produced in the United States immediately after 9/11, where "good" Americans appear as white, living in a nuclear family (Lampert, 2008). Textually mediated ruling relations:

> form a complex field of coordinated activities, based in technologies of print, and increasingly in computer technologies. They are activities in and in relation to texts, and texts coordinate them as relations. Text-mediated relations are the forms in which power is generated and held in contemporary societies.
>
> *(p. 79)*

For us, then, disparate people are connected through texts and textually mediated ruling relations as they are connected through everyday experiences of climate change.

The texts that serve to coordinate are imbued with an ideological code that replicates itself across sites. A great deal of scholarship now exists that documents the impact of global neoliberal policies on education, from the explosion of standardized assessment (Stobart, 2008) with concomitant didactic pedagogies (Hayes et al., 2017) and neo-conservatization of literacy curricula (Apple, 2014) to teachers' critical digital literacies mediating their efforts to speak out (Stewart & Boggs, 2019). In Smith's terms, there is now a set of dominant ruling relations that organizes the social relations, work, and lives of teachers.

While Smith's research has tended to focus on texts that are produced as part of the functioning of institutions, such as the hospital or the justice system, we can consider the picture book as a key text of early education sites and of introduction to the local and global experiences of climate change.

It is not only the text itself which is of significance but also how it is used as a part of everyday social relations. Baker and Freebody (1989) demonstrated decades ago now, how children's first school books, often picture books, are employed by teachers to instruct children in normative ways of classroom participation and moral training. It is the talk around the text that tells children what counts as proper reading in a particular situation. Similarly, Luke (1992) showed how participation in shared book literacy lessons can simultaneously prepare young children to become docile classroom members/readers who sit, look, and act according to directions specified by the teacher. In these materially embodied practices, children are learning the work of behaving as school children learning to read (Luke, 2018).

Books, even wholesome children's picture books with a young female as the protagonist and nice messages about saving the world from climate disaster, are not neutral. We can ask many questions about such texts, their publication, and uses in context. *The Tantrum* is of course just one of many picture books designed to instruct children about climate change, biodiversity, and the risks for people in particular places around the planet. It is always worth asking: Who is the ideal reader of such a text? Who might read this book to which kinds of listeners in which kinds of places to what ends? Why did Sophia have "a tantrum"? Why might the author have described her behavior as a "tantrum"? How else might it be understood? What else might be read or viewed alongside this book? For example, it would, in a range of classroom contexts, make sense to view some of Greta Thunberg's speeches and the responses of various politicians, featured in the media, to her specifically, and to young people becoming involved in climate change protests instead of attending school. Students might be invited to re-write the story from the point of view of their own context, for example after the 2019/2020 bushfires in Australia that devastated significant places such as Kangaroo Island and the Gondwana rainforests.

If we read the text itself in ways fostered by Smith (see Stanley, 2018), we might first define its ideological code. We might then examine how the characters in the picture book behave/speak/dress, how they are described by the narrator; who is positioned as a knower; who is silenced; which places are seen as "Other" and so forth. By way of example, the protagonist Sophia opens her door to various "unwelcome arrivals" including a polar bear whose ice cap has melted, bees, a flamingo, a tiger, farmers, a seaman, and a family who is described as "out-of-towners" with children who are "quite out of hand." This ethnocentric view of the visitors ultimately leads Sophia to conclude that "She had to give those who'd been silenced a voice" (p. 31). This position of power, in which Sophia is authorized to take the lead is interesting when we consider how texts might be activated by real people in real places around the world who are experiencing climate change. How, for example, might a classroom teacher in Kiribati (where the unwanted family with unruly children came from) activate this text within the context of a critical literacy discussion?

Critical literacy researchers and educators have no doubt worked to disrupt dominant views of how literacy is constituted, and how it should be taught. However, in reflecting on the work of critical literacy educators, and how they might activate a text such as *The Tantrum* in their classrooms, we underline with Smith the importance of assessing how a text has been and is being activated to understand its *accomplishments* in the world. What work is this text being asked to do? Is it functioning as a token of multiculturalism, a gateway to further inquiry, a climate change anxiety anodyne? Attending to the ways in which texts are activated can help expose a text's ideological code and its role in upholding hidden power relations.

Responses to Any Critiques and Current Research in the Area

Smith's concern about the role of text in replicating ruling relations draws us onward through *The Tantrum* to a critical look at our own scholarly stances. Sophia's re-voicing human and nonhuman challenges in her own terms reminds us how hidden pressures and traditions in academic research affect us at a deep level and threaten to undercut core principles of critical literacy. Critical perspectives trouble justifications for the analyst's voice over and against that of the author, the characters, and, indeed, those they ostensibly re-present. We may ask, extending this metaphor of ensemble performance, "Why is this microphone volume pre-set to be so loud relative to others' mics?"

Questions such as this one draw our journey into another level, where we recognize our attitudes, understandings, and motivations as researchers are themselves features of an economic system that functions within and replicates the very inequalities we aspire to disrupt. At the core of the urge to write and publish must be a kind of faith in the way one's own knowledge production is networked in the world (Carrette, 2007). In this view, researchers may "go along" with accepted ethical rationales for engaging in specific research ventures to get along with institutional expectations, without reckoning with the ethical quandaries of trafficking the experiences of others for the benefit of still others without a local value proposition and with little or no local accountability. A critical stance, we argue, may become available as researchers learn to work against the inertia of their discipline by not-knowing, by refusing to assert knowledge, and by embracing meaningful uncertainty (Boggs, 2011).

Michel Foucault's philosophy reinforces Smith's perspectives through awareness that contemporary concepts of personhood are features of a social system of coercion and control. This concern is not at all impractical. It is simply a recognition that every shred of human consciousness exists within the world and among "others" as a *product* of the power relations at work in the world. Any conceivable representation of human identity (Rowsell & Abrams, 2011) or experience may be productively understood as an outgrowth of power relations in a given context. Foucault and others have used a concept of networked mathesis to explain the importance of this interconnection among the worlds of thought, action, and material. For our critical literacy research journey, this concept means that our research attitudes, products, and aspirations may be as much parts of the landscape of the current economic and political systems as they are critiques of them.

The basic parameters of critical philosophy offer to challenge the justice of social justice agendas that so readily cling to critical literacy research. If *The Tantrum* were read as a parable of critical literacy research, the story might be darkly humorous: Those advanced industrialized states whose civilizations prospered to the extent they were able to efficiently extract and use natural resources of all kinds, including humans, may indeed welcome the world's climate refugees and they may indeed produce the best-known and loudest voices calling for change. But it won't be because of the orderliness of a cosmic narrative of righting wrongs, or because human lives or the lives of polar bears are sacred. It will be because globalization, including its academic apparatus, has conditioned individuals themselves to accept this evolution of power relations. A particularly pointy barb in the imagined parable is that Sophia is only aware of her subjectivity in the most naive and unwieldy way. She senses disturbances in *her* environment, but sees *others* as the problem, yet still sees *herself* alone as the source of remedy.

The fetishization of the lone, authoritative voice dramatized by Sophia's tantrum is a chilling reminder of the precarious position of the researcher and the teacher—that these "cultural workers," as Freire called them, may be expected to talk loudly and with authority as mouthpieces for evolving power relations shifting from one form of oppression and inequality to another. At the core of the urge to teach and publish must be a kind of faith in the way one's own knowledge production conforms to networked knowledge in the world, and it is here that Foucault (1997) offers the clearest pivot point in asserting critical literacy perspectives. One's personhood is *not* the right kind for making a difference, but certain forms of personhood in certain societies might be expected to believe thus despite tragic and ironic historical unfolding cycles of oppression. Instead, however, the critical stance can become an institutional *tactic* rather than philosophical, ethical, or even textual *strategy*.

Implications for Pedagogy

We think it is timely for critical literacy scholars to reflect on how we advocate for an approach to text activation of resources such as *The Tantrum* in ways that have the potential to stimulate meaningful discussion and critical thinking, while not rejecting or threatening that which people hold sacred. Our approach to critical literacy involves problematizing *all* texts, including those authorized and used by educational institutions, respecting the everyday language and literate practices of marginalized peoples, and repositioning students as researchers of language and literacy practices, so that every text is open to question (Comber, 1994).

We also think it is timely to consider what knowledges, texts and pedagogical approaches are currently orchestrating the work of teachers. Given the high-stakes nature of standardized testing and other accountability measures, we think it is worth considering how we might best advocate for teachers to make space for powerful, critical, satisfying and socially responsible literate practices. As researchers working with teachers, we have sometimes felt marginalized ourselves. Perhaps by contesting taken-for-granted assumptions about literacy has put us outside of dominant views around how literacy is constituted and taught as well as how we use data–driven evidence as researchers. Like many of the teachers we have worked with, we have found it difficult to make the case for alternative approaches towards literacy instruction or to have an impact in a system where quantified data and standards-based instruction dominate.

Implications for Research

In reflecting on critical literacy research, and our earlier questions around whose mics are pre-set to be the loudest, we pause to consider how research is produced. As Smith (1990b) writes, the social organization and accomplishment of knowledge is often obscured by traditional forms of academic inquiry. She asks, "how can there be 'knowledge' that exists independent of knowers? What are the socially organized practices of knowers who in concerted ways obliterate their presence as subjects from the objectified knowing we call *knowledge*?" (p. 63). We therefore conclude by reflecting on the embodied and situated knowledge of those who produce knowledge of and about critical literacy. We are aware, for instance, of the growing number of researchers and academics who are employed precariously. To date, insufficient data have been collected on this population (cf. Connell, 2019; UCU, 2019), which means their stories and their involvement in critical literacy research are often obfuscated. For example, consider a research project Nerida has worked on in recent years that explored the experiences of contingent researchers in the UK and Australia (Spina, Bailey, Harris, & Goff, 2020). In that study, Nerida spoke with a non-tenured researcher who has worked on various literacy research projects (including critical literacy research) over more than a decade. Ruby [pseudonym], whose employment has been sustained by short-term and casual contracts at various universities (mostly in Australia) talked of the disjuncture she felt as someone working at the "front-line" of research.

In Ruby's experience, because tenured professors are typically under significant pressure to publish and generate grant funding, she often undertook responsibility for a majority of the data collection, working for extended periods of time in schools and early childhood settings. Ruby talked of conducting literacy-based research interventions, interviewing, observing, and working closely with teachers, families and children. The impact of this systematized and inequitable structure of employment meant Ruby's involvement with participants was often only for the period of data collection. Once tenured academics had collected what they needed from the participants, Ruby's work would come to an end, leaving her with a sense that "you go and you do research and you leave. I hate it." In another situation, a Chief Investigator decided that findings from a critical literacy research project should not be shared with anyone, including the research participants. Ruby stated "I get the feeling sometimes that [tenured professors] are too far removed from what actually *is* . . . . I was seeing it from the *teacher's* point of view, not a research point of view." In contrast (we can only assume that) the Chief Investigator may have been more oriented towards typical research expectations and demands such as producing publications in prestigious journals. This disjuncture is built on what Smith describes as a kind of "intellectual housekeeping," in which the organization and production of knowledge "is not apparent in the final product" (pp. 62–63). We believe Smith's insistence on understanding the production of knowledge is relevant for those engaging in critical literacy scholarship.

Implications for Our Social Responsibility as Academics

Ruby's vignettes highlight the need for practicing social responsibility among all academics. Her unease about how tenured and non-tenured academics work with teachers as well as with families and children points to Smith's (1990a) concern regarding a disjuncture between those at the front lines of teaching (educators), non-tenured researchers and tenured academics. Ruby explained the situation this way: "I feel like I always seem to be getting all the [research data] and handing it over [to tenured academics]. [I] get nothing out of it." Influenced by the gravity of Ruby's situation, we recognize in ourselves (as teachers and researchers) that the lenses we have employed in this chapter point to an embarrassment of riches for ethical reflection and integrity too readily sacrificed as we *go along* with institutional and neoliberal accounts of knowledge production *to get along* as economically and politically self-interested adults. A time of unprecedented displacement of the world's inhabitants by political and environmental instability calls for action, but action appropriate to our capacity to render meaningful contributions. Ruby's story illustrates a vital point: that participants in the research process may see through the veil of social science in the public interest to underlying systems of extraction and networking of knowledge that further unequal power relations.

Recommendations for Future Research and Praxis

Pausing to consider critical literacy from the standpoint of those at the frontlines offers a new perspective—one that potentially could make a difference to frontline teachers as well as to tenured and non-tenured academics. If we continue to go along with the ethical rationale that critical literacy research is inherently justice oriented—without taking into account how that proposition subjugates those with whom we work—the notion of mutual support between teachers, researchers, and policymakers may be reckoned a ruse perpetrated by researchers hiding their economic and ideological self-preservation efforts. Educational researchers should be able to explain how the pressures they face—to publish or perish, for example—place community sovereignty and well-being at risk.

Finally, to trouble some of the assumptions underlying Ruby's sense of subjugation, we propose engaging with Hall, Murphy, and Soler's (2008) practice pedagogy and its correlate, cultural identity formation. Their approach to studying culturally discursive practices—like Foucault's genealogical approach to deconstructing relations of power—hold implications for future research and praxis. Though working from a different time and theoretical perspective, Hoffman and Alvermann's (2020) use of a Foucauldian approach to answer their question regarding the subjugation of present-day reading instruction in the United States by forces at work since the early 1930s have direct ties to Ruby's sense of subjugation. Specifically, those ties reside in what Hoffman and Alvermann identified as enabling conditions for ensuring that institutional influences and revolving relations of power contribute to whose voices are heard initially, how they historically continue to be heard, and the consequences of such hearings for contemporary critical literacy educators and researchers. As part of our continuing journey to address issues of critical literacies and practice pedagogies, the four of us commit to keeping Smith's standpoint theory and Foucault's philosophy of power relations alive. For as Foucault reminds us, "People know what they do; they frequently know why they do what they do; but what they don't know is what *what* they do *does*" (Foucault, as cited in Dreyfus & Rabinow, 1983, p. 187, italics added). Critical literacy work framed in this way may be thought of as kind of *katabasis*, where we descend and accept knowledge of the jarring difference between our efforts and the work our efforts are doing.

References

Alvermann, D. E. (2019). The power of discourse: CML and "The Tantrum that Saved the World." *International Journal of Critical Media Literacy, 1*(1), 128–136.

Apple, M. W. (2014). *Official knowledge: Democratic education in a conservative age.* Routledge.

Baker, C. D., & Freebody, P. (1989). *Children's first schoolbooks.* Basil Blackwell.

Boggs, G. L. (2011). The reordering of knowledge. *Mind, Culture, and Activity: An International Journal, 18*(1), 89–92.

Carrette, J. (2007). *Religion and critical psychology: Religious experience in the knowledge economy.* Routledge.

Carroll, W. K. (2010). 'You are here': Interview with Dorothy E. Smith. *Socialist Studies/Etudes Socialistes*, *6*(2), 9–37.

Comber, B. (1994). Critical literacy: An introduction to Australian debates and perspectives. *Journal of Curriculum Studies*, *26*(6), 655–668.

Connell, R., 2019, *The good university*. Monash University Publishing.

Doyle, K., & Deeley, S. (2017). *The worms that saved the world*. Kevin Doyle Books.

Dreyfus, H. L., & Rabinow, P. (1983). *Michel Foucault: Beyond structuralism and hermeneutics* (2nd ed.). University of Chicago Press.

Foucault, M. (1990). *The history of sexuality: An introduction, Volume 1* (R. Hurley, Trans.). Vintage Books. (Original work published 1976)

Foucault, M. (1997). The hermeneutic of the subject (R. Hurley et al., Trans.). In P. Rabinow (Ed.), *Michel Foucault: Ethics, subjectivity and truth* (Vol. I, pp. 93–106). The New Press.

Garland, D. (2014). What is a "history of the present"? On Foucault's genealogies and their critical preconditions. *Punishment & Society*, *16*(4), 365–384. https://doi.org/10.1177/1462474514541711

Gill, M. C. (2017). *The fart that saved the world*. M. C. Gill.

Hall, K., Murphy, P., & Soler, J. (Eds.). (2008). *Pedagogy and practice: Culture and identities*. Sage.

Hayes, D., Hattam, R., Comber, B., Kerkham, L., Lupton, R., & Thomson, P. (2017). *Literacy, leading and learning: Beyond pedagogies of poverty*. Routledge.

Herbert, M., & Mann, M. E. (2017). *The tantrum that saved the world*. World Saving Books.

Hoffman, J. V., & Alvermann, D. E. (2020). What a genealogical analysis of Nila Banton Smith's *American Reading Instruction* reveals about the present through the past. *Reading Research Quarterly*, *55*(2), 251–269.

Lampert, J. (2008). Picturing whiteness: The events of 9/11 in children's storybooks. In M. Casey, F. Nicoll, & A. Moreton-Robinson (Eds.), *Transnational whiteness matters* (pp. 39–55). Lexington Books.

Luke, A. (1992). The body literate: Discourse and inscription in early literacy instruction, *Linguistics and Education*, *4*, 107–129.

Luke, A. (2012). Critical literacy: Foundational notes. *Theory into Practice, 51*(1), 4–11. https://doi.org/10.1080/00405841.2012.636324

Luke, A. (2018). *Critical literacy, schooling, and social justice: The selected works of Allan Luke*. Routledge.

Rowsell, J., & Abrams, S. S. (2011). (Re)conceptualizing I/identity: An introduction. *Teachers College Record*, *113*(13), 1–16.

Smith, D. E. (1990a). *Texts, facts and femininity: Exploring the relations of ruling*. Routledge.

Smith, D. E. (1990b). *The conceptual practices of power: A feminist sociology of knowledge*. Northeastern University Press.

Smith, D. E. (1997). Comment on Hekman's 'Truth and method: Feminist standpoint theory revisited'. *Signs*, *22*(2), 392–398.

Smith, D. E. (2005). *Institutional ethnography: A sociology for people*. Rowman Altamira.

Spina, N., Bailey, S., Harris, J., & Goff, M. (2020). *Making it as a contract researcher: A pragmatic look at precarious work*. Routledge.

Stanley, L. (2018). *Dorothy E. Smith feminist sociology & institutional ethnography*. X Press.

Stewart, T. T., & Boggs, G. L. (2019). Urban teachers' online dissent produces cultural resources of relevance to teacher education. *The Urban Review*, *50*, 1–18.

Stobart, G. (2008). *Testing times: The uses and abuses of assessment*. Routledge.

University and College Union (UCU). (2019). *Stamp out casual contracts*. Retrieved August 30, 2019, from www.ucu.org.uk/stampout

3.4

PLANETARY LITERACIES FOR THE ANTHROPOCENE

Karin Murris and Margaret J. Somerville

Introduction

In this chapter, we develop the concept of 'planetary literacies' and suggest it is useful for think-ing through critical literacies for the planet in response to the urgency of children's concerns about climate change, as expressed in international protests led by Greta Thunberg. We draw on the concept of 'the Anthropocene', the proposed new geological age, prompted by human induced changes to the Earth's biosphere (Crutzen, & Stoermer, 2000). The concept of 'entanglement' is central to the age of the Anthropocene, described as 'a new phase in the history of both humankind and of the Earth, when natural forces and human forces became intertwined, so that the fate of one determines the fate of the other' (Zalasiewicz, Williams, Steffen, & Crutzen, 2010, p. 2231). Anthropocene scholarship focusses on posthuman and new materialist methodologies that aim to develop 'new concepts of the human, new figures of life, and new understandings of what counts as thinking' (Colebrook, 2010, p. 15). 'The Anthropocene' has acted as a provocation to more sus-tainably connect nature and culture, economy and ecology, and the natural and human sciences, in order to address species loss, environmental destruction and global warming. Through an example from teacher education in South Africa, we show how our concept of planetary literacies aims to incorporate new 'post human' understandings of subjectivity in which 'Animals, insects, plants, cells, bacteria, in fact the planet, and the cosmos, are turned into the political arena' (Braidotti, 2017, p. 26). In this sense, we propose that in pushing the boundaries, critical literacies could significantly include new posthuman, and new materialist approaches, to address the urgency of climate change.

Posthuman Scholarship and the Anthropocene

Attending to posthuman theories and how they interact with understandings of language, literacy and cultural diversity offers a catalyst for extending current understandings and applications of criti-cal literacy.

Posthuman Theory and Language

Many contemporary philosophers have contributed to theorizing new planetary literacies for the Anthropocene. They focus on human entanglement in the fate of the planet, seek to de-centre the human being, and are generally referred to as 'post-human' or 'new materialist'. Post-human

DOI: 10.4324/9781003023425-39

Anthropocene scholarship has rapidly risen to prominence across all disciplines in response to the imperative to find new ways to bring human and natural systems together in language, thought and action. These approaches seek ways to re-think the human subject as co-constituted with the more-than-human-world. In terms of a potential posthuman approach to critical literacies, language and literacy could be reconceptualized as co-emergent with the world, as evident in young children's world-making play (Hackett & Somerville, 2017; Powell & Somerville, 2019).

Quantum physics philosopher, Karen Barad, one of the most influential of these new posthuman theorists, proposed the concept of intra-action, describing how 'to be entangled is not simply to be intertwined with another as in the joining of two separate entities, but to lack an independent self-contained existence' (Barad, 2007, p. x). In this understanding, the individual subject emerges only through the mutual intra-actions of different bodies of matter, each with their own force or agency. A child, for example, is playing at a river, and language emerges as a new planetary literacy in the intra-action of river water, rocks, sticks, bird call, blue sky and child song:

> (Water gurgling, birds twittering)
> child singing high bird-like sounds
> child walks into water with fine stick balancing on stones
> flicking stick at water and at stones
> wobbles back to stones on island, humming,
> sings to rocks, 'that's a daddy (low sing song voice, lifting a rock),
> that's a daddy, that's a daddy, that's a bigger daddy (patting a rock each time)
> that's a little baby (picking up a small pebble), that's a little baby
> got babies cousins dadda (arms wide open in expansive gesture
> walks away lifts hands to sky, loud sound to sky
> comes back to rock pile singing)
> a-gugu a-gugu a-gugu (sing-song to birds trilling)
> you're a baby, and I'm a mama kangaroo
> I'm a mama kangaroo, you're a baby kangaroo
> that's my fire (loudly, pointing to rocks)
> that's my fire, baby kangaroo, that's my fire, baby kangaroo
> that's my fire, baby kangaroo (Charmain, 3 years at river).

(Somerville & Green, 2013)

Language and Cultural Diversity

Other theorists propose that languages encode collective knowledge bases in a way that is often non-translatable, but links its speakers to their landscape inextricably. This is true of the many Indigenous languages throughout the world, many of which are in danger of extinction, often impacted by the dual erosion of biological and cultural diversity. More than 250 Indigenous Australian languages, including 800 dialectal varieties, were spoken on the continent at the time of European settlement in 1788. Only 13 traditional Indigenous languages are still acquired by children (AIATSIS, 2019). At least 50 languages are now believed to be extinct, with another 100 facing imminent extinction. There is, however, a national move by Indigenous Australians towards language and cultural revitalization in Country, which recognises the crucial entanglement of language and land. A significant issue for critical literacy is that, 'Linguistic diversity is, then, our treasury of historically developed knowledge—including knowledge about how to maintain and use sustainably some of the most vulnerable and most biologically diverse environments in the world' (Pretty et al., 2009, p. 42).

In the following, we discuss three related topics—new education theorising; global applications; and the sympoietic system—and suggest implications for research and pedagogy throughout.

New Educational Theorising Relevant to Planetary Literacies: Implications for Research and Education

Globally, new theories are emerging which have important implications for planetary literacies as a form of critical literacy. Canadian Marcelina Piotrowski proposes thinking alongside an 'elemental Deleuze' in which 'subjectification includes the classical elements of air, water, earth, fire' (2019, p. 9). David Rousell (United Kingdom), offers the pedagogical potential of what he calls 'little justices', for those interested in 'thinking-with students', through animals, rivers, mountains, etc., and exploring 'the speculative possibilities of life, politics, sociality, and experience beyond the human' (Rousell, 2018, p. 13). Greg Mannion (Scotland), suggests 'assemblage pedagogies' as emergent in engagement with the world, 'to create openings that allow for new relations among people and place so that more sustainable ways of life might emerge' (2019, p. 11). McPhie and Clarke, (Cumbria, UK), highlight the significance of concepts themselves, proposing attention to what a concept is capable of, what a concept can do: 'We are interested in the type of experiments that allow us, and our learners, to become philosopher physicians, critically playing with the everyday concepts we pick up in literature and our daily lives to literally create new material-conceptual worlds'. Monroe et al. recommend in their review of climate change education, that the task is to seize 'the learning moment to think about what really and profoundly matters, to collectively envision a better future, and then to become practical visionaries in realizing that future' (Monroe, Plate, Oxarart, Bowers, & Chaves, 2017, p. 17).

Global Applications of Planetary Literacies: Implications for Pedagogy

South Africa is among the developing countries predicted to experience the most severe impacts of the anthropogenic global warming of the Anthropocene. Posthuman and new materialist approaches are envisioned as offering possibilities for a different future in relation to the Anthropocene, requiring opportunities for the child to touch, feel, and smell their environment, and the material world: 'Environmental education should be all-pervasive; interdisciplinary, integrated into all subject areas, and foundational to all teaching' (Blyth & Meiring, 2018, pp. 112–113). A posthuman approach is proposed to 'foster wider concerns of ecojustice, ecological thought and life processes, that are relevant to everyday South African urban living, offer[ing] a promise of justice-to-come' (Blyth & Meiring, 2018, pp. 112–113).

The widely advocated Ubuntu *ecosophy* is a distinctive Indigenous contribution from South Africa. Ubuntu is 'inextricably bound up in the human being's connectedness with other human beings and with an ever-changing and complex (biophysical) world' (Le Grange, 2012, p. 63). Ubuntu 'would require teachers to identify ruptures within existing curriculum frameworks and school arrangements to invigorate lines of escape along which sustainability can be developed through placed-based education' (Ontong & Le Grange, 2014, p. 35). In Australia, the Aboriginal and Torres Strait Islander Histories and Cultures priority of the Australian Curriculum provides a pedagogical framework for 'an understanding of the interconnected elements of Country/Place, Culture and People', and for development of knowledge about 'law, languages, dialects and literacies, linked to the deep knowledge traditions and holistic world views to provide a context for learning' (ACARA, 2017).

An Example of Planetary Literacies in Teacher Education Pedagogy in South Africa

Examples of a posthuman shift in teacher education practices in South Africa that do not assume western notions of progress and teleological development are now becoming more noticeable (see, e.g., Giorza, 2018; Murris, Reynolds, & Peers, 2018; Murris & Muller, 2018; Murris, 2020; Murris & Borcherds, 2019). Affect and other transcorporeal knowledges, previously excluded from the domain of what counts as knowledge, are now having attention paid to them (Anwarrudin, 2015; Lewis, 2014). Prior to the posthuman ontological return, language was seen as the prime medium for knowledge construction and thus put up a barrier in terms of judging students' abilities. For example, the 100 languages' of children (clay, dance, photography, digital technology, painting, etc.) of the Reggio Emilia approach in early childhood education, have been theorised and applied using posthumanism as a navigational tool in early childhood education (Lenz Taguchi, 2010; Giorza, 2018), are now also influencing higher education, inspired by early childhood education pedagogies (Murris, 2016; Murris et al., 2018). If the human is understood as with and part of the world and not separate from it, the challenge is to find other, more tacit ways of experiencing the world that also account for more-than-human experiences.

Posthumanism as Sympoietic System: Implications for Pedagogy

Central to planetary literacies is the notion of ontological entanglement. This ontological shift has implications for epistemology—what counts as knowledge—who or what does the knowing, and where knowledge is located, for example, not 'in' human consciousness as mental states as pre-supposed by cognitive social scientists. Posthumanism attempts to rethink relationality *without* the Nature/Culture binary—as a *sympoietic* system that lack boundaries. *Sympoiesis* is a word appropriate 'to complex, dynamic, responsive, situated, historical systems. It is a word for worlding-with, in company' (Haraway, 2016, p. 58).

The ontological turn is a return to Indigenous onto-epistemologies and makes us think differently about what it means to know or 'give' students 'experiences' in higher education. In sympoietic pedagogies, knowing is a direct material and moving engagement with/in the world as a worlding process. Individuals do not *have* experience, but rather, subjects are constituted *through* experience, always in flux and in the process of becoming. Texts and theories in this approach to planetary literacies are important too, as we will show, when explored dynamically, through transmodal movement and activity. In sympoietic knowledge production, more complex relational elements are given credit as playing their own part in knowledge production. This includes nonhuman bodies, such as sand, glass, paper, atmosphere, curriculum, rape, murders, and an impending exam (an art installation), as we show in the case-study that follows. The complexity of sympoiesis or 'making-with' (Haraway, 2016, p. 58) includes Karin remembering what happened during a course she was lecturing, and both of us entangled authors: 'being-with', 'making-with', 'thinking-with' as a '*sympoietic* system' as we return to the event as storied in the following.

Enacting and Researching a Sympoietic Pedagogy

Karin was convener of a one-year Postgraduate Certificate in Education (PGCE) Foundation phase.[1] She conceptualised and co-designed the curriculum of this teacher education programme at the University of Cape Town (UCT). In this chapter, we draw on one visual exam essay while researching

Karin's experimentation with posthuman sympoietic teaching in a childhood studies course. In 2019, instead of teaching three hours a week over a period of seventeen weeks, different lecturers worked across courses in blocks of intensive one-week teaching. Each morning over a whole week, the class of 27 students engaged with only one of the courses. Such deliberate restructuring of the curriculum can enable deeper immersion in the subject and disrupts the usual fragmentation and disjointedness. In this case-study, researching Karin's teaching, the concept of 'tidying up' kept returning, expanding and reverberating throughout the childhood studies course, but because of lack of space, only a few threads are made explicit here.

Tidying Up

Pre-service teachers engaged with the concept of the Anthropocene in a philosophical enquiry session.[2] They had just started their third block of teaching and watched a video Karin had made on holiday of two young girls playing with little bits of sand in a park in Beijing. One student remarks that the children 'were tidying up the park' and an enquiry ensues after Karin asks them whether 'tidying up' can also be a form of 'play' (linking it to the field trip to a local park some months earlier and the concept 'play'). The next day, Karin picks up the concept again and reads and explores the picture book *Tidy* (2016) by Emily Gravett with the students. In this hilarious story, a badger takes the concept 'tidying up' to the extreme by hoovering up the leaves from the trees in the autumn, polishing, scouring and scrubbing the rocks. Still unhappy, he digs up every single tree and covers up the soil with cement until he realises that this also means he has no longer anything to eat and then tries to reverse the damage!

Linking the concepts with/in the story with their own experiences, the students volunteer many ideas about how 'tidying up' in their schools during teaching practice was a pervasive concept, also creating much anxiety, as standards differ, and some principals had been really strict and demanding. One student's remark that 'organised mess' should be allowed, is built upon by another student who argues that untidiness can be a way of expressing one's identity (e.g., how you wear your school uniform or your hair). Subsequently, Karin invites the students to take the concept of 'tidying up' into how education introduces children to a tidied-up world through pre-existing categories and binary opposites.

The next day she brings in photocopies of the picture book *Elephant Elements* (2001) by Pittau and Gervais and in small groups they explore over two mornings how the categories big/small, long/bottom, behind/front, boy/girl, closed/open, fat/thin, lucky/unlucky, intelligent/stupid, etc. work in the early years classroom. This deceptively simple, but very clever and witty picture book shows what these pairing opposites could mean for an elephant. The students discuss the opposites in small groups through a range of materials (playdough, thick felt tip pens, paper, fabric, glue, etc.). But their discomfort increases when they start to realise how the binary logic implied in the book, include some and exclude others, and normally speaking without opportunities for children to question the ethics of, for example, teaching 'living/dead' as uncontroversial. Talking about how to decide what is alive and dead, was particularly poignant as one of their peers at university, a first year female student, had just been raped and murdered, and a week later after her burnt body had been found another (male) student had been knifed to death (for his phone) at the beach where we had planned our last field trip for the year.

Some do not want to go to the beach. Karin reminds them that there are twenty-seven people in the group and three teacher educators (so they should be safe in numbers) and invites them to take an empty yoghurt jar Karin had been collecting during the year to the beach. The idea was that they would put sand from the beach in the jar and intra-act with/in it as part of a final exam essay. When they walk onto the beach Karin invites them to tidy up the beach (see Figure 3.4.1).

Figure 3.4.1 An assemblage of 'tidying up' at Clifton beach and the university exam space

A Layer of 'Nothing'

Two weeks' later, one student, let's call her Ayanda, presents her jar with sand as exam requirement for the final exhibition and explains her reasoning under the title '*the formation of sand is dynamic*' (see Figure 3.4.1). Here are some extracts as relevant for this chapter:

> *Beaches are like fingerprints . . . [T]his is particularly true of the dynamic formation of its sand. At first glance, sand may be seen as a single unit, a large mass of a uniform substance covering an area where land meets sea. However, if we take the time to breakdown the composition of the sand we hold we can quickly see how it is made up of lots of differently shaped objects and particles . . . I will be exploring how the composition of sand can be compared to the composition of how we understand and visualise the 'child' and the concept of childhood . . . I would like to investigate how societal factors shape and influence the concept of childhood in the same way the ocean influences the creation of the sand. My installation is a representation of the different elements that make up sand. To demonstrate this, I have deconstructed the material into layers. Namely, rock, shells and pollutants . . . we cannot ignore that the sand I have collected is likely contaminated with micro and macro pollutants . . . 'Bay of Sewage', a short documentary film, discusses the dangers of the untreated wastewater that is pumped into the water of the Camps Bay area on the surrounding environment, including the sand on the beaches*
>
> *(JacksonFilmSA, 2016).*

> *The pollution, or the injustice, children face also contributes to the makeup of sand, or our view of childhood [and here she refers to Donald Trumps' denigrating tweets about Greta Thurnberg]. I think it is important here to reflect on another layer present in my installation. You may not notice it initially. There is, however, a layer of 'nothing' between where the pollution level ends and the jar of the lid. I think this can act as an important reminder of what might be unknown to us. There are so many factors we are unaware of that shape children's experience and how we view childhood . . . Childhood*

and our perception of what it means to be a child is not created in a vacuum. Rather, there are historical, cultural, social, political, economic and environmental influences that affect how we identify childhood and in turn, how society treats children as part of this society.

The atmosphere had been heavy on the beach. Ayanda explains why this was and traces how the sand is entangled with the murders of the two UCT students:

> *It feels unjust to be discussing the concept of childhood, entwining it with the formation of sand on Clifton Beach without discussing the beach as a sight of violence against young people. Cebo Mheli Mbatha, an 18-year-old UCT student, was murdered on Clifton 3rd last month.*

Quoting an extract from a newspaper article (Hodes, 2019), Ayanda points out how the violence against young people and particularly women is deeply engrained in South African society and 'mixed in with [the] sand':

> *The violence against Uyinene and Cebo has brought to the surface something that lies deeper, much deeper than the shallow grave that Uyinene's murderer dug for her corpse. It is deeper than Clifton's boulders—Plutons—the chunks of broken-off magma that graze the coast. This violence is mixed in with sand, diamonds, coal and silica. And for Cebo, the sand of Clifton, which is especially sticky. It lodges itself in your feet and thighs and buttocks. It finds its way into crevices. It is sloughed off rock and mollusc, shiny bits of shell and mother of pearl. You'll find it later, in your shoes, your pockets, your bed. Some of it may even make its way into Cebo's grave.*

Like the heavily polluted sand, invisible to the human eye, nose or touch, violence is diffracted through the sand, 'we cannot escape its presence'—maybe 'visibly not discernible', but 'not intangible' (Barad, 2017, p. G106). Ayanda concludes how the way she tidied up her jar has made it possible to take something so overlooked as sand and to reimagine its dynamic possibilities to reconfigure adult/child and human/nonhuman relationalities.

Tidying Up Some Threads

Researching Karin's sympoietic teaching suggests the impact a concept such as 'tidying up' can have to more sustainably connect nature and culture, economy and ecology, and the natural and human sciences in teacher education. Including a posthuman shift in critical literacies is urgently needed in order to address species loss, environmental destruction and global warming. As an approach to teaching and researching planetary literacies, critical posthumanism was proposed as a different *relational ontology*—an ontological return to African Indigenous scholarship and ways of living—that reconfigures subjectivity and brings into existence the notions of sympoietic teacher education as generative in the Anthropocene.

Supported by an assemblage of photographs of one student's work for her final childhood studies exam, this chapter shows how Karin, as lecturer, responded to the students' interest in the concept 'tidying up' by providing transmodal opportunities for the students to make-with and think-with the concept 'tidying up', productively taking the concept generated inside the university classroom, to a picture book, then outside to the beach and then back inside the classroom again. One student made an intricate connection with the materiality of sand as always already entangled with local histories of violence and environmental damage. Karin's posthuman teacher education programme in South Africa shows how as Mcphie and Clarke (2018, p. 14) put it earlier, it is possible to literally create 'new material-conceptual worlds'. The example of the concept of 'tidying up' (common in early childhood education settings) highlights how a concept can work and what it is capable of, by paying attention to what a concept can do (Mcphie & Clarke, 2018).

Implications for Social Responsibility as Academics and Educators

Sympoietic pedagogy is about doing justice that also includes the more-than-human. It is about 'proceeding responsibly', which involves the impossible task of allowing the response of the 'between' that Barad (2012, p. 81) says she is trying to gesture toward. Barad (2012) explains:

> (Doing justice is a profound yearning, a crucially important if inevitably unachievable activity, an always already inadequate attempt to respond to the ethical cry of the world.) Or, rather, perhaps I can put it this way: It is the very question of justice-to-come, not the search for a final answer or final solution to that question, that motivates me. The point is to live the questions and to help them flourish.
>
> *(p. 81)*

This aesthetic, epistemological, political and ethical move is therefore not about *truths about a just future* as perceived by the educator to be taught (transmitted) to the learner, but to continue to ask the awkward questions together and to respond to, and to be touched by, the world that includes, but also moves beyond the human senses. Human subjects come into existence through intra-action and emerge through their intra-relating; time and space, matter and meaning. Planetary literacies offers a radical proposal to respond to the 'ethical cry of the world' and getting entangled with/in the world for 'justice-to-come' (Barad, 2012, p. 81). Through the 'tidying-up-the-beach' case-study we have shown what difference the profound shift in planetary literacies from individual subjectivity to a relational ontology makes to teacher education epistemologically, ontologically and ethically in the Anthropocene. The enactment of a critical posthuman pedagogy illustrates how pre-service teachers and teacher educators can learn to pay attention in a dis/embodied way to the more than human in their teaching and research practices.

Critical literacy needs to explore afresh the territory in between the human and more-than-human and challenge notions of individual subjectivity, human superiority and exceptionalism. Critical literacy is an evolving project and including a posthuman focus on the Anthropocene enables us to be even more affected by the ethical and political nature of the worldly entanglements we humans are always already a part.

Acknowledgements

We would like to thank the students of the PGCE Foundation Phase of 2019 at the University of Cape Town and their consent to write about and publish part of an exam script and the images. Moreover, we would like to thank the educators and researchers Karin worked closely with in 2019: two postdoctoral scholars from Brazil, Luzia de Souza and Heloisa da Silva, and in particular Rose-Anne Reynolds, lecturer in the PGCE at UCT.

Notes

1. This one-year programme used to prepare graduate students for the teaching profession (of 5–9 year olds).
2. The teacher education programme featured in this chapter worked with Philosophy with Children (P4C) with/in an emergent curriculum, inspired by the Reggio Emilia approach to early childhood education (for this powerful diffractive combination, see: Murris, 2016).

References

ACARA. (2017). *The Australian curriculum (Cross-curricular priorities)*. Retrieved April 27, 2019, from www.australiancurriculum.edu.au/f-10-curriculum/cross-curriculum-priorities/

Anwarrudin, S. (2015). Why critical literacy should turn to 'the affective turn': Making a case for critical affective literacy. *Discourse: Studies in the Cultural Politics of Education, 37*(3), 381–396.

Australian Institute of Aboriginal and Torres Strait Islander Studies. (2019). *Indigenous Australian languages celebrating 2019 international year of indigenous languages*. Retrieved from https://aiatsis.gov.au/explore/articles/indigenous-australian-languages

Barad, K. (2007). *Meeting the universe halfway: Quantum physics and the entanglement of matter and meaning*. Duke University Press.

Barad, K. (2012, June). Intra-actions: An interview with Karen Barad by Adam Kleinman. *Mousse*, #34, 76–81.

Barad, K. (2017). No small matter: Mushroom Clouds, ecologies of nothingness, and strange topologies of spacetimemattering. In A. Tsing, H. Swanson, E. Gan, & N. Bubandt (Eds.), *Arts of living on a damaged planet*. University of Minnesota Press.

Blyth, C., & Meiring, R. (2018). A posthumanist approach to environmental education in South Africa: Implications for teachers, teacher development, and teacher training programs. *Teacher Development, 22*(1), 105–122.

Braidotti, R. (2017). Four theses on posthuman feminism. In R. Grusin (Ed.), *Anthropocene feminism* (pp. 21–48). University of Minnesota Press.

Colebrook, C. (Ed.). (2010). *Extinction: Framing the end of the species*. Open Humanities Press.

Crutzen, P., & Stoermer, E. F. (2000, May). The 'Anthropocene'. *The IGBP Newsletter, 41*, 17–18.

Giorza, T. (2018). *Making kin and taking care: Intra-active learning with time, space and matter in a Johannesburg preschool* (Unpublished PhD thesis). University of Cape Town.

Gravett, E. (2016). *Tidy*. Two Hoots.

Hackett, A., & Somerville, M. (2017). Post-human literacies: Young children moving in time, place and more-than-human worlds. *Journal of Early Childhood Literacy, 17*(3), 374–391.

Haraway, D. (2016). *Staying with the Trouble: Making Kin in the Chthulucene*. Duke University Press.

Hodes, R. (2019). *Violence unveiled: Blood and sand: The murder of UCT students*. Retrieved October 17, 2019, from www.dailymaverick.co.za/article/2019-10-07-blood-and-sand-the-murder-of-uct-student

JacksonFilmSA. (2016). *Bay of Sewage—a short documentary* [Video]. Retrieved from www.youtube.com/watch?v=tEh5JpoH9qo&t=31

Le Grange, L. (2012). Ubuntu, Ukama and the healing of nature, self and society. *Educational Philosophy and Theory, 44*, 56–67.

Lenz Taguchi, H. (2010). *Going beyond the theory/practice divide in early childhood education. Contesting early childhood Serie*. Routledge.

Lewis, C. (2014). Affective and global ecologies: New directions for critical literacy. In J. Zacher Pandya & J. Ávila (Eds.), *Moving critical literacies forward: A new look at praxis across contexts* (pp. 187–193). Routledge.

Mannion, G. (2019). Re-assembling environmental and sustainability education: Orientations from new materialism. *Environmental Education Research*. https://doi.org/10.1080/13504622.2018.1536926

Mcphie, J., & Clarke, D. (2018). Nature matters: Diffracting a keystone concept of environmental education research—just for kicks, *Environmental Education Research*. https://doi.org/10.1080/13504622.2018.1531387

Monroe, M., Plate, R., Oxarart, A., Bowers, A., & Chaves, W. (2017). Identifying effective climate change education strategies: A systematic review of the research. *Environmental Education Research, 25*(6), 791–812.

Murris, K. (2016). *The posthuman child: Educational transformation through philosophy with picturebooks*. Contesting Early Childhood Series. Routledge.

Murris, K. (2020). Posthuman de/colonising teacher education in South Africa: Animals, anthropomorphism and picturebook art. In P. Burnard & L. Colucci-Gray (Eds.), *Why science and art creativities matter: STEAM (re-)configurings for future-making education* (pp. 52–78). Brill Publishers.

Murris, K., & Borcherds, C. (2019). Body as transformer: 'Teaching without Teaching' in a teacher education course. In C. Taylor & A. Bayley (Eds.), *Posthumanism and higher education: Reimagining pedagogy, practice and research* (pp. 255–277). Palgrave Macmillan.

Murris, K., & Muller, K. (2018). Finding child beyond 'child': A posthuman orientation to foundation phase teacher education in South Africa. In V. Bozalek, R. Braidotti, M. Zembylas, & T. Shefer (Eds.), *Socially just pedagogies: Posthumanist, feminist and materialist perspectives in higher education* (pp. 151–171). Palgrave Macmillan.

Murris, K., Reynolds, R., & Peers, J. (2018). Reggio Emilia inspired philosophical teacher education in the Anthropocene: Posthuman child and the family (tree). *Journal of Childhood Studies: Interdisciplinary Dialogues in Early Childhood Environmental Education Special Issue, 43*(1), 15–29.

Ontong, K., & Le Grange, L. (2014). The role of place-based education in developing sustainability as a frame of mind. *Southern African Journal of Environmental Education, 30*, 27–38.

Piotrowski, M. (2019). 'An atmosphere, an air, a life:' Deleuze, elemental media, and more-than-human environmental subjectification and education. *Environmental Education Research.* https://doi.org/10.1080/1350 4622.2018.1485134

Pittau, F & Gervais, B. (2001). *Elephant elements.* Chrysalis Books Group.

Powell, S., & Somerville, M. (2019). Drumming in excess and chaos: Music, literacy and sustainability in early years learning. *Journal of Early Childhood Literacy.* https://doi.org/10.1177/1468798418792603

Pretty, J., Adams, B., Berkes, F., de Athayde, F., Dudley, N., Hunn, E., . . . Pilgrim, S. (2009). The intersections of biological diversity and cultural diversity: Towards integration. *Conservation and Society, 7*(2), 100–112.

Rousell, D. (2018). Doing little justices: Speculative propositions for an immanent environmental ethics. *Environmental Education Research, 10*(23), 1–15.

Somerville, M., & Green, M. (2013). Sustainability education: Researching practice in primary schools. *Environmental Educational Research, 21*(6), 832–845.

Zalasiewicz, J., Williams, M., Steffen, W., & Crutzen, P. (2010). The new world of the Anthropocene. *Environmental Science and Technology, 44*(7), 2228–2231.

3.5

CRITICAL LITERACY, DIGITAL PLATFORMS, AND DATAFICATION

T. Philip Nichols, Anna Smith, Scott Bulfin, and Amy Stornaiuolo

Introduction

In this chapter, we examine key ideas associated with platform studies and datafication, and their relation to critical literacy. We contend that platform technologies present a challenge for critical literacy scholars: while critical literacy is a powerful resource for identifying and analyzing certain digital practices, it can strain to explain or intervene in the broader social, technical, and economic forces whose entanglements animate digital platforms. Rather than undermining the project of critical literacy, we suggest such limitations help to clarify where critical literacy can contribute as part of a wider repertoire of tactics for mapping, critiquing, and transforming digital ecosystems, and we outline implications for research, teaching, and practice.

Definitions of Key Concepts

Platforms refer to (1) infrastructures on which applications are built (e.g. a video game console is a platform for playing its compatible software); and (2) online networks that facilitate economic and social exchanges (e.g. a social media site is a platform for connecting with others).

The first of these meanings reflects the concept's lineage in video game studies, where scholars explore relations between hardware and software environments. Bogost and Montfort (2009) define a platform as "a computing system of any sort upon which further computing can be done" (p. 2). This framing spotlights the centrality of *relation* to platform studies: platforms never exist in isolation, and are best understood in relation to the other systems with which they interoperate. Importantly, these relations are often mediated through hidden mechanisms. A smartphone, for instance, is functional only in relation to less-visible hardware and software infrastructures (e.g. batteries and silicon chips, or algorithms and code). As designed elements, these components inherit particular interests and values from those who produce them. This is why media theorists refer to these components as the "socio-technical" dimension of platforms (van Dijck, 2013).

The second meaning of "platform" signals how this technical dimension is mobilized in social and economic exchanges. Gillespie (2010) argues, "Platforms are platforms not necessarily because they allow code to be written or run, but because they afford opportunity to communicate, interact, and sell" (p. 351). In other words, platforms are not just technical constructs; they are shaped by social actors whose asymmetrical relations (e.g. public/private, consumer/producer) give shape to the "socio-economic" dimension of platforms (van Dijck, 2013). This dimension is visible in

 DOI: 10.4324/9781003023425-40

the growing "platformization" of the Internet (Helmond, 2015): where once-decentralized digital spaces like message boards and personal websites are now consolidated in the hands of a few platform operators (e.g. Amazon, Apple, Facebook, Google, and Microsoft). The simultaneous rise of platformization and the interdependence of users' work and leisure on digital systems has increasingly led to a social situation where the logic and economy of platforms are extending into spheres of life once spared from digital connectivity and control.

Crucially, this proliferation of platform logics is dependent on *datafication*—or, the translation of social activity into quantifiable, extractable data (Sadowski, 2019). Since platforms can only centralize social and economic exchanges legible to their underlying code, their scalability demands the conversion of everyday activities into calculable measures amenable to prediction and tracking. Facebook, for instance, relies on datafication of users' social ties to people ("friends") and things ("likes") to structure what news and advertisements are accessible to them (Bucher, 2012). This information is often termed *Big Data*—a phrase that indexes the staggering volume of data-points collected and analyzed to make such calculations. While it is often argued that Big Data surfaces patterns and associations that can tailor technical-systems to users (Mayer-Schoenberger & Cukier, 2013), it also raises ethical questions: What is omitted when social activities are reduced to numbers; and how does the funneling of user-data to private interests leave individuals vulnerable to surveillance and exploitation? Zuboff (2019), for instance, shows how commercial platforms sell user-data to third-parties to "nudge, coax, tune, or herd behavior toward profitable outcomes" (p. 8)—or share information with government agencies and creditors. As such, the promise of platforms and datafication must be weighed against their capacities to centralize user-data, erode expectations for privacy, and expand state and corporate mechanisms for raced and classed surveillance (cf. Benjamin, 2019; Browne, 2015).

Critiques of Critical Literacy in Digital Platforms

In literacy studies, platforms and datafication are beginning to emerge in research on "critical digital literacy." This area of inquiry extends "critical literacy"—the reading and re-writing of the word and world in ways that confront, resist, or upend power hierarchies (Freire & Macedo, 1987)—to digital media (Ávila & Pandya, 2013). While "digital literacy" holds multiple, competing meanings (Nichols & Stornaiuolo, 2019), critical digital literacy has centrally focused on analysis and use of digital media as it relates to social reproduction or transformation. Numerous studies explore how youth use digital tools and platforms to engage in critical literacy: leveraging mobile devices in political protest (Smith, Stornaiuolo, & Phillips, 2018); critiquing racialized representations in popular media (Baker-Bell, Stanbrough, & Everett, 2017); or orienting new media technologies toward civic action projects (Jocson, 2015). Such work is instructive for understanding the capacities of digital media in disrupting power asymmetries within and across social worlds.

Increasingly, however, scholarly attention to the technical and economic dimensions of platforms is surfacing new complexities in the transformative power of such practices (Sefton-Green, 2021). This work highlights how young people's agentive ingenuity can be amplified or subverted by the design constraints and commercial interests that drive platform technologies. For example, the same mobile devices youth may use in political protest are inextricably linked to the governance policies and data practices of cell-service providers and third-party applications. These firms not only extract personal and geolocation data from users, but recycle (or sell) that data for new development projects—including the training of algorithms that can monitor or disrupt future protests (Nichols & LeBlanc, 2021). Such relations do not obviate the necessity of political action; but do suggest that familiar critical digital literacy tactics may need to be augmented or reimagined in a media ecosystem where algorithmic rationality is being deployed to foreclose horizons of political possibility.

Education scholars have mapped these tensions in the integration of "transformative" technologies (Selwyn, Nemorin, Bulfin, & Johnson, 2017) and personalized learning software (Robinson, 2020) in schools—each of which promise adaptive, student-centered outcomes, yet mediate these potentials through mechanisms aimed at ranking and controlling students. These findings suggest platformatization in education often extend existing regimes of standardization to increasingly refined and invasive scales, like clicks, swipes, and biometrics (e.g. heart-rate, eye-movements, moods, etc.) (Williamson, 2018). This has led critical digital literacy scholars to grapple with the incongruity between the revolutionary power of digital technologies and their regressive tendencies toward surveillance, control, and market-optimization (Garcia & Nichols, 2021; Golden, 2017). Such tensions raise questions about critical literacy's possibilities and limits as a resource for clarifying and intervening in platform relations.

Responses to Critiques and Current Research

One way critical literacy scholarship has attended to this challenge involves engaging work in peripheral fields like platform, critical algorithm, and media studies. These literatures explore micro- and macro-level phenomena implicated in platform architectures: from physical hardware (Dourish, 2017) and algorithms (Noble, 2018) to shifts in human labor (Irani, 2015) and transnational governance (Bratton, 2015). Literacy scholars have drawn on such work both to map more expansive frames for co-articulating literacy and platform studies (Nichols & Stornaiuolo, 2019) and to explore particular facets of digital practice. For instance, Noble's (2018) research on racialized bias in Google's search engine has inspired studies that consider the hidden work of algorithms in conditioning everyday literacy activities (Bhatt & MacKenzie, 2019; Nichols & Johnston, 2020). Likewise, analysis of datafication (Kitchin, 2014) has propelled examinations of the data literacy practices that teachers and students might leverage to resist or speak back to predatory data extraction and surveillance (Pangrazio & Selwyn, 2019; Stornaiuolo, 2019). These studies extend critical literacy to particular technical and economic substrates at work in digital platforms.

Even so, it remains a challenge for critical literacy frameworks to capture the simultaneity of competing relations that animate platform activities. To return to our previous example: when the same mechanisms that allow protesters to take political action also enroll their data into systems whose predictive capacities can be used to thwart future protests, it is not immediately clear where forms of critical analysis and action can be mobilized. This is because, as Dixon-Román and colleagues (2020) argue, platforms are not static or stable contexts, but performative entanglements: their multiple dimensions are mutually constitutive and in-motion. Applying a critical lens to one part of the assemblage (e.g. "algorithmic bias") can easily elide other contingencies that overdetermine that component's performance and impacts (e.g. code, standards, institutional practices, human labor, broader forces of racial capitalism, etc.). This has led some critical literacy scholars to work at capturing this performativity in digital reading and writing. Smith, Cope, and Kalantzis (2017), for instance, trace the construction of "quantified writers" as platforms enfold student composing into datafied feedback loops to mold future practice. Others, similarly, map how the competing interests of developers, instructors, and students intermingle in digitally mediated literacy activities (Scott & Nichols, 2017; Sobko, Unadkat, Adams, & Hull, 2020). Such studies draw on critical literacy traditions, while highlighting the frictions such frames face when applied to platform relations. They suggest, in other words, there is a need to crystalize which relations in platforms' performative ecology are amenable to analysis and intervention using existing frames for critical literacy—and which might require additional, or alterative, resources for studying, resisting, or reimagining such dynamics.

Implications for Pedagogy

One generative avenue that critical literacy scholars have pursued involves pedagogical orientations focused on unmasking and critiquing less-visible dimensions of platforms. Recent scholarship advocates for critical engagement with the "software space" that operates "beneath the screen" where literacy practices occur (Lynch, 2015). This could involve, for instance, mapping how the use of a Google document in a classroom assignment conditions teaching and learning as it circulates through hardware and software (e.g. code, interfaces, databases, Wi-Fi) and broader cultural and commercial relations. Such forms of critical digital literacy pedagogy help to concretize otherwise abstract, or obscured, technical and economic flows that structure "free" learning platforms like Google Classroom, Edmodo, or Schoology (Nichols & LeBlanc, 2020). Importantly, this also invites inquiry into how these mechanisms work in practice. Writing in HTML or JavaScript, analyzing metadata, or setting up a server, for example, adds texture to "critique" by situating it within deeper knowledge of how connective technologies operate and the ways they underwrite observable literacy practices. By engaging in such systemic analyses, educators act as change agents (Morrell, 2017), supporting learners in assessing how educational technologies actively participate in the co-construction of literacies in ways that may exacerbate already-existing injustices.

A second intervention, parallel to interrogating platform architectures, involves educators engaging in such critical reflection themselves. Before literacy educators can help students use digital tools or software—for instance, producing data visualizations in R to understand thematic patterns in a text—there is a need for them to examine the assumptions and ideologies inherited in the design of such technologies. Lynch (2015) suggests this includes critical attention to the entanglements of human, machine, and computational languages that make these designs possible. Developing this knowledge involves investment in teacher preparation and professional learning that stresses interdisciplinary collaboration—not to prepare youth for narrow economic futures (a neoliberal rationale), but to better understand and intervene in the world-making capacities (utopian and dystopian) of platforms and data. Part of this orientation includes self-examination, by educators, of the educational technologies they use—that is, how certain platforms invite predictive logics and commercial interests into classrooms which can work against their pedagogical values and commitments. Such an approach helps foreground ethical questions about the ways platforms enroll teachers and students into the involuntary co-authorship of data, which can have impacts that ripple well beyond the walls of classrooms (de Roock, 2021).

A third area to build on is critical literacy's emphasis on people's agentive efforts to create media that challenge oppressive systems and work toward justice-oriented social transformation (Mirra, Morrell, & Filipiak, 2018). Recent efforts to examine young people's data literacy practices (Wilkerson & Polman, 2020) have taken a critical turn, highlighting data's racialized and political dimensions (Philip, Schuler-Brown, & Way, 2013) and positioning young people as active participants in generating, representing, interpreting, and communicating about data (Hardy, Dixon, & Hsi, 2019). This shift denotes a significant pedagogical aim of critical data literacies, particularly in facilitating youth's uses of data to take social action (Pangrazio & Selwyn, 2019; Stornaiuolo, 2019). Such efforts take up the broader aims of critical literacy to center communities of color and non-dominant ways-of-knowing in order to re-imagine and re-make the conditions under which we live, work, and learn (Paris & Alim, 2017)—an arena that increasingly calls for critical examination of platform and data practices that permeate everyday life, and that are implicated in the struggle for justice, educational and otherwise (Philip, Olivares-Pasillas, & Rocha, 2016).

Implications for Research

With the steady creep of platforms and datafication into all aspects of social life, researchers, too, face challenges analyzing and intervening in those dimensions of digital ecosystems that have historically fallen outside the scope of literacy studies. As we suggest, the invisibility of platform infrastructures and the performativity their social, technical, and economic dynamics are two glaring dilemmas for those studying such systems. They demand that literacy researchers be equipped with nimble approaches for conducting and mobilizing inquiry as they navigate participation across opaque systems and processes (Stornaiuolo, Smith, & Phillips, 2017). From timestamps to versioning, the metadata of literacy activity has become "smaller, and the recording continuous" (Cope & Kalantzis, 2016, p. 2). As scholars engage in research using digital platforms, their activity also contributes to the datafication of literacy, generating new data-streams that are recursively utilized in the refining of commercial products or as a salable commodity. Responding to the common misapprehension of such data architectures as instrumental rather than ideological, Noble and Tynes (2016) call for an intersectional critical race technology studies as:

> but one means of doing a closer reading of the politics of the internet, from representation to infrastructure . . . to allow us to interrogate naturalized notions of the impartiality of hardware and software . . . [and] to examine how information, records, and evidence can have great consequences for those who are marginalized.
>
> *(p. 3)*

Such an approach reorients the emphasis of critical digital literacy toward the ways that digital literacy practices—including research itself—always unfold with, within, and against platform infrastructures (Star & Bowker, 2002). This suggests a need for scholars to interrogate the assumed autonomy of their methods: considering, instead, how their chosen modes of inquiry are mutually shaped by the platform architectures that underwrite the research process. As a reflexive stance, this pushes researchers outside the familiar territory of casting certain digital practices as "dangerous" or "liberatory" (Bulfin & McGraw, 2015), and encourages, by contrast, an ecological view of the relations between observable practices and their attachments to other scales of platform activity—from the micro (e.g. forms of precision data-processing) to the macro (e.g. the environmental impacts of hardware production and energy-hungry cloud servers) (cf. Bowers, 2016).

Platforms also have implications for research ethics. Beyond established guidelines, like the Institutional Review Board's familiar protocols for privacy, consent, and anonymity, the Association of Internet Researchers (franzke et al., 2020) provides internationally informed recommendations for addressing emerging ethical dilemmas in digital scholarship. These include suggestions for mitigating risk for researchers and participants due to threats, doxing, and harassment, as well as cautions about the limits of conventional approach to informed consent in media landscape driven by datafication. Specific to online literacy research, Curwood, Magnifico, Lammers, and Stornaiuolo (2019) delineate a range of ethical considerations which scholars ought to attend: from the shifting dynamics of participant and platform access; to the unequal researcher-participant reciprocity in many online spaces; to the expanding availability of personal data online, often at (or beyond) the edges of traditional research consent.

To nurture more equitable digital research methods, some scholars have used "infrastructuring" (Ehn, Nilsson, & Topgaard, 2014; West-Puckett, Smith, Cantrill, & Zamora, 2018) as a mode of participatory design through which teams of researchers and participants, together, analyze how systems perpetuate or exacerbate inequitable relations. They then work to remake these systems, inserting flexible and responsive structures to better support the autonomy and flourishing of those impacted by it. Researchers are also intervening in these systems by taking their scholarship public, addressing legislators and general audiences about the need for regulation (or even dismantlement) of platform architectures that presently work against the public good (see, for example, Saheli Singh, 2019; www.screeningsurveillance.com).

Implications for Social Responsibility as Academics

Given what we have argued earlier about the challenges of doing critical digital literacy in an increasingly platform and datafied educational reality, how might academics and educators continue to think productively about their social responsibilities in relation to these issues?

For starters, a more capacious understanding of critical (digital) literacy is needed—one that can account for more than changes to the representational and textual dimensions of platforms and the ways these shape opportunities, identities, and social participation. Approaches to critical literacy, and even critical digital literacy, have been largely shaped in response to the world of late print capitalism, and can be stretched thinly when they are grafted onto different epistemological contexts. Acknowledging these limitations helps clarify something fundamental in the shift to established and emerging forms of digital capitalism, where digital infrastructures are pegged to a global market system that caters primarily to corporate actors and interests, often in increasingly intractable and untraceable ways (Schiller, 2000; Fuchs & Mocso, 2016). In this context, scholars need to ask whether familiar modes of criticality (or critical literacy) are adequate for understanding and intervening in the social, technical, and economic forms of life now taking shape.

As we suggest, negotiating these complex "digital infrastructures" (Srnicek, 2017) is increasingly difficult. Acknowledging this complexity means looking beyond the social dimensions of platforms and understanding, as well, the technical and economic DNA. Doing so can elucidate how social inequities are reproduced and reinscribed through systems that are subtler, and more automated, than we might be accustomed to reading through existing frames for critical literacy. For instance, understanding how platform logics are dependent on modes of categorization that, themselves, have epistemic roots in eugenics; or how "connectivity" folds everyday practices into webs of extractive and exploitative relations with no immediate options for resistance or escape. Understanding how platforms encode such forms of knowing demands an ethical reflexivity that extends to scales with which scholars, educators, and others (e.g. designers, developers, users) might become much more familiar. Indeed, not taking careful and critical account of these dimensions of platforms has already become an ethical problem and challenge, and a series of "blind" and "blank" spots (Wagner, 1993), for scholars, educators and others.

An additional ethical problem, which we have already hinted at, is the ease with which scholars can be unwittingly caught up in the race to understand and explain the new and shiny, while ignoring the challenging realities. Researchers interested in education, literacy, and the digital have long traded on a focus and analysis of the latest digital "advance"—typically arguing that such developments, and their accompanying digital practices, are more or less key aspects of many young people's digital literacies and identities. Such techno-determinism "lite" contributes to a powerful discursive field where significant commercial interests are served, as educational institutions become willing—and sometimes unwilling, of course—consumers of an ever-expanding array of technology products (Bulfin & Koutsogiannis, 2012).

When the focus is on the "new," and not the importance of infrastructures, education is reduced to fuel for the digital economy. This association has, in recent years, become a significant facet of neoliberal and market-driven educational policy (Nichols, 2020). It is not just that digital economies require significant financial investment—although, of course, they do. Digital, platform, and data capitalism also require certain kinds of people—subjects with the capacity for creativity, innovation, and collaboration. These are positive-sounding abilities; but abilities, in turn, which are also important goals of critical literacy. Given the ease of co-option into the design of social futures presently being imagined by platform architects, big data merchants, and edu-preneurs, researchers would do well to continue to ask, what is critical (digital) literacy? As evidenced by this very handbook, the practice and aims of critical literacy have always been contested and debated. In the context of platformization and datafication of social and educational life, the debate about the role of critical literacy must continue urgently.

Recommendations for Future Research and Praxis

A hallmark of critical literacy praxis is its thoroughly contextualized nature. As such, a recommendation for future research and praxis is to recognize the limitations of critical literacy in addressing the simultaneity and recursivity of platform architectures not as something that obviates or undermines it as a political project, but as something that can attune educators to the places critical literacy can best contribute in a world increasingly mediated by data technologies. Such an orientation invites us to ask where "critical literacy" might fit within a wider repertoire of tactics—drawn from a broad coalition of scholars, artists, organizers, and agitators; and rooted in diverse modes of inquiry and ways of knowing—that is capable of critiquing, resisting, reimagining, and transforming platform ecologies. As we have suggested, studies of platforms and datafication offer promising avenues for surfacing the possibilities and limitations of our existing frameworks for critical literacy. In doing so, they can also provide guidance for new directions in research, teaching, and practice that are attuned to the ethical and political questions that the emerging media environment makes urgent.

References

Ávila, J., & Pandya, J. Z. (2013). *Critical digital literacies as social praxis: Intersections and challenges.* Peter Lang.

Baker-Bell, A., Stanbrough, R. J., & Everett, S. (2017). The stories they tell: Mainstream media, pedagogies of healing, and critical media literacy. *English Education, 49*(2), 130–152.

Benjamin, R. (2019). *Race after technology: Abolitionist tools for the New Jim Code.* Polity Press.

Bhatt, I., & MacKenzie, A. (2019). Just Google it! Digital literacy and the epistemology of ignorance. *Teaching in Higher Education, 24*(3), 302–317.

Bogost, I., & Montfort, N. (2009). Platform studies: Frequently questioned answers. *Digital Arts and Culture.* Retrieved from http://escholarship.org/uc/item/01r0k9br.pdf.

Bowers, C. (2016). *Digital detachment: How computer culture undermines democracy.* Routledge.

Bratton, B. (2015). *The stack: On software and sovereignty.* MIT Press.

Browne, S. (2015). *Dark matters: On the surveillance of blackness.* Duke University Press.

Bucher, T. (2012). Want to be on the top? Algorithmic power and the threat of invisibility on Facebook. *New Media & Society, 14*(7), 1164–1180.

Bulfin, S., & Koutsogiannis, D. (2012). New literacies as multiply placed practices: Expanding perspectives on young people's literacies across home and school. *Language and Education, 26*(4), 331–346.

Bulfin, S., & McGraw, K. (2015). Digital literacy in theory, policy and practice: Old concerns, new opportunities. In M. Henderson & G. Romeo (Eds.), *Teaching and digital technologies: Big issues and critical questions* (pp. 266–281). Cambridge University Press.

Cope, B., & Kalantzis, M. (2016). Big data comes to school: Implications for learning, assessment and research. *AERA Open, 2,* 1–19.

Curwood, J. S., Magnifico, A. M., Lammers, J. C., & Stornaiuolo, A. (2019). Ethical dilemmas within online literacy research. *Literacy Research: Theory, Method, and Practice, 68*(1), 293–313. https://doi.org/10.1177/2381336919870264

de Roock, R.S. (2021). On the material consequences of (digital) literacy: Digital writing with, for, and against racial capitalism. *Theory into Practice, 60*(2), 183-193.

Dixon-Román, E., Nichols, T. P., & Nyame-Mensah, A. (2020). The racializing forces of/in AI educational technologies. *Learning, Media, and Technology.* https://doi.org/10.1080/17439884.2020.1667825.

Dourish, P. (2017). *The stuff of bits: An essay on the materialities of information.* MIT Press.

Duncan-Andrade, M., & Morrell, E. (2008). *The art of critical pedagogy: Possibilities for moving from theory to practice in urban schools.* Peter Lang.

Ehn, P., Nilsson, E. M., & Topgaard, R. (2014). *Making futures: Marginal notes on innovation, design, and democracy.* MIT Press.

franzke, a. s., Bechmann, A., Zimmer, M., Ess, C., & the Association of Internet Researchers. (2020). *Internet research: Ethical guidelines 3.0.* Retrieved from https://aoir.org/reports/ethics3.pdf

Freire, P., & Macedo, D. (1987). *Literacy: Reading the word and the world.* Paradigm Publishers.

Fuchs, C., & Mocso, V. (2016). *Marx in the age of digital capitalism.* Brill.

Garcia, A., & Nichols, T.P. (2021). Digital platforms aren't mere tools – they're complex environments. *Phi Delta Kappan, 102*(6), 14-19.

Gillespie, T. (2010). The politics of 'platforms'. *New Media & Society, 12*(3), 347–364.

Golden, N. A. (2017). Critical digital literacies across scales and beneath the screen. *Educational Media International.* https://doi.org/10.1080/09523987.2018.1391523.

Hardy, L., Dixon, C., & Hsi, S. (2019). From data collectors to data producers: Shifting students' relationship to data. *Journal of the Learning Sciences, 29*(1), 104–126. https://doi.org/10.1080/10508406.2019.1678164

Helmond, A. (2015). The platformization of the web: Making web data platform ready. *Social Media + Society, 1*(2), 1–11.

Irani, L. (2015). The cultural work of microwork. *New Media & Society, 17*(5), 720–739.

Jocson, K. (2015). New media literacies as social action: The centrality of pedagogy in the politics of knowledge production. *Curriculum Inquiry, 45*(1), 30–51.

Kitchin, R. (2014). *The data revolution.* Sage.

Lynch, T. L. (2015). Where the machine stops: Software as reader and the rise of new literatures. *Research in the Teaching of English, 49*(3), 297–304.

Mayer-Schoenberger, V., & Cukier, C. (2013). *Big data: A revolution that will transform how we live, work, and think.* John Murray Publishers.

Mirra, N., Morrell, E., & Filipiak, D. (2018). From digital consumption to digital invention: Toward a new critical theory of multiliteracies. *Theory into Practice, 57*(1), 12–19.

Morrell, E. (2017). Toward equity and diversity in literacy research, policy, and practice: A critical, global approach. *Journal of Literacy Research, 49*(3), 454–463. https://doi.org/10.1177/1086296X17720963

Nichols, T. P. (2020). Innovation from below: Infrastructure, design, and equity in literacy classroom makerspaces. *Research in the Teaching of English, 55*(1), 56–81.

Nichols, T. P., & Johnston, K. (2020). Rethinking 'availability' in multimodal composing: Frictions in digital design. *Journal of Adolescent and Adult Literacy.* https://doi.org/10.1002/jaal.1107.

Nichols, T. P., & LeBlanc, R. J. (2020). Beyond apps: Digital literacy in the platform society. *The Reading Teacher.*

Nichols, T.P., & LeBlanc, R.J. (2021). Media education and the limits of "literacy": Ecological orientations to performative platforms. *Curriculum Inquiry.* DOI: 10.1080/03626784.2020.1865104.

Nichols, T. P., & Stornaiuolo, A. (2019). Assembling 'digital literacy': Contingent pasts, possible futures. *Media & Communication, 7*(2), 1–10.

Noble, S. (2018). *Algorithms of oppression.* New York University Press.

Noble, S., & Tynes, B. M. (2016). *The intersectional internet: Race, sex, class, and culture online.* Peter Lang.

Pangrazio, L., & Selwyn, N. (2019). 'Personal data literacies': A critical literacies approach to enhancing understandings of personal digital data. *New Media & Society, 21*(2), 419–437.

Paris, D., & Alim, S. (Eds.). (2017). *Culturally sustaining pedagogies: Teaching and learning for justice in a changing world.* Teachers College Press.

Philip, T. M., Olivares-Pasillas, M. C., & Rocha, J. (2016). Becoming racially literate about data and data-literate about race: Data visualizations in the classroom as a site of racial-ideological micro-contestations. *Cognition and Instruction, 34*(4), 361–388. https://doi.org/10.1080/07370008.2016.1210418

Philip, T. M., Schuler-Brown, S., & Way, W. (2013). A framework for learning about big data with mobile technologies for democratic participation: Possibilities, limitations, and unanticipated obstacles. *Technology, Knowledge and Learning, 18*(3), 103–120. https://doi.org/10.1007/s10758-013-9202-4

Robinson, B. (2020). The ClassDojo app: Training in the art of dividuation. *International Journal of Qualitative Studies in Education.* https://doi.org/10.1080/09518398.2020.1771460.

Sadowski, J. (2019). When data is capital: Datafication, accumulation, and extraction. *Big Data & Society, 6*(1), 1–12.

saheli singh, s. (2019). Screening surveillance: Mapping, monitoring, and future-ing Big Data surveillance. In G. T. Donovan & J. Reich (Eds.), *Proceedings of the mapping (in)justice symposium.* Fordham University. Retrieved from https://mappinginjustice.org

Schiller, D. (2000). *Digital capitalism: Networking the global market system.* MIT Press.

Scott, J., & Nichols, T. P. (2017). Learning analytics as assemblage: Criticality and contingency in online education. *Research in Education, 98*(1), 83–105.

Sefton-Green, J. (2021). Towards platform pedagogies: Why thinking about digital platforms as pedagogic devices might be useful. *Discourse: Studies in the Cultural Politics of Education.* DOI: 10.1080/01596306.2021.1919999.

Selwyn, N., Nemorin, S., Bulfin, S., & Johnson, N. (2017). Left to their own devices: The everyday realities of one-to-one classrooms. *Oxford Review of Education, 43*(3), 289–310.

Smith, A., Cope, B., & Kalantzis, M. (2017). The quantified writer: Data traces in education. In K. Mills, A. Stornaiuolo, A. Smith, & J. Pandya (Eds.), *Handbook of writing, literacies, and education in digital cultures* (pp. 235–248). Routledge.

Smith, A., Stornaiuolo, A., & Phillips, N. (2018). Multiplicities in motion: A turn to transliteracies. *Theory into Practice*, *57*(1), 20–28.

Sobko, S., Unadkat, D., Adams, J., & Hull, G. (2020). Learning through collaboration: A networked approach to online pedagogy. *E-Learning and Digital Media*, *17*(1), 36–55.

Srnicek, N. (2017). *Platform capitalism*. Polity Press.

Star, S. L., & Bowker, G. C. (2002). How to infrastructure. In L. A. Lievrous & S. Livingstone (Eds.), *The handbook of new media* (pp. 230–245). Sage.

Stornaiuolo, A. (2019). Authoring data stories in a media makerspace: Adolescents developing critical data literacies. *Journal of the Learning Sciences*, *29*(1), 81–103.

Stornaiuolo, A., Smith, A., & Phillips, N. (2017). Developing a transliteracies framework for a connected world. *Journal of Literacy Research*, *49*(1), 68–91.

van Dijck, J. (2013). *The culture of connectivity: A critical history of social media*. Oxford University Press.

Wagner, J. (1993). Ignorance in educational research or, how can you not know that? *Educational Researcher*, *22*, 15–23.

West-Puckett, S., Smith, A., Cantrill, C., & Zamora, M. (2018). The fallacies of open: Participatory design, infrastructuring, and the pursuit of radical possibility. *Contemporary Issues in Technology & Teacher Education*, *18*(2).

Wilkerson, M. H., & Polman, J. L. (2020). Situating data science: Exploring how relationships to data shape learning. *Journal of the Learning Sciences*, *29*(1), 1–10. https://doi.org/10.1080/10508406.2019.1705664

Williamson, B. (2018). *Big data in education*. Sage.

Zuboff, S. (2019). *The age of surveillance capitalism. The fight for a human future at the new frontier of power*. Profile Books.

3.6

CONNECTING CRITICAL LITERACY AND DIS/ABILITY STUDIES

Opportunities and Implications

David I. Hernández-Saca

Introduction

The purpose of this chapter is to connect critical literacy studies (CLS) and critical dis/Ability studies in education (CDSE) in order to promote a productive cross-fertilization between these important areas of study. This cross-fertilization is vital, given that these two bodies of work have not been systematically connected before. Although each is grounded in critical theory and pedagogy and explore the sociocultural construction of literacy and dis/Ability, I articulate a broader, complementary understanding of CLS and CDSE.

To highlight this potential for cross-fertilization of CDSE and CLS to strengthen the study of dis/Ability in education, I focus on discourses about high-incidence dis/Abilities such as specific Learning Disabilities (LD) in special education and its need for ideological critique. Ideological critique is indispensable given the academic, social, and emotional impacts that high-incidence special education disability labels have on students' sense of self, and in particular, Black, Indigenous and People of Color (BIPOC) and youth (Iqtadar, Hernández-Saca, & Ellison, 2020).

A History of Key Concepts

Critical Literacy

Critical literacy skills empower "people to interpret messages in the modern world through a critical lens and challenge the power relations within those messages" (Coffey, 2010, para. 2). Critical literacy educators position students to "interrogate societal issues and institutions like [the state,] family, poverty, education, equity, and equality in order to critique the structures that serve as norms [and] how these norms are not experienced by all members of society" (para. 2). In turn, Critical Literacy Studies (CLS) scholars and students engage in paradigmatic critique at the epistemological level, which in turn has implications for the ontological, axiological, and etiological dimensions of the phenomena or text under study. They interrogate the social and emotional construction of reality toward achieving justice. Reexamining "reality" for justice is crucial since critical theory and pedagogy is also a theory of happiness (Ingram & Simon-Ingram, 1992). Undoing the ideological struggle of re-thinking and re-feeling our experiences of the world, we interrogate our thoughts and feelings about the texts of our lives. Through this dialectical process, one can begin to refute and

DOI: 10.4324/9781003023425-41

nullify oppression at the intersections to keep hope, love, and happiness alive towards the possibilities of individual and societal transformation. In doing so, humans can be agentive in their social practices within institutions like education (Ingram & Simon-Ingram, 1992).

The unraveling of dehumanization through the humanizing power of critical literacy education, teaching, and learning can then have the potential to create an activist imperative of literacy. Critical literacy theory centers "on the relationships between language, power, social practice, and access to social goods and services, . . . numerous methods of engaging students in becoming critical members of their society" (Coffey, 2010, para. 12). By doing so, CLS generates new knowledge and counter-narratives that re-mediate how we see, know, feel, do, and become concerning a given subject-matter with the hope of speaking truth to power. CLS generates critical emotion praxis and privileges silenced discourses and materialities in order to re-frame the hegemonic emotion discursive practices that reproduce the status quo.

Critical Dis/Ability Studies in Education

Critical disability studies (CDS) interrogate how dis/Ability is understood for theory, research, and practice for the benefit of people with impairments. CDS is an interdisciplinary field of study that conceptualizes "disability" through a social, cultural, and political lens ("social model" of disability), as opposed to the previously accepted medical, biological, or psychological frameworks ("medical model" of disability). The medical model of disability situates "disability" as a deficit and intrinsic to the person's body, brain, or mind. The social model of disability challenges this medicalization that locates the "disability" within the individual, and instead investigates the social construction of both ability and disability, hence, "dis/Ability." According to Rice (2007), CDS troubles "the idea of the normal/abnormal binary" and suggests that a range of human variation is "normal" in local and global contexts (Meekosha & Shuttleworth, 2009) (p. 466).

Disability Studies in Education (DSE) is the application of CDS in education. DSE emerged as an alternative to the hegemony of special education as the main domain in which disability was understood by educational institutions. However, in the 1990s, before DSE, special educators who were "critical special educators" and leaders of the Society of Disability Studies focused on issues at the nexus of CDS and educational research. It's important to note that critical special education as a study and discipline was one of "other forms of education research" that were applied to the domain of CDS scholarship (Connor, 2012) at that time. DSE scholars provided a counter paradigm to challenge "traditional" frameworks that animated the dominant special education view towards disability. This resistance against positivist underpinnings of special education led to a counter-disability or non-positivist, non-empiricist, and non-objectivist discourse, which has had less influence and power within the academy (Connor, 2012).

Since their inception, the fields of critical special education, CDS and DSE have critically examined dis/Ability at the intersections of race, gender, class, and other categories. However, only recently has an explicit intersectionality framework been applied to the theory, research, and practice of disability in education and society broadly, albeit sometimes in limited ways (Artiles, 2013). The critical fields of study of disability in society and education were also at risk of reproducing the larger hegemonic order of white supremacy—in this case, perpetuating a narrative of non-intersectional disability. David Connor's body of work (2008) is an exception. More recently, Annamma, Connor, and Ferri (2016) employed DSE as well as Critical Race Theory to explore disability and race, and more specifically, how racism based on Western cultural norms and ableism mutually constitute educational spaces and other social institutions.

Furthermore, the interdisciplinary and intersectional nature of DSE has produced critical special education and DSE scholars who have contributed to the interdisciplinarity spirit of the field. For example, the body of work by interdisciplinary critical studies of disability (CSD) scholar Alfredo J. Artiles (2013) has contributed to our understanding of the problem of over- and under-representation of students of color labeled with special education high-incidence disability categories within the United States. Socially and emotionally constructed identities such as race, class, gender, ability, and disability have particularly impacted the lives of BIPOC and youth in U.S. public schools. Given the legacies of racism and ableism in U.S. schools, students of color and their ways of communicating and forms of literacy have been pathologized and stigmatized in educational contexts since the founding of the country (Patton Davis & Museus, 2019). Racism and ableism have been enacted emotionally, spatially, materially, linguistically, culturally, socially, and politically within schools. Literacy has also been used by dominant institutions to perpetuate racist and ableist practices disguised behind a cloak of benevolence and masquerading as the "official" purpose of U.S. school's mission to create "literate citizens." However, movements to create literate citizens have been uncritical, reproducing hegemonic master narratives and a status quo that does not support the lives of BIPOC and youth and their communities and in turn reproduces systematic whiteness and ableism. Historical deficit-oriented ideologies have been attached to particular identity groups to which youth belong. Justice dilemmas such as the disproportionate representation of youth of color in special education and the discursive, material, and emotional consequences of this misrepresentation compared to their white-peers with the same high-incidence disability label have resulted in civil and educational rights violations (Artiles, 2013). The lived experiences of BIPOC and youth labeled with special education high incidence disabilities have led to the following problematic outcomes:

1. Low-expectations
2. Denial of access to the general education curriculum
3. Physical segregation and denial of access to their least restrictive environment both in terms of placement in the general education classroom and quality of participation with their non-labeled peers, which is guaranteed through the Individuals with Disabilities Education Act (IDEA) of 2004
4. Stigmatization leading to intersectional discrimination based on disability and another category of difference

Such negative documented outcomes of disproportionality in special education have led to psycho-emotional disablism, "a form of social oppression involving the social imposition of restrictions of activity on people with impairments and the socially engendered undermining of their psycho-emotional well-being" (Thomas, 2007, p. 73). Furthermore, a qualitative research synthesis by Iqtadar et al. (2020) found that K–16 BIPOC and youth with disabilities at their intersections of other forms of difference a) experience disability labels as an assigned identity, which limited their educational opportunities and left a psychological and emotional impact on their well-being. BIPOC youth with disabilities used a variety of strategies and acts of resistance to negotiate the stereotypical master narratives surrounding their intersectional identities.

Critiques of Critical Literacy in This Domain

Summarizing DSE scholars Kliewer, Biklen, and Kasa-Hendrickson (2006), Keefe and Copeland (2011) characterize how literacy has been considered for students and people with extensive support needs "as a narrative of pessimism," that is, "the belief that individuals with extensive needs for support cannot acquire literacy skills often results in a lack of opportunity to learn these skills and therefore, becomes a self-fulfilling prophecy" (p. 92). According to Carol Thomas (2007), this narrative of pessimism is rooted in the medical-psychological model of disability that creates psycho-emotional disablism.

I further understand such narratives as master narratives that constrain not only students but all stakeholders surrounding students with literacy-based learning disabilities. It also constitutes a form of deficit thinking and language. According to Patton Davis and Museus (2019), deficit thinking and language "holds students from historically oppressed populations responsible for the challenges and inequalities that they face . . . Overall, these perspectives serve as tools that maintain hegemonic systems" (p. 119). Similarly, the "narrative of pessimism," like the medical-psychological model, blames students for their "lack of literacy skills" and does not provide a narrative of hope or life. Keefe and Copeland (2011) call for a "narrative of optimism" based on a long-standing CDSE core-principle of presumed competence (Biklen & Burke, 2006) "for individuals regardless of label or perceived ability" or literacy (p. 92). Biklen and Burke (2006) define presumed competence as a verb, inter-action and co-constructing ability and competence as education-as-dialogue not only for students with disabilities, but all students, and its connection to inclusive education. Biklen and Burke (2006) therefore provide a counter-narrative to the master narrative of pessimism of the abilities of students with intellectual disabilities when they asserted that: "In light of the pessimism that surrounds autism and the intellectual abilities of persons so classified, to presume competence is a step outside of conventional theory and practice" (p. 167). Presuming competence also leads to democratic schooling that centers the student and teacher relationship and student voice about educational processes, practices, and student experience in school (Biklen & Burke, 2006). Presuming competence, in turn, leads to systemic school reform and change efforts based on a kind of optimistic lived-narrative-in-interaction with students and teachers for inclusive education that foregrounds systemic change.

Consequently, according to CSE and DSE scholars, national and global educational literacy policies such as the U.S. National Reading Panel and the United Nations' Educational, Scientific and Cultural Organization (UNESCO) disregard local literacy theories and practices and do not adequately account for students with disabilities and their communication and literacy needs. Keefe and Copeland (2011) traced the historical trajectory of notions of literacy, from understanding literacy as a human right with the inception of UNESCO and the Program for International Student Assessment to the following types: (a) traditional skilled-centered functional literacy (*e.g., decoding the written word through phonetics and other basic-skills for comprehension*), (b) critical literacy (e.g., *reading and writing involves the reading and writing of the world from a Freirean type of problem-posing that leads to critical consciousness*), and lastly, (c) a broader understanding of literacy that center the students with disabilities expansive understanding of literacy as multimodal (e.g., "*literacy as the construction (which includes interpretation) of meaning through visually or tactually crafted symbols that compose various forms of text*" (Kliewer, 2008, p. 106, as cited in Keefe & Copeland, 2011, p. 96).

Keefe and Copeland (2011) synthesized these multiple definitions of literacy and proposed the following core principles for students with significant literacy needs:

1. All people are capable of acquiring literacy.
2. Literacy is a human right and is a fundamental part of the human experience.
3. Literacy is not a trait that resides solely in the individual person. It requires and creates a connection (relationship) with others.
4. Literacy includes communication, contact, and the expectation that interaction is possible for individuals; literacy has the potential to lead to empowerment.
5. Literacy is the collective responsibility of every individual in the community; that is, to develop meaning making with all human modes of communication to transmit and receive information (p. 97).

On the one hand, critical literacy studies have not systematically included the role of the social construction of dis/Ability at its intersections of power, identities and emotionality for theory, research and practice. On the other hand, CDSE, which has focused on the intersections of power, identities, and emotionality, has not cross fertilized with CLS. Although a Freirean approach to literacy within critical literacy studies has also been a part of DSE regarding critical consciousness raising (Connor, 2008), a more systematic cross-disciplinary collaboration within and across both fields would generate new theory, research, and practice.

Current Research in the Area

Similar to Keefe and Copeland's definition of literacy principles, other interdisciplinary critical studies of disability scholars have focused on the role of culture in the historical problem of racial disproportionality of special education diagnoses in U.S. schools. More African American and Latinx students are diagnosed with subjective special education categories such as learning disabilities and categorized as "struggling readers."

Within the large body of research, not one accepted version of reading interventions for struggling readers exists. They range from interventions that focus on explicit instruction of technical skills (phonemic awareness, word-recognition, etc.) to connecting those skills to literature (i.e., embedded literacy) to combining technical skills with whole language approaches. Researchers like Wyatt, Phillips, and Lonigan (2009) developed an approach to reading intervention as a prevention program, such as the Get Ready to Read! emergent literacy screener. The state of research on this topic has been prolific and diverse but the focus remains on developing discrete skills as a means to early and later literacy acquisition. There is hardly any attention to culture, sociocultural, and historical variables that influence human language and literacy development (Artiles, 2002; Gutierrez, Zepeda, & Castro, 2010).

According to Sharon Vaughn, the state of reading research and instruction for struggling readers has made great strides in identifying best practices for prevention, instruction and re-mediation for children who struggle to read. Vaughn states: "much of what we've learned from research is being translated into materials, practice, policy, and decision-making . . . there's much to be excited about" (as cited in Chamberlain, 2006, p. 169). Nevertheless, there is a cautionary tale, "our knowledge about reading instruction for students who are most at need, some of whom are English Language Learners and many of whom are individuals with disabilities" needs more research for practice (Vaughn, as cited in Chamberlain, 2006, p. 169). I concur with Vaughn, however, additional research is needed to offer innovative tools and practices for BIPOC and youth, including English Learners, students with disabilities, speakers of African American Vernacular English and other regional dialects, and students who have historically been marginalized and/or privileged within U.S. society. It's imperative to examine the complexity and diversity of the U.S. student population since it has implications for educational equity. Sample populations within empirical studies of reading interventions mostly comprise students who come from socioeconomic backgrounds that label them as "poor" (Donovan & Cross, 2002).

Gutierrez et al's (2010) critique of the National Early Literacy Panel (NELP) report of 2008 illuminated the types of alternative perspectives and issues that are important for BIPOC and youth. Gutierrez et al. (2010) interrogated NELP for its culture-free (e.g., lack of attention to the simultaneous relationship and salience of oral language and literacy development, etc.) and over-generalizing based on sample sizes that do not consider dual language learners (DLLs) ages four years old and younger. Gutierrez et al. (2010) like Artiles (2002) in his response to Wise and Snyder's (2002) literature review on the nature and treatment of language-based reading difficulties, namely specific reading disabilities (SRDs)—highlight the problematic nature of treatment and interventions based on discrete psycholinguistic processes that minimize opportunities to learn for BIPOC and youth who come to school with out-of-school literacy practices that combine both oral language and literacy repertoires of practice (Gutierrez & Rogoff, 2003).

The types of measures conducted within reading interventions consist of quantitative assessments that measure psychometric processes of students' literacy. These typically measure letter name fluency, initial sound fluency, phoneme segmentation fluency, nonsense word fluency, oral reading fluency, and retell fluency. Typical reading intervention studies begin with a battery of tests to determine if students qualify as part of the sample or the pool of participants included in the intervention. Tests include, but are not limited to: *Woodcock Reading Mastery Test Revised* and *Dynamic Indicators of Basic Early Literacy Skills*. Oftentimes these tests are used in isolation, but used in a combination of ways by researchers to help them identify the specific "deficits" and progress, or "lack thereof," in their sample populations or participants.

The early reading characteristics of children who are both represented in reading interventions and are "unresponsive" to treatment in part constitute what is targeted in early literacy interventions outlined by the National Reading Panel ([NRP]2000) from the National Institute of Child Health and Development. The purpose of the NRP report, *Teaching Children to Read Reports of the Subgroups*, was to examine the scientific evidence relevant to the impact of phonemic awareness instruction on reading and spelling development (NRP, 2000). The areas of early literacy of struggling and "unresponsive" readers are as follows: (1) phonological awareness; (2) phonological encoding in memory and phonological discrimination; (3) rapid naming; (4) intelligence, verbal IQ, and disability status; (5) attention and behavior problems; and (6) orthographic processing (Al Otaiba & Fuchs, 2002). In their meta-analysis, Nelson, Benner, and Gonzalez (2003) found that "the primary learner characteristics that influenced the treatment responsiveness of early literacy interventions were, in order of magnitude, rapid naming, problem behavior, phonological awareness, alphabetic principle, memory, IQ, and demographics" (p. 255). Al Otaiba and Fuchs (2002) found that children who were "non-responders" showed "slow" letter-naming speed, difficulty encoding, storing, and organizing phonological information into memory, had IQ "deficits," attention or problem behaviors and found students demographics (age, level of English proficiency, and parental education levels and occupation) had an influence on children's responsiveness to interventions. Al Otaiba and Fuchs (2002) analyzed five studies that investigated if children's demographics (e.g., children's age, parent's education and occupation, level of English proficiency, etc.) effect responsiveness to treatment and found these to "correlate with treatment unresponsiveness" (Al Otaiba & Fuchs, 2002, p. 312). In contrast to Al Otaiba and Fuchs (2002), who further argue that English proficiency and other sociocultural variables lead to classifying students as "non-responders," Artiles (2002), Artiles and Kozleski (2010), Gutierrez and Rogoff (2003) and Gutierrez et al. (2010) argue that cognitive and psycholinguistic processes as well as sociocultural and historical variables mediate literacy and language use from a sociocultural and historical approach to human development.

These sociocultural and historical variables are not seen as a "liability" but as part and parcel of the repertoires of literacy practices that students bring to school. However, scholars would agree that these outside-of-school variables should be taken into account in the definition of literacy, "response," and intervention within reading intervention studies for the literate lives of BIPOC and youth. Comparing and contrasting BIPOC and youth to monolingual students and applying universal and over-generalizing forms of intervention studies about literacy without considering culture, history, power, and emotion is misguided.

Within reading interventions studies, some defining characteristics of historically multiply marginalized students for early literacy are "problem behavior," memory, IQ, and demographics (Al Otaiba, & Fuchs, 2002). Although these factors may cause barriers to historically multiply marginalized students, "problem behaviors" and how they are interpreted can and should be contested. If we only define memory in its neurological, cognitive, and psycholinguistic sense, it can certainly be a barrier to the acquisition of reading and writing. Foregrounding memory as simply an individual process is problematic. What we remember most does not only involve discrete cognitive and psycholinguistic skills. How we make sense involves what we do together: *what, how, and why* we communicate, talk, eat, interact, feel, and build community. In particular, from a Freirean and critical literacy perspective what we do in classrooms and out of classrooms can center a more boundless meaning of literacy in relation to memory by highlighting the dialectical relationship between meaning making and what I call the *sociocultural and emotional repertoires of practices* in which we engage with ourselves, others, and the world.

Implications for Pedagogy

This exploration of the nexus of CLS and CDSE holds many implications for pedagogy. These implications include an expansive understanding of literacy beyond the written word. However, such a connection would underscore the fact that all human beings, regardless of a label or ability, are critically literate with texts and the world. This understanding of literacy highlights the structural and political nature of literacy for liberation, emancipation, and hope. A pedagogy of critical dis/Ability literacy studies, where our abilities to communicate are not only honored, but enabled in multimodal ways with assistive technologies, such as Augmentative Alternative Communication (AAC) and devices such as Picture Exchange Communication Systems (PECS). However, such devices would be used in culturally sustaining and counter-hegemonic ways to enable all human beings, instead of reifying whiteness and ableism (Lewis, 2020). Through Keefe and Copeland's (2011) definition of literacy principles, a pedagogy of critical dis/Ability literacy studies would anchor the *sociocultural and emotional repertoires of practices* of BIPOC and youth with/out disabilities at their intersections of power, identities and emotionalities inside and outside of education. Such a pedagogy would include a narrative of optimism that would radically shift our understanding of what counts as dis/Ability and literacy for individuals living with impairments and their competency to be self-determining and self-advocating for their wants and needs. One starting point would be the use of education-as-dialogue through an optimistic lived-narrative-in-interaction approach.

Implications for Research

Given the interdisciplinary and intersectionality within CDSE there are several implications for research based on the cross-fertilization between CLS and DSE. One way of bridging these fields for a *Critical Dis/Ability Literacy Studies (CDLS)* would be to operationalize the tenets of Critical Race and Disability Studies (Annamma et al., 2016) to center the critical voices of students with multi-dimensional identities to explore how BIPOC and students with/out dis/Abilities counter-narrate their lived experiences in literacy practices in K-16 and beyond education and life. Operationalizing such a *CDLS* lens would enable critical social science research to have personal, interpersonal, structural, and political dimensions (Crenshaw, 1990). One case study would be the disproportionality of BIPOC and youth with disabilities in subjective categories like specific learning disabilities or students who are categorized as "struggling readers." The nomenclature would need a paradigmatic shift away from a deficit-oriented understanding of students that places dis/Ability within their neurology and bodies. A critical literacy lens accounts for the interrelationships between these research theoretical and methodological tools, which could be culled from a range of critical theories that can operationalize *CDLS* based on the researcher's participants and the goals of the research as a transformative praxis for emancipation and hope.

Implications for Our Social and Emotional Responsibility as Academics

As academics we need to critically think and feel before we act as educational equity researchers and acknowledge our responsibility to not only our discipline, and the academy, or to our professional identity, but as human beings first and foremost. In so doing, we can activate a politics of *CDLS* that disrupts global, ableist hegemony for personal and professional development as it relates to being a citizen within one's local and global communities of practice for justice for all. Centering the lives and voices of BIPOC and youth with special education disability labels and impairments that range the full spectrum of the human condition is critical for our individual and collective pursuits for theory, research, and practice, which is in the spirit of liberatory critical literacy. This is especially so given the raise of neoliberalism and Right-Wing populist movements, within the U.S. and across the globe that have influenced the culture of K-16 education (Ellison, 2019; Maskovsky, 2012). Academics, especially critical educational equity social scientists have had to oppose:

> the advent of consumerist, market-driven learning; the privatization, corporation, and branding of the university; the decline in public spending on higher education; the speed-up of the academic assembly line; audit culture; outcomes assessment and other efficiency-oriented interventions; and the casualization of academic labor . . . glossed as neoliberal.
>
> *(Maskovsky, 2012, p. 819)*

Although, academics are not a monolithic and have responded to neoliberalism in diverse ways given their social positioning and issues of power and privilege, we cannot consider the raise of neoliberalism in isolation from other movements and crises (Ellison, 2019; Maskovsky, 2012). But part and parcel of what Ellison (2019) would have us critically analyze as the "discipline of the conjuncture" at the nexus of historical, contemporary and futurity of global ableist hegemonic and non-hegemonic moments for individual and collective resistance.

Recommendations for Future Research and Praxis

The following recommendations for future research and critical emotion praxis are paramount for the life-chances of BIPOC and youth with/out dis/Abilities for their literate lives and are intended for all involved in BIPOC and youth's with/out dis/Abilities literacy education:

1) Center the voices, literacies and capabilities of BIPOC and youth with/out dis/Abilities.
2) Presume competence of BIPOC and youth with/out dis/Abilities.
3) Co-construct learning, teaching, and research ecologies and literacy practices with BIPOC and youth with/out dis/Abilities that are multimodal and incorporate the full range of cultural signs to counter-Eurocentric and Eugenics consciousness and practices for liberation, emancipation, and hope.

References

Al Otaiba, S., & Fuchs, D. (2002). Characteristics of children who are unresponsive to early literacy intervention: A review of the literature. *Remedial and Special Education, 23*(5), 300–316.

Annamma, S. A., Connor, D. J., & Ferri, B. A. (2016). A truncated genealogy of DisCrit. In D. J. Connor, B. A. Ferri, & S. A. Annamma (Eds.), *DisCrit: Disability studies and critical race theory in education* (pp. 1–8). Teachers College Press.

Artiles, A. J. (2002). Culture in learning: The next frontier in reading difficulties research. In R. Bradley, L. Danielson, & D. P. Hallahan (Eds.), *Identification of learning disabilities: Research to policy* (pp. 693–701). Lawrence Erlbaum Associates.

Artiles, A. J. (2013). Untangling the racialization of disabilities: An intersectionality critique across disability models. *DuBois Review, 10*, 329–347.

Artiles, A. J., & Kozleski, E. B. (2010). What counts as response and intervention in RTI? A sociocultural analysis. *Psicothema, 22*(4), 949–954.

Biklen, D., & Burke, J. (2006). Presuming competence. *Equity & Excellence in Education, 39*(2), 166–175.

Chamberlain, S. P. (2006). Sharon Vaughn: The state of reading research and instruction for struggling readers. *Intervention in School and Clinic, 41*(3), 169–174.

Coffey, H. (2010). *Critical literacy.* Learn NC.

Connor, D. J. (2008). *Urban narratives: Portraits in progress, life at the intersections of learning disability, race, & social class* (Vol. 5). Peter Lang.

Connor, D. J. (2012). *History of disability studies in education.* Hunter College.

Crenshaw, K. (1990). Mapping the margins: Intersectionality, identity politics, and violence against women of color. *Stanford Law Review*, *43*, 1241.

Donovan, M. S., & Cross, C. T. (2002). *Minority students in special and gifted education.* National Research Council.

Ellison, S. (2019). Against fragmentation: Critical education scholarship in a time of crisis. *Educational Studies*, *55*(3), 271–294.

Gutierrez, K. D., & Rogoff, B. (2003). Cultural ways of learning: Individual traits or repertories of practice. *Educational Researcher*, *32*(5), 19–25.

Gutierrez, K. D., Zepeda, M., & Castro, D. C. (2010). Advancing early literacy learning for all children: Implications of the NELP Report for dual-language learners. *Educational Researchers*, *39*(4), 334–339.

Iqtadar, S., Hernández-Saca, D. I., & Ellison, S. (2020). "If it wasn't my race, it was other things like being a woman, or my disability": A qualitative research synthesis of disability research. *Disability Studies Quarterly*, *40*(2).

Ingram, D., & Simon-Ingram, J. (Eds.). (1992). *Critical theory: The essential readings.* Paragon House.

Keefe, E. B., & Copeland, S. R. (2011). What is literacy? The power of a definition. *Research and Practice for Persons with Severe Disabilities*, *36*(3–4), 92–99.

Kliewer, C. (2008). Joining the literacy flow: Fostering symbol and written language learning in young children with significant developmental disabilities through the four currents of literacy. *Research and Practice for Persons with Severe Disabilities*, *33*(3), 103-121.

Kliewer, C., Biklen, D., & Kasa-Hendrickson, C. (2006). Who may be literate? Disability and resistance to the cultural denial of competence. *American Educational Research Journal*, *43*(2), 163–192.

Lewis, T. (2020, January 25). *Ableism 2020: An updated definition.* [Blog]. https://www.talilalewis.com/blog/ableism-2020-an-updated-definition

Maskovsky, J. (2012). Beyond neoliberalism: Academia and activism in a nonhegemonic moment. *American Quarterly*, *64*(4), 819–822.

Meekosha, H., & Shuttleworth, R. (2009). What's so 'critical' about critical disability studies? *Australian Journal of Human Rights*, *15*(1), 47–75.

National Reading Panel (US), National Institute of Child Health, & Human Development (US). (2000). *Teaching children to read: An evidence-based assessment of the scientific research literature on reading and its implications for reading instruction: Reports of the subgroups.* National Institute of Child Health and Human Development, National Institutes of Health.

Nelson, J. R., Benner, G. J., & Gonzalez, J. (2003). Learner characteristics that influence the treatment effectiveness of early literacy interventions: A meta-analytic review. *Learning Disabilities Research & Practice*, *18*(4), 255–267.

Patton Davis, L., & Museus, S. D. (2019). What Is deficit thinking? An analysis of conceptualizations of deficit thinking and implications for scholarly research. *Currents*, *1*(1), 117–129.

Rice, N. (2007). Disability studies. In G. L. Anderson & K. G. Herr (Eds.), *Encyclopedia of activism and social justice*, *1*, 466–466. Sage.

Thomas, C. (2007). *Sociologies of disability and illness: Contested ideas in disability studies and medical sociology.* Macmillan International Higher Education.

Wise, B., & Snyder, L. (2002). Clinical judgments in identifying and teaching children with language-based reading difficulties. In R. Bradley, L. Danielson, & D. Hallahan (Eds.), *Identification of learning disabilities: Research to practice* (pp. 653–692). Erlbaum.

Wyatt, M. A., Phillips, B. M., & Lonigan, C. J. (2009). Predictive validity of the get ready to read! Screener: Concurrent and long-term relations with reading-related skills. *Journal of Learning Disabilities*, *42*(2), 133–147.

3.7

CRITICAL LITERACY AND ABOLITION

Justin A. Coles, Roberto Santigo de Roock, Hui-Ling Sunshine Malone, and Adam D. Musser

Introduction

Literacy has long been tied to enslavement and domination, but also the abolition of institutions and systems of domination. In the United States of America (U.S.) and across the world, these relationships are particularly poignant during the dual pandemics of COVID-19 and racial domination (Kendi, 2020; Pirtle, 2020). Although nothing new, recent events highlight disproportionate harm and premature death to Black, Brown, and Indigenous communities at the hands of police, public health policy, and other structural and material violence. This ascendant fascism relies heavily on a manipulation of critical literacy (or lack thereof) among the white electorate through media manipulation, misinformation, and disinformation. On the other hand, communities continue to resist, leveraging years of organizing and social media while drawing on sophisticated critical community and ancestral literacies. Still, most schools continue as spaces that disenfranchise minoritized communities, including through literacy ideology and pedagogy. This occurs through restrictions, sorting, and criminalization tied to the denial of literacy opportunities, biased literacy assessments, constant racialization, the production of surplus populations, and persistent antiblackness under racial capitalism (de Roock, 2021; Gilmore, 2007; Robinson, 2000).

This chapter surveys literacy theory and practice connected to the carceral continuum. We regard racial capitalism's antiblackness and white supremacy as the underlying ideologies of life, literacy, and schooling in the U.S., and we highlight the abolitionist literacies working against them. Recognizing that abolition is not a singular movement or approach, we cover writing from a number of areas including intersectionality and Black feminism; literacy praxis of the incarcerated and against racist policing; policing and discipline in schools; and around punitive school testing and sorting with their roots in eugenics. We maintain that literacy praxis not directly supporting abolition and collective liberation works in the service of captivity and domination.

Definitions of Key Concepts

Abolition and Antiblackness

Abolition traces back to movements to end the violent bondage of African people in the Americas. In particular, abolition refers back to work by formerly enslaved Blacks and the general strike carried out by enslaved Blacks on Southern plantations that precipitated the defeat of the Confederacy and

DOI: 10.4324/9781003023425-42

end of the Civil War (Robinson, 2000). Though during the period of enslavement many could not imagine a world without slavery, abolitionists like Frederick Douglass and Harriet Tubman made it possible through their determined vision of liberation expressed through writing and action. Dery (1994) helps us understand how Black abolitionists were grounded in afrofuturism, imagining and then creating alternative ways of life "in unlikely places, constellated from far-flung points" (p. 182). Abolitionists, then, are engaged in "technologies of the sacred," or what we might conceptualize as technologies of escape (p. 182). Current thinking builds on the pioneering work of W. E. B. Du Bois and praxis of Black feminists such as Angela Y. Davis and Audre Lorde over the last 50 years, calling for ending harmful systems that enact domination while envisioning new, radically democratic, liberatory systems. Abolition is, therefore, a critique, a call to action, and a future-facing imagination.

Abolition, like decolonization, is not a metaphor (Tuck & Yang, 2012). The term abolition is now most popularly used in ending the system of mass incarceration that is intricately linked to racism and capitalism, which are closely coupled and theorized together as racial capitalism (Pirtle, 2020; Roberts, 2019; Robinson, 2000). Abolition stands in contrast with liberal multiculturalism that dominates sociocultural educational theory and fetishizes "diversity" along with individual student voice and social mobility (de Roock, 2021; de Roock & Baildon, 2019; Tuck & Yang, 2012). In the spirit of reimagining new realities without prisons, Angela Y. Davis (2003) and other prison abolitionists argue that we must uproot all oppressive institutions for a more just society. One major reason is the endemic antiblackness of these institutions. We define antiblackness as the:

> Legacy of U.S. chattel and plantation style slavery, which represents the human races structurally embedded degradation of Black people and communities through imagining Blackness as inherently negative, needing to be policed and/or neutralized, and as outside the realms of humanity.
>
> *(Coles, 2019, p. 2)*

Antiblackness, "renders people of African descent categorically unacceptable as human beings, irrespective of their intelligence, character, competence, creativity, or achievements" (Washington, 1981, p. 146). As a transplant regime characterized by the "disgust and disdain for Black bodies" (Dumas, 2016, p. 8), antiblackness renders Black ideals of freedom (abolition) in the form of control over one's existence as unimaginable; such unsurveilled Black freedom runs counter to the logics of antiblackness. Antiblackness forms the paradigmatic and material foundation of racial capitalism, resting in the absence of true Black self-rule.

Intersectionality and Black Feminist Politics

We cannot discuss abolitionist work and praxis without acknowledging Black Feminist Thought and Black women who, given their vulnerable positionality in this world, continuously uplift and transform our society. The foundational Combahee River Collective (Collective, 1982) statement emphasized a commitment to "struggling against racial, sexual, heterosexual, and class oppression, [seeing] as our particular task the development of integrated analysis and practice based upon the fact that the major systems of oppression are interlocking" (Taylor, 2017, p. 1). Freedom for Black women would mean freedom for all, since it would require the destruction of all these systems of oppression.

Intersectionality (Crenshaw, 1991) describes how the intersection of race and gender "highlights the need to account for multiple grounds of identity when considering how the social world is constructed" (p. 1245). Audre Lorde, Black feminist lesbian academic and poet, connects to Freire's idea of "praxis" (reflection and action), through "transformation of silence into language and action" (Lorde, 1984, p. 43). Lorde points particularly to Black women to share a commitment to language and to reclaim language that has worked against them toward liberation. A Black feminist praxis demands expanding critical literacy into abolitionist literacies that brings liberation to the most vulnerable of us, to free all of us. As Black civil rights activist Fannie Lou Hamer (1971) stated, "Nobody's free until everybody's free" (n.p.).

School-Prison Nexus, Educational Enclosures, and the Carceral Continuum

There are a number of ways to conceptualize the problem space of abolitionist literacy theory and practice under racial capitalism. The relationship between schools and youth detention centers, jails, and prisons is popularly known as the school-to-prison pipeline, "a system of educational policies and practices that increase the likelihood of incarceration for some youths, [which has been] useful for explaining the structural logics upholding the literacy crisis" (Kirkland, 2017. p. 1). With Meiners (2007) and others (e.g. Kirkland, 2017; Sojoyner, 2016; Winn, 2018), we reject the linear duality of the pipeline metaphor in favor of understanding the relationship between schools and the carceral state as a school-prison nexus. The linkages between schools and incarceration are more like a web of intertwined, punitive threads (Meiners, 2007, p. 32). Literacy forms one of these threads.

While many good teachers teach so that Black children never encounter the physical site of prison, schools themselves often operate as "enclosures" of Black youth and Black liberation (Sojoyner, 2016). Some young people attend schools where the doors lock automatically so that no one may enter without permission and are chained from the inside so that no one may leave without authorization, where Black and Brown boys are suspended for missing too many school days, where there are "no pipelines to prison" because it is "all prison" (Kirkland, 2017, p. 468). The carceral continuum (Shedd, 2011) describes the ways that "racist and classist forms of social control [. . .] are not limited to obvious forms of incarceration and punishment; rather, they entail [. . .] a 'carceral continuum' that scales over prison walls" (Benjamin, 2019, p. 2). We understand literacy practices, ideologies, assessments, labels, restrictions, etc. to be central aspects of the school-prison nexus and carceral continuum, and thus a crucial element in their abolition.

Abolitionist Perspectives on Critical Literacy

Within education there is powerful work calling for abolitionist teaching (Love, 2019) and education for transformation (de los Ríos et al., 2019; Winn & Winn, 2019). Abolitionist critiques and imaginaries have transferred into education, within a growing understanding of schooling as a "site for Black suffering" (Dumas, 2013). Love (2019) calls on educators to enact "abolitionist teaching" to dismantle the "spirit murdering" and "educational survival complex" that leaves children languishing under the white gaze with severe material impacts to their lives and communities (Morrison, 1998). Black freedom struggles and dreams have been appropriated into liberal multiculturalist discourse to propel forth the struggles (and ideas, discourse, power/authority) of others (Wilderson, 2020), including within critical literacy. Critical literacy has been critiqued for hanging on to the ideas of the universal subject, in particular from a feminist perspective, but an abolitionist critique goes even further. Abolitionist work poses a challenge to critical literacy praxis that has generally remained within the liberal imagination that fetishizes the immediately possible at the expense of more radical, humanizing possibilities.

Abolitionist Critique of Literacy Praxis

We are specifically concerned with antiblackness as a permanent and embedded feature within the socio-political contexts of the U.S. (and elsewhere) and the ways it operationalizes as a structure that seeks to deny Black people's right to have a voice. To resist the dangers of antiblackness, especially the ways anti-Black logics and systems (e.g. anti-literacy laws and de jure segregation) have worked to stunt Black voice, literacy learning, and Black education broadly (Anderson, 1988; Bell, 2004; Moss, 2010; Rickford, 2016; Warren & Coles, 2020), Black people still boldly engage in literacy because they still see that literacy "is a tool of empowerment to be acquired and skillfully employed" (Barrett, 1995, p. 430).

Within the socio-political confines of the continental U.S., particularly through the period of chattel slavery to present-day, struggles toward abolition have been enacted through the terrain of literacy. Understanding literacy broadly as "the development of the capacity for expression" (Freire, 1970a, p. 225), Black people have relentlessly sought to develop these capacities for expression, often in the face of great danger, in order to assert themselves and their humanity in efforts to fight for control over their own minds and bodies (Williams, 2007).

Struggling toward the development of Black capacities for expression, or simply Black critical literacies, has historically been a struggle for sovereignty. A great part of U.S. history has operated under the position that Black people did not own their bodies (a history that exists beyond the formal institution of slavery). Through this lack of control of one's own body, Blackness was socially constructed as illiterate, outside the realms of capacity for meaningful, critical expression. To counter the false rendering of a perpetual and unfixable Black illiteracy, many scholars have detailed the ways that Blacks were not inherently incapable of literacy, but rather how they were systematically barred from all matters of the mind and engaged with matters of the body in efforts to obliterate abolitionist existences. It was understood that Black expression, especially under the dehumanizing system of slavery, would lead to a subversion of the system and the larger racial project of antiblackness. Thus, literacy became inextricably linked with Black life early on as it embodied "the mind's ability to extend itself beyond the constricted limits and conditions of the body" (Barrett, 1995, p. 419). For Black Americans, the power of literacy was well known "to be strong medicine if for no other reason than the fact that it was in large measure legislated away from them" (Gilyard, 1996, p. 23). Engaging in literacy by any means was a necessity to have control over one's own life, to get free and remain free.

In particular, Black literacy resistance against the dominance of white supremacy has mitigated the marginalization of Black people, which in the U.S., operationalizes through the ongoing socio-structural regime of antiblackness and racial capitalism (Robinson, 2000; Smith, 2012). Despite Black lived experience unfolding within the boundaries of antiblackness, Black people have not let antiblackness exist unchallenged. Through the interconnected theorizing of literacy and abolition, the goal is not to obscure what Watson (2009) refers to as the "vexed nature of literacy" for Blacks, which stems from literacy's relation to "race, slavery, and Christianizing campaigns throughout the eighteenth-century Atlantic world and the burgeoning black Diaspora" (Watson, 2009, p. 68).

It remains true that "the social construction of Blacks as non writers, non-enactors of literacy, is structurally embedded within American society and its social institutions, such as the urban school" (Coles, 2018, p. 77). This can be seen in the numerous ways literacy is intertwined with the school-prison nexus. Literacy is central to punitive school testing and sorting with roots in eugenics, "the attempt to engineer a supposedly stronger, more intelligent population by selective breeding and other approaches" (Gillborn, 2010, p. 244). For at least two centuries, standardized testing has impeded the social progress of Black people within the U.S. (Fleming, 2000). The ways racialized standardized testing bias has concretized within our nation's schools stems directly from a history of overtly racist theories of racial intelligence, which used variations of pseudo-science to project Black mental inferiority as an absolute and objective fact. Creating tests to *standardize* intelligence meant that the networks of white scientists, philosophers, and government officials responsible for setting the standards had the power and privilege to decide what qualified as superior or inferior, academically.

Formal and informal raciolinguistic judgments of non-dominant students' language and literacy practices from teachers and testing regimes leads to the further marginalization of the youth, and further denial of quality literacy instruction through remediative pedagogies (Alim, Rickford, & Ball, 2016). This is also evidenced in the disproportionate application of language and learning disability labels (indicative of overdiagnosis and misdiagnosis) on Black, Indigenous, and Latinx students (Annamma, 2017; Annamma, Morrison, & Jackson, 2014). Literacy remediation and special education labels are closely connected to the ways Black youth are also subject to vastly disproportionate discipline measures and other violence within and outside of schools, even at young ages (Annamma, 2016). Underlying these logics is a dismissal of the value, sophistication, and validity of Black language and literacy practices.

Black/Abolitionist Literacies

We center and prioritize the liberatory nature of Black literacies and conceptualize how Black enactments of literacy, as a struggle for sovereignty and against anti-Black resistance, have been embodiments of abolition in spite of totalizing antiblackness. We theorize the valorization of Blackness as abolition and a site of critical literacy. To inhabit Blackness is to inhabit an orientation towards abolition, given that to inhabit Blackness means to inhabit a social positioning where one is birthed being considered unfree and/or socially dead (Wilderson, 2020).

Critical literacy, just like Black life, "aims to challenge the status quo by disrupting commonplace notions of socially constructed concepts" (Wallowitz, 2008, p. 1). Moreover, linking critical literacy to Black life makes sense when considering that to be critically literate is a mindset characterized by "a way of viewing and interacting with the world" (p. 16). In a society where "anti-black racism is the fulcrum of white supremacy" (Nakagawa, 2012), Black people had to develop and embody a mindset that was critical of all aspects of U.S. social life. Revisiting Vizenor's (2008) ideals on survivance prove to be useful in this moment to critique critical literacy through the lens of abolition: "Survivance stories are renunciations of dominance, detractions, obtrusions, the unbearable sentiments of tragedy, and the legacy of victimry" (p. 1). Since antiblackness has constructed Blackness in opposition to the nation's status quo, embodying critical literacy as an identity has been crucial to the ways Black people have survived the continuous occupation of slavery's ongoingness (Sharpe, 2016).

Literacy has always served as a tool of refusal and liberation, centering "Black cultures, histories, and identities" (Lyiscott, 2017, p. 52), in a world predicated on the devaluation of Black life. This can be seen in ways literacy was used during slavery for Black self-emancipation (Mitchell, 2008), how Black expressive culture was constructed during the Harlem Renaissance to expand the form and content of the larger expressive culture of the U.S. (Smethurst, 2011), to the current ways Black people use their expressivities to articulate the value of Black life (e.g., #BlackLivesMatter and #SayHerName). The historicity of Black literacies are tethered to abolition, characterized by refusing the ongoing conditions of capture. Black literacies function specifically as a critical literacy—an engagement in expressive refusal that seeks to challenge the world that currently exists, while simultaneously using this challenge as a basis or starting point to reimagine new and more liberatory Black existences. Herein lies the key theorizing of abolitionist critiques of critical literacy: Antiblackness creates the conditions for Black people to experience routine and unimaginable violences (material and psychic), which catalyzes an embodiment of Black textual expressivities rooted in critique and refusal of antiblackness as a totalizing structural regime.

As the foundation for the ways all peoples come to make sense of themselves and the world/s around them, literacy has been a historic platform where Black people and other minoritized communities have resisted such dominance (Coles, 2021; Gates, 1988; King, 1992; Muhammad, 2019; Smitherman, 1999; Watson, 2009). Central to critical literacy and/as abolition has been literacy's function as a way to "improve and elevate" Black lives (Muhammad, 2019, p. 8). Conceptualizing literacy as an elevation of life pairs particularly well with Kirkland and Jackson's (2009) view of literacy as "the practice of shaping identities and as a tool for participating in culturally valued experiences" (p. 279). As Shor (1999) outlined, "the way we speak and are spoken to help shape us into the people we become" (p. 2). In order to improve how we exist in the world/s around us, it is imperative that we understand the uniqueness of our identities and the ways larger social contexts influence how we shape and re-shape who we are continuously un/becoming.

The historical relationship between Black people and literacy has always "included the goals of identity meaning-making and criticality" (Muhammad, 2019, p. 10). Indeed, leveraging criticality through literacy or engaging in critical literacy is at the core of the kinship between Black lived experience and literacy as means to author oneself outside of dominance. Through critical literacy, "the literacy process must relate speaking the word to transforming reality" (Freire, 1970a, p. 213) and to our collective role in this transformation. Bent towards transformation, critical literacy can be understood as much more than obtaining the basics of becoming a literate person, but rather inspiring people to take ownership over their lives and voices in the face of ongoing oppression.

Implications and Recommendations

Taking to heart an abolitionist critique and imagination on critical literacy has major implications for our social responsibility as academics. In this chapter, we have focused on a provocative approach to analyzing the ties between literacy and Black captivity and liberation, believing that "we don't lack information about abolition; we lack imagination about abolition" (Laura, 2018, p. 20). While the implications for academics are largely subsumed under teaching and research, we argue we need to be engaged beyond both. If we believe in critical literacy, then this demands direct participation in social movement and being in the streets, shoulder-to-shoulder with those struggling towards an abolitionist vision of self-determination and collective power. We seek to abolish the white gaze over our value and our work. This means no longer viewing testing and other artificial and oppressive standards as measurements of worth, particularly on Black and other vulnerabilized communities. This means disrupting the normalization of whiteness and resisting dangerous deficit perspectives placed upon Black and other vulnerabilized communities. Abolition is something to be lived, not just researched, taught, or summed up in our "Monday morning pedagogy." Following Angela Y. Davis (2003):

> Positing decarceration as our overarching strategy, we would try to envision a continuum of alternatives to imprisonment—demilitarization of schools, revitalization of education at all levels, a health system that provides free physical and mental care to all, and a justice system based on reparation and reconciliation rather than retribution and vengeance.
>
> *(p. 107, cited in Benjamin, 2019, pp. 3–4)*

Implications for Pedagogy

We align with those who have documented the need for literacy and English Language Arts classrooms to be(come) spaces of healing in which historical and contemporary harms are acknowledged and the needs produced by such harms are addressed (de los Ríos et al., 2019; Johnson, Jackson, Stovall, & Baszile, 2017; Winn, 2013). To begin, this means centering pedagogies that, for example, teach confinement and captivity literature (Hill, 2013), work with the incarcerated and push against policing, develop restorative justice in literacy contexts (Winn, 2013), and center youth voices and imaginaries (hooks, 1994).

In this sense, we are particularly critical of literacy projects that proclaim to "give voice" to Black and Brown students. In pursuing literacy that claims to give voice to students, these projects position students as voiceless. This pedagogy participates in a dehumanizing education (Freire, 1970b). We reject the notion of voiceless students who are given voice through schooling and education. Rather, we look to literacy practices and projects that affirm students' voices (along with their bodies, accents, dialogues, and rhythms) through centering their knowledges (Annamma, 2016; Baker-Bell, 2020; de los Ríos, 2019; Gonzales & González Ybarra, 2020; Gutiérrez, 2008; Martinez, 2017; Paris, 2011; Player, Coles, & González Ybarra, 2020; Winn, 2010; Winn & Winn, 2021). We work to sustain the communities our students emanate from and take the lead from local leaders that emphasize community power and control, taking a decolonial approach toward schooling (Tuck & Gaztambide-Fernández, 2013; Winn & Winn, 2021). We align with literacies that amplify students' already-articulate voices and provide spaces "where their voices, ideas, and lived experiences can be heard" (Winn & Behizadeh, 2011, p. 167) by those of us who believe that we have a responsibility to be listening.

Implications for Research

We write from an ethical/radically transformative perspective for the research community that we love, that we are a part of, and that has fallen short of its potential. Rather than prescribing interventions for individuals and communities already resisting everyday racism and colonization, literacy research must be for and toward abolition and must advance interventions for our "racist society predicated on colonization" (Patel, 2016, p. 23). We call for research that understands every gap in test scores and punishment rates as both consequence and reification of an "education debt" that must be repaid and repaired (Ladson-Billings, 2006). Such research must be attuned to the variously productive and problematic ways young people resist the school-prison nexus, the hypercarceral social systems, and racial capitalism of the United States and beyond (Alim et al., 2016; Coles & Powell, 2020; Meiners, 2007; Sojoyner, 2016; Tuck & Yang, 2014; Winn, 2012). We encourage all researchers to interrogate the theories of change at work in their research and to clarify how proposed research advances humanizing social systems and relationships (Patel, 2016; Tuck, 2009). Finally, we call for an increase in the quantity and quality of educational research that engages directly with those who have experienced incarceration. Their visions of how to achieve and sustain an abolitionist practice are vital to the humanizing project of abolition for all.

References

Alim, H. S., Rickford, J. R., & Ball, A. F. (2016). Introducing raciolinguistics. *Raciolinguistics: How Language Shapes Our Ideas about Race*, 1–30.

Anderson, J. D. (1988). *The education of Blacks in the South, 1860–1935*. University of North Carolina Press.

Annamma, S. A. (2016). Disrupting the carceral state through education journey mapping. *International Journal of Qualitative Studies in Education*, *29*(9), 1210–1230. https://doi.org/10.1080/09518398.2016.1214297

Annamma, S. A. (2017). *The pedagogy of pathologization: Dis/abled girls of color in the school-prison nexus* (1st ed.). Routledge. https://doi.org/10.4324/9781315523057

Annamma, S. A., Morrison, D., & Jackson, D. (2014). Disproportionality fills in the gaps: Connections between achievement, discipline and special education in the school-to-prison Pipeline. *Berkeley Review of Education*, *5*. https://doi.org/10.5070/B85110003

Baker-Bell, A. (2020). Dismantling anti-black linguistic racism in English language arts classrooms: Toward an anti-racist black language pedagogy. *Theory Into Practice*, *59*(1), 8–21. https://doi.org/10.1080/00405841.2019.1665415

Barrett, L. (1995). African-American slave narratives: Literacy, the body, authority. *American Literary History*, *7*(3), 415–442.

Bell, D. (2004). *Silent covenants: Brown v. Board of Education and the unfulfilled hopes for racial reform.* Oxford University Press.

Benjamin, R. (Ed.). (2019). *Captivating technology: Race, carceral technoscience, and liberatory imagination in everyday life.* Duke University Press.

Coles, J. A. (2018). *A BlackCrit ethnography on the co-creation of textual sanctuary as means to understanding and resisting antiblackness at a US urban high school* (Dissertation). Michigan State University.

Coles, J. A. (2019). The Black literacies of urban high school youth countering antiblackness in the context of neoliberal multiculturalism. *Journal of Language & Literacy Education, 15*(2), 1–35.

Coles, J. A. (2021). "It's really geniuses that live in the hood": Black urban youth curricular un/makings and centering Blackness in slavery's afterlife. *Curriculum Inquiry,* 1–22. Advance online publication.

Coles, J. A., & Powell, T. (2020). A BlackCrit analysis on Black urban youth and suspension disproportionality as anti-Black symbolic violence. *Race Ethnicity and Education, 23*(1), 113–133.

Combahee River Collective. (1982). A Black feminist statement: The Combahee River collective. In G. T. Hull, P. Bell-Scott, & B. Smith (Eds.), *All the women are White, all the Blacks are men, but some of us are brave: Black women's studies* (pp. 13–22). The Feminist Press.

Crenshaw, K. (1991). Mapping the margins: Intersectionality, identity politics, and violence against women of color. *Stanford Law Review, 43(6),* 1241–1299. https://doi.org/10.2307/1229039

Davis, A. Y. (2003). *Are prisons obsolete?* Seven Stories Press.

de los Ríos, C. V. (2019). "Los músicos": Mexican corridos, the aural border, and the evocative musical renderings of transnational youth. *Harvard Educational Review, 89*(2), 177–200. https://doi.org/10.17763/1943-5045-89.2.177

de los Ríos, C. V., Martinez, D. C., Musser, A. D., Canady, A., Camangian, P., & Quijada, P. D. (2019). Upending colonial practices: Toward repairing harm in English education. *Theory Into Practice, 58*(4), 359–367. https://doi.org/10.1080/00405841.2019.1626615

de Roock, R. S. (2021). On the material consequences of (digital) literacy: Digital writing with, for, and against racial capitalism. *Theory Into Practice, 60*(2), 183–193. https://doi.org/10.1080/00405841.2020.1857128

de Roock, R. S., & Baildon, M. (2019). *MySkillsFuture* for students, STEM learning, and the design of neoliberal citizenship in Singapore. *Cognition & Instruction, 37*(3), 285–305.

Dery, M. (1994). Black to the future: Interviews with Samuel R. Delany, Greg Tate, and Tricia Rose. In M. Dery (Ed.), *Flame wars: The discourse of cyberculture* (pp. 179–222). Duke University Press.

Dumas, M. J. (2013). 'Waiting for Superman' to save black people: Racial representation and the official antiracism of neoliberal school reform. *Discourse: Studies in the Cultural Politics of Education, 34*(4), 531–547. https://doi.org/10.1080/01596306.2013.822621

Dumas, M. J. (2016). Against the dark: Antiblackness in education policy and discourse. *Theory Into Practice, 55*(1), 11–19. https://doi.org/10.1080/00405841.2016.1116852

Fleming, J. (2000). Affirmative action and standardized test scores. *Journal of Negro Education, 69*(1/2), 27–37.

Freire, P. (1970a). The adult literacy process as cultural action for freedom. *Harvard Educational Review, 40*(2), 205–225.

Freire, P. (1970b). *Pedagogy of the oppressed* (M. B. Ramos, Trans.). Continuum.

Gates Jr, H. L. (1988). *The signifying monkey: A theory of African American literary criticism.* Oxford University Press.

Gillborn, D. (2010). Reform, racism and the centrality of whiteness: Assessment, ability and the 'new eugenics'. *Irish Educational Studies, 29*(3), 231–252.

Gilmore, R. W. (2007). *Golden gulag: Prisons, surplus, crisis, and opposition in globalizing California.* University of California Press.

Gilyard, K. (1996). *Let's flip the script: An African American discourse on language, literature, and learning.* Wayne State University Press.

Gonzales, L., & González Ybarra, M. (2020). Multimodal cuentos as fugitive literacies on the Mexico-US borderlands. *English Education, 52*(3), 223–255.

Gutiérrez, K. D. (2008). Developing a sociocritical literacy in the third space. *Reading Research Quarterly, 43*(2), 148–164.

Hamer, F. L. (1971). "Nobody's free until everybody's free". Speech delivered at the founding of the national women's political caucus, Washington, DC, July 10, 1971

Hill, M. L. (2013). A world without prisons: Teaching confinement literature and the promise of prison abolition. *English Journal, 102*(4), 19–23.

hooks, b. (1994). Confronting class in the classroom. *The Critical Pedagogy Reader,* 142–150.

Johnson, L. L., Jackson, J., Stovall, D. O., & Baszile, D. T. (2017). "Loving Blackness to death": (Re) Imagining ELA classrooms in a time of racial chaos. *English Journal, 106*(4), 60–66.

Kendi, I. X. (2020). What the racial data show: The pandemic seems to be hitting people of color the hardest. *The Atlantic*. Retrieved from www.theatlantic.com/ideas/archive/2020/04/coronavirus-exposing-our-racial-divides/609526/

King, J. E. (1992). Diaspora literacy and consciousness in the struggle against miseducation in the Black community. *The Journal of Negro Education, 61*(3), 317–340.

Kirkland, D. E. (2017). A dance of bars: Rethinking the role of literacy education in the age of mass incarceration. *Journal of Adolescent & Adult Literacy, 60*(4), 467–470. https://doi.org/10.1002/jaal.615

Kirkland, D. E., & Jackson, A. (2009). "We real cool": Toward a theory of black masculine literacies. *Reading Research Quarterly, 44*(3), 278–297.

Ladson-Billings, G. (2006). From the achievement gap to the education debt: Understanding achievement in US schools. *Educational researcher, 35*(7), 3–12.

Laura, C. T. (2018). Against prisons and the pipelines to them. In E. Tuck & K. W. Yang (Eds.), *Toward what justice: Describing diverse dreams of justice in education* (pp. 19–28). Routledge.

Lorde, A. (1984). *Sister outsider: Essays and speeches* (Reprint edition). Crossing Press.

Love, B. (2019). *We want to do more than survive: Abolitionist teaching and the pursuit of educational freedom*. Beacon Press.

Lyiscott, J. (2017). Racial identity and liberation literacies in the classroom. *English Journal, 106*(4), 47–53.

Martinez, D. C. (2017). Imagining a language of solidarity for Black and Latinx youth in English language arts classrooms. *English Education, 49*(2), 179–196.

Meiners, E. R. (2007). *Right to be hostile: Schools, prisons, and the making of public enemies*. Routledge.

Mitchell, A. B. (2008). Self-emancipation and slavery: An examination of the African American's quest for literacy and freedom. *Journal of Pan African Studies, 2*(5), 78–98.

Morrison, T. (1998). *Toni Morrison* [Public Broadcasting Service]. Retrieved from www.youtube.com/watch?v=F4vIGvKpT1c

Moss, H. J. (2010). *Schooling citizens: The struggle for African American education in antebellum America*. University of Chicago Press.

Muhammad, G. (2019). *Cultivating genius: An equity framework for culturally and historically responsive literacy*. Scholastic Teaching Resources.

Nakagawa, S. (2012, May 4). *Blackness is the fulcrum*. Race Files. Retrieved from www.racefiles.com/2012/05/04/blackness-is-the-fulcrum/

Paris, D. (2011). 'A friend who understand fully': Notes on humanizing research in a multiethnic youth community. *International Journal of Qualitative Studies in Education, 24*(2), 137–149.

Patel, L. (2016). *Decolonizing educational research: From ownership to answerability*. Routledge.

Pirtle, W. N. L. (2020). Racial capitalism: A fundamental cause of novel coronavirus (COVID-19) pandemic inequities in the United States. *Health Education & Behavior*, 1–5.

Player, G. D., Coles, J. A., & González Ybarra, M. (2020). Enacting educational fugitivity with youth of color: A statement/love letter from the fugitive literacies collective. *The High School Journal, 103*(3), 140–156.

Rickford, R. (2016). *We are an African people: Independent education, black power, and the radical imagination*. Oxford University Press.

Roberts, D. E. (2019). Abolition constitutionalism. *Harvard Law Review, 133*(1), 3–122.

Robinson, C. J. (2000). *Black Marxism: The making of the Black radical tradition*. University of North Carolina Press.

Sharpe, C. (2016). *In the wake: On blackness and being*. Duke University Press.

Shedd, C. (2011). Countering the carceral continuum: The legacy of mass incarceration. *Criminology & Public Policy, 10*(3), 865–871.

Shor, I. (1999). What is critical literacy? *Journal of Pedagogy, Pluralism, and Practice, 1*(4), 1–32.

Smethurst, J. (2011). *The African American roots of modernism: From reconstruction to the Harlem Renaissance*. University of North Carolina Press.

Smith, A. (2012). Indigeneity, settler colonialism, white supremacy. In D. Martinez HoSang, O. LaBennett, & L. Pulido (Eds.), *Racial formation in the twenty-first century* (pp. 66–90). University of California Press.

Smitherman, G. (1999). *Talkin that talk: Language, culture and education in African America*. Routledge.

Sojoyner, D. M. (2016). *First strike: Educational enclosures in Black Los Angeles*. University of Minnesota Press.

Taylor, K.-Y. (Ed.). (2017). *How we get free: Black feminism and the Combahee River Collective*. Haymarket Books.

Tuck, E. (2009). Suspending damage: A letter to communities. *Harvard Educational Review, 79*(3), 409–427.

Tuck, E., & Gaztambide-Fernández, R. A. (2013). Curriculum, replacement, and settler futurity. *Journal of Curriculum Theorizing, 29*(1).

Tuck, E., & Yang, K. W. (2012). Decolonization is not a metaphor. *Decolonization: Indigeneity, Education & Society, 1*(1), 1–40.

Tuck, E., & Yang, K. W. (2014). R-words: Refusing research. In D. Paris & M. T. Winn (Eds.), *Humanizing research* (pp. 223–248). Sage.

Vizenor, G. (Ed.). (2008). *Survivance: Narratives of native presence*. University of Nebraska Press.

Wallowitz, L. (Ed.). (2008). *Critical literacy as resistance: Teaching for social justice across the secondary curriculum* (Vol. 326). Peter Lang.

Warren, C. A., & Coles, J. A. (2020). Trading spaces: Antiblackness and reflections on Black education futures. *Equity & Excellence in Education*, 1–17. https://doi.org/10.1080/10665684.2020.1764882

Washington Jr, J. R. (1981). The religion of antiblackness. *Theology Today*, *38*(2), 146–151.

Watson, S. E. (2009). "Good will come of this evil": Enslaved teachers and the transatlantic politics of early Black literacy. *College Composition and Communication*, *61*(1), W66–W89.

Wilderson III, F. (2020). *Afropessimism*. Liveright Publishing.

Williams, H. A. (2007). *Self-taught: African American education in slavery and freedom*. The University of North Carolina Press.

Winn, M. T. (2010). 'Our side of the story': Moving incarcerated youth voices from margins to center. *Race Ethnicity and Education*, *13*(3), 313–325.

Winn, M. T. (2012). The politics of desire and possibility in urban playwriting:(Re) reading and (re) writing the script. *Pedagogies: An International Journal*, *7*(4), 317–332.

Winn, M. T. (2013). Toward a restorative English education. *Research in the Teaching of English*, *48*(1), 126–135.

Winn, M. T. (2018). *Justice on both sides: Transforming education through restorative justice*. Harvard Education Press.

Winn, M. T., & Behizadeh, N. (2011). The right to be literate: Literacy, education, and the school-to-prison pipeline. *Review of Research in Education*, *35*(1), 147–173. https://doi.org/10.3102/0091732X10387395

Winn, M. T., & Winn, L. T. (2019). This issue. *Theory Into Practice*, *58*(4), 305–307. https://doi.org/10.1080/00405841.2019.1626621

Winn, M. T., & Winn, L. T. (2021). *Restorative justice in education: Transforming teaching and learning through the disciplines*. Harvard Education Press.

3.8

CRITICAL DIGITAL LITERACY

Alexander Bacalja, Earl Aguilera and Edison Ferney Castrillón-Ángel

Definitions of Key Concepts

Definitions of CDL have their genesis in the nexus between sociocultural understandings of literacy, digital literacy and critical literacy. As a result of the 'sociocultural turn' among researchers and educators, conceptualizations about literacy have shifted from something which is the sole domain of schools, to something that takes place everywhere, and from the singular "literacy" to the plural "literacies." This has created space for thinking more broadly about what it means to be literate and reconsidering how literacy educators prepare learners for the literacy demands of adult life (Luke & Freebody, 1999).

With the shift to literacies in the plural have come efforts to explore the social and cultural factors associated with new technologies and their relationship to self-making and identity practice (Alvermann, 2004). Early interest in digital literacies tended to focus on the provision of computers and the skills necessary to operationalize this technology (Molnar, 1978). However, the notion that digital literacy is more than the skills which operationalize new technologies has become central to the thinking of those who argue that what we do with the digital is always sensitive to contextual factors and tied to negotiations of identity and self (Alvermann, 2004; Hagood, 2009; Lankshear, Green, & Snyder, 2000). For Bulfin and North (2007), digital literacy practices are never simply at-school or at-home. Rather, they are traced and sourced across our whole lived experiences, and intricately tied to ongoing identity work.

Critical dimensions of digital literacies can be understood in terms of the critical movement and its emphasis on education for social change and the emancipatory capacity of schooling (Freire, 1972). Allan Luke defines critical literacy as the "use of the technologies of print and other media of communication to analyze, critique and transform the norms, rule systems and practices governing the social fields of everyday life" (2012b, p. 5). This definition addresses two important aspects of this movement, developing understanding and action. The former is interested in all kinds of technologies, old and new, at-school and out-of-school, and understanding how they are designed and how they position us. The hope is that developing new understandings about how texts are constructed will impact how they are consumed. The latter is focused on the transformational capacity that arises from this new knowledge. It emphasizes the importance of literacies as tools that have the capacity to change power relations between people and systems.

Critical digital literacies (CDL), as a broad, descriptive term brings together digital technologies with a dual interest in knowing the world and acting upon the world. As Avila and Pandya state,

 DOI: 10.4324/9781003023425-43

CDL practices are "those skills and practices that lead to the creation of digital texts that interrogate the world; they also allow and foster the interrogation of digital, multimedia texts" (2013, p. 3). Understanding and critiquing the digital world which we inhabit includes knowing how that world is constructed and how language and power are mediated through a range of technologies that often mask the nature of the systems (Eubanks, 2018). Beneath the screens of a digitally mediated society lies issues of data storage and manipulation, agency and control, ownership, the trustworthiness of information, access, and sustainability. These hidden characteristics of digital literacies are often shrouded by surface features (Golden, 2017; Lynch, 2017).

CDL has been used to describe social practices that lead to the creation of digital texts that interrogate issues of power, access, and agency in the world. We can see an example of this in the ways that activist movements have mobilized on social media to exchange ideas, disseminate information, and publicly critique oppressive systems and institutions (Carney, 2016).

CDL has also been used to describe social practices aimed at critically interrogating digital media and technologies themselves. One argument for interrogating contemporary online systems is made by Virginia Eubanks (2018), who has explored the ways that computational algorithms designed into software have been a part of the automation of inequality through the disproportionate surveillance, profiling, and punishment of poor and working-class people in the U.S. Understanding how these algorithms shape online media practices would require, at the very least, attentiveness to the ideologies that are enacted through the outputs of these algorithms.

Critiques of Critical Digital Literacies in This Domain

Arguments against expanding critical literacy imperatives to ever-more popular digital technologies have centered around three concerns.

Firstly, debates around "screen time," which entered into the public discourse between the 1960s and 1970s, when televisions were becoming widespread household technology in the United States, now manifest in terms of concerns about young people spending too much time engaging with a wide-range of devices, including computers, video game consoles, and mobile devices (Turkle, 2017). There has been a tendency, in both media and public discourse, to focus disproportionately on the negative effects of these technologies and to develop ways to mitigate their impacts (Orben & Przybylski, 2019). These concerns are tied to debates about the purpose of schooling and literacy, and whether already limited time for formal learning is the best place for more engagement with the digital. The fear is that time spent studying digital technology will detract from traditional foundational literacy skills and from developing the knowledge of literature necessary to develop a shared cultural heritage.

Secondly, critiques relating to issues of unequal access to the technology necessary to pursue CDL objectives have been raised. As contemporary scholarship has demonstrated, digital divides manifest in different ways across global contexts, and these inequities can impact the work of educators and researchers interested in exploring CDL. For example, while access to digital resources across students from different socio-economic backgrounds has narrowed, not all students have the knowledge and skills to be able to benefit from the digital resources available to them (OECD, 2015). Thus, while educators consider the benefits of engaging students in CDL as a means for educational and social transformation, they must also keep in mind these issues of access and equity.

Thirdly, concerns have been raised regarding the impact of developing critical dispositions towards the everyday digital texts from which people gain so much pleasure. What happens when we demystify the everyday world? Is there a risk of minimizing the aesthetic enjoyment associated with the uncritical consumption and production of digital texts? What will be the consequences of CDL instruction on positive affective responses? Misson and Morgan (2006) have discussed these concerns with regards to bringing critical literacy to young people's everyday aesthetic texts and the potential impact on individual identity, human emotion, and creativity. Similarly, Pangrazio (2016) expresses concern with the impact of developing dispositions of critique that may alienate an individual's personal affective response. The crucial challenge is reconciling the development of an ideological critique with an individual's right to personal and affective experiences with digital media (p. 168).

Responses to Any Critiques and Current Research in the Area

In response to those who problematize young people's engagement with digital technologies, or who link excessive screen time with all of society's ills, scholars have highlighted the diversity of today's media landscape, criticizing the tendency to treat all information and entertainment-based screen media as equivalent. Contemporary digital media enable social, participatory, and youth-organized spaces for creativity, collaboration, and activism online, and the ever-expanding body of literacy practices associated with digital media (Jenkins, Shresthova, Gamber-Thompson, Kligler-Vilenchik & Zimmerman, 2018). The tendency for many popular media outlets to treat all digital practices homogeneously simplifies complex social and cultural interactions.

While issues of access to digital technologies continue to produce obstacles for those seeking to understand CDLs, researchers emphasize the need to push forward with efforts to both examine the complexity of these in-school and out-of-school digital practices and produce pedagogic responses so that educators can work with learners to develop critical understandings. Despite the differential access to the technologies necessary to engage in digital literacy, there is much the educational community can still do to ensure that all literacy learners are given opportunities to engage in cultures of digital consumption and production (Rowsell, Morrell, & Alvermann, 2017).

In response to back-to-basics rhetoric which rejects the value of spending time on digital literacies, frameworks have been developed demonstrating the multidimensionality of all literacy experiences, and the importance of pedagogy which supports moving beyond a focus on operational literacy practices. With emphases on a reader's role as a participant in the meaning-making of a text (Luke & Freebody, 1999), practices involved in navigating, interpreting, designing, and interrogating multimodal texts (Serafini, 2012), and pedagogies which invites students and teachers to engage with the content, computational, and contextual dimensions of these media from critical perspectives (Aguilera, 2017), these scholars recognize the importance of a range of practices which are essential to engaging with digital media and multimodal texts.

Current research relating to CDL seeks to address many of the critiques raised earlier, focusing on both out-of-school digital literate practices, as well as pedagogical responses aimed at formal learning contexts.

Research suggests that one affordance of digital literacy practices associated with contemporary life is the tendency for new forms of political participation. For example, Jenkins et al. (2018) have explored the potential of the media and the advances of digital language to explore new forms of citizen participation activities that emerge from the practice of participatory culture in the youth population. Through the term *hacker literacies*, Santo (2013) describes the ways that digital media technologies have been critically repurposed, remixed, or reconfigured by individuals and groups seeking more equitable shifts in power relations in social and virtual worlds. Santo's examples include the Arab Spring, the Occupy Wall Street movement, the development of the Twitter hashtag, and public responses to Facebook's changes in privacy policy. Finally, Mundt, Ross, and Burnett (2018) provide exploration of the use of social media to *scale up* the Black Lives Matter movement in the U.S., though the authors caution that "careful management of online media platforms is necessary to mitigate concrete, physical risks that social media can create for activists" (p. 1).

Research has also sought to understand how these predominantly out-of-school digital literate practices might become the objects of critical study in formal educational contexts. In the context of teacher-education, Castrillón-Ángel (2020) investigated podcasting as a CDL practice to capture the life narratives of preservice teachers and inform their own pedagogical praxis. Within classroom settings, Sealey-Ruiz and Haddix (2018) have discussed the ways that teachers and schools can use purposefully positioned digital media to empower the learning of urban youth of color, including centering students' interests through media production, shifting power relations by reconfiguring digital assessment practices, and reframing classroom policies to better respect youths' existing media practices. While Bacalja's (2018) research into the critical study of digital games in English classrooms addressed some of the challenges associated with recontextualizing youth literacy practices in institutionalized settings, especially in terms of questioning how these texts position their audiences.

Implications for Pedagogy

Focusing on CDL in formal learning contexts has raised a number of pedagogical issues that all educators will need to consider, including: recognizing local contexts, encouraging transformative practice, shifting classroom power dynamics, and the misappropriation digital literacies for educational purposes.

Situating CDL pedagogy in local contexts reflects arguments made by critical literacy advocates who have long stated that developing critical dispositions should start with where students are at and born out of their contexts (Freire, 1972). This sentiment is expressed in Paolo Freire's description of his first experiences of reading, drawing connections between the sights and sounds of his home as a child, a place where the texts, words and letters were incarnated in everyday things; the old house, the songs of birds, the thunder and rain, and his experience and construction of self. By carefully considering the context of the learner, and the dynamically intertwined relationship between language and reality, contemporary critical literacy advocates remind us that critical literacy is less about any single text, or in the case of CDL, any single digital technology, and more about the issues that matter locally (Alford, Schmidt, & Lyngfelt, 2019).

Much like research associated with participatory culture, which argues that empowerment comes from meaningful decisions within real civic contexts (Jenkins et al., 2009), educators will have to consider how they make CDL learning individually meaningful. Given the many ways that young people now negotiate their identities through digital media, CDL instruction which is locally situated, authentic and relevant will need to be prioritized. As Luci Pangrazio (2019) has found in her fieldwork with young people investigating what they do with digital media, digital narratives are a product of personal background and life experience. These narratives develop through a complex interplay between place and space, which young people navigate as a part of their everyday digital practice. While there will be a temptation to formalize CDL goals into policy and curricula, this is territory that will need to be carefully traversed and localized.

Another consideration for educators is how to move learners from roles as critical consumers to critically conscious producers of text. The forms of Participatory Democracy advocated by Freire, where the pursuit of *conscientização* entails comprehending our relationship in and with the world, involve being able to express the world's reality through creative language and simultaneously transforming the world through actions (1972). At a time when the global reform movement with its emphasis on standards and accountability, has closed off creative opportunities for language and literacy learning (Pandya, 2011), CDL theorists continue to emphasize developing a new critical consciousness towards digital technologies which shift learners from new knowledge and new consciousness towards new and meaningful activity. Research into critical literacy and popular culture has shown that young people can be scaffolded towards literacy practices in the real world that seek to disrupt power, authority and "truth-telling" (Ávila & Zacher Pandya, 2014; Hagood, 2009).

Critical literacies' interest in issues of power and authority also requires thinking carefully about the dynamics of teacher to student relations. As Avila and Pandya state, many critical digital literacies context produce power relationships between learners and teachers that are fluid (2013). Teachers give up their control as boundaries between "us" and "them" blur, and as the roles of experts and teachers are shared with learners. Students and teachers become "joint seekers of knowledge and joint producers of new media," (p. 5) and in some cases as the creation of podcasting as a CDL practice, students and teachers work together with the same level of participation. Here students and teachers forge their own paths to authority and they become designers, builders, and broadcasters of their experiences. This is especially important given research findings which suggest that the more teachers seek to retain control, the less room available for student choice and fewer critical literacy skills fostered (Ávila & Zacher Pandya, 2014, p. 10).

For some educators, classroom teaching which focuses on CDL will be liberating, placing students' digital literacies at the center of learning will constitute an act of resistance against centralized and high-stakes forms of teaching that relegate students to passive recipients of knowledge. For others, this will be a challenge, the success of which will be at least partially tied to beliefs about the value of what students bring with them to the classroom.

Lastly, while some proponents of digital technologies highlight the value of these tools and media to promote "boundary-crossing" between the everyday lives of students and the worlds of school and work (Gee, 2013), there is concern regarding recent trends in formal schooling where digital practices are appropriated and taught in ways that standardize, commodify, or otherwise recontextualize them—in some cases alienating the same students that engage in these practices beyond their schooled lives (Sefton-Green, 2014).

Implications for Research

While current research in CDL suggests a number of implications for literacy research and educational research more broadly, a particular area that this chapter will highlight are some of new ethical dilemmas being raised as scholars explore digital-age affinity spaces (Gee, 2005), distributed teaching and learning systems (Holmes, 2017), online communities (Fields, Giang & Kafai, 2013), virtual worlds (Steinkuehler & Duncan, 2008), and other examples of what Lammers, Curwood, and Magnifico (2012) call "literacies on the move" (p. 4). One framework for thinking through such dilemmas comes from Curwood, Magnifico, Lammers & Stornaiuolo (2019), who identify issues of *accessibility*, *positionality*, *relationality*, and *temporality* as key areas of consideration for expanding institutionalized ethics and considering new ways of thinking about and doing research.

In this framing, accessibility focuses on the ways that researchers recruit participants in digital literacies research. Gaining access to a digital affinity space or online communities, for example, may involve learning about the participation of individuals who have not necessarily consented to being a part of the research study, but through their contact with recruited participants, risk having their own expressions and communications unwittingly exposed through research.

Curwood et al.'s (2019) framework considers of issues of positionality including the ways participants may choose to represent themselves and construct identities within and across digital contexts, as well as the ways researchers might position themselves in these spaces. Ethical dilemmas of positionality also touch on issues of privacy, anonymity, and safety. These issues relate to the ways that participants, researchers, and the broader social context of research are positioned in relation to one another in ways that place-based research has not yet had to consider in the same ways.

Issues of positionality impact relationality, that is, the ways that researchers develop, maintain, and critically interrogate relationships between participants. One key feature of online affinity spaces, for example, is their porous nature—participants can freely come and go in a given space—which will raise complications for researchers who must consider how participants form part of that space or community (Hayes & Duncan, 2012).

Finally, this framing highlights issues of temporality as something that might be experienced in digital spaces in qualitatively different ways than physical place-based research has established.

"Studying online spaces asks us to consider time in multiple, layered ways," posit Curwood et al. (2019, p. 304), alluding to the ways that participants in online communities and affinity spaces can quite literally link back to discussions of the past, revise and update digital artifacts for a more current audience, and program future events and changes that can impact the literacy practices in a given context. Considering temporality as a dimension of methodological focus can drive deeper explorations of how this sense of altered time can inform the ways that participants engage in critical literacy practices.

Implications for Our Social Responsibility as Academics

Educators and academics have been challenged by CDL research to transform their pedagogical practice toward more equitable partnerships with students. Not only must those in positions of authority reconsider their roles as supposed gatekeepers of existing power structures, but they are also being called upon to question how they mobilize areas of expertise to empower meaningful social change on behalf of the communities they serve. Two ways that have been suggested include questioning the "siloed" nature of disciplines, seeking out interdisciplinary collaborations that yield new directions for knowledge building and social transformation, and challenging the purpose and effect of scholarship which will entail asking CDL researchers to ask; *for whom, toward what ends*, and *under what conditions* our efforts to generate knowledge in the field occur (Luke, 2012b).

In response, researchers have begun to suggest ways that research in these sites might take place with a greater sensitivity to social responsibilities discussed previously. With regard to the limits of place-based methodologies for studying digital literacy practices, Leander and McKim (2003) have proposed approaches such as "connective ethnography" as a way to trace "flows of objects, texts, and bodies, analyzing the construction of boundaries within and around texts, and focusing upon the remarkable ways in which texts represent and embed multiple contexts" (p. 211). The mobile nature of literacy practices in contemporary times requires continuously revisiting the analytical framework for understanding the transliteracy practices of adolescents as they move across spaces, communities, and contexts.

Recommendations for Future Research and Praxis

Given the speed with which new digital technologies are being conceived, and the changes in literate practices that follow their rapid uptake, there is a need for research that responds to these new communication forms. Current vocabulary advocated for study, such as "free," "friend," "like," terms typically associated with social media use, and concepts such as platforms, algorithms, interface and privacy will soon be replaced with new terms as digital technologies evolve, demonstrating the need to constantly evaluate novel digital media (Pangrazio, 2019). Similarly, given community concerns regarding data protection, online identity issues, and cyber crime, research will need to address these aspects of digital literacy and the need to develop critical dispositions towards the digital which Freebody and Freiberg (2010) argue should be the outcome of all critical literacy education.

Likewise, we need to continue to expand literacy frameworks to explicitly address exactly what it is that makes digital texts, and the literacy practices associated with them, unique from other kinds of representational media. Initial thinking which explores digital literacy frameworks has already begun, for example, in Janet Murray's (1997) work on computational media as *participatory, encyclopedic, procedural*, and *spatially navigated*, in Katie Salen-Tekinbas and Eric Zimmerman's (2003) frames for digital game design, and in Pangrazio's (2016) thinking regarding digital design literacy. However, the speed with which the COVID-19 global pandemic has shifted literacy practices into digital spaces for work and life requires continually reassessing how literacy frameworks support critical practices.

While a focus on the productive capacities of CDL practices has been commonplace in popular and academic press (Vee, 2017; Lankshear & Knobel, 2008), scholars express concern that this focus might crowd out research investigating social and political understandings of digital technologies (Pangrazio, 2016).

As issues associated with algorithmic bias, data extraction, and digital systems of surveillance and punishment evolve, there is value in working with educators and learners to raise awareness of the ways digital technologies are imbued with the perspectives, biases, and agendas of their creators (Eubanks, 2018). Scholars of CDL are well positioned to engage in participatory action research that aims to transform the social and technological worlds we all inhabit (Mirra, Garcia & Morrell, 2015).

References

Aguilera, E. (2017). More than bits and bytes: Digital literacies on, behind, and beyond the screen. *Literacy Today, 35*(3), 12–13.

Alford, J., Schmidt, C., & Lyngfelt, A. (2019). Critical Literacy as legitimate knowledge. In S. Riddle & M. Apple (Eds.), *Re-imagining education for democracy* (pp. 92–111). Routledge.

Alvermann, D. (2004). Media, information communication technologies, and youth literacies: A Cultural Studies perspective. *American Behavioral Scientist, 48*(1), 78–83.

Ávila, J., & Zacher Pandya, J. (2013). Traveling, textual authority, and transformation: An introduction to critical digital literacies. In J. Avila & J. Z. Pandya (Eds.), *Critical digital literacies as social praxis: Intersections and challenges* (pp. 1–14). Peter Lang.

Ávila, J., & Zacher Pandya, J. (2014). *Moving critical literacies forward: A new look at praxis across contexts.* Routledge.

Bacalja, A. (2018). What critical literacy has to offer the study of video games. *Australian Journal of Language and Literacy, 3*(41), 144–154.

Bulfin, S., & North, S. (2007). Negotiating digital literacy practices across school and home: Case studies of young people in Australia. *Language and Education, 21*(3), 247–263.

Carney, N. (2016). All lives matter, but so does race: Black lives matter and the evolving role of social media. *Humanity & Society, 40*(2), 180–199.

Castrillón-Ángel, E. F. (2020). Podcasting as a CDL practice to promote preservice teachers' narratives in Colombia (Unpublished Master's thesis). Universidad Pontificia Bolivariana.

Curwood, J. S., Magnifico, A. M., Lammers, J. C., & Stornaiuolo, A. (2019). Ethical dilemmas within online literacy research. *Literacy Research: Theory, Method, and Practice, 68*(1), 293–313.

Eubanks, V. (2018). *Automating inequality: How high-tech tools profile, police, and punish the poor.* St. Martin's Press.

Fields, D. A., Giang, M., & Kafai, Y. B. (2013). Understanding collaborative practices in the Scratch online community: Patterns of participation among youth designers. *To see the world in a grain of sand: Learning across levels of space, time, and scale: CSCL 2013 Conference Proceedings, 1,* 200–207.

Freebody, P., & Freiberg, J. M. (2010). The teaching and learning of critical literacy. In M. L. Kamil, D. P. Pearson, E. B. Moje, & P. P. Afflerbach (Eds.), *Handbook of reading research* (Vol. IV, pp. 432–452). Routledge.

Freire, P. (1972). *Pedagogy of the oppressed.* Penguin.

Gee, J. P. (2005). Semiotic social spaces and affinity spaces. In D. Barton & K. Tusting (Eds.), *Beyond communities of practice: Language, power, and social context.* Cambridge University Press.

Gee, J. P. (2013). *The anti-education era: Creating smarter students through digital learning.* Palgrave Macmillan.

Golden, N. A. (2017). Critical digital literacies across scales and beneath the screen. *Educational Media International, 54*(4), 373–387.

Hagood, M. C. (Ed.). (2009). *New literacies practices: Designing literacy learning.* Peter Lang.

Hayes, E. R., & Duncan, S. C. (Eds.). (2012). *Learning in video game affinity spaces.* Peter Lang.

Holmes, J. B. (2017). Video games, Distributed teaching and learning systems, and multipedagogies. In E. Gee & F. Serafini (Eds.), *Remixing multiliteracies: Theory and practice from New London to New Times* (pp. 134–137). Teachers College Press.

Jenkins, H., Clinton, K., Purushotma, R., Robison, A. J., & Weigel, M. (2009). *Confronting the Challenges of participatory culture: Media education for the 21st century.* MIT Press.

Jenkins, H., Shresthova, S., Gamber-Thompson, L., Kligler-Vilenchik, N., & Zimmerman, A. (2018). *By any media necessary: The new youth activism.* New York University Press.

KhosraviNik, M., & Unger, J. W. (2016). Critical discourse studies and social media: Power, resistance and critique in changing media ecologies. In R. Wodak & M. Meyer (Eds.). *Methods of critical discourse studies* (3rd ed., pp. 206–233). Sage.

Lammers, J. C., Curwood, J. S., & Magnifico, A. M. (2012). Toward an affinity space methodology: Considerations for literacy research. *English Teaching Practice and Critique, 11*(2), 44–58.

Lankshear, C., Green, B., & Snyder, I. (2000). *Teachers and technoliteracy: Managing literacy, technology and learning in schools.* Allen & Unwin.

Lankshear, C., & Knobel, M. (Eds.). (2008). *Digital literacies: Concepts, policies and practices.* Peter Lang.

Leander, K. M., & Mckim, K. K. (2003). Tracing the everyday "sitings" of adolescents on the internet: A strategic adaptation of ethnography across online and offline spaces. In *Education, Communication & Information, 3*(2), 211–240.

Luke, A. (2012a). After the testing: Talking and reading and writing the world. *Journal of Adolescent & Adult Literacy, 56*(1), 8–13.

Luke, A. (2012b). Critical literacy: Foundational notes. *Theory Into Practice, 51*(1), 4–11.

Luke, A., & Freebody, P. (1999). A map of possible practices: Further notes on the four resources model. *Practically Primary, 4*(2), 5–8.

Lynch, T. L. (2017). Soft (a) ware in the English Classroom: Below the Screen: Why multiliteracies research needs to embrace software. *English Journal, 106*(3), 92.

Mirra, N., Garcia, A., & Morrell, E. (2015). *Doing youth participatory action research: Transforming inquiry with researchers, educators, and students.* Routledge.

Misson, R., & Morgan, W. (2006). *Critical literacy and the aesthetic: Transforming the English classroom.* National Council of Teachers of English.

Molnar, A. R. (1978). Computer literacy in the classroom. *THE Journal, 5*, 35–38.

Mundt, M., Ross, K., & Burnett, C. M. (2018). Scaling social movements Through social media: The case of Black Lives Matter. *Social Media + Society, 4*(4).

Murray, J. H. (1997). *Hamlet on the Holodeck: The future of narrative in cyberspace* (1st ed.). MIT Press.

OECD. (2015). Implications of digital technology for education policy and practice. In *Students, computers and learning: Making the connection.* OECD Publishing.

Orben, A., & Przybylski, A. K. (2019). The association between adolescent well-being and digital technology use. *Nature Human Behaviour, 3*(2), 173–182.

Pandya, J. Z. (2011). *Overtested: How high-stakes accountability fails English language learners.* Teachers College Press.

Pangrazio, L. (2016). Reconceptualising critical digital literacy. *Discourse, 37*(2), 163–174.

Pangrazio, L. (2019). *Young people's literacies in the digital age: Continuities, conflicts and contradictions.* Routledge.

Rowsell, J., Morrell, E., & Alvermann, D. E. (2017). Confronting the digital divide: Debunking brave new world discourses. *The Reading Teacher, 71*(2), 157–165.

Santo, R. (2013). Hacker literacies: User-generated resistance and reconfiguration of networked publics. In J. Avila & J. Z. Pandya (Eds.), *Critical digital literacies as social praxis: Intersections and challenges* (pp. 197–218). Peter Lang.

Sealey-Ruiz, Y., & Haddix, M. M. (2018). 21st century new literacies and digital tools as empowering pedagogies for urban youth of color. In *Information and technology literacy: Concepts, methodologies, tools, and applications* (pp. 1331–1345). IGI Global.

Sefton-Green, J. (2014). From 'othering' to incorporation: The dilemmas of crossing informal and formal learning boundaries. In K. Sanford, T. Rogers, & M. Kendrick (Eds.). *Everyday youth literacies: Critical perspectives for new times* (pp. 175–189). Springer.

Serafini, F. (2012). Expanding the four resources model: Reading visual and multi-modal texts. *Pedagogies: An international journal, 7*(2), 150–164.

Steinkuehler, C., & Duncan, S. (2008). Scientific habits of mind in virtual worlds. *Journal of Science Education and Technology, 17*(6), 530–543.

Turkle, S. (2017). *Alone together: Why we expect more from technology and less from each other.* Hachette UK.

Vee, A. (2017). *Coding literacy: How computer programming is changing writing.* MIT Press.

Zimmerman, E., & Salen, K. (2003). *Rules of play: Game design fundamentals.* MIT Press.

3.9

CRITICAL LITERACY AND ADDITIONAL LANGUAGE LEARNING

An Expansive View of Translanguaging for Change-Enhancing Possibilities

Sunny Man Chu Lau, Zhongfeng Tian and Angel M. Y. Lin

Definitions of Key Concepts

We use **additional language** (AL) education to refer to education contexts that involve the teaching and learning of a new language—be they sheltered instruction to support learners' mastery of English to transition to mainstream programs, or two-way Spanish-English bilingual classrooms, or immersion contexts with content and language integrated learning (CLIL) in a target language. The term AL aims to shift the prevailing deficit-orientation toward English language learners to one that highlights combined bi/multilingual resources and their reciprocal influences (Jarvis & Pavlenko, 2010), a dynamic perspective promulgated by some scholars as early as the 1990s to challenge the restrictive monolingual view of bilingualism (e.g., Leung, Harris, & Rampton, 1997). Research in sociolinguistics (Blommaert, 2010), linguistic ethnography (Creese, 2008), and psycholinguistics and neurolinguistics (Wu & Thierry, 2012) have all pointed to fluid cross-language interdependence, described as, for example, cognitive underlying proficiency (Cummins, 2001), or multicompetence (Cook, 1995, 2016), which contributed to the theoretical basis for translanguaging.

Translanguaging (TL), a translated term from Welsh (*trawsieithu*) by Baker (2001), first describes a strategic pedagogic approach in alternating input and output between English and Welsh to support students' bilingualism. It has since been further theorized (García & Li, 2014; García & Lin, 2017) beyond the context of minority language education. TL theory highlights the dynamic interconnections among languages and cultures. It is built on the notion of "languaging" that describes a cognitive *process* of ongoing negotiation and mediation through which thoughts and experience are given shape (Swain, 2006). Languaging shares a similar emergentist view with the Dynamic Systems Theory (Herdina & Jessner-Schmid, 2002) which recognizes language use and learning as complex, continual processes of co-adaptation and co-construction through a myriad of cognitive and social variables. TL theory also draws on sociolinguistic research that documents language in action, demonstrating that diversity and hybridity are often the norm than exception. Language mixing, borrowing, switching or co-mingling long existed in pre-colonial port cities, marketplaces, and borderlands (Canagarajah & Liyanage, 2012) and still do in urban centres, except that diversity now operates anew on unprecedentedly globalized spatiotemporal scales (Vertovec, 2007), with super hybrid and fluid multilingual and multimodal communicative practices that produce, resist or

 DOI: 10.4324/9781003023425-44

redefine the complex relationships between culture, ethnicity, and nationality. TL as a pedagogic approach articulates a critical stance to leverage and legitimize these outside-school multilingual and multimodal repertoires and practices for meaningful learning (García & Kleyn, 2016) to disrupt language hierarchies and academic monolingualism and promote minoritized students' education and identities (Flores & Rosa, 2015). Particularly, enlisting students' full semiotic repertoires allow for greater engagements in complex, critical learning (García & Li, 2014) that is often precluded from AL classrooms operating from monolingual standards.

Critical literacy (CL) aims to foster a critical stance in students as they learn to read and write (Freire & Macedo, 1987). While CL theory and practice have been further expanded and developed by many literacy scholars (Leland, Lewison, & Harste, 2013; Morrell, 2015; Vasquez, 2010; Zacher Pandya & Ávila, 2014), SLA has been slow in responding to these developments. Up until the late 1990s, SLA research and practice were still predominated by cognitive-oriented methodologies and processes of reading and writing, focusing on discrete linguistic structures perceived as disconnected from students' lives (Graman, 1988). Responding to this imbalance, Pennycook (2001) proposes a "critical applied linguistics" (CAL) that involves:

> a constant skepticism [. . .] and demands a restive problematisation of the givens of applied linguistics, [. . .] and seeks to connect it to questions of gender, class, sexuality, race, ethnicity, culture, identity, politics, ideology and discourse.
>
> *(p. 10)*

AL learning entails a dual socialization (Pennycook, 1996) as students learn to re-read and re-write the world in a different language that reshapes, modifies, juxtaposes and/or complements the cultural and ideological framings embedded in their first language. By extension, learning an AL requires one's ability to "translate, transpose and critically reflect on social, cultural and historical meaning conveyed by the grammar and lexicon" (Kramsch, 2006, p. 103). Hence, CAL articulates an explicit focus on *critical language awareness* (Fairclough, 1992), which, built on Halliday's systemic functional linguistics, aims to promote consciousness of how lexical and grammatical operations are used to construct "ideological representations (field), social relations (tenor), and textual formations (mode)" (Luke, 2000, p. 453) that altogether shape "selective versions of the world" (Janks, 2010, p. 22). Apart from textual critique, another common CAL approach is aligned more broadly with critical pedagogy, engaging students in critical social practice (Luke, 2013). Diversity and difference are included in texts and curricula as real issues faced by students to invite sharing, problematization and critical reflections on these experiences to collaboratively find alternatives and enact change (e.g., Benesch, 2009; Kubota & Lin, 2009; Motha, 2014; Nelson, 2015; Norton & Toohey, 2004)

Among different CL approaches, Janks'(2010) synthesis model brings together not only critical language and cultural awareness but also cross-language and modal engagements for critical learning, which resonates the core principles of TL. She proposes four interdependent orientations for CL: to ensure students' mastery of designs or grammars across modes and modalities to understand how linguistic and semiotic features are assembled to construct meaning (*access*); to analyze and critique how linguistic/modal choices are made in texts to uphold or silence certain worldviews or voices (*domination*); to include students' multiple linguistic and cultural practices as legitimate and valuable resources for critical discussions and reflections on diverse perspectives (*diversity*); and to engage with different semiotic systems to find creative, transformative solutions to issues of concerns to students (*design*). Janks urges these four dimensions be constantly kept in a dynamic, productive balance because highlighting access alone perpetuates English hegemony while deconstructing dominance without redesigning overlooks human agency and creativity as problem-solvers. Similarly, critique without access further marginalizes disadvantaged students (the access paradox, Janks, 2004), while celebrating diversity alone without access and critique respectively ghettoizes diversity and reifies identity.

Critiques of the "Criticality" of TL

Janks' integrated model dovetails the core principles of TL pedagogy (see Lau, 2019 for a full discussion). Articulating a political stance against English dominance and purity, both CL and TL argue for a dynamic integrated use of linguistic and non-linguistic resources for socially meaningful learning and affirmation of minoritized identities and practices. The transformative potential of TL is strongly underscored by its proponents, as it connects to linguistic human rights, empowerment of minoritized subjectivities and voices, and their creative, critical re-mediation of semiotics to learn and perform beyond the mono-lingual norms (García & Li, 2014; Li, 2018). TL is taken up as a promising critical approach to AL education as it fosters an inclusive learning environment for minoritized learners whose diversity is affirmed as assets, voices amplified, and positive bi/multilingual identities cultivated (García-Mateus & Palmer, 2017). TL pedagogy is also shown to assist deeper conceptual learning (Durán & Henderson, 2018), promote reading comprehension (Vaish & Subhan, 2015) and writing skills (Machado & Hartman, 2019), and facilitate metacognitive and metalinguistic awareness (Goodwin & Jiménez, 2016). Exponential research on TL has further triggered a paradigmatic shift in SLA from one driven by mono-lingual standards to one that validates heteroglossic, multimodal communication and meaning construction.

Many scholars stand for the critical potential of TL as it provides the needed scaffolds for minoritized students to navigate the "codes of power", enabling more equitable academic and social engagements. However, for some scholars, operating from a mere scaffolding stance, TL runs the risk of further perpetuating English hegemony. For example, Flores (2014) argues that some TL practices are increasingly "disconnected from the larger political struggles" (n.p.), and Flores and Rosa (2015) remind us that transformation cannot be achieved solely through supporting minoritized students' access to the dominant language but also through active dismantling of the raciolinguistic hierarchies. Similarly, other scholars (Kubota, 2016; McNamara, 2011) caution against an overly celebratory attitude toward plural approaches to AL education, as recognition of multilingual abilities is often restricted to more prestigious named languages, which are often tied to discourses of global capitalism and cosmopolitanism. Flores and Rosa hence call for a *critical heteroglossic perspective* in TL to not only valorize marginalized identities and communicative practices for knowledge construction but also to raise awareness about language and power to critically interrogate dominant structures. This resonates with Janks' (2010) integrated approach to CL, begging the question of how we can hold valorization of multilingualism in productive tension and balance with support for students to negotiate gatekeeping and access to powerful social opportunities and positions.

Responses to Critiques and Current Research

In this section, we review some recent studies of TL in AL classrooms that adopt a more overt critical focus on social issues commensurate with a critical heteroglossic perspective (Flores & Rosa, 2015) and Janks' (2010) integrated model. This is by no means to define or restrict what criticality looks like in AL education, but rather to underscore how "a restive problematisation" (Pennycook, 2001) of TL practices can bolster possibilities for change without reducing it to another neoliberal project of celebratory pluralism (Kubota, 2016). We also bring in some most recent articulations of TL that encompass an expansive, ecological, distributed view of language, offering new lenses/dimensions for CL engagements in AL classrooms.

Critical Translanguaging

López-Gopar and colleagues (2020) in Oaxaca, Mexico engaged their student teachers in developing a critical theme-based unit for elementary children to address real social issues while learning English. Based on the theme of nutrition and healthy habits, TL practices were used to build knowledge and foster full participation, while challenging the school's monolingual standards in raising students' awareness about the common hybrid use of languages and borrowed words (e.g., Spanish and Mixe, English, and Spanish). Using songs, games, flash cards, and physical activities as well as visual and narrative text production, the teachers invited students to problematize and co-construct knowledge about healthy eating and exercising habits in multimodal and multisensory ways. In the process, TL engagements helped disrupt both the children's and the student teachers' internalized sense of inferiority about their indigenous languages and identities, decolonizing monolingual English as the only legitimate pathway to learn and perform. The study demonstrates a critical TL approach, operating with Janks' dynamic intersection of access, domination, diversity and design orientations.

Seltzer's (2020) study similarly adopts what she calls a *critical translingual approach* to writing pedagogy, in which she and the participating Grade 11 teacher co-developed a yearlong ELA curriculum in a New York City high school to read and discuss translingual mentor texts, examining particularly how TL is used as a rhetorical device to tell a certain story. Students also studied radio/TV interviews and articles where the authors discussed their language choices and responses to censorships and pushbacks, which revealed aspects of their identity and positionality as racialized writers. Throughout the process, students read and produced multimodal texts (blog posts, podcasts, spoken word performances, etc.) to co-construct and demonstrate their developing understanding of the topic. In the cumulating project, students used translingual writing to craft their personal reflections in the genre of a college entrance essay, which traditionally upholds English monolingualism. This study's TL engagements not only made possible for meaningful communication and personal reflections but also critique on academic monolingualism. Of great importance is the teacher/researcher's attention to students' emotional investment and self-determination about language and identity. Given the highly regulated nature of high-stake assessments (college entrance essays in this case), students had mixed responses as to whether they would submit their translingual essay to an actual college. Students' complex and competing emotions and desires, as in their enthusiasm about translingual writing practice and cautiousness about what and/or whether to reveal about their multilingual identities, reflect the enduring challenges of the access paradox. Nonetheless, Seltzer asserts that student engagements in meta-talk about language use and choice can enhance agentic self-determination about what elements of their identities to bring forth (and to what degree) without further putting them in marginalized positions.

Poststructuralist and feminist scholars have long called for attention to desires and identity work beyond reason—not to treat reason and emotions as binary opposites but rather corollaries mutually informing, shaping, and constituting each other (Benesch, 2012; Motha & Lin, 2014). Attending to these corporeal sensations deepens understanding how embodied memories, experiences and feelings shape behaviors, beliefs, and values, and vice versa. CL in this sense should involve both intellectual and emotional engagements, expanding the traditionally logo- and verbo-centric CL work (Janks, 2002) to alternative modalities and avenues that allow for embodied experiences and somatic means of knowing and sensing (Holmes, 2010), to maximize and diversify change-enhancing possibilities.

An example of critical embodied TL engagements is from Lau, Juby-Smith, and Desbiens' (2016) collaborative action research study in Quebec which draws particular attention to students' raw emotions towards social differences. Reading children's storybooks in English and French alternately, the teachers and children discussed and analyzed social stereotypes in both languages. Despite their articulate critique of social stigma, the children's sharing of their fear and avoidance towards the homeless points to their complex, conflicting attitudes towards people different from them. Their honest dialogues allowed for more nuanced understanding of how ideologies work and incited greater reflexivity on individuals' complicity in inequitable social relations. TL was used in a coordinated way by the teachers who provided target language models while crafting a TL space (Li, 2018) to enhance trans-systemic mean-making possibilities and discuss how linguistic and visual cues were assembled in texts to construct ideas. From their embodied TL experiences in class, they also came to question the arbitrary language and curricular boundaries between English and French, an enduring sociopolitical and historical divide inherent in the wider Quebec/Canadian context, raising awareness and affording alternative avenues for critical, reflexive knowing and being.

An Expansive View of Translanguaging

The latest articulations of TL theory show an increasing attention to not only affective and bodily affordances but also an expansive, ecological, and human de-centering view of language. Thibault (2011) argues that TL involves highly complex, heterogeneous interactions among the mind, body and culture across spatiotemporal scales. TL is seen as "an assemblage of diverse material, biological, semiotic and cognitive properties and capacities" (2017, p. 82) that interlocutors as co-acting agents orchestrate in real-time across diverse contexts. In other words, TL involves sensorimotor (auditory, vocal, and visual activities, facial expressions, and gestures, etc.), cognitive, and affective processes to dialogically negotiate meaning and to affect (and be affected by) other TL bodies. These added biological, material, and ecological dimensions highlight language as distributed across the minds, bodies, and sociocultural and physical world. The neural, affective and sociocultural engagements emphasize TL as "whole-body" (2011, p. 211) sense-making processes that are intersubjective and socio-culturally and ecologically embedded with affordances from the environment, artifacts and technologies (p. 216).

This distributed view of language is increasingly adopted by AL scholars. For example, both Canagarajah (2017) and Pennycook (2010) draw attention to the idea of *spatial repertoires* to extend understanding of language beyond language-to-language and language-to-person relations to those between semiotic resources, artifacts, activities, and space (Pennycook & Otsuji, 2014). An anthropocentric view often relegates space as "dead matter to be shaped by human cognition and language" (Canagarajah, 2017, p. 33), but a spatial orientation reevaluates how language and literacy practices are "situated, holistic, networked, mediated, and ecological, thus integrated with diverse conditions, resources, and participants" (ibid). Lin (2019), building on these understandings of language as "embodied, emplaced, and ensembled" (p. 8) further theorizes TL as trans-semiotization (TS) and flows. Drawing on Lemke (2016), Lin argues that communication or meaning making is materialized through speech in conjunction with all non-speech actions and physical responses of non-human mediums; in other words, "all processes and flows which contribute to the unfolding of an activity or event [. . .] constituted and constrained on and across multiple time scales" (Lemke, as cited in Lin, 2019, p. 11). Following this expanded, distributed view of language, Wu and Lin (2019) documented how a Grade 10 Hong Kong biology teacher engaged his Cantonese-speaking students in a multimodal and multisensory exploration of the interlocking processes in transpiration pull in plants. Building on students' Cantonese wordings and everyday logic of "no water—then get water" (p. 262), the teacher co-constructed understanding of the scientific concepts (e.g., cell structure and mechanisms of diffusion, evaporation and osmosis) by interanimating (Bakhtin & Holquist, 1981) between and among Cantonese and English, everyday and scientific registers, intonation textures, embodied actions and gestures, as well as visuals (hand-drawn diagrams in conjunction with projected scanned textbook image on the board). The study illustrates how teachers and students as speaking/acting bodies were entangled in the collective flows of linguistic, multimodal, bodily and material resources, tools, and artifacts all contributing dynamically to their evolving understanding of the focal scientific concepts.

Lin (2019) argues that TL/TS practices are more than mere scaffolding for mastery of academic and scientific learning. Rather, student engagements in the continuing flows of inter- and intra-actions with linguistic (registers, varieties, and styles), semiotic, material, and bodily resources, allow for the Bakhtinian "dialogic encounters with otherness" (p. 13). In other words, learning an academic term or using a word in an AL is to interact with and enter into the "other" way of being, thinking, and relating to the world that is tied to sociohistorical dimensions and ideologies. The critical goal is hence not to replace but expand students' multiple communicative means in their continual encounters with othernesses to create own meaning and find own words, a goal resonating with the Seltzer's (2020) emphasis on students' capacity building and self-determination in their decision to comply with or resist institutional expectations.

Another study built on an ecological, distributed view of language is Comber and colleagues' (Comber, 2016; Comber & Nixon, 2013) place-based inquiry with children in a diverse neighborhood in Adelaide, Australia with families of immigrant, refugee, and Aboriginal backgrounds. Guided by an inquiry into the concept of belonging, the focal teacher took the children out for routine neighborhood walks (sometimes virtually through Google Earth), and invited reflections on what mattered to them in the community, including both animate and inanimate objects and activities (e.g., houses, families, facilities, trees, and pets). Apart from learning to read and draw maps, the children documented their emergent learning through various tools and technologies (camera, KidPix, or iMovie). For a culminating task, they wrote and drew wishes for the neighborhood, which revealed both their fears (big dogs or bullying kids) and desires for future changes (e.g., a greener or quieter neighborhood and more responsible behaviors from children and adult alike). Class discussions and sharing of the final product allowed the children (and the teacher) to get to know each other and reflect on their sense of self and relationships with the social and physical environment, facilitating a better understanding of difference and possible actions to enhance their sense of belonging in the community. Such place-conscious pedagogy engages with students' whole-body sense-making repertoire to co-act with the space, tools and material for enhanced critical reflections and reconstruction of desirable and hopeful socio-spatial relationship, foregrounding an expansive, ecological CL approach for students to learn, experience, sense, and be touched in multiple, alternative ways for greater transformative possibilities.

Implications for Pedagogy and Research

The latest expansive view of TL as assemblages of diverse cognitive, affective, social, and material affordances reflects an uptake on posthumanist, ecofeminist (Bennett, 2010; Davion, 2009) understandings of language and learning in the field of SLA and AL education. In fact, the Douglas Fir Group (2016), formed by leading scholars in SLA related fields, proposed a transdisciplinary framework for the 21st century, which also highlights language as multimodal, embodied, and mediated social practices with power, identity, emotions and affect playing crucial roles in teaching and learning. They call for research and practice that acknowledge multilingual realities in translocal spaces and trajectories and the emergent, dynamic, and open-ended negotiated nature of language use and learning.

Appleby and Pennycook (2017) argue that the new ecological and posthumanist approaches are not to replace but rather to build on the existing critical perspectives (rooted in historical materialism as an analytical lens for socioeconomic and political structures) to reconsider how language intersects with class, gender, race as well as bodies, things, and space as wider assemblages, promoting critical citizenship as ethical interdependence between the human and material world. This expansive but resolute problematizing stance helps address scholars' worries about TL pedagogy's gradual loss of political rigor and its assimilation into neoliberal cosmopolitanism that might further aggravate the global and local socioeconomic divide (Flores & Rosa, 2015; Kubota, 2016). Attention to hybridity and plurality is not to forget how inequity plays out in local practices (Otsuji & Pennycook, 2010) as minoritized groups are still constantly struggling with alienation and immobilization by fixed mono-lingual and racialized ideologies in legal, medical, education, and immigration systems. Researchers and teachers should examine both hybridity and fixity in tandem, not as dichotomies, but as complex hybrid and fixed forms of practices that are adopted, adapted, resisted, and/or integrated into each other in different spatiotemporal scales. Attending to the material, corporeal, and affective processes would require systematic research and teaching engagements in contextualized spaces. Both university and school-based researchers should work closely alongside with their students in localized places to collaboratively and collectively analyze and experience issues and concerns that matter to them and to co-act with linguistic, semiotic, technological tools to create, imagine, and enact alternative ways of being, behaving, thinking, and feeling about these issues. This entails a political stance undertaken by university- and school-based actors to engage in inquiry as praxis, co-developing more eco-ethical social and physical relationships and disrupting the boundaries between education and research (Smythe, Hill, MacDonald, Dagenais, Sinclair, & Toohey, 2017).

Implications for Social Responsibility as Academics and Recommendations for Future Research and Praxis

Systematic contextualized research engagements entail a moral commitment to praxis with the local communities that is fueled by genuine care and relational connectedness. Researchers' engagements with the education communities require humility and reflexivity in ongoing interrogation of (a) how we position ourselves as all-knowing researchers or as co-learners with teachers and students with distributed expertise, (b) whose research agenda that we pursue—what likely gets funded or what matters to the communities, and (c) what changes are desirable and to whom. This connects to the enduring question feminist scholars raise about how to do critical work without being imposi-tional (Lather, 1991). Park (2006) argues for relational knowledge in collaborative research engage-ments with the community that is grounded in both cognitive and affective understanding of the other's needs and desires so that change-enhancing context can be co-created on equitable terms.

This also brings us back to the perpetual question of what criticality means in AL research and practice. In this chapter, we take Pennycook's (2001) principle of CAL as "a constant skepticism" and "a restive problematisation" (p. 10) of language and power. Janks (2010) reminds us to find ways to hold access, critique of domination, diversity and design in dynamic balance, weaving them together as complex moves. This does not mean we cannot work with students on a certain dimension at a time, providing that other dimensions are brought in later. Jaspers (2019) further argues that transfor-mation or empowerment can take different forms. For example, it can be an important breakthrough for a teacher whose teaching is largely informed by monolingualism to become more positive toward using students' multilingual and multimodal repertoires to promote learning, or for a school who is not ready yet to allow students' home languages in formal classrooms to have them included in extracurricular activities to support student engagement. What Jaspers argues is not to close off alter-natives but rather widen options so that possibilities for more critical engagements can be brokered (see also Canagarajah and Dovchin's [2019] urge for a non-essentialized view of TL in relation to resistance, power and identity). There is no easy solution to fix the access paradox—as global English expands its hegemony on the material lives of minoritized languages and subjectivities, access and critique cannot be held as either-or options. The key is to treat them as "both-and" imperatives and to engage in constant skepticism and problematization of TL and CL work as continuous, not one-off or add-on, endeavors to balance and critique moves across access, domination, design and diversity at all times. The idea is to heighten and expand students' embodied awareness and experiences of oppression and change so that they come to determine for themselves what they are ready to fight for and/or compromise given their unique circumstances.

Meanwhile, more research on assessment that moves away from monolingual practices should be conducted to catch up with changes in ecological, pluralist pedagogies. Kubota (2016) critiqued that it would hypocritical for educators and researchers to promote multilingual repertories while similar practices are absent or disallowed in actual high-stake examinations and scholarly publications. All these research, teaching and assessment engagements require long-term commitment and care in collaborative inquiry with practitioners, which however runs contrary to the current audit culture in the academia and the immense pressure for fast publications. It begs the question of how scholars can collectively fight against the corporate culture of speed and "productivity" for more eco-ethical ways of teaching and research.

References

Appleby, R., & Pennycook, A. (2017). Swimming with sharks, ecological feminism and posthuman language politics. *Critical Inquiry in Language Studies, 14*(2), 239–261.

Baker, C. (2001). *Foundations of bilingual education and bilingualism* (3rd ed.). Multilingual Matters.

Bakhtin, M. M., & Holquist, M. (1981). *The dialogic imagination: Four essays.* University of Texas Press.

Benesch, S. (2009). Theorizing and practicing critical English for academic purposes. *Journal of English For Academic Purposes, 8*, 81–85.

Benesch, S. (2012). *Considering emotions in critical English language teaching.* Routledge.

Bennett, J. (2010). *Vibrant matter: A political ecology of things.* Duke University Press.

Blommaert, J. (2010). *The sociolinguistics of globalization.* Cambridge University Press.

Canagarajah, A. S. (2015). Clarifying the relationship between translingual practice and L2 writing: Addressing learner identities. *Applied Linguistics Review, 6*(4), 415–440.

Canagarajah, A. S. (2017). Translingual practice as spatial repertoires: Expanding the paradigm beyond structuralist orientations. *Applied Linguistics, 39*(1), 31–54.

Canagarajah, A. S., & Dovchin, S. (2019). The everyday politics of translingualism as a resistant practice. *International Journal of Multilingualism, 16*(2), 127–144. https://doi.org/10.1080/14790718.2019.1575833

Canagarajah, A. S., & Liyanage, I. (2012). Lessons from pre-colonial multilingualism. In M. Martin-Jones, A. Blackledge, & A. Creese (Eds.), *The Routledge handbook of multilingualism* (pp. 49–65). Routledge.

Comber, B. (2016). *Literacy, place, and pedagogies of possibility.* Taylor & Francis.

Comber, B., & Nixon, H. (2013). Urban renewal, migration and memories: The affordances of place-based pedagogies for developing immigrant students' literate repertoires. *REMIE Multidisciplinary Journal of Educational Research, 3*(1), 42–68.

Cook, V. (1995). Multi-competence and the learning of many languages. *Language, Culture, and Curriculum, 8*(2), 93–98. https://doi.org/10.1080/07908319509525193

Cook, V. (2016). Premises of multi-competence. In V. Cook & L. Wei (Eds.), *The Cambridge handbook of linguistic multi-competence* (pp. 1–25). Cambridge University Press.

Creese, A. (2008). Linguistic ethnogrpahy. In N. H. Hornberger (Ed.), *Research methods in language and education* (Vol. 10, pp. 229–242). Springer.

Cummins, J. (2001). *Negotiating identities: Education for empowerment in a diverse society* (2nd ed.). California Association for Bilingual Education.

Davion, V. (2009). Feminist perspectives on global warming, genocide, and card's theory of evil. *Hypatia, 24*(1), 160–177. https://doi.org/10.1111/j.1527-2001.2009.00012.x

Douglas Fir Group. (2016). A transdisciplinary framework for SLA in a multilingual world. *The Modern Language Journal, 100*(S1), 19–47. https://doi.org/10.1111/modl.12301

Durán, L., & Henderson, K. (2018). Pockets of hope: Cases of linguistic flexibility in the classroom. *EuroAmerican Journal of Applied Linguistics and Languages, 5*(2), 76–90.

Fairclough, N. (Ed.). (1992). *Critical language awareness.* Longman.

Flores, N. (2014). *Let's not forget that translanguaging is a political act.* Retrieved from https://educationallinguist. wordpress.com/2014/07/19/lets-not-forget-that-translanguaging-is-a-political-act/

Flores, N., & Rosa, J. (2015). Undoing appropriateness: Raciolinguistic ideologies and language diversity in education. *Harvard Educational Review, 85*(2), 149–171.

Freire, P., & Macedo, D. (1987). *Literacy: Reading the word and the world.* Bergin & Garvey.

García, O., & Kleyn, T. (Eds.). (2016). *Translanguaging with multilingual students: Learning from classroom moments.* Routledge.

García, O., & Li, W. (2014). *Translanguaging: Language, bilingualism and education.* Palgrave Macmillan.

García, O., & Lin, A. M. Y. (2017). Translanguaging in bilingual education. In O. García, A. M. Y. Lin, & S. May (Eds.), *Bilingual and Multilingual Education* (pp. 117–130). Springer International Publishing.

García-Mateus, S., & Palmer, D. (2017). Translanguaging pedagogies for positive identities in two-way dual language bilingual education. *Journal of Language, Identity & Education, 16*(4), 245–255.

Goodwin, A. P., & Jiménez, R. (2016). TRANSLATE: New strategic approaches for English learners. *The Reading Teacher, 69*(6), 621–625.

Graman, T. (1988). Education for humanization: Applying Paulo Freire's pedagogy to learning a second language. *Harvard Educational Review, 58*(4), 433–448.

Herdina, P., & Jessner-Schmid, U. (2002). *A dynamic model of multilingualism: Perspectives of change in psycholinguistics.* Multilingual Matters.

Holmes, M. (2010). The emotionalization of reflexivity. *Sociology, 44*(1), 139–154.

Janks, H. (2002). Critical literacy: Beyond reason. *Australian Educational Researcher, 29*(1), 7–26. https://doi.org/10.1007/BF03219767

Janks, H. (2004). The access paradox. *English in Australia, 139,* 33–42.

Janks, H. (2010). *Literacy and power.* Taylor & Francis.

Jarvis, S., & Pavlenko, A. (2010). *Crosslinguistic influence in language and cognition.* Routledge.

Jaspers, J. (2019). Authority and morality in advocating heteroglossia. *Language, Culture and Society, 1*(1), 83–105. https://doi.org/10.1075/lcs.00005.jas

Kramsch, C. (2006). From communicative competence to symbolic competence. *The Modern Language Journal, 90*(2), 249–252. https://doi.org/10.1111/j.1540-4781.2006.00395_3.x

Kubota, R. (2016). The multi/plural turn, postcolonial theory, and neoliberal multiculturalism: Complicities and implications for applied linguistics. *Applied Linguistics, 37*(4), 474–494.

Kubota, R., & Lin, A. M. Y. (Eds.). (2009). *Race, culture, and identities in second language education: Exploring critically engaged practice.* New York: Routledge.

Lather, P. (1991). *Getting smart: Feminist research and pedagogy with/in the postmodern.* Routledge.

Lau, S. M. C. (2019). Convergences and alignments between translanguaging and critical literacies work in bilingual classrooms. *Journal of Translation and Translanguaging in Multilingual Contexts, 5*(1 [Special Issue] Positive synergies: Translanguaging and critical theories in education), 67–85. https://doi.org/10.1075/ttmc.00025.lau

Lau, S. M. C., Juby-Smith, B., & Desbiens, I. (2016). Translanguaging for transgressive praxis: Promoting critical literacy in a multiage bilingual classroom. *Critical Inquiry in Language Studies,* 1–29. https://doi.org/10.1080/15427587.2016.1242371

Leland, C., Lewison, M., & Harste, J. C. (2013). *Teaching children's literature: It's critical!* Routledge.

Lemke, J. (2016). *Translanguaging and flows.* Unpublished research manuscript.

Leung, C., Harris, R., & Rampton, B. (1997). The idealised native speaker, reified ethnicities, and classroom realities. *TESOL Quarterly, 31*(3), 543–560. https://doi.org/10.2307/3587837

Li, W. (2018). Translanguaging as a practical theory of language. *Applied Linguistics, 39*(2), 9–30.

Lin, A. M. Y. (2019). Theories of trans/languaging and trans-semiotizing: Implications for content-based education classrooms. *International Journal of Bilingual Education and Bilingualism, 22*(1), 5–16. https://doi.org/10.1080/13670050.2018.1515175

López-Gopar, M. E., Sughrua, W. M., Córdova-Hernández, L., López Torres, B. P., Aldaz, E. R., & Morales, V. V. (2020). A critical thematic unit in a teaching praxicum: Health issues and plurilingualism in the "English" classroom. In S. M. C. Lau & S. Van Viegen (Eds.), *Plurilingual pedagogies: Critical and creative endeavors for equitable language in education.* Springer International.

Luke, A. (2000). Critical literacy in Australia: A matter of context and standpoint. *Journal of Adolescent & Adult Literacy, 43*(5), 448–461.

Luke, A. (2013). Regrounding critical literacy: Representation, facts and reality. In M. R. Hawkins (Ed.), *Framing languages and literacies: Socially situated views and perspectives* (pp. 136–148). Routledge.

Machado, E., & Hartman, P. (2019). Translingual writing in a linguistically diverse primary classroom. *Journal of Literacy Research, 51*(4), 480–503. https://doi.org/10.1177/1086296x19877462

McNamara, T. (2011). Multilingualism in education: A poststructuralist critique. *Modern Language Journal, 95*(3), 430–441.

Morrell, E. (2015). *Critical literacy and urban youth: Pedagogies of access, dissent, and liberation.* Routledge.

Motha, S. (2014). *Race, empire, and English language teaching: Creating responsible and ethical anti-racist practice.* Teachers' College Press, Columbia University.

Motha, S., & Lin, A. M. Y. (2014). "Non-coercive rearrangements": Theorizing desire in TESOL. *TESOL Quarterly, 48,* 331–359. https://doi.org/10.1002/tesq.126

Nelson, C. D. (2015). LGBT content: Why teachers fear it, why learners like it. *Language Issues, 26*(1), 6–12.

Norton, B., & Toohey, K. (Eds.). (2004). *Critical pedagogies and language learning*. Cambridge University Press.

Otsuji, E., & Pennycook, A. (2010). Metrolingualism: Fixity, fluidity and language in flux. *International Journal of Multilingualism*, 7(3), 240–254. https://doi.org/10.1080/14790710903414331

Park, P. (2006). Knowledge and participatory research. In P. Reason & H. Bradbury (Eds.), *The handbook of action research* (pp. 83–93). Sage.

Pennycook, A. (1996). TESOL and critical literacies: Modern, post, or neo? *TESOL Quarterly*, 30(1), 163–171. https://doi.org/10.2307/3587613

Pennycook, A. (2001). *Critical applied linguistics: A critical introduction*. Lawrence Erlbaum Associates.

Pennycook, A. (2010). *Language as a local practice* (1st ed.). Routledge.

Pennycook, A., & Otsuji, E. (2014). Metrolingual multitasking and spatial repertoires: 'Pizza mo two minutes coming'[This paper]. *Journal of Sociolinguistics*, 18(2), 161–184. https://doi.org/10.1111/josl.12079

Seltzer, K. (2020). Translingual writers as mentors in a high school "English" classroom. In S. M. C. Lau & S. V. Viegen (Eds.), *Plurilingual pedagogies: Critical and creative endeavors for equitable language in education*. Springer International.

Smythe, S., Hill, C., MacDonald, M., Dagenais, D., Sinclair, N., & Toohey, K. (2017). *Disrupting boundaries in education and research*. Cambridge University Press.

Swain, M. (2006). Languaging, agency and collaboration in advanced language proficiency. In H. Byrnes (Ed.), *Advanced language learning: The contribution of Halliday and Vygotsky* (pp. 95–108). Continuum.

Thibault, P. J. (2011). First-order languaging dynamics and second-order language: The distributed language view. *Ecological Psychology*, 23(3), 210–245.

Thibault, P. J. (2017). The reflexivity of human languaging and Nigel Love's two orders of language. *Language Sciences*, 61, 74–85.

Vaish, V., & Subhan, A. (2015). Translanguaging in a reading class. *International Journal of Multilingualism*, 12(3), 338–357. https://doi.org/10.1080/14790718.2014.948447

Vasquez, V. M. (2010). Critical literacy isn't just for books anymore. *The Reading Teacher*, 63(7), 614–616. https://doi.org/10.1598/RT.63.7.11

Vertovec, S. (2007). Super-diversity and its implications. *Ethnic and Racial Studies*, 30(6), 1024–1054.

Wu, Y., & Lin, A. M. Y. (2019). Translanguaging and trans-semiotising in a CLIL biology class in Hong Kong: Whole-body sense-making in the flow of knowledge co-making. *Classroom Discourse*, 10(3–4), 252–273.

Wu, Y. J., & Thierry, G. (2012). Unconscious translation during incidental foreign language processing. *NeuroImage*, 59(4), 3468–3473. https://doi.org/10.1016/j.neuroimage.2011.11.049

Zacher Pandya, J., & Ávila, J. (Eds.). (2014). *Moving critical literacy forward: A new look at praxis across contexts*. Routledge.

3.10

INDIGENOUS YOUTH DIGITAL LANGUAGE ACTIVISM

Kristian Adi Putra and Lusia Marliana Nurani

The Key Concepts of Indigenous Language Activism

Language activism is not a new topic in Indigenous language revitalization efforts but has relatively recently been theorized formally by scholars including Florey (2008) and Combs and Penfield (2012). Early Hawaiian language activism, for instance, took place in 1896 after the use of Hawaiian in public education was suppressed by the Government of the United States at that time (Kawai'ae'a, Housman, & Alencastre, 2007). But this activism was not yet fruitful until the early 1980s when the language was almost extinct with fewer than 50 speakers under the age of 18 (Kawai'ae'a et al., 2007; Nämähoe & Barcarse, 2007). To bring back the vitality of Hawaiian language, an immersion preschool called *Pünana Leo* was established through grassroots movement (Kawai'ae'a et al., 2007; Nämähoe & Barcarse, 2007). Now, the immersion school not only provides early childhood education but also elementary, secondary, and tertiary education resulting in the sharp increase of Hawaiian speakers (Kawai'ae'a et al., 2007; Nämähoe & Barcarse, 2007). The most important achievement from this activism is that the language has reclaimed its important position not only as the symbol of Native Hawaiian identity but also as a means of communication (Kawai'ae'a et al., 2007; Nämähoe & Barcarse, 2007).

In other countries, similar grassroots movements also took place around the same time or later, such as Hebrew beginning in the 1880s in Palestine prior to the formation of the state of Israel (Zuckerman & Walsh, 2011), Sami in Norway in 1960s (Hirvonen, 2008), Navajo in the United States in 1960s (Lomawaima & McCarty, 2006), Maori in New Zealand in 1970s (Harrison, 2005), and minority language groups in Zimbabwe in 1980s (Nyika, 2008). Language activists involved in these movements, very often including Indigenous youth, did not only advocate for the place and voice of Indigenous languages in educational settings, and the use of the language at home and public domains, but also for the documentation of the endangered Indigenous languages, the development of strategic community language planning and policies, the development of teaching and assessment materials, and the officialization of the Indigenous languages, as in the case of Hawaiian as the official language of the State of Hawaii (Kawai'ae'a et al., 2007).

Combs and Penfield (2012) specifically define language activism as "energetic action focused on language use in order to create, influence and change existing language policies" (p. 462) while language activists as "individuals or groups who, through various means, actively defend their right to venerate and freely use their languages in multiple, often in the public domain" (p. 462). Therefore, language activism can be defined as any energetic efforts done by language activists to revitalize

DOI: 10.4324/9781003023425-45

or to maintain the vitality of an Indigenous language, which according to Florey (2008) can range from "language documentation, language training, skill sharing to materials development, language programs, raising community awareness, and encouraging participation in language work" (p. 121).

Language activists, thus, can be anyone and people of all ages, as well as people from inside and outside of the community, linguists and non-linguists, and researchers and non-researchers, as long as the activism that they do is for the sake of the well-being of the language and the culture in the community. In multiple studies, for instance, scholars have pointed out how youth and elders (Kral, 2010, 2011) and community members and researchers from outside and inside of the community (e.g., Davis & Phyak, 2015; Thorne, Siekmann, & Charles, 2015; Villa, 2002) collaborate in the maintenance of Indigenous language and culture in Indigenous communities in both offline and online settings. The activism also does not necessarily take place only in remote or rural Indigenous communities, but also in diverse urban areas. In addition, the advancement of digital technology today opens up the possibility for language activists to be more connected and make efforts together.

Critiques and Misperception Toward Indigenous Youth

Over the last two decades, Indigenous language scholars, employing different research methodologies ranging from ethnography to case study to narrative inquiry, have looked at ways youth can be involved and encouraged to take part in Indigenous language revitalization efforts, particularly how they initiated language activism projects (e.g., Cru, 2015; Jimenez-Quispe, 2013; Kral, 2012; Messing, 2009; Nicholas, 2009; Witherspoon & Hansen, 2013). These studies also found that Indigenous youth's grassroots initiatives often took place in endangered language settings and commonly started from the youth reflections on their lived experiences and growing awareness on what was happening within their community.

However, it is worth noting that young people are commonly accused of not being loyal to their Indigenous language and culture by their older counterparts. In fact, the phenomenon of language shift among the youth have been reported in a number of studies (e.g., Himmelmann, 2010; Katubi, 2007; King, 2001; Nurani, 2015; Setiawan, 2013; Suharsono, 1995; Tuominen, 1999; Wong Fillmore, 1991; Zentz, 2012). These studies highlighted the fact that interference in intergenerational language transmission was prevalent in the second or the third generation. Youth opted the dominant language over their own native language primarily because the former opened more socioeconomic opportunities.

Despite the negative perception of the older generation toward the youth, many young people actually do care about their Indigenous language and culture. This finding was unraveled by Nicholas (2009) who examined language and identity among the Hopi youth in the United States. In her study, she found that the Hopi youth perceived maintaining language as not the only factor to maintain one's Indigenous identity, but included alongside maintaining the Hopi culture "to live Hopi" (p. 321). Active participation in their Indigenous way of life is a mandatory condition to become a Hopi and they were willing to make efforts to maintain their language and culture. Similar to Nicholas' finding, Nurani's study (2015) also showed how the youth were eager to nurture their Indigenous language, namely Javanese language, by pursuing their passion to teach Javanese to middle school students.

Indigenous language and culture maintenance by the youth can also be found on the Australian continent. An ethnographic study done by Kral (2012) shows how rural Warlpiri youth in Australia shared the videos that they created on social media to educate the public about what was right and not right about their community. Similarly, the practices of activism were also found in different parts of the world, such as in Mexico (Cru, 2015) and Bolivia (Jimenez-Quispe, 2013) where Indigenous youth created videos and used Hip Hop culture to deliver their message and critics about social injustice around them to the public in their Indigenous language as well as Spanish and

English. In Ontario, Canada (Witherspoon & Hansen, 2013), Indigenous youth used social media, such as a web page, a hashtag on Twitter, and Facebook, to organize various events for their "Idle No More" movement, a campaign to honor Indigenous sovereignty, land, and water. These studies have shown that the youth did seriously take part in the efforts to defend the vitality of their language and culture. Hence, these studies are clearly the counternarratives of the common misperceptions about the Indigenous youth that they assimilate much more into the mainstream culture instead of defending their own. Given the pivotal role of youth in Indigenous language revitalization efforts (Wyman, McCarty, & Nicholas, 2013), there is still a need to understand what makes Indigenous youth initiate their language activism and how community members can encourage other youth to participate in the efforts.

Moreover, previous studies on language activism carried out within this decade indicated the preference of the Indigenous youth to incorporate digital aspects in their activism. The inclusion of critical digital literacies is of course unavoidable due to the emergence of the digital natives. It is therefore important to take into account the extent to which the youth's critical digital literacies will matter in executing language activism. Specifically, we need to understand how technology, as a part of youth contemporary culture, plays a role in young peoples' involvement in Indigenous language revitalization. We still need to look at how these Indigenous youths incorporate their critical digital literacies for their activism and what changes they envision for their communities through their projects.

The Counternarratives to the Critiques and Misperceptions: Examples From Indonesia

In September 2019 or at the end of the first term of President Joko Widodo's administration, the House of Representatives of the Republic of Indonesia (DPR RI) controversially approved a legislation that according to many would weaken Indonesia's Corruption Eradication Commission. This led to a series of massive demonstrations not only in the capital city, Jakarta, but also in different cities in Indonesia, such as Yogyakarta, Surakarta, Makassar, Surabaya, among many others. The demonstrations were mainly organized by college students' unions across the country and participated by students and the general public. Following the demonstrations, different hashtags, such as *#GejayanMemanggil* (Gejayan is calling) and *#SoloBergerak* (Solo is moving), also appeared and even became worldwide trendings in social media, especially Twitter. Through social media, the youths across the country united and voiced the rejection of the newly approved legislation and forced it to be revoked.

In the history of Indonesian politics, this was not the first time college students, in this case youths, criticized the government's unpopular policies and proactively got involved in politics. In May 1998, for instance, huge student demonstrations were also taking place forcing President Soeharto to step down after 32 years in power. He was accused of abuse of power and practicing collusion, corruption and nepotism. The students gathered in DPR RI's building, expressed their dissatisfaction with the regime, and demanded the total reformation of the national political system and leadership. On May 21, 1998, President Soeharto finally gave up and let his vice president, B.J. Habibie, take over his presidency.

Although similarly initiated by college students, there was a fundamental difference between the two movements. In 1998, social media was still in its infancy, and it had not been used by youths as prevalent as it is today. Mainstream media, such as television, radio and newspaper, had already been around, but the contents were mostly stirred by the political agenda of a particular group of people in power. Therefore, the voices of the people in majority were always not represented and, at times, were actively marginalized. Today, although social media also possibly have the same challenges with such a political agenda, everyone also has more control over what they want to express in it.

Therefore, it opens up the possibilities for them, including youths, not only to (re)connect, but also to update, be updated, and reflect upon what is happening today as well as in the past and future. It, thus, offers youths a space to engage more actively in politics.

Indigenous youths in Indonesia are no exception. In what follows, we will share stories of two Indigenous youths from Indonesia and their language activism projects through social media. We will focus particularly on describing their lived experiences as an Indigenous youth witnessing the reduced and limited numbers of speakers and space to use their language as well as a language activist trying to maintain the survivance of their language and culture. Using social media as the space to enact their projects, they are similarly targeting their peers, or younger generations of their respective Indigenous communities, raising awareness of what is happening with their language and culture, and inviting them to join the efforts to defend them. In line with the re-conceptualization of critical digital literacies theory as proposed by Pangrazio (2016), the Indigenous youths here are thus not only assimilating, evaluating and re-integrating information (see for instance Thorne et al., 2015) or accepting conditions as they are, but also challenging them critically and doing something to reverse and improve them.

In reference to the definition of youths, we refer to the Republic of Indonesia Law on Youth (Number 40 of 2009 or *Undang-Undang Republik Indonesia Nomor 40 Tahun 2009 tentang Kepemudaan*) in chapter I article 1, which mentions that youths are the Indonesian citizen aged 16–30 years old. With regard to the term Indigenous people of Indonesia, we adopt the definition coined by the International Labor Organization (ILO) Convention 169 article 1 of 1989 and adapt to the Indonesian context. Therefore, Indigenous People of Indonesia refers to people in this country who are the descendants of the populations which inhabited the country pre, during, and post colonization. In brief, they are natives of the country, and the examples that follow refer to natives of Indonesia.

Translation:

How calm it is in the Port of Belawan,
The sea wave splashes in the morning.
The magical eclipse is covered by the cloud,
The angry star where you are going.

First Reply:

You are moon you are star,
Beautifying the calm night cloud.
Waiting for girlfriend that still has not come,
(Your) soul is telling (you) are missing her.

Second Reply:

You are moon,
You are star,
Because of you,
I have a lot of debt.

Picture 1 was typical Encik's posts on his social media. Recognized as a young poet among his friends, Encik frequently posted poems in Malay. His friends also often replied to his posts using poems.

Picture 1. A poem written by Encik (30 years old, a Malay poet) and the replies in his Facebook

Growing up in Malay community, Encik told us how *Gurindam*, a type of classic Malay poetry consisting of two lines of sentences with the same number of syllables and rhyme, was deeply rooted in the life of the people of Malay. Modern Malay poetry, as in his aforementioned poems in social media on the other hand, has four lines of sentences, and similarly each sentence in the poetry has the same number of syllables and rhymes, for example, AAAA, AABB, or ABAB. Historically, in the golden era of the Islamic Malay Kingdom of Penyengat, there was a legendary historian, scholar and poet, Raja Ali Haji (1808–1873), who wrote a gurindam titled "Gurindam 12," which remains a very influential literary work for the Malay people.

It is still common to hear people read gurindam and modern Malay poetries in traditional ceremonies and official events organized by the local government in Tanjungpinang. Similarly, in schools, government offices, and public places in the city, we also can still easily see the texts of Gurindam 12 on the wall of the buildings. It has been influenced by the way the City of Tanjungpinang labeled themselves as *Kota Gurindam* or the City of Gurindam. All the activities and the linguistic landscapes in public spaces, therefore, need to be designed to better represent this identity.

However, Encik pointed out that recently, the Malay cultural gatekeepers were mostly dominated by elders. The participation of the younger generations was still relatively low. Encik's intention of posting his poems in his social media was, thus, to make it more accessible for his younger Malay and non-Malay friends. Additionally, he also wanted to encourage his friends to practice replying to his poems with a poem to him, in the hopes that later his friends would do the same in their social media with their friends. He argued that someday after the older generation of the Malay people died, he and his peers would be the one who was responsible for the maintenance of Malay traditions, including poetries. Therefore, he felt that he needed to do something to encourage the younger generation of the Malay people to be more proactive in the community efforts to maintain Malay poetry. He realized that the way people used Malay poetry in Tanjungpinang might have changed a lot today, but it did not mean that Malay poetry did not have a place anymore in informal conversation. He felt that the presence of social media, in which many youth in Tanjungpinang

Picture 2. Instagram post of Novri (26 years old, a solo classic Lampung guitarist) showing his solo classic Lampung guitar performance

might spend hours on a daily basis, needed to be used to revitalize the sociocultural function of the Malay poetry, but that someone needed to initiate it. Encik convincingly told us that he wanted to be the one to do so.

The translation of the caption:

> I don't have a lot of wishes. I just want Lampung arts and cultural traditions to survive and not to be eroded due to modernization. So, let us, young people, the nation's next generation, take an active role in the preservation of our cultural traditions in this beloved land of Lampung. Hopefully later, Lampung can become a role model for other provinces on the preservation of the arts and cultural traditions in Indonesia.

In Picture 2, Novri posted a video of his performance in his Instagram account. In the post, he wrote a caption in Lampung language to remind and invite his friends to join his efforts to preserve Lampung language and culture.

Novri was originally from the City of Liwa, West Lampung Regency. He was born and grew up there, until he finally decided to move to Bandar Lampung for college in 2015. In Liwa, he spoke Lampung language with his family at home, people in the neighborhood and friends at schools. In majority, people in Liwa are Lampung ethnic, so they still maintain the use of the language and practice their traditional culture in the community. He learned how to play a solo classic Lampung guitar from a relatively early age. When he was in senior high school, he started performing regularly and established himself as a solo classic Lampung guitarist in his hometown.

Solo classic Lampung guitar performance is one of the traditional music performances of the Lampung people. It comes with songs that have poetic lyrics in Lampung language and that contain a lot of moral values, particularly about life and love (Rahman, 2019). It is commonly performed in traditional ceremonies in the community, such as in a wedding ceremony. Novri mentioned how nowadays, the existence of this tradition as well as the community enthusiasm to continuously listen to it was quite worrying. People did not really know traditional songs anymore, because of their preference and the massive exposure to the mainstream music industries in television, radio and internet. Lampung traditional music performances in these spaces were limited, so that access to Lampung traditional music was not equal to mainstream music.

Novri told us that he started to realize how Bandar Lampung was different from Liwa. A lot of Lampung traditions were no longer practiced in Bandar Lampung. In percentage, there were about 25% of Lampung people in the city (Statistics Indonesia, 2015), but not all of them necessarily spoke Lampung language, particularly the younger generation in the community. They mostly spoke in Indonesian, as their parents at home and the elders in the community also spoke in Indonesian. This is in line with the findings of some previous studies (Gunarwan, 2006; Putra, 2018) that showed diglossia in the home domain of Lampung language families in Bandar Lampung. Today's Lampung youth, therefore, could be the second or the third generation in the family who do not speak Lampung language.

This situation made him decide to step up and do something. When he moved to Bandar Lampung, he continuously maintained communication with his family and peers back home in Liwa in Lampung language via social media. Eventually, he also added his fellow college students and other new friends from the City of Bandar Lampung as friends in his personal social media accounts. Although he used primarily Indonesian language on a daily face to face interaction with his new friends in Bandar Lampung, except with Lampung speaking friends, he decided to frequently maintain the use of Lampung language in social media. He wanted to make his social media posts a space for his friends in Bandar Lampung, both Lampung and non Lampung ethnics, to use the language. He believed that his new friends would eventually learn and try to comment in Lampung language, especially as his family and peers from Liwa still frequently commented and used the language.

Not only through his personal social media accounts, Novri also did his activism through the Lampung guitarist community's Instagram and YouTube accounts that he created with his fellow guitarists in Bandar Lampung. He established the community because he believed that the impact of his activism would be more massive if he worked together with others who had the same interests and concerns. Recently, with his colleagues, he also started offering his services to plan and organize Lampung traditional wedding ceremonies in the City of Bandar Lampung, allowing him to better promote Lampung cultural traditions in the city.

Implications for Language Revitalization and Maintenance Efforts

Encik's story gives us insight into how youth can participate in Indigenous language revitalization and maintenance both collaboratively and individually and in formal and informal settings, while considering specific, intergenerational target audiences for their efforts. In the formal setting, Encik worked collaboratively with the Mayor of the City of Tanjungpinang whose audiences were mostly young adults and elders. In comparison, in the informal setting, in this case via his social media, Encik engaged in language activism as an individual, targeting younger audiences, particularly his close friends. From the story, we also can learn how the vision of the local government to represent the Province of Riau Islands as the Motherland of Malay language and the City of Gurindam influenced collective efforts from the local government and the local community in the region to collaboratively or individually participate and innovate. Encik's story also provides us insight in how youth may also connect to traditional literary art forms and invest in this particular form and cultural practice. Additionally, it is also striking that Encik used Indigenous language poetry for multiple contemporary purposes in ways that made sense for this context.

Novri's story gives us insights into how migration allows Indigenous youth to reflect upon their identity and the future of their community. Migrating from a predominantly Lampung speaking rural area to a diverse urban area where most Lampung people did not speak Lampung anymore raised Novri's awareness of the complex challenges faced by their community and encouraged him to do something for his community. Novri believed that their Lampung peers in Bandar Lampung wanted to learn and use Lampung, as it is a part of their cultural identity, but they just did not have enough support to do it. Appreciations that he received from both his Lampung and non-Lampung peers showed us that this was really the case. This is thus in line with previous studies that showed how Indigenous youth continued to have a positive attitude toward their Indigenous language and indicated their willingness to (re)learn and (re)use the language even after they experienced complex language shifts in their family and community (Lee, 2009; McCarty, 2014; Nicholas, 2009).

Implications for Pedagogy

In general, the findings of Indigenous youth studies have been conclusive in showing that these youth want to be able to speak in their language, to reclaim their Indigeneity, and to be involved and proactively initiate language activism projects. However, the studies also reported cases of misperceptions about Indigenous youth on their inability to speak the language. It added to the vicious circle of linguistic insecurities experienced by the youths that were not only discouraging for them, but also dangerous for the future of the community. Here, we would like to stress the need to continuously value the important role and contribution of each youth taking part in transformative praxis through their contemporary digital culture within their community and within themselves. Indigenous communities need to accommodate the voices of their youth, more patiently guide them, and involve them in what Davis (2014) called "engaged language policy and practices."

Pedagogically, we will refer to what Smith (2015) has proposed to decolonize schooling for Indigenous communities. Smith (2015) mentioned, "schooling (has) become important sites of struggle" and that we need to "redevelop schooling and education away from the inevitability of the reproduction of dominant cultural, social, and economic norms" (p. 55). Drawing on Freire's Pedagogy of the Oppressed (Freire, 1972), Smith (2015) proposes the notion of critical analysis and transformative praxis to transform the inequity experienced by Indigenous communities taking place in educational settings and in contemporary society. Smith describes and discusses the cases that he encountered in Maori communities in New Zealand. Smith highlights that although colonialism ended in a literal sense, it is now taking into new forms through the hegemony of neoliberal economy, and continuously oppressing Indigenous communities, people, languages, and cultures to make them assimilate into dominant, monolingual, and monocultural society.

As hegemony is commonly introduced through schools, Smith asserts that "schooling become important sites of struggle" and that we need to "redevelop schooling and education away from the inevitability of the reproduction of dominant cultural, social, and economic norms" (p. 55). In facing such oppression, Indigenous communities need "first to recognize these new formations of colonization and second to do something about them" (Smith, 2015, p. 64), and thus recognize that the struggle is "both cultural (referring to agency) and structural (referring to economic, ideological, and power structures)" (p. 74). In the conception of transformative praxis, Smith emphasizes three elements of praxis: conscientization, resistance, and transforming, in an interdependent and sustaining relationship, which might not necessarily take place in such exact order.

Drawing on Smith's statement, educators play an important role to foster conscientization, to maintain resistance, and to transform pedagogical practices to promote Indigenous language and culture by reflecting on what the Indigenous people need and want to achieve through schooling. To reach their goals, educators must take into account the Indigenous youth's participation and make them their collaborators. That is, to decolonize schooling will require educators to be the agents and students to be the collaborators so that the tripartite cycle of decolonization (conscientization, resistance, and transforming) will occur effectively. Referring back to the theme of this chapter, in each step of such critical analysis and transformative praxis, we need to always include Indigenous youths and value what they know and what they can do, as they are the ones who will continue defending their community in the future.

Implications for Research

Thematically, previous Indigenous youth studies have in majority focused on describing the perspectives of Indigenous youth on language shift, endangerment, and revitalization as well as showing what Indigenous youths have initiated and how Indigenous youths collaborated with academics and elders in their communities. While scholars have repeatedly mentioned the need to build top down and bottom up as well as home, school, and community collaborations in Indigenous language revitalization efforts (see Wyman, Galla, & Jiménez-Quispe, 2016), studies that show such collaborative practice is still relatively rare in the literature. There is also still a need to conduct more action research studies, in addition the one done by Putra (2018), that connects language activists with Indigenous youths at schools and in the communities. Such studies are important as the presence of language activists can inspire and encourage Indigenous youth to take part or initiate their own language activism projects. Additionally, they will also have someone that they can seek guidance from as they share their stories.

Implications for Our Social Responsibility as Academics

Collaboration projects involving academic scholars, communities, and Indigenous youth have been done and continue to progress (e.g., Galla, 2010; Kral, 2012; Lee, 2009; Thorne et al., 2015; Villa, 2002). In addition to assisting the formulations of ideal language planning and policies for the communities and being with them to document their language, there have also been a lot of other efforts that academics have done with Indigenous youth. The rationales of such projects commonly include raising the awareness of Indigenous youth about their endangered Indigenous language situation and equipping them with academic and technical skills needed to participate and help revitalize their Indigenous language. Some of the activities that have been done included documenting the language, developing authentic instructional materials, designing web-based language learning, teaching the language, among many others.

Such collaboration and training are crucial because it is often challenging for researchers who are considered outsiders to gain access to an Indigenous community. Therefore, providing Indigenous youth with these skills will enable these youth to determine what should be done and what information to share with the public in the efforts to maintain their language (Villa, 2002; Thorne et al., 2015). Take a study conducted by Villa (2002) in the Southwestern United States as an example. The Navajo youth from different colleges were invited to New Mexico State University (NMSU) in Summer 1999 and 2000 to take part in several NMSU faculty members' research projects related to Indigenous language issues and to participate in language documentation training. First, they discussed the critical issues related to Indigenous language shift and endangerment in their community with faculty members in the project; then, they together determine what needs to be done to help their community. The final product of the project itself was the audio and video recording of oral history from their community.

To end this chapter, we would like to debunk misconceptions about Indigenous youths' ignorance toward their language. We would like also to highlight the need for academics to nourish and continue collaborations with the Indigenous youth in order to empower Indigenous youth and their communities by equipping them with academic and technical skills to revitalize their language in the hope to ensure the future of diversity and humanity.

References

Combs, M. C., & Penfield, S. D. (2012). Language activism and language policy. In B. Spolsky (Ed.). *The Cambridge handbook of language policy* (pp. 461–474). Cambridge University Press.

Cru, J. (2015). Language revitalization from the ground up: Promoting Yucatec Maya on Facebook. *Journal of Multilingual and Multicultural Development, 36*(3), 284–296. http://doi.org/10.1080/01434632.2014.921184

Davis, K. A. (2014). Engaged language policy and practices. *Language Policy, 13*(2), 83–100. http://doi.org/10.1007/s10993-013-9296-5

Davis, K. A., & Phyak, P. (2015). In the face of neoliberal adversity: Engaging language education policy and practices. *L2 Journal, 7*(3), 146–166. http://doi.org/10.5070/L27323494

Florey, M. (2008). Language activism and the 'new linguistics': Expanding opportunities for documenting endangered languages in Indonesia. *Language Documentation and Description, 5,* 120–135.

Freire, P. (1972). *Pedagogy of the oppressed.* Penguin Books.

Galla, C. K. (2010). *Multimedia technology and indigenous language revitalization: Practical educational tools and applications used with native communities* (Doctoral dissertation). The University of Arizona, Tucson, Arizona.

Gunarwan, A. (2006). Kasus-kasus pergeseran bahasa daerah: Akibat persaingan dengan Bahasa Indonesia? *Linguistik Indonesia, 24*(1), 95–113.

Harrison, B. (2005). The development of an Indigenous knowledge program in a New Zealand Maori-language immersion school. *Anthropology & Education Quarterly, 36*(1), 57–72. http://doi.org/10.1525/aeq.2005.36.1.057

Himmelmann, N. P. (2010). Language endangerment scenarios: A case study from northern Central Sulawesi. In M. J. Florey (Ed.). *Endangered languages of Austronesia* (pp. 45–72). Oxford University Press.

Hirvonen, V. (2008). 'Out on the fells, I feel like a Sami: Is there linguistic and cultural inequality in the Sami school? In N. H. Hornberger (Ed.), *Can schools save Indigenous languages? Policy and practice on four continents* (pp. 15–41). Palgrave Macmillan.

International Labor Organization. (1989). *Indigenous and tribal peoples convention* (No. 169). Retrieved from www.ilo.org/dyn/normlex/en/f?p=NORMLEXPUB:12100:0::NO:12100:P12100_ILO_CODE:C169

Jimenez-Quispe, L. (2013). *Indians weaving in cyberspace, Indigenous urban youth cultures, identities and politics of languages* (Unpublished doctoral dissertation). The University of Arizona, Tucson, Arizona.

Katubi, O. (2007). Lampungic languages: Looking for new evidence of language shift in Lampung and the question of its reversal. *Studies in Philippine Languages and Cultures, 16,* 1–10.

Kawaiʻaeʻa, K. K. C., Housman, A. K., & Alencastre, M. (2007). Pūʻā i ka ʻōlelo, ola ka ʻohana: Three generations of Hawaiian language revitalization. *Hūlili: Multidisciplinary Research on Hawaiian Well-Being, 4,* 183–238.

King, K. A. (2001). *Language revitalization process and prospects: Quichua in the Ecuadorian Andes.* Multilingual Matters.

Kral, I. (2010). *Plugged in: Remote Australian Indigenous youth and digital culture.* Center for Aboriginal Economic Policy Research, Australian National University.

Kral, I. (2011). Youth media as cultural practice: Remote Indigenous youth speaking out loud. *Australian Aboriginal Studies, 1*(1), 4–16.

Kral, I. (2012). *Talk, text and technology: Literacy and social practice in a remote Indigenous community.* Multilingual Matters.

Lee, T. S. (2009). Language, identity, and power: Navajo and pueblo young adults' perspectives and experiences with competing language ideologies. *Journal of Language, Identity, and Education, 8*(5), 307–320. http://doi.org/10.1080/15348450903305106

Lomawaima, K. T., & McCarty, T. L. (2006). *"To remain an Indian": Lessons in democracy from a century of Native American education.* Teachers College Press.

McCarty, T. L. (2014). Negotiating sociolinguistic borderlands—Native youth language practices in space, time, and place. *Journal of Language, Identity & Education, 13*(4), 254–267. http://doi.org/10.1080/15348458.2014.939031

Messing, J. H. E. (2009). Ambivalence and ideology among Mexicano youth in Tlaxcala, Mexico. *Journal of Language, Identity, and Education, 8,* 350–364. http://doi.org/10.1080/15348450903307680

Nämähoe, L., & Barcarse, K. (2007). ʻAha Pūnana Leo. *Cultural Survival Quarterly, 31*(2), 44–47.

Nicholas, S. E. (2009). "I live Hopi, I just don't speak it"—The critical intersection of language, culture, and identity in the lives of contemporary Hopi youth. *Journal of Language, Identity, and Education, 8,* 321–334. http://doi.org/10.1080/15348450903305114

Nurani, L. M. (2015). *Changing language loyalty and identity: An ethnographic inquiry of societal transformation among the Javanese people in Yogyakarta, Indonesia* (Unpublished doctoral dissertation). Arizona State University, Tempe, Arizona.

Nyika, N. (2008). Language activism in Zimbabwe: Grassroots mobilisation, collaborations and action. *Language Matters, 39*(1), 3–17. http://doi.org/10.1080/10228190802320998

Pangrazio, L. (2016). Reconseptualising critical digital literacy. *Discourse: Studies in the Cultural Politics of Education, 37*(2), 163–174. http://doi.org/10.1080/01596306.2014.942836

Putra, K. A. (2018). *Youth, technology and Indigenous language revitalization in Indonesia* (Unpublished doctoral dissertation). The University of Arizona, Tucson, Arizona.

Rahman, N. (2019). *Nilai karakter syair lagu gitar tunggal Lampung Pesisir* (Unpublished undergraduate thesis). Universitas Lampung, Bandar Lampung, Indonesia.

Setiawan, S. (2013). *Children's language in a bilingual community in East Java* (Unpublished doctoral dissertation). The University of Western Australia, Perth, Western Australia, Australia.

Smith, G. H. (2015). Equity as critical praxis: The self development of Te Whare Wananga O Awnuiarangi. In M. A. Peters & T. Besley (Eds.), *Paolo Freire: The global legacy*. Peter Lang.

Statistics Indonesia. (2015). *Provinsi Lampung dalam Angka 2015*. Badan Pusat Statistik.

Suharsono. (1995). *Attitudes of young Javanese towards their native language* (Unpublished master thesis). Murdoch University, Perth, Western Australia, Australia.

Thorne, S. L., Siekmann, S., & Charles, W. (2015). Ethical issues in Indigenous language research and interventions. In P. I. De Costa (Ed.), *Ethics in applied linguistics research: Language researcher narratives* (pp. 142–160). Routledge.

Tuominen, A. (1999). Who decides the home language? A look at multilingual families. *International Journal of the Sociology of Language, 140*(1), 59–76. http://doi.org/10.1515/ijsl.1999.140.59

Undang-Undang Republik Indonesia Nomor 40 Tahun 2009 tentang Kepemudaan (The Republic of Indonesia Law on Youth Number 40 of 2009). Retrieved from www.dpr.go.id/dokjdih/document/uu/UU_2009_40.pdf

Villa, D. J. (2002). Integrating technology into minority language preservation and teaching efforts: An inside job. *Language Learning and Technology, 6*(2), 92–101. doi.org/10125/25163

Witherspoon, T., & Hansen, J. (2013). The "Idle No More" movement: Paradoxes of First Nations inclusion in the Canadian context. *Social Inclusion, 1*(1), 21–36. doi.org/10.17645/si.v1i1.107

Wong Fillmore, L. (1991). When learning a second language means losing the first. *Early Childhood Research Quarterly, 6*, 323–346. doi.org/10.1016/S0885-2006(05)80059-6

Wyman, L. T., Galla, C. K., & Jiménez-Quispe, L. (2016). Indigenous youth language resources, educational sovereignty and praxis: Connecting a new body of language planning research to the work of Richard Ruiz. In N. H. Hornberger (Ed.), *Honoring Richard Ruiz and his work on language planning and bilingual education* (pp. 396–430). Multilingual Matters.

Wyman, L. T., McCarty, T. L., & Nicholas, S. E. (Eds.). (2013). *Indigenous youth and multilingualism: Language identity, ideology, and practice in dynamic cultural worlds*. Routledge.

Zentz, L. (2012). *Global languages identities and ideologies in an Indonesian university context* (Unpublished doctoral dissertation). University of Arizona, Tucson, Arizona.

Zuckerman, G., & Walsh, M. (2011). Stop, revive, survive: Lessons from the Hebrew revival applicable to the reclamation and empowerment of Aboriginal language and cultures. *Australian Journal of Linguistics, 31*(1), 111–127. http://doi.org/10.1080/07268602.2011.532859

3.11

CRITICAL LITERACY AND ENGLISH LANGUAGE TEACHING

Seonmin Huh, Lílian Vimieiro Pascoal, and Andréa Machado de Almeida Mattos

Key Concepts

In the area of ELT, especially in terms of teaching methodology, a triad of concepts has made history throughout time: approach, method, and technique—and the differences among them. Richards and Rogers (2001) discuss such differences and consider approaches as the broader concept that can involve method and techniques. The approach is the underlying guide to teachers' planning and practices; it is linked to their set of beliefs, assumptions, values, and theories about ELT. The approach informs the method, which is a step-by-step plan of what a teacher normally does in the classroom. Techniques, on the other hand, are the procedures teachers use in their daily practices, and they are often method-specific.

McDonough, Shawn, and Masuhara (2013) discuss these definitions in terms of how approach, design and procedure, respectively relating to approach, method, and technique, can be pinpointed in language teaching practice. The approach would be the moment of planning materials and the mobilization of the teachers' views on language. Planning demands decisions that are based on the teachers' views. This is when the design comes to fruition, when decisions are made regarding what is to be included in the language teaching process. The procedures are the proposals and actions taken in the classroom in order to put the planning into practice.

Discussions around methodology in ELT have also indicated the limitations posed by the end of the millennium and how it "has brought new challenges as well as new opportunities for the profession to venture beyond methods" (Kumaravadivelu, 2006, p. 161). There is no definition and, therefore, selection of one method that works in every single context of ELT. Consequently, it is not sufficient to uncritically follow one method only. Teachers face specificities in their contexts of language teaching when considering their practices in a more local reference. To name a few, classroom conditions, cultural and socio-economic aspects are some of the many contextual specificities. These make way to the possibility and urgency of teachers' choices over their practices, and, more importantly, their postmethod pedagogy, as Kumaravadivelu (2006) highlights:

> Any actual postmethod pedagogy has to be constructed by the classroom teacher. The pedagogic frameworks [presented as the foundation of postmethod pedagogy] offer certain options and certain operating principles. Based on them, and on their own attempt to theorize what they practice and to practice what they theorize, practicing teachers may be able to develop their own location-specific postmethod pedagogies.
>
> *(Kumaravadivelu, 2006, p. 213)*

DOI: 10.4324/9781003023425-46

By the same token, critical literacy is a perspective in the pedagogical field that yields the connection between the teaching and learning processes with the social contexts in which they are taking place. It views students as co-creators of society, therefore, actors who should understand and have the necessary tools to increase their participation in society.

Insofar as critical literacy is the focus, many researchers are concerned in not defining it as one more method that has lately become a fad. On the contrary, researchers emphasize that CL is not a method *per se*, but a perspective, or a point of view (Janks, 2013), a proposal or plan for critical education (Monte-Mor, 2013), an attitude of the teacher (Duboc, 2012, 2013; Jordão, 2013; Valério & Mattos, 2018), a way to read the word and the world, as Freire and Macedo (1987) have proposed.

Instead of proposing a step-by-step script through which language may be taught, CL allows teachers and students to change practices to attend to matters that would otherwise be overlooked. According to the prominent work of Cervetti, Pardales, and Damico (2001), language is a possibility of exposure and reconstruction of inequalities. Learning the language and the ways in which societies communicate promotes reading the word and the world in terms of existing social relations.

More recently, Luke (2014) defined critical literacy as "the use of the technologies of print and other media of communication to analyze, critique, and transform the norms, rule systems, and practices governing the social fields of institutions and everyday life" (Luke, 2014, p. 21). Luke argued teaching and learning are always political, and that research must focus on textual and discourse analysis. Luke argued that ethical and moral issues in and out of texts should also be key components of critical literacy teaching and learning. In ELT body of research, text analysis and discourse analysis are still the main foci as students learn English and dominant curricula center around developing communicative competence over analyzing developing intercultural citizenship through critical literacy and being able to address ethical or moral issues around their everyday life.

Critiques of Critical Literacy in ELT

In ELT, most research is done qualitatively and focused on specific teaching practices and their impacts on students' learning. Most ELT research also dominantly comes from university or elementary level research.

First, arguments have been made for implementing critical literacies for Multilingual Learners (English language learners). Research to date has mainly investigated perceptions of teachers and students, the effectiveness of pedagogical practices for using critical literacies, and special concerns that arose when critical literacies perspectives are implemented in ELT settings.

Since critical literacies have been an exploratory domain in ELT, the dominant body of research has focused on participants' perceptions of critical literacies. One body of research on teachers investigated how teachers of English perceived critical literacies approaches.

CL defies some well-established assumptions regarding language teaching and learning; some ELT practices can be seen as antagonistic to critical literacy approaches. These include the teacher-centered method, in which the teacher has more control, is the provider of knowledge, and chooses topics that are neutral. Potentially-controversial topics, such as power relations or relations among different racial groups are not seen as being within the scope of a language classroom. For instance, teachers reflected on detailed use of control in the classroom (Jeyaraj & Harland, 2014), to the extent that they limit students' perspectives (Kubota, 2014), and their intentional choice of safe topics over controversial social issues and resistance to provoking social actions (Bender-Slack, 2010; Sangster, Stone, & Anderson, 2013).

Another body of research on teacher perception details teachers' beliefs that contradict critical literacies; these educators believe that students should master print-based literacy skills before they are able to engage critical literacies (Curdt-Christiansen, 2010; Ko & Wang, 2009; Park, 2011; Tan &

McWilliam, 2009). Research by Curdt-Christiansen (2010), Masuda (2012), and Tan, Bopry, and Lido (2010) illustrate challenges to teachers implementing critical literacies that stem from constraints of a standardized curriculum and national examinations that devalue critical literacies. Teachers often believe that they should pay more attention to raising their students' English language proficiency or test scores (Ko & Wang, 2009; Masuda, 2012; Tan & Guo, 2009).

An important line of discussion in ELT critical literacies research is addressing ELT-specific educational issues. Some ELT critical literacies research demonstrates students' potential growth and improvement of critical literacies without explicit connections to students' traditional language skills development (Allison, 2011; Dooley, 2009; Dooley & Thangaperumal, 2011; Hammond & Macken-Horarik, 1999; Huang, 2011a, 2012; Huh, 2016; Ko, 2013; Lau, 2012, 2013).

Second, the persistent deficit-orientation towards students' linguistic and cultural backgrounds was identified as a barrier for CL engagements. Teachers pointed out that students' cultural backgrounds that discourage the raising of student voices and challenging the author hindered the implementation of critical literacy practices (Ko, 2010; Kuo, 2009; Park, 2011), which highlights the need for such critical practices in terms of agency, active engagement and citizenship in order to confront and raise issues of power.

There are also some concerning observations of a lack of teacher education to support critical literacy praxis. For instance, Choi (2016) implemented the Freirean critical literacy approach and found herself to be not fully capable of using the teaching approach that would actually work in a classroom setting to help her EFL learners in Korea. We learn that systematic teacher development programs are required, especially those that can incorporate particular issues of ELT, such as raising students' English proficiency as well as critical literacies, addressing ELT learners' cultural backgrounds that possibly conflict with the principles of critical literacies, and possible ways to deal with ELT teachers' resistance or hesitation to work on critical literacies with their students.

Other issues include the barriers perceived by students. Multilingual learners of English had difficulty engaging in critical literacy practices due to the lack of access to deeper understanding required for critical analysis of the socio-cultural issues presented in the texts (Park, 2011; Zyngier & Fialho, 2010), and their inability to critically question the authors' choice of text design and discourse features related to power inequity (Black, 2010; Weninger & Kan, 2013). Students generally agree with the authors' opinions (Kaura & Sidhub, 2013; Huh & Suh, 2015) and do not see literacy practices as social critique, but as information-gathering and entertainment (Huang, 2011a). The variety of perceptions of literacy practices and social contexts indicates the complexity of pedagogical concerns when considering critical perspectives in the ELT field.

Lastly, the lack of interdisciplinary approaches to CL limits the ability to draw upon students' multimodal and multilingual resources for critical learning and to reposition them as agentive learners. Studies in the ELT area point out that, as Bobkina and Dominguez (2014) mention, CL is one of the teaching perspectives that is not sufficient in and of itself in terms of implementation in a classroom. In this vein, Valério and Mattos (2018) have proposed the use of CL together with the communicative approach in order to promote students' critical thinking and citizenship education, as well as communicative competence in the target language.

This is also clear when we consider that CL does not attempt to be a method or a set of procedures. On the contrary, it is a perspective that allows seeing and understanding texts and practices beyond the word. In its roots, current research and practices, it is possible to notice that CL calls for interdisciplinarity.

In Brazil, Monte-Mor (2015) refers to three generations of literacy practices. The first generation was based on Paulo Freire's ideas and challenged the previous view of literacy as embedded in phonics methodology, which was seen as dislocated from students' reality. During this first generation of literacy practices, being able to read and write meant simply to decode isolated phrases and their respective words and syllables. The second generation was based on New Literacy Studies and Street's (1984) proposals for the autonomous and ideological models of reading and started viewing literacy as a social practice instead of a neutral skill which could be separated from its social context. The third generation started when the New Literacy Studies began to be incorporated by several other disciplines, such as science literacies, numeracy and critical literacy in ELT. It also incorporated multiliteracies proposals which reflected changes in Brazilian society due to globalization and digital technology (Monte-Mor, 2015). Technology has contributed to the changes in texts which are more evidently multimodal, as Kress (2003) considers. It also allows students and citizens in general to participate more actively in society and be the sources of change in it (Kalantzis & Cope, 2012). This third generation view of literacies shows potential for fostering transdisciplinarity across the various academic disciplines in school contexts.

In first language learning contexts, strong efforts to move beyond one academic discipline tend to be reflected in critical literacies research. Statistical literacy education in mathematics with a critical approach (Weiland, 2016), music education with critical literacy (Beach & Bolden, 2018), social studies and critical literacy (Demoiny & Ferraras-Stone, 2018), visual literacies (Ferraz, 2014) and social media pedagogy with interdisciplinary approach to teaching multimodal critical digital literacy (Talib, 2018) are some of the examples. Following this trend, more attention has been paid to interdisciplinary education for ELT learners (Kumagai & Kono, 2018; Huh & Suh, 2015). For instance, literature and English curricula have been integrated into the first language studies and an interdisciplinary approach, including both social studies and English, has been explored to develop students' critical literacies. Kumagai and Kono (2018) discussed how involving more than one academic discipline helps to disrupt the commonplace knowledge boundaries in one subject area and broaden the horizon to explore creative ways to engage students in critical literacies (teaching critical thinking skills through analysis of a fictional literature example from Bokkina & Steganova, 2016). ELT critical literacies should explore potential interdisciplinary education to help students learn critical literacies.

Responses to Any Critiques and Current Research in the Area

In a critique of the lack of clear connection between language development crucial for multilingual learners and critical literacies, some studies discuss how critical literacies contribute to the ELT-specific issue of students' language skill development, and how both language skills development and critical approach to literacy education enrich students' acquisition of English language as well as their critical awareness of social issues and power (Gómez Jiménez & Gutiérrez, 2018; Huang, 2011b; Huh, 2016). Huang (2011b) emphasized the importance of not sacrificing conventional skills-based literacy instruction over critical literacy and Huh (2016) defined an instructional model of CL that addresses the balance between conventional skills-based and critical literacies. In Huh's study, students learned conventional literacy skills and built upon CL skills of questioning the authors' perspective as well as raised their critical awareness of social issues. Mattos (2012, 2014) reports on two different contexts where CL perspectives are integrated with the teaching of language skills. Mattos (2012) discusses CL as it was implemented by a high school teacher of English in Brazil together with the development of the main language skills (reading, writing and oral skills) and citizenship education. The second study reports on a Brazilian university experience using critical literacy and the communicative approach to language teaching in the context of a pre-service English teachers' development course (Mattos, 2014). Gómez Jiménez and Gutiérrez (2018) more recently reported that Columbian university students showed evidence of learning new vocabulary and expressions in English even with some challenges of expressing themselves in the target language. Gómez Jiménez and Gutiérrez (2018) mainly dealt with speaking skill improvement through critical literacies.

Developing both traditional conventional language skills as well as critical literacies is an important line of ELT research. Liu (2019) explicitly argued that critical literacies can contribute to general language proficiency. While there seems to be a disagreement whether language learning should proceed (Allison, 2011; Hammond & Macken-Horarik, 1999) or should be taught concurrently with critical engagement (Dooley, 2009; Dooley & Thangaperumal, 2011; Huang, 2011b, 2012; Huh, 2016; Ko, 2013; Lau, 2012, 2013; Mattos, 2012, 2014; Suh & Huh, 2014), there is a commonplace agreement that teaching both critical literacies and language learning is necessary. For instance, Suh and Huh (2014) taught decoding and comprehension, personalizing the reading contents, critiquing and reflecting on the reading texts from marginalized cultural perspectives. Students demonstrated competent use of more diverse reading strategies and to develop critical sensitivity and paid attention to organization of ideas, tone and language use to foreground particular ideologies over others. Duboc (2013) and Valério and Mattos (2018) contend that it is in the hands of the teacher to bring critical literacies perspectives into the language classroom and to integrate critical literacies into the teaching of language skills.

We learn that recent educational efforts in CL involve the complex meaning-making skills through multimodal literacies, critical media literacies, as well as interdisciplinary literacy skills for critical awareness. ELT research, however, does not seem to reflect this complexity of teaching and learning of critical literacies in that research on the effectiveness of critical literacies mainly focuses on print-based literacy materials as well as implanting particular teaching approaches only within English subject area. Previous research implies that students should be able to read and write critically beyond one mode of literacy and this requires strong collaboration across academic disciplines. Interdisciplinary collaboration to encourage ELT critical literacies is needed to re-conceptualize critical literacies in ELT.

Second, there is a lack of establishment of a theoretical framework of ELT critical literacies teaching and learning and ELT research depends on a theoretical framework of critical literacies and critical literacy pedagogy that are based upon first language and literacy teaching and learning settings. The teaching and learning contexts play an important role here. The lack of a theoretical framework has to do with the context because, as Ferraz (2018) remarks, some aspects may be studied as critical in some contexts but may be interpreted differently in other contexts. In ELT research contexts, it may be proven to be difficult to follow ELT students throughout their learning processes, which is a different reality from first language research. As we can observe the unique educational issues raised in the ELT contexts in the body of ELT research on critical literacies, there is a need and space to develop, explore and share experiences and research-based findings.

Implications for Pedagogy

We learn that pedagogical considerations for ELT involve the complexity of addressing both general language skills improvement as well as critical literacies skills. We need to construct professional development programs for teachers to be able to broaden their knowledge base to teach critical literacies. As discussed in Mattos (2012), professional development programs may potentially provide space for teachers to re-imagine critical identities, making them better "prepared to work in global contexts and allowing them to develop professional agency, renewed pedagogical attitudes and critical consciousness that will also lead them to enhance critical awareness in their students" (p. 209). Teachers should also learn to collaborate across different academic disciplines and create a professional community to expand their teaching methodologies.

Instead of founding upon the pedagogical models from the first language teaching and learning contexts, ELT pedagogical and instructional models of critical literacies need to be developed and discussed further. We contend that teacher educators in professional development contexts will often act as models for pre-service and in-service teachers. However, these models need not be static or fixed. On the contrary, pedagogical and instructional models should be flexible, evolving and capable of accommodating the diversity of learners in the innumerable ELT contexts around the world. Therefore, pedagogical efforts around different linguistic and cultural contexts should be compiled and shared to expand our knowledge foundation for ELT critical literacies pedagogy.

Implications for Research

A more mixed method design is needed to theoretically frame ELT-specific critical literacies. We should identify multiple issues and dimensions that impact on teachers and learners when teaching and learning about critical literacies in ELT educational contexts. Both longitudinal qualitative research and quantitative research design may support conceptualizing diverse ELT pedagogical models of critical literacies and practices.

More empirical research on different age groups will also benefit the ELT field, as age factors do impact educational practices, and requires different considerations that need to be reflected in ELT policy design, curriculum, teaching methodologies and interaction patterns in classroom, as well as in classroom testing cultures and practices.

Implications for Our Social Responsibility as Academics

ELT education and research in the field of critical literacies tend to be quite limited in scope and boundaries. It is important to disrupt the perceived boundaries of professional knowledge considered appropriate and required for developing critical literacies and to encompass the synthesis of knowledge across various academic disciplines. We as academics should be responsible to collaborate with those with other ways of thinking and with other academic traditions and therefore add to literacy and ELT critical education.

Recommendations for Future Research and Praxis

An important line of research in ELT-related issues with critical literacy—and one that, in our view, has been very much neglected both in research and teacher education—is assessment. Pascoal (2018) conducted research with classroom teachers who often used critical literacy practices in their English classes. However, these teachers did not use the same critical perspectives in their testing and assessment practices. Among the different possible ramifications of study are the ones that relate to teacher education, assessment tools and the stakeholders' views. There is a need for promoting and researching teacher education courses that highlight the importance of critical literacy in the integrated processes involved in ELT, namely teaching, learning, and assessing; developing, studying and applying assessment tools that explore language as the word and the world; and finally, there is much to explore in terms of teachers' and students' views regarding assessment practices in a critical perspective of ELT.

More robust research, both quantitative and qualitative, is required for the critical literacies component to be included in educational policy, school curriculum, ELT teacher development and ELT learners' literacy acquisition. Longitudinal action research with mixed method design may contribute to expand the edge of knowledge and to construct an ELT-specific theoretical framework of critical literacies and pedagogical methods to build upon. Policy and curriculum transformation will require the support of future research.

References

Allison, D. (2011). Learning our literacy lessons: EAL/D students, critical literacy, and the national curriculum. *The Australian Journal of Language and Literacy, 34,* 181–202.
Beach, P., & Bolden, B. (2018). Music education meets critical literacy: A framework for guiding music listening. *Music Education Journal, December,* 43–50.

Bender-Slack, D. (2010). Texts, talk . . . and fear? English Language Arts teachers negotiate social justice teaching. *English Education, 42*(2), 181–203.

Black, R. W. (2010). Online fan fiction and critical media literacy. *Journal of Computing in Teacher Education, 26*(2), 75–80.

Bobkina, J., & Dominguez, E. (2014). The Use of Literature and Literary Texts in the EFL Classroom; Between Consensus and Controversy. *International Journal of Applied Linguistics & English Literature, 3*(2), 249–260.

Bokkina, J., & Steganova, S. (2016). Literature and critical literacy pedagogy in the EFL classroom: Towards a model of teaching critical thinking skills. *Studies in Second Language Learning and Teaching, 6*(4), 677–696.

Cervetti, G., Pardales, M. J., & Damico, J. S. (2001). A tale of differences: Comparing the traditions, perspectives, and educational goals of critical reading and critical literacy. *Reading Online, 4*(9).

Choi, S. J. (2016). Critical literacy in the EFL classroom: Perspectives of undergraduates on reading beyond the text. *English Language & Literature Teaching, 22*(3), 35–58.

Curdt-Christiansen, X. L. (2010). Competing priorities: Singaporean teachers' perspectives on critical literacy. *International Journal of Educational Research, 49*, 184–194.

Demoiny, S. B., & Ferraras-Stone, J. (2018). Critical literacy in elementary social studies: Juxtaposing historical master and counter narratives in picture books. *The Social Studies, 109*(2), 64–73.

Dooley, K. T. (2009). Re-thinking pedagogy for middle school students with little, no or severely interrupted schooling. *English Teaching: Practice and Critique, 8*, 5–20.

Dooley, K. T., & Thangaperumal, P. (2011). Pedagogy and participation: Literacy education for low-literate refugee students of African origin in a western school system. *Language and Education, 25*, 385–397.

Duboc, A. P. M. (2012). *Atitude Curricular: Letramentos Críticos nas Brechas da Formação de Professores de Inglês* (Doctoral dissertation), Faculdade de Filosofia, Letras e Ciências Humanas, University of São Paulo, São Paulo. https://doi.org/10.11606/T.8.2012.tde-07122012-102615.

Duboc, A. P. M. (2013). Teaching with an attitude: Finding ways to the conundrum of a postmodern curriculum. *Creative Education, 4*(12B), 58–65.

Ferraz, D. M. (2014). Visual literacy: The interpretation of images in English classes. *Eventos Pedagógicos, 5*(1), 16–28.

Ferraz, D. M. (2018). Os sentidos de 'crítico' na educação linguística: problematizando práticas pedagógicas locais. In D. M. Ferraz & C. J. Kawachi-Furlan (Eds.), *Educação linguística em línguas estrangeiras* (pp. 39–62). Pontes.

Freire, P., & Macedo, D. (1987). *Literacy: Reading the word & the world.* Routledge & Kegan Paul.

Gómez Jiménez, M. C., & Gutiérrez, C. P. (2018). Engaging English as a foreign language students in critical literacy practices: The case of a teacher at a private university. *Profile: Issues in Teachers' Professional Development, 21*(1), 91–105.

Hammond, J., & Macken-Horarik, M. (1999). Critical literacy: Challenges and questions for ESL classrooms. *TESOL Quarterly, 33*, 528–544.

Huang, S. (2011a). "Critical literacy helps wipe away the dirt on our glasses": Towards an understanding of reading as ideological practice. *English teaching: Practice & Critique, 10*(1), 140–164.

Huang, S. (2011b). Reading "further and beyond the text": Student perspectives of critical literacy in EFL reading and writing. *Journal of Adolescent & Adult Literacy, 55*, 145–154.

Huang, S. (2012). The integration of "critical" and "literacy" education in the EFL curriculum: Expanding the possibilities of critical writing practices. *Language, Culture, and Curriculum, 25*, 283–298.

Huh, S. (2016). Instructional model of critical literacy in an EFL context: Balancing conventional and critical literacy. *Critical Inquiry in Language Studies, 13*, 210–235.

Huh, S., & Suh, Y.-M. (2015). Becoming critical readers of graphic novels: Bringing graphic novels into Korean elementary literacy lessons. *English Teaching, 70*(1), 123–149.

Janks, H. (2013). Critical Literacy in teaching and research. *Education Inquiry, 4*(2), 225–242.

Jeyaraj, J. J., & Harland, T. (2014). Transforming teaching and learning in ELT through critical pedagogy: An international study. *Journal of Transformative Education, 12*(4), 343–355.

Jordão, C. M. (2013). Abordagem comunicativa, pedagogia crítica e letramento crítico: farinhas do mesmo saco? In C. H. Rocha & R. Maciel (Eds.), *Língua estrangeira e formação cidadã:* entre discursos e práticas (pp. 69–90). Pontes.

Kalantzis, M., & Cope, B. (2012). *Literacies.* Cambridge University Press.

Kaura, S., & Sidhub, G. K. (2013). Evaluating the critical literacy practices of tertiary students. *Procedia- Social and Behavioral Sciences, 123*, 44–52.

Ko, M. Y. B. (2010). *Critical literacy development in a college-level English reading class in Taiwan* (Doctoral dissertation), Indiana University, Bloomington, IN.

Ko, M. Y. B. (2013). A case study of an EFL teacher's critical literacy teaching in a reading class in Taiwan. *Language Teaching Research, 17*(1), 91–108.

Ko, M. Y. B., & Wang, T. F. (2009). Introducing critical literacy to EFL teaching: Three Taiwanese college teachers' conceptualization. *The Asian EFL Journal Quarterly, 11*, 174–191.

Kress, G. (2003). *Literacy in the new media age.* Routledge.

Kubota, R. (2014). "We must look at both sides—but a denial of genocide, too? Difficult moments on controversial issues in the classroom. *Critical Inquiry in Language Studies, 11*(4), 225–251.

Kumagai, Y., & Kono, K. (2018). Collaborative curricular initiatives: Linking language and literature courses for critical and cultural literacies. *Japanese Language and Literature, 52*, 247–276.

Kumaravadivelu, B. (2006). *Understanding language teaching: From method to post-method.* Lawrence Erlbaum Associates.

Kuo, J. M. (2009). Critical literacy and a picture-book-based dialogue activity in Taiwan. *Asia Pacific Education Review, 10*, 483–494.

Lau, S. M. C. (2012). Reconceptualizing critical literacy teaching in ESL classrooms. *Reading Teacher, 65*, 325–329.

Lau, S. M. C. (2013). A study of critical literacy work with beginning English language learners: An integrated approach. *Critical Inquiry in Language Studies, 10*, 1–30.

Liu, S. (2019). Using science fiction films to advance critical literacies for EFL students in China. *International Journal of Education & Literacy Studies, 7*(3), 1–9.

Luke, A. (2014). Defining critical literacy. In J. Avila & J. Pandya (Eds.), *Moving critical literacies forward: A new look at praxis across contexts* (pp. 19–31). Routledge.

Masuda, A. (2012). Critical literacy and teacher identities: A discursive site of struggle. *Critical Inquiry in Language Studies, 9*(3), 220–246.

Mattos, A. M. A. (2012). Education for citizenship: Introducing critical literacy in the EFL classroom. In R. M. Gillies (Ed.), *Pedagogy: New developments in the learning sciences* (pp. 191–212). Nova Science Publishers.

Mattos, A. M. A. (2014). Educating language teachers for social justice teaching. *Interfaces Brasil-Canada, 14*(2), 125–151.

McDonough, J., Shaw, C., & Masuhara, H. (2013). *Materials and methods in ELT: A teacher's guide* (3rd ed.). Wiley-Blackwell.

Monte-Mor, W. (2013). The development of agency in a new literacies proposal for teacher education in Brazil. In E. Junqueira & M. E. K. Buzato (Eds.), *New literacies, new agencies? A Brazilian perspective on mindsets, digital practices and tools for social action in and out of school* (pp. 126–146). Peter Lang.

Monte-Mor, W. (2015). Learning by Design: Reconstructing knowledge processes in teaching and learning practices. In B. Cope & M. Kalantzis (Eds.), *A pedagogy of multiliteracies: Learning by design* (pp. 186–209). Palgrave Macmillan.

Park, Y. (2011). Using new articles to build a critical literacy classroom in and EFL setting. *TESOL Journal, 2*, 24–51.

Pascoal, L. A. V. (2018). *Avaliações escritas de Língua Inglesa em contextos de extensão e formação de professores: possíveis relações com letramento crítico* (MA thesis). Federal University of Minas Gerais, Belo Horizonte, Brazil.

Richards, J., & Rogers, T. (2001). *Approaches and methods in language teaching* (2nd ed.). Cambridge University Press.

Sangster, P., Stone, K., & Anderson, C. (2013). Transformative professional learning: Embedding critical literacies in the classroom. *Professional Development in Education, 39*(5), 615–637.

Street, B. (1984). *Literacy in theory and practice.* Cambridge University Press.

Suh, Y.-M., & Huh, S. (2014). Possibilities and challenges of a critical approach to reading instruction with Korean university students. *English Language Teaching, 26*(3), 39–62.

Talib, S. (2018). Social media pedagogy: Applying an interdisciplinary approach to teach multimodal critical digital literacy. *E-learning & Digital Media, 15*(2), 55–66.

Tan, L., Bopry, J., & Lido, G. (2010). Portraits of new literacies in two Singapore classrooms. *RELC Journal, 41*(1), 5–17.

Tan, L., & Guo, L. (2009). From print to critical multimedia literacy: One teacher's foray into new literacies practices. *Journal of Adolescent & Adult Literacy, 53*(4), 315–324.

Tan, L., & McWilliam, E. (2009). From literacy to multiliteracies: Diverse learners and pedagogical practice. *Pedagogies: An International Journal, 4*(3), 213–225.

Valério, K. M., & Mattos, A. M. A. (2018). Critical literacy and the communicative approach: Gaps and intersections. *Brazilian Journal of Applied Linguistics, 18*(2), 313–338. http://dx.doi.org/10.1590/1984-6398201812252.

Weiland, T. (2016). Towards a framework for a critical statistical literacy in high school mathematics. In M. B. Wood, E. E. Turner, M. Civil, & J. A. Eli (Eds.), *Proceedings of the 38th annual meeting of the North American chapter of the international group for the psychology of mathematics education*. The University of Arizona.

Weninger, C., & Kan, K. H. Y. (2013). (Critical) language awareness in business communication. *English for Specific Purposes, 32*(2), 59–71.

Zyngier, S., & Fialho, O. (2010). Pedagogical stylistics, literary awareness, and empowerment: A critical perspective. *Language and Literature, 19*(1), 13–33.

3.12

PROPOSING A POLITICS OF IMMEDIATION FOR LITERACY STUDIES, OR WHAT IS POSSIBLE FOR LITERACY STUDIES BEYOND CRITICAL THEORY'S MEDIATIONS?

Christian Ehret, Kelly C. Johnston, and Jennifer Rowsell

> Theories of ideology rest on the thesis that there is a power of conformity already in place prior to experience.
>
> *(Massumi, 2019, p. 505)*

Massumi's poststructural provocation informs our searching title and hones our chapter's focus: If structuralist theories of mediation give ideologies too much power, then what new concepts do poststructurally oriented literacy researchers need to practice their critiques of power? If mediation overly determines our analyses of emergent moments, then what new concepts are necessary to weaken such powers of conformity, which operate incessantly and create inequities in the diverse lives of those alongside whom we research? Working forward from these questions, our goal in this short chapter is not to rehash poststructural critiques of mediation that have developed through the latter half of the 20th century and continue through this day.[2] Neither do we present concepts and insights from the full range of poststructural theory that has grown through the same period of time. Rather, we rouse our propositions for continuing to attend to power in poststructural literacy research from a history of process philosophy that has moved through the philosophies of, for example, Spinoza, Whitehead, Deleuze, Guattari, and, more recently, Massumi.

Defining Key Concepts

We choose this particular line of thought for two reasons relevant to our work in this chapter. First, it has galvanized critical literacy researchers participating in a current turn to affect (Leander & Ehret, 2019). Through a Spinozaian lineage of thought, these literacy scholars, as well as the process philosophers upon whom they draw, conceptualize affect via Spinoza as bodies' emergent capacities to affect and be affected. Because it is thereby conceptualized as a dimension of life—because its force diminishes or amplifies capacities to act—affect is inherently political (Massumi, 2015b). The question is not *whether* affect is political but how ideologies inflect experience through its emergent,

DOI: 10.4324/9781003023425-47

affective dimensions. What more moving a concept could literacy researchers desire in their efforts to open potentials for youth to read, write, speak, and make media beyond the powers of conformity that may limit such potentials, that may diminish capacities for practicing literacies and using literacies to move others?

Critiques of Critical Literacies in This Domain

Second, the implicit, and often explicit (e.g., Manning, Munster & Thomsen, 2019), critique of theories of mediation that undergird critical and sociocultural theories of literacy offers an opportunity to ask what else is possible for literacy researchers interested in questions of politics and power. Outlined briefly at the beginning of the next section, we see specific concepts this critique spawned as particularly crucial at this moment in history, where power operates more and more through logics that affect fear of the uncertain futures—futures human beings face in the Anthropocene, and in relation to global migration, weaponized social media, and technologies such as AI that touch at the core of what it means to be human and humanity's potentially diminished role in our conceptions of existence. We therefore urgently review the concepts of immanence and immediation, including their relation to mediation in the next section. We use these concepts to propose one technique for attuning to power in literacy events, conceptualized poststructurally (Ehret, 2019), and to the affective conditions through which bodies practice literacy. We then bring these concepts into relation with current work in the field in order to generate propositions for pedagogy and practice more attuned to the politics of affect.

Responses to Critiques: Immanence and Immediation

> A politics of immediation orients around a concept of the political that itself must be invented anew with each occasion of experience.
>
> *(Manning, 2019, p. 10, emphasis in original)*

A process-oriented ontology of immanence posits that what exists is existing now, in the moving, decentered relations between bodies[3] affecting each other with varying degrees of intensities. In this ontology immediations may be thought of as the unpredictable gestures, made by any*body* (see again footnote 3), that inflects experience toward this or that potential. This is why Manning argues that the concept of the political must be invented anew with each occasion of experience: What gestures, right *here*, right *now*, might disrupt assumptions about what *these* racialized youth might do with their literacies in school? What gestures, right *here*, right *now*, might open new potentials for classed youth to use their literacies toward activist ends? What gestures, right *here*, right *now*, might decenter human primacy in making meaning of the environment as a problem rather than a multiplicity of bodies to live alongside? Any answer must be the gesture operating in *this* literacy event, the immediation, the thought in the act: the answer middling.

Mediation operates through a different ontology of time that places mediation "in the middle" between "cause" and "effect". In critical, sociocultural approaches to literacy studies, researchers investigate the mediating means in literacy events. We can think of this in a few ways, each of which inserts mediation into the "middle" between cause and effect: cultures and histories mediate meaning-making with texts; categories of race, gender, sexualities, and class mediate how bodies are read in particular social contexts in which they are practicing literacies. With mediation, the causes (cultures, histories, categories), indeed the politics, were already at stake before the event began, and critiquing the causes requires standing outside of the event and looking back. Mediation limits recourses for becoming-differently in the moment.

Affective Conditions for Relating to Futurity

Immanence allows us to ask how power works to maintain control in any set of emergent relations, and immediation compels us to act and to speculate conditions that mitigate power's ability to control and to determine in advance what is possible and for what bodies. A politics of immediation for literacy studies therefore asks how to create future affective conditions for more bodies, for every*body*, to move and be moved in relation to texts. In the current epoch of ontopower, where the politics of preemption dominate, never has it been more important to develop our techniques for speculating more just futures beyond the critique of just-past presents. Massumi's (2015) developed the concept of ontopower from Foucault's (1978; see also, 1977) notion of biopower. In Foucault's analysis, an era of bio-power began in the late 18th century, where power came to be exercised over the "life" of communities and individuals with the aim of either "foster[ing] [it] or disallow[ing] it to the point of death" (1978, p. 138). In an analysis of the George W. Bush administration, Massumi pushed this idea further to show how states' use nebulous threat and emergency to make a future, unrealized threat affect and control lives in the present. Massuumi's logic is: If we feel a threat, there is a threat, and therefore the irrational sense of an unreal threat can create a mechanism for social control (Imagine any number of T★★★pian threats that control policy and affect our embodied interactions).

In these current conditions, the politics of affect require relating to futurity, to the mobilization of future "facts" that affect what is possible in the present. What fears create the normative conceptions of literacy and what bodies can do with literacy?: That humanity will lose print literacy. That literacies "on screen" harm capacities for empathy. That literacies of the global south and from Indigenous communities will never be accepted as "Literacy" and so what is the point? That if we accept that literacy is a more-than-human practice, then human beings will lose their unique standing in the center of the universe. The future birth of the affective fact (Massumi, 2015a) limits the potentials for literacy, for bodies capacities to affect and to be affective through literacy events—this is the politics of affect for literacy studies.

A question that gestures toward what is possible for literacy studies beyond critical theory's mediations: How, immanently, can literacy, and literacy researchers, immediate ontopower's attempt to control potentials for more just, sustainable futures?

Implications for Research and Pedagogy: Meeting the Literature in the Middle

In the following, we take this question to current poststructural literacy research participating in the affective turn. We do so not in a review looking backward in time asking what is there, or what the literature has said. Rather, we write in relation to research that has immediated our own capacities for doing and thinking literacy differently, as well as our capacities to think how politics and power work to stifle difference through literacy events. Our review is therefore theoretically aligned with our process philosophical orientation, and it is necessarily only a partial view of the field. As we review each piece and sets of pieces, we work to relate: how does this research itself, or in relation with our present reading, produce new concepts and techniques to immediate affective conditions toward more just potentials and possibilities? We therefore hope to meet the research we review in the middle of our own experience with it and through an ethics of speculating more just, sustainable futures whenever possible.

Implications for Social Responsibility as Academics: Becoming-Otherwise

Becoming-otherwise refers to a relationality that is oriented toward futurity as opposed to a relationality already determined, fixed or idealized to fit a hegemonic norm. Extending an understanding of relationality with immanence in mind affords pedagogical potential to immediate affective conditions for justice-oriented possibilities related to students, literacies, and classrooms. An affective lens on relationality, then, works toward affective potentials seeking to disrupt the territorialized control placed on relationality through the affective fact that subsumes the workings of so many literacy classrooms.

Ehret and MacDonald (2019), for instance, refer to the minor gestures—the undercurrents always at flow—that generate relational transformation integral to literacy practice that disrupt "major infringing upon moments with students" (p. 46) that tend to over-structure human relationality, particularly in classroom spaces. In effort to open up such an imposed, limited relationality, Zapata, Van Horn, Moss, and Fugit (2019) suggest improvisational teaching as a method for creating affective conditions that build from the immanent connections of texts, bodies, and meaning moving and working to produce student learning. An improvisational method fosters the mediation of sociocultural practice yet also immediates the something more that cannot be fully represented or fully named. Through their research with middle and high school students, the interrelation of "feelings, connections, and confusion" (p. 181) produced the critical moments that made critical literacies possible. Positioning "critical literacy" as the intention or goal would not have been enough on its own to include the emerging responses that fostered critical thought. When affective potentials are overlooked or stifled, imposed control is apt to creep in.

As Zapata et al. (2019) demonstrate in their analysis, the affected and visceral moments "produced a new reality for students and new conditions of literacy possibilities" (p. 182). As students engaged with texts and current events around the killing of unarmed teenager Michael Brown and the local protests that followed, teachers leaned into improvisational teaching to be more attuned to affect as a part of students' literacies. These included embodied tensions, reflexivity on uncertainty, and listening to students. Teachers were initially worried about how to attend to affect and felt connections related to justice-oriented work—the affective fact—produced through fear, worried if there is space for such critical stances in classrooms comprised of culturally, racially, and linguistically diverse students who were already labeled as "under-performing," a worry that we believe resonates with many pedagogically. Yet they found a merging of the major and the minor: "Being with the major resources that students brought to learning not only meant reading their body language more deeply alongside their literacy work but also attending to the emotional charge produced around those resources" (p. 185), a charge inherent to relationality that flows as a minor current.

Relationality, then, extends beyond human interactions to the materials that also act on human bodies to influence how they feel, act, and make. Pushing beyond the limits of traditional writing as a linearly conceived act limited to words and paper by extending to materials that compel humans to act and make in responsive ways, poststructural literacy scholars continue to examine relationality through multimodal literacies and materials. Kuby and Rucker (2016), for instance, expand upon young children's writing through the concept of literacy desiring, examining how children become as writers through intra-activity with materials, other children, and open-ended compositional forms.

This understanding of relationality has extended into makerspaces demonstrating affect as a "becoming through modalities" (Rowsell & Shillitoe, 2019, p. 1555). Rowsell and Shillitoe examine youths' engagement with materials and how this produced craftivism with "what if" possibilities that open up potentials for activist creations and meanings. Craftivism is one way to push forward the critical potentials of affect through the interrelationality of people and materials as a way for new potentials to become-other than before. In their research, for example, youth analyzed games and created their own, moving them to consider structures of power and how they might reimagine things differently, "compelling young people to think beyond their everyday and to problematize work-place stereotypes as well as reassess their own projected futures" (p. 1557). Relationality becomes significant through the time, place, and way these things and bodies come together to create the relational becoming-other.

Sense-Making Through Felt Sensations

Becoming-otherwise through relationality, however, extends beyond bodies; it is also propelled through felt intensities. These are the felt sensations that occur before language can actually represent the feeling, yet they are embodied and experienced nonetheless. These sensations are a part of our sense-making, and thus a part of literacies, and are essential for thinking about potentials of sustainable, just futures.

Pedagogically, this means attuning to felt sensations, and how these may be produced through the literacy event (Ehret, 2019). Dutro (2013) discusses the visceral potentials moving through children's literacies, often destabilizing the structures imposed on children and what stories they are invited (or not) to tell. In her work on students' trauma and pedagogy of critical witness to these, Dutro's scholarship propels us to expect the affective in students' stories. If we know stories offer a counter-narrative, how might the non-representational support a deconstruction of power and control in the literacy classroom? Franklin-Phipps and Rath's (2018) work with pre-service teachers demonstrate the ways such emergent, sense-making practices might disrupt such norms, which in their research is framed around whiteness. They attend to affect through collage-making, and how the senses attuned to these practices might support "unsticking from whiteness and sustain a becoming racially literate" (p. 146).

Sense making through felt intensities hold implications for pedagogy related to the multimodal nature of literacies. Just as bodies form relational assemblages that produce felt effects, multiple modes are always at work in literacies producing embodied, felt intensities. Johnston (2020) referred to these sensuous flows through modes and signs as a "feeling power . . . enhanced through students' meaning-making related to their own lives" (p. 196). The felt, though not always seen, cannot be ignored as an integral aspect of literacy practices. Attuning to these felt intensities humanizes literate acts, making literacy about the people who make it what it is as opposed to being about structured practices intended to box people in or shut them out. Felt intensities are always charging through us and into the world to deconstruct, dismantle, and reconfigure the structures that continue to control, impose and limit possibilities for just futures.

Reconfiguring Power

The becoming-other relationality and felt sensations are immanently produced through literacies, potentially pushing against norms, totalities, and ideal outcomes. How do these perspectives shift practices and purposes of literacy pedagogy so that power might be worked against and reconfigured for more just, sustainable futures? Leander and Ehret (2019) urge us to consider how starting with affect to disrupt the norms that impose hegemonic structures and systems might alter how we understand the seemingly stable systems that currently work against equitable relations of power.

To reposition and reimagine race, gender, and difference in relation to literacy pedagogy, Jocson and Dixon-Román (2021) discuss racializing affect "as a sociopolitical process of hierarchizing and differentiating bodies, a process that is situated in a sociohistorical and material history of colonialism that becomes flesh shaping bodily movement and intensities" (p. X). Racializing affect attunes to the relationality produced through the Black and Brown high school girls they worked alongside as they become-technologist in a technology-based high school program. This was an act toward reconfiguring the racializing affect with technology in relation with the students and how they could become-other through their "rhythm, relationality, movement, and intensities" as they engaged with literacies in the program.

Through this example, reconfiguring power is about attending to affect to redistribute power and afford equitable futures. This involves attuning to relationality, the becoming-other that is always possible, and the felt, nonrepresentational sensations always flowing in literacies.

Recommendations for Future Research and Praxis

Inherent to the literature and implications suggested in this chapter is a teacher and researcher reflexivity on affective dimensions of literacies. This involves time, space, and informed thought to reflect on the "feeling" side of things, including felt attachments to classrooms and practices that might actually hinder students' enactments of literacies and even more so, harm vulnerable students already marginalized through normed practices (Nichols & Coleman, 2021). Humanizing literacy education with students means humanizing teachers to support them in the reflexive work of attuning to their own affectivities. This act alone is a dismantling of the control imposed on teachers' time and demands and how it should be appropriated.

For students, implications in this chapter point to a continued examination of how Black and Brown bodies racialize affect to become-other in a way that embraces all of their sociocultural resources while immanently being moved to disrupt literacy practices overcoded by whiteness. Drawing on Ehret (2019), we ask how are students' lives becoming with literacies? And how are those lives valued (or not) in this process and in spaces, such as schools? Affect affords a critical lens questioning power that limits desire and following how the amodal desire immanently immediates for a becoming-other to move beyond limitations of the "now" by what might be in the future.

Implications for Literacy Research

Orienting literacy to affect and embodiment awakens senses and practices in critical ways. As Burnett and Merchant (2018) have identified, locating affective intensities within literacy "troubles the idea of reading as individualised and transportable" and instead presents iconic literacy acts such as reading "as embedded in complex networks of people and things, as part of what happens from moment to moment" (2018, p. 67). Harking back to the history and lineages of critical literacy (Janks, 2000; Freire, 1993; Luke, 2004; Morrell, 2006) should remind us as literacy researchers that the politics of literacy is about the intensities of senses and affect. Disrupting racism, sexism, classism to name a few fundamental goals of critical literacy involve being in the middle of power imbalances and hegemonic forces to deconstruct, hopefully expose, maybe even if we are lucky, topple them. To enact political movements through literacy events means being in and of the world and pushing against the grain, the accepted, the powerful.

Turning to the world to frame things differently and to have more difficult conversations has allowed critical literacies, as a pedagogical movement, to create dialogic spaces. There is no one method for a politics of immediation within literacy studies; there are however some well-formed routes that have developed over time that identify some further implications and pathways. Classic critical literacy scholarship asks what and who gets privileged as definitions of literacy (Street, 1985). The field then moved from actions to spaces and temporal rhythms to locate power and privilege (Lemke, 2000; Leander & Sheehy, 2004). More modern renditions of power and politics in literacy scholarship has now shifted the conversation to objects, technologies, bodies, emotions, and experiences (Leander & Ehret, 2019).

Nonetheless, if we are to truly be critical as literacy researchers we need to do a better job reaching more marginalized perspectives in the global south and we need to listen far more to less visible populations of learners. Sitting and simmering beneath the surface of visible ideologies and injustices inherent to literacy are emotions such as anger, sadness, belonging, insecurities and there needs to be much greater account of these felt intensities within our work as literacy scholars attuned to power and politics. In this chapter, we called for research to open up to everything, everyone, and every moment. What are routes into these felt intensities and forms of becoming? Thinking about a seminal figure within critical literacy, Freire (1993), called on educators to read the *word* and the *world*, which ultimately entails a sharp focus on bodies' emergent capacities to affect and be affected—to live literacy as immanent and immediate.

Notes

1. For perspectives from philosophy and communication studies drawn upon in this chapter, see Massumi (2019, 2020)
2. For perspectives from philosophy and communication studies drawn upon in this chapter, see Massumi (2019, 2020)
3. We use bodies inclusively of all "things" moving in an event, including human bodies, and to avoid fixed categories of human and non-human that have histories in colonialism and categorical exclusion.

References

Burnett, C., & Merchant, G. (2018). Affective encounters: Enchantment and the possibility of reading for pleasure. *Literacy, 52*(2), 62–69. https://doi.org/10.1111/lit.12144

Dutro, E. (2013). Towards a pedagogy of the incomprehensible: Trauma and the imperative of critical witness in literacy classrooms. *Pedagogies: An International Journal, 8*(4), 301–315.

Ehret, C. (2019). Propositions from affect theory for feeling literacy through the event. In D. E. Alvermann, N. J. Unrau, M. Sailors, & R. Ruddell (Eds.), *Theoretical models and processes of literacy* (pp. 563–581). Routledge.

Ehret, C., & MacDonald, R. (2019). How minor gestures generate relational transformations in the act of literacy teaching and learning. *Affect, Embodiment, and Place in Critical Literacy: Assembling Theory and Practice, 43*.

Foucault, M. (1977). *Discipline and punish: The birth of the prison* (A. Sheridan, Trans). Vintage.

Foucault, M. (1978). *The history of sexuality, volume 1: An introduction* (R. Hurley, Trans). Vintage.

Franklin-Phipps, A., & Rath, C. L. (2018). Collage pedagogy: Toward a posthuman racial literacy. In *Posthumanism and literacy education* (pp. 142–155). Routledge.

Freire, P. (1993 [1970]). *Pedagogy of the oppressed*. Continuum.

Janks, H. (2000). Domination, access, diversity and design: A synthesis for critical literacy education. *Educational Review, 52*(2), 175–186.

Jocson, K. M., & Dixon-Román, E. J. (2021). Becoming Shuri: CTE, racializing affect, and the becoming-technologist. *Reading Research Quarterly, 56*(2), 257–271.

Johnston, K. C. (2020). Tapping into the feeling power: Considering the affordances of the affective nature of multimodal literacies. *Language Arts, 97*(3), 194–197.

Kuby, C. R., & Rucker, T. G. (2016). *Go be a writer! Expanding the curricular boundaries of literacy learning with children*. Teachers College Press.

Leander, K. M., & Boldt, G. (2013). Rereading "A pedagogy of multiliteracies" bodies, texts, and emergence. *Journal of Literacy Research, 45*(1), 22–46.

Leander, K. M., & Ehret, C. (Eds.). (2019). *Affect in literacy learning and teaching: Pedagogies, politics and coming to know*. Routledge.

Leander, K. M., & Sheehy, M. (Eds.). (2004). *Spatializing literacy research and practice*. Peter Lang.

Lemke, J. L. (2000). Across the scales of time: Artifacts, activities and meanings in ecosocial systems, *Mind, Culture and Activity, 7*(4), 273–290.

Luke, A. (2004). Two takes on the critical. In B. Norton & K. Toohey (Eds.), *Critical pedagogies and language learning* (pp. 21–29). Cambridge University Press.

Manning, E. (2019). Toward a Politics of Immediation. *Frontiers in Sociology, 3*, 42.

Manning, E. (2020). *For a pragmatics of the useless*. Duke University Press.

Manning, E., Munster, A., & Thomsen, B. M. S. (2019). *Immediation*. Open Humanities Press.

Massumi, B. (2015a). *Ontopower: War, powers, and the state of perception*. Duke University Press.

Massumi, B. (2015b). *Politics of affect*. Polity Press.

Massumi, B. (2019). Immediation unlimited. In E. Manning, A. Munster & B. M. S Thomsen, *Immediation II* (pp. 501–543). Open Humanities Press.

Morrell, E. (2006). Critical participatory action research and the literacy achievement of ethnic minority youth, in J. V. Hoffman, D. L. Schallert, C. M. Fairbanks, J. Worthy, & B. Maloch (Eds.), *55th Annual Yearbook of the National Reading Conference*. Oak Creek, WI: National Reading Conference.

Nichols, T. P., & Coleman, J. J. (2021). Feeling worlds: Affective imaginaries and the making of democratic literacy classrooms. *Reading Research Quarterly, 56*(2), 315–335.

Rowsell, J., & Shillitoe, M. (2019). The craftivists: Pushing for affective, materially informed pedagogy. *British Journal of Educational Technology, 50*(4), 1544–1559.

Street, B. (1985). *Literacy in theory and practice*. Cambridge University Press.

Zapata, A., Van Horn, S., Moss, D., & Fugit, M. (2019). Improvisational teaching as being with: Cultivating a relational presence toward justice-oriented literacies. *Journal of Adolescent & Adult Literacy, 63*(2), 179–187.

3.13

THE SITUATIONAL IN CRITICAL LITERACY

Catarina Schmidt, Ninni Wahlström, and Amy Vetter

Introduction

In this study, we draw from pragmatism and transactional realism to conceptualize the meaning of critical literacy. As Sundström Sjödin (2019) writes, "[t]he critical stands for moments which are radical and urgent, political, challenging, transformative and liberating" (p. 87). Transactional realism refers to John Dewey's version of realism, in which realism is experienced as a function of the organism–environment transaction (Biesta & Burbules, 2003). The aim of this chapter is to contribute to expanding the meaning of critical literacy in line with, for example, "reconstruction" (Janks, 2010, p. 19), "access and equity" (Luke, 2000, p. 459) or critical literacy as "embodied" (Johnson & Vasudevan, 2012, p. 34) to also include the unforeseen critical moments occurring in oral and written text situations in classrooms. These critical moments are not planned beforehand; rather, these moments emerge through interactions in the environment constituted by the teacher, the students, the teaching content, and physical objects. We argue that a transactional understanding of text situations is helpful to understand how certain situations turn into "critical moments"; that is, when students pay attention to critical aspects in text situations and act upon it. Such moments can be acknowledged, rejected, or go unnoticed by the teacher. Such critical thinking and acting might increase possibilities for equity and justice within society, resisting what Freire (1970) referred to as the culture of silence.

In this chapter, we describe how this "renewed" concept of critical literacy can be understood as critical moments. We ask: What kinds of critical situated moments appear and what characterizes these critical situated moments? In the following sections, we present current interpretations of critical literacy and perspectives on critical literacy in relation to pragmatism and transactional realism. Next, we outline the methodology and analysis of the situated moments of critical literacy within two classrooms. Lastly, we present the findings and discussion.

Current Interpretations of Critical Literacy

Reading texts in critically reflective ways relates to the field of critical literacy (CL) (e.g. Janks, 2010; Comber, 2013; Lankshear & McLaren, 1993). CL is solidly grounded within classroom practices and closely connected to New Literacy Studies (NLS), where literacy is and has been studied as situated within social practices (e.g. Barton, 1994; Heath, 1983; Rowsell & Pahl, 2007). To help students critically examine textual information, teachers must help students learn how to recognize

DOI: 10.4324/9781003023425-48

and investigate issues of power within texts and to use their existing and new discourse resources for social exchange in the social fields where texts and discourses matter (Luke, 2004). According to Janks (2010), critical literacy work means holding the interdependent elements of power, access, diversity, and design in productive tension. The concept of power highlights the dominant discourses which a certain text represents, produces and distributes, and which might have both positive and negative consequences for different individuals (Foucault, 1978). The concept of access raises the question of which texts students have access to and should have access to in various social practices. Diversity, according to Janks (2010), involves reading and writing in the broadest sense, including a variety of semiotic systems and modalities, but also a multiplicity regarding social identities, languages, literacies, and cultures. Redesign in this context refers to processes involving reflections about the design of the content of texts as well as about underlying conditions, like senders and their motives. Comber (2013) argues that critical approaches with the goal of redesign involve moving "between micro features of texts and the macro conditions of institutions, focusing upon how relations of power work through these practices" (p. 589). Recently, the concept of critical literacy has been expanded to recognize how texts and responses are embodied (Johnson & Vasudevan, 2012), how the critical in text situations can be analyzed as transactional effects in the assemblages of heterogeneous actors (e.g. individuals, signs, and material objects) (Sundström Sjödin, 2019; Leander & Burriss, 2020).

Educators have provided critiques of critical literacy over the years (Bacon, 2018; Behrman, 2006; Luke & Woods, 2009). Consistently, there have been questions about how critical literacy affects classroom-based instructional decisions, including consistent teaching strategies that apply the theory into practice (Behrman, 2006). Scholars argue that teachers should not use a set of strategies to foster critical literacy in their classroom (Luke, 2000; McLaughlin & DeVoogd, 2004) and Comber (2001) stated that "critical literacy needs to be continually redefined in practice" (p. 100). Other criticisms include critical literacy's tendency to situate the teacher as the critical conscious hero whose job is to enlighten and empower students (Luke & Woods, 2009). In addition, some educators experience pressures of high-stakes exams and scripted curriculum that hinder the integration of critical literacy into their classrooms. Overall, teachers and students tend to engage in the following practices when engaging in critical literacy: (1) reading supplementary texts, (2) reading multiple texts, (3) reading from a resistant perspective, (4) producing countertexts, (5) conducting student-choice research projects, and (6) taking social action (Behrman, 2006). All of these practices require conversations about critical issues. Navigating those conversations can be difficult and include tensions related to silences from students and teacher (Castagno, 2008; Haddix, 2012; San Pedro, 2015), dichotomizing of truth versus falsehood over substantive power-analysis (Bacon, 2018), difficulty recognizing underlying systems of oppression (DiAngelo, 2018; Schaffer & Skinner, 2009), and a desire to maintain "safe" spaces that inhibit the brave and courageous work needed in critical literacy (Arao & Clemens, 2013; Leonardo & Porter, 2010; Staley & Leonardi, 2016). Thus, more research needs to be done to unpack how critical literacy occurs during classroom interactions in classrooms.

Critical Literacy as Critical Moments

The case for examining critical literacy as critical moments stems from a broader framework of study that argues for the importance of paying attention to improvised interactions in relation to learning and development (Cole & Engeström, 1993; Erickson, 2004; Vygotsky, 1997). Specifically, research has illustrated that classroom interactions are the medium by which teaching and learning occurs (Cazden, 1988) and shape how students situate themselves as learners within a classroom (Bloome et al., 2008). Critical discourse analysis has also shaped this area of study by examining interactions at the meso-, macro-, and micro-level in ways that focus on how talk and text operate in relationship to power, with a goal of fostering positive social change (Fairclough & Wodak, 1997; Rogers, 2011; Van dijk, 2015).

Thus, the way humans interact with their environment is through communication. Language and communication have implications on other events, "physical and human, giving them meaning or significance" (Dewey, 1929/1958, p. 173). Transactional realism, then, is a helpful theoretical perspective for understanding how humans and non-humans are affecting one another, and for creating space and forms of expressions for critical literacy in classrooms. Dewey's philosophy goes beyond a dualism of subject and object by asserting that our knowledge of the world is both constructed and "real," because it is constructed through human communication in an environment of human and nonhuman objects (Biesta & Burbules, 2003). The core concept in this integrated view of subject and object is experience. Transaction implies that we, as well as teachers and their students, are always settled in relation to our experiences. Such experiencing includes processes of thinking, or what Dewey termed reflective inquiry. Reflective forms of thinking "transforms confusion, ambiguity and discrepancy into illumination, definiteness and consistency" (Dewey, 1929/1958, p. 67). Since knowledge is understood as a relation between actions and consequences, there is a temporal dimension in a pragmatism understanding of experience (Biesta, 2014). Environment is not a stable place; instead, the environment is shaped by what matters to an individual.

This focus opens up an understanding of the situation as performative, that is, not assuming beforehand what becomes important. Moreover, every situation has a potential for change, both regarding the individual and his or her environment (Sundström Sjödin & Wahlström, 2017). The potentiality of a situation, formed by an individual's interaction with matters of concern, which defines the environment, offers an analytic framework for perceiving occurrences when text situations become critical. From this perspective, what is critical in literacy cannot be assumed on beforehand. Instead, "the critical" emerges in situations where the critical is experienced and felt by the students. Such an understanding implies a displacement from critical literacy to when literacy becomes critical (Sundström Sjödin, 2019).

Teachers' ways of talking and of organizing classroom conversations have an impact on their student's possibilities of participation and development of critical thinking. Drawing on Alexander's (2001, 2008) data regarding international classroom discourse, recitation is the overall dominant category of teaching talk, i.e. sequences of teacher-led questions and answers to explore students' knowledge or gain new knowledge. At the same time, Alexander (2001, 2008) stresses teacher-led discussions (exchange of ideas and shared information) and dialogues (achievement of common understanding through structured conversation and questioning) as crucial for students' learning. The importance of discussions and dialogue is highlighted by Alexander (2008), because these categories of teaching talk are equivalent to what he apprehends as transformation. Transformation refers to how students are supported in learning to reflect and develop as people and as such revise knowledge or solve problems. Such transformation, as a consequence of education, relates to highly qualitative and complex aspects of teaching and learning, where dialogue and active use of content and language become crucial (Cummins, 2001; Schmidt & Skoog, 2018). However, fostering critical literacy moments through talk, or critical conversations, is complex and requires sophisticated practices from teachers. For example, research with teachers learning to better foster critical conversations with high school students in the United States (Schieble, Vetter, & Martin, 2020) showed that teachers needed to engage in five interrelated concepts to be prepared: (a) knowledge about power (Foucault, 1978), (b) critical self-reflection (Sensoy & DiAngelo, 2017), (c) critical pedagogy (Freire, 1970; Lankshear & McLaren, 1993), (d) vulnerability (Sensoy & DiAngelo, 2017), and (e) critical talk moves (Thomas, 2013, 2015). These concepts illustrate the complexity involved in preparing and maintaining critical conversations with students. The examples of classroom talk in the next section is organized through whole class talk, and appear mainly through sequences of the teacher's posed questions and/or comments, followed by the students answers and/or comments. However, we will examine to what extent the teacher's recitation opens up opportunities for critically situated moments. In these moments, the teachers partly take on the role of being an explorer of what the students know, think, and understand of what is being discussed in the classroom (Wahlström, 2018).

Two Examples From Classroom Research

We include examples from two classrooms. In the first, data sources include 12 video recorded lessons and field notes collected over one year (2015–2016) from one Swedish classroom with 23 students in Grade 6. In the second, our data included 10 audio recorded lessons and field notes collected over one year (2016–2017) from one U.S. classroom with 28 students in Grade 10. Drawing on the video observations and field notes from the classroom conversations and the teaching content described in the following, we investigate what kinds of critical moments appear during whole class interactions and what characterizes these moments. In the analysis, we draw on transactional realism and, in relation to the identified critical moments of teachers of teacher and student talk, explore in what text situations literacy becomes "critical."

Critically Situated Moments—Information and Commercials

The teaching content was focused on how to critically examine television advertisements. During some lessons, the teacher and the students watched eight video clips. Between these clips, the students were encouraged to discuss in pairs regarding the sender and the message behind the ads with the aim of developing source criticism. The discussions in pairs were followed by whole-class conversations regarding the content in each video, including a discussion about the target audience and the use of persuasive techniques. One video that was discussed was the Volvo commercial (2019) in which the Swedish football player Zlatan recites the Swedish national anthem.

Sequence 1

TEACHER: Well, then one might wonder, Volvo that is so big, why do they have to take on a person like Zlatan?

TIM: Because they can.

TEACHER: It is a Swedish company and he is Swedish, yes. Do you think more people will buy Volvo cars?

TIM: Zlatan chooses Volvo and other brands, yes I want Volvo as well, I want to be as Zlatan!

TEACHER: But he never sings [referring to the Swedish national anthem] otherwise.

REBECCA: But he does sing the anthem [referring to the commercial].

In this recitation event, the supposed aspect of being critical is to take a critical stance on advertisements. However, what becomes important in this situation is not the Volvo advertisement as such, but the question of identity and who is considered Swedish. It is the teacher who more or less consciously creates the critical moment by questioning the involvement of "a person like Zlatan." The teacher does not introduce the Swedish football player as a famous person, but as a "Swedish person." Next, the teacher notes that Zlatan does not participate when the Swedish team sings the national anthem. This comment reinforces the theme on national identity, against a Swedish social background of the spread of a xenophobic view that Zlatan is "not really" Swedish. Zlatan, although born in Sweden, has parents who are Bosnian and Croatian. Tim, who thinks of Zlatan as an admired football player, whom he wants to be like, does not notice the critical moment. Instead, it is Rebecka who draws attention to the implied aspect and takes a stance; she notes that Zlatan recites the national anthem in the commercials, although not singing, and ends the underlying discussion (he recites the anthem, thus, he is Swedish). It is an irony that the brand of Volvo is still unreflectively considered Swedish, even though the company has Chinese owners. People's national identity is, by contrast, an ever-present issue, not the least on social media, a fact that Zlatan himself is aware of. In one of the largest Swedish daily newspapers (Svenska Dagbladet, 2014), Zlatan comments on his recitation of the anthem: "I do not talk perfect Swedish, but this is how it is" and continues:

> I can be Swedish anyway. We are all different but anyway alike. Dad is from Bosnia and Muslim. Mum is from Croatia and Catholic. But I am born in Sweden and a Swedish citizen. This is not changeable.
>
> *(Translated from Swedish by the authors)*

In the classroom, the aforementioned contextualization is not made clear. The students do not get access to the background information about Zlatan, and as a result, do not fully understand the teacher's comment that "he never sings otherwise." In addition, a third of the students in this class-room have a similar background as Zlatan, in terms of being children to migrants. These students remain silent, a pattern that is visible throughout the school year. In fact, it is mainly boys, most often Tim and Bill, and a few girls that participate during whole class conversations.

Drawing on the conversation that is framed by the teacher's recitation, the students seem to be aware of masked advertising as well as the dubious trustworthiness of various ads. One student says, for example: "That Red Bull gives you wings is rather exaggerated." The teacher draws on this utterance, saying: "One shall not make use of you as consumers to buy an item because you do not understand better." Then the teacher continues, adding social possibilities of diverse identities: "Not degrading someone because of gender, looks, ethnicity or age."

Critically Situated Moments—Deconstructing Masculinity

In this discussion, a high school English teacher in the U.S. asked students to examine masculinity to better understand Okonkwo in the novel *Things Fall Apart* by Chinua Achebe. After being asked to make a list of "manly" characteristics, several students shared that they wrote down physical strength. In response, Sarah argued that some women are physically stronger than men and reminded the class that strength can also be emotional. The teacher responded with a clarification question, as seen in the following.

Sequence 2

TEACHER: So are you saying that a characteristic of a man might be that he is emotionally weak?

SARAH: Not really emotionally weak, but say he is. Okonkwo didn't have a good relationship with his dad, so he is trying to fill that void with his famous lifestyle and money and wives. So, he is trying to fill that part in his heart, I guess you could say, where his dad didn't say it.

TEACHER: Okay. So, are you saying that a woman who had a similar issue with her dad or her mom—she doesn't want to be like her dad or her mom—would respond differently than Okonkwo because women respond differently to emotion? [Sarah indicates that she is not ready to answer. The teacher calls on Earl.]

EARL: Someone who is so comfortable with his manhood is able to go outside of his comfort zone. Like playing an instrument . . . I think that someone who is able to step outside of their comfort zone is considered to be more manly than someone who is afraid.

TEACHER: Okay. And I think that Mr. W. mentioned this idea of ancient Greeks and even this idea of the Renaissance. You were manly if you were able to do all of this creative stuff and that is what defined manhood and many of us might have a very different idea about that. That was how it used to be.

THAD: I don't think he (Okonkwo) can be considered a man because a man does not cover up situations he can't face. I just think that a man doesn't cover up his problems; he faces them.

TEACHER: So, you are saying that Okonkwo is not a man?

THAD: I wasn't saying that. I just think that a man doesn't cover up his problems; he faces them.

TEACHER: Okay. And you think that Okonkwo is doing some of the things he does to cover up things that he is afraid of. Can you think of something specifically?

THAD: Most of the time when people are confident or cocky, they are trying to hide something.

TEACHER: So, by definition, you are saying that people who do that are not manly?

THAD: I'm not saying that, well . . .

SARAH: These questions are so hard to answer.

In this transcript, the teacher asked students to engage in a critical conversation by challenging them to make sense of manliness as it relates to their own experience and the experience of Okonkwo. Throughout the conversation, the teacher and students engaged in a similar discourse pattern that included students sharing multiple perspectives about masculinity that tended to be static (i.e., all men are . . .). In response, the teacher asked clarification questions to help students deconstruct their ideas of masculinity. For example, at the beginning of the excerpt, the teacher asked Sarah if she intended to say that all men are emotionally weak. In response, Sarah clarified and related her comment to Okonkwo. As a result, students shared differing perspectives about manliness. For example, Earl stated that manhood meant not being afraid to step outside of stereotypes. Thad added another perspective by saying that a man faces his problems and related that statement to Okonkwo's experience. In response, the teacher pressed Thad by asking him to clarify his responses about what it means to be a man. At this point, Thad ("I'm not saying that, well") and Sarah ("These questions are so hard to answer") express a *critical moment* when they begin to realize how problematic it can be to develop a fixed definition of masculinity and then use that definition to label someone a man (or not). This critical moment, then, was an unexpected shift for Thad and Sarah who started to question their previously confident responses. Throughout the rest of the discussion, the teacher and students continued to deconstruct masculinity and as a result, reconstructed what it meant to them in relation to the character in *Things Fall Apart*.

Limitations and Opportunities—Critical Literacy as Critical Moments

Janks (2010), who is a prominent researcher in the field of critical literacy, claims that critical literacy is focused on power and on the unraveling of social dominance and injustice in literacy practices. This interpretation represents the mainstream in critical literacy. Critical literacy as critical moments does not object to this main focus of critical literacy; however, it shifts the focus to "burning" situations that arise in the moment (Sundström & Sjödin, 2019). Such moments are unpredictable and hard to catch; yet, they express a matter of potential controversy, intuitively perceived by one or more of the actors in the specific situation. As researchers, we can observe such moments in how students indicate a question in passing, shift the perspective in a recitation or dialogic situation, or express critical moments with the body. Because of their unpredictability, these moments are difficult for teachers to capture and exploit to address urgent issues in a common discussion. Thus, critical literacy as emerging critical moments is about approach, rather than method. However, these moments are invaluable because they are visible evidence of how students actually interact with their environment when they experience it as urgent. If these moments are met with inattention or silence, a fledgling of engagement risks being lost. While critical literacy in a more traditional understanding is easier for teachers to plan, conduct, and evaluate, critical literacy as critical moments are important for teachers who strive to make the classroom a critical environment for the students.

Implications for Pedagogy and Research

Classroom research offers striking examples of situated critical moments, characterized by elusive critical issues, in whole class situations of recitations and dialogues. If critical literacy researchers direct their attention to these situated critical moments occurring in daily classroom conversations, such moments can be identified, analyzed and conceptualized to, in turn, help teachers to become attentive to these critical situations and their inherent potential. Thus, educators would benefit from seeing more examples of what it looks like to navigate these critical moments during classroom discussion. In addition, more research is needed in relation to specific analytic guides that teachers could use as tools to examine critical moments in conversations.

The potential consists in the authenticity of the students' comments or questions. The spontaneity that characterizes these moments are derived from an instantaneous critical observation that raises the student's genuine interest in the issue. In practice, this means that teachers might need to let go of what was planned for the lesson and instead take up a critical moment that students share. The second implication is a need to broaden the learners' repertoires for partaking. To participate is not necessarily to formulate an answer or utter an opinion. Participation might also be to think, listen, reflect, agree, or disagree, with others' views. As Schultz (2009) points out, learning occurs in classrooms through both silence and talk. There are various ways to participate in teaching situations, provided the different approaches are intentional. The task of the teacher is to create safe or brave spaces for students to take part. Finally, students would benefit from follow-up questions from teachers that encourage them to develop their thoughts in critical and reflective ways.

Conclusions

The term of "transaction" denotes that experiences are not merely inner activities that individuals undergo; experiences also have an active side which, to some extent, has an impact on the environment (Dewey, 1916/2008). This means that one student's genuine experience has the potential to influence the learning environment for the other students. Authentic reflective experiences might challenge and inspire other students to pose critical questions, thereby creating an active space for joint exploratory conversations. Situated critical moments in everyday classroom conversations are elusive and quickly passed by. However, if captured in the current situation, these moments have a genuine potential to encourage students to think critically.

References

Alexander, R. (2001). *Culture and pedagogy: International comparisons in primary education.* Blackwell.

Alexander, R. (2008). *Essays on pedagogy.* Routledge.

Arao, B., & Clemens, K. (2013). From safe spaces to brave spaces. In L. M. Landreman (Ed.), *The art of effective facilitation* (pp. 135–150). Stylus.

Bacon, C. K. (2018). Appropriated literacies: The paradox of critical literacies, policies, and methodologies in a post-truth era. *Education Policy Analysis Archives, 26*, 147.

Barton, D. (1994). *Literacy. An introduction to the ecology of written language.* Blackwell Publishers Ltd.

Behrman, E. H. (2006). Teaching about language, power, and text: A review of classroom practices that support critical literacy. *Journal of Adolescent & Adult Literacy, 49*(6), 490–498.

Biesta, G. (2014). Pragmatising the curriculum: Bringing knowledge back into the Bloome, D., Carter, S. P., Christian, B. M., Madrid, S., Otto, S., Shuart-Faris, N., & Smith, M. (2008). *On discourse analysis in classrooms: Approaches to language and literacy research.* Teachers College Press.

Biesta, G., & Burbules, N. C. (2003). *Pragmatism and educational research.* Rowman & Littlefield.

Castagno, A. E. (2008). "I don't want to hear that!": Legitimating whiteness through silence in schools. *Anthropology & Education Quarterly, 39*(3), 314–333.

Cazden, C. B. (1988). *Classroom discourse: The language of teaching and learning.* curriculum conversation, but via pragmatism. *The Curriculum Journal, 25*, 29–49.

Cole, M., & Engeström, Y. (1993). A cultural-historical approach to distributed cognition. *Distributed Cognitions: Psychological and Educational Considerations*, 1–46.

Comber, B. (2001). Classroom explorations in critical literacy. In H. Fehring & P. Green (Eds.), *Critical literacy: A collection of articles from the Australian Literacy Educators' Association* (pp. 90–102). International Reading Association.

Comber, B. (2013). Critical literacy in the early years: Emergence and sustenance in an age of accountability. In J. Larson & J. Marsh (Eds.), *The SAGE handbook of early childhood literacy* (pp. 587–601). Sage/Paul Chapman.

Cummins, J. (2001). *Negotiating identities: Education for empowerment in a diverse society* (2nd ed.). California Association for Bilingual Education.

Dewey, J. (1929/1958). *Experience and nature*. Dover Publications.

Dewey, J. (1916/2008). Democracy and education. In J. A. Boydston (Ed.), *John Dewey: The middle works, 1899–1924* (Vol. 9, pp. 3–355). Southern Illinois University Press.

DiAngelo, R. (2018). *White fragility: Why it's so hard for White people to talk about racism*. Beacon Press.

Erickson, F. (2004). *Talk and social theory*. Polity Press.

Fairclough, N., & Wodak, R. (1997). Critical discourse analysis. In T. van Dijk (Ed.), *Discourse as social interaction* (pp. 258–284). Sage.

Foucault, M. (1978). *The history of sexuality* (Vol. 1). Penguin.

Freire, P. (1970). *Pedagogy of the Oppressed*. Penguin Books.

Haddix, M. (2012). Talkin in the company of sistas: The counterlanguages and deliberate silences of Black female students in teacher education. *Linguistics and Education, 23*(2), 169–181.

Heath, B. S. (1983). *Ways with words. Language, life and work in communities and classrooms*. Cambridge University Press.

Janks, H. (2010). *Literacy and power*. Routledge.

Johnson, E., & Vasudevan, L. (2012). Seeing and hearing students' lived and embodied critical literacy practices. *Theory Into Practice, 51*, 34–41.

Lankshear, C., & McLaren, L. P. (1993). *Critical literacy. Politics, praxis, and the postmodern*. SUNY Press.

Leander, K. M., & Burriss, S. K. (2020). Critical literacy for a posthuman world: When people read, and become, with machines. *British Journal of Educational Technology, 51*(4), 1262–1276.

Leonardo, Z., & Porter, R. K. (2010). Pedagogy of fear: Toward a Fanonian theory of "safety" in race dialogue. *Race Ethnicity and Education, 13*(2), 139–157.

Luke, A. (2000). Critical literacy in Australia: A matter of context and standpoint. *Journal of Adolescent & Adult Literacy, 43*, 448–461.

Luke, A. (2004). On the material consequences of literacy. *Language and Education, 18*(4), 331–335.

Luke, A., & Woods, A. F. (2009). Critical literacies in schools: A primer. *Voices from the Middle, 17*(2), 9–18.

McLaughlin, M., & DeVoogd, G. (2004). Critical literacy as comprehension: Expanding reader response. *Journal of Adolescent & Adult Literacy, 48*, 52–62.

Rogers, R. (2011). *An introduction to critical discourse analysis in education*. Routledge.

Rowsell, J., & Pahl, K. (2007). Sedimented identities in texts: Instance of practice. *Reading Research Quarterly, 42*(3), 388–401.

San Pedro, T. J. (2015). Silence as shields: Agency and resistances among Native American students in the urban southwest. *Research in the Teaching of English, 50*(2), 132–153.

Schaffer, R., & Skinner, D. G. (2009). Performing race in four culturally diverse fourth grade classrooms: Silence, race talk, and the negotiation of social boundaries. *Anthropology & Education Quarterly, 40*(3), 277–296.

Schieble, M., Vetter, A., & Martin, K. M. (2020). *Classroom talk for social change: Critical conversations in English language arts*. Teachers College Press.

Schmidt, C., & Skoog, M. (2018). The question of teaching talk. Targeting diversity and participation. In N. Wahlström & D. Sundberg (Eds.), *Transnational curriculum Standards and classroom practices. The new meaning of teaching* (pp. 81–97). Routledge.

Schultz, K. (2009). *Rethinking classroom participation: Listening to silent voices*. Teachers College Press.

Sensoy, O., & DiAngelo, R. (2017). *Is everyone really equal? An introduction to key concepts in social justice education*. Teachers College Press.

Staley, S., & Leonardi, B. (2016). Leaning into discomfort: Preparing literacy teachers for gender and sexual diversity. *Research in the Teaching of English, 51*(2), 209–229.

Sundström Sjödin, E. (2019). *Where is the critical in literacy? Tracing performances of literature reading, readers and non-readers in educational practice*. Örebro Studies in Educational Sciences with an Emphasis on Didactics, 8: Örebro University.

Sundström Sjödin, E., & Wahlström, N. (2017). Enacted realities in teachers' experiences: Bringing materialism into pragmatism. *Journal of Curriculum Studies, 49*(1), 96–110.

Svenska Dagbladet. (2014, January 24). Zlatan sågar nationalsången [Zlatan disrespect the national anthem]. Retrieved February 16, 2020, from www.svd.se/zlatan-sagar-nationalsangen.

Thomas, E. E. (2013). Dilemmatic conversations: Some challenges of culturally responsive discourse in a high school English classroom. *Linguistics and Education, 24*(3), 328–347.

Thomas, E. E. (2015). "We always talk about race": Navigating race talk dilemmas in the teaching of literature. *Research in the Teaching of English*, 154–175.

van Dijk, T. A. (2015). Critical discourse analysis. In D. Tannen, H. E. Hamilton, & D. Schiffrin (Eds.), *The handbook of discourse analysis* (pp. 466–485). John Wiley & Sons.

Volvo. (2019). *Du gamla du fria*. Retrieved from www.youtube.com/watch?v=_bFM4KSJSyo [retrieved 2019–12–22].

Vygotsky, L. (1997). *The collected works of L. S. Vygotsky (Volume 4: The history of the development of higher mental functions)* (M. Hall, Trans.). Plenum. (Complete Russian edition published in 1987).

Wahlström, N. (2018). When transnational curriculum policy reaches classrooms—teaching as directed exploration. *Journal of Curriculum Studies, 50*(5), 654–668.

3.14

SUPPORTING CRITICAL LITERACIES THROUGH CULTURALLY SUSTAINING PEDAGOGY WITHIN YOUTH-LED SPACES

Casey Philip Wong and Tanja Burkhard

Setting the Stage and Defining Key Concepts

When Paris (2012) first invoked culturally sustaining pedagogy (CSP), he defined his conceptualization as an extension of Ladson-Billings' (1995) culturally relevant pedagogy. CSP was a change in "stance, terminology, and practice" with the "explicit goal [of] supporting multilingualism and multiculturalism in practice and perspective for students and teachers" (p. 95). Paris (2012) sought to push forward his argument that culturally relevant pedagogy had often been misapplied in disservice to the vision laid out by Ladson-Billings (1995). The goal of CSP was for teachers to go beyond merely being relevant and responsive to the languages and cultures of students to teach U.S. state-sanctioned curricula. Rather, Paris (2012) argued for valuing, perpetuating, and fostering the languages and cultures of students and communities as goods unto themselves, for the purpose of building toward a more socially just society and future.

Building on emerging and intergenerational theorizing from Black, Indigenous, Latinx, Asian, Pacific Islander, and intersecting and overlapping communities of color, CSP has come to invoke the White and hegemonic gazes to describe the figurative and literal violence and influence that emerge from the institutions and relations of respectively White supremacy and interlocking systems of oppression. The White and hegemonic gazes discipline and/or eliminate people depending on their identified structural position within European-rooted social hierarchies in order to accumulate capital, land, life, and/or increased influence for those elevated as socially, culturally, linguistically, and/or biologically superior. Accordingly, Alim, Paris, and Wong (2020) invoked CSP as "necessarily and fundamentally a critical, anti-racist, anti-colonial framework that rejects the white settler capitalist gaze and the kindred cisheteropatriarchal, English-monolingual, ableist, classist, xenophobic and other hegemonic gazes."

Decentering the White and hegemonic gazes has become the critical literacies project of CSP, whereby critical literacies can be defined in the manner elucidated by Freire (1985):

> reading the world is not only preceded by reading the word, but also by a certain form of writing it or rewriting it. In other words, of transforming it by means of conscious practical action . . . this dynamic movement is central to literacy.
>
> *(p. 18)*

DOI: 10.4324/9781003023425-49

For CSP, the ultimate goal becomes developing critical literacies that understand personal liberation as inseparable from collective liberation. Collective liberation *decenters* the White and hegemonic gazes in favor of *centering*, sustaining, and building socially just communities; communities that cooperatively strive for joy, love, pleasure, hope, and freedom from oppression and suffering, which is only possible together (Wong, 2019). Bearing in mind this genealogy of CSP, and its relation to understandings of critical literacy and collective liberation, we return to how educational researchers and community-rooted educators alike have "always already" been concerned with questions about who decides how and what education should take place in our spaces of teaching and learning (Simpson, 2014).

In this chapter we draw on teaching, learning, and research within the One World[2] after-school program at a large suburban high school in the Northeastern region of the U.S. nation-state. We generatively take on how difficult the CSP project of supporting critical literacies can be in educational practice as we aim to sustain youth and communities. Specifically, we examine the role of adults within *youth-led* and *transnational* educational spaces as deserving of attention and critical inquiry (i.e. "adult ally" within the One World program, what we refer to as a "lifeway sustainer" within the realm of CSP). We question what it means to enact CSP to decenter the White and hegemonic gazes, and reflect upon how power was spoken about, felt, enacted, and imagined. We aim to push forward what it means to engage in decentering as a process rather than as a stance, considering how pedagogical theory often neglects the real-time social exchanges that result in contested visions of collective liberation.

So How Do We Decenter?: Loving Critique of Culturally Sustaining Pedagogy's Engagement With Critical Literacies and Transnational Systems of Oppression

Ten students in the One World after-school program sit together at four square tables in Wright High School's library. One of the student facilitators for the week hands out a picture. Each group discusses what they see. One student ("Amita") stands up. She holds a childhood picture of Damba Koroma of Sierra Leone for all to see. Amita lets the group know that Damba is a student whose arm was cut off by rebels. Her emotion is palpable. Amita movingly explains how the picture touched her. She explains that although she has not lost a limb, the picture compelled her to reflect on the loss of her childhood. Before migrating to the United States, Amita too had spent years living in refugee camps. Then, she and her family moved about in the United States until she eventually moved to the school district that serves Wright High. The room grows quiet. Following Amita's testimony, a White student walks over and embraces her tearfully.

After Tanja observed the exchange described in the previous vignette, she was left wondering about the politics of this after-school space, one of 23 chapters of the One World program. The One World program was lovingly founded by Sarah, a student at a different high school, and taken up by students at "Wright High School" in 2017. Tanja was a postdoctoral fellow working at a nearby university and had been invited to join as an "adult ally." Within this chapter of One World, Tanja took on the role of a culturally sustaining pedagogue and lifeway sustainer (Alim et al., 2020). Accessing her pedagogical expertise and experiences as a Transnational Black Feminist scholar (Burkhard, 2018), Tanja aimed to sustain, revitalize, and support the evolving knowledges and practices that the young people used to decenter the White gaze as they "read the word and world" (Freire, 1985).

Since The One World program was student created and led, Tanja did her best to honor the sanctity of the students' autonomy and purpose for coming together. Each week, the students met to understand and question the attitudes, values, and beliefs of written, visual, and spoken texts about global issues, including wealth inequality, migration, and issues of human rights and injustice. However, it must be noted that the founder, Sarah, primarily created One World for students to have an opportunity to cross institutional barriers, get to know each other, and build friendships that extended beyond the confines of their classrooms, which were often insulated from each other. This was felt as particularly needed by students at Wright High School.

Wright High School was socially and structurally managed such that students classified as "English Language Learners" (ELL) hardly, if ever, interacted with students who were tested and reclassified as no longer ELL. This was also the case for students in "mainstream" classes who rarely engaged with students who attended English as a Second Language (ESL) courses. Wright High School maintained a *de facto* segregation and tracking of its students.

In this way, nationality and migration/diaspora status were central facets constructing social and physical boundaries at their school. These boundaries often mirrored and made local the xenophobic discourses pervading, structuring, and constituting global politics of Eurocentric modernity in the 21st century (Rosa, 2014). Reflecting on how institutional segregation impacted their relationships, the founders of One World at Wright High wished for an affirming space to co-create understandings of their differing life experiences. Tanja, as the designated adult ally, was both hopeful about their aspirations and increasingly concerned about how the group of students was navigating each other's racialized, classed, gendered, languaged, and migratory/diasporic backgrounds as they participated in activities like the one described in the previous anecdote. Like many youth programs that center "youth voice," youth were often celebrated for sustaining and engaging in passionate, earnest, and organic practices of critical literacy, just as their problematic and oppressive renderings of themselves and the world were often overlooked in favor of their intentions and accomplishments.

Throughout her time at One World, Tanja acknowledged the power struggles the youth experienced with other adults, and therefore carefully considered when to step in with questions to guide critical questioning, and when to step back; at times failing to consider the complexities of interpersonal and intercultural dynamics at play. The youth-led transnational educational space of the One World after-school program, then, became both a place in which critical literacies were developed and practiced, *and* a place where the White and hegemonic gazes were maintained and used to evaluate *the Other* (i.e. in the form of globally *and* locally situated politics of race, nationality, class, gender, ableism, migration/diaspora, etc.; Burkhard, 2018; Alim et al., 2020). Contradicting simplified narratives of critical literacies and pedagogies, U.S. exceptionalism and systems of oppression were often simultaneously questioned and reinforced, complicating what it means to enact CSP's goal of decentering the White and hegemonic gazes in educational practice.

As Tanja considered the processes of teaching and learning in the situated social context of the One World program, she frequently confronted globalized issues of injustice linked to migration/diaspora, nationality, sovereignty, and transnational systems of oppression that remain undertheorized by scholars of CSP in the problem-space[3] of the early 2020s. In many ways, these issues are still in their early phases of being taken up from research by Alim (2011) and Paris (2012) in the 2010s, and operationalized within educational practice (Alim & Haupt, 2017; Lee & McCarty, 2017): How do we approach decentering the White and hegemonic gazes within educational spaces where students and educators are making sense of experiences, beliefs, language varieties, and ways of being from living within, and migrating across, multiple nation-states and contested lands? Remaining one of the most prominent empires in the early 21st century, the U.S. nation-state continues to play a large role in how White Supremacy and systems of oppression are constructed and imposed across the globe. However, at the same time, understandings of White Supremacy and systems of oppression are managed by locally situated institutions and relations that are dependent upon the specific nation-state with its role in the global order, and its respective designs for accumulating land, capital, and influence through systemic processes of violence.

Response to Loving Critique: An Approach to Decentering the White and Hegemonic Gazes Within a Youth-Led Transnational Space in Educational Practice

The One World program was often a powerful youth-led transnational space. Students worked together to generate radical possibilities for collective learning and attaining critical literacies. However, the space also frequently centered the White gaze in ways that pervade many classrooms. While the White gaze is sometimes spoken about as necessarily and literally attached to White-identified bodies, the White gaze is better understood as a semiotic rendering of the projected ideologies of White Supremacy that impact and control social and material relations (Morrison, 1998; Alim et al., 2020; Yancy, 2008). This meant that it was possible for students of color to look out upon girls like Damba through the White gaze, which happened in the One World program. The same could be said about other intersecting and overlapping hegemonic gazes. White girls and girls of color sometimes looked out upon each other and others through cisheteropatriarchal ways of seeing the world, just as immigrant youth at times took up U.S. exceptionalism (Lachica Buenavista, 2018). While many One World students offered notable critiques of processes of capitalism, they often did so without taking into account interlocking systems of race and colonialism (i.e. racial capitalism; Robinson, 2000 [1983]).

This was the case as the activity unfolded in the opening anecdote. The student facilitators created an activity which was intended to expose the violence and harm happening to children around the world, and to raise awareness for violence and conflict among the One World youth. They collectively looked at pictures of war, cruelty, and suffering, and were then invited to affectively connect with the immediate pain portrayed through the lens of the camera. While having the intended impact of creating sympathy for the people in the images, like Damba Koroma from Sierra Leone, Tanja also felt that the activity reinforced White Supremacy and racial capitalist ideologies by not unpacking the systems of oppression that created the conditions for and enabled the violence in the pictures. The harm of this obscuring specifically impacted youth like Amita.

Amita grappled with her connection to Damba through her own lived experiences as a girl of color who had gone through various dimensions of life in refugee camps and migration in Nepal, eventually ending up in the U.S. Tanja witnessed how Amita's level of connection was not shared or reciprocated by students like Anna, a white girl who grew up middle-class as a U.S. citizen. Amita was struggling with her feelings as youth like Anna were still trying to understand what it meant to be complicit in and benefit from systemic processes of injustice. The One World program was in fact partially designed to reckon with how students did not receive opportunities during their schooling to generatively grapple with their complicity in systems of oppression. While compulsory state-sanctioned schooling[4] in the U.S. is often imagined as providing youth with opportunities to develop the critical literacies needed to make sense of global politics and understand the world, this was rarely the case, and the situation for both Anna and Amita. Students in the Wright High chapter of One World acknowledged this weakness in their schooling, and made critiquing and questioning their education a consistent practice. The students often pulled up news articles and videos, and expressed their thoughts about education and justice as part of guided activities.

However, without the guidance to understand the picture of Damba and the larger context of processes of colonialism in Sierra Leone, as well as Amita's subsequent response, what was designed as an activity to build co-conspiracy with each other and marginalized peoples across the world instead had the impact of reifying racialized hierarchies of difference between students like Anna and Amita. The student facilitators designed an activity that revealed how they lived within a society that individualizes experiences, disaligns communities, and refuses responsibility for violence occurring outside the country. The activity also reinforced ideologies of White Supremacy and ongoing processes of colonialism; they left unquestioned how youth like Damba even came to experience violence from an unidentified and seemingly faceless group of "rebels."

The activity organized by the One World program did not interrogate the politics that had driven the rise of "rebels" and Damba's limblessness in Sierra Leone (Banya, 1993). Damba was a child who came from the more than 16 interconnected assemblages of people who courageously came together to combat British imperialism, including the Temne, Mende, Limba, Loko, Fula, Mandingo, Krio, Sherbro, Kuranko, Kono, Susu, Kissi, Yalunka, Vai, and Kru (Sengova, 2006). Following a prolonged struggle for sovereignty and the founding of Sierra Leone as a nation-state, elites in the territory had taken over the same institutions and structures created by the previous British colonizers. The "rebels" alluded to by Amita had fought the elites for a share of the wealth of this maintained system. The brutal images of the civil war overlooked how it was propelled by continuing racial capitalist demand for natural resources by British and Western interests that did not stop at the so-called "independence" of Sierra Leone.

Often imagined as a violent and insignificant territory, Sierra Leone has one of the world's largest deposits of rutile, and is among the world's greatest suppliers of diamonds, titanium, and bauxite (Bermúdez-Lugo, 2008). Incursions by U.S., British and Western corporations and interests have fueled conflict among people who are still grappling with all they lost to fight a brutal British administration and colonial rule. The Indigenous people have been systematically robbed of compensation for the extraction of natural resources by local elites and warlords who come from their own communities, as well as outside interests which have quite literally propelled industries and made everyday life possible for youth like Amita and Anna. While seeing a child without limbs should propel an affective sadness, without context, youth like Damba become limbless simply due to isolated circumstances in their own respective society. Although factions within Sierra Leone were the actors committing violence, this situation was only made possible by ongoing racial capitalist exploitation and processes of colonialism by the U.S. and Western world which made Damba's limblessness collateral damage; as ultimately tragic, but worthwhile and profitable.

A knowledge of this history and context would have likely produced another affective state that centered the oppressed: anger. The sadness in the room was predominantly driven by a helplessness about what was occurring in what was perceived as a less privileged world outside of their reach. While some students embraced and felt sadness for the injustices experienced by girls like Damba, and their peers like Amita, this sadness was primarily made meaningful by understanding the safety of white children as unrelated to the violence and lack of safety experienced by children of color. The white student who hugged Amita did not experience feelings like anger and disgust, which are made possible when you realize that you, your peers, and your ancestors could take actions to address your own complicity in the historical and ongoing injustices that produce violence against children. Instead of compassion and empathy driving a need to tackle White Supremacy, racial capitalism, and ongoing processes of colonialism, Damba and Amita became ahistorical victims of violence.

White Supremacy is often maintained through the enactment of affective states (e.g. objectifying pity and sadness) that do the work of exceptionalizing and celebrating the lives of White people and children as ideal and perfect, and *the Other* as inferior and in need of sympathy, affection, and saving from imagined uncivilized cultures of poverty and violence (Ahmed, 2014). The ahistorical understanding of the photo in the activity suggested that violence was taking place because of a lack of caring and empathetic white saviors to save Damba and Amita, rather than White Supremacy, racial capitalism, and ongoing processes of colonialism that produced the conditions driving the atrocities experienced by Damba and Amita. While the students intended to use the specially selected photos to engage in radical empathy building and to interrogate the harm and atrocities that go overlooked by the White gaze, instead, the activity had the impact of affectively reinforcing and objectifying *the Other*. The *Other* became Damba. The *Other* became Amita. Amita became a body who was in need of affection, rather than justice from the violence that she and Damba experienced from the White cisheteropatriarchal, ableist, racial capitalist order.

At this moment Tanja debated about whether to intervene and contest what she felt was a lack of questioning and critical literacy into the circumstances facing Damba and Amita. Amidst promising practices and pedagogies emerging amongst the students in the program, Tanja knew she was an adult who held power in spite of the "adult ally" role she had been given. Without being a teacher, she was able to develop relationships with students that could blossom outside of the rules and regulations of school. Tanja's unique positioning meant that she served multiple roles, including as a chaperone, adult presence, and record-keeper. Tanja had to negotiate power dynamics between the student leaders, members and herself as she fulfilled these multiple roles, as a Black immigrant woman from Germany. She had a close relationship with some students, and a more passing cordiality with others. This was further complicated as students joined and attended meetings, and had to get acclimated to the norms of the space, Tanja's presence, and their differing relations to existing members. In spite of how Amita and the other youth ran the space, Tanja had to remind students that this was their program. The One World program was voluntary, and not under the jurisdiction and control of normative school protocols.

While one of the very strengths of youth-led educational spaces like the One World program is that students lead and control, and can decide how to center CSP and developing critical literacies, it also means that students have to make hard decisions and act on fewer experiences with and ways of knowing the world. This was one of the motivations for Sarah and her peers in appointing an adult ally like Tanja. These tensions with their adult ally, Tanja, and their school were often generative in helping the students gain a deeper understanding of their agency. Negotiating this relationship with Tanja enabled the students to further develop critical literacies, knowledges, organizing and leadership skills that could help them learn how to impact the school and the wider world. However, this youth-led space often became constrained by what gave it its power. The students knew, and Tanja knew.

Decentering Is a Process, Not a Position: Implications for Pedagogy and Praxis

Later reflecting upon what happened in the opening anecdote, Tanja felt that as a culturally sustaining pedagogue, she should have stepped in to help the youth question their gazes, especially considering Damba and Amita. However, Tanja's reflections and regrets on what she witnessed happened after this experience, which is often the case in educational practice. While we can usually sense that something is not quite right, in that moment, we regularly do not have the attention within a room full of children to immediately know what and how to respond. We also need to give ourselves grace in youth-led spaces, just as we need to constantly consider better approaches to issues that arise.

While we have each been serving in the role of lifeway sustainers within youth-led after-school and out-of-school educational spaces for quite some time, rarely, if ever, do we finish a session with students where we do not have regrets about small or large failures of our educational practice. However, this does not have to result in our feeling inadequate, depressed, or otherwise unworthy. What is needed is: (1) an ongoing commitment to the potential of education to contribute to developing the critical consciousness needed for working toward social justice; (2) a humility and willingness to admit and be rigorously accountable to one's mistakes and actions; (3) grace with one's own and others shortcomings; and (4) ongoing critical reflection and research into better ways to understand social justice, teaching and learning.

One of the most common assumptions among activists and educators is that all they need to do is work hard to develop social justice ways of knowing, being, teaching and learning, and then they can walk into a space, ready. This is especially the case for educators who identify as embodying a personhood further away from the locally situated center of power. However, we cannot fall into the politics of believing we can *embody what is right; this is the very logic undergirding White Supremacy*. As we have been taught by elders like Anzaldúa (1987), just because we embody positions of oppression does not mean we cannot enable, further, and operate from the White and hegemonic gazes. As culturally sustaining educators, we have to understand that decentering the White and hegemonic gazes is an ongoing process, not a position that we can embody, claim, and occupy.

Implications for Future Research and Social Responsibility as Academics

CSP is linked with a rich legacy of scholars who have written from the asset-based and critical pedagogy traditions from the vantage point and intention of supporting classroom teachers within U.S. compulsory state-sanctioned schooling. We have only just begun to consider what it means to engage CSP in educational practice within out-of-school and after-school youth-led educational spaces.

Relatedly, we too often attribute the success of both classroom teachers, as well as after-school and out-of-school educators to their degree(s) or "formal" training. We have a social responsibility as educational researchers to justly explore this education and training that happens outside of institutions certified through the White and hegemonic gazes, and do justice to education as a process of teaching and learning (Alim et al., 2020); not just an event that only occurs within ratified educational spaces (e.g. compulsory state-sanctioned schooling or universities). Doing so holds broader implications for not only harm reduction in compulsory state-sanctioned schooling, but in fostering, sustaining, and revitalizing educational *otherwises* that will arise as we move toward a future of collective liberation.

Next Steps for New Researchers and Educators

We have complicated CSP's call to decenter the White and hegemonic gazes in order to call attention to the all encompassing and often inescapable complicity that we have with systems of oppression. However, we have done so not as an embrace of hopelessness, but rather to optimistically hone the strategies and tactics that we pedagogically deploy. Following Lyiscott (2020) who contends that confronting systemic violence enacted upon Black, Brown and marginalized youth in schooling requires the sustenance of "fugitive literacy practices—where youth develop the tools to liberate themselves from whiteness and anti-Blackness," Tanja argues that one of the central duties of new research should be to investigate fugitive literacy practices with the goal of understanding what is needed to sustain, encourage, and give power to youth and communities in disrupting systems of oppression (p. 259). Expanding from a U.S.-centric lens, Tanja also asserts that these fugitive literacy practices have to consider the global reach of systemic processes of violence and injustice.

For new educators who are committing to social justice-based education and supporting critical literacies through CSP, Casey has often recommended starting with three relational building blocks as a foundation for establishing the relationships needed to engage in teaching and learning that honors, lovingly critiques, sustains, builds, revitalizes and (re)imagines communities for collective liberation. These three relational building blocks have long been passed on in various ways through the lifeways of educators from Black, Indigenous, Latinx, Asian, Pacific Islander and intersecting and overlapping communities of color (Simpson, 2014), and have enabled the relationships needed within an educational community to approach decentering the White and hegemonic gazes: (1) courage, (2) honesty, and (3) vulnerability. If you do not have the courage to admit when you're wrong, question your assumptions, lovingly call out injustices, and attempt educational practices that may be uncomfortable to you, you will not be prepared to have the serious conversations and interactions needed to develop critical literacies through CSP. Further, if you are not honest with yourself and others as you engage in these moments of courage, your efforts will falter as you compromise the possibility of co-generating an educational community that supports vulnerability; decentering as a process is not possible without vulnerability. Vulnerability means politicizing the personal, and consensually and publicly linking that personal to the collective (Nash, 2013); it means revealing and giving up power in ways that create the relational and structural conditions needed to teach and learn for collective liberation.

Notes

1. "One World" is a pseudonym to protect the identities of the respective after-school program and high school.
2. "One World" is a pseudonym to protect the identities of the respective after-school program and high school.
3. "A problem-space . . . is an ensemble of questions and answers around which a horizon of identifiable stakes (conceptual as well as ideological-political stakes) hangs." (Scott, 2004, p. 4).
4. We refer to compulsory state-sanctioned schools as the public and private schools that fulfill the educational mandate of the U.S. nation-state, and are accountable to the U.S. government through the Department of Education.

References

Ahmed, S. (2014). *Cultural politics of emotion*. Edinburgh University Press.

Alim, H. S. (2011). Global ill-literacies: Hip hop cultures, youth identities, and the politics of literacy. *Review of Research in Education, 35*(1), 120–146.

Alim, H. S., & Haupt, A. (2017). Reviving soul (s) with Afrikaaps: Hip Hop as culturally sustaining pedagogy in South Africa. In H. S. Alim & D. Paris (Eds.), *Culturally sustaining pedagogies: Teaching and learning for justice in a changing world* (pp. 157–174). Teacher's College Press.

Alim, H. S., Paris, D., & Wong, C. P. (2020). Culturally sustaining pedagogy: A critical framework for centering communities. In N. S. Nasir, C. Lee, R. Pea, & M. M. De Royston (Eds.), *Handbook of the cultural foundations of learning*. Routledge.

Anzaldúa, G. (1987). *Borderlands/la frontera* (Vol. 3). Aunt Lute Books.

Banya, K. (1993). *Implementing educational innovation in the third world: A West African experience*. The Edwin Mellen Press.

Bermúdez-Lugo, O. (2008). The mineral industries of Liberia and Sierra Leone. In U.S. Geological Survey (Ed.), *2008 Minerals Yearbook: Liberia and Sierra Leone*. U.S. Department of Interior.

Burkhard, T. (2018). I need you to tell my story: Qualitative inquiry for/With transnational black women. *Cultural Studies - Critical Methodologies, 19*(3), 184–192. https://doi.org/10.1177/1532708618817883

Freire, P. (1985). Reading the world and reading the word: An interview with Paulo Freire. *Language Arts, 62*(1), 15–21. Retrieved March 2, 2020, from www.jstor.org/stable/41405241

Lachica Buenavista, T. (2018). Model (undocumented) minorities and "illegal" immigrants: Centering Asian Americans and US carcerality in undocumented student discourse. *Race Ethnicity and Education, 21*(1), 78–91.

Ladson-Billings, G. (1995). But that's just good teaching! the case for culturally relevant pedagogy. *Theory into Practice, 34*(3), 159–165. https://doi.org/10.1080/00405849509543675

Lee, T. S., & McCarty, T. L. (2017). Upholding Indigenous education sovereignty through critical culturally sustaining/revitalizing pedagogy. In D. Paris & H. S. Alim (Eds.), *Culturally sustaining pedagogies: Teaching and learning for justice in a changing world* (pp. 61–82). Teachers College Press.

Lyiscott, J. (2020). Fugitive literacies as inscriptions of freedom. *English Education, 52*(3), 256–263.

McCarty, T., & Lee, T. (2014). Critical culturally sustaining/revitalizing pedagogy and Indigenous education sovereignty. *Harvard Educational Review, 84*(1), 101–124.

Morrison, T. (1998, March). *From an interview on Charlie Rose*. Public Broadcasting Service. Retrieved from www.youtube.com/watch?v=F4vIGvKpTlc

Nash, J. C. (2013). Practicing love: Black feminism, love-politics, and post-intersectionality. *Meridians, 11*(2), 1–24.

Paris, D. (2012). Culturally sustaining pedagogy: A needed change in stance, terminology, and practice. *Educational Researcher, 41*(3), 93–97.

Paris, D., & Alim, H. S. (2014). What are we seeking to sustain through culturally sustaining pedagogy? A loving critique forward. *Harvard Educational Review, 84*(1), 85–100. https://doi.org/10.17763/haer.84.1.982l873k2ht16m77

Paris, D., & Alim, H. S. (Eds.). (2017). *Culturally sustaining pedagogies: Teaching and learning for justice in a changing world.* Teachers College Press.

Robinson, C. (2000 [1983]). *Black Marxism: The making of the black radical tradition.* University of North Carolina Press.

Rosa, J. (2014). Learning ethnolinguistic borders: Language and diaspora in the socialization of US Latinas/os. *Diaspora Studies in Education: Toward a Framework for Understanding the Experiences of Transnational Communities, 39*–60.

Scott, D. (2004). *Conscripts of modernity: The tragedy of colonial enlightenment.* Duke University Press.

Sengova, J. (2006). Aborigines and returnees: In *Search of linguistic and historical meaning in delineations of Sierra Leone's ethnicity and heritage'. New perspectives on the Sierra Leone Krio* (pp. 167–199). Peter Lang.

Simpson, L. B. (2014). Land as pedagogy: Nishnaabeg intelligence and rebellious transformation. *Decolonization: Indigeneity, Education & Society, 3*(3), 1–25.

Wong, C. P. (2019). *Pray you catch me: A critical feminist and ethnographic study of love as pedagogy and politics for social justice* (Doctoral dissertation). Retrieved from Proquest Dissertations & Theses Global database.

Yancy, G. (2008). *Black bodies, white gazes: The continuing significance of race.* Rowman & Littlefield.

3.15

CRITICAL COMMUNITY LITERACIES IN TEACHER EDUCATION

Pooja Dharamshi, Laura Ruth Johnson, and Judy Sharkey

Introduction

We situate our chapter within the growing literature to decenter, decolonize, and reclaim a more humanizing approach to language and literacy teacher education and research by positioning community members—youth, families, and community organizers—as faculty and architects in designing and supporting the development of community-responsive teachers and researchers (e.g., Martin, Pirbhai-Illich, & Pete, 2017). Supporting and nurturing critical community literacies is integral to this larger project and greatly facilitated by robust collaborations between community-based researchers/organizers and university-based language and literacy teacher educator scholars.

Community-engaged teacher education begins with interrogating the project of school and its relationship to communities. It requires consideration of how larger schooling systems can be radically reimagined, configured, and held accountable for the damage they have perpetrated on minoritized communities. Discourses of schooling, teaching, and learning are entangled in the ideology of coloniality. The project of schooling itself is bound to leverage "students' lives and communities" to reach goals already determined by the settler colonial nation-state (Dominguez, 2019). Although social justice and equity are oft-stated goals in their programs, teacher education remains largely a colonial endeavor framed by Eurocentric ways of knowing and being. Epistemic and ontological shifts are needed to decenter Whiteness of teacher education (Milner & Howard, 2013; Sleeter, 2016), and to "disrupt the frameworks with which our teachers see the world and reject the hubris of the zero point which we have held to for far too long" (Dominguez, 2019, p. 59).

Definitions of Key Concepts

Our views of critical community literacies are informed by our individual and collective understanding of "critical," "community," and "literacy," how they interact, and how the different disciplines within and across the humanities and social sciences define and enact these concepts. Communities are multi-layered and complex spaces, existing in specific and bounded geographical locales, as well as in virtual settings, and populated by a variety of knowledge, experiences, and textual resources. "Community" is a value-laden, contested concept used by varying groups to welcome or prohibit entry to particular spaces: physical, virtual, ideological (Delanty, 2010). In its most inclusive and expansive sense, "community" draws on notions of cosmopolitanism, where difference is welcomed and valued, and the transmigrant and translocal realities of the 21st century expand rather than threaten perspectives and traditions. In its most exclusive and parochial sense, "community" weaponizes difference to stoke fear and justify exclusionary, racist, xenophobic policies and actions, Trump's border wall campaign and Modi's "anti-Muslim" policy in India being two recent examples (Norris & Inglehart, 2019; "Citizen Amendment Bill," 2019). Integral to these multiple conceptualizations of community are notions of belonging and solidarity (Delanty, 2010), which parallel similar conceptions of literacy.

We define *literacies* as situated, cultural practices that permit or bar participation in social worlds (Kalman, 2003; Vygotsky, 1986; Wenger, 1998) and highlight their plurality to capture the multilingual, multimodal realities of what it means to participate in and across personal, professional, and/ or the aesthetic communities (Cope & Kalantzis, 2009). *Critical* literacies contest inequities, material and social, and broaden access to and participation in various communities. Paulo Freire's literacy campaigns in Brazil more than 60 years ago remain an illustrative example whereby gaining print literacy allowed participation in democratic practices (Freire, 1974). Further, curriculum must always be locally generated, co-created by learners, and afford opportunities to critique and transform their realities (Freire, 1970).

A concept we find particularly useful in our work is Communities as Intellectual Spaces (CIS) (Community as Intellectual Space: Preliminary Program, 2005; Johnson, 2017; Johnson & Rodriguez-Muniz, 2017). Initially developed to articulate and guide university-community partnerships and collaborative research within a particular community in Chicago, CIS recognizes and values community members as savvy theoretical interlocuters and creators of sophisticated theoretical knowledge. For academic researchers interested in critical community literacy practices, this means working reciprocally and collaboratively with community organizations and residents within the research process, and being accountable to community stakeholders at all stages of the research, from design to dissemination. Such approaches to research upend models to studying critical literacy in communities that view academic researchers as the sole theoretical experts and purveyors of knowledge. Using a CIS orientation, researchers work collaboratively with community members and organizations to design robust studies of critical literacy, and community members are more than sources of data, but integral generators of theory and possessors of essential knowledge and experiences that make sense of local and community literacy practices. The collaboration between the Kateri Center of Chicago, an urban indigenous community organization and the teacher education program at Loyola University (Lees, 2016) is an illustrative example. Here, Indigenous community leaders work as co-teachers to help develop the kinds of teachers urban indigenous children need and deserve.

Another important source and site for critical community literacies exists in social media and the use of hashtags (Bonilla & Rosa, 2015) which have provided opportunities for a variety of community residents to participate in broader debates and activism and engage in a wide range of discursive practices. For youth, in particular, social media is a regular facet of their daily lives, and smartphones are now accessible to individuals at all socioeconomic levels; however, use of phones and social media is often viewed by educators as at odds with literacy development, as distractions and hindrances to learning rather than as contexts for literacy practices and the transmission of literacy knowledge and skills. For example, Latino/a/x and African American Pregnant and Parenting Youth (PPY) used social media to challenge and speak back to negative stereotypes and stigma about PPY—in ways that were safer and that made them less vulnerable than, say, confronting individuals and family members in person—employing the hashtag #noteenshame and #teen parent pride to index images of themselves marching in a contingent at a local parade and attending and/or graduating from high school (Johnson, 2019, April). Social media allowed them to engage in advocacy efforts on behalf of themselves and their children. Literacy research that examines the intertextual facets and semiotic potential of social media for particular communities can lead to better understandings of how critical community literacies develop and are then used for specific purposes.

Decolonizing, decentering teacher education also means seeking out and valuing the vast repertoires of literacies that youth engage in to claim membership and shape the communities they inhabit. Thus, critical community literacies are key starting points for teacher education. Connecting curriculum to students' lives is not a new idea but the punitive effects of the accountability and standardization movement in addition to the damaging legacy of coloniality have meant that critical scholars of teacher education have had to be even more vigilant and vocal in insisting that children's out of school lives be connected to content and pedagogy in schools (Ladson-Billings, 2006; Paris, 2011; Villegas & Lucas, 2002).

Critiques of Community Critical Literacy in This Domain

Two principal critiques of community engaged literacies in teacher education programs are the ways they can lead to reinforcing stereotypes and deficit perspectives of traditionally minoritized communities and the positing of "community knowledge" as less than "real school knowledge." Meaningful engagements in communities are critical to understanding children's home cultures, allowing teachers to better align children's existing knowledges and skills to new content (Villegas & Lucas, 2002). However, global migration patterns and shifting demographics have created a significant diversity gap between PK–12 teachers and their students in numerous urban centers worldwide (Sharkey, Olarte, & Galindo, 2016). As a result, many pre- and in-service teachers come from realities and social identities different from their students.

In response, several teacher preparation programs have made gaining community knowledge and investigating local literacies an explicit and intentional part of their curriculum (e.g., Dharamshi, 2019; Khasnabis & Reischl, 2018; Olarte & Galindo, 2019; Sharkey, 2016). These practices are wide ranging, from experiences in the community to community-based teacher education programs. Despite their promising potential, these approaches have not been without troubling consequences, including when teachers' observations and interpretations lack critical analysis and/or when participants' conceptions of "community" are left undefined.

The "community walk," for example, has become a common experience in teacher education programs with intentions of broadening student teacher conceptions of literacy by exploring community literacy events and practices in traditional (e.g., schools, libraries, museums) and non-traditional (e.g., laundromats, parks) learning spaces. But entering previously unknown communities for observation or student teaching without meeting an adult community member poses risks of superficial engagements and re-inscribing stereotypes and deficit orientations (Noel, 2016). Counter-productive discourses may emerge after experiences such as a community walk as in Dharamshi's (2019) study of community literacies in teacher education: a literacy teacher educator recalled student teachers' deficit views when debriefing the walk:

> [The students] had noticed there was a lot of trash on the floor. . . [but] sometimes when student [teachers], try to be open-minded, they re-inscribe a certain relativism. . . "Well garbage, it bothers me to have the neighborhood look like that, but maybe, that's just how they live."
>
> *(p. 96)*

Although well-intentioned, community-based experiences devoid of critical reflection both perpetuate harmful stereotypes and leave pre-service teachers unprepared for the social, political, and economic conditions impacting the lives of their students, families, and communities. After realizing that her predominantly White, middle-class, monolingual English-speaking teachers were defining "community" as code for "urban, poor, and non-English speaking," Sharkey (2012) began having her teacher learners openly share and question each other's understanding of "community." Humanizing pedagogies, such as those advocated by Carter Andrews, Brown, Castillo, Jackson, and Vellanki (2019) counter the damage-centered pedagogies (Tuck, 2009) that define marginalized communities as broken and in need of fixing, and promote a strengths-based approach to teaching and learning.

Another critique of community literacies, when local literacies are not deemed school worthy, reflects Freire's (1970) notion of cultural invasion whereby subjects doubt or devalue their own knowledge. In their report on a rich family histories project with Gujarati students and families in a Canadian school, Marshall and Toohey (2010) lamented that the parents and children saw the project "'as something special,' not really school" (p. 37). Maribel Ramirez, a secondary Spanish arts teacher in Bogotá, Colombia reported that parents strongly objected to her unit on graffiti until they saw and heard the students' sophisticated linguistic and semiotic analysis produced (Sharkey et al., 2016).

Current Research in the Area

Within research on/with multiliteracies, methods that capture "both regularity and variance" within communities (Gutierrez & Orellana, 2006, p. 503) help us move beyond methods that rely on descriptive statistics and take a monolithic approach to studying communities, often contributing to static and deficit-oriented views of communities and residents. Gutierrez and Orellana (2006) urge for a consideration of ecological validity when conducting literacy research in communities and caution against the "analytical reductiveness" (p. 504) that can occur when researchers focus on "a narrow range of what constitutes. . . [a learner's] literacy toolkit or repertoires" (p. 504) and emphasize narrative difference and "mismatches" between non-mainstream youth and dominant literacy practices and institutions, rather than being attentive to the potentially banal and everyday practices, and the ways that community members' literacy knowledge and repertoires both draw upon and diverge from mainstream practices.

In order to develop robust and authentic studies of community critical literacy, academic researchers must build asymmetrical relationships with communities and community-based organizations that are weighted towards community expertise and knowledge, thereby "redistribut[ing] intellectual authority" (Campano, Ghiso, & Welch, 2015, p. 30). This is especially important because of historical inequities between universities and marginalized and non-mainstream communities. Researchers should also be attentive to the distribution of power and privilege within communities, and the ways that inequities and discrimination functioning in the broader society are reproduced within community settings to silence certain voices, experiences, and practices. This entails adopting more complicated and complex notions about what a community is and paying attention to the diversity of populations, sub-communities, and identities within communities. Some ways that researchers might redistribute knowledge and authority is through shared project leadership with community partners and the integration of "structured and situated forms of and opportunities for critical inquiry and discussion into the project" (Johnson, 2017, p. 23). More specifically, research questions should be developed collaboratively and data collection and analysis should be conducted by teams which include community members and stakeholders.

Researchers conducting critical literacy research within communities are also often contending with their own complex identity categories as they collaborate with community members, engaging in what Green (2014) has termed "Double Dutch" methodology, as researchers navigate and negotiate shifting roles as an engaged participant and the "objective observer," sought for in much research, with their own subjectivities and experiences that may overlap and intersect with those of community members. Dmitriadis (2001) speaks to the multiple roles academic researchers may play in studies within community organizations, and how their relationships with participants may shift throughout the course of a study, thus underscoring the dynamic nature of this work.

If teacher education is truly committed to community-engaged work, deep and sustained shifts in power are required. By troubling notions of expertise, content and epistemologies of learning (Zeichner, Payne, & Brayko, 2015), knowledge-power relationships in teacher education will be disrupted. This includes decentering of university-based teacher educators as experts, seeking out and integrating the practices and ways of being of historically marginalized communities (Battiste & Youngblood Henderson, 2009), and enacting pedagogies of literacy teacher education that engage student teachers in interrogating their own social positions and the ways they inform their views and practices of teaching and learning.

Implications for Pedagogy

Decentering and decolonizing teacher education and naming it as a site for social justice and equity, requires that strategies and methods include meaningful recognition, integration and collaborations with and for local communities. Pedagogies of literacy teacher education must engage pre-service teachers in a process of "critical interrogation of their social locations and the ways they engage with the realities of teaching and learning" (Haddix, 2015, p. 66). Recognizing the hierarchical nature related to issues of "whose knowledge counts in the education of teachers" contemporary scholars are calling for a paradigm shift in teacher education where "academic, practitioner, and community-based knowledge respect and interact to develop new solutions to the complicated process of preparing teachers" (Kretchmar & Zeichner, 2016, p. 428).

In some cases, teacher educators are taking important steps in enacting community-engaged pedagogies of literacy education. For example, Cipollone, Zygmunt, and Tancock (2018), who study their own teacher education program in the Midwestern US, illustrate how community voices and knowledges are reflected in the preparation of teachers. They deliberately broaden the term "teacher educator" to include community mentors in the preparation of teachers. For one school term, pre-service teachers are paired with community mentors who are active members in the community. Mentors include community elders, members of local community council, pastors, and families within the community. The aim is to facilitate cultural immersion and build relational ties between local communities and student teachers to develop community-engaged and culturally responsive teachers via authentic engagements. For example, community mentors along with faculty host community history days where residents share community artifacts, such as photos with student teachers. These experiences allow for space and time for relation building, which practices described earlier such as the community walk lack, and thus counter superficial and dangerous interactions with the community. By structuring a program around mentorship, engagements in the community are sustained over a substantial period of time, allowing for authentic engagements to emerge and deep learning and unlearning to occur.

By drawing on community literacies and community voices, teacher educators actively work towards decentering themselves as the only "experts." Literacy teacher educators develop practices which center community voices/perspectives- community mentors, drawing on voices not in mainstream (e.g., twitter). By valuing the role of community mentors in the preparation of teachers, teacher learning is situated in historical and cultural contexts while centering and elevating the voices of families and communities. Two current collaborative projects that illustrate this commitment at the University of New Hampshire involve teacher education students learning to develop curriculum based on the expertise and knowledge of community leaders from the Indigenous New Hampshire Collaborative Collective (https://indigenousnh.com) and the Black Heritage Trail of New Hampshire (http://blackheritagetrailnh.org).

To help student teachers see past superficial impressions of "there's lots of trash here," teacher education programs must take up the pedagogical work that develops critical observation and critical inquiry skills, as well as authentic and sustained relations in the communities and worlds that youth and families inhabit.

In order to accomplish this and move beyond superficial (and potentially harmful) engagements with the community, some teacher education programs have transformed their focus and strategies to work more intimately with communities and community-based organizations, positioning the programs directly into communities (Noel, 2016). In their study on literacy teacher educators' practices and pedagogies in preparing student teachers for culturally and linguistically diverse student populations, Dharamshi (2019) reported teacher educators' pedagogies challenged assumptions about the "site" or "place" of where literacy practices occurred (traditionally taking place in schools). They understood literacy learning as a situated practice that is specific to a learner's socio-cultural context. The literacy teacher educators designed learning opportunities for their student teachers to immerse themselves in local community initiatives, as well as the day-to-day occurrences of the community in which they would later teach. Some teacher educators delivered their courses in community centers, churches and elementary schools. One teacher educator's course, for example, was largely based in a Catholic church that had a school attached to it. By engaging with community members in a place where they were regarded as knowledgeable and successful, the student teachers in his class were able to experience first-hand expansive literacy practices taking place outside of traditional sites of literacy learning.

By situating programs directly in communities trust is built (Noel, 2016) and pre-service teachers have opportunities to deeply understand community literacies and develop critical literacies practices that are responsive to the local community (Ladson-Billings, 2006).

Graduate and undergraduate students studying literacy could also be introduced to community-based qualitative research (CBQR) (Johnson, 2017) as a methodology particularly well suited to pursuing questions related to critical community literacies. CBQR provides opportunities to engage in sustained and immersive ways within community settings. Thus, university literacy education courses could include conducting community-based research as part of class projects and working with community organizations and particular community groups to better understand the critical literacy knowledge and practices in local contexts. Coursework might be held within community contexts and in collaboration with local organizations, making use of community residents and leaders as co-instructors, to engage students in critical dialogues about the community's literacy practices. This collaborative process is inherently pedagogical and involves mutual processes of teaching and learning (Johnson, 2017).

Inviting community experts and professionals into courses as co and/or lead instructors also alleviates some of the fear that pre- and in-service teachers may express when asked to do community investigations while also highlighting the value of professional collaborations across various sectors (Sharkey et al., 2016). Social workers, public health workers, local artists, and housing advocates are often eager to forge partnerships with teachers and schools.

Implications for Research

The views of community that we describe here have substantial implications for academic researchers investigating critical community literacies, requiring collaboration at all phases of the study. For example, in a study of youth civic engagement and critical literacy, Rosario-Ramos and Johnson (2013) collaborated with teachers and community members who worked with an alternative high school to develop interview guides; the sorts of questions they generated reflected their innate and insider knowledge of the community and the experiences of youth attending the school. Studies which take a more traditional approach, wherein data collection instruments and materials are developed outside of the community setting and without community collaboration and input, often discount local experiences and understandings. Findings in these studies may be premised on inaccurate concepts of literacy practices and notions of where literacy takes place. For example, academic researchers unfamiliar with a community may focus on institutions such as libraries and community centers as the sole sites for studies of community literacy, rightly viewing them as outside of the formal educational system of public schools, but still possibly providing a limited view of a community's literacy practices and knowledge. More appropriate contexts could include businesses and workplaces. For example, in a summer community-based research class taught by one of the authors, through conversations with community members, a student learned that a bikeshop hosted a homework class and reading group and that the library was inaccessible to many community youth due to limited hours, their own work schedules, and location in a hostile gang territory. This sort of awareness of social and economic factors and constraints would likely be unavailable to academic researchers not from the community. The early work of Fisher (2006) examined the role of Black bookstores as participatory learning communities and part of "a culture of literate practices" that allowed community residents to earn "dual degrees" (p. 83). These formal and informal community spaces can serve as essential contexts for literacy. Also notable here is Gutierrez and Orellana's (2006) critique of studies which have looked at alternative knowledge spaces, such as gangs, lowrider culture, and graffiti, but possibly in reductive, essentializing, and romanticizing ways which focus on deficits, emphasize "exotic" differences and reify stereotypes and monolithic views of particular marginalized communities.

When researchers genuinely value a community's knowledge about critical literacy, there is a rethinking of dissemination efforts, in order to reach and engage broader audiences and participate in substantive and critical dialogue with community members and stakeholders about research findings. This includes organizing community research forums, publishing findings in local publications, and/or creating flyers and posters highlighting findings for posting in local businesses. Furthermore, in these sorts of studies research findings might be used to support and expand programs, through the preparation of grant proposals or design of curricula. Social media might play a critical role in these efforts, particularly in studies that involve youth, resulting in the launching of hashtag campaigns to share key research findings, communicate with the wider public, and participate in advocacy efforts.

Decentering and decolonizing teacher education means doing the same for research and this entails collaborations that invite the expertise and participation of people from and across multiple organizations and entities: academic, professional, civic, in formal and non-formal settings. To develop capacity for community engaged research and collaborative initiatives, universities and funding agencies should support faculty collaboration across departments, develop relationships with community members, and engage more with equity-based principles and approaches.

Implications for Our Social Responsibility as Academics

As university-based academics our professional responsibilities—as defined by our employers—entail teaching, scholarship, and service. Our social responsibilities as academics cut across all three as well. In our courses, from foundations to curriculum and research methods, we model the pedagogies we advocate for our students, future teachers, researchers, and/or community-involved professionals. This means engaging in critical self-reflexivity (Kubota & Miller, 2017), examining what kinds of knowledge/literacies are featured in our syllabi, working to decolonize our readings, inviting students, teachers, and community members to shape our syllabi and attending to the ways our identities are always part of our pedagogies (Peercy, Sharkey, Baecher, Motha, & Varghese, 2019). As researchers, we seek to establish collaborative and non-hierarchical relationships with our community partners. This can entail recentering academic and intellectual authority in a study, stepping aside as experts. We co-author and co-present with students, teachers, and community members and pursue funding to support their participation in activities that are outside of their typical responsibilities. In terms of our professional service, we have tremendous responsibility as gatekeepers acting as editors and peer reviewers for journals and conference presentations. In this capacity we can challenge traditional hierarchies of knowledge and research methodologies, broaden participation in academic and scholarly venues and support the promotion and tenure cases of colleagues who conduct engaged scholarship. While community-engaged research is increasingly encouraged in universities, particularly at US public land grant institutions (see APLU, 2015), criteria for "research productivity" for tenure and promotion often do not align with the nature of this scholarship. Thus, we can use our service and membership on various institutional level committees to expand expectations to recognize engaged scholarship as legitimate and valuable.

Furthermore, building the sorts of relationships required to conduct engaged scholarship entails a commitment on the part of researchers, towards interrogating their own positions of privilege and becoming authentically involved in certain aspects of community life, through participation in community events and regular engagement in the life of the community. The sorts of roles include teachers and facilitators within community settings; ambassadors and allies who work in solidarity to support community initiatives; and advocates and activists working within the community (Johnson, 2017). Community members in one of the author's projects offered advice to researchers interested in working within the community, to "check their privilege," respect the knowledge and experiences of community members, and become involved: "So if you are here in the community to do research here. Go to events . . . and just be willing . . . to give your time . . . Lend a hand" (Johnson, 2017, p. 49).

Recommendations for Future Research and Praxis

We opened this chapter by stating our commitment to decentering and decolonizing teacher education and seeing critical community literacies as integral to this project. In addition to the recommendations woven throughout the chapter we see the engaged scholarship movement as having potential for future research and praxis in critical community literacies. Engaged scholarship values social justice and civic engagement and its core principles include reciprocity, boundary-crossing and democratizing of knowledge (Beaulieu, Breton, & Brousselle, 2018). It redefines the roles of faculty, students, and community members in pursuit of knowledge that improves social and material conditions. Relationships built on mutual respect are central to this work but take trust and time to develop. Although universities claim to value engaged research they continue to struggle in efforts to recognize and reward collectivist and collaborative research. The research and pedagogies of critical community literacies we have highlighted here share epistemological and ontological affinity with engaged scholarship. A potentially powerful praxis could be the more formal linking of these two areas: critical community literacies can serve as illustrative examples of engaged scholarship and the discourse of engaged scholarship could help community-based researchers gain access to new levels of support and recognition.

References

APLU. (2015). *Annual report of the association of public land-grant universities.* Retrieved from https://www.aplu.org/library/2015-annual-report/file

Battiste, M., & Youngblood Henderson, J. (2009). Naturalizing Indigenous knowledge in Eurocentric education. *Canadian Journal of Native Education, 32*(1), 5–18.

BBC. (2019, December 11). Citizenship amendment bill: India's new 'anti-Muslim' law explained. *BBC News.* Retrieved from www.bbc.com/news/world-asia-india-50670393

Beaulieu, M., Breton, M., & Brousselle, A. (2018). Conceptualizing 20 years of engaged scholarship: A scoping review. *PLoS One, 13*(2), e0193201. https://doi.org/10.1371/journal.pone.0193201

Bonilla, Y., & Rosa, J. (2015). #Ferguson: Digital protest, hashtag ethnography, and the racial politics of social media in the United States. *American Ethnologist, 42*(1), 4–17.

Campano, G., Ghiso, M. P., & Welch, B. (2015). Ethical and professional norms in community-based research. *Harvard Educational Review, 85*(1), 29–49.

Carter Andrews, D., Brown, T., Castillo, B. M., Jackson, D., & Vellanki, V. (2019). Beyond damage-centred teacher education: Humanizing pedagogy for teacher educators and preservice teachers. *Teachers College Record, 121*(6), 1–28.

Cipollone, K., Zygmunt, E., & Tancock, S. (2018). "A paradigm of possibility": Community mentors and teacher preparation. *Policy Futures in Education, 16*(6), 709–728.

"Community as intellectual space: Preliminary program, [Symposium]." (2005, June 17–19). http://conferences.illinois.edu/cis/cis.program.draft7.pdf.

Cope, B., & Kalantzis, M. (2009). "Multiliteracies": New literacies, new learning. *Pedagogies: An International Journal, 4*(3) 164–195.

Delanty, G. (2010). *Community* (2nd ed.). Routledge.

Dharamshi, P. (2019). "I remember being aware of how I was being positioned by my school": How early experiences with deficit views of education influence the practice of teacher educators. *Teaching and Teacher Education, 77*, 90–99.

Dmitriadis, G. (2001). Coming clean at the hyphen: Ethics and dialogue at a local community center. *Qualitative Inquiry, 7*(5), 578–597.

Dominguez, M. (2019). Decolonial innovation in teacher education development: Praxis beyond the colonial zero-point. *Journal of Education for Teaching, 45*(1), 47–62.

Fisher, M. (2006). Black bookstores as alternative knowledge spaces. *Anthropology & Education Quarterly, 37*(1), 83–99.

Freire, P. (1970). *Pedagogy of the oppressed.* Continuum.

Freire, P. (1974). *Education for critical consciousness.* Continuum.

Green, K. (2014). Doing double Dutch methodology: Playing with the practice of participant observation. In D. Paris & M. T. Winn (Eds.), *Humanizing research: Decolonizing qualitative inquiry with youth and communities* (pp. 147–160). Sage.

Gutierrez, K. D., & Orellana, M. F. (2006). The "problem" of English learners: Constructing genres of differences. *Research in the Teaching of English, 40*(4), 502–507.

Haddix, M. (2015). Preparing community-engaged teachers. *Theory Into Practice, 54*, 63–70.

Johnson, L. R. (2017). *Community-based qualitative research: Approaches for education and the social sciences.* Sage.

Johnson, L. R. (2019, April). *Proving them wrong: Reproductive justice, engagement, and advocacy for and by Pregnant and Parenting Youth.* Paper presented at Annual Meeting of American Educational Research Association, Toronto, ON.

Johnson, L. R., & Rodriguez-Muniz, M. (2017, November). *Community as intellectual space: Reflections from research on Puerto Rican Chicago.* Paper presented at Annual Meeting of American Studies Association, Chicago, IL.

Kalman, J. (2003). El acceso a la cultura escrita: La participación social y la apropiación de conocimientos en eventos cotidianos de lectura y escritura. *Revista Mexicana de Investigación Educativa, 8*(17), 37–66.

Khasnabis, D., & Reischl, C. (2018). Six blocks down, take a left at the corner: Learning to teach English learners outside the school walls. *TESOL Journal, 9*(4), 1–13.

Kretchmar, K., & Zeichner, K. (2016). Teacher prep 3.0: A vision for teacher education to impact social transformation, *Journal of Education for Teaching, 42*(4), 417–433.

Kubota, R., & Miller, E. (2017). Re-examining and re-envisioning criticality in language studies: Theories and praxis. *Critical Inquiry in Language Studies, 14*(2), 129–157. https://doi.org/10.1080/15427587.2017.1290500

Ladson-Billings, G. (2006). It's not the culture of poverty, it's the poverty of culture: The problem with teacher education. *Anthropology and Education Quarterly, 37*(2), 104–109.

Lees, A. (2016). Roles of urban indigenous community members in collaborative field-based teacher preparation. *Journal of Teacher Education, 67*(5), 363–378.

Marshall, E., & Toohey, K. (2010). Representing families: Community funds of knowledge, bilingualism, and multimodality. *Harvard Educational Review, 8*(2), 221–242.

Martin, S., Pirbhai-Illich, F., & Pete, S. (2017). *Culturally responsive pedagogy: Working towards decolonization, indigeneity and interculturalism.* Palgrave Macmillan.

Milner, R. H., & Howard, T. (2013). Counter-narrative as method: Race, policy and research for teacher education. *Race, Ethnicity, and Education, 16*(4), 536–561.

Noel, J. (2016). Community-based urban teacher education: Theoretical frameworks and practical considerations for developing promising practices. *The Teacher Educator, 51*(4), 335–350.

Norris, P., & Inglehart, R. (2019). *Cultural backlash: Trump, Brexit, and authoritarian populism.* Cambridge University Press.

Olarte, A. C., & Galindo, M. (2019a). *Las pedagogías de la communidad en contextos urbanos: Un enfoque de formación docente a través de investigaciones locales* (pp. 259–261). Bogotá, Colombia: Fondo de Publicaciones Universidad Distrital Francisco José de Caldas.

Olarte, A. C., & Galindo, L. (2019b). *Las pedagogías de la comunidad a través de investigaciones locales en el contexto urbano de Bogotá.* Bogatá, Colombia: Universidad Distrital Francisco José de Caldas.

Paris, D. (2011). Culturally sustaining pedagogy: A needed chance in stance, terminology, and practice. *Educational Researcher, 41*(3), 93–97.

Peercy, M., Sharkey, J., Baecher, L., Motha, S., & Varghese, M. (2019). Exploring TESOL teacher educators as learners and reflective scholars: A shared narrative inquiry. *TESOL Journal, 10*(4). https://doi.org/10.1002/tesj.482

Rosario-Ramos, E. M., & Johnson, L. R. (2013). Communities as counter-storytelling (con)texts: The role of community-based educational institutions in the development of critical literacy and transformative action. In J. C. Zacher-Pandya & J. A. Avila (Eds.), *Moving critical literacies forward: A new look at praxis across contexts* (pp. 113–126). Routledge.

Sharkey, J. (2012). Community-based pedagogies and literacies in language teacher education: Promising beginnings, intriguing challenges. *Íkala, revista de lenguaje y cultura, 17*(1), 9–13.

Sharkey, J. (2016). Addressing the relational gap through community connections: Examples of language teacher learning in Colombia and the United States. In M. A. Celani (Ed.), *Tendências e desafios na formação de professores de línguas no século 2* (pp. 29–47). Pontes Editores.

Sharkey, J., Olarte, A. C., & Galindo, L. (2016). Developing a deeper understanding of community-based pedagogies with teachers: Learning with and from teachers in Colombia. *Journal of Teacher Education, 67*(4), 363–378.

Sleeter, C. (2016). Wrestling with the problematics of whiteness in teacher education. *International Journal of Qualitative Studies in Education, 29*(8), 1065–1068.

Tuck, E. (2009). Suspending damage: A letter to communities. *Harvard Educational Review, 79*(3), 409–428.

Villegas, A. M., & Lucas, T. (2002). *Educating culturally responsive teachers: A coherent approach.* SUNY Press.

Vygotsky, L. S. (1986). *Thought and language* (A. Kozulin, Ed.). MIT Press.

Wenger, E. (1998). *Communities of practice: Learning, meaning, and identity.* Cambridge University Press.

Zeichner, K., Payne, K., & Brayko, K. (2015). Democratizing teacher education. *Journal of Teacher Education, 66*(2), 122–135.

3.16

DISRUPTING XENOPHOBIA THROUGH COSMOPOLITAN CRITICAL LITERACY IN EDUCATION

Rahat Zaidi and Suzanne S. Choo

A dominant phenomenon that has emerged, as the world headed into the third decade of the 21st century, is the rise of xenophobia alongside increasing instances of ultranationalism and fascism. Xenophobia can be defined as possessing an excessive fear, or intense negative feelings towards anything different or "foreign" that is outside of one's own culture or social group (Philippas, 2014). As countries all over the world scrambled to contain the global spread of COVID-19, a parallel epidemic of "coronaracism" has intensified with reports of Asians being ostracized, denied access to public areas and transportation, verbally and physically abused.

Michael Peters (2020) has observed how fascist behavior has returned with the rise of anti-immigration and white supremacists movements across Europe and the United States. In 2020, the director of the Federal Bureau of Investigation in the United States highlighted ethnically motivated extremists as a "national threat priority" given that this group now comprises a large portion of domestic terrorism investigations (Donaghue, 2020). In recent history, targeting of specific races has been on most political agendas. As an example, the United States' travel ban prohibiting specific (Muslim) countries from entering the U.S. has been formalized into law. More recently, in India, a law has been passed that grants citizenship to religious and persecuted minorities with the exception of Muslims. Opposition parties argue the law "is discriminatory as it singles out Muslims in an officially secular nation of 1.3 billion people. Muslims form nearly 15 percent of the population" (Kuchay, 2019, para. 4). Further violence against Muslims has provoked a worldwide debate around religious xenophobia and, in particular islamophobia, and how certain races are being framed and marginalized.

Further contributing to the xenophobic reaction against Muslims is the dynamic flow of immigrants to countries all over the world, including North America and Europe. This transborder migration has become a global reality and, as a result, societal stereotypes and predictive opinions have begun to dominate politically, religiously, and culturally. These xenophobic reactions are often related to the mistrust and suspicion created whenever there is a substantial movement of people and cultures from place to place. Since immigration first began to occur, host societies have often demonstrated unwelcome attitudes towards immigrants. In modern day history, Muslim immigrants have witnessed significantly high levels of prejudice and discrimination as they emigrate from their home countries—sometimes to an extent that threatens to place the orderly functioning of a society into disarray (Kaya, 2015).

DOI: 10.4324/9781003023425-51

The socio-political situation in which the world now finds itself has led to concrete issues of the effects of war, immigration, and the specific challenges of relationships to the Islamic world. Any talk of peace essentially interacts with possibilities for justice and human flourishing. Provoked by Judith Butler's question "What is a life," as explored in her (2010) book *Frames of War*, Smits and Naqvi (2015) gathered a diverse set of reflections on how society might think about and enact curriculum in the face of polarizing frames of apprehension in the context of global conflicts. The challenge they suggest is how people might think in terms of "frames of peace," implying a re-framing of under-standing *the other* and the responsibility of education. The opportunity exists now to examine how living together in a world where difference, regard for *the other*, and the responsibilities for renewal become important foundations for curriculum.

In this chapter, we begin by conceptualizing cosmopolitan critical literacy and its fundamental role in education. We then provide examples of its use as a pedagogical intervention to disrupt xenophobia (with a particular emphasis on Islamophobia) and to foster more inclusive and hospitable mindsets.

History and Features of Cosmopolitan Critical Literacy

While literacy had largely been discussed from a cognitive psychological perspective, there was increasing pressure to globalize the field from the 1970s. This social turn brought attention to the ways reading, writing and other meaning-making practices are embedded in social and material contexts (Gee, 2015). The work of Paulo Freire was particularly influential in calling for a peda-gogy that "makes oppression and its causes objects of reflection by the oppressed [so that] from that reflection will come their necessary engagement in the struggle for their liberation" (Freire, 1970, p. 30). Central to the Freireian model of "emancipatory literacy" is the dialectical relation-ship between human beings and the world on one hand and language and transformative agency on the other (Giroux, 1987, p. 7). Reading the word must be integrally bound up with reading the world as a means for empowering oppressed groups to transform realties of oppression and injustice (Freire & Macedo, 1987). The 1970s which saw the heightening of neoliberalism also corresponded with the popularity of Poststructuralism in Humanities and Philosophy departments in the universities as well as Critical Discourse Analysis as a methodological approach to critiquing social realities particularly in relation to power discourses in the workings of the state and of capital-ism (Fairclough, 2015).

Today, the notion of literacy must account for both social and global processes while affirming the cultural and linguistic diversity of students. Traditional conceptions of literacy originating from the Latin *littera* referring to the letter of the alphabet and denoting the ability to read and write, have now given way to active rather than passive meaning-making practices in which students engage critically, aesthetically and ethically with information, digital, multimodal and other discourses in the world.

The notion of cosmopolitanism or *kosmopolites*, translated from the Greek as citizen of the world, stretches back to Cynic and Stoic philosophers who expressed concern about how the state privi-leged particular citizens over foreigners. They critiqued the injustices arising from parochialism and sought to articulate a vision of belonging that extended to all human beings (Brown, 2006). Simi-larly, cosmopolitan ideals have also been located in the writings of Confucius who subscribed to an "anthropocosmic worldview" in which heaven, earth, and human beings are interconnected (Tucker, 1998). Multiple conceptions of Muslim Cosmopolitanisms have also been articulated throughout the history of Islam (Hassim, 2020).

Since the late 20th century, there has been a renewed scholarly interest in cosmopolitanism partly because it is perceived as an ethical response to the exigencies arising from globalization. The result is a myriad of adjectives that have become associated with the term. Cosmopolitanism focuses on the naturalized ways in which identities are dynamic, plural, connected, local and global (Zaidi & Rowsell, 2017).

Critical cosmopolitan literacy refers to reading, writing, and other meaning-making practices aimed at facilitating critical ethical engagements with diverse cultures and values in our world (Choo, 2018). This entails three dominant characteristics.

The first characteristic involves an intentional focus on countering narratives that facilitate the continued commodification, exploitation and ideological colonization of others. Akin to what Bruce Robbins (2012) terms "new, dirty cosmopolitanism," such literacy practices foregrounds unequal power relations and how these may arise from global flows of capital or the consequence of hypercapitalism (Hawkins, 2018). Consideration is given to the ways meaning is constructed and negotiated with global others leading to the re-organization and re-distribution of knowledge and resources (Canagarajah, 2013). Critical cosmopolitanism lends attention also to the persistence of Eurocentrism and how colonial difference is reproduced and maintained by global corporations and other dominant forces (Mignolo, 2000).

The second characteristic accommodates a more aspirational quality arising from the need to re-imagine new dialogic possibilities with others. Critical cosmopolitan literacy seeks to "train the imagination to be tough enough to test its limits" (Spivak, 2012, p. 290) which includes training the imagination to problematize ideological representations of others and question one's own epistemological readings of others. The training of the imagination also encompasses what Arjun Appadurai (2013) terms, the ethics of possibility involving:

> ways of thinking, feeling, and acting that increase the horizons of hope, that expand the field of the imagination, that produce greater equity in . . . the capacity to aspire, and that widen the field of informed, creative and critical citizenship.
>
> *(p. 295)*

The expansion of the imagination ultimately leads to the formation of transnational affinity groups that contribute to normative critiques of systemic injustices and that drive social/global movements driven by the hope of more democratically inclusive and just worlds (Gills, Goodman, & Hosseini, 2017; Strydom, 2012).

The third characteristic is its bottom-up as opposed to top-down approach to critical cosmopolitanism. Critical cosmopolitanism emerges from encounter, exchange, and dialogue with others (Delanty, 2012). Terms such as "everyday cosmopolitanism" (Noble, 2009), "ordinary cosmopolitanisms" (Lamont & Aksartova, 2002) and "relational cosmopolitanism" (Baildon & Damico, 2011) capture the dynamic, ground-up ways in which individuals navigate diverse intercultural realities. Such relations embody the kind of deliberative democracy envisioned by Habermas (1984) as organically driven by transnational solidarity and struggle (Delanty, 2014). Not only can schools provide opportunities for intercultural encounters with others, they can also empower students to see how their lives are interconnected with wider social, political and economic contexts (Rizvi & Choo, 2020). As students examine how their lives are situated within global webs of power, this can facilitate bottom-up responses that disrupt everyday oppression that they and their communities may face (Oikonomidoy, 2018).

Criticisms and Responses to Critiques of Cosmopolitan Critical Literacy

The main criticisms of cosmopolitan critical literacy concern the dangers of universalism and anarchy.

First, cosmopolitan critical literacy can implicitly propagate universalistic values that mask imperialistic agendas often in the guise of critical readings of other cultural discourses. This was predominantly the problem associated with "old cosmopolitanism" that perpetuated a monolithic, universal view of citizenship popularized during the period of 18th-century Enlightenment by the German philosopher Immanuel Kant and more recently by Martha Nussbaum. Scholars have critiqued how the term promotes Eurocentrism and Colonization in the name of universalism. For example, rights-based discourses are premised on the recognition of an inherent dignity in others. This presumes a common understanding of what the protection of dignity entails but differing metaphysical and teleological conceptions generate diverging pespectives of moral standards needed to uphold the dignity of others (Islam, 2018). Further, when cosmopolitan critique becomes fixated on the dangers of particularistic belonging, this also diminishes the value of local values and traditions.

Second, cosmopolitan critical literacy can lead to extreme anti-state views. This can occur when critical reading becomes solely focused on "strategic cosmopolitan" practices of the state and those in power. Strategic cosmopolitanism is typically associated with Marx and Engels' (1848) observation of the cosmopolitan nature of capital and how the bourgeoisie who own the means of production seek to exploit the world market by forging global networks for the profit-making. Strategic cosmopolitanism is aligned with the ideas of "tactical globalization" and "selective globalization" (Chong, 2006; Koh, 2007) in which governments or corporations perpetuate inequality and systemic injustices in the country such as through the selling of national resources to foreign corporations that lead to the impoverishment of locals. When cosmopolitan critique is narrowed to critiquing the abuses of state or corporate power, this indirectly perpetuates a vision of a transnational world order in which individuals are connected to diverse others around the world without need for state intervention or protection. Further, cosmopolitan critique may result in reifying groups into categories such as those who perpetrate, defend, and are victims of injustice (Adami, 2014). Such simplistic categorization inhibits one group from understanding the other thus limiting productive dialogues across groups.

Both criticisms of cosmopolitan critical literacy, highlighted previously, point to the dangerous assumption that individuals can forge relations with strangers without need for attachments to local communities and without the protection accorded by the state. Such a view is unrealistic and has been replaced by scholars who propose a "new cosmopolitanism" that recognizes the interplay between universal ideals and ideals emanating from specific sociohistorical contexts (Delanty, 2014).

In this paper, we focus on the ways new cosmopolitanism can inform multimodal literacy practices in our global age. Cosmopolitanism alludes to a process of identity formation that involves gathering up and assembling disparate properties into an identity that people project into the world. (Gee, 2007). Snapchat and Instagram provide good avenues for people to project their identities in terms of different ideologies, discourses, and forms of being. Stornaiuolo, Hull, and Sahni (2011) and Vasudevan (2011) view cosmopolitanism as a means of understanding how people forge identities, orienting their beliefs, convictions and goals in a global manner, as opposed to having these rooted in only one culture or nation. Nussbaum (2008) has framed this as a commitment to humanity over nationhood. The term has changed even more recently, exuding a more active, animated feeling of *doing* as opposed to *being*. Hansen (2011) talks about people's capacities as cosmopolitan agents. Cosmopolitanism also sees identity framing as being complex and accomplished through linguistic, discursive and multimodal practices, within physical as well as online spaces. We think of cosmopolitanism as a forging or framing of identity in complex ways and as the projecting of identities (Gee, 2007).

Implications for Pedagogy: Practices of Cosmopolitan Critical Literacy in Countering Xenophobia

In spite of all the rhetoric around immigration, phobic reaction and how new immigrants self-identify, it remains important to acknowledge that cosmopolitanism still remains a common goal of all curricula, whether in Canada, Australia, the UK or Europe. Today, foreign policy, ideologies of war and groups like ISIS exerting world-wide influence, all contribute to the necessity for a new type of curriculum—a curriculum that helps to address how new immigrants to a country can embrace their culture, while at the same time affording them the opportunity to be counted as one of the many cultural components that help define who we are as a global entity, wherever we may live. The following exemplifies how cosmopolitan critical literacy practices are enacted through an online, open-access resource for educators.

Example 1: Anti-Islamophobic Curriculum

In Canada, an anti-phobic curriculum entitled "Living Together: Muslims in a Changing World" (Naqvi, 2015) aims to help young students (Grades 1–6) become more aware of other cultures beyond the predominant English–French–Indigenous Canadian cultural experience. Activities in the curriculum include cultural lessons revolving around the recognition of cultural diversity, individual and multiculturality, Muslim contributions to civil society, and basic knowledge about immigrant culture. Although the emphasis is on the Islamic culture and the sociophobic reactions its members often experience, the conclusions drawn are applicable to any culture (Zaidi, 2017). Young students are engaged, simply and gently, in basic knowledge and information. The purpose is not conversionary but friendly, and represents an opportunity for non-Muslim young people to better understand and gain insight into the cultural practices and identity of their Muslim friends and neighbors. Including Muslim characters and traditions in the curriculum in an integrative way gives students the opportunity to learn about Muslim practices and to be sensitive to the issues that affect Muslims in a context that does not single them out. In some sense, being Muslim is normalized.

The example provided here expands on the notion of cosmopolitan critical literacy in that, as immigration patterns alter global demographics, curricula can be altered as well to perpetuate the awareness of cultural shifts that is becoming increasingly necessary in today's world. The curriculum described deliberately notices the face of multiculturalism and how this can be used to embrace change by integrating both religious differences and cultural dynamics into the school system. Using curricula to counter sentiments of Islamophobia successfully within the classroom encourages cosmopolitanism and it is important to unpack literacy questions at a base level, meeting young people where they are (e.g. school).

Example 2: Dual Language Books in the Classroom

Furthermore, through cosmopolitan critical literacy practices, students can be engaged in open, honest dialogue in the hopes of dispelling some of the myths and fears around Islam and Muslim culture, as an example. These practices can include the use of resources such as dual language books (DLBs) to encourage students to ask questions and be informed as they increase their literacy.

A DLB is a book written in two languages, with English on one page and a second language on the other. DLBs have been published world-wide in 30 different languages and are being used in many classrooms where a large percentage of the students identify from other languages and cultures. Using DLBs, teachers, students, and guest readers are encouraged to become cosmopolitan as they interact with the books, using play and language awareness in an attempt to counteract potential feelings of xenophobia within their classroom, school and immediate cultural vicinity. By encouraging literacy through the use of this type of book, the teacher is exploring the cultural capital of immigrant children and encouraging them to think, act and be within a more diverse paradigm.

The following example illustrates cosmopolitan critical literacy development through the reading of a dual language book, *The Swirling Hijaab* (Figure 3.16.1). The book (read in Urdu, Punjabi, French, and English) was written by Na'ima Bint Robert (2002) and illustrated by Nilesh Mistry.

Using colorful illustrations, the book highlights the story of a young girl's imaginative uses of her mother's hijab. The hijab is a head covering in Islamic cultures; however, it is also a religious

Figure 3.16.1 Book cover of *The Swirling Hijaab* by Nilesh Mistry, illustrator and Na'ima bint Robert, author (reprinted with permission from Mantra Lingua UK, www.mantralingua.com)

garment worn during prayer. Through the reading of this book, both students and the teacher are able to explore the text, and "play" with the languages represented in the DLB. The entire process encourages critical literacy and demonstrates the important role it has through playful imagination and social relationships, both of which are highly valued as part of the development of literacy practices. Hall's (2004) "cultural flows" are very evident here as the students and the DLB reading merge to transcend time and cultural spaces.

Example 3: Class Discussion on Cultural Spaces and Contributions

Exploring cultural spaces includes class discussion on various physical elements of a particular culture or race. Given the current socio-political climate in the world, there have been renewed calls for curricular change to include more awareness of race, historical accountability and how these factor into society's behavior. As an example, a classroom discussion could involve examining Islamic architecture with background information given on the decoration of Islamic buildings. As an example of this type of cosmopolitanism, one such resource was developed for older students (Grades 3–6) and has a primary focus on the Muslim contributions towards the arts, sciences and civil society. In this resource, students look at Muslim cultural contributions as they relate specifically to the Arts. The class examines mosque décor and design, as well as textile development and its use both within and outside the home. Students look at examples of calligraphy and learn about its historical use in language development. They are also given the opportunity to view different accessories used in Muslim culture, like headdresses, jewelry and perfume.

A culture's contributions to the arts, sciences and civil society display recognition of its place in the world and its history, encouraging cosmopolitanism at a different level.

Through critical literacy practices, students are given the opportunity to become more culturally aware and cosmopolitan in their thinking. Awareness activities include understanding a culture's legacy left throughout the world (e.g. the Muslim historical legacy). The resource helps the teacher to explain xenophobia, giving their students critical awareness as to how people develop social systems, order and civility in their society, and this leads to quality discussion around diverse forms of decision making. Students also engage in activities that help them to understand historical events that have contributed to a particular culture's faith (Muslim) and how it spreads around the world. With this understanding, teachers can hopefully counteract feelings of xenophobia and bring about a more cosmopolitan view in their literacy instruction (Zaidi, 2017).

Using Bernstein's (1990) reflections, cosmopolitan learning must factor in "a pedagogically open framework that explores the dynamics of cultural interactions in an on-going fashion" (p. 267). This would suggest that learning takes place in a less hierarchical manner as to what counts as valued knowledge and ensuring that how that knowledge is imparted be within a less centralized mechanism of control.

Implications for Research and Future Directions

When curricula are shaped around the notion that identity is not formed in conflict with others (Turner, 2002), we can have cosmopolitan learning, which encourages students to reflect on their responsibilities towards changing relationships within and beyond our national borders. Turner (2002) further reiterates "cosmopolitan virtue also requires self-reflexivity with respect to both our own cultural context and other cultural values" (p. 57). A decade ago, it was argued that the diversification of societies around the world in the 21st century demanded literacy education that was not only digital and hybrid (mixing signs, symbols and genres), but also included discussion around language, culture and identity. Today, our society is evolving again, and the concept of race (rather than simply the word "immigrant") has become a focal point of the discussion on identity and what each person represents and brings to the table. There are huge implications for research, a brand new field of exploration that spans the globe in its complexity, providing ample opportunity to accelerate the work needed to find solutions to a growing problem of where people fit in this world. All of this has resulted in a renewed surge in demand for curricula to change again, paving the way for how cosmopolitanism can help society and, specifically education, to better understand how we can live together in a changing world.

Much research on cosmopolitan critical literacy has centered on curriculum and pedagogy. Future research would need to attend to the teleological ends of the curriculum which, in this case, refers to the cosmopolitan ends of education. In particular, we need to examine different philosophical visions across cultures of what human flourishing entails. Related to this is the question of what cosmopolitan values and dispositions should educators seek to foster and how do we guard against cosmopolitan values becoming another nomenclature for Western liberal values that discounts the values from other cultures including those from Muslim societies.

Implications for Social Responsibility

Finally, in relation to social responsibility, there is an urgent need for educators and scholars to foreground the ethics of cosmopolitanism in all facets of education from teacher training, research, to the development of policies and curriculum. Given that language mediates one's encounter with the other, there is then a need to critically examine how the other is represented and misrepresented in discourses as well as to consider ways to de-represent and re-represent interpretations of the other. In short, critical literacy practices premised on the ethos of ethical cosmopolitanism disrupts strategic uses of language that objectify marginalized others to reinforce hegemonic values that then hinders hospitable ways of imagining the other as well as dialogue that embraces difference (Choo, 2016).

In conclusion, we argue that integrating cosmopolitan critical literacy presents a more progressive and proactive way of empowering students to engage with the multiplicity of cultures and cultural differences in our global age. Within a culturally and linguistically diverse classroom, a focus on cosmopolitan critical literacy affords rich opportunities for students and teachers alike to examine identity, its processes of construction, change, and interconnection with local and global cultures.

Cosmopolitan critical literacy provides opportunities to interrogate past cultural practices and traditions in order to problematize the fixity and authenticity of cultures and engage with ethical questions underlying cultural value systems. Through active meaning-making practices, students can also create and redefine new visions of living and flourishing in the world. Introducing texts, for example, that do not fit into a typical, English-only mode, produces examples of cultural images that are not consistently found in traditional curricula. Tying in cultural symbols with students' own stories and further examining xenophobic reaction to any of these symbols further promotes awareness of the other and cultivates a stronger cosmopolitan consciousness. The social implications for teachers are critical within this context. By being more aware of cosmopolitanism and critical literacy, the curricula used in the classroom is better defined through the lens of what society's new reality entails. This is a reminder that we live in an age when, by definition, the teaching of language and literacy have become fundamentally transcultural in nature.

References

Adami, R. (2014). Re-thinking relations in Human Rights education: The politics of narratives. *Journal of Philosophy of Education, 48*(2), 293–307.

Appadurai, A. (2013). The future as cultural fact. In A. Appadurai (Ed.), *The future as cultural fact: Essays on the global condition.* Verso.

Baildon, M., & Damico, J. S. (2011). *Social studies as new literacies in a global society: Relational cosmopolitanism in the classroom.* Routledge.

Bernstein, B. (1990). *The structuring of pedagogic discourse: Class, codes, and control, Volume IV.* Routledge.

Brown, E. (2006). Hellenistic cosmopolitanism. In M. L. Gill & P. Pellegrin (Eds.), *A companion to ancient philosophy* (pp. 549–558). Blackwell.

Butler, J. (2010). *Frames of war: When is life grievable?* Verso.

Canagarajah, S. A. (2013). Negotiating translingual literacy: An enactment. *Research in the Teaching of English, 48*(1), 40–67.

Chong, T. (2006). Singapore globalizing on its own terms. In D. Singh & L. C. Salazar (Eds.), *Southeast Asian affairs* (pp. 263–282). Institute of Southeast Asian Studies.

Choo, S. S. (2016). Fostering the hospitable imagination through cosmopolitan pedagogies: Re-envisioning literature education in Singapore. *Research in the Teaching of English, 50*(4), 400–421.

Choo, S. S. (2018). The need for cosmopolitan literacy in a global age: Implications for teaching literature. *Journal of Adolescent and Adult Literacy, 62*(1), 7–12.

Delanty, G. (2012). The idea of critical cosmopolitanism. In G. Delanty (Ed.), *Routledge handbook of cosmopolitan studies* (pp. 38–46). Routledge.

Delanty, G. (2014). The prospects of cosmopolitanism and the possibility of global justice. *Journal of Sociology, 50*(2), 213–228.

Donaghue, E. (2020, February 5). Racially-motivated violent extremists elevated to "national threat priority," FBI director says. *CBS News.* Retrieved March 26, 2020, from www.cbsnews.com/news/racially-motivated-violent-extremism-isis-national-threat-priority-fbi-director-christopher-wray/

Fairclough, N. (2015). *Language and power* (3rd ed.). Routledge.

Freire, P. (1970). *Pedagogy of the oppressed* (M. B. Ramos, Trans.). Continuum.

Freire, P., & Macedo, D. (1987). *Literacy: Reading the word and the world.* Bergin & Garvey.

Gee, J. P. (2007). *What video games have to teach us about learning and literacy.* Palgrave Macmillan.

Gee, J. P. (2015). The new literacy studies. In J. Rowsell & K. Pahl (Eds.), *The Routledge handbook of literacy studies* (pp. 35–48). Routledge.

Gills, B. K., Goodman, J., & Hosseini, S. A. H. (2017). Theorizing alternatives to capital: Towards a critical cosmopolitanist framework. *European Journal of Social Theory, 20*(4), 437–454.

Giroux, H. A. (1987). Introduction: Literacy and pedagogy of political empowerment. In P. Freire & D. Macedo (Eds.), *Literacy: Reading the word and the world* (pp. 1–36). Bergin & Garvey.

Habermas, J. (1984). *The theory of communicative action. Vol. 1: Reason and the rationalization of society* (T. McCarthy, Trans.). Beacon Press.

Hall, K. (2004). The ethnography of imagined communities: The cultural production of Sikh ethnicity in Britain. *ANNALS, 595,* 108–120.

Hansen, D. T. (2011). *The teacher and the world: A study of cosmopolitanism as education.* Routledge.

Hassim, E. (2020). Muslim cosmopolitanisms in a transnational world: Implications for the education of Muslims, *Asia Pacific Journal of Education*, *40*(1), 10–19. https://doi.org/10.1080/02188791.2020.1725434

Hawkins, M. A. (2018). Transmodalities and transnational encounters: Fostering critical cosmopolitan relations. *Applied Linguistics*, *9*(1), 55–77.

Islam, J. S. (2018). A critique of liberal universalism: The concept of secular philosophical grounding. *Theoria*, *154*(65), 48–74.

Kaya, S. (2015). Islamophobia in Western Europe: A comparative, multilevel study. *Journal of Muslim Minority Affairs*, *35*, 450–465.

Koh, A. (2007). Living with globalization tactically: The metapragmatics of globalization in Singapore. *Sojourn: Journal of Social Issues in Southeast Asia*, *22*(2), 179–201.

Kuchay, B. (2019, December 16). What you should know about India's 'anti-Muslim' citizenship law. *Aljazeera*. Retrieved March 26, 2020, from www.aljazeera.com/news/2019/12/india-anti-muslim-citizenship-bill-191209095557419.html

Lamont, M., & Aksartova, S. (2002). Ordinary cosmopolitanisms: Strategies for bridging racial boundaries among working-class men. *Theory, Culture and Society*, *19*(4), 1–25. https://doi.org/10.1177/0263276402019004001

Marx, K., & Engels, F. (1848). *Manifesto of the communist party* (S. Moore, Trans.). Cosimo.

Mignolo, W. D. (2000). The many faces of Cosmo-polis: Border thinking and critical cosmopolitanism. *Public Culture*, *12*(3), 721–748. https://doi.org/10.1215/08992363-12-3-721.

Naqvi, R. (Ed.). (2015). *Living together: Muslims in a changing world*. Retrieved March 26, 2020, from www.living-together.ca

Noble, G. (2009). Everyday cosmopolitanism and the labour of intercultural community. In A. Wise & S. Velayutha (Eds.), *Everyday multiculturalism* (pp. 46–65). Palgrave Macmillan.

Nussbaum, M. C. (2008). Toward a globally sensitive patriotism. *Daedalus*, *137*(3), 78–93.

Oikonomidoy, E. M. (2018). *Critical cosmopolitanism in diverse students' lives: Universal and restricted expressions*. Routledge.

Peters, M. A. (2020). 'The fascism in our heads': Reich, Fromm, Foucault, Deleuze and Guattari—the social pathology of fascism in the 21st century. *Educational Philosophy and Theory*. https://doi.org/10.1080/00131857.2020.1727403

Philippas D. (2014). Xenophonis. In A. C. Michalos (Eds.), *Encyclopedia of quality of life and well-being research*. Springer.

Rizvi, F., & Choo, S. S. (2020). Education and cosmopolitanism in Asia: An introduction. *Asia Pacific Journal of Education*, *40*(1), 1–9. https://doi.org/10.1080/02188791.2020.1725282

Robbins, B. (2012). *Perpetual war: Cosmopolitanism from the viewpoint of violence*. Durham, NC: Duke University Press. https://doi.org/10.1215/9780822395188

Robert, N. B. (2002). *The swirling hijab*. Mantra Lingua.

Smits, H., & Naqvi, R. (Eds.). (2015). *Framing peace: Thinking about and enacting curriculum as "radical hope"*. Peter Lang.

Spivak, G. C. (2012). *An aesthetic education in the era of globalization*. Harvard University Press.

Stornaiuolo, A., Hull, G. A., & Sahni, U. (2011). Cosmopolitan imaginings of self and other: Youth and social networking in a global world. In J. Fisherkeller (Ed.), *International perspectives on youth media: Cultures of production and education* (pp. 263–280). Peter Lang.

Strydom, P. (2012). Modernity and cosmopolitanism: From a critical social theory perspective. In G. Delanty (Ed.), *Routledge Handbook of Cosmopolitan Studies* (pp. 25–37). Routledge.

Tucker, M. E. (1998). Religious dimensions of Confucianism: Cosmology and cultivation. *Philosophy East and West*, *48*(1), 5–45.

Turner, B. S. (2002). Cosmopolitan virtue, globalization and patriotism. *Theory, Culture & Society*, *191*(2), 45–64.

Vasudevan, L. (2011). An invitation to unknowing. *Teachers College Record*, *113*(6), 1154–1174.

Zaidi, R. (2017). *Anti-Islamophobic curriculums*. Peter Lang.

Zaidi, R., & Rowsell J. (Eds.). (2017). *Literacy lives in transcultural times*. Routledge.

3.17

BORDER LITERACIES

A Critical Literacy Framework From Nepantla

Enrique David Degollado, Idalia Nuñez, and Minea Armijo Romero

> Nosotros los Chicanos straddle the borderlands. On one side of us, we
> are constantly exposed to the Spanish of the Mexicans, on the other
> side we hear the Anglos' incessant clamoring so that we forget our
> language. . . . Neither eagle nor serpent, but both. And like the
> ocean, neither animal respects borders.
>
> *(Anzaldúa, 1987, p. 84)*

Borne out of the ashes of conquest, the borderlands represent the 2,000 mile stretch between the United States and Mexico where, "the Third World grates against the first and bleeds," creating "una herida abierta"—an open wound (Anzaldúa, 1987, p. 25). For those who inhabit this in-between space, the epigraph encapsulates their way of life: straddling epistemologies and ontologies that are neither here nor there but both, and contradictory at the same time. In this chapter, we examine the unique role the borderlands play in birthing a border literacy. Grounded in the work of Gloria Anzaldúa (1987) and Walter Mignolo (2000), we argue that border literacies are critical literacies embodied and employed for *reading the word* and *world* (Freire & Macedo, 2005). In doing so, those who practice and manifest a border literacy navigate systems of oppression like hegemonic whiteness (Hooks, 1992; Flores, 2013). We also discuss the implications for border literacy in research and practice and the need to recognize these practices as social justice, anti-racist, and anti-colonial practices in our schools and society.

Definitions of Key Concepts

Anzaldúa (1987) advanced the concept of the borderlands by articulating the new mestiza consciousness whereby border crossers engage in deterritorialzing and remapping practices that rearticulate boundaries and margins within the power contexts, fashioning a way life within the confines of those limits (Gruzinski, 2013; Roemer, & Sharma, 1993; Keating, 2006). In this sense, worlds are recreated, and cultural frameworks are consequently disrupted and readapted to a new lived reality. Anzaldúa (1987) takes up the use of the word *nepantla*, a Náhuatl (Aztec) word meaning "in the middle" to illustrate how nepantla identities are in a "perpetual transition", thereby intersecting with literacies that thrive in the boundary (Lizárraga & Gutiérrez, 2018). For Anzaldúa, to be in nepantla is to be caught in the middle where we learn to embrace contradiction, and where hybrid forms and

DOI: 10.4324/9781003023425-52

border-crossing practices are born out of necessity. As such, nepantla is visible in hybrid forms and cross-border practices of reading and writing.

Correspondingly, couched in the legacies of colonialism in which certain language and epistemologies were/are subalternized, Mignolo (2000) theorizes that a disjuncture from Euro-western epistemologies manifests *border thinking*. Specifically, Mignolo defines border thinking as "a double consciousness, a double critique operating on the imaginary of the modern/colonial world system of modernity/coloniality" (p. 87). Cervantes-Soon and Carrillo (2016) elucidate a *pedagogy of border thinking* that includes testimonios, translanguaging, subaltern knowledge, Mestiz@ Theory of Intelligences (MTI), Straddling, and resistance. Mignolo's theory of bilanguaging—another aspect of border thinking—in which thinking between epistemologies and languages becomes the "necessary corrective" to a world dealing with the oppression of colonial legacies (p. 274). In what follows we argue that scholars build on the foundational work of Anzaldúa and Mignolo to further explicate border literacies as a critical literacy.

Critiques of Critical Literacy

Despite the critical perspective and much-needed political stance of critical literacies (Luke, 2014), Giroux (1988) reminds us that this orientation to literacy still offers a western patriarchal view of the struggles of marginalized communities. We contend that engaging in critical literacy is an act of questioning, challenging, and pushing boundaries, but the boundaries need to be deterritorialized. To accomplish this, critical literacy must recognize the knowledge that derives from the margins that can serve to delink from goals of settler colonialism and modernity (Cervantes-Soon & Carrillo, 2016; Mignolo, 2000)—what scholars describe as border literacies. As such, border literacy deterritorializes, or remaps, in the way it privileges subaltern knowledge and eradicates borders, recentering the locus of enunciation (Mignolo, 2002).

According to Janks and Vasquez (2011) critical literacy involves understanding "the relationship between texts, meaning-making, and power to undertake transformative social action that contributes to the achievement of a more equitable social order" (p. 1). Border literacies, however, center on *theory of the flesh* (Moraga & Anzaldúa, 2015); meaning, how the brown body reads, feels, and views the world, bearing in mind the colonial legacies of those who have inhabited the border. Vila (2000) argues that the border serves as a double mirror in which border identities manifest based on how (trans)fronteriza/o/xs[1] perceive themselves in relation to people on both sides of the border. Border literacies, therefore, derive from the constant negotiation of identity and subjectivity of living colonial legacies—that is, Americanness and Mexicanness, English, and Spanish—an epistemic authenticity that is not captured by critical literacies.

If central to border literacies is the idea of experience over curricular practice, then we must be attuned to the notion of difference. In a critique of critical pedagogy, Elenes (1997) cautions this arguing that, "living in the borders and breaking away from specific boundaries are conditions we all live by; however, critical pedagogy does not specify how differences are incorporated into their projects" (p. 370). Thus, while critical literacy can teach us to deconstruct notions of power at play within literacy, there always remains a residual colonial difference that is created by white patriarchal society. As an example, push-back from critics that privilege colonial languages to integrate hybrid literacy practices, or translanguaging, into the curriculum fail to account for this colonial difference (García, Flores, & Chu, 2011). In other words, translanguaging as a border literacy practice is the result of multiple colonial projects at play whereby a speaker from a position of privilege cannot fully apprehend as they elect to participate in the speaking practices of historically marginalized people; (trans)fronterizx/a/os, on the other hand, have historically been forced to accommodate to privileged speakers to *sobrevivir* (Trinidad Galván & La Vereda, 2006), or survive (Rosa & Flores, 2017).

A Borderland Response to Critical Literacy

Border literacies are critical literacies that stem from an anti-colonial (Cervantes-Soon, 2018; Nuñez & Urrieta, 2021; Tuck & Yang, 2012) and critical perspective that exists on the margins. It is the border thinking and subaltern knowledge that derives from living and experiencing delegitimization caused by unnatural borders that were fundamentally built from the history of colonization, imperialism, and the hegemony of eurocentric, western thought (Anzaldúa, 1987; Mignolo, 2000). According to Anzaldúa (1987), "The prohibited and forbidden" are the inhabitants of margins—the border cross- ers; they do not define themselves by the borders, but, instead, see themselves in the in-betweeness or nepantla (p. 27)—"ni de aquí, ni de allá," neither from here or there (Anzaldúa, 1987, p. 81). Border crossers possess critical border literacies that are perceived as deficient and/or deviant because their border thinking "a process of *doing* decoloniality" (Mignolo, 2011, p. 282) against hegemonic epistemologies (Grosfoguel, 2008). This kind of knowledge critiques eurocentrism from the voices and perspectives of those who have been silenced (Mignolo, 2000; Grosfoguel, 2008), and is a critical response to deficit and marginalizing discourses that exist. For example, Chicana Feminist researchers (Cervantes-Soon, 2014; de los Ríos, 2017; Delgado Bernal, 1998; Delgado-Gaitan, 1993; Saavedra, 2011; Villenas, 1996), have used border theory to recognize the cultural, linguistic, and political knowledge of communities of color. de los Ríos (2017), for instance, explores corridos—a Spanish ballad—as a type of critical literacy, which involves critical consciousness, stories of resistance and oppression, and transnational and translingual knowledge that is important to transnational youth. In a similar way, *platicás* (González, 1998), *testimonios* (Delgado Bernal, 1998), and *saberes* (Urrieta, 2016), among other border literacies have been documented to reveal the powerful and meaningful ways in which subaltern communities have sustained their ways of being despite discriminatory and marginal- izing experiences.

Border literacies provide an understanding of the limits produced by boundaries and provides the creativity to survive marginal realities (Mignolo, 2011). To illustrate this, Nuñez's (2018) study illuminated the everyday uses of language and literacy of three transfronterizo children who face daily national, institutional, and social borders. Informed by their surveillance consciousness and border thinking, the children recognized the limits set by the borders they faced daily—at home, school, community, and across national borderlines. For example, as they crossed the international bridge into the U.S., the children "legitimized" their identity by embodying language based on the Border Patrol agent's expectations. Strategically, the children responded to the border agent in the language—English or Spanish—in which they were addressed. Though the children were bilingual, and U.S. citizens, they recognized the rigidity and surveillance of language borders, and its signifi- cance to entering the United States. Here, speaking Spanish only, or being bilingual is demonized, and the children have developed the critical border literacies to understand that in this situation, as well as other spaces. Their critical border literacies are critical literacies that allow them to recognize and navigate linguistic borders that aim to surveil them.

Additionally, border literacies provide the opportunity to (re)imagine and to transform futures within and across borders. Cervantes-Soon (2016), for instance, demonstrates how young women from Ciudad Juarez, Mexico embody and (re)conceptualize smartness. Used their experiential knowledge to recognize "systems of oppression," this group of women, straddled gender, class, and race borders (Cervantes-Soon, 2016, p. 7). Recognizing the asymmetrical relations between the U.S. and Mexico—and the effect it had on cartel violence experienced on the border—the socially con- structed, gendered discourses imposed on women, they embodied the necessary knowledge to live on the borderlands: self-defense, being bold, self-motivation, and how to self-generate the resources needed to survive everyday life in Juarez. These women deemed themselves *mujeres truchas*, or criti- cally conscious women. A mujer trucha understands "the assumption that society is an unequal playing field, that struggle is part of every woman's life, and that advancement is not real unless it is part of a collective" (Cervantes-Soon, 2016, p. 1215). Hence, border literacies are necessary every day critical literacies for subaltern communities.

Implications for Pedagogy

Border literacies compel us to reimagine pedagogy in a way that recognizes and empowers subaltern knowledge in the context of a racialized reality. Here, we build on neplantera and border pedagogy. For Reza-López, Charles, and Reyes (2014) neplantera pedagogy acknowledges human dignity via conscientization (critical consciousness), conocimientos (knowledges), dialogism, and ideological becoming. Prieto and Villenas (2012) deem that "nepantla [pedagogy] speaks to and informs the difficulty and often overlapping spaces cultural dissonance, conciencia con compromiso, and cariño" (consciousness with commitment, and love) (p. 425). Similarly, Cervantes-Soon and Carrillo (2016) define border pedagogy as the "scaffolding power, naming inequities through critical dialogue, and involving students in their growth and critical consciousness" (p. 288). Taken together, these ideas create a space where marginalized enunciated-voice is acknowledged and constructed beyond binarisms deriving from location and power-language to bear border literacy.

We consider the following examples to be part of a neplantera and border thinking pedagogy. Testimonio brings the mind, body, spirit, and political urgency to the fore to theorize and learn from experiences of oppression and resistance (Delgado Bernal, Burciaga, & Flores Carmona, 2012; Saavedra, 2011). In classrooms, testimonio disrupts silence, invites connection, and entices collectivity—it is social justice pedagogy. Nuñez (2019), for example, highlights the pedagogies of Latina mothers who challenged static notions of literacy by incorporating Spanish multimodal texts (e.g. Mexican websites and Spanish captions on English videos) to foster biliteracy at home. Degollado, Bell, and Salinas (2019) document how Texas escuelitas were spaces of nepantlera possibility in how they focused on Spanish literacy and Mexican culture, fostering resistance and resilience in Mexican American children, allowing them to traverse the hegemony of English in U.S. schools. In all these examples, the locus of enunciation resides outside normative schooling literacy practices, and necessitates the humility, vulnerability, and wherewithal to foster and appreciate subaltern knowledge. To advance border literacies as a critical literacy through our pedagogy, we must follow Elenes (1997) who asks us to recenter the experiences of those who live and embody the borderlands—both physical and psychological. A process that involves looking beyond our understanding of best practices and seeing how (trans)fronterizx/a/o (i.e. parents, children, and communities) are reading, writing, and shaping their world.

Implications for Research

Much of the research on borderland theory has taken place within the context of the physical border. Historically, however, Latinxs have lived beyond border communities. Moreover, borderland thinking largely emerges out of the Texas-Mexico context. In fact, Anzaldúa informs her theories from her lived experience growing up in south Texas. Transnational youth may offer insight into the ways in which border thinking plays out beyond the geographic border. Skerrett and Bomer (2013), among other literacy scholars, have started to push the nation-state ideational boundaries regarding language and literacy knowledge to demonstrate the hybrid, border-crossing, and multimodal affordances of transnational experiences. We contend that scholars should identify the relationship border literacies play in the language and literacy practices of transnational youth (García, 2015; Dworin, 2003; Hornberger & Link, 2012).

Smith and Murillo (2012) claim that:

> By focusing on colonias as a specific type of hybrid community along the border, one that is continuously under construction by residents, we have identified a platform for theorizing about the spatial dimensions of language and literacy practices in other multilingual, multiliterate communities.
>
> *(p. 649)*

Similarly, Degollado (2019) demonstrated how space informed the language and literacy ideologies of bilingual maestras who have lived and been educated in the borderlands. Put together, we learn that the borderlands exemplify how to straddle two worlds. At the same time, border literacies are not unique to this space; nepantla can exist outside these spaces (Kasun, 2014, 2016). Thus, more research is needed to determine how neplanterxs make sense of their distinctive lived experiences outside the physical borderlands.

Furthermore, we maintain that borderlands theories should be applied to name border literacies in classrooms. Much of the literature cited in this chapter draws on sociocultural theories of literacy (i.e. Gee, 1991; New London Group, 1996; Street, 1995; Vygotsky, 1978). While we recognize that these scholars have historically informed literacy education, we join other scholars of color (Cervantes-Soon & Carrillo, 2016; Degollado, 2019; de los Ríos, 2017; Nuñez, 2018) who engage in theorizing with nepantla and border thinking to better articulate the ways in which border literacies disrupt the hegemony of how literacy research is conducted. Consider how Anzaldúa's (1987) mestiza consciousness and Mignolo's (2000) border thinking are theorized. Their attention to the colonial projects and legacies that produced border literacies have been pivotal to centering the knowledges of indigenous communities, transnational communities, communities of color, and the Global South.

Implications for Our Social Responsibility as Academics

In Trump's pronouncement to the world that he was running for the presidency of the United States, he claimed that Mexicans are "not sending their best," thereby bringing to foreground in our national discourse the latent racist, anti-immigrant, and xenophobic attitudes that have plagued Latinxs and minoritized population throughout US history. His words reverberate in the hearts and minds of those who are most vulnerable—that is, undocumented people, people of color—and must not be forgotten. For those who work with the fronterizxs, his words were a call to action to engage in anti-racist pedagogies and advocate for students' well-being. Because we have come to realize that many support his xenophobic attitudes, our social responsibility as educators and research is to foster, encourage, and validate the use of *border literacies* (Nuñez & Urrieta, 2021) as they continue to be forms of resistance and resilience in times of adversity (Degollado et al., 2019).

de los Ríos (2018) writes that "as the socio-political climate intensifies and manifests hostility toward immigrant and transnational communities, it is an urgency to connect contemporary linguistic practices as these reveal the tensions and also the resistance of Latinx communities" (p. 457). To be sure, border literacies are the manifestation of resistance and resilience. Schools however are dominant institutions where education is ideologically bound by the nation-state of which they are part. According to Abu El-Haj (2007), "Schools play a very important role in the way boundaries are allegorically constructed within these learning spaces. Moreover, these spaces attribute or take away national identity" (p. 288). We must ensure that students feel that their border literacies are welcome in these spaces, allowing for agency and innovation in how students use their border literacies to make sense of the world they are inhabiting (Cashman, 2019; Lizárraga & Gutiérrez, 2018).

Just as important is the need to be in community with fronterizos and be an advocate and ally. Trinidad Galván (2011) attests that we coexist with our participants, through the process of convivencia, experiencing humanity. Learning from others how they go beyond surviving Therefore, by attending ourselves to the acute ways that fronterizos employ their border literacies to transform this world allows us to be in community with them. This demands humility, an open mind, and an open heart (Freire, 1970; Mignolo, 2000) to be able to listen and humanize the experiences of fronterizos and restructure how we conduct ourselves in spaces where educators and scholars are privileged and hold institutional power.

Recommendations for Future Research and Praxis

To better understand border literacies, we must first contemplate their utility in the classrooms as a set of critical literacy practices. While border literacies cannot be part of fixed curriculum, border literacies are practiced on an every-day basis on the part of the teachers and the students. Border literacies deepen our understanding of critical literacies in that they consider the epistemologies and ontologies of those who have traversed a physical and metaphorical in-between space. *Borderlands/La Frontera* (Anzaldúa, 1987) continues to serve as a model for what it means to read, write, and speak from an authorial voice that is uniquely a borderlands practice. In this sense, we must augment our curriculums to allow for this style of writing and expression to happen. This entails us using translanguaging as a legitimate literacy practice. Cervantes-Soon and Carrillo (2016) argue that translanguaging is border thinking practice. Indeed, for many fronterizxs translanguaging is their everyday practice. However, it is seldom recognized and validated in schools (Martínez, Hikida, & Durán, 2015). In Degollado's (2019) study of fronteriza maestras, however, he shows how translanguaging was a pedagogical practice that was heavily leaned on. He postulates that it was the bilingual maestras' abuelita epistemologies (Gonzales, 2015) that fortified them with the notion that "Spanglish"—as his participants named it—to be a legitimate form of communication and meaning making practice. In that sense, teachers and researchers alike must continue to push for translanguaging as a teaching practice to undo monoglossic ideologies.

As previously mentioned, border literacies are part of a larger framework for teaching and preparing future teachers within a social justice framework. In short, it is a social justice act to practice and honor border literacies. Scholars have laid the theoretical foundation for this work through culturally relevant pedagogies (Ladson-Billings, 1995), cultural sustaining pedagogies (Paris & Alim, 2014), humanizing pedagogies (Freire, 1970) and the like. de los Ríos and Molina (2020) offer compelling insight into these pedagogies by documenting literacies of refuge that connects the Mexican Christmas posadas to immigration issues. That said, teachers must be equipped with these practices in their training. Cervantes-Soon (2018) reveals this in her Xicana Feminists framework for bilingual education, arguing that the basis for teacher preparation should be the lived experiences of Chicanas.

Lastly, we must consider and push ourselves to name border literacies beyond the physical border. For Anzaldúa (1987), nepantla was not only a physical representation of the border but also a psychological one—one that fronterizos carry beyond the immediate U.S.–Mexico borderlands. Indeed, Latinx communities live in spaces all over the continental United States and beyond. Thus, their border thinking (Mignolo, 2000) allows them to navigate the spaces where the hegemonic whiteness pervades the psyche. Scholars, then, must task themselves with working with and for these communities to (re)imagine the possibilities of positioning these communities as border pedagogues and embracing anti-racist, anti-colonial, etc. literacies that are rooted border knowledge.

Note

1. We use the term (trans)fronterizx/x/a/o to capture the lived experiences of those who have both crossed the literal border (trans) and those who have only lived the border.

References

Abu El-Haj, T. R. (2007). "I was born here, but my home, it's not here": Educating for democratic citizenship in an era of transnational migration and global conflict. *Harvard Educational Review, 77*(3), 285–316.

Anzaldúa, G. (1987). *Borderlands/La frontera.* Aunt Lute Books.

Cashman, T. G. (2019). Transnational Educational Research in four countries: Promoting Critical Border Praxis. *Journal of Research, Policy and Practices of Teachers, 9*(1), 46–57.

Cervantes-Soon, C. G. (2014). The U. S.-Mexico border-crossing Chicana researcher: Theory in the flesh and the politics of identity in critical ethnography. *Journal of Latino/Latin American Studies, 6*(2), 97–112.

Cervantes-Soon, C. G. (2016). Mujeres truchas: Urban girls redefining smartness in a dystopic global south. *Race Ethnicity and Education, 19*(6), 1209–1222.

Cervantes-Soon, C. G. (2018). Using a Xicana feminist framework in Bilingual teacher preparation: Toward an anticolonial path. *The Urban Review, 50*(5), 857–888.

Cervantes-Soon, C. G., & Carrillo, J. F. (2016). Toward a pedagogy of border thinking: Building on Latin@ students subaltern knowledge. *The High School Journal, 99*(4), 282–301.

Degollado, E. D. (2019). *The storied lives of fronteriza bilingual maestras: Constructing language and literacy ideologies in nepantla* (unpublished doctoral dissertation). The University of Texas at Austin.

Degollado, E. D., Bell, R. C., & Salinas, C. S. (2019). "No Había Bilingual Education:" Stories of negotiation, Educación, y Sacrificios from South Texas Escuelitas. *Journal of Latinos and Education,* 1–15.

Delgado Bernal, D. (1998). Using a Chicana feminist epistemology in educational research. *Harvard Educational Review, 68*(4), 555–579.

Delgado Bernal, D., Burciaga, R., & Flores Carmona, J. (2012). Chicana/Latina testimonios: Mapping the methodological, pedagogical, and political. *Equity & Excellence in Education, 45*(3), 363–372.

Delgado-Gaitan, C. (1993). Researching change and changing the researcher. *Harvard Educational Review, 63*(4), 389–412.

de los Ríos, C. V. (2017). Picturing ethnic studies: Photovoice and youth literacies of social action. *Journal of Adolescent & Adult Literacy, 61*(1), 15–24.

de los Ríos, C. V. (2018). Toward a corridista consciousness: Learning from one transnational youth's critical reading, writing, and performance of Mexican corridos. *Reading Research Quarterly, 53*(4), 455–471.

de los Ríos, C. V., & Molina, A. (2020). Literacies of refuge:"Pidiendo Posada" as ritual of justice. *Journal of Literacy Research,* 1086296X19897840.

Dworin, J. E. (2003). Insights into biliteracy development: Toward a bidirectional theory of bilingual pedagogy. *Journal of Hispanic Higher Education, 2*(2), 171–186.

Elenes, C. A. (1997). Reclaiming the borderlands: Chicana/o identity, difference, and critical pedagogy. *Educational Theory, 47*(3), 359.

Flores, N. (2013). The unexamined relationship between neoliberalism and plurilingualism: A cautionary tale. *TESOL Quarterly, 47*(3), 500–520.

Freire, P. (1970). *Pedagogy of the oppressed.* Continuum International Publishing Group, Inc.

Freire, P., & Macedo, D. (2005). *Literacy: Reading the word and the world.* Routledge.

García, O. (2015). Translanguaging and abecedarios ilegales. In T. M. Kalmar (Ed.), *Illegal alphabets and adult biliteracy: Latino migrants crossing the linguistic border* (pp. 131–136.). Routledge.

García, O., Flores, N., & Chu, H. (2011). Extending bilingualism in US secondary education: New variations. *International Multilingual Research Journal, 5*(1), 1–18.

Gee, J. P. (1991). What is literacy? In C. Mitchell & K. Weiler (Eds.), *Rewriting literacy: Culture and the discourse of the other* (pp. 5–11). Bergin & Garvey.

Giroux, H. A. (1988). Border pedagogy in the age of postmodernism. *Journal of Education, 170*(3), 162–181.

Gonzales, S. M. (2015). Abuelita epistemologies: Counteracting subtractive schools in American education. *Journal of Latinos and Education, 14*(1), 40–54.

González, F. E. (1998). *The formations of Mexicannes: Trenzas de identidades multiples: The development of womanhood among young mexicanas: Braids of multiple identities* (PhD dissertation). University of California, Davis.

Grosfoguel, R. (2008). Transmodernity, border thinking, and global coloniality. *Eurozine: Decolonizing Political Economy and Postcolonial Studies.* http://www.eurozine.com/articles/2008-07-04-grosfoguel-en.html

Gruzinski, S. (2013). *The mestizo mind: The intellectual dynamics of colonization and globalization.* Routledge.

hooks, b. (1992). *Teaching to transgress*. Routledge.

Hornberger, N. H., & Link, H. (2012). Translanguaging and transnational literacies in multilingual classrooms: A biliteracy lens. *International Journal of Bilingual Education and Bilingualism, 15*(3), 261–278.

Janks, H., & Vasquez, V. (2011). Critical literacy revisited: Writing as critique. *English Teaching, 10*(1), 1.

Kasun, G. S. (2014). Hidden knowing of working-class transnational Mexican families in schools: Bridge-building, Nepantla knowers. *Ethnography and Education, 9*(3), 313–327.

Kasun, G. S. (2016). Interplay of a way of a knowing among Mexican-origin transnationals: Chaining to the border and to transnational communities. *Teachers College Record, 119*(9), 1–32.

Keating, A. (2006). From borderlands and new mestizas to nepantlas and nepantleras: Anzaldúan theories for social change. Human architecture: *Journal of the Sociology of Self-knowledge, 4*(3), 3.

Ladson-Billings, G. (1995). Toward a theory of culturally relevant pedagogy. *American Educational Research Journal, 32*(3), 465–491.

Lizárraga, J. R., & Gutiérrez, K. D. (2018). Centering Nepantla literacies from the borderlands: Leveraging "in-betweenness" toward learning in the everyday. *Theory Into Practice, 57*(1), 38–47.

Luke, A. (2014). Defining critical literacy. In J. Z. Pandya & J. Ávila (Eds.), *Moving critical literacies forward: A new look at praxis across contexts* (pp. 19–31). Routledge.

Martínez, R. A., Hikida, M., & Durán, L. (2015). Unpacking ideologies of linguistic purism: How dual language teachers make sense of everyday translanguaging. *International Multilingual Research Journal, 9*(1), 26–42.

Mignolo, W. D. (2000). *Local histories/global designs: Coloniality, subaltern knowledges, and border thinking*. Princeton University Press.

Mignolo, W. D. (2002). The geopolitics of knowledge and the colonial difference. *The South Atlantic Quarterly, 101*(1), 57–96.

Mignolo, W. D. (2011). Geopolitics of sensing and knowing: On (de) coloniality, border thinking and epistemic disobedience. *Postcolonial Studies, 14*(3), 273–283.

Moraga, C., & Anzaldúa, G. (Eds.). (2015). *This bridge called my back: Writings by radical women of color*. SUNY Press.

Nuñez, I. (2018). *Literacies of surveillance: transfronterizo children translanguaging identity across borders, inspectors and surveillance* (Unpublished doctoral dissertation). The University of Texas at Austin.

Nuñez, I. (2019). "Le Hacemos La Lucha": Learning from Madres Mexicanas' multimodal approaches to raising bilingual, biliterate children. *Language Arts, 97*(1), 7–16.

Nuñez, I., & Urrieta Jr, L. (2021). Transfronterizo children's literacies of surveillance and the cultural production of border crossing identities on the US–Mexico border. *Anthropology & Education Quarterly, 52*(1), 21–41.

Paris, D., & Alim, H. S. (2014). What are we seeking to sustain through culturally sustaining pedagogy? A loving critique forward. *Harvard Educational Review, 84*(1), 85–100.

Prieto, L., & Villenas, S. A. (2012). Pedagogies from Nepantla: Testimonio, Chicana/Latina feminisms and teacher education classrooms. *Equity & Excellence in Education, 45*(3), 411–429.

Reza-López, E., Charles, L. H., & Reyes, L. (2014). Neplantera pedagogy: An axiological posture for preparing critically conscious teachers in the borderlands. *Journal of Latinos and Education, 13*, 107–119.

Roemer, M., & Sharma, V. (1993). Reviewed Work(s): Border crossings: Cultural workers and the politics of education. *The Journal of the Midwest Modern Language Association, 26*(1), 82–85.

Rosa, J., & Flores, N. (2017). Unsettling race and language: Toward a raciolinguistic perspective. *Language in society, 46*(5), 621–647.

Saavedra, C. M. (2011). Language and literacy in the borderlands: Acting upon the world through "testimonios". *Language Arts, 88*(4), 261–269.

Skerrett, A., & Bomer, R. (2013). Recruiting languages and lifeworlds for border-crossing compositions. *Research in Teaching of English, 47*(3), 313–337.

Smith, P. H., & Murillo, L. A. (2012). Researching transfronterizo literacies in Texas border colonias. *International Journal of Bilingual Education and Bilingualism, 15*(6), 635–651.

Street, B. V. (1995). *Social literacies: Critical approaches to literacy in development, ethnography and education*. Longman.

The New London Group. (1996). A pedagogy of multiliteracies: Designing social futures. *Harvard Educational Review, 66*(1), 60–93.

Trinidad Galván, R. T. (2011). Chicana transborder Vivencias and Autoherteorias: Reflections from the field. *Qualitative Inquiry, 17*(6), 552–557.

Trinidad Galván, R. T., & La Vereda, G. U. N. U. (2006). Campesina epistemologies and pedagogies of the spirit: Examining women's Sobrevivencia. In D. Delgado Bernal, C. Elenes, F. E. Godines, & S. Villenas (Eds.), *Chicana/Latina education in everyday life: Feminista perspectives on pedagogy and epistemology*. SUNY Press.

Tuck, E., & Yang, K. W. (2012). Decolonization is not a metaphor. *Decolonization: Indigeneity, Education & Society, 1*(1).

Urrieta Jr, L. (2016). Diasporic community smartness: Saberes (knowings) beyond schooling and borders. *Race Ethnicity and Education, 19*(6), 1186–1199.

Vila, P. (2000). *Crossing borders, reinforcing borders: Social categories, metaphors, and narrative identities on the US-Mexico frontier.* University of Texas Press.

Villenas, S. (1996). The colonizer/colonized Chicana ethnographer: Identity, marginalization, and co-optation in the field. *Harvard Educational Review, 66*(4), 711–732.

Vygotsky, L. S. (1978). *Mind in society: The development of higher psychological processes.* Harvard University Press.

3.18

CONCLUSION

Critical Literacy and the Challenges Ahead of Us

Raúl Alberto Mora, Jessica Zacher Pandya, Jennifer Helen Alford,
Noah Asher Golden, and Roberto Santiago de Roock

In bringing this Handbook to a close, we as editors reflect on the privilege it has been to gather these chapters together in one volume as a contribution to the scholarship and activism in the field. The five of us came to this Handbook positioned as both scholars and learners. As we noted in the Preface, we are aware of and grateful for the giants on whose shoulders this Handbook stands. Some appear as authors in our chapters, and others have influenced our paths to critical literacy since graduate school; we are honored to be their students and mentees, as well as their friends and colleagues. We came to this Handbook with the certainty that critical literacy was the cornerstone or core of our work. As we explained in the Introduction, we all shared the belief that critical literacy is not just a buzzword or something we *do*. Critical literacy shapes who we *are* as teachers, as researchers, as scholars, as community members, and as family members. However, we were also fully aware that we still had so much more to learn about the field. We know we have segmented vision based on conceptual affinities, geographical locations, and other epistemological positionalities. We know that our field can only grow if we expand our horizons through radical linguistic, cultural, and geographic inclusivity.

An ethos to discover and rediscover what critical literacy is, what it looks like all over the world, and what it should or could be guided this project. We know of no other effort in critical literacy research gathering such a polyphony of voices from different places, many traditionally in the periphery (Haddix, 2020), "forgotten" (Friedrich & Berns, 2003) regions. Each of the chapters in this handbook offered valuable insights about different authors' journeys with critical literacies. Chapters cover new textual practices, modes of analysis, spaces, and platforms that offer insights into where the critical literacies praxis is going. This volume welcomed scholars from the places where scholars built the tradition (e.g., Australia, South Africa, United States, United Kingdom), places whose scholars have already added their contributions to the field (e.g., Brazil, Canada, Mexico, Aotearoa New Zealand) and places with their own scholarly traditions that resonate with, enrich, and extend Western conceptions of critical literacy on their own terms (e.g., Colombia, Russia, Central Africa, Middle East). We joined experienced scholars who built the field as we know it with emerging scholars on the rise from around the world, scholars we hope you will keep referencing in the near future. We are proud of this polyphony, of the recentering of critical literacy works we discovered in the process.

This conclusion to the Handbook is a moment for our individual and collective reflexivity about the challenges that critical literacy as a field will face in the future. The historic circumstances forming the backdrop to this volume highlight the unparalleled urgency of our work. They

 DOI: 10.4324/9781003023425-53

include the COVID-19 pandemic that has further entrenched power and material inequalities, with deadly consequences for those at the margins. The pandemic has shifted the ways we think about education, highlighting the perils of reverting to economy-driven online models that can easily foster and justify functional literacy practices, leaving little room for bigger questions about society and the world. It has come on the heels of and been exacerbated by another pandemic: the gradual resurgence of neo fascist, ethnonationalist movements around the world and their attacks on science, facts, and truth. We continue to face the risks and material reality of a climate crisis (Carrington, 2019) that increasingly transforms dystopian movie scenarios into news headlines (Carrington, 2021; Thunberg, 2019). However, in the midst of this despair, we have also seen how different generations, older and newer, have risen to the occasion, thinking of solutions for these problems, turning online classrooms and public spaces into arenas to creatively challenge the world, as well as moments for small-scale and global resistance and bravery. It is in this tension that critical literacy praxis needs to rethink itself as a force that can fuel change in and outside of our classrooms (Freire, 1972).

Lessons from the Past and Present

The Meaning of "Critical Literacy" Is in Flux

In their own ways and with diverse ideologies, the chapters in this Handbook provide an invitation to rethink what exactly is meant by critical literacy. One striking feature of the contributions is the broad range of theoretical and conceptual lenses used to interrogate critical literacies practice and to argue for new directions. Today, critical literacy *is* a transnational, translingual affair and the network we started in 2018, the Transnational Critical Literacies Network (TCLN), is a consequence of that reality, not a catalyst. This ongoing project of bringing together critical literacy researchers and practitioners from across the globe has shown the momentum and importance of the frameworks. This work immediately surfaced the nuanced and contextually-bound nature of critical literacy in terms of languages, epistemologies, and sociocultural specificity. The domination of scholarship by the Global North — and especially by white, Anglophone discourses — sometimes obscures the tensions that scholars in non-Anglophone regions face when they move across the different languages they use to talk about literacy. This is a tension that has been long evidenced in Spanish (2.5, 2.10, 2.11) and Portuguese (2.3) speaking countries and communities (see Mora, 2016 for a brief discussion), but chapters in Area 2 also highlighted tensions in French (2.20), Norwegian, Finnish (2.19), Arabic (2.8), Hindi (2.6), Mandarin and Cantonese Chinese (2.18), and Russian (2.12) speaking countries; struggles of Indigenous peoples in relation to languages are also examined (2.1, 2.14, 2.22). The meaning and use of critical literacy as a transnational and translingual affair warrant further scrutiny as we explore the different layers that literacy definitions have across languages other than English, and how geographical and cultural diversity creates new understandings of text and its position in society.

Finally, authors have mapped out challenging new territory where critical literacies can be extended beyond current boundaries and understandings. For instance, a common thread of Area 3, Critical Literacies in Motion, is one of emergence: criticality cannot be seen as an identity or position we occupy, but an ongoing process in which we engage. Authors point to the need for more discussion of emergent topics and critical production as actors explore new tools, platforms, and fresh perspectives on literacy practices. They challenge utopian visions of "21st-century literacies" while marking out new fields of inquiry and seeking to address theoretical and practical conundra. The range of topics highlight the key challenges of our era: decentering the human in service of the planet's survival; critiquing the ideologies surrounding learning disabilities; subverting the dominance of standard versions of English in schooling through translanguaging; and dismantling xenophobia. The future of critical literacies is being painted on multiple canvases, offering possibilities for more equitable conditions, civic engagement, and more sustainable futures.

The Scope of Critical Literacy Has Grown Beyond Traditional Notions and Settings

Handbook chapters surfaced a number of complexities and tensions, in particular as a result of the transnational scope and framing. It is certainly true that work defined explicitly as critical literacy is happening in classrooms across the globe, even if in sometimes limited ways or scattered pockets. Additionally, there is ample indication that pedagogies and practices we would call critical literacies, even if not explicitly described as such, are happening everywhere, including far beyond the reach or influence of the authors of this handbook or other critical literacy practitioners. In many countries, schools may be the least likely sites in which to encounter critical literacies. This reality is perhaps the most fascinating, frustrating, and compelling aspect of critical literacies research. Chapters in all areas demonstrate the need to contest normative critical literacy discourse (i.e., what is seen, research, taught, etc. as "Critical Literacy") as resembling what happens in Western contexts. This formation is typically seen in schools or empowerment organizations, explicitly teaching a skill sometimes called "critical thinking", one that is almost inevitably seen autonomously (Street, 1984) to some degree, especially in Western contexts with liberal arts training traditions. We contend that it is possible the most powerful critical literacy praxis is least likely to be labeled as such, since it would be organic, situated, grounded in local social movements, contesting traditional understandings of top-down globalization. In a sense, its authenticity might render it invisible.

Chapters in Area 2 show a constant tension between the hegemonic Western, the "transnational" (see Chapter 1.1 for our extended discussion), and the local. Case studies such as those of Indonesia (2.7) and Iran (2.8) push us to think past pedagogies that are normatively critical literacy to look at alternate and local versions, often with religion in mind. They lead us to wonder whether the secular orientation of critical literacies in the West is not only culturally specific but actually myopic and constitutive of our own ongoing crises. Chapters also indicate how critical literacy is easily subsumed under the neoliberal notions of critical thinking concerned with increasing human capital for workforce development, as opposed to critical engagement with power structures. Questions linger about the legacies that have built the field and the residual effect of patriarchal, heteronormative, colonial, and monolingual discourses that still permeate the conversations around critical theories and literacies. How we break these cycles of social and conceptual reproduction will be an issue for our field in the immediate future.

Finally, many countries are still struggling with (so-called) basic education, often getting caught up in the discourse that "basic" needs to be addressed first and that the "critical" comes later (even in more "advanced" or high-performing systems). These and other related issues often arise from the influence of Western NGOs and international organizations (see Chapter 2.21), and (neo)colonialism more broadly. There are also clear tensions inherent in the limits of public schooling as state-linked (liberal or illiberal) institutions, where objectivity and the apolitical is normative whereas subjectivity, activism, and political approaches are discouraged or even banished. Such notions of critical literacy, still dominant within the West, hearken back to Enlightenment notions of the thinking person and the universal political subject.

A Blueprint for the Unknown

Chapters throughout the Handbook make it clear we must move forward towards justice. This includes the everyday work of preservice teacher education (1.9) in which many of us engage. Critical literacies should be present throughout teacher preparation programs, not as isolated modules but as the structures for courses themselves (1.6). This includes the possibilities of a queer critical literacy framework to interrogate texts and design QCL curriculum (with reliance on Janks' [2010] model (1.8)), which could easily be part of a larger scale teacher preparation program overhaul. The implementation of such changes is needed not only in coursework for teachers but in teacher practice; they need support in the classroom as they learn to support sustained criticality in classrooms and educational systems. Indeed, one major critique of critical literacy is its failure to gain a foothold, much less a sustained presence, in teacher education contexts.

Other chapters in Area 1 emphasize that critical digital media literacies production must be continuously reshaped given the increasingly mobile nature of some of our lives (1.10), and that the body, and its readings, are central to the work of critical literacy (1.7). The chapter on Youth Participatory Action Research argues for critical and intergenerational participatory research as a form of critical literacy praxis, and pushing against traditional adult–youth binaries and power relations in our work (1.5). Authors in chapter 1.2 and 3.7 ask if we even need more scholarship; perhaps, they suggest, the time for scholarship is past, and now it is time for organizing to make change. That is one of the clearest implications for our social responsibility as academics. We are complicit in the neoliberal education systems that continue to shape the lifeworlds of children, youth, and adults in increasingly unequal ways. Within such a reality, a transformative approach seems the only ethical way forward.

Area 2 chapters make clear the need to consider how we engage different constituencies, communities, and peoples around the world. As inclusive as this effort has been, there are far too many areas that are not represented within the Handbook. This is, first and foremost, a shortcoming of our editorial team's limited scholarly networks, but also an indication of our field's limits arising from gatekeeping and myopic scholarly gaze. To make literacy a truly global affair we need to move beyond Englishes and embrace the need for multilingual work, making space for other ethnolinguistic groups in these conversations. We need to work more closely with communities around the world and serve as discourse brokers and find ways to share all of our histories, epistemic stances, and counterstories (Solórzano & Yosso, 2001).

This transnational perspective highlights the need for more inclusive frameworks in theorizing critical literacy around the globe. For example, as we put together the chapters, we wrestled with questions about to what extent the idea of "country" normatively used to construct global affairs makes sense to talk about critical literacy especially given the nation-state's fundamental and historic ties to ethnonationalist formations. We sought to bring critical literacy advocates around the world together through various "scapes" of cultural flows (Appadurai, 1996) that avoid separating by (neo) colonial boundaries and instead congregate around commonalities.

From Area 3, the recommendations for future practice and research disrupt entrenched ways of thinking about critical literacies. These proposals spearhead new trajectories that will not be achieved without challenge, and even, perhaps, ideological conflict. The diversity among and the contradictions between these chapters is remarkable. These trajectories begin from common concerns yet offer a wide range of possibilities for critical literacies praxis. Chapters throughout this Area emphasize how in the shifting literary and media landscape of this century, critical educators should prioritize texts that use many modes to represent experience (including posthuman), that delve into the major socio-political issues of our times, and invite readers to experience a range of both critical and emotional responses (3.1; 3.4). Given this ever-shifting landscape, Chapter 3.8 authors encourage critical analysis of the digital media, platforms, and technologies used to produce digital texts that themselves can interrogate issues of power, representation, and access. Chapter 3.2 authors recommend critical arts-literacies centered in research designs that speak back to dominant forms of knowing—logic, mathematics, the verbal—to emphasize abductive, imaginative, and emotional ways of understanding literacies learning and teaching. Chapter 3.14 authors stress that criticality is a process and not a position, and offer narratives stressing the need for humility and accountability as we engage in dialogue in youth-led spaces. Similarly, Chapter 3.15 authors offer approaches to decentering teacher educators' voices by drawing on community literacies and enacting sustained dialogues that value community-based knowledge, as teacher educators partner with community members in the complex work of preparing literacy educators.

Robust implications for the social responsibility as academics are outlined in all Area 3 chapters but one in particular stands out. The authors of Chapter 3.3 argue that there are many opportunities for teachers and scholars to reflect on the ethics and integrity of our work, but that we often ignore them as we accept, out of economic and political self-interest, institutional and neoliberal accounts of knowledge production and distribution, among other things. Many of us were perhaps first attracted to critical literacies work for its transformative potential in people's lives, including our own. However, as the "neo-liberal juggernaut" (Doherty, 2015) tightens its grip, we find ourselves less and less able to make the stand we want to make, or the change we want to see. How, then, do we maintain the momentum for critique and social action when our institutional livelihoods are structured around their undoing? This occurs in such processes as the casualization of faculty and lack of tenure, increasing and ever-changing work roles and workloads, and standardization of curriculum at all levels. Despite these constraints, the long-term critical literacies project requires that we actively seek new ways of being socially responsible.

The chapters in this area provide a roadmap to work our way into positions of greater collective agency and power to sustain our commitment to critical literacies in forms old and new. As Chapter 3.9 authors argue, there is a need for "constant skepticism" and "restive problematization" in collectively working to change the conditions that minoritize people based on their language practices and literacies. There is a great need to shift from describing these processes and mobilizing to interrupt the "persistent deficit orientation" (3.11) that is grounded in monolingual and racialized language ideologies. Chapter 3.16 authors see cosmopolitan pedagogies as a way to counter the longstanding and rising xenophobia, encouraging the value of multiple languages, identities, and literacy practices. With some parallels, Chapter 3.17 authors see the possibility of reimagining our pedagogies by centering Border literacies that disrupt silences and create opportunities for connection and collectivity. Throughout Area 3, the wellspring of approaches to critical analysis and production, and the opportunities they engender for collective actions and interruptions of existing hierarchies and systems, offer us pathways forward as we seek new ways of living and interacting in our biosocial world.

Entering Uncharted Territory: A Coda

The 108 authors in the 50 chapters penned for this Handbook provide a unique opportunity to gain a deeper understanding of critical literacy around the world. They represent strong and diverse understandings of what critical literacy *is*, but most importantly, powerful ideas of what critical literacy *should be*. Undoubtedly, this is the challenge for our field beyond this Handbook. Through this project, the idea of the *social responsibility of academia*, once again resonating with the ideas and challenges that critical theorists over the decades have posed for education (e.g. Giroux, 2011; How, 2003; Leonardo, 2005; Ndimande, 2010; Nieto, 2010) was the compass and guiding light. Without a sense of social responsibility to help craft a better world (Céleste Kee & Carr-Chellman, 2019; Goodman & Cocca, 2014; Janks, 2014; Stevens & Stovall, 2010; Willis, 2015) critical literacy rings hollow. All the authors in this volume seemed to agree that the future of critical literacy as a space for research, scholarship, and advocacy will depend on how we live by that social responsibility.

The ideas in this Handbook move us, as the title in this section says, into unchartered territory. The field has moved from thinking about the "possible" (Morgan, 1997) and started thinking of the *impossible*. Critical literacy is very clearly not just about *transforming* but about completely *reinventing* education. It is not just about *questioning* inequity (social, economic, linguistic), but about *combating* it by creating real spaces for counterhegemony (Gramsci, 1975) through language and other means. Critical literacy, true to its roots, is most powerful when moving past critique to mobilize resources, both at grassroots (Blommaert, 2008) and formalized levels, towards social and political transformation. Granted, a great deal of transformation is yet to happen, but we hope the Handbook may open new avenues for collaboration and research. This collective effort, then, is just the beginning for all of us, both the editors and the contributing authors.

We offer our gratitude to all of the authors for their inspiration and commitment to literacy, to education, to justice, to a better world. We felt it in their words and the literature from their areas of expertise and the countries and regions they represent. As editors, we are truly humbled by the rigorous and thoughtful contributions they have made to this Handbook. We want to especially thank those authors who also doubled as chapter reviewers for their insightful feedback. Their comments and suggestions made all of the chapters even stronger. For our readers, we hope that the chapters that comprise this volume afford insights and stimulation as you either embark on or continue your work for social, cultural, political and economic justice in your own contexts. If the work introduced here inspires you to propose new avenues for critical literacy, the field needs to hear more about your work.

In this endeavor, we were able to find compelling voices and activist, engaged scholarship, but we are also well aware that many voices were left out. Some because they could not join us at this time, some because we were not able to find you. If someone's work is not represented in this Handbook, if you are reading this and are not an author or have not had your work cited by these 108 authors, know that the fault is ours as editors. Your scholarship is most valuable and we want, to paraphrase Shirley Chisholm's famous quote, to assure you that there is no need to bring a folding chair to this table. There is a seat already waiting for you and we do not want that seat to remain empty. Critical literacy as a field is poised for a moment of reckoning. We are reinventing what we mean by "critical" and by "literacy" and we need to keep amplifying more voices and efforts. Finally, for researchers who have felt somewhat comfortable in this field, the lesson is: the field is expanding, and expansive. There is room for all of us--especially if we are willing to argue our positions, listen to others, and make some concessions.

The TCLN Founding Five (Jessica, Raúl, Jennifer, Noah, Roberto)

References

Appadurai, A. (1996). *Modernity at large: Cultural dimensions of globalization.* University of Minnesota Press.

Blommaert, J. (2008). *Grassroots literacy: Writing, identity and voice in Central Africa.* Routledge.

Carrington, D. (2019, May 17). Why the Guardian is changing the language it uses about the environment. *The Guardian.* Retrieved from xwww.theguardian.com/environment/2019/may/17/why-the-guardian-is-changing-the-language-it-uses-about-the-environment

Carrington, D. (2021, January 27). Climate crisis: World is at its hottest for at least 12,000 years—study. *The Guardian.* Retrieved from www.theguardian.com/environment/2021/jan/27/climate-crisis-world-now-at-its-hottest-for-12000-years

Céleste Kee, J., & Carr-Chellman, D. J. (2019). Paulo Freire, critical literacy, and indigenous resistance. *Educational Studies, 55*(1), 89–103. https://doi.org/10.1080/00131946.2018.1562926

Doherty, C. (2015). Tracking the neoliberal juggernaut: A virtual edition. *Critical Studies in Education, 56*(3), 395–401

Freire, P. (1972). *Pedagogy of the oppressed* (M. B. Ramos, Trans.). Penguin.

Friedrich, P., & Berns, M. (2003). Introduction: English in South America, the other forgotten continent. *World Englishes, 22*(2), 83–90. https://doi.org/10.1111/1467-971X.00280

Giroux, H. A. (2011). Paulo Freire and the courage to be political. *Our Schools/Our Selves, 20*(2), 153–163.

Goodman, S., & Cocca, C. (2014). Spaces of action: Teaching critical literacy for community empowerment in the age of neoliberalism. *English Teaching: Practice and Critique, 13*(3), 210–226. https://eric.ed.gov/?id=EJ1050185

Gramsci, A. (1975). *Prison notebooks* (J. A. Buttigieg & A. Callari, Trans.). Columbia University Press.

Haddix, M. M. (2020). This is us: Discourses of community within and beyond literacy research. *Literacy Research: Theory, Method, and Practice, 69*(1), 26–44. https://doi.org/10.1177/2381336920937460

How, A. (2003). *Critical theory*. Palgrave Macmillan.

Janks, H. (2010). *Literacy & power*. Routledge.

Janks, H. (2014). Critical literacy's ongoing importance for education. *Journal of Adolescent & Adult Literacy, 57*(5), 349–356. https://doi.org/10.1002/jaal.260

Leonardo, Z. (2005). Critical social theory and transformative knowledge: The functions of criticism in quality education. *Educational Researcher, 33*(6), 11–18. https://doi.org/10.3102/0013189X033006011

Mora, R. A. (2016). Translating literacy as global policy and advocacy. *Journal of Adolescent & Adult Literacy, 59*(6), 647–651. https://doi.org/:10.1002/jaal.515

Morgan, W. (1997). *Critical literacy in the classroom: The art of the possible*. Psychology Press.

Ndimande, B. S. (2010). Critical theory as social justice pedagogy. In T. K. Chapman & N. Hobbel (Eds.), *Social justice pedagogy across the curriculum: The practice of freedom* (pp. 89–103). Routledge.

Nieto, S. (2010). *Language, culture, and teaching: Critical perspectives* (2nd ed.). Routledge.

Solórzano, D. G., & Yosso, T. J. (2001). Critical race and LatCrit theory and method: Counter-storytelling. *Qualitative Studies in Education, 14*(4), 471–495. https://doi.org/10.1080/09518390110063365

Stevens, L. P., & Stovall, D. O. (2010). Critical literacy for xenophobia: A wake-up call. *Journal of Adolescent & Adult Literacy, 54*(4), 295–298. https://doi.org/10.1598/JAAL54.4.8

Street, B. V. (1984). *Literacy in theory and practice*. Cambridge University Press.

Thunberg, G. (2019). *Speech at the climate action summit, New York* [Video]. Retrieved from www.npr.org/2019/09/23/763389015/this-is-all-wrong-greta-thunberg-tells-world-leaders-at-u-n-climate-session?jwsource=cl

Willis, A. I. (2015). Literacy and race: Access, equity, and freedom. *Literacy Research: Theory, Method, and Practice, 64*, 23–55. https://doi.org/10.1177/2381336915617617

LIST OF CONTRIBUTORS

A

Arman Abednia is a lecturer in Education at Murdoch University, Perth, Australia, where he teaches research methodology and literacy units in undergraduate and graduate programs. Arman also serves as the academic literacy development advisor at Edith Cowan College, Perth. His research areas include teacher education, teacher identity, and critical pedagogy/literacy. His most recent publication is a book entitled *Starting Points in Critical Language Pedagogy* that he has co-authored with Professor Graham V. Crookes (Information Age Publishing, 2021). https://orcid.org/0000-0002-9402-9845

Earl Aguilera is an assistant professor in the Department of Curriculum and Instruction at California State University, Fresno, located on the ancestral and traditional lands of the Yokuts and Mono peoples. He has recently published in the *Handbook of Research on Cultivating Literacy in Diverse and Multilingual Classrooms* and the *Handbook of Research on Integrating Digital Technology with Literacy Pedagogies*. https://orcid.org/0000-0002-3694-1406

Anwar Ahmed is an assistant professor in the Department of Languages, Literatures and Linguistics at York University in Canada. He is co-editor of *Mobility of Knowledge, Practice and Pedagogy in TESOL Teacher Education: Implications for Transnational Contexts* (Palgrave Macmillan, 2021). https://orcid.org/0000-0002-5883-3238

Jennifer Helen Alford is associate professor in Education at Queensland University of Technology, Brisbane, Australia. She is interested in how language education policies articulate criticality; and how teachers mobilize critical approaches with English learners amid increasingly acritical education priorities. Her book *Critical Literacy with Adolescent English Language Learners: Global Policy and Practice* was published in 2021 by Routledge. She is a co-editor of *Literacy Research: Theory, Method & Practice* journal for the Literacy Research Association (LRA). http://orcid.org/0000-0001-9238-0933

Donna E. Alvermann is the Omer Clyde and Elizabeth Parr Aderhold Professor in Education and the Appointed Distinguished Research Professor of Language and Literacy Education at the University of Georgia, USA. Her research focuses on young people's critical digital literacies, their uses of popular culture, and a Foucauldian approach to genealogy involving historical texts. She is lead editor on the 7th edition of *Theoretical Models and Processes of Literacy* published in 2019 by Routledge. https://orcid.org/0000-0001-6881-0657

DOI: 10.4324/9781003023425-54

Grant Andrews is a lecturer at the University of the Witwatersrand School of Education in Johannesburg, South Africa. His research interests include queer theory, queer visual cultures in South Africa, and gender and sexuality studies. https://orcid.org/0000-0001-5268-0800

Minea Armijo Romero is a Ph.D. candidate in the Language Literacy and Sociocultural Studies program at the University of New Mexico, and Faculty at the Education Department at Central New Mexico Community College. Her research looks at the intersection of transnationalism, border theory, and intercultural educational models in Latin America. https://orcid.org/0000-0003-1087-2577

B

Alexander Bacalja is a lecturer in Language and Literacy and member of the Language and Literacy Research Hub in the Melbourne Graduate School of Education, The University of Melbourne. His research focuses on critical digital literacies in both school and non-school contexts, and the potential for pedagogy to move users to more critical understandings of contemporary texts, technologies, and platforms. His recent work on digital game literacies and critical digital literacies can be found in *The Australian Journal of Language and Literacy* and *Game Studies*. https://orcid.org/0000-0002-2440-1488

George Lovell Boggs investigates the development of specialized literacies, often considering how learning processes intersect with formal education. Recent projects seek to understand the practical economic significance of literacy against a backdrop of cultural myths. He loves to make music, farm, gather firewood, and cook with his family in the Georgia mountains.

Scott Bulfin is a senior lecturer in English education at Monash University in the Faculty of Education. His research focuses on new literacies, the sociology of educational technology and secondary English education. His latest book is *Everyday Schooling in the Digital Age*. Routledge, 2018. https://orcid.org/0000-0001-9083-5236

Cassie J. Brownell is an assistant professor of Curriculum, Teaching, and Learning at the Ontario Institute for Studies in Education of the University of Toronto. Her research takes up issues of educational justice and equity in early childhood. https://orcid.org/0000-0002-8640-2777

Mardiana Abu Bakar is a lecturer with the Policy, Curriculum and Leadership Academic Group at the National Institute of Education, Nanyang Technological University. She is also programme leader in the Master of Education, Curriculum, Teaching and Learning. In these roles, she teaches and partly administers the core programmes on curriculum policy and theory; and an elective on curriculum implementation. She is currently PI in a Funds of Knowledge research in Singapore schools as well as co-PI in three research projects: 1. Diversity and intercultural mindedness amongst secondary school students; 2. The role of a child support model for low-income families; and 3. The pathways and life trajectories narratives of vocational students in Singapore. A critical scholar interested in issues of curriculum access and equity, Mardiana believes that schools are places of possibilities and constraints; and her main passion is to contribute towards the nurturing of self-critical communities of reflexive educators.

Tanja Burkhard is an assistant professor in the Department of Human Development at Washington State University. Her research interests focus on qualitative methodologies, race, immigration, language, and postcolonial theories. She has recently co-edited a volume titled *Race, Justice, and Activism in Literacy Instruction*. https://orcid.org/0000-0003-4960-676X

Lavern Byfield is an associate professor in the School of Education at Southern Illinois University Carbondale (Carbondale, Illinois, USA). Her publications and research are in the areas of language acquisition, English Language Arts instruction for diverse populations, English as a Second Language (ESL) instruction, and culturally responsive pedagogy. https://orcid.org/0000-0003-1756-6097

C

Claudia Cañas is an English teacher at Universidad Pontificia Bolivariana (UPB) Elementary School, where she has served as academic coordinator in the English department. She is also an adjunct professor at the School of Education and Pedagogy at the same university, where she teaches Communicative Competence courses in the BA in English-Spanish, and graduate courses on linguistics for English teachers and literacies in second languages and supervises master's students. She is also the associate chair at the Literacies in Second Languages Project (LSLP) research lab at Universidad Pontificia Bolivariana. Her current research explores and characterizes children's personal literacies in and out of school, using multimodality and multiliteracies as conceptual underpinnings. She has already presented her research in international conferences such as AERA and LRA and some of her recent work was also featured in Research in the Teaching of English. https://orcid.org/0000-0003-1978-1567

Edison Ferney Castrillón-Ángel is a full-time instructor at Universidad Católica Luis Amigó in Medellín and a member of the Literacies in Second Languages Project (LSLP) research lab at Universidad Pontificia Bolivariana. He is also pursuing his PhD at the Federal University of Piauí in Brazil. Edison's research and scholarship adopts a multidisciplinary strategy that incorporates the fields of educommunication, languages, critical digital literacy, technologies, ICT, and cultural behaviors. He holds a BA in Social Communication from Corporación Universitaria Minuto de Dios (UNIMINUTO), a Graduate Specialization in ELT and a MA in Learning and Teaching Processes in Second Languages, both from Universidad Pontificia Bolivariana. https://ORCID.org/0000-0001-9237-1084

Benjamin "Benji" Chang is an associate professor of Equity Education at the University of North Carolina, Greensboro. His work applies intersectional approaches to teacher education, community engagement, and language, literacy and culture with minoritized communities from around the Asia-Pacific Rim. He has been published in venues like *Linguistics & Education* and *Curriculum Inquiry*, and is Co-Editor of the journal *Critical Inquiry in Language Studies*. https://orcid.org/0000-0002-4054-8738

Chris K. Chang-Bacon is an assistant professor of Education at the University of Virginia. His research on critical literacies in multilingual contexts has been featured in *Journal of Literacy Research* (2017) and *Journal of Teacher Education* (2020). https://orcid.org/0000-0002-5584-189X

Suzanne S. Choo is an associate professor in the English Language and Literature Academic Group at the National Institute of Education, Nanyang Technological University, Singapore. Her research has been published in various peer-reviewed journals including *Harvard Educational Review, Critical Studies in Education*, and *Discourse: Studies in the Cultural Politics of Education*. Her book, *Reading the World, the Globe, and the Cosmos: Approaches to Teaching Literature for the Twenty-First Century*, was awarded the 2014 Critics Choice Book Award by the American Educational Studies Association. Her most recent book is *Teaching Ethics Through Literature: The Significance of Ethical Criticism in a Global Age* (Routledge, 2021). https://orcid.org/0000-0001-7446-3372

James S. Chisholm is an associate professor in the College of Education and Human Development at the University of Louisville. His current research projects focus on sociopolitical discourses in the teaching of writing, social justice and arts integration, and social capital in a student-led bilingual mentoring program. With Kathryn F. Whitmore, he co-authored *Reading*

Challenging Texts: Layering Literacies Through the Arts (NCTE and Routledge, 2018). https://orcid.org/0000-0002-0988-9315

Justin A. Coles is an assistant professor in the division of Curriculum and Teaching at Fordham University, Graduate School of Education in Manhattan, NY. His research agenda converges at the intersections of critical race studies, urban education, language and literacy, and Black studies. https://orcid.org/0000-0002-6232-8939

Barbara Comber is a research professor in the Centre for Research in Educational and Social Inclusion, Education Futures at the University of South Australia. Her research interests include teachers' work, critical literacy, social justice, and creative pedagogy. Two recent books reflect these interests and her long-term collaborations with front-line educators—*Literacy, Place and Pedagogies of Possibility* (Comber, 2016) and *Literacy, Leading and Learning: Beyond Pedagogies of Poverty* (Hayes, Hattam, Comber, Kerkham, Thrupp & Thomson, 2017).

Anne Crampton is the academic program director of Teacher Education for Inclusive Environments at Western Washington University, in Bellingham, Everett, and Bremerton, WA, USA. She researches, writes, and teaches about critical literacy practices, affective experiences and learning, and digital and multimodal literacies.

Susan Cridland-Hughes is an associate professor of English Education at Clemson University, South Carolina, USA. Her most recent publications include "Fostering Critical Participatory Literacy through Policy Debate" in *English Teaching: Practice and Critique* (2018) and "We don't wanna strait-jacket you: Community, Curriculum and Critical Literacy in Urban Debate" in the *Journal of Language and Literacy Education* (2018). https://orcid.org/0000-0002-4209-5197

Graham Crookes is professor, Department of Second Language Studies, University of Hawai'i at Mānoa. He has spent most of his professional life in the Asia-Pacific region; his work is focused on critical language pedagogy, critical literacy, and teachers' values. His most recent publication book is *Starting Points in Critical Language Pedagogy* (co authored with Arman Abenia (Information Age Publishing, 2021). https://orcid. org/0000-0002-9402-9845

D

Roberto Santiago de Roock is an assistant professor of Learning Sciences & Technology at University of California, Santa Cruz. His interdisciplinary work examines the relationships between literacy, technology, and liberation under racial capitalism. He primarily does this through ethnographic design work, but also in pioneering critical digital discourse analysis and participatory methods. https://orcid.org/0000-0002-4844-4386

Enrique David Degollado is an assistant professor in Multilingual Education at The University of Iowa. His research focuses on the influence of bilingual education teachers' lived experiences on their language and literacy ideologies and pedagogical practices. https://orcid.org/0000-0001-9052-5596

Alexandre Dessingué is professor of Literacy Studies and History Education at the University of Stavanger, Norway. His research interests focus on cultural and collective memory studies, cultural representations of WW1, WW2, the Holocaust and of the colonial period, memory theories, critical literacy/awareness and history education. His last publications include a co-edited volume with Jay Winter, *Beyond Memory: Silence and the Aesthetics of Remembrance* (Routledge, 2016), the book chapters "Paul Ricoeur: Understanding the Past and Writing the Future" (Routledge, 2017), "The Ethics of Memory" (Verlag, 2017) and the article "Developing Critical Historical Consciousness:

Re-thinking the Dynamics between History and Memory in History Education" (Nordidactica, 2020). ORCID: https://orcid.org/0000-0002-3171-2719

Pooja Dharamshi is an assistant professor in the Faculty of Education at Simon Fraser University (Vancouver, Canada). Her research explores the ways in which teacher educators conceptualize and enact critical literacies practices in an era of increasing neoliberal reforms. Her new book is entitled "*Advancing Equity and Social Justice in Teacher Education: Transformative Practices and Pedagogies of Literacy*" which is part of the Literacies as Resistance series for DIO Press. https://orcid.org/0000-0003-2917-6897

Lynn Downes is a lecturer in the School of Education and Leadership at the Queensland University of Technology, Australia. Her research interests focus on language and linguistics, specifically language change and sociolinguistics in the area of taboo linguistics. Lynn's interests also include Critical Discourse Analysis and English language and literacies in the primary school context, with a focus on the use of multimodal texts and critical literacies. Her most recent article is *Critical discourse analysis in transcultural spaces* (2019). https://orcid.org/0000-0002-4393-620X

Ana Paula Duboc is a professor of Language Teaching Methodology at the School of Education from the University of Sao Paulo, Brazil. In 2016, she co-authored the decolonial-oriented English curricular guidelines within the Municipal Secretariat of Education in Sao Paulo. Her research interests comprise language and literacy education, educational policies, language teacher education, critical literacies, decoloniality. She coordinates the ELCo—*Grupo de Estudos Educação, Linguagem e Colonialidade* (Research Group on Education, Language, and Coloniality). https://orcid.org/0000-0002-3136-3504

E

Christian Ehret is an associate professor in the Faculty of Education at McGill University in Montréal, Québec. He develops social theory toward more affective, material, and embodied understandings of literacy and learning with digital media. His volume, co-edited with Kevin Leander, *Affect in Literacy Teaching and Learning: Pedagogies, Politics, and Coming to Know* was published in 2019. https://orcid.org/0000-0002-7589-1974

Grace Enriquez is a professor of Language and Literacy at Lesley University, Cambridge, MA, USA. She centers her teaching and research on intersections of literacies, identities, and embodiment; critical literacies; reader response; and children's literature for social justice. Most recently, she is co-author of *The Reading Turn-Around with Emergent Bilinguals: A Five-Part Framework for Powerful Teaching and Learning* (2019) and co-editor of *Literacies, Learning, and the Body: Putting Theory and Research into Pedagogical Practice* (2016). https://orcid.org/0000-0002-6556-4021

F

Jennifer Farrar is a lecturer at the University of Glasgow, Scotland, in children's literature and literacies. Her research interests include student teachers' knowledge and use of children's literature and its potential as a vehicle for critical literacies. Her current research explores the intersection of political and critical literacies within initial teacher education. Recently published articles have explored the status of critical literacies in Scottish Educational Policy (2019) and critical literacy's role in Scotland's new LGBTI-inclusive curriculum (2020). https://orcid.org/0000-0002-7128-6355

Daniel Ferraz is a professor at the Department of Modern Languages from the University of São Paulo, Brazil. He centers his teaching and research on teacher education, language education, literacies, and cultural studies. He is the coordinator of the *Grupo de Estudos sobre Educação Linguística em Línguas Estrangeiras* (GEELLE). https://orcid.org/0000-0002-8483-2423

Rafael Filiberto Forteza Fernández is an associate professor at the Ural Federal University, Ekaterinburg, Russia. He centers his teaching and research on issues of critical discourse, teacher language awareness, and ideology in English language teaching. He co-authored the papers on critical literacy *Language and Cultural Awareness of a non-native ESP teacher* (2019) and *Content Edulcoration as Ideology Visualization in an English language coursebook* (in print 2020), and authored *Critical Discourse Analysis of Key Concepts in Obama's Statement: Cuba Policy Changes* (2016) as well as others on issues pertaining ELT in the Russian context. https://orcid.org/0000-0001-5356-5337

G

Antero Garcia is an assistant professor in the Graduate School of Education at Stanford University. Antero received his Ph.D. in the Urban Schooling division of the Graduate School of Education and Information Studies at the University of California, Los Angeles. Prior to completing his Ph.D., Antero was an English teacher at a public high school in South Central Los Angeles. His work explores how technology and gaming shape learning, literacy practices, and civic identities. His recent books include *Everyday Advocacy: Teachers who Change the Literacy Narrative, Good Reception: Teens, Teachers, and Mobile Media in a Los Angeles High School,* and *Compose Our World: Project-Based Learning in Secondary English Language Arts.* https://orcid.org/0000-0002-8417-4723

Carlos Andrés Gaviria is a language teacher in Spanish language academies in Medellín and a researcher at the Literacies in Second Languages Project (LSLP) research lab at Universidad Pontificia Bolivarian, Medellín-Colombia. His current research interest explores the use of second languages in virtual and online spaces to propose alternative ways to understand how people interact and communicate in these places. His publications and presentations include work in digital and gaming literacies as well as language education. He graduated with honors from his BA in English and Spanish Education at Universidad Pontificia Bolivariana. https://orcid.org/0000-0002-0302-5284

Noah Asher Golden is an assistant professor of Teacher Education at California State University, Long Beach. His scholarship contributes to knowledge on the identity enactments and (re)positioning practices of minoritized youth and is situated within critical and sociocultural approaches to literacies research and teaching/learning practice. https://orcid.org/0000-0002-5296-5803.

Polina Golovátina–Mora is an associate professor of Film and Media in Education at the Norwegian University of Science and Technology (NTNU). She has taught and guest lectured in Russia, Czech Republic, and Poland. Her research covers the intersections between narratives, language, and power, critical theories, social theory and qualitative methodologies, and individual–nature relations. Some of her featured research has appeared in *International Journal of Cultural Studies and Qualitative Inquiry.* She was a grantee of a number of fellowships, including Fulbright Graduate Scholarship (University of Illinois), AFP Open Society Returning Scholar Fellowship, Robert Bosch Tandem Program, and an Erasmus Mundus Post-doctoral Fellowship and pursued her studies in the United States, Poland, and Russia. She has a track record of publications and presentations delivered in Russian, English, Spanish, Czech, and Polish. https://orcid.org/0000-0002-7686-9699

Steve Goodman is the founding executive director emeritus of the Educational Video Center in New York City, and media education instructional coach for K–12 schools, colleges, and community-based organizations. His research and practice focuses on critical literacy, youth media, civic engagement, and youth participatory action research. He is the author of numerous publications, including *It's Not About Grit: Trauma, Inequity and the Power of Transformative Teaching* (Teachers College Press, 2018). https://orcid.org/0000-0003-3129-784X

Navan Govender is a lecturer at the University of Strathclyde in Glasgow, United Kingdom, where they teach on the PGDE English programme. Working in the field of Applied (English) Language and Literacy Education, Navan's research explores the relationship between language and power in education by working at the interface of critical literacies, multimodality and transmodality, and diverse (queer) identities. Their two most recent articles include *Critical Literacy & Critically Reflective Writing: Navigating Gender & Sexual Diversity* and *Critical Transmodal Pedagogies: Student Teachers Play with Genre Conventions*. https://orcid.org/0000-0001-6764-1169

Margarita Gudova is a professor at the Ural Federal University, Ekaterinburg, Russia, the leader of Ural Research team Multilingualism and interculturalism in the era of Post-literacy, the director of scientific laboratory New Literacy and Cognitive Technology. Her recent publications include *Analyzing the Intercultural and Multilingual University Space: Methodological Foundations* (2018) and *Synesthetic Artistic Perception in the Era of Post-Literacy* (2017). https://orcid.org/0000-0002-9628-0451

Gloria Gutiérrez-Arismendy is the research coordinator at The New School, a private school in Medellín. She is also involved in thesis supervision at the MA in Learning and Teaching Processes in Second Languages at Universidad Pontificia Bolivariana. She is an affiliated researcher at the Literacies in Second Languages Project (LSLP) research lab at Universidad Pontificia Bolivariana. She has experience working with vulnerable populations from different ages. Her research interests intersect her teaching background and her work as a professional stage actress to propose an arts-based approach to language and literacy development. https://orcid.org/0000-0002-8357-6907

Maria Guzikova is an associate professor at the Ural Federal University, Ekaterinburg, Russia. Her research focuses on the area of multiculturalism and multilingualism in the era of post-literacy. Her recent publications include *Questioning the conventional language teaching methods: transformational teaching approach* (2019) and *Analyzing the Intercultural and Multilingual University Space: Methodological Foundations* (2018). https://orcid.org/0000-0001-6550-4814

H

Christianti Tri Hapsari is currently a lecturer at the English Department, Faculty of Languages and Arts, Universitas Negeri Semarang (UNNES), Indonesia. She is a Researcher at the Literacy Research Centre of UNNES. She is also a reviewer for ELT Forum: Journal of English Language Teaching, English Department, Universitas Negeri Semarang (UNNES). Her fields of interest are on Teaching English as a Foreign Language (TEFL), literacy (reading and writing). https://orcid.org/0000-0002-1548-3952

Donna Hazzard is a principal lecturer at St Mary's University College, Belfast. Her research interests include critical literacy and the work of Pierre Bourdieu. Her most recent publications include "Challenging Misrecognition: A Case for Critical Literacy" (2021), International Journal of Educational Research, and Creating Young News Readers: The Irish News Critical Literacy Project, (2021) (second edition), Belfast, The Irish News. https://orcid.org/0000-0002-4301-9567.

David I. Hernández-Saca is an assistant professor of Disability Studies in Education within the Department of Special Education, at the University of Northern Iowa. His work in the field of Learning Disabilities (LD) interrogates the emotional impact of LD labeling on conceptions of self at the intersections of power and identities. He is the author of *Sophia Cruz's Emotional Construction of Learning Disabilities: A Liberation DisCrit Emotion Narrative and Community Psychology Approach* (2021, Palgrave Macmillan). https://orcid.org/0000-0002-3070-4610

Gregorio Hernandez-Zamora is a professor of Education, Design, and Communication at Autonomous Metropolitan University (UAM) in Mexico City. He received his PhD in Language, Literacy, and Culture from UC Berkeley. His work in the field of language and literacy education explores the connections between language, culture and cognition, with a focus on issues of educational inequality. He is author of *Decolonizing Literacy: Mexican Lives in the Era of Global Capitalism* (2010, Multilingual Matters) and *From New Literacy Studies to Decolonial Perspectives in Literacy Research* (2019, *Íkala: Revista de Lenguaje y Educación*) among other chapters, articles, and books. https://orcid.org/0000-0003-3364-0939

Seonmin Huh is an invited professor at Chungbuk National University, Korea. Her research focuses on critical literacies, critical perspectives to English education for foreign language learners of English, innovative teaching methodologies and the development of learning and teaching model. Her most recent articles are "Pedagogical Efforts to Encourage Students' English Oral Discussions in University Reading Classes" (2019) and "Preparing elementary readers to be critical intercultural citizens through literacy education" (2019). https://orcid.org/0000-0002-1654-7604

Betina Hsieh is an associate professor of teacher education at California State University, Long Beach (California, United States). Her work on critical literacies has been featured in *English Teaching, Practice and Critique* and *Pedagogies: An International Journal*. https://orcid.org/0000-0003-1456-765X.

J

Radha Iyer is Senior Lecturer in Education at Queensland university of Technology, Brisbane, Australia. She teaches in the sociology of education, postgraduate teacher training programs and in the Master of Education courses. Her research interests include critical discourse analysis, applied linguistics, critical literacy, media literacy, multiliteracies, gender and educational issues. She is currently one of the co- editors of International Education Journal: Comparative Perspectives.

Hilary Janks is a professor emerita in the School of Education at the University of the Witwatersrand, Johannesburg, South Africa. She is the author of *Literacy and Power* (2010) and the editor and author of *Doing Critical Literacy* (2014). Her teaching and research are in the areas of language and literacy education in multilingual classrooms, critical literacy and the literacies and spatialities of childhood. Her work is committed to a search for equity and social justice in contexts of poverty. https://orcid.org/0000-0002-9992-9623

Elisabeth Johnson is an independent educational consultant who teaches, researches, and writes about youth, teachers and critical literacies through an ethnographic lens attuned to theories of embodiment. In 2016, she co-edited *Literacies, Learning and the Body* with Grace Enriquez, Stavroula Kontovourki, and Christine Mallozzi. Her most recent work is in *English Teaching Practice and Critique* (2020), *Australian Journal of Language and Literacy* (2018), and *Hacking Education in a Digital Age* (2018). https://orcid.org/0000-0001-7602-2888

Laura Ruth Johnson is an associate professor in the Department of Educational Technology, Research and Assessment in the College of Education, Northern Illinois University, DeKalb, IL, where she teaches classes in qualitative research methods, with a focus on ethnographic and community-based research. Her recent book is entitled *Community-Based Qualitative Research: Approaches for Education and the Social Sciences* (2017). https://orcid.org/0000-0001-9629-9016

Kelly C. Johnston is an assistant professor of Literacy in the Department of Curriculum & Instruction at Baylor University, Waco, TX, USA. Her research focuses on intersections of literacies, children and youth, and interdisciplinary education. Dr. Johnston's recent scholarship can be found in *Journal of Research in Childhood Education* (2021), *English Teaching: Practice and Critique* (2020), and *Language Arts* (2020). https://orcid.org/0000-0002-9287-8237

Miriam Jorge is the Dr. Allen B. & Mrs. Helen Shopmaker Endowed Professor of Education and International Studies at the University of Missouri St. Louis, USA, and associate editor of the *Brazilian Journal of Applied Linguistics*. Her current research interests include critical literacies, social justice education, the internationalization of teacher education, and academic literacies for international students and scholars. http://orcid.org/0000-0001-8397-4916

K

Jean Kaya is an assistant professor in the Teacher Education Program at Colorado Mountain College in Colorado, USA. His publications and research are in the areas of language teaching and learning, discourse analysis, critical literacies, identities, teacher education, and international education. https://orcid.org/0000-0002-3382-3180

Nihal Khote is an assistant professor of TESOL at the Inclusive Education Department, Kennesaw State University, Atlanta, Georgia. His research focuses on implementing culturally sustaining and critical literacy frameworks with linguistically marginalized students through the intersection of translanguaging and systemic functional linguistics. https://orcid.org/0000-0003-2453-2813

Stavroula Kontovourki is an assistant professor of Literacy and Language Arts Education at the University of Cyprus, focusing on literacy and embodiment, multimodality, and literacy teachers, curricula, and educational policy. She co-edited "*Literacies, Learning and the Body*" (Enriquez, Johnson, Kontovourki, & Mallozzi, 2016) and recently published in *English Teaching: Practice and Critique* (2020), *Curriculum Journal* (2018), and edited volumes. http://orcid.org/0000-0001-8994-7222

Amoni Kitooke is a graduate student of Educational Research at the University of Gothenburg, Sweden. His academic interest is in critical educational research, managing cultural diversity and critical literacy. He is the Deputy Executive Director at the Cross-Cultural Foundation of Uganda, and the Chairperson of the Uganda National English Language Teachers' Association.

Kristiina Kumpulainen is Professor of Education at the University of Helsinki, Finland and Associate Professor in Educational Technology and Learning Design at Simon Fraser University, Canada. She has published widely on communication, learning and education in the digital age including publications on digital literacies and learning, as well as agency and identity. She is the Co-Editor of Elservier's journal Learning, Culture and Social Interaction.

L

Heidi Layne is a University Lecturer in Sustainable and Global Education at the Faculty of Education and Psychology, University of Jyväskylä, Finland. She gained her PhD in the Philosophy of Education from the University of Helsinki and has worked as a Research Scientist in the Nanyang Technological University, National Institute of Education in Singapore. Her background is in social context of education, teacher education and qualitative research methods. Currently, she is engaged in a research project on early interventions for children with low-income family background in Singapore and on everyday multiculturalism and racism in schools in Singapore and in Finland. ORCID ID: https://orcid.org/0000-0003-0346-3062

Sunny Man Chu Lau is an associate professor at Bishop's University in Quebec, Canada, is a nominee for Tier 2 Canada Research Chair in Integrated Plurilingual Teaching and Learning. She is the co-editor of the book *Plurilingual Pedagogies: Critical and Creative Endeavors for Equitable Language in Education* (Lau & Van Viegen, 2020) and for the journal *Critical Inquiry in Language Studie*s. https://orcid.org/0000-0001-7626-4473

Cynthia Lewis is Professor and Chair of Education at the University of California, Santa Cruz. She has published widely on the sociocultural and sociopolitical dimensions of literacy learning in and out of school, with a special focus on critical literacy and critical media analysis and production. Recent publications have examined how youth mobilize emotion to transform texts and signs, practices that are widely understood to be central to critical (media) literacy. She is author and co-editor of two award-winning books and is co-editor (with Jennifer Rowsell and Carmen LIliana Medina) of the Routledge book series Expanding Literacies in Education.

Angel M. Y. Lin is a professor and Tier 1 Canada Research Chair in Plurilingual and Intercultural Education at Simon Fraser University, Canada. She has published widely in critical discourse analysis, trans/languaging (TL), trans-semiotizing (TS), classroom analysis, and language and identity studies. Her book, *Language Across the Curriculum and CLIL in English as an Additional Language Contexts: Theory and Practice*, was published by Springer in 2016. orcid.org/0000-0002-6204-8021

Mario López-Gopar (PhD, OISE/University of Toronto) is a professor at *Universidad Autónoma Benito Juárez de Oaxaca*. Mario's main research interest is intercultural and multilingual education of Indigenous peoples in Mexico. He has received over 15 academic awards. His PhD thesis was awarded both the 2009 AERA second language research dissertation award and the 2009 OISE Outstanding Thesis of the year award. He has published numerous articles and book chapters in Mexico, USA, Canada, Argentina, Brazil and Europe. His latest books are *Decolonizing Primary English Language Teaching* (Multilingual Matters, 2016) and *International Perspectives on Critical Pedagogies in ELT* (Palgrave MacMillan, 2019). https://orcid.org/0000-0001-5121-3901

David E. Low is an associate professor of Literacy Education at California State University, Fresno. A former secondary English teacher, David conducts research on how young people's multimodal reading and composing practices—particularly through the medium of comics—facilitate various enactments of critical literacy. Recent articles have appeared in *Written Communication, Literacy, English Journal, Language Arts, JoLLE* and *Gender & Education*. David is also a past chair of the Literature SIG of AERA.

Anna Lyngfelt is a professor of Literacy Education at School of Humanities and Media Studies, at Dalarna University in Sweden. Her research includes various aspects of literacy and literacy development—see digital text production as narratives: an analysis of text production in a multilingual classroom at primary school, in *Educational Role of Language Journal* (2019), Reading in your first and second language. On the use of prior knowledge when processing fictional texts at school, in *Social Sciences and Education Research Review* (2018) and Fiction at school for educational purposes. What possibilities do students get to act as moral subjects?, in *Ethical Literacies and Sustainability Education: Young People, Subjectivity and Democratic Participation* (Routledge, 2017). https://orcid.org/0000-0003-3048-5603

M

Hui-Ling Sunshine Malone is a visiting assistant professor of English Education at Michigan State University. Hui-Ling's research interests center on culturally sustaining pedagogies, critical pedagogy and community oriented African epistemologies in order to advance equity in schools and their surrounding neighborhoods. Her work surrounds young people and draws on community centric pedagogies to strengthen relationships between students, schools and surrounding community members to address immediate social issues for the greater good of the collective.

David Martínez-Prieto is an Assistant Professor at the Department of Bilingual and Literacy Studies at the University of Texas Rio Grande Valley. He holds a PhD in Culture, Literacy, and Language from the University of Texas-San Antonio. David's research focuses on the impact of curricular ideologies among transnational populations. He has co-edited, *In Search of Hope and Home: Mexican Immigrants in the Trinational NAFTA Context* (Peter Lang, in press). His recent publications appeared in *TESOL Quarterly*, the *TESOL Journal*, and the *Journal of Latino Education*, among others. https://orcid.org/0000-0001-8227-9831

Andréa Machado de Almeida Mattos is an associate professor of Applied Linguistics at the School of Languages and Linguistics, Federal University of Minas Gerais, Brazil, and editor-in-chief of the Brazilian Journal of Applied Linguistics. She holds a Productivity Researcher Grant from the National Council for Scientific and Technological Development—CNPq (Process n. 308243/2020-0) and has published widely both in Brazil and abroad. Her research focuses on Critical Literacies, Critical Teacher Education, Narratives and Memory. https://orcid.org/0000-0003-3190-7329

Carolyn McKinney is an associate professor of Language Education, School of Education, University of Cape Town, South Africa. Carolyn's teaching and research focuses on language ideologies; multilingualism as resource for learning; critical literacies and the intersections of language and race. Co-founder of bua-lit, language and literacy advocacy collective (www.bua-lit.org.za), she authored *Language and Power in Post-Colonial Schooling: Ideologies in Practice* (2017, Routledge).

Carmen Liliana Medina is an associate professor in the Department of Literacy, Culture and Language Education at Indiana University. She does research in the areas of literacy/biliteracy as social and critical practices, embodied/performative pedagogies, and Latino/a (bilingual) children's literature. Recently she has been working on a research project examining Puerto Rican children critical engagement and imaginative literacy practices at the intersection of transnational landscapes and colonization politics. She is co-author with Dr. Karen Wohlwend of the book, *Literacy, Play and Globalization: Converging Imaginaries in Children's Critical and Cultural Performances* (2014, Routledge Research Series) and co-editor of the volume entitled *Methodologies of Embodiment* with Dr. Mia Perry (2015, Routledge Research Series).

Rohit Mehta is an assistant professor of secondary curriculum with instructional technology at Kremen School of Education and Human Development, California State University, Fresno, established on the occupied lands of Yokuts and Mono people. He conducts inquiries on the intersections of creativity, decolonization, literacies, and technology. Some of his interdisciplinary writings were published in the *Thinking Skills and Creativity, Journal of Digital Learning in Teacher Education, Journal of Technology and Teacher Education*, and *Handbook of Research on Literacy and Digital Technology Integration in Teacher Education*. https://orcid.org/0000-0003-0686-9877

Seyyed-Abdolhamid Mirhosseini is an associate professor at Alzahra University, Tehran, Iran. His research areas include the sociopolitics of language education, qualitative research, and critical discourse studies. He has recently co-edited *English Language Education Worldwide Today: Ideologies,*

Policies and Practices (Routledge, 2020) and *The Sociopolitics of English Language Testing* (Bloomsbury, 2020), and has written *Doing Qualitative Research in Language Education* (Palgrave Macmillan, 2021). https://orcid.org/0000-0001-8758-1175

Nicole Mirra is an assistant professor of urban teacher education at Rutgers, The State University of New Jersey. Her research explores the intersections of critical literacy and civic engagement with youth and teachers across classroom, community, and digital learning environments. She is the author of *Educating for Empathy: Literacy Learning and Civic Engagement* (Teachers College Press, 2018) and a co-author (with Antero Garcia and Ernest Morrell) of *Doing Youth Participatory Action Research: Transforming Inquiry with Researchers, Educators, and Students* (Routledge, 2015). https://orcid.org/0000-0003-4225-2209

Walkyria Monte Mór has a Doctor's degree in Language and Education (University of São Paulo), a Master's degree in Philosophy of Education (PUC-SP) and is a senior associate professor at the Department of Modern Languages, University of São Paulo. She co-directs the Nation-wide Project on Literacies: Language, Culture, Education and Technology, DGP-CNPq. Recent research: literacies, multiliteracies, critical literacy, critique and meaning making, teacher education. https://orcid.org/0000-0003-0303-8664

Raúl Alberto Mora is an associate professor of Literacy Studies and Language Education at Universidad Pontificia Bolivariana in Medellín. He has also served as visiting and guest faculty in Colombia, the US, Brazil, Czech Republic, Spain, Poland, and Russia. At Universidad Pontificia Bolivariana, he teaches courses on language teaching methods, research, literacy, and critical theory. He chairs the Literacies in Second Languages Project (LSLP) research lab at this university, where he and his "Legion" study second language literacies in urban and digital spaces and retheorize literacies research for second language learning and teaching from a Global South perspective. He holds the top rank of Senior Investigator from the Colombian Ministry of Science (Minciencias) and received the Divergent Award for Excellence in 21st Century Literacies Research in 2019. In addition to his publications in peer-reviewed journals and book chapters, he has guest edited for *International Journal of Cultural Studies, Social Semiotics, and Pedagogies*. https://orcid.org/0000-0003-0479-252X

Karin Murris is a professor of Early Childhood Education at the University of Oulu (Finland) and Emerita Professor of Pedagogy and Philosophy, University of Cape Town (South Africa). She is a teacher educator and grounded in academic philosophy and a postqualitative research paradigm, her main interests are in philosophy of education, childhood studies, ethics, democratic postdevelopmental pedagogies, children's literature and digital play. She is principal investigator of various projects, including *The Post-Qualitative Research in Higher Education Collective* (2021–2023), *Children, Technology and Play* (2019–2020) and *Decolonising Early Childhood: Critical Posthumanism in Higher Education* (2016–2019) in South Africa. Her books include: *The Posthuman Child* (2016), and (with Joanna Haynes) *Literacies, Literature and Learning: Reading Classrooms Differently* (2018), *Picturebooks, Pedagogy and Philosophy* (2012). She is co-editor of the *Routledge International Handbook of Philosophy for Children* (2017) and editor of *Navigating the Postqualitative, New Materialist and Critical Posthumanist Terrain Across Disciplines* (2021). She is Chief Editor of the Routledge Postqualitative, New Materialist and Critical Posthumanist Research series. https://orcid.org/0000-0001-9613-7738

Adam D. Musser is an abolitionist educator and restorative justice practitioner. His research elevates the literacy practices of young people experiencing incarceration and centers youth knowledges in movements toward freedom and justice. Adam is a Dissertation Year Fellow at the University of California, Davis. https://orcid.org/0000-0002-1752-8472

N

Lusia Marliana Nurani is an assistant professor of Literacy, Media, and Culture in the Faculty of Arts and Design at Institut Teknologi Bandung (ITB), Indonesia. She currently also holds the position of Head of Human Resource Development Unit of ITB, has served as the Advisor of American Corner ITB since 2016, and is currently developing the first Writing Center in ITB. She was the recipient of the Fulbright PhD Presidential Scholarship for her Doctoral study in Applied Linguistics at Arizona State University while for her Master's study in Applied Linguistics at the University of Melbourne she received Australia Development Scholarship (ADS). Her research interests include linguistic anthropology, language and literacy, and Indigenous language policy and planning.

Hossein Nazari holds a PhD in English from the University of Canterbury. He is currently an Assistant Professor of English Language and Literature at the University of Tehran, Iran, where he teaches English and American literature, as well as translation courses. His main areas of research include Postcolonialism, (Neo-)Orientalism, and Subaltern Studies. His forthcoming book (Bloomsbury, 2021) investigates contemporary literary representations of Iran and Islam in mainstream US literary discourses. email: nazarih@ut.ac.ir. https://orcid.org/0000-0001-6429-3779

T. Philip Nichols is an assistant professor of Literacy Education at Baylor University. His research explores how science and technology condition the ways we practice, teach, and talk about literacy. Recent articles have appeared in *Teachers College Record, Learning, Media, and Technology, Reading Research Quarterly*, and *Research in the Teaching of English*. https://orcid.org/0000-0002-8648-1276

Silje Normand is an associate professor of English at the University of Stavanger, Norway. Her current research interests include critical literacies and pedagogies, interculturality, inclusive participatory research, and performative practices within schools and teacher education. She heads the research group Democracy and Citizenship (DEMCI) focused on inclusive citizenship education and practices and is actively involved in the Erasmus+ project Critical Literacy and Awareness in Education (CLAE). https://orcid.org/0000-0001-8551-8199

Idalia Nuñez is an assistant professor of Language and Literacy at the University of Illinois at Urbana-Champaign. Her research focuses on addressing linguistic equity in teaching and learning to support the education of emergent bilinguals from marginalized backgrounds. https://orcid.org/0000-0002-1102-3609

P

Jessica Zacher Pandya is Dean of the College of Education and Professor of Liberal Studies at California State University, Dominguez Hills. A former kindergarten teacher in the California Bay Area who received her PhD at UC Berkeley, her early research focused on children's literacy and identity work in diverse urban classrooms. Her latest book is *Exploring Critical Digital Literacy Practices: Everyday Video in a Dual Language Context* (Routledge, 2018). Pandya has published in journals such as *Research in the Teaching of English, Written Communication, Teachers College Record, Language Arts* and *The Australian Journal of Language and Literacy*. https://orcid.org/0000-0001-7125-4006

Lílian Vimieiro Pascoal is a Brazilian researcher that is involved and interested in the different levels of citizenship education. She is a school teacher working with teenagers, and a professor of Applied Linguistics at the School of Languages and Linguistics at the Federal University of Minas Gerais where she works with teachers' education. https://orcid.org/0000-0003-3706-4860

Robert Petrone is an associate professor of literacy education and critical youth studies at the University of Missouri in the United States. His research focuses on the intersections of learning and literacy in youth cultures and English (teacher) education. He is co-author (with Sophia Sarigianides and Mark A. Lewis) of *Re-thinking the "Adolescent" in Adolescent Literacy* (National Council for Teachers of English, 2017) and (with Allison Wynhoff Olsen) *Teaching English in Rural Communities: Toward a Critical Rural English Pedagogy* (Rowan & Littlefield). https://orcid.org/0000-0002-7647-5833

Prem Phyak is an assistant professor at the Department of English in the Chinese University of Hong Kong. Previously, he worked in Tribhuvan University, Nepal where he was heavily involved in the leadership positions, teacher training/education and research at the Faculty of Education. His research interests include language policy, multilingual education, sociolinguistics, language ideology, critical pedagogy, and politics of English. He has co-authored (with Kathryn A. Davis) a book *Engaged Language Policy and Practices* (Routledge) and published articles in various journals such as *Language Policy, Current Issues in Language Planning*, and *Language in Society*. https://orcid.org/0000-0001-7032-1027

Kristian Adi Putra is an assistant professor of applied linguistics at the Deanship of Preparatory Year, Prince Sattam Bin Abdulaziz University, Saudi Arabia. Prior to that, he trained pre-service and in-service English language teachers at the Department of English Language Education, Universitas Sebelas Maret, Indonesia and taught Indonesian language and culture at the Defense Critical Language and Culture Program, University of Montana, USA. He is primarily interested in the study of Indigenous language planning and policy and critical discourse analysis, and secondarily in language teacher education and technology-enhanced language teaching and learning. https://orcid.org/0000-0002-4451-3778

Q

Rosa María Quesada-Mejía currently works as a literacy teacher at Universidad Iberoamericana in Mexico City. She has combined her teaching in both elementary and college levels. She is very interested in Children's literature and literacy and has carried out research about it. She has been Editor of Didac, Universidad Iberoamericana's journal for teachers, and has also authored educational materials for the teaching of Spanish language from preschool to high school levels. Her last article is Overseen presence of critical literacy in Mexico: Eight cases to be analyzed, in sinectica.iteso.mx

R

Natalia Andrea Ramírez is an English instructor at the Theodoro Hertzl school in Medellín, Colombia. She is an affiliated researcher at the Literacies in Second Languages Project (LSLP) research lab at Universidad Pontificia Bolivariana. Her current research interests explore the infusion of critical literacies in preservice teacher education. She is particularly invested in exploring the overt and covert presence of critical literacy practices in both instructional practices and curricula as the basis to develop a stronger critical literacies perspective for teacher preparation. Natalia holds an Honors M.A. in Learning and Teaching Processes in Second Languages from Universidad Pontificia Bolivariana (UPB) in Medellín and her track record already includes book chapters and major international conference presentations. https://orcid.org/0000-0001-5716-5998

Rebecca Rogers is the E. Des Lee Endowed Professor of Tutorial Education and Curators' Distinguished Research Professor at the University of Missouri-St. Louis. Her scholarship centers on educational literacies, teacher education, community and family literacies, and lifespan learning ecologies. She has actively been involved in contributing to and studying communities of practice in the pursuit of educational and racial justice. She has written many journal articles and books. Her new book is called *Reclaiming Powerful Literacies: New Directions for Critical Discourse Analysis* (Routledge, 2017) and focuses on positive approaches to discourse analysis in educational and community contexts.

Minea Armijo Romero is a PhD candidate in the Language Literacy and Sociocultural Studies program at the University of New Mexico, and Faculty at the Education Department at Central New Mexico Community College. Her research looks at the intersection of transnationalism, border theory, and intercultural educational models in Latin America. https://orcid.org/0000-0003-1087-2577

Jennifer Rowsell is a Professor of Literacies and Social Innovation at University of Bristol's School of Education in the United Kingdom. She is a co-editor of the *Routledge Expanding Literacies in Education* book series with Carmen Liliana Medina (Indiana University and Co-Editor of *Digital Cultures and Education.* https://orcid.org/0000-0002-9062-8859

S

Pramod K. Sah is a PhD Candidate and Killam scholar in the Department of Language and Literacy Education at the University of British Columbia, Canada. His research interests include English-medium instruction, language policy and planning, critical literacies, critical pedagogies, TESOL, social class, and language ideology. His recent research has appeared in journals, such as *International Journal of Bilingual Education and Bilingualism, Journal of Multilingual and Multicultural Development, International Multilingual Research Journal,* and *Asia Pacific Journal of Education.* https://orcid.org/0000-0002-6200-8898

Zulfa Sakhiyya is an assistant professor at the English Department, Faculty of Languages and Arts, Universitas Negeri Semarang (UNNES), Indonesia. She is the Director of Literacy Research Centre in UNNES while actively involved in the New Literacy Studies group in Indonesia. Her research interests span from critical literacy, educational policies and gender studies addressing the question of how knowledge is produced and represented. Her works appear in journals, such as *Pedagogy, Culture and Society; Gender and Education;* and *Globalisation, Societies and Education.* She is the chief editor of "Education in Indonesia: Critical Perspectives" (Springer, 2021). http://orcid.org/0000-0003-4183-977X

Susan Sandretto is an associate professor in the University of Otago College of Education, Dunedin, New Zealand. Her research interests include critical literacy and critical multiliteracies. She is a co-author of *Planting Seeds: Embedding Critical Literacy into Your Classroom Programme* (with Scott Klenner, NZCER, 2011). She has published in *Journal of Adolescent and Adult Literacy, Discourse: Studies in the Cultural Politics of Education, Journal of LGBT Youth,* and *Gender and Education.* https://orcid.org/0000-0001-6106-1032

Cassandra Scharber is an associate professor of Learning Technologies in the Department of Curriculum and Instruction at the University of Minnesota, USA. Her research focuses on K–12 computer science education, technology integration, and digital literacies within formal and informal learning settings. https://orcid.org/0000-0003-2965-3307

Robin Schell is a visiting assistant professor of TESOL and Literacy at Miami University in Oxford, Ohio. Her research focuses on educational equity for English learners and literacy development through critical and culturally sustaining pedagogy. Her recent work on English learners and participatory literacy can be found in the *Journal of Adolescent and Adult Literacy*.

Derek Shafer is a lecturer at the Division of Education, University of Waikato, New Zealand, and specialises in secondary initial teacher education, English curriculum practice, critical literacies and culturally responsive pedagogies. His current PhD research focuses on the impacts of professional development in supporting in-service secondary teachers' critical thinking and pedagogy in practice. https://orcid.org/0000-0002-2128-030X

Jeff Share is a faculty advisor in the Teacher Education Program at the University of California, Los Angeles (UCLA), USA. His research and practice focus on preparing educators to teach critical media literacy in K–12 education for the goals of social and environmental justice. He is author of *Media Literacy is Elementary: Teaching Youth to Critically Read and Create Media* (Peter Lang, 2015) and co-author (with Douglas Kellner) of *The Critical Media Literacy Guide: Engaging Media and Transforming Education* (Brill Sense, 2019). https://orcid.org/0000-0001-6593-817X

Judy Sharkey is the John & H. Irene Peters Professor & Chair of the Education Department at the University of New Hampshire (USA). Within critical second language and literacy education, her research focuses on teacher/teacher educator learning and development in plurilingual, transmigrant and diaspora communities in the US, Colombia, and Pakistan. Recent research has appeared in *Language Teaching Research, TESOL Journal*, and *Journal of Teacher Education*. She is the co-editor (with Megan Madigan Peercy) of *Self-Study of Language and Literacy Teacher Education Practices: Culturally and Linguistically Diverse Contexts* (Emerald, 2018). https://orcid.org/0000-0002-0332-9712

Catarina Schmidt is an associate professor in Pedagogy at Jönköping University, Sweden and University of Gothenburg, Sweden. Her research focuses on conditions and possibilities for children's and young people's literacy learning and citizenship in relation to multilingualism and critical literacy, including ecological and social sustainability. A recent publication is the article "Enhancing children's literacy and ecological literacy through critical place-based pedagogy (published online 28 Aug 2020), *Environmental Education Research*, co-authored with Margaretha Häggström. https://orcid.org/0000-0002-3925-9656

Rob Simon is an associate professor at the Ontario Institute for Studies in Education of the University of Toronto. His research explores critical literacy, social justice education, and participatory research. More information available at: www.addressinginjustices.com. https://orcid.org/0000-0003-0569-3531

Anna Smith is an associate professor at Illinois State University. She is co-author of *Developing Writers: Teaching and Learning in the Digital Age* and co-editor of the *Handbook of Writing, Literacies, and Education in Digital Cultures*. Her recent research on writing development, transliteracies, and the intersection of teaching and learning can be found in journals such as *Learning, Culture and Social Interaction, Theory into Practice*, and *Journal of Literacy Research*. https://orcid.org/0000-0002-6448-5620

Margaret Somerville is a professor of Education at Western Sydney University and leader of the Planetary Wellbeing and Human Learning Program of Research and Cohort of doctoral students. She is interested in alternative and creative approaches to research and writing with a focus on relationship to place and planetary well-being. Her research has been carried out in collaboration with Aboriginal communities, educational practitioners and doctoral students. She recently led an international ARC funded study, Naming the world: enhancing early years literacy and sustainability learning, involving collaboration with young children in 10 sites in New South Wales, Queensland, Victoria, and Finland, exploring their extraordinary capacities in world naming. She has continued this work, developing the concept of planetary literacies in a project involving young children's experience of Australia's catastrophic bushfires, and learning about bushfire recovery. Her new book, *Rivers of the Anthropocene* was published in Routledge's Environmental Studies series in 2020. https://orcid.org/0000-0001-8804-5825

Sandra L. Soto-Santiago is an associate professor in Language and Education in the Department of English at the University of Puerto Rico at Mayagüez and her research interests focus on issues of social justice and education, transnational youth and translanguaging practices in Puerto Rico. She is co-author of Con confianza: The emergence of the zone of proximal development in a university ESL course (2015). https://orcid.org/0000-0002-8078-7063

Nerida Spina is a senior lecturer in Education at Queensland University of Technology, Brisbane, Australia. Her research interests include teachers' work, social justice, education and literacy policy, practitioner inquiry and the sociology of numbers. Her research explores the everyday work of teachers, pre-service teachers and school leaders, and the impact of policy on their practices and lives. Her book *Data Culture and the Organisation of Teachers' Work* will be published in 2021 by Routledge. https://orcid.org/0000-0002-2923-0104

Olivia G. Stewart is an assistant professor of Literacy at St. John's University in Queens, NY, USA. Her multiliteracies-framed and critical digital literacies-framed research interests center around multimodal authoring paths to expand notions of "what counts" as writing, particularly for academically marginalized students. She has recently published in the *Handbook of Research on Integrating Digital Technology with Literacy Pedagogies.* https://orcid.org/0000-0003-2093-2182

Kelly Stone is a lecturer in early literacies with teaching experiences across undergraduate and postgraduate programmes in Initial Teacher Education. Her research is primarily concerned with issues of equity and social justice, and specifically with critical literacies and the use of children's literature as a platform for social justice and sustainability. Recently published articles have explored the status of critical literacies in Scottish educational policy (2019) and critical literacy's role in Scotland's new LGBTI-inclusive curriculum (2020). https://orcid.org/0000-0002-2693-5539.

Amy Stornaiuolo is an associate professor of literacy education at the University of Pennsylvania. Her research examines adolescents' multimodal composing practices, teachers' educational uses of digital technologies, and relationships between authors and audiences in online, networked spaces. She is co-editor of the book *Handbook of Writing, Literacies, and Education in Digital Cultures* (Routledge, 2018) and is currently serving as co-editor of the journal *Research in the Teaching of English.* https://orcid.org/0000-0003-0633-7117

Sneha Subramaniam is a teacher educator and curriculum developer in Bangalore, India. She works on programs that reposition children as imaginative thinkers and creators of language through Literature. Her research interests include literature in education, critical literacy, teacher education and inclusive education through education technology.

T

Yuya Takeda (@yuyapecotakeda) is a PhD Candidate at the Department of Language and Literacy Education at University of British Columbia. In his dissertation, Yuya studies conspiracy theories through philosophical and discourse analytic approaches and speculates on how critical media literacy education can respond to them. He posits that rationalistic debunking is not an effective way to teach conspiracy theories. Instead, he takes existentialist and critical pragmatist stances and examines conspiracy theories in relation to cults and counter-culture movements. https://orcid.org/0000-0002-2171-3355

Shinya Takekawa is an associate professor at Aichi University of Education in Aichi, Japan. His focus of research and teaching is in equity and quality issues of literacy, pedagogy and curriculum. His current research includes a theoretical and practical investigation on critical inquiry literacy, reconstructing theories of critical literacy within the current Japanese context, and a study of teacher training to develop critical awareness. His publications include "Effects of Globalised Assessment on Local Curricula: What Japanese Teachers Face and How They Challenge It" in *The SAGE Handbook of Curriculum, Pedagogy and Assessment* (SAGE, 2016). https://orcid.org/0000-0002-8337-1792

Siao See Teng is a sociologist working at the Centre for Research in Pedagogy and Practice (CRPP), National Institute of Singapore, Nanyang Technological University. She is also Co-Program Director of the Schools, Leadership and Systems Studies at CRPP. She currently leads a funded study on the intercultural mindedness of secondary school students and another on the life trajectories and educational pathways of vocational students in Singapore, and is involved in other projects researching into immigrant parents' educational involvement and funds of knowledge. She serves as a Managing Editor for the Asia-Pacific Journal of Education.

Angela Thomas is a senior lecturer in English Education at the University of Tasmania, Australia. Her research interests include children's literature, social semiotics, multimodal discourse analysis, critical literacies and the fusion of literature and new media. She is the author of *Youth Online*, and co-editor of *English teaching and new literacies pedagogy: Interpreting and authoring digital multimedia narratives*. Angela is a co-recipient of the PETAA grant *Language and Literacy Learning through Augmented Reality*, and is an associate editor for the *Australian Journal of Language and Literacy*. https://orcid.org/0000-0003-4508-2874

Zhongfeng Tian is an assistant professor in TESOL/Applied Linguistics at the University of Texas at San Antonio, USA. He has co-edited a special issue "Positive Synergies: Translanguaging and Critical Theories in Education" (2019) with Holly Link for *Translation and Translanguaging in Multilingual Contexts*. He is also the co-editor of two books: "Envisioning TESOL through a Translanguaging Lens: Global Perspectives" (*Springer*, 2020) and "English-Medium Instruction and Translanguaging" (*Multilingual Matters*, 2021). https://orcid.org/0000-0003-0233-0284

Jane Tilson is a lecturer at the University of Otago College of Education, Dunedin, New Zealand. Her research interests include critical literacy, critical multiliteracies, reflective practice and video. She is co-author of Integrating critical multiliteracies using the *Four resources model: A New Zealand guide* (with Susan Sandretto 2016). She has published in *Teacher and Teacher Education, Discourse: Studies in the cultural politics of education, Journal of Adolescent & Adult Literacy*. https://orcid.org/0000-0002-6972-4088

Lina Trigos-Carrillo is an associate professor in the Department of Psychology of Development and Education at Universidad de la Sabana in Chia, Colombia. Her research focuses on community and family literacies, critical perspectives to literacies, popular education, multilingual education, and professional development. Her most recent articles are "Social impact of a transformative service-learning experience in a post-conflict setting" (2020) and "Community Cultural Wealth and Literacy Capital in Latin American Communities" (2019). https://orcid.org/0000-0003-2297-3906

V

Lisa van Leent is a senior lecturer in the School of Teacher Education and Leadership at Queensland University of Technology, Australia. Lisa has recently been the guest editor for English in Australia on the special issue "Love in English" (2018). Lisa published an article in 2018 titled "A queer critical media literacies framework in a digital age." https://orcid.org/0000-0002-8720-545X

Saskia Van Viegen is an assistant professor in the Department of Languages, Literatures and Linguistics at York University. Her research engages with language in education, bi/multilingualism and language and content integrated teaching and learning. She is co-editor of the book *Plurilingual Pedagogies: Critical and Creative Undertakings for Equitable Language (in) Education* (Springer, 2020) and is currently serving as co-editor of the international journal *Critical Inquiry in Language Studies*. https://orcid.org/0000-0002-3748-1990

Vivian Maria Vasquez is a professor in the School of Education at American University. She has worked in the field of education for over 30 years. Her research interests are in critical literacy, early literacy, and information communication technology. Her publications include eleven books and numerous book chapters and articles in refereed journals. Her awards include the 2019 NCTE Outstanding Elementary Educator in the English Language Arts Award, the NCTE Advancement of People of Color Award (2013), the AERA Division B Outstanding Book of the Year Award (2006) and The James N. Britton Award (2005).

Amy Vetter is a professor in English education in the School of Education at the University of North Carolina Greensboro, where she teaches undergraduate courses in teaching practices and curriculum of English and literacy in the content area, and graduate courses in youth literacies, teacher research, and qualitative research design. Dr. Vetter has developed a scholarly record that underscores the significance of classroom interactions for impacting the development of reader/writing identities and teacher identities, the role critical conversations play in identity work within secondary and undergraduate classrooms, and the importance of learning from youth's writing identities. Her most recent book, written with Melissa Schieble and Kahdeidra Martin, is *Classroom Talk for Social Change: Critical Conversations in English Language Arts Classrooms*. https://orcid.org/0000-0002-2481-5007

Aslaug Veum is Associate Professor at Department of Language and Literature, University of South-Eastern Norway, Norway. Her research interests are critical literacy, critical discourse analysis and multimodality. She has published work on immigrant students' identity texts, school textbooks, social media and newspaper texts. From 2020-2023 she is leading the project *Critical Literacy in a Digital and Global Textual World (CritLit)*, funded by The Research Council of Norway.

W

Marianna Vivitsou is postdoctoral researcher at the Faculty of Educational Sciences, University of Helsinki. She is member of Helsinki Institute of Sustainability Science (HELSUS) and Global Education Research in Finland. Her work draws from the theory of narratology, metaphor theory, the new materialist thinking and feminist studies. She is interested in policies and practices for sustainable university future-oriented hybrid pedagogies, multimodal literacies, and the imaginaries that emerge with the use of digital technologies.

David-Alexandre Wagner is an associate professor in History and Leader of the History Group at the Department of Cultural Studies and Languages at the University of Stavanger, Norway. He is a founding member of the Future-Pasts Group (FPG), a research unit in public history and history education. His current research interests are connected to critical literacy and the use of visual media in history education. He is a member of the steering group of the Erasmus+ CLAE project (Critical Literacies & Awareness in Education—https://clae.no/**),** involving schools in France, Norway and Spain. https://orcid.org/0000-0002-2060-3816

Ninni Wahlström is a professor of Education at Linnaeus University, Sweden. Her current research focuses on national curriculum and classroom teaching from a perspective of educational philosophy and curriculum theory. A recent publication is the article "Reading in the wing chair: The shaping of teaching and reading bodies in the transactional performativity of materialities" (published online 01 Sept 2020), *Educational Philosophy and Theory*, co-authored with Elin Sundström Sjödin. https://orcid.org/0000-0001-5554-6041

Ty Walkland is a PhD candidate in Curriculum and Pedagogy at the Ontario Institute for Studies in Education of the University of Toronto, where his dissertation research explores critical and holistic approaches to school-based drug education at the intersections of critical literacy, public health, and teacher education. https://orcid.org/0000-0003-1230-1954

Kathryn F. Whitmore is a professor and chair of the Special Education, Early Childhood Education, and Culturally and Linguistically Diverse Education Department at Metropolitan State University of Denver. Her most recent book is *Reclaiming Literacies as Meaning Making* (co-edited with R.J. Meyer, 2020, Routledge). She is a co-lead editor of *Literacy Research: Theory, Method and Practice*. https://orcid.org/0000-0002-5982-2047

Csilla Weninger is an associate professor in the department of English Language and Literature at the National Institute of Education, Singapore. Her research examines the imprint and impact of political and institutional ideologies on the conduct of schooling, including its material dimensions such as textbooks as well as everyday pedagogies. Her publications have appeared, among others, in *Teaching and Teacher Education, Discourse, TESOL Quarterly, Linguistics and Education*, and *ELT Journal*. https://orcid.org/0000-0001-5874-8757

Casey Philip Wong is a post-doctoral scholar in the UCLA Department of Anthropology and a visiting scholar at the USC Rossier School of Education. His research focuses broadly on studying how communities understand and organize against racialization and interrelated systems of oppression through education. He has recently co-edited a volume titled *Freedom Moves: Hip Hop Knowledges, Pedagogies, and Futures*. https://orcid.org/0000-0002-1412-4317

Annette Woods is a professor in the School of Early Childhood and Inclusive Education, in the Faculty of Education at the Queensland University of Technology, Brisbane, Australia. She teaches and researches in the fields of literacies, social justice, and curriculum, pedagogy and assessment. Her most recent edited collection is entitled *Literacies in Early Childhood: Foundations in Equity and Quality* (OUP, 2020) with Beryl Exley. She is a chief investigator in the Australian Research Council Centre of Excellence for the Digital Child based at QUT and Immediate Past President of the Australian Association for Research in Education (AARE). https://orcid.org/0000-0003-1585-5688

Rahat Zaidi is a professor and chair of Language and Literacy in the Werklund School of Education at the University of Calgary. Her research expertise focuses on multilingual literacies that clarify intersectional understandings across sociophobia, diversity, immigration, and pluralism. Through her research, she advances social justice and equity, transculturalism, and identity positioning in immigrant and transcultural contexts, all of which are particularly relevant and pertinent to the intertwining social, cultural, and political contexts in which society functions today. Dr. Zaidi's recent publications include "Dual Language Books: Enhancing Engagement and Language Awareness" published by the *Journal of Literacy Research*, "Digitizing Dual-Language Book Pedagogies in Uncertain Times" published by *The Reading Teacher*.

INDEX

Note: Page numbers in *italic* indicate a figure, and page numbers in **bold** indicate a table on the corresponding page.

of nothing 340–341; new educational theorising 337; posthuman scholarship and 335; posthuman theory and language 335–336; social responsibility as academics 343; tidying up 339, 341–342
antiblackness 363–364
Anti-ELAB Movement 263, 268
anti-Islamophobic curriculum 451
anti-racist disruption 206–207
Anwaruddin, S. M. 294
Anzaldúa, G. 434, 456, 458, 459, 461
Aotearoa New Zealand: action literature 119–120; colonialism 398; critical literacy mandate 118; critical literacy praxis 119–121; educational policy 118; introduction 117; language activism in 391; reflection literature 120–121; social landscape 117–118; theory literature 121
Appadurai, A. 449
Appleby, R. 386
Aragaki, N. 187–189
Aranda, J. A. 199
Arce, L. C. *153*
Archer, A. 230
Arendt, H. 314
Arnot, M. 240
Arrancando mitos de raíz (Godreau et al.) 207
artful pedagogy 320
Artiles, A. J. 355, 358, 359
Art of Critical Pedagogy, The (Duncan-Andrade and Morrell) 53
arts-literacies: abduction 317–318; academic rigor 319–320; concept dilution 319; emotion 318–319; imagination 318; introduction 317; literal transmediation 320; overview 320–323; research and pedagogy 323–324
Asakereh, A. 179
Ashcroft, C. 87
assemblage pedagogies 337
Attick, D. 32
Aukerman, M. 64
Australia: Chalkface Press 100; critical digital literacy 130; curriculum in 101; educational system 126; Indigenous language activism 392; indigenous perspectives 129; intercultural understanding 129–130; literature survey 126–129; low-income backgrounds 63; research suggestions 130; social responsibility as academics 130–131; sociopolitical context 125–126; testing 30; translanguaging in 386; transnational and other critical work 129–130
autobiographical poems 10–15
"Average Black Girl, The" (Morrison) 322
Ávila, J. 109, 373, 376
Ayllu de Warisata School 16
Azim Premji Foundation 164
Azza, F. 294

Bacalja, A. 373, 376
Baer, P. 147, 321

Baird, A. 241
Bakar, M. A. 218
Baker-Bell, A. 231, 249
Baker, C. D. 329
Baker, E. 19
Bakhtin, M. M. 138, 265
Bangladesh 292, 293, 294
Barad, K. 336, 343
Barden, O. 241
Barron, B. 110
Barton, D. 138, 293
Batista-Morales, N. S. 44
Baude-e-sabaa 35
becoming-otherwise 413–416
Begoray, D. 146
Belcher, D. 97
Bell, R. C. 459
Benavides Buitrago, C. *153*
Benner, G. J. 359
Bernaldez, C. 196
Bernstein, B. 453
Bertanees, C. 121
Bhattacharya, U. 165
Bhimayana 293
Bhola, H. S. 292
Bhutan 293, 294
Big Data 346
Biklen, D. 356, 357
Bildung 277, 278, 285
bilingualism 146, 256–257; *see also* additional language learning; English as a Foreign Language (EFL); English as a Second Language (ESL)
biopower 413
Bishop, J. 119
Bishop, R. S. 311
Black/abolitionist literacies 367–368
Black feminist politics 364
Black Freedom Movement 19
Black girls' literacies 248–249
Black Heritage Trail of New Hampshire 441
Black male experiences 63, 75
Black women and girls: Black girls' literacies 78, 248–249; embodiment and 72, 74
blanqueamiento 207
blogging 173–174
body as social text 71
body-poems 75
Boggs, G. L. 327
Bogost, I. 345
Bokkina, J. 404, 405
Boler, M. 145–146
Bolívar, S. 15
Bolivian language activism 392
Bomer, R. 459
Bonnar, M. 119
Bopry, J. 404
borderlands 456, 458–459; *see also* border literacies
Borderlands/La Frontera (Anzaldúa) 461